Rebooting Policy Analysis

Strengthening the Foundation, Expanding the Scope

Peter Linquiti

The George Washington University

FOR INFORMATION:

SAGE Publications, Inc.
2455 Teller Road
Thousand Oaks, California 91320
E-mail: order@sagepub.com

SAGE Publications Ltd.
1 Oliver's Yard
55 City Road
London, EC1Y 1SP
United Kingdom

SAGE Publications India Pvt. Ltd.
B 1/I 1 Mohan Cooperative Industrial Area
Mathura Road, New Delhi 110 044
India

SAGE Publications Asia-Pacific Pte. Ltd.
18 Cross Street #10-10/11/12
China Square Central
Singapore 048423

Printed in the United States of America

ISBN 978-1-5443-7260-0

This book is printed on acid-free paper.

SUSTAINABLE FORESTRY INITIATIVE
Certified Sourcing
www.sfiprogram.org
SFI-01028

Acquisitions Editor: Anna Villarruel
Product Associate: Tiara Beatty
Production Editor: Vijayakumar
Copy Editor: Benny Willy Stephen
Typesetter: TNQ Technologies
Proofreader: Christobel Colleen Hopman
Indexer: TNQ Technologies
Cover Designer: Scott Van Atta
Marketing Manager: Jennifer Jones

22 23 24 25 26 10 9 8 7 6 5 4 3 2 1

For Teri and Megan, the twin lights of my life.

CONTENTS

PART III • LOOKING AT POLICY ISSUES THROUGH DIFFERENT LENSES 267

CHAPTER 8 • The Equity Lens 273

CHAPTER 9 • The Economics Lens 317

PREFACE

This book is meant for graduate students and advanced undergraduates in the fields of public policy, public administration, and other subjects related to public affairs. In particular, the book is suitable for courses in policy analysis, design, and delivery.

The fundamental premise of the book is that although the classical models of policy analysis—the linear progression from problem to 'solution' and the iterative cycle of design, implement, evaluate, redesign—provide a solid foundation for policy analysis, they are not enough. These models, as typically taught:

- Are often out of sync with real-world policy discourse, overemphasizing microeconomics and statistics at the expense of political, institutional, legal, and sustainability considerations;

- Rarely offer methods for rigorously analyzing matters of equity, justice, fairness, and liberty;

- Are too optimistic about the ability of policy analysis to deliver an optimal policy choice that will 'solve' a problem;

- Have little to say about how powerful stakeholders manipulate policy analysis to serve their narrow interests;

- Underemphasize the constrained environments in which policy analysis is often done and contain scant guidance on dealing with time, resource, and information constraints;

- Pay insufficient attention to the application of inclusive user-centric design principles in the development of public policy;

- Encourage a reductionist, rather than holistic, view of the systems in which policy problems arise and into which policy interventions are introduced; and

- Rest on an academic perspective about how decisions *should* be made, rather than how decisions *are* made.

Post-truth was the Oxford Dictionary's 2016 Word of the Year; it describes situations in which objective facts have less impact on our understanding of the world around us than do appeals to our emotions and personal beliefs (Oxford University

Press, 2016). A post-truth world can make it feel like policy discourse is untethered from reality. At times, we can lose sight of what a well-informed, outcome-oriented, and rigorous policy discussion even sounds like.

Can we develop actionable policy-relevant truths in a post-truth world? This book argues that, with a rebooted version of policy analysis, the answer is yes. My proposed vision of the field aspires to strengthen its existing foundations while also expanding its scope. In short, the book aspires to answer the challenge issued by Lee Friedman (2017), from UC Berkeley's Goldman School of Public Policy:

> Policy analysis surely does matter. … But … [p]olicy analysis can and should be made better … [by] … understanding it as part of an organizational or institutional process that embodies specific constraints and obstacles that policy analysts must recognize and confront.
>
> (pp. 201–202)

How do we move forward? I don't propose a break with the decades-long history of policy analysis, but an extension of it. In my view, we need to help students master a reimagined version of policy analysis. Doing so entails equipping students with the skills needed to do high-quality policy analysis even when their work looks nothing like the classical models. And, ultimately, we need to help students embrace the mindset of an effective policy analyst, a mindset built on critical thinking, pragmatism, competence, tough mindedness, a service orientation, and self-awareness.

The book, which can be covered in a single semester, is organized into 15 chapters, comprising four parts:

- *Part I* provides a sympathetic portrayal of the classical models of prospective policy analysis and retrospective program evaluation, but concludes with a critique of these models that motivates the rebooting of the field proposed in the remainder of the book.

- *Part II* describes four core competencies that all aspiring policy analysts need to master: metacognition, use of logic to identify tentative truths, collection of evidence to anchor analysis in real-world conditions, and a mindset appropriate to the successful execution of policy analysis.

- *Part III* aims to rebalance the standard public policy curriculum by going beyond microeconomics and quantitative methods to provide a panoptic view that also looks at policy issues through the lenses of justice and equity, political and institutional processes, the law, sustainability, and scientific and technological change.

- *Part IV* provides the building blocks of a rebooted version of policy analysis, including systems thinking, policy design, visualizing future outcomes, and an approach to daily life for an analyst who wants to have a meaningful impact while preserving his or her integrity.

Each chapter includes specific learning objectives, a chapter summary, and a set of discussion questions.

There are a few other important things to know about this book. It reflects a normative commitment to the principles of representative democracy and generally focuses on public policy in the United States (although the principles described in it are broadly applicable to any democracy). The book is not a textbook for the fields of statistics, economics, law, public administration, or political science. These fields are all relevant to policy analysis and discussed to some degree in the book, but a deep dive into each would produce an unmanageably long text. The book is also not an instruction manual for aspiring political activists, although it will give such students many of the skills needed to be a more effective advocate. Finally, if students want to learn how to develop analyses to support foregone conclusions, this is not the right book for them.

REFERENCES

Friedman, L. (2017). *Does Policy Analysis Matter? Exploring Its Effectiveness in Theory and Practice*. Oakland, CA: University of California Press.

Oxford University Press. (2016, November 11). *Oxford Dictionary*. Retrieved January 10, 2017, from https://www.oxforddictionaries.com/press/news/2016/11/17/WOTY-16

ACKNOWLEDGMENTS

I have learned much of what I know about policy analysis by working directly with public sector clients. I have watched firsthand as these public servants navigated—sometimes successfully, sometimes not—their own home institution and its political leaders, while trying to develop and implement programs that respected the rule of law, brought innovation to government, and reflected political constraints imposed by stakeholders. Their commitment to public service, especially in an era of partisan polarization, inspires me on a daily basis.

I would like to acknowledge with gratitude the many GW students whose enthusiasm for public policy, tough questions, and thoughtful comments have motivated and pushed me to refine my views on policy analysis.

I also thank my colleagues here at GW's Trachtenberg School of Public Policy and Public Administration for creating a great environment in which to work. The School exhibits a true sense of community and mutual support. I especially appreciate feedback from faculty participants in two discussion sessions organized by Leah Brooks in which I presented portions of early work on this book. Their comments—including those provided by Burt Barnow, Stephanie Cellini, Dylan Conger, Nina Kelsey, and Sanjay Pandey—were particularly valuable. I also received helpful advice from Sarah Anzia, Henry Brady, and Mia Bird at UC Berkeley's Goldman School of Public Policy in Spring 2021. Theresa Gullo read and carefully edited many of the chapters of the book. Finally, I am grateful to GW for a two-semester sabbatical in 2020–2021, which gave me the time and freedom to prepare the manuscript.

I appreciate the comments of Pete Fontaine and Mark Hadley on an essay on policy analysis that I wrote for my students in 2017. That essay—at Mark's suggestion—eventually morphed into the book you're now reading.

Graphic artist Mark Hill deserves credit for the wonderful illustrations that appear in the introductions to each of the four parts of the book.

Special thanks are owed to several research assistants who, over the past few years, supported work that eventually became part of this book including Nathan Cogswell, Philip Gilman, Mitali Mirle, Jeremiah Mitoko, Carolyn Nixon, and Stephanie Palmer. In addition, beginning in 2017, I had the pleasure of serving as the chair of Daniel Kim's doctoral committee. Dan's work helped me better appreciate the treatment of scientific uncertainty in policymaking, and especially, in the legal system.

Writing these acknowledgments gave me the opportunity to take a walk down memory lane to recall those teachers, mentors, and colleagues who have contributed in one way or another to my intellectual and professional development. The following folks have my deep appreciation: Chris Achen, Paul Bailey, Margaret Baker, Eugene Bardach, Henry Brady, Jack Citrin, Clayton Daughenbaugh, Randy Freed, Lee Friedman, Michael Harmon, Donna Infeld, Sudhakar Kesavan, David Kirp, Ken Kolsky, George Lowden, Arun Malik, Herb McCloskey, Kathy Newcomer, Hannah Pitkin, Philippe Nonet, Isabel Reiff, Bob Stoker, David Strelneck, Alex Triantis, Nick Vonortas, John Wasson, Russell Westrup, and Ray Wolfinger.

I would also like to thank the team at SAGE/CQ Press, especially Anna Villarruel, Tiara Beatty, Scott Greenan, and Jerry Higgins, for their help and guidance.

The following reviewers also provided valuable feedback during the development of the book.

Alexandre Couture Gagnon, The University of Texas Rio Grande Valley

Richard Greggory Johnson III, University of San Francisco

Joel Hicks, George Mason University

Gary E. Hollibaugh, Jr., University of Pittsburgh

Sara McClellan, Sacramento State University

Brian S. Nakamura, University of Arkansas

Bruce Ransom, Clemson University

Jasmine Renner, East Tennessee State University

Diane E. Schmidt, California State University, Chico

Christy D. Smith, University of New Haven

Geoffrey Willbanks, University of Texas at Tyler

Robert (Bo) Wood, University of North Dakota

In acknowledging these folks, I don't mean to suggest that they would endorse all of the ideas herein. I alone bear responsibility for the content of the book, and for any shortcomings it may contain.

Peter Linquiti
Arlington, Virginia
November 2021

ABOUT THE AUTHOR

Peter Linquiti is an Associate Professor at the Trachtenberg School of Public Policy and Public Administration at the George Washington University in Washington, DC. He joined GW's faculty in 2012 after a 23-year career as a policy analyst at ICF International, where he supported clients on a wide variety of assignments related to the design, implementation, and evaluation of policies at the Environmental Protection Agency, Federal Emergency Management Agency, Department of Energy, Occupational Health and Safety Administration, United Nations Environment Program, the World Bank, and the governments of Thailand, Philippines, Malaysia, and Indonesia. His final position at ICF was as an Executive Vice President and one of four executives leading the firm of about 600 consultants. At GW, Dr. Linquiti teaches graduate courses in policy analysis, environmental policy, and decision modeling. He holds a PhD in Public Policy and Public Administration from GW, an MPP from the Goldman School of Public Policy at UC Berkeley, and a BA in Political Science from UC Berkeley.

THE CLASSICAL MODELS AND THEIR LIMITATIONS

SCHOOL BOY EINSTEIN FINDS THE INTERSECTION OF TWO STRAIGHT LINES	PROFESSOR EINSTEIN DERIVES THE AGE, SIZE, AND DENSITY OF THE COSMOS

$$2y + 2x = 6$$
$$4y - 3x = 5$$
$$2x = 6 - 2y$$
$$x = 3 - y$$
$$4y - 3(3-y) = 5$$

$$7y = 14$$
$$y = 2$$
$$x = 3 - 2 = 1$$

$$D = \frac{1}{P} \cdot \frac{1}{C} \cdot \frac{dP}{dt}$$
$$D = \frac{1}{P^2} \cdot \frac{P_0 - P}{P} \sim \frac{1}{P^2}$$
$$D^2 = \frac{1}{3}\kappa\rho \cdot \frac{P_0 - P}{P} \sim \frac{1}{3}\kappa\rho$$
$$D^2 = \sim 10^{-53}$$
$$\rho \sim 10^{-26}$$
$$P \sim 10^{-8}$$
$$T \sim 10^{10}$$

TO BE AN EXPERT, YOU FIRST NEED TO MASTER THE BASICS

In this part of the book, I introduce the two classical models of policy analysis that are routinely taught in public policy programs in the United States. Chapters 1 and 2, respectively, describe the conventional versions of prospective policy analysis and retrospective program (or impact) evaluation. While both models have flaws, they offer a valuable point of departure for the discussion in later chapters of the book. In the same way that I imagine Einstein learning linear algebra before he could explain the cosmos, I would suggest that you first need to master these classical models if you want to maximize your impact as a policy analyst.

Why bother studying flawed models? Over the last century, scholars and practitioners in fields like political science, public policy and administration, decision sciences, economics, sociology, and law have studied how we can make better decisions about matters of public policy and more rigorously assess existing policies. In starting with the classical models, I aspire to "stand on the shoulders of giants," which was Isaac Newton's way of saying that we are always indebted to those who come before us and advance the fields in which we currently work (1675).

Notwithstanding this impressive body of knowledge, the final chapter of Part I lays out several areas where these two classical models are insufficient to meet the needs of policymaking in the 21st century. As such, Chapter 3 motivates the reboot of policy analysis offered in the remainder of the book. Before diving into Chapter 1, however, it's important to define a few key terms.

What Is Policy Analysis?

The phrase policy analysis pops up in a lot of places, including the cover of this book. While arguments about the best way to organize human affairs undoubtedly date back tens of thousands of years to the earliest days of communal living, many scholars trace the modern version of policy analysis to Harold Lasswell's work in the post–World War II era (deLeon, 2006; Dryzek, 2006; Stone, 2012). Imbued with a sense of optimism after the Allies' defeat of fascism, Lasswell sought to bring systematic thinking to public affairs in the form of what he called the **policy sciences**.

Lasswell's version of the policy sciences was built around three core elements (deLeon & Martell, 2008). First, policy analysis should be problem-oriented; its goal is not universal and generalizable knowledge, but rather the specific knowledge needed to address a particular problem. Second, because most policy problems have multiple causes and several possible responses, analysis should not be confined to a single discipline like law or economics, but instead, should be broadly multidisciplinary. Third, Lasswell argued that analysis should be explicitly rooted in normative notions of democratic governance.

Lasswell's work started a decades-long debate about contradictions, omissions, and limitations in the concept of the policy sciences. The debate continues today. To maintain the pragmatic focus of this book, I won't describe the ins and outs of these often-theoretical arguments. Instead, I will offer a version of policy analysis that has its roots in the work of both Lasswell and his critics, but which is updated to reflect the practical realities faced by today's working policy analysts.

Fast forward from Lasswell's work in the 1950s to the 2020s: Over 300 colleges and universities now offer master's degrees in public policy or public administration (NASPAA, 2019). Accreditation standards for these programs require that students develop the ability to "analyze, synthesize, think critically, solve problems and make evidence-informed decisions in a complex and dynamic environment" (NASPAA, 2019). Here at the George Washington University, one of the ways we meet this NASPAA standard is with a course simply entitled Policy Analysis.

What's more, virtually every US Federal agency has an internal unit devoted to conducting policy analysis (deLeon, 2006). Friedman calculates that about 440,000 people have been "trained in public policy analytic skills" and are currently using that training in government jobs or the nonprofit or commercial sectors in the United States (2017, p. 11). A Google search for the phrase policy analysis returns 12.30 million results while the same search in the much narrower, academically oriented Google Scholar search engine still yields 1.91 million hits.

Given the ubiquity of the phrase, I want to give you my definition of policy analysis. In doing so, I don't aim to settle debates about what these words should mean. Instead, my goal is simply to create a mutual understanding of what I mean when I refer to policy analysis. The phrase policy analysis comprises two words: policy and analysis. Let's look at each in turn.

What Is Policy?

First, you should recognize that the words *policy, program, activity, function, and project are often used interchangeably* and, at least in the United States, lack formal government-wide definitions (GAO, 2012). In my experience, both scholars and practitioners alike use these words to capture similar meanings but do so inconsistently. To simplify matters, let's focus on only two of these terms: policy and program. You can think of *policy* as a broad construct that describes the basic approach by which we tackle a public problem while *program* is a narrow construct that refers to specific initiatives, projects, and activities through which we implement policy. For example, a school district may have a policy of providing pre-K education to four-year-olds. The program would then be the specific curriculum and mode of delivery. Similarly, the US Navy may have a policy to patrol the Persian Gulf to protect oil tankers while the program would be the deployment of specific numbers and types of vessels and the tactics used.

Next, you should insert the word public before the word policy, meaning that *policy analysis focuses on public policy*. In this book, I'm not talking about policies developed and implemented by private companies, nonprofit institutions, or community or religious groups. While there exists a substantial overlap between the types of techniques we'll discuss in this text and the types of analyses done to support decisions made by these nongovernmental organizations, there are also some important differences. Accordingly, we can deepen our definition of public policy by differentiating the *private* and *public* spheres of human activity.

Let's start with the private sphere. In our lives, we make thousands of decisions about what to do with our time, whether and where to work, how to relate to family, friends, and neighbors, how to express our sense of identity, where to live, if and how to practice a spiritual life, what types of food to eat, what to spend our money on, whether to drive, take the bus, or walk to wherever we're going, and so on. The list of such decisions is literally endless and covers a spectacularly large array of choices we might make. What unites all these decisions, however, is that they are private decisions.

By way of illustration, consider a simple thought experiment. Imagine for a minute a society without public policy. In this imaginary society, we would arrange our lives based solely on choices we make for our families and ourselves. The only commitments and obligations to others would be those that we had entered into voluntarily, based on mutual agreement among the relevant parties.

Of course, in most societies, we don't live in a world without public policy. In the United States, for example, policies emanate from about 90,000 units of government, comprising localities, tribal authorities, states, and the federal government (U.S. Bureau of Census, 2019). The US federal government alone has issued over 186,000 pages of regulation (Regulatory Studies Center, 2019). And when it comes to the states, there are 4.6 million instances of restrictive language in the text of state administrative codes (McLaughlin, Sherouse, Francis, & Nels, 2018). Collectively, the activities of these governments are the essence of public policy, the means by which policy is made tangible in the real world.

The one thing that unites these activities—that is the defining characteristic of **public policy**—is that they represent the *substitution of collective choice for private choice*. For now, we'll set aside questions about how those collective choices are made—whether they're transparent, just, and democratic or opaque, corrupt, and authoritarian—and instead focus on the fact that once collective choice is rendered as public policy, the vast array of private choices to which I alluded earlier are no longer unconstrained. Collective decisions, i.e., public policy, now limit private decisions.

Moreover, the types of constraints created by public policy are different from other constraints we face. Sure, the employers we work for, the schools we attend, the organizations we belong to, and the religious traditions to which we may subscribe all have rules that constrain our behavior. And breaking those rules can have consequences. We can be denied pay raises or be given poor grades. If our breach of the rules is substantial, we can be fired, expelled, or excommunicated. But, for the most part, none of these rules is backed by the power of government to compel certain behaviors.

On the other hand, *public policies rest on the coercive power of the state*. If you don't show up for work, your boss can't order the company's security staff to find you and drag you to your job. On the other hand, if you're summoned for jury duty and fail to appear, in most cases, a judge can issue a bench warrant for your arrest. Similarly, if you tell a charity that you intend to make a $500 donation but then renege, there's not much the charity can do. But try to shortchange the Internal Revenue Service $500 on your income taxes, and you'll find that the money can be taken from your bank account or your paycheck without your consent. In short, it is the ability to use the police powers of government to compel compliance that distinguishes public policy from other efforts to constrain our behavior.

Having defined public policy as *the substitution of collective choice for private choice backed by the coercive power of the state*, we can further deepen our definition by looking at the concrete forms that public policy may take. A number of scholars including Lowi (1972), O'Hare (1989), and Bardach (2016) among others, have developed taxonomies to organize the types of public policies that are available to government decisionmakers.

Consider the eight roles of government shown in Exhibit I-1. These roles are not mutually exclusive; a single policy may span multiple categories. In addition, not all governments undertake policies in all areas and, for those policies that *are* undertaken, successful implementation is often elusive. Finally, bear in mind that depending on your politics and ideological preferences, you might feel that my list includes roles that government ought not play or, conversely, that some of these government activities are absolute necessities. Accordingly, don't look at this list as the set of activities that governments *should* undertake. Rather, think of it as an empirically based menu of activities that at least some governments *do* undertake.

Exhibit I-1   Public Policies Typically Entail One or More of the Following Types of Government Activity

1. Implement infrapolicies to maintain societal systems and facilitate other policies

2. Regulate the behavior of individuals, firms, institutions

3. Provide services

4. Allocate rights to public resources

5. Redistribute wealth and income

6. Levy taxes, spend money, provide subsidies

7. Endeavor to foster economic development

8. Facilitate the flow of information

First, governments **implement infrapolicies that maintain societal systems and facilitate other policies**.[1] Infrapolicies comprise the rules of the game—the foundations upon which other policies rest. Without effective infrapolicies, achieving success with other public policies is much harder. Governments create infrapolicies by, for example, setting and administering property rights, endeavoring to protect civil liberties, maintaining court systems and legislatures, enforcing criminal law and civil court judgments, running elections, punishing corruption among government officials, and engaging in diplomacy with other countries to facilitate international trade and travel and to mitigate conflict. Unfortunately, not all infrapolicies operate in a benign fashion. Though more than a matter of public policy, the systematic mistreatment of

---

[1] My use of the word infrapolicy is inspired by Tassey's definition of an infratechnology as a basic technology without which other technologies would be infeasible (2005).

indigenous peoples and institutionalized racism are examples of how a collection of infrapolicies might become instruments of oppression or disenfranchisement.

Second, governments may **regulate the behavior of individuals, firms, and institutions**. For example, law enforcement officers implement traffic rules, police a variety of violent and nonviolent offenses, and guard the border. Zoning laws dictate what landowners can and cannot do with their property. Corporate behavior may be regulated in diverse areas like wages and working conditions, pollutant emissions, and anticompetitive activity. Sector-specific regulations also abound. Banks are required to maintain certain financial reserves, airlines must meet safety and operating requirements, importers must ensure shipments are free of agricultural pests, and so on.

Third, governments may **provide services** like national defense, education, firefighting, transit, roads and highways, mail delivery, food, shelter, and medical care for the indigent, water and sewage treatment, and so on. Sometimes, responsibility for services is shared across levels of government (e.g., Medicaid, which provides health services to the poor, is a shared state and federal responsibility). Not all services take a tangible form; for example, government may provide flood insurance, student loans, and loan guarantees. Private firms may provide similar services, either under contract to government or as a commercial transaction between two private entities.

Fourth, governments may **allocate rights to public resources**. Governments own, operate, or control a great many resources, from roads and bridges to oil, gas, and coal reserves to forests, fisheries, and public lands. Deciding whether to allow access to these resources, to whom access should be allowed, and on the price to be charged (if any) reflect public policy choices. Examples of policies where government allocates rights to public resources include road congestion pricing (where drivers pay a fee in crowded urban areas at busy times of day), a moratorium on coal mining on Federal land (an Obama administration policy later reversed by President Trump), and deciding whether the Dakota Access Pipeline can cross the Missouri River near the Standing Rock Sioux Reservation.

Fifth, governments may **redistribute wealth and income**. Some policies redistribute resources to the poor in the form of tax credits, free services, or cash transfers. In other cases, middle-income citizens benefit from redistribution, when, for example, the mortgage interest tax deduction reduces taxes for homeowners but not for renters. Wealth can also be redistributed up the income ladder by policies that impose lower tax rates on income from capital (dividends and capital gains) than on income from labor (wages and salaries). Some corporate sectors benefit from policies that protect them from market competition, such as tariffs on imported products. In such cases, redistribution occurs when consumers pay more for goods and services than they otherwise would, to the benefit of firm owners and their employees. Finally, resources may be redistributed from one corporate sector to another by policies that create favorable business conditions for the latter but not the former.

Sixth, governments may **levy taxes, spend money, and provide subsidies** in ways that change the relative costs of activities undertaken by firms, consumers, workers, investors, and other levels of government. Taxes typically finance government operations, while spending in the form of subsidies and tax credits is intended to increase the level of the subsidized activity or to compensate a party, at least partially, for a cost incurred. Decisions about how much tax revenue to raise and the specific activities to be taxed, along with the size and nature of subsidies and tax credits, can be powerful instruments of public policy. Raising taxes on an activity makes it less likely that firms and individuals will engage in that activity, while lowering taxes (or providing subsidies) makes it more likely. For example, a tax on carbon emissions will likely reduce use of fossil fuels while subsidies for solar and wind energy will likely increase use of renewable energy. Finally, intergovernmental grant making is another financing operation through which policy is set. Federal grants to states, for example, often come with strings attached as exemplified by the fact that ten percent of highway funding is withheld from states that don't set their minimum drinking age at 21 years (U.S. Congress, 1984).

Seventh, governments may **endeavor to foster economic development**. Whether it's a stadium for the local sports team, offering tax relief to a firm looking to locate a new facility, or passing trillion-dollar stimulus packages, governments at all levels often enact policies to stimulate (or maintain) private economic activity. Their motivations can be diverse: to expand a tax base to generate government revenue, to support unemployed workers, to redevelop a blighted area, to maintain social stability, or to earn political support from beneficiaries of such policies. At the national level, government uses monetary and fiscal policy to manage inflation, growth, employment, and interest rates. The federal government may also use trade policy to protect domestic industry and workers from foreign competition. In an international context, economic development often entails efforts to help less developed nations enhance human capital, build public infrastructure, and increase economic output.

Eighth, governments may, for a variety of reasons, attempt to **facilitate the flow of information**. Sometimes, the aim is to reduce the risk of a bad outcome. Mandatory product warning labels alert consumers to, for example, the risks of smoking, the dangers of pesticide misuse, and the potential side effects of medications. In other cases, the purpose of additional information is to improve the working of private markets. For example, mandatory efficiency labels (like those that provide the gas mileage of new cars) give buyers access to more information than they otherwise might have at the time of purchase. Regulations requiring plain language disclosures for financial firms issuing credit cards and making loans can help borrowers be better informed before deciding to take on new financial obligations.[2]

---

[2]Government-mandated disclosures are not the only information in the marketplace. A lot of information is conveyed through other channels, like advertising, word of mouth, and third-party services like Consumer Reports or Yelp.

For the sake of brevity, I have described these eight types of government policy in very broad terms. Of course, in reality, when it comes to designing, implementing, and evaluating policy, we need to be more specific. In short, the details matter … a lot. We'll come back to this topic repeatedly throughout the book. But for now, having both developed a working definition of public policy and described a broad menu of the eight forms that policy can take, let's turn to the concept of analysis.

What Is Analysis?

Exhibit I-2 provides the dictionary definition of the word **analysis** which, for our purposes, works quite well.[3] The analytic process entails going beyond the overall appearance of something—in our case, a public policy issue—and digging deeply into the elements that comprise the whole. The original Greek word *analuein*, meaning to unloose, is a particularly apt interpretation of what we aim to do with policy analysis. We're trying to first *break apart* the motivations, assumptions, evidence, and reasoning that lurk beneath the surface of policy debates, *examine* them from a critical, skeptical, and neutral perspective, and then *integrate* what we've learned into a holistic view of things that can be used to improve the quality of the policymaking process.

Exhibit I-2 "Analysis"

Detailed examination of the elements or structure of something, typically as a basis for discussion or interpretation … the process of separating something into its constituent elements. Often contrasted with synthesis …
   ORIGIN late 16th century: via medieval Latin from Greek analusis, from analuein 'unloose,' from ana- 'up' + luein 'loosen.' (The New Oxford American Dictionary, 2001)

Policy analysis is composed of two closely connected intellectual paradigms. The first is *prospective analysis* in which we consider the future consequences of today's decisions. Prospective analysis has the potential to improve the results of these decisions by raising the likelihood of favorable future outcomes and reducing the chances of adverse or unanticipated consequences.[4] The second form of policy analysis is retrospective in nature. *Retrospective analysis* examines the status quo and asks whether existing policies are meeting their original objectives and creating meaningful impacts; this type of analysis may also lead to recommendations for changes in current programs or provide evidence to inform the design of new programs.

---

[3] Other dictionary definitions of analysis related to psychoanalysis, linguistics, and mathematics are omitted.

[4] Later we'll discuss the many obstacles that lay between a well-executed prospective policy analysis and a well-designed, effectively implemented, and successful policy in operation.

Because there isn't a single agreed-upon definition of these two types of analysis, the vocabulary can sometimes be confusing. Analytic work oriented toward the future (i.e., prospective investigation) is often referred to as policy analysis but could just as easily be called decision analysis or program planning. Conversely, work examining the status quo (i.e., retrospective investigation) is routinely referred to as program evaluation but could also be called impact evaluation, program analysis, or even policy evaluation. To keep it simple, you can think about two types of analysis: retrospective and prospective.

Whether retrospective or prospective in nature, policy analysis aims to articulate the pros and cons of alternative answers to the question 'What should we do next?' In this context, before policymakers who have the power and authority to make public policy decide how to proceed, they often but not always want to consider the wisdom, desirability, and impacts of the choices before them. And even if policymakers are indifferent to the consequences of their decisions, members of society who will experience those consequences—positive and negative—have a vested interest in ensuring that their concerns, preferences, and points of view are well understood during the policymaking process.

Put more formally, **policy analysis** is the *consideration of available evidence, coupled with well-reasoned inferences, to illuminate trade-offs among available choices for exercising government power*. There is a lot packed into this definition and, in the next two chapters, we'll go over it in detail. For now, just keep in mind that the basic rationale behind policy analysis is that it can facilitate better decisions and more effective policies than an alternative approach in which we ignore evidence about the results of existing programs, fail to verify the logic behind claims made during policy debates, and neglect to consider the potential pros, cons, and trade-offs of new policies.

While policy analysis can bring clarity to a complicated world and help policymakers better understand the consequences of their choices, it lacks the precision of fields like engineering, math, and the natural sciences. In particular, policy analysis often requires the ability to *imagine* alternative states of the world. The impacts of an existing policy, or the costs and benefits of a potential new policy, for example, cannot be assessed in isolation. We're usually interested in two situations—one with and one without the policy we're analyzing. If, for example, we're evaluating the impact of a government program, it's not enough to study the details of its operations and describe its results. To know whether the program is making a difference, we also have to consider how things would have turned out in the absence of the program (i.e., an imagined state of the world); only then can we isolate the program's impact.

With retrospective analysis, we at least have the luxury of knowing that one of the two states of the world we're comparing actually exists. We have a historical record of what really happened with the existing program, meaning that we only need to imagine one world—a past without the program. Prospective policy analysis is more demanding because it calls on us to imagine not just one world that doesn't yet exist, but two such worlds. We need to consider a future world with the policy under analysis *and* a future world without that policy. Both are a matter of projection.

This process of conjuring and characterizing worlds that do not exist is an integral part of policy analysis and is responsible for many of its challenges. Definitive information about conjured worlds, of course, does not exist. Even current conditions that exist in reality may not be well understood or may have been subjected to insufficient study to allow the policy analyst to draw definitive conclusions. Moreover, given the constraints of the policymaking process, there may not be enough time or resources to gather more information about the status quo or to develop more precise projections of the future. In short, uncertainty about current conditions and about imagined states of the world is an intrinsic and inescapable feature of policy analysis.[5] We'll talk more about such issues later in the book.

What Role Does the Client Play in Policy Analysis?

A definition of policy analysis would be incomplete without a discussion of the **client**. As mentioned above, policy analysis aims to illuminate potential answers to the core question 'what do we do next?' Accordingly, policy analysis is inherently associated with a decisionmaking process, and perhaps more importantly, with a decision-*maker*. The use of the pronoun *we* in the core question is what I'm talking about here. To be clear, however, 'we' doesn't necessarily refer to a particular person of authority, deliberative body, or government agency (though it often does), it could also refer to 'we the people' who, as a community are trying to decide what to do next (Stone, 2012).

Think of the client as the ultimate audience for the policy analyst's work. If your boss is a decisionmaker, then your client is likely your boss. But often the client—the audience for your analysis—is outside your immediate organization. You might be employed by an agency like the California Legislative Analyst's Office whose work usually treats the state legislature writ large as its client. Sometimes, you have two clients. For example, you might work for a political interest group advocating a particular point of view. Your boss is one client, and the policymaker(s) that the group aspires to influence are another. Alternatively, you could be an academic or public intellectual writing op eds or posting to social media in an effort to inform and perhaps influence the governmental policymaking process. In such cases, the analyst doesn't have a personal relationship with the client, but instead relies on the media to transmit their advice to the client.

I think about it this way: If your work is meant to directly inform a pending decision about public policy, then it meets the definition of policy analysis. And if there's a decision to be made, then you should be able to figure out who the decisionmaker is. In the vocabulary of this book, the audience for your work is your client.

---

[5]Learning to be comfortable with uncertainty and ambiguity is a key step in becoming a professional policy analyst. If you don't think you can do so, then you may want to consider a different career. Seriously.

If you can't envision a client, then it's not policy analysis. Instead, it is more likely to be policy research.

What Is the Difference between Policy Analysis and Policy Research?

You can think of **policy research** as a deep dive into one, or a few, aspects of a particular policy issue. A policy researcher aspires to apply sophisticated analyses to carefully collected evidence to characterize policy-relevant phenomena and the causal connections among them. Policy analysis and policy research have a lot in common and often focus on the same types of issues. But policy analysis faces constraints that often don't affect policy research. For example, policy analysis is linked to a particular policy decision whereas policy research often occurs in a scholarly setting farther removed from the policymaking process. Moreover, policy analysis is, of necessity, holistic in nature, trying to reflect all decision-relevant factors in a single effort while policy research is more granular, trying to develop the best, most credible, characterization of one, or at most a few, decision-relevant factors.

Because policy analysis is directly linked to real-world decisionmaking, the *schedule for doing policy analysis is usually set not by the analyst but by the demands of the decisionmaking process.* In contrast, policy researchers typically set their own schedules. Work is complete when the scholar becomes confident that a valid answer to a research question has been derived. Not so for policy analysts. If, for example, a vote on a new ordinance will be taken by the city council on Friday, then a policy analysis delivered the following Monday can't inform the decision. In short, policy analysis has to be delivered on a schedule that works for the decisionmaking process, not the other way around.

In addition, the principles of academic freedom typically mean that policy scholars get to call the shots with respect to their own research. Yes, they often have to find grant funding, but the ultimate authority to decide on research questions, data sources, methodology, and the interpretation of findings rests with the researcher. The life of a policy analyst is not so free. With a client to serve, policy analysts operate in a more constrained environment. Limitations on the subject of the analyst's work, the set of policy options to be evaluated, the nature of evidence deemed credible, the types of arguments considered persuasive, and the interpretation of results are just a few examples of the constraints faced by policy analysts that are usually not encountered by academic scholars.

Policy analysis often relies heavily on the results of policy research, and on the work of other disciplines like microeconomics, political science, law, and data analytics. These disciplines inform policy analysis but are not themselves policy analysis. Don't get me wrong. Just because your work doesn't meet my definition of policy analysis, that doesn't mean it isn't vitally important.[6]

---

[6]I once had a professor who memorably told us: "It's a free country. Believe whatever you want." I appreciated his willingness to argue for his own point of view, while making it easy to disagree.

To recap, public policy is the substitution of collective choice for private choice, backed by the coercive power of the state, while policy analysis is the consideration of available evidence, coupled with well-reasoned inferences, to illuminate trade-offs among available choices for exercising government power. The key constraints on policy analysis, especially in contrast to policy research, are that it exists in the context of a policy decision, that the needs and preferences of a client have a profound effect on the structure and nature of the work, and that it must accommodate tight schedules, information gaps, and other resource constraints.

Having reviewed the definitions of public policy and of policy analysis that shape the book to come, we turn now to the three chapters that comprise Part I of the book. Chapter 1 describes the classical model of prospective policy analysis, while Chapter 2 does the same thing for retrospective program evaluation. Chapter 3 then describes the intrinsic limitations of these two models as a preface to the subsequent twelve chapters, in which I attempt to address these limitations and provide practical solutions for successfully navigating them.

CHAPTER ONE

THINKING ABOUT THE FUTURE
Prospective Policy Analysis

The classical model of prospective policy analysis is traditionally presented as a linear process in which you work through a series of analytic steps that lead you to a policy recommendation for addressing the problem at hand. In Chapter 3, you will see that this model has several shortcomings that limit its applicability, one of which is that policy analysis rarely proceeds in a linear fashion. Nonetheless, as an aspiring policy analyst, you need to master this model and understand the logic upon which it was built. Despite its flaws, the model is a powerful tool for clarifying messy and confusing policy debates. It also reflects the kinds of careful and disciplined thinking that is a prerequisite for success as a policy analyst. Although you'll find variations in the literature (Bardach & Patashnik, 2016; Patton, Sawicki, & Clark, 2013; Stone, 2012; Weimer & Vining, 2017), the classical model is usually built on the six steps listed in Exhibit 1-1. Each subsection of this chapter corresponds to one of these steps and later chapters of the book take a deeper dive into several of the steps.

Exhibit 1-1   Steps in Prospective Policy Analysis

1. Characterize the Policy Problem
2. Specify Policy Alternatives
3. Identify Evaluation Criteria
4. Create a Criteria-Alternatives Matrix and Predict Performance of Alternatives
5. Analyze Trade-offs Across Alternatives
6. Communicate Results

Learning Objectives

By studying this chapter, you should be able to:

- Describe the sequential approach to policy analysis in classical models of prospective policy analysis.

- Define a policy problem as a gap between a descriptive, as-is, condition and a normative, to-be, condition.

- Create policy alternatives that are actionable, detailed, realistic, and matched to the problem at hand and its context.

- Identify evaluation criteria that surface all of the important pros and cons of all policy alternatives being considered.

- Predict the performance of each alternative with respect to each criterion, and summarize the results in a criteria-alternatives matrix.

- Characterize the trade-offs across alternatives using cost–benefit, cost-effectiveness, multiattribute analysis, or narrative prose.

- Describe some key features of policy writing and communication.

1.1 CHARACTERIZE THE PROBLEM

The point of departure in classical policy analysis is the **problem definition**.[1] The basic idea is that before we can discuss the pros and cons of different policy options, we need a clear understanding of exactly the problem we're trying to address.

Imagine a debate about building a new community recreation center. Planners have rolled out the design. It's expensive but packed with features that the community has asked for—a pool, basketball courts open late at night, a running track, and a weight room. One group of residents is adamantly opposed to the project while its supporters are equally fervent. The opposition claims that the costly new center is just another example of the tax-and-spend attitude of unelected bureaucrats. Some proponents don't care much about the center's expensive features but really want to make sure teenagers have a supervised place to hang out in the evening. On the other hand, fitness buffs aren't really worried about the teenagers but want a high-quality and free alternative to a commercial gym.

As you try to make sense of this debate, you begin to realize that these advocates are coming from very different places. Before the community can decide what to do, it has to figure out what it's actually trying to accomplish. Is the problem a lack of safe spaces for teenagers? Or is it that the community doesn't offer residents affordable opportunities for health and fitness? Or might it be that there are other pressing community needs on which the money would be better spent? Depending on the answers, the appropriate policies may differ radically.

Starting your policy analysis with a problem definition is intended to give you an intellectual destination, namely, the best way of approaching the problem at hand. If it helps, think of it as your North Star; you can use it to navigate your way through the policy analysis. Doing so will help you avoid the quandary faced by Alice in Wonderland when she went down the Rabbit Hole:

> Alice: Would you tell me, please, which way I ought to go from here?
> The Cheshire Cat: That depends a good deal on where you want to get to.
> Alice: I don't much care where.
> The Cheshire Cat: Then it doesn't much matter which way you go.
> (Carroll, 1865)

Without a crystal-clear problem definition, like Alice, your policy analysis will begin to wander aimlessly as you get distracted by all the things that *might* be relevant.

---

[1]Most versions of the classical model don't provide much guidance about the process of deciding which specific policy problems deserve our attention in the first place.

So, let's drill down on this idea. What, exactly, is a policy problem? The word problem implies that something is amiss, that the current state of affairs—the status quo—is somehow not what it should be. Maybe, for example, our military is not properly equipped for the threats it's been asked to address.

Regardless of the issue, all well-reasoned claims about a policy problem comprise two elements. The first element of a policy problem is an assertion about the status quo, a descriptive statement about the **as-is condition**. When it comes to the readiness of the military, the descriptive as-is condition might be characterized in terms of the types of threats from enemy actors, the dangers posed by those threats, and the capability of existing military technology and tactics to neutralize them.

By itself, however, a descriptive as-is statement about the status quo is insufficient to fully define a policy problem. We need a second ingredient: a normative, **to-be condition**. This element of a policy problem is normative because it embeds a value judgment, not about what the world currently *does* look like, but about what it *should* or *ought to* look like. Military readiness is a policy problem only if we think that our military *should* be stronger than it currently is. If we find the status quo—the current state of affairs—normatively acceptable, then we don't have a policy problem.

This leads us to a working definition: *A policy problem exists when there is a gap between the descriptive as-is condition that exists now and a normative to-be condition that we believe ought to exist in the future*. Keep in mind that these gaps can take on different forms. It might be that the status quo is horrendous, but we can imagine ameliorating its worst features even though we can't quite envision attaining a trouble-free to-be condition. Alternatively, the status quo could be working reasonably well, but opportunities for further improvement might be within easy reach.

Accordingly, your first task is to *come up with a clear problem definition* that reflects a gap between the as-is and to-be conditions. But be careful about locking on to a specific formulation of the problem until you've done sufficient research to understand whether your first intuitions were right. It's a lot like trying on clothes in a store; something might look good on the mannequin, but you don't want to hand over your debit card until you're sure it looks good on you. Similarly, policy analysis is a highly iterative process, and you should become comfortable with the process of trying on and discarding multiple versions of the problem definition until you're confident that you've got it right.

Another word of advice: *Don't embed an implicit solution* into the problem definition. For example, if you define the problem along the lines of "there are too few homeless shelters," you are unnecessarily steering the analysis toward the foregone conclusion that we should build more shelters. A more neutral problem definition—"there are too many homeless persons"—opens up the conversation in ways that let you consider a broader, and potentially more effective, set of approaches to the problem.

Moreover, you'll need to *decide who has standing* to be considered in your analysis. Standing defines the people, institutions, and groups whose problems, concerns, and experiences are deemed relevant to the analysis. If you're studying homelessness, for example, you'll need to decide on your geographic scope. You could focus on one neighborhood, the whole city, or an entire metro area. In short, standing delineates the scope of the problem definition. The condition of folks without standing is irrelevant to your analysis whereas folks with standing are at the center of your work.

To develop your problem definition, start with some *context*. Is this a big problem, affecting many people or wasting a lot of time, money, or resources, or is it a small problem? When did the problem first arise? Did it just pop up, or has it been around for as long as anyone can remember? Is the problem getting better or worse over time? How does the nature and structure of the problem *here* compare to the problem *there*, in the next town, state, or region? Have we tried to solve this problem before? If so, why are we unhappy with that solution? What went wrong?

Once you've characterized the context of the problem and decided who has standing, you're ready to move on to **causal reasoning**. The rationale for doing so is that before you tackle a problem, it's best to understand why the problem is occurring in the first place. Think about a doctor who sees a patient with symptoms that could be caused by two different maladies, each with its own treatment. Misidentifying the cause of the symptoms will lead to the wrong treatment. So too with policy problems.

How do you go about figuring out the causal drivers of the problem that concerns you? In my class, I talk about Taiichi Ohno and the Toyota Production System he helped develop in the 1950s. Mr. Ohno was well known for his work to improve the quality and efficiency of Toyota's auto manufacturing plans (Card, 2017). In particular, he is credited for developing the **Five Whys** approach to problem diagnosis. Take a look at Exhibit 1-2, which depicts the process of figuring out production problems on a factory assembly line. When a problem is detected, we don't settle for the first explanation of its cause, but dig deeper to get closer to the root cause of the problem. Every time we get an answer to the question of why a driver of a problem exists, we ask why *that* driver exists. The rationale for doing so is that addressing the underlying drivers of a problem increases the chances of successfully mitigating the problem. In the simple example depicted in Exhibit 1-2, each cause produces one effect, and each effect subsequently causes one consequence. In Chapter 12, we'll look at more sophisticated ways of simultaneously considering the interaction of multiple causes and effects.

An example may help here. I live in Northern Virginia, in the suburbs of Washington, DC. Many jurisdictions in the area are struggling with the loss of affordable housing. Long-term, low- and middle-income residents are moving out of the area to more affordable locations. Amazon's recent decision to locate its second headquarters in the area has heightened concern about the cost of housing (Lytle, 2019). Imagine you're working for a local or state policymaker who thinks that the loss of affordable housing is a serious problem worthy of policy action. She asks you to suggest some policy options.

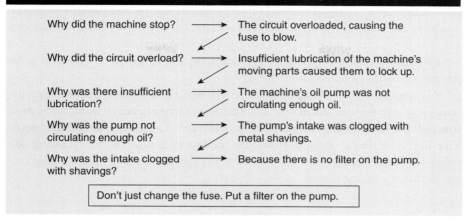

Exhibit 1-2   Diagnosing Causality: The "Five Whys" at Toyota

Why did the machine stop? → The circuit overloaded, causing the fuse to blow.

Why did the circuit overload? → Insufficient lubrication of the machine's moving parts caused them to lock up.

Why was there insufficient lubrication? → The machine's oil pump was not circulating enough oil.

Why was the pump not circulating enough oil? → The pump's intake was clogged with metal shavings.

Why was the intake clogged with shavings? → Because there is no filter on the pump.

Don't just change the fuse. Put a filter on the pump.

Source: Adapted from Toyota Motor Asia Pacific Pte Ltd, 2006

Before you can do so, however, you need greater clarity on the cause of the problem. Perhaps it's an influx of highly paid workers who have moved into the area for its amenities (parks, schools, nightlife) and are willing to pay much higher rents than current residents. Maybe its profit-seeking developers who have built high-end apartments and condominiums close to the area's subway stations. It could be that existing zoning rules strongly favor low density development in most areas; it could also be that many neighborhoods are fully 'built-out' with virtually no open land on which more housing could be built. Perhaps it's cold-hearted employers who refuse to pay low-skill labor a living wage. Depending on what's causing the problem, the preferred policy option is likely to differ.

Let's imagine that with sufficient research and careful thinking, you develop a solid understanding of the causal drivers of the problem. You're not done with the problem definition, however, until you can articulate the consequences of the problem. In policy analysis, *characterizing the effects of a policy problem is as important as identifying its causes*. Why? Because the consequences of the problem are what motivate citizens and policymakers to 'care' about the problem. Identifying the specific effects of a problem may also point the way to policy alternatives which, while they don't eliminate the problem, might mitigate its impacts. The doctor may not be able to cure you of the cold virus you've come down with, but she can treat your symptoms with, say, a cough suppressant and a decongestant.

Let's return to our example of affordable housing in Northern Virginia. Rather than applying the Five Whys approach, you can use what I call the **Five So-Whats** method. Housing has become unaffordable. So what? We might think it's just wrong to force out long-time residents, and we want our elected officials to do something about it. Maybe folks who play a key role in society—nurses, teachers, fire fighters, and police officers—can't afford to live in the community they serve. Perhaps employers won't be able to find the workers they need for lower-paid jobs like hotel housekeepers, landscapers, day care staff, and fast-food workers. Maybe the number of homeless people living on the street will increase, creating a moral quandary and a jump in the demand for social services.

Having articulated a gap between the as-is and to-be conditions, asked *why* five times, and asked *so-what* five times, you undoubtedly have uncovered a great deal of material that could be relevant to the policy problem of interest. What should you do with all this stuff? A good test of whether you have a sufficient understanding of a policy problem is to try to write a *succinct problem definition* of only two to three sentences that does three things:

- Describes the *most important causes* of the problem, typically in just a few words each,
- Articulates the *core problem that arises from the gap* between the as-is and to-be conditions, without getting bogged down in details, and
- Identifies the *most important consequences*, again in just a few words each.

One formulation of a problem definition for our unaffordable Northern Virginia city might look something like this:

Increases in the number of highly paid workers throughout the region, improved community amenities for residents, zoning rules that limit housing density, and static wages for low-skill jobs have caused a continuing loss of affordable housing in the area. Consequently, there has been a spike in homelessness, displacement of long-time residents, and an inability for public servants and low-skill workers to live in the communities they serve.

Notice how we move progressively along a chain of causation. We start with the drivers of the problem, move on to articulate the core problem, and conclude with the major consequences of concern. To link back to our earlier discussion, this progression is created first by asking "why?" several times, then articulating the gap between the descriptive as-is and the normative to-be conditions, and finally by asking "so what?" several times.

For practice, try crafting a problem definition for an issue you care deeply about. Try to copy the style of the example above. Really, take out a piece of paper and give it a try. I'll wait.

Now look at what you've written and ask two questions. First, do you suspect all of the statements are likely true? Don't worry if you're not 100% sure; after all, at this point, you haven't yet done your analysis. Second, do you your words capture the most important aspects of the causes and consequences of the problem? If the tentative answer to both questions is yes, then you have a workable problem definition upon which to base the rest of your analysis. If not, you need to go back and, perhaps repeatedly, revise your problem definition until you *can* answer yes to both questions. Remember, the problem definition is the foundation upon which your analysis will be built. If your problem definition is flawed, then the quality of your subsequent analytic work will suffer.

The final task in the problem definition process is to select the potential **point(s) for policy intervention**. Will you try to attack the root causes of the problem or focus on treating its symptoms? If the former, will you tackle all of the causes of the problem, or just one or two? If the latter, which of the problem's consequences will get your attention? There is no right answer here, but these questions must be asked and answered before you move forward with your policy analysis. Aaron Wildavsky (1979), the founding Dean of what is now the Goldman School of Public Policy at UC Berkeley, offers some advice:

> Policy analysis is an art [and] must create problems that decision-makers are
> able to handle with the variables under their control and in the time available.
> … Policy analysis, to be brief, is an activity creating problems that can be
> solved. (pp. 15–17)

Putting Wildavsky's advice into practice requires you to think about your client—the policymaker—and consider their *legal authority*, *political power*, *and ability to command resources* when you are deciding where to target your policy interventions. You should also think about how quickly you need to come up with potential responses to the problem. Do you have two weeks, two months, or two years? If you have limited time and resources, you might choose to work on only one aspect of the problem. If you have a lot of time and resources, you might go for more fundamental reforms that tackle the problem's underlying root causes.

1.2 SPECIFY POLICY ALTERNATIVES THAT MIGHT MITIGATE THE PROBLEM

With a solid understanding of the policy problem you hope to address, it's time to start thinking about policy options that deserve consideration as potential approaches to the problem. Let's start with Exhibit 1-3 and the characteristics of policy alternatives that facilitate further analysis.

Exhibit 1-3   Characteristics of a Strong Policy Option

1. Actionable

2. Described in detail

3. Matched to problem and context

4. Described, not evaluated

5. Not a dummy alternative

First, a policy option needs to be *actionable*. An aspirational statement along the lines of 'parents should read more to their kids so they will do better in school' is not an actionable policy option. A reasonable alternative might be something like 'hold Saturday morning workshops for parents at local libraries and teach kids how to use the library.' In short, we must be able to imagine that the policy can be turned into a concrete and tangible statement of how it would work.

Second, each policy alternative should be *specified in enough detail* so that it's possible to project the consequences of its adoption. Imagine we are considering a policy to end incarceration of nonviolent drug offenders. Are we talking about changing sentencing guidelines so that fewer people go to prison in the first place? Or about releasing folks currently in prison; if so, what are the criteria for who is to be released? What services, if any, will be offered to facilitate prisoners' return to their communities? Are we talking about Federal, state, or local prisons? I could go on with more questions, but the point should be clear: Vague and ambiguous language now—while specifying policy alternatives—will come back to haunt us later when we're try to figure out the pros and cons, and the costs and impacts of the policy alternatives that we are evaluating.

Third, *match the policy alternatives to the problem* at hand and the *context in which solutions will be attempted*. Imagine you work for the city manager who, in consultation with the Fire Chief, has determined that for budgetary reasons, one of the city's five fire stations must be closed. In this case, the set of options has been predetermined for you: Close station 1, 2, 3, 4, or 5. While you might ask your boss and the Chief if they'd like you to consider other ways of closing the budget gap, if their answer is no, then you're done with the process of specifying policy alternatives. As you finalize your list of alternatives, inject a *dose of pragmatism*. Your options need to be within the power your client has (or aspires to have), come with a price tag that is in the realm of the possible, and comply with relevant constitutional or statutory constraints.

Fourth, your goal—at this point in the analysis—is simply to *describe the policy alternative, not evaluate it*. Novice policy analysts often find it difficult to follow this advice. Consider this policy alternative: "The Federal government will levy an excise tax of $5 per ton on coal used by electric power plants so that emissions of greenhouse gases will fall." The first part of the sentence is fine; the policy is specific and actionable. The trouble comes with the second part of the sentence, which makes a causal claim about the effect of the tax. Yes, the *rationale* for the policy *is* to decrease emissions, but at this point in the process, we have yet to actually do the work to predict the impact of the tax. Our subsequent analysis might reveal that a $5 tax is too low to have a material effect on emissions.

Finally, *stay away from dummy alternatives*. A dummy option is a policy option that you know to be deeply flawed; yet, you include it anyway. Sometimes, such options are referred to as straw men because they are easily knocked down. Why might you be tempted to include a straw man option in your analysis? Sometimes, before you even begin the analysis, you already have a favorite option that you think is best suited to addressing the policy problem at hand. By comparison, a dummy option can make your option appear stronger. Until you actually do your analysis, however, you do not have a basis for having a definitive opinion. To be blunt: If you already know the answer, why are you wasting time and resources doing an analysis to reach a foregone conclusion?

Once you've assembled your list of alternatives, you will usually want to add one more option: *continue current policies*. As bad as current conditions are, there might not be any policy intervention that would appreciably improve the situation. Failure to consider the option of leaving existing policies unchanged creates an inappropriate bias for action. In other words, if maintaining the status quo is omitted from the analysis, you run the risk of deciding on an option that actually makes matters worse. The only exception to the rule is when you're told that *something* must be done. In this case, inaction is not an option. This can happen for political reasons; perhaps your boss is loath to be perceived as uncaring, indecisive, or unable to tackle problems. Other times, you're handed a constrained problem definition, like which of the five fire stations should be closed. In such cases, there's no need for a current policy option because business as usual is not a choice.

Exhibit 1-4 shows a hypothetical set of options that might be used in an analysis of our illustrative Northern Virginia affordable housing situation. Let's assume that our client is the city manager, so we are interested only in policies that can be implemented at the local level. We give each alternative a short name to help us keep track of it in our subsequent analysis and then succinctly describe its key features.

Current Policy: Under this option, the city would not change existing policy. Zoning regulations would remain unchanged. Rents and home prices would be dictated only by market forces, or by policies implemented by other levels of government.

Rent Control: Under this option, landlords would be prohibited from raising rents faster than the cost-of-living. Conversions from rental housing to individually owned units would be banned.

Public Housing: Under this option, the city would build and operate three low-rise apartment complexes in separate neighborhoods, comprised of two- and three-bedroom units suitable for families. Rents would be permanently limited to no more than 30% of the median family income for the city. A total of 500 units would be constructed.

Vouchers: Under this option, the city would issue vouchers to families with incomes below three times the poverty level. Vouchers would have a value of $1,000 per month and could be applied to the rent on any residential property in the city. Landlords would redeem vouchers for cash.

Developer Regulations: Under this option, zoning regulations would require that all new multiunit residential rental buildings set aside 25% of the units as affordable. Rents would be permanently limited to no more than 30% of the median family income for the city.

Your goal is to have four to seven alternatives. Including three or fewer options is probably a sign that you're not being expansive enough in your thinking about how to approach the problem. More than seven and you risk analytic overload, trying to cover too much terrain in a single project. It's also ideal to have policy alternatives are distinctly different from, rather than slight variations of, each other. The idea is to creatively consider a conceptually wide range of options. All this notwithstanding, if there are only a couple of options with any prospect of being adopted, or if your client instructs you to focus on a particular option, then you should do whatever the situation requires rather than heeding my advice!

1.3 IDENTIFY CRITERIA FOR EVALUATING ALTERNATIVES

Virtually *all policy options have both pros and cons*. If someone tells you that they've found a policy that doesn't—all upside and no downside—you should treat their claim with deep skepticism. Ask them how it's possible that their amazingly great option has not already been adopted (Bardach & Patashnik, 2016). An honest answer to your question will undoubtedly reveal someone—people, institutions, firms, or politicians—who prefer the status quo to the proposed policy. And therein lies at least one downside of the proposed policy, the need to use the coercive power of public policy to override preferences of proponents of the status quo (while you may not see doing so as a problem, rest assured that the parties on the receiving end of the coercion will).

Here's another way to think about it: *By choosing one policy option over another, we experience the pros and cons of the selected option and forego the pros and cons of the other, unselected, option.* Consider a simple example. Imagine a pre-K program (like Head Start) that a large school district is thinking about adopting. It's been proven very effective but has a high cost per pupil. The School Board could roll out the program district wide for 6,000 students at a cost of $30 million or it could offer the program to only 2,000 students at low-performing schools for $10 million. The first option helps a lot more students (a pro), but at a higher cost (a con), than does the less costly (a pro) second option which helps fewer students (a con). On the other hand, the second option addresses those most in need of help (a pro for those lucky enough to get into the program, but a con for those who don't).

Most situations are not so simple. Without some sort of organizing framework, keeping track of all the pros and cons of multiple complex policy proposals can be very difficult, especially during heated debates. This challenge was well articulated by Benjamin Franklin two and a half centuries ago:

> When these difficult Cases occur, they are difficult chiefly because while we have them under Consideration all the Reasons pro and con are not present to the Mind at the same time; but sometimes one Set present themselves, and at other times another, the first being out of Sight. Hence the various Purposes or Inclinations that alternately prevail, and the Uncertainty that perplexes us. (Franklin, 1772)

The classical model of policy analysis has a practical suggestion for Mr. Franklin: the *systematic application of a set of evaluation criteria to each policy option* under consideration. Think of criteria as "mental standards for evaluating the results of action" (Bardach & Patashnik, 2016, p. 45). Applying each criterion—in the same way, with the same method—to each alternative ensures that we use an intellectually consistent approach to evaluate the alternatives against a common set of benchmarks. Evaluation criteria also give us a way to discipline our personal preferences. If we're already inclined toward or away from one of the options, systematically taking a hard look at each alternative in light of each criterion may help us control our own biases.

It's one thing to say that systematic application of evaluation criteria will help us keep track of pros and cons. It's another to explain where evaluation criteria come from, particularly in light of Nienaber and Wildavsky's wry observation that evaluation criteria "invariably may be distinguished by three outstanding qualities: they are multiple, conflicting, and vague. They mirror, in other words, the complexity and ambivalence of human social behavior" (1973, p. 10). What follows below is my advice about developing evaluation criteria.

While the set of relevant criteria will vary from analysis to analysis, four evaluation criteria should be considered for inclusion in all policy analyses. I think of them as **off-the-shelf criteria** because once you master them, you can insert them in any analysis and in doing so, quickly jumpstart the process of getting your policy analysis sorted out. The four criteria are efficacy, cost, equity, and administrability. Let's look at each one in turn.

The first off-the-shelf criterion is **efficacy**, which means the degree to which the policy alternative is likely to mitigate the core policy problem. To be more specific, an efficacy-based criterion captures the extent to which adoption of a policy alternative might narrow the gap between the descriptive as-is and the normative to-be conditions. You probably won't use the word efficacy in your criterion; rather, you should aim for a more intuitive phrase. If the core problem is lack of community mental health services, for example, then an efficacy-based criterion might read, "maximize the number of mental health practitioners." It's also possible to have more than one efficacy-based criterion. For example, you might add a second criterion—"maximize the number of spaces in in-patient mental health facilities"—to get at another aspect of the problem.

The second off-the-shelf criterion is **cost**, which is often broken into two subcriteria: cost to the government and cost to nongovernmental parties. Governmental costs matter because policymakers are invariably allocating a limited budget across a number of competing priorities. Predicting government costs under alternative policies is usually a conceptually straightforward process: figure out the scope and magnitude of the activities that government will undertake and put a price tag on each.

Nongovernmental costs comprise two components. First, there may be **direct costs** paid by consumers, workers, firms, and institutions as a consequence of the policy. Second, there may be **indirect opportunity costs** experienced by these groups when policy limits their ability to engage in an activity to the same extent as they otherwise would in the absence of the policy. Even though they don't directly affect the public treasury, nongovernmental costs are important in policymaking because they are typically incurred by the constituents of those making policy decisions.

While important, nongovernmental costs can get tricky to calculate. If we compel a firm to install a $1 million pollution control device, for instance, we might be tempted to tally the cost at $1 million but doing so would not capture the full cost. The cost of production will go up for the directly regulated firm and its production will likely drop somewhat, thereby costing the firm the returns it would have earned on those lost sales and depriving customers of the value they would have received from consuming those additional units of production. We also need to consider the value of the environmental benefit created by the pollution reduction. In short, we have to take care to count all costs, avoid double counting, and compute only net costs when we're assessing policy alternatives. Microeconomists have developed sophisticated ways of sorting out these issues (with a technique called cost–benefit analysis, or CBA); we'll touch on CBA later in this chapter and take a close look at it in Chapter 9.

The third off-the-shelf criterion is **equity**. The term equity is a container for several related concepts like equality, liberty, justice, and security (Stone, 2012). As you develop criteria related to equity, you may want to start with a series of questions like the following, which are adapted from Stone's work, to stimulate your thinking.

- *Rights and Duties:* What demands can a person legitimately make of other people or of society in general? What obligations legitimately bind people to act on behalf of others?

- *Equality:* To what degree do people enjoy equal opportunities? Can inequality of results be satisfactorily explained?

- *Liberty:* To what degree are individual liberties unnecessarily limited? Is the power of governments, firms, and institutions appropriately limited?

- *Justice:* Are people treated fairly by governments and institutions? To what degree is there meaningful participation in collective decision-making?

- *Stability, Security, and Safety:* Are important social systems reasonably stable or are they changing rapidly in disruptive ways? Are people secure in their economic situation with resources to cover the costs of daily life? Do people enjoy physical and emotional safety?

As you develop answers to these questions and ponder their relevance to your analysis, you'll need to convert them into the form of evaluation criteria, along the lines of 'minimize racial disparities in criminal sentencing,' 'maximize freedom of landowners to develop their property as they choose,' or 'ensure that all workers receive a living wage.' We'll take a deep dive into the process of applying normative thinking to policy analysis in Chapter 8.

The final off-the-shelf criterion is **administrability**. Here, our focus is on the ease with which a particular policy can be readily implemented in the real world. Why focus on administrability? Simple: words on a page don't matter. We only reap the benefits of programs that are successfully implemented. Similarly, good intentions don't matter; if a program has a convoluted, hard-to-understand structure, requires sophisticated expertise, is intolerant of small mistakes, or makes unrealistic assumptions about folks' ability to implement it, the program will likely fail to deliver all of the hoped-for positive outcomes.

Logic and experience suggest that big, complex programs are harder to administer than are small, straightforward programs. Think also about which agencies and levels of government will be involved in implementation. A program under the control of a single entity within one level of government will be easier to administer than one where staffing, budget, and authority are spread across multiple agencies at the Federal, state, or local levels, and perhaps also to nonprofit organizations. You'll also need to think about whether agencies charged with implementation responsibilities have the staff skills, physical infrastructure, and requisite budget to successfully execute the tasks they've been given. Finally, consider whether the program structure allows for continuous improvement so that managers can try different approaches, keeping what works and discarding what doesn't. Such a program will be easier to administer than one where policymakers have set a rigid structure and made it very hard to adjust the program without going all the way back through the policymaking process.

You'll note that there is one potential criterion—maximize political feasibility—that doesn't make my list of off-the-shelf criteria. That doesn't mean that politics is irrelevant to policy analysis. To the contrary, very few polities are put in place except as the result of a political process (Eggers & O'Leary, 2009; Mead, 2013). It's just that *doing a good job of political analysis within policy analysis is almost impossible*. There are at least two reasons why this is true.

First, political bargaining about policy adoption doesn't always follow a predictable pattern. You might think a particular policy option simply isn't politically feasible, but behind closed doors, one vote may be traded for another and suddenly the option becomes viable. As former Congressman Barney Frank put it "The key to understanding deal making in Congress is to remember that the ankle bone is connected to the shoulder bone. Anything can be the basis of a deal" (Binder & Lee, 2015, p. 246).

Second, the politics behind a policy may change not only because of deal making among politicians but because of persuasive policy arguments, coupled with an effective lobbying campaign by the policy's proponents (and perhaps an ineffective campaign by its opponents). In other words, even though your initial appraisal of a promising policy option might be that it's politically infeasible, it could gain political support over time as its merits become apparent to larger and more powerful audiences (rendering your initial judgment incorrect). Conversely, a policy proposal that initially enjoys strong political support may be subjected to relentless attacks by its opponents and become politically infeasible over time. The bottom line? The political feasibility of a particular policy option is a dynamic and fluid concept that can be very hard to capture in a policy analysis.

What's more, an overemphasis on what is politically feasible may distort the analytic process. *Just because a policy is politically popular, that doesn't make it a good idea; likewise, just because a policy option lacks political support, that doesn't make it a bad idea.* In short, adding political feasibility as an evaluation criterion may bias your analysis toward popular policies and away from unpopular policies that are strong on their merits.

Mead suggests a way out of this dilemma. He recommends that, initially, politics be left out of policy analyses so that options can be judged solely on the basis of their intrinsic pros and cons. After identifying the most promising policy option, the policy analyst then investigates how the political world might react to that option. If the reaction is likely positive, great! If not, the analyst revisits the preferred option to assess whether it can be adjusted to mollify its political critics without undermining its fundamental effectiveness. The analyst may also choose to revisit the second- and third-best options to determine whether, if politically acceptable, they still might be worthy and reasonable responses to the policy problem of concern. Alternatively, he or she might choose to wait for the politics to change, rather than moving forward with a politically acceptable, but likely ineffective, option. Finally, the analyst might opt to back off and allow time for politicians, lobbyists, and/or citizens to change their minds (Mead, 2013).

While these four off-the-shelf criteria can jump start your development of the evaluation criteria for your analysis, you'll need to do more work before you can finalize the set of criteria for your analysis. At this point, you want to think about possible **unintended consequences** of your policy options and, rather than letting them surprise you after implementation, find a way to explicitly factor them into your analysis. Shift into brainstorming mode and try to come up with as many ways as possible to evaluate your list of policy alternatives. Write down everything that comes to mind without prejudging whether they're good or bad ideas. Here are some suggestions to get you started.

- Think about each policy alternative. Pretend you're a consultant being paid first to viciously tear it down and then to enthusiastically promote it. What would you say?

- Think about your favorite alternative. What do you like about it? Think about your least favorite alternative. What do you dislike about it?

- What do advocates claim are the strengths and weaknesses of policies being debated?

- Assume each alternative affected you directly, and that you don't like it. Where are the loopholes? How would you avoid compliance? What if everyone behaved like that?

- To what degree will the effects of each option change over time, for better or worse?

Jot down answers to these questions and then look at what you have in the context of our four off-the-shelf criteria. Perhaps the four criteria will adequately surface all the issues that you just brainstormed. If not, you may need additional criteria to permit a full understanding of *all* the pros and cons of *all* the options. You may have to cut and paste, delete, merge, and rearrange your messy notes but, with a little work, you should have a working draft of your evaluation criteria.

One last step remains before you can finalize your criteria: you must *ensure that you have a complete list of evaluation criteria*. All factors that might affect the policy decision must be captured in the criteria. Imagine you're working on a plan to modify local bus routes and fares to deal with budget cutbacks. Aiming to minimize impact on transit riders, you include criteria related to cost, convenience, and ridership. Failing to recognize the connection between transit and car use, you neglect to include a criterion to capture impacts on local drivers. Based on your recommendation, bus fares are raised but riders desert the system and start driving, leading to increased traffic congestion. Leaving out an important criterion can leave you regretting the conclusion you drew from your analysis. By way of illustration, Exhibit 1-5 provides a set of evaluation criteria that could be used to assess policies for our hypothetical Northern Virginia city facing a loss of affordable housing.

Exhibit 1-5 Hypothetical Set of Evaluation Criteria

Maximize Affordable Housing: Measured as the estimated number of rental units in 2025 with rents that do not exceed 30% of the income of a family at three times the poverty level.

Minimize Cost: Measured as the cost to the city over ten years of operating the program.

Maximize Development Incentives: Measured using a qualitative scale of high, moderate, and low. Metric is intended to capture city's desire for ongoing increases in amount of housing.

Maximize Administrability: Measured using a qualitative scale of high, moderate, and low. Metric is intended to reflect the likelihood of successful program implementation by the city.

Minimize Social Disruption: Measured using a qualitative scale of high, moderate, and low. Metric is intended to reflect degree of stigmatization of program participation and potential segregation of low-income residents.

1.4 CREATE A CRITERIA-ALTERNATIVES MATRIX AND PREDICT THE PERFORMANCE OF EACH ALTERNATIVE

You've settled on a problem definition, identified policies that deserve scrutiny, and selected the evaluation criteria to systematically assess the pros and cons of the alternatives. In short, you've framed the analysis by setting boundaries on what you will and won't consider. Create a **Criteria-Alternatives Matrix** (or CAM[2]) like the one shown in Exhibit 1-6. Use the short titles of your policy alternatives and evaluation criteria as row and column headers. You might want to identify the client and provide a brief version of the problem definition to title the matrix. For now, the cells

---

[2]Rhymes with ham. Note that there are other names for a CAM, including a decision matrix and a policy scorecard.

Exhibit 1-6   Illustrative Criteria-Alternatives Matrix

Client: **City Manager**

Problem: **Loss of Affordable Housing in Northern Virginia**

		Evaluation Criteria				
		# of Affordable Housing Units in 2025	Incremental Cost to City over 10 Years	Continued Incentives for Development	Ease of Administration by City	Extent of Social Disruption
Policy Options	Current Policy					
	Rent Control					
	Public Housing					
	Vouchers					
	Developer Regulations					

of the matrix are empty but eventually, they will be filled in with short statements about the performance of the alternatives.

By the way, if you asked me to single out the most important feature of the classical model of policy analysis, I would name the Criteria-Alternatives Matrix. Why? A *thoughtful and carefully constructed CAM can be a powerful tool for organizing the debate* about how to address a policy problem.

While the CAM, by itself, can't tell you what to do about a particular policy problem, it will provide a structure that helps people focus on what's important and avoid talking past one another. One of the most important contributions a policy analyst can make is to bring clarity to the complexity of policy debates. For this reason, learning to build and use CAMs that are complete, clear, and user-friendly is a skill worth mastering.

Once you've created the (as yet incomplete) CAM, look it over and double check that you're satisfied with it. Is anything missing? Have you left out an important alternative or criterion? Did you include an alternative or criterion that, on second thought, should be dropped or perhaps revised? If so, now is the time to fix problems with the CAM. Because you haven't yet done the hard work of predicting the performance of each alternative and making trade-offs across alternatives, changing the

CAM now can save you pain and suffering later if you try to revise it midway through your analysis.

After you have finalized the structure of your CAM, it's time to methodically work through each of its cells and think about how each policy alternative will perform with respect to each criterion. Ultimately, you will be inserting only a short phrase into each cell, but don't think that doing so is an easy process. Your task is to transport your mind into the future and *imagine a world where the policy alternative has been fully implemented*. When you're in that imaginary world, take a look around and figure out to what extent the alternative is meeting each evaluation criterion. Take some notes and move onto another imaginary world in which a different alternative has been put in place. Look again at each criterion and judge the performance of *that* alternative. Sometimes the process is easier if, as you travel to the imaginary future, you work through the matrix one criterion at a time (rather than one alternative at a time). Doing so may help you apply the criteria in a more consistent fashion across alternatives.

There are several techniques for making this process as rigorous as possible. If your criterion lends itself to quantification, your predicted outcome might be a specific number. For instance, if your criterion focuses on governmental costs, perhaps you can build up a cost estimate for each policy option by looking at all the activities that an agency would undertake to implement that option and then attach a price tag to each one. The sum of all the cost detail is then entered in the CAM.

Another way to predict the performance of an option in your analysis is to look for analogous existing policies that have already been implemented elsewhere, in another jurisdiction.[3] If you can find policies like the one you're assessing, you may be able to extrapolate from the performance of those other policies to predict how a similar policy might perform in your jurisdiction. As you do the extrapolation, however, be sure to take account of differences, both in context and in content. By context, I mean the ways in which the two jurisdictions might differ—bigger or smaller, wealthier or poorer, more rural or more urban—in ways that could affect the degree to which results in the other jurisdiction are predictive of the results you can expect in your jurisdiction. As regards content, be sure to think about whether the policy as implemented elsewhere is really the same as the policy you're contemplating for your situation. Seemingly small differences in program design may have big effects on results. If you are thinking about implementing a different version of the policy option in your jurisdiction, be sure to adjust your predicted outcomes accordingly. Don't let an inability to quantify a policy outcome deter you from including it in your CAM. Instead, try to cobble together evidence and logic

---

[3]We'll revisit the nature of inferential reasoning in Chapter 5 and the process of extrapolating from other jurisdictions in Chapter 13.

to draw conclusions about how each policy option will perform. Your carefully considered judgment is almost certainly more instructive than no information at all. In short, don't be afraid to populate your CAM with narrative predictions such as

- High, medium, or low cost,
- Simple, somewhat challenging, or very difficult to implement, or
- Equal, disproportionate, or very disproportionate impacts across socioeconomic lines.

As you fill in your matrix with the predicted performance of each option, there are three things to keep in mind. First, if you are uncertain about the accuracy of a particular prediction, don't hide your uncertainty. It's fine to say something like 'the cost of Option A is likely to be somewhere between $10 million and $20 million' or 'Option B will probably be very difficult to implement, but with a strong management team and adequate resources, effective implementation is possible.' And, while you do want to characterize uncertainty, take care not to impose your own risk preferences on the analysis. You may be a risk-averse person who would shy away from an option with highly uncertain outcomes, but your client may feel differently about risk and not worry so much about it. It's best to leave those judgments to the policymaker.

Second, decide at the outset whether you will report **absolute or incremental results**. By way of simple example, consider a large city that currently has 2,500 drug overdoses per year. Under Option A, you believe the number would drop to 2,000 and under Option B, to 1,500. You could either report that Option A reduces overdoses *by* 500 per year (incremental) or *to* 2,000 overdoes (absolute). Neither number is incorrect, but whichever approach you use, be consistent. Offering a conclusion that Option A reduces overdoses by 500 while Option B reduces overdoses to 1,500 is needlessly confusing.

Third, recall that above all, policy analysis is an applied and pragmatic process that takes place in the context of specific pending decisions. If time is short, data are sparse, and a decision is looming, you *may need to content yourself with completing the CAM with your best guess* of each outcome (sometimes referred to as a 'quick and dirty analysis' or a 'back of the envelope' estimate). In such cases, annotate your CAM with language that makes clear the tentative and uncertain nature of your results. Do so on the same page as the CAM, to avoid separating these important caveats from your results. When you're finished, you should have something that resembles the Criteria-Alternatives Matrix shown in Exhibit 1-7 for our hypothetical Northern Virginia city.

Exhibit 1-7 Illustrative Criteria-Alternatives Matrix Including Predicted Outcomes[a]

Client: **City Manager**

Problem: **Loss of Affordable Housing in Northern Virginia**

		Evaluation Criteria				
		# of Affordable Housing Units in 2025	Incremental Cost to City over 10 Years	Continued Incentives for Development	Ease of Administration by City	Extent of Social Disruption
Policy Options	Current Policy	1,000 (+0 units)	$0	High	High	Moderate
	Rent Control	2,250 (+1,250 units)	$0	Low	Moderate	Low
	Public Housing	1,500 (+500 units)	$350 million	Moderate	Low	High
	Vouchers	2,000 (+1,000 units)	$240 million	High	Moderate	Low
	Developer Regulations	2,500 (+1,500 units)	$0	Moderate	High	Low

[a]The information in this matrix is purely hypothetical, intended only to illustrate the process of completing a criteria-alternatives matrix.

1.5 MAKE THE TRADE-OFFS ACROSS ALTERNATIVES

What, exactly, do I mean by the word **trade-off**? It may be helpful to think of a transaction that involves a *get and a give*. For example, you go to the grocery store to stock up for the coming week. You *get* a bag's worth of groceries and you in turn you *give* a chunk of your hard-earned cash to the store.

Let's apply this concept to the policy world with another example. I recently heard a news story about bike and pedestrian safety near a subway station. On-street parking didn't leave enough space for everyone to get by safely, leading to accidents. The city decided to remove 29 parking spots on the streets around the station. Doing so sounds like it was probably a good idea, but even in this simple case, there was a trade-off, a get *and* a give. The get was lower risks for bikers and walkers, while the give was reduced convenience and mobility for drivers, who could no longer park near the station.

Your trade-off analysis will be built upon the completed criteria-alternatives matrix. The first step in trade-off analysis is to revisit the CAM and investigate whether there are any ways to simplify it. You should begin by checking whether you've inadvertently given a policy alternative more credit than it deserves because its predicted outcome exceeds a desired performance **threshold**. By way of example, consider two approaches to a post-disaster assistance program. Suppose that Option A can deliver 500,000 meals per day while Option B can deliver 600,000. Option B is better, right? Perhaps not. If there are only 500,000 people who need to be fed, then both options clear the threshold and we should be indifferent between the two (at least with respect to number of meals per day).

After adjusting the CAM to ensure that all options are treated similarly with respect to relevant thresholds, the next check is for **dominated options**. A policy option is dominated when its performance is *inferior to another option on at least one evaluation criteria, and equal to or inferior to, that same option on all other criteria*. If a policy option is dominated, it can be dropped from analysis on the grounds that there is at least one unambiguously better option available.

Take a look at Exhibit 1-7, where you will find two dominated options. The Rent Control option is dominated by Developer Regulations: it provides fewer affordable units, has the same cost, has a greater adverse impact on incentives for development, is more difficult for the city to administer, and has the same impact on social disruption. In other words, there is no criterion on which Rent Control outperforms Developer Regulations, and at least one criterion where its performance is worse. As long as we're sure we haven't left out any important evaluation criteria, we can safely say that Rent Control is a dominated alternative, not worth continued analysis. The Public Housing option is also dominated, both by Vouchers and by Developer Regulations. Take a minute to review Exhibit 1-7 and make sure you understand why this option is dominated.

New analysts sometimes make the mistake of incorrectly identifying an alternative as dominated. This typically occurs when, as they consider each criterion, they find other options—but not always the same option—that are superior. Remember, *the check for dominance is a series of pairwise tests*; you compare one option in its entirety—across all criteria—to another, one pair of options at a time.

Having eliminated dominated alternatives from your CAM, you next want to see if one or more criteria can be dropped. *If all options are rated equally on a criterion, then that criterion is no longer relevant to the decision-making process*. Again, consider Exhibit 1-7, but this time imagine that Ease of Administration had been rated as 'High' rather than 'Moderate' for the Vouchers option. Then, after eliminating the Public Housing and Rent Control options as dominated, the three remaining alternatives would all be rated the same on Ease of Administration (i.e., 'High'). In this example, no matter which option we select, we would be left with a program where the Ease of Administration is 'High,' meaning that our desire to maximize administrability will not help us select among the available alternatives.

Having cleaned up the CAM by recalibrating options that exceed threshold levels, discarding dominated alternatives, and removing any evaluation criteria on which all alternatives perform identically, you can begin the process of making **trade-offs**.

When it comes to trade-off analysis in the classical model, there are at least four methods you might use. Some scholars refer to the first three as **solution methods** (Weimer & Vining, 2017). The implication is that, having started with a problem definition, our ultimate goal is to solve the problem. While this vocabulary has an internal logic to it, it can also be misleading. Rarely, if ever, can a policy analysis alone be used to *solve* social problems. It's more appropriate to characterize a well-executed policy analysis as a helpful product that can inform policymakers' thinking about what actions they might take.

The first approach to evaluating a completed criteria-alternatives matrix—shown at the top of Exhibit 1-8—is **cost–benefit analysis** (CBA). This approach is used when

Exhibit 1-8 Illustrative Examples of Trade-off Analysis

Cost–Benefit Analysis
All Impacts Monetized
Decision Rule: Select Alternative With Highest Net Benefit

Alternative	Total Benefit	Total Cost	Net Benefit
A	$50 million	$100 million	−$50 million (net cost)
B	$200 million	$75 million	$125 million
C	$150 million	$50 million	$100 million

Cost-Effectiveness Analysis
All Impacts but One Monetized
Decision Rule: Select Alternative With Highest Cost Effectiveness

Alternative	Net Cost	Benefit Metric	Cost per Unit of Benefit
Q	$15 million	10,000	$1,500
R	$25 million	7,500	$3,333
S	$18 million	12,500	$1,440

Multiattribute Analysis
All Impacts Scored From 1 to 10
Decision Rule: Select Alternative With Highest Aggregate Score

Alternative	Metric 1	Metric 2	Metric 3	Metric 4	Total Score
X	8.0	6.2	2.3	9.7	26.2
Y	4.2	8.8	9.5	7.8	30.3
Z	6.5	7.3	5.5	8.2	27.5

all aspects of the problem can be convincingly monetized. In CBA, you replace every entry in the CAM with a dollar figure, positive for benefits or negative for costs. Once everything has been monetized, you add up the costs and benefits of each alternative. The decision rule is to *select the alternative with the highest net benefits* (or lowest net costs, depending on how the problem is framed). In Exhibit 1-8, Alternative B, with net benefits of $125 million, would be preferred to Alternative C (net benefits of $100 million) and to Alternative A (net benefits of *negative* $50 million, meaning that it has more costs than benefits).

The second approach—shown in the middle of Exhibit 1-8—is **cost-effectiveness analysis** (CEA). With CEA, all attributes except one are monetized. The remaining attribute—usually the one where monetization would be most conceptually difficult or politically controversial—is left in its natural units. A classic application of the cost-effectiveness method is in traffic and highway safety programs where various infra-structure projects affect the probability of a fatal accident. In such cases, the metric of interest is a statistical estimate of the number of lives that would likely be saved by the alternatives under consideration. When combined with the net cost of the project, we can compute the cost-per-life-saved (i.e., the cost-effectiveness metric), and *select the option with the highest cost-effectiveness* (i.e., with the lowest cost per life saved). In the case of Exhibit 1-8, this would be Alternative S.[4]

The third technique—shown in the lower portion of Exhibit 1-8—is **multiattribute analysis** (MAA) where, instead of monetary metrics, a score (typically from 1 to 10) is used to capture the performance of each policy alternative with respect to each evaluation criterion. For the method to work, you must ensure that a "10" always represents the most advantageous result for all criteria. The scores of each alternative with respect to each criterion are then summed to generate an aggregate score for each alternative. The decision rule is then to *select the option with the highest score*. In Exhibit 1-8, Alternative Y, with its score of 30.3, is thus preferred over Alternatives X (26.2) and Z (27.5).

These three techniques (CBA, CEA, and MAA) are intended to create **commensurability** across options. *Commensurability ensures that each predicted outcome is valued with a metric that has the same intrinsic meaning regardless of the alternative or criterion being assessed.* In CBA, it is ensured because all results are reported in monetary terms (e.g., a dollar of benefit under one option has the same value as a dollar of benefit under another). With CEA, everything is also monetized except for the effectiveness metric, which itself is calculated in a commensurable fashion for all

---

[4]A cost-effectiveness metric, however, doesn't capture the scale of the policy option. A very cost-effective highway safety measure may, for example, only be applicable to a very small part of the roadway system.

alternatives (i.e., we use the same methodology in a consistent way to estimate the effectiveness of each alternative).

Finally with MAA, the scoring system aims to ensure that a one-point difference in the rating of one option has the same value, or importance, to the decision as a one-point difference in another option's rating. If we succeed in ensuing commensurability, then finding the optimal decision is simply a matter of selecting the option with the highest net benefit, cost-effectiveness, or score.

You will, however, *often find it impossible to combine all relevant aspects of a policy alternative into a single, commensurable metric*. Sometimes, the problem is a technical one. Suppose you hope to use CBA to identify the right policy choice. There may not be sufficient data or a suitable method, or perhaps simply not enough time, for a microeconomist to attach a dollar figure to policy outcomes like the gentrification of a neighborhood and the displacement of long-time residents. More often, the problem is a paradigmatic one. You may convince yourself that your adroit and sophisticated use of CBA, CEE, or MAA has established commensurability across options and pointed to a singularly optimal alternative, but you may very well find that your audience—the policymakers you aspire to advise—don't find your methods intuitively understandable, or at worst, reject them as fundamentally flawed.

Nonetheless, even if you can't use CBA, CEE, or MAA as a solution method for your analysis, all is not lost—far from it. Your CAM is a gold mine of insight from which you can extract a great deal of information that will help you frame a clear trade-off statement.

Take another look at the completed Criteria-Alternatives Matrix in Exhibit 1-7 and think about how you might describe the get and the give of the policy options for addressing affordable housing. Recall that we dropped Public Housing and Rent Control as dominated options. Our task now is to describe the decision choice (and its attendant trade-offs) in succinct, plain language. There is no one right way to do this, but take a look at what I came up with:

> If the city chooses to address the affordable housing issue, it could use Vouchers or Developer Regulations. Developer Regulations are predicted to add 500 more units of affordable housing than would Vouchers, while also avoiding the $240 million cost and increased administrative burden of Vouchers. This regulatory approach will, however, likely undermine incentives for development—a city priority—in a way that vouchers probably won't. Strong incentives for development can also be preserved by the current policy, though at a cost of 1,000 to 1,500 fewer affordable units. The city must trade off the importance of protecting development incentives against fewer affordable units and against the cost and burden of administering the vouchers program.

Clearly, these 125 words of narrative prose on trade-offs lack the precision of a solution method that simply identifies *the* optimal policy choice. On the other hand, *prose-based trade-off statements bring to the fore the kinds of information that almost all policymakers are likely to care deeply about.*

So, am I saying that the three solution methods—CBA, CEE, and MAA—have no value? Absolutely not. All three methods impose a discipline and rigor on the analytic decision-making process that are antecedents to a well-crafted narrative trade-off statement. And, in many cases, the analytic assumptions and data needs of these methods can be satisfactorily addressed. In such cases, the optimum solution identified by the method may indeed be the best choice for policymakers to adopt.

At this point in the sequential approach of classical policy analysis, many policy analysis textbooks tell readers that it is now time to recommend a preferred option. For reasons detailed in Chapter 3, I argue that it is rarely possible to use policy analysis to unambiguously identify *the* optimal response to a policy problem. So, *if you do make a recommendation, don't oversell it.*

1.6 COMMUNICATE THE RESULTS

The final step in the classical policy analysis framework is to convey your results to the appropriate audience, usually your client but often other interested folks as well. A traditional mechanism for doing so is the "policy memo," a short communication of two to three pages (certainly less than 1,500 words) from you to your client or boss.

Policy writing is very different from the academic writing that appears in scholarly journals or the essays you wrote in Freshman English. It's also unlike fiction writing, where intricate plotting, broad scene-setting, and rhetorical flourishes are common-place. Instead, a policy memo is meant to be read and understood quickly. It is written in a succinct and to-the-point fashion, with simple wording, short sentences, brief paragraphs, and explanatory headings. Jargon that the reader may not understand should be avoided. The analyst's conclusions are traditionally presented in the first paragraph of a policy memo rather than at the end. A more extensive written report describing the analysis might also be required.

Either in lieu of or in addition to a policy memo, you may need to provide the results of your analysis in a verbal briefing, often supported by a set of slides. A policy analysis presentation is not like the Gettysburg Address or a Shakespearean soliloquy. You need to get and hold the audience's attention *without manipulating their emotions.* At the same time, you need to deliver complex analytic results *without putting the audience to sleep.* In short, you need an engaging yet substantive style as you deliver a credible but neutral and evenhanded presentation.

Communicating your results also happens to be the final step in the retrospective policy analysis framework described in the next chapter. The guiding principles of clear communication are similar in both cases. Rather than repeat the same material, I've integrated the discussion of how best to present analytic results—prospective and retrospective—into a single section that appears in Chapter 7.

CHAPTER SUMMARY

This chapter began by noting that even though the classical model of prospective policy analysis has multiple shortcomings, all aspiring policy analysts need to master it. By doing so, analysts can take advantage of the model's many capabilities while being careful not to apply it in situations to which it is not well suited.

We then worked through the six steps of the classical model, starting with the problem definition process. We next looked at some suggestions for developing potential policy alternatives that might mitigate a problem and considered the process of coming up with a comprehensive set of evaluation criteria to sort out the pros and cons of the alternatives being debated.

We then considered how a criteria-alternatives matrix can be used to systematically capture our predictions of how each alternative might perform with respect to each criterion. Four methods of making trade-offs across alternatives were described. The chapter closed with some of the key features of policy writing and communication, noting that Chapter 7 takes a deeper dive into the process of effectively sharing analytic results.

DISCUSSION QUESTIONS

1. Pick a policy issue you care about. What do you think the problem is? How does the status quo differ from your preferred situation? Why does the problem exist? What are its most important consequences?

2. What are some of the ways you think we could tackle the problem you identified? Do you already have a favorite proposal? Can you get past your predispositions to identify other reasonable options? Can you identify each policy choice in a detailed but succinct fashion?

3. What are the most important considerations relevant to the choice of a policy option to tackle your problem of concern? Will the set of criteria you've identified surface all of the important pros and cons of all the options under consideration?

4. Try to predict the future performance of each alternative with respect to each criterion. How would you defend the validity of your predictions? Where did you encounter difficulty in coming up with a prediction? How confident are you in your predictions?

5. Develop a succinct trade-off statement that captures the consequences of picking one alternative over another. Were you able to admit the shortcomings of the alternative you most prefer? Were you able to acknowledge the strengths of the alternative you most dislike?

6. How helpful do you think the classical model of prospective policy analysis will be during your career? What are its strengths and weaknesses?

CHAPTER TWO

THINKING ABOUT THE PAST
Retrospective Program and Impact Evaluation

Having reviewed prospective policy analysis in Chapter 1, we now turn from the future to the past. Although you'll find variations in the literature, the classical model of retrospective evaluation is usually built on the six steps listed in Exhibit 2-1. The model focuses on existing programs and policies, and helps us figure out how well they are working. As with prospective analysis, there are often real-world impediments to the successful execution of retrospective analysis. But even if you can't always complete all of the steps in the model or end up completing them in a nonsequential order, having a framework for examining existing programs in your professional toolkit can be very helpful.

Exhibit 2-1 Steps in Retrospective Policy Analysis

1. Delineate Program and Identify its Purpose
2. Build Logic Model based on a Theory of Change
3. Decide on Scope of Evaluation
4. Identify Evaluation Questions and Select Research Design
5. Define Counterfactual for Impact Evaluation (if needed)
6. Conduct Evaluation, Draw Conclusions, and Communicate Results

---

In this chapter, we first review the rationale for retrospective evaluation by locating it within a bigger cycle of policy analysis, enactment, implementation, and evaluation. The remaining subsections of this chapter then walk through the steps in Exhibit 2-1, describing each in more detail and offering some suggestions to help you execute it.

Learning Objectives

By studying this chapter, you should be able to:

- Explain the rationales for retrospective analysis.

- Describe a stylized policy cycle that provides context for retrospective evaluation while noting shortcomings of policy cycle models.

- Discern the goals and objectives of an existing program or policy.

- Use Theory of Change thinking to build a program-specific logic model.

- Define and distinguish the emphasis on efficiency in a program evaluation from the emphasis on effective-ness in an impact evaluation.

- Define and differentiate a formative assessment and a summative assessment.

- Explain how evaluation questions drive the design of a retrospective analysis.

- Describe methods for defining a counterfactual for impact evaluation.

- Describe common challenges that may arise when communicating the results of a retrospective evaluation.

2.1 RETROSPECTIVE EVALUATION IN CONTEXT OF THE POLICY CYCLE

There are many reasons why you might conduct a retrospective analysis. You might simply be responding to a broad government-wide or agency-wide mandate for ongoing program evaluation. Or there might be a more program-specific reason that a particular program is being evaluated. A supporter of the program may be interested in doing everything possible to improve its day-to-day operations so that it can deliver more powerful results. A neutral party might be genuinely wondering whether the program is worth the money being spent on it. More cynically, a program opponent might have reached the foregone conclusion that the program is a bad idea and wants evidence to prove it's not working. Your client might also request a retrospective analysis of a program that is working well in order to identify the drivers of its success so that it can be replicated elsewhere. Moreover, in the face of constrained budgets, program evaluation of multiple programs can be used to allocate scarce resources to the most cost-effective programs. Finally, the motive for analysis may be a normative belief that because the government is spending taxpayer money, we should always monitor existing programs and use the results to hold their public sector managers accountable for successes and missteps.[1]

Another, less specific, use of retrospective evaluation is to help break out of what Eggers & O'Leary (2009) call the **Complacency Trap**, a phenomenon that arises when the status quo becomes so entrenched that we become blind to whether current programs are still producing benefits. In their words, "the Complacency Trap is the dangerous tack of staying the same when the circumstances of the world around you change" (p. 171). Routine application of retrospective evaluation to existing policies, even those that appear to be working just fine, can ferret out situations where programs no longer serve a valuable purpose or where there are new and innovative ways of achieving our objectives.

Although it looks to the past, *retrospective policy analysis shares its intellectual foundation and ultimate purpose with future-oriented prospective analysis*. In both cases, we gather and use evidence, coupled with carefully reasoned inferences, to help answer the perennial question of public policymakers: what should we do next? There are, however, two important differences.

First, in retrospective analysis, we are almost always studying *a single existing policy or program*. We focus on the status quo (i.e., the program that has actually been put in place) and try to answer two basic questions. First, if we weren't already operating this program, would we still think it's a good idea? And second, if the program is a good

---

[1]Private foundations and other grant makers also often use retrospective program evaluation to better understand whether their funding activities are producing intended results.

idea, would we run it the same way, or would we make changes? (Drucker, 1995). By contrast, prospective analysis usually studies *multiple policy options that might be put in place going forward*, and tries to answer one basic question. What's the best way to deal with an existing policy problem?

Second, another important difference between retrospective and prospective analysis relates to the role of **counterfactual reasoning** (i.e., conjuring the state of the world in the absence of a policy). In a prospective study, the imaginary states of the world (one for each policy alternative under consideration) are all in the future. When it comes to a retrospective study, however, one state of the world (the one with the policy in place) doesn't have to be conjured at all. We have a track record of program implementation, and if we're lucky, a collection of evidence on which to base our analysis. Moreover, the single counterfactual world that we do have to conjure (what the world would have looked like in the absence of the policy or program) occurs in the past, meaning that we have a base of historical information that may help us better characterize that counterfactual.

The traditional point of departure for prospective policy analysis is the problem definition, while for retrospective analysis the point of departure is an existing policy or program. Before diving into the mechanics of retrospective evaluation, it may be helpful to provide a broader context. In both scholarly research and in policy text-books, there is a long tradition of describing policymaking as a circular process that relates prospective and retrospective evaluation to the processes of policy imple-mentation (Weible, 2017). In keeping with that tradition, I offer my version of the policy cycle in Exhibit 2-2.

Exhibit 2-2   The Policy Cycle: A Stylized Representation

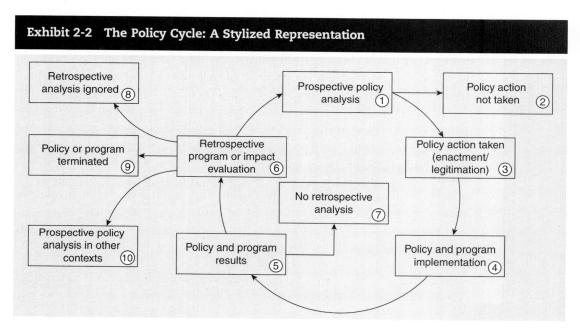

But, before you study the diagram, please consider a large caveat: *most of the time, the world doesn't actually work in this neat and stylized way* (Cairney & Weible, 2017). In reality, multiple cycles covering a wide range of related problems and existing programs are underway at any given time, competing for policymakers' limited attention. What's more, the power and authority of these policymakers is shared (often unwillingly) among branches and agencies of government and fragmented across national, state, and local governments. As a consequence, the ostensibly circular process often gets derailed by the preferences of stakeholders and decisions of policymakers, by election results and shifting electoral coalitions that shape the political landscape, and by real-world events, such as program successes and failures, evolving public opinions and social norms, scandals and disasters. In short, policies and programs often rise and fall for reasons that are only loosely connected to their intrinsic effectiveness or to the societal significance of the problems that they purportedly address.

You should also recognize that an important step precedes any prospective analysis or retrospective evaluation: the **agenda setting** process (Dye, 2011; Parsons, 1995). Agenda setting is the mechanism by which social concerns and issues with existing programs become salient enough to gain the attention of policymakers, in turn leading to a debate about an appropriate course forward. To put it bluntly, the mere existence of a profound problem does not automatically spawn a prospective policy analysis process to tackle the problem. Similarly, the fact that a major government program is dysfunctional doesn't mean policymakers will be interested in a retrospective evaluation to sort things out.

Scholars of policy processes are well aware of the deficiencies of the neat and stylized cyclical model and have been working assiduously for decades to build theoretically sound and empirically tested models of how the policy process really works (Weible & Cairney, 2018; Weible & Sabatier, 2017). The theoretical policy literature is home to several lively and fascinating debates; in fact, there are at least seven prominent theories of the policy process (Weible & Sabatier, 2017).

In my 30+ years of experience as a policy analyst, however, I have found that *these theoretical debates don't directly affect the day-to-day lives of most working policy analysts.* The endless stream of public issues, practical problems, and questions of governance that demand policymakers' attention doesn't wait for definitive theoretical explanations—either of the policy process writ large or of the specific drivers of particular problems. I think that pragmatist philosopher Michael Harmon got it right when he rejected the "assumption that practical problems require a prior theoretical basis from which to address and solve them. … For pragmatists, *all* problems, in order to qualify *as* problems, necessarily entail practical concerns about 'what we ought to do'" (Harmon, 2006, p. 137), *emphasis in original.*

Accordingly, I'll skip over competing theories of the policy process in favor of a set of analytic tools that I believe will stand the test of time as relevant no matter which all-encompassing theory of the policy process is (if ever) broadly accepted as the definitive explanation of how things work. Why, then, am I bothering to give you a graphic depiction of a process that we know is not quite right? As one scholar—who refers interchangeably to the policy cycle model and the stagist model—puts it:

> As a heuristic device the policy cycle enables us to construct a model with which we can explore public policy. But, as with all heuristic models, it must be treated with caution. … [W]e must be wise to the fact that such maps have grave limitations and may distort our understanding. … [But] given the sheer range of frameworks and models which are available as analytical tools, we need some way in which this complexity can be reduced to a more manageable form. … [C]ontemporary policy analysis is a multiframed activity. The strength of the stagist approach is that it affords a rational structure within which we may consider the multiplicity of reality. Each stage therefore provides a context within which we deploy different frames. … The idea of breaking down the making of public policy into phases … may well be to impose stages on a reality that is infinitely more complex, fluid and interactive. … [U]nderstanding and explaining this complexity is a matter which involves appreciating that reality exists within the context of a multiplicity of frameworks. (Parsons, 1995, pp. 80–81), *internal references omitted*

Despite its imperfections, the stage-based policy cycle model offers a roadmap for visualizing how the pieces notionally fit together and, equally important, provides a framework for further analysis.

Let's take a close look at the nine steps in the policy cycle illustrated in Exhibit 2-2. We pick up where the last chapter left off—with *prospective policy analysis (Step 1)* that explores how we might address a current policy problem. Again, as mentioned above, we're skipping the agenda setting process which drives the selection of the policy problem in the first place. Speaking in general terms, two things can follow prospective policy analysis. First, it's possible that *no policy action is taken (Step 2)*; perhaps consensus couldn't be reached on an appropriate policy option or on whether the problem was even worth attempting to address in the first place. Maybe all the available options were too expensive or had major shortcomings. The second possibility is that policymakers do *enact some form of new policy (Step 3)*. Scholars sometimes refer to this step as legitimation (Cairney, 2020; Dye, 2011), implying that the policy has been properly endorsed by those who control the power of the state. The enacted policy may fully incorporate the insights of the prospective policy analysis, or conversely, it may completely ignore the analysis and instead reflect a mix of political compromises and parochial interests. Of course, it could also lie between these extremes.

Once the policy is in place, *implementation begins (Step 4)*, and specific program activities are launched. Some programs may get up and running quickly; others may take years to become operational. Some may be well-funded and fully staffed from the beginning; others may suffer chronic resource shortages. Over time, program *results accumulate (Step 5)*. Well-designed programs typically establish, track, and monitor performance metrics that help folks understand program results. In many cases, however, results remain opaque and are hard to discern because evidence about program operations is not systematically collected or consistently archived.

At some point after its launch, a program *may or may not be subjected to retrospective analysis (Steps 6 and 7)*. There are several reasons why a program might not be evaluated; perhaps there is no institutionalized requirement to conduct an evaluation. Even if there is, there may be no funding to cover its cost. It could also be the case that program managers are so focused on implementation that evaluation feels like an unnecessary distraction or it might be that government executives and politicians are not interested in hearing potentially bad news about the effectiveness of a program that they and their constituents support. But many programs are subjected to retrospective evaluation and the remainder of this chapter takes a deep dive into the mechanics of doing such an evaluation.

But before moving on, let's finish this discussion of the policy cycle. There are essentially four things that can happen in the aftermath of a program evaluation. Not infrequently, the evaluation *results are ignored (Step 8)*. Why might this happen? There are usually stakeholders inside government whose jobs depend on the program and stakeholders outside government who benefit from the program. So, negative findings notwithstanding, the status quo may remain unchanged. Alternatively, if the evaluation of the program is highly critical or if program opponents contrive to use the findings to undermine support for the program, then the evaluation may lead to *termination of the policy (Step 9)*. Sometimes, retrospective evaluation has consequences beyond the studied program, when the results of the evaluation are used as *evidence for prospective policy analyses in other contexts (Step 10)*. Finally, the circle may be closed as we cycle back to where we started. In this case, the findings of the retrospective evaluation of a particular program become the foundation of a new prospective analysis in which policymakers decide if and how to modify the existing program going forward in response to the results of the program evaluation.

Again, we know that the real-world often does not play out in alignment with this stylized representation of the policy cycle. Nonetheless, the cycle should help you see at least three important themes. First, whenever we are thinking about future policy options, we are not painting on a blank canvas. There is often—though not always—a potential *body of evidence from the evaluation of similar existing programs* on which we can draw to inform our analysis. Our clients are well served if we seek out such evidence as we help them decide how to move forward. Second, because a defining feature of prospective analysis is uncertainty about the future, if we are able to implement and then evaluate a new policy, we may be able to limit the consequences of that uncertainty when, as the result of our program evaluation, we can *adjust the policy to reflect what we've learned during program implementation*. Finally, even if we never close the loop after a program evaluation to adjust the specific program we've studied, we have at least *documented our findings so that others can take what we've learned and use it* to inform and improve the design of programs in other locations at other points in time.

2.2 DELINEATE PROGRAM BOUNDARIES AND IDENTIFY ITS PURPOSE

Within the broader context set by this notional policy cycle, let's turn now to the first step in retrospective program analysis. To start, if we aim to understand how well an existing program is working, we first need to define what we mean by the **program**. You may recall from the introduction to Part I, there is no commonly accepted definition of the word program. Accordingly, the initial step in a retrospective evaluation is the careful delineation of the program to be studied and its boundaries. Our scope could be broad if, for example, we want to study whether a police department is achieving its goal of protecting and serving all citizens across socioeconomic lines, or it might be narrow, if we want to evaluate whether a specific officer training program to address implicit bias is producing results. Similarly, we might study all aspects of a program or only one component of it. Responsibility for air pollution control in the United States, for instance, is shared between the Federal government and the states. We might do an evaluation of the Federal role, of one or more states, or of the system in its entirety. We also need to identify the relevant time frame of our analysis. We might assess the program's performance over the past year, the past ten years, or since the last time major changes were made to the program.

Once you and your client have defined the boundaries of the program to be studied, the next step is to settle on a working definition of the **program's purpose**—its goals and objectives—that will guide your study. Think about it. If we want to figure out if a program is successful, we first must know what success would look like. In the same way that the problem definition is the North Star of prospective policy analysis, the purpose of an existing program is the North Star of a retrospective policy analysis. Every component of the evaluation needs to contribute to your understanding of the degree to which the program is achieving its goals and objectives.

To figure out a program's goals and objectives, you might start with a series of questions:

- Who or what is the *target* of the program? Is it trying to affect or influence the public, civil servants, communities and neighborhoods, corporations, nongovernmental organizations, other agencies or levels of government, or other countries?

- What *changes in existing conditions* do we expect the program to have? Do we expect changes in the knowledge, attitudes, or behavior of people or organizations? Or in the condition of the built environment (e.g., public infrastructure or commercial, residential, or industrial property), the condition of the natural environment (e.g., land, air, or water resources), or the condition of the social environment (e.g., poverty, education, or equality)?

- What is the expected *timing and magnitude* of the program's impacts? Does the program aim to affect a large swath of the community, country, or population or is this a small, specialized program? Do we expect change to happen quickly, or do we think that change can only be expected to come slowly, perhaps in fits and starts?

- Did we expect a *binary* all-or-nothing result leading to either complete success or outright failure? Or, did we anticipate a *continuum* of potential results with a mix of successes and failures?

These sorts of questions will help you frame your definition of goals and objectives, but this process isn't just up to you. There are always other points of view to consider, other stakeholders who have an opinion about what the program you're evaluating should be doing. So, where else should you look? Try to locate and review the following sorts of information for more insight into the core purpose of an existing program. As you do, *take care to be intentionally inclusive and make sure you hear all the voices that can give you insight* into what folks think the program should be doing.

- Statutory, regulatory, and policy documentation that formally launched the program.

- Records of policy debates (legislative or administrative) that took place when the program was being established.

- Prospective policy analyses or other background materials that might have been developed at the time policymakers were deciding whether to establish the program.

- Program mission statements, strategic plans, or similar plans or documents developed during program operation.

- Ongoing reports about the program including audits, reviews, or evaluations which may contain statements about program goals and objectives, and their evolution over time.

- Prior program evaluations done in the past.

- Statements by issue advocates (supporters *and* opponents) who have argued about what the goals and the objectives of the program should be.

- Comments from program managers and staff, as well as from beneficiaries and other participants in the program's operations.

- Any evidence of public opinion on the purpose of the program; you shouldn't expect unanimity here, but you may be able to expand your set of potential goals and objectives for the program by taking care to hear the public's voices.

- Any commentary from the person or organization that asked for the program evaluation (i.e., your client) and what they believe the goals and objectives of the program to be.

Having assembled this information, you need a way to make sense of it. The first consideration is whether all the material you've found is internally consistent. In other words, is there uniform agreement as to the program's goals and objectives? If so, great. Your next step is to synthesize the material and articulate a concise list of the program's top priorities. Depending on what you've come up with, you might find there are some primary priorities, and some secondary ones; there might also be a natural taxonomy (or classification) of the priorities, with some better fitting in one category and others fitting a different category.

On the other hand, let's suppose that different stakeholders or sources of information about the program suggest *divergent, potentially competing goals* for the program. How might that happen? A group of policymakers might support the same policy measure but may do so for very different reasons. For instance, some might argue that the US military ought to build more F-35 aircraft to secure the country's safety in a dangerous world. Others might argue that the United States needs more F-35 fighters to solidify the nation's industrial base and provide a large number of well-paying, high-tech jobs. Though they disagree on the rationale, both points of view suggest building more F-35s.

Now imagine that you're asked to do an evaluation of the F-35 program. How would you characterize the goals and objectives of the program? You could *select one definition of the program's purpose* and narrow your evaluation accordingly. In other words, you would evaluate either the F-35's contribution to national security or its contribution to economic development. Alternatively, though it will make the analysis more complex, you could *try to incorporate both visions of the program into your evaluation* and reach a conclusion about how well the program is doing in achieving each of the two purposes. If it's any consolation, *there is no right answer here*. Mindful of schedule, resource, and information constraints, you and your client will need to decide how to proceed when it comes to specifying the program's purpose—its goals and objectives—to incorporate in your evaluation.

Irrespective of whether everyone agrees on the purpose of the program or there are divergent points of view, remember the metaphor of the North Star. *Your clear, concise statement of program goals and objectives will guide the remainder of your evaluation.* It's worth taking time now to ensure that you've got this nailed down.

Finally, one last thing to consider is whether you've been asked to evaluate a program which has a **symbolic purpose** rather than an **instrumental purpose**. The former is primarily meant to signal a normative value while the latter aims to directly affect real-world conditions. Think about a small city that decides to purchase only electric vehicles for its municipal fleet. The performance of such cars is virtually identical to that of gas-powered cars but if their batteries are charged using electricity from renewable resources, then the city's fleet no longer creates any greenhouse gas emissions. The city's policy thus directly serves an instrumental purpose: fewer emissions will in turn reduce global warming. The reality, of course, is that the city's contribution to global emissions is so small that its policy (taken in isolation) will have an immaterial effect on global warming. Instead, the purpose of such a program is likely largely symbolic, intended to send a signal to citizens, the corporate sector, other levels of government, and other nations that action on greenhouse gas emissions is both feasible and desirable. If we limit ourselves to the instrumental goal of reducing global warming, we'd probably judge this program to have failed. But if we broaden our view to include the symbolic statement being sent, we could evaluate the degree to which the program has motivated other jurisdictions to take climate action. Accordingly, when it comes to deciding on the goals and objectives of a symbolic policy, you will want to take care not to mix up instrumental and symbolic constructs. Both may be present in one program, but it's best to treat them separately.

2.3 BUILD A PROGRAM-SPECIFIC LOGIC MODEL BASED ON A THEORY OF CHANGE

By specifying the purpose of a program—its goals and objectives—you define *what* the program is trying to achieve. Your next challenge is to describe *how* the program aspires to achieve those goals and objectives (Pressman & Wildavsky, 1984). We could it leave to fate, chance, or some other magic force to connect a program's purpose to the changes we aim to create in real-world conditions. Most of us, however, would probably prefer a more thoughtful and careful consideration of the path forward, an articulation of the rationale, or theory, that links programs and policies to results and impacts.

Accordingly, at this step of the process, you should try to articulate a **Theory of Change** that explains the program you are evaluating. There is no single, widely accepted, definition of this phrase (Ringhofer & Kohlweg, 2019). There *is* broad consensus, however, that building a Theory of Change for a public policy or program entails an articulation of a *causal theory about how actions taken within the program will lead to changes outside the program*. What's more, practitioners of Theory of Change analysis emphasize the importance of critical reflection on the assumptions (valid or not) made by program designers, on the motives and incentives of *all* relevant stakeholders, and on the broad context into which the program has been introduced. Patricia Rogers offers this summary:

> Every programme is packed with beliefs, assumptions and hypotheses about how change happens—about the way humans work, or organisations, or political systems, or ecosystems. Theory of change is about articulating these many underlying assumptions about how change will happen in a programme. (Vogel, 2012, p. 4)

Methods for developing and applying Theories of Change in the context of program evaluation comprise an extensive literature. See, for example, texts by Vogel (Review of the Use of 'Theory of Change' in International Development, 2012) and by Funnell and Rogers (Purposeful Program Theory: Effective Use of Theories of Change and Logic Models, 2011).

Even though this literature represents a large body of knowledge regarding Theory of Change thinking, the core idea—at least for us here—is a simple one. If your retrospective analysis aspires to understand how and why a policy or program is (or is not) having an effect, then you need a working hypothesis about the Theory of Change that underlies it. As you investigate the program's purpose (see Section 2.2 above), be on the lookout for information that will help you characterize proponents' arguments about how and why the program is expected to produce intended results. Though they may not refer to it as such, those arguments represent the building blocks of a Theory of Change.

A widely used technique for describing the Theory of Change embedded in a particular policy or program entails construction of a **logic model**, so named because it is built on a series of logical if-then statements (GAO, 2012; Kellogg Foundation, 2004). In short, a logic model describes a chain of causality: if we do Q, then the result will be R; if R occurs, then the result will be S; if S occurs, then the result will be T; and so on.

There are different forms of logic models in the literature (Kellogg Foundation, 2004), but a typical approach relies on a model with five sequential components:

- *Inputs* are generally the human, physical, financial, and intellectual resources made available to operate the program. You may want to think of inputs as the raw materials that program managers can tap into in order to operate the program.

- *Activities* are the tasks, processes, actions, and operations that are completed within the confines of the program itself using the inputs provided. To identify relevant activities, take a look at the day-to-day operations of the program and figure out how the folks associated with it spend their time each day.

- *Outputs* are the direct result of the activities undertaken by the program and might include the deliverables created by project activities, the services provided by the program to its clients, or tangible physical products. Outputs have a clear, unbroken, and unambiguous causal link to program activities.

- *Outcomes* are created by program outputs but stand apart from the program itself and constitute the initial consequences of the program for its target audience. They are changes experienced by individuals, companies, nonprofit organizations, or government agencies as a result of the program's outputs. Because of their indirect nature, causal links from outputs to outcomes may be ambiguous and can be affected by factors beyond the program's boundaries.

- *Impacts* result from the outcomes created by the program but are usually observed over longer time frames than outcomes and, importantly, are the point in the logic model where counterfactual reasoning is explicitly introduced. In other words, the impact of a program is measured as the difference between the actual state of the world with the program and a conjured state of the world in which the program didn't exist.

Finally, the logic model framework also lets you identify **contextual features** or **mediating factors** that affect the behavior both of individual elements within the model and of the relationships among the model's major components. There are two reasons for characterizing mediating factors. First, they provide context for understanding how a program is operating. Knowing, for example, that a specific agency program is of special interest to an important politician or that another agency with relevant resources has declined to support the program may help you understand how and why certain program decisions have been made. Second, a program's results typically depend on more than just the program itself. For example, we may be evaluating a program to reduce the duration of a hospital stay for a certain medical procedure. The health of incoming patients is not controlled by the hospital directly, but the patients' health almost certainly will affect the duration of their stay irrespective of how well the evaluated program has performed (Productivity Commission, 2013). Paying careful attention to mediating factors during a program evaluation can yield more accurate analytic results.

If it helps, you might think about the first three steps in the logic model (inputs, activities, and outputs) as occurring **inside the studio** while the last two steps (outcomes and impacts) occur **outside the studio**. The metaphor of a studio is meant to capture the idea that there exists a place in which creative work (art, film, architecture, or, in our case, a public program) is developed prior to its broader distribution to the public at large.[2] When we evaluate a program, it's a good idea to remember that the program's manager and staff have direct control only over things within the confines of the program (i.e., inside the studio) and have much less control over how the program plays out in society over time (i.e., outside the studio).

This terminology may make more sense with an example. Exhibit 2-3 displays a logic model that I put together for an analysis of Federal research and development (R&D) programs intended to foster the deployment of new clean energy technologies (Linquiti, 2015). Reading from left to right, we start with the *inputs* to the program. Inputs include, of course, funding, but also the scientists and engineers who conduct the research, the facilities in which they do their work, and the existing state of the art with regard to technical and scientific knowledge.

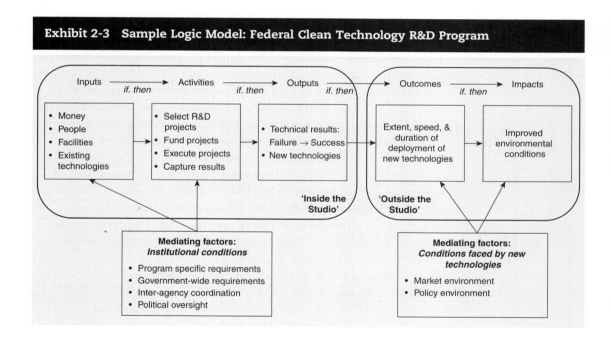

Exhibit 2-3   Sample Logic Model: Federal Clean Technology R&D Program

---

[2]One could argue about whether program outputs should be described as inside or outside the studio. Because outputs occur at the intersection of the program itself and the larger community, perhaps it's more accurate to say that outputs stand in the doorway of the studio.

The program then engages in *activities* that make use of these inputs. Based on the current state of the field, a set of potential R&D projects is identified and then narrowed to a shorter list for funding. Projects are staffed and set in motion. Once projects are underway, they are monitored and perhaps revised midstream. Once projects are complete, results are recorded with some form of documentation that can be shared with others.

These activities, in turn, create the program's *outputs* which may include new technical knowledge relevant to innovation, and if things go well, tangible new working technologies. Even if an R&D project fails, there is still an output: knowledge about what doesn't work, thereby saving another research team the time and effort of working on a fruitless endeavor in the future. At this point, we might be tempted to end our evaluation of the program; after all, creating new technologies is the reason we started the program in the first place.

But, a moment's thought should convince you that we really don't care about new technologies sitting in some research facility. We've got to go beyond the confines of the program itself and look at its *outcomes* more broadly in society. In short, we care about whether these technologies are actually deployed and how quickly and deeply they penetrate the market for energy technologies. Perhaps a new technology is more expensive than its predecessor, and as a consequence of market realities, is rarely deployed. Perhaps the new technology is so complex and capital-intensive that it takes several years to fully penetrate the market.

Having characterized outcomes, we're still not quite done; we need to keep our eyes on our North Star—the purpose of the program. In this case, the ultimate goal of the program is to observe that the new technologies have a meaningful *impact* on the quality of the environment compared to a scenario in which the program did not exist (i.e., the hypothetical counterfactual). If the program ends up developing a widely deployed new technology that the private sector would have developed on its own anyway—in the absence of the government R&D program—it would be a mistake to credit the program with having had a significant impact. The states of the world with and without the program would be the same, and the change in the quality of the environment as a consequence of the new technology, would also be the same. On the other hand, of course, if the size and scope of the R&D project were such that a risk-averse private sector would never have undertaken the project, then the environmental improvement can be reasonably characterized as a program impact.

Finally, Exhibit 2-3 identifies two sets of *mediating factors* that provide additional context for our program evaluation. The first relates to the program itself and addresses the political, bureaucratic, and institutional conditions that affect both the level of inputs provided to the program and the ways in which the day-to-day operations of the program are conducted. The second set of mediating factors affects conditions relevant to, but distinct from the program itself (e.g., market conditions that affect whether firms find it profitable to pay for the new technologies). These factors are beyond the direct control of the program's administrators but nonetheless affect the prospects for the success or failure of the program.

Building a logic model before you dive into your retrospective evaluation has a number of advantages. First, the act of creating it will force you to develop a deep understanding of the rationale behind the program and assess whether it's even plausible that a causal link exists between inputs and impacts. Second, the model can serve as a map of the terrain you might study with your program evaluation. You could, for example, endeavor to study the entire program or just one part of it; with a logic model in hand, sorting this out will be easier. Finally, characterizing mediating factors that create the context for the program serves as an important reminder of the complex systems in which public programs operate and the often large and powerful forces that can affect their prospects of success.

Before reading on, I suggest you think about an existing program with which you are familiar, take out a sheet of paper, and try to describe its Theory of Change in a sentence or two and then sketch the associated logic model. Lay out the five boxes from left to right and try to fill in each with a couple bullet points to describe its content. Take a crack at listing the mediating factors—both inside and outside the studio—that affect the program. Think about how the Theory of Change that may have driven the program's structure. Don't worry if you can't actually create a model that you're confident is right. This is simply a quick exercise to give you some hands-on practice with the concepts we've just reviewed.

2.4 DECIDE ON THE SCOPE OF YOUR RETROSPECTIVE ANALYSIS

There are two fundamental dimensions that define the scope of a retrospective policy analysis. The first is whether the study focuses primarily inside the studio (a program evaluation) or outside the studio (an impact evaluation). The second dimension is whether the study is part of the learning process during program development (a formative evaluation) or whether the study is being used to render a more definitive verdict on the performance of a mature program that has been fully implemented (a summative evaluation). Let's tackle each dimension separately.

The first dimension of the scope of a retrospective analysis is whether it's an inside-the-studio program evaluation or an outside-the-studio impact evaluation. As shown in Exhibit 2-4, an analysis focused inside the studio addresses the implementation of the first three elements of the logic model—inputs, activities, and outputs—and is referred to as a **program evaluation**. When it comes to an analysis focused outside the studio, however, the nomenclature has been evolving in recent years. Previously, all aspects of retrospective evaluation were usually lumped together

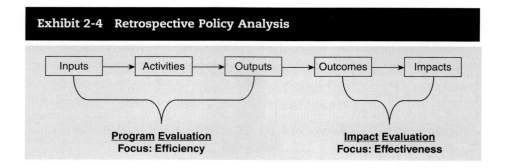

Exhibit 2-4   Retrospective Policy Analysis

Inputs → Activities → Outputs → Outcomes → Impacts

Program Evaluation
Focus: Efficiency

Impact Evaluation
Focus: Effectiveness

and characterized as program evaluation. It's now increasingly common to refer to an evaluation that addresses outcomes or impacts as an **impact evaluation**.

Another difference between program evaluation and impact evaluation is that the former focuses on the efficiency of the program while the latter addresses its effectiveness. The efficiency of a program is measured by comparing inputs and outputs and asking *whether we're getting the maximum output for a given level of inputs*[3] or, conversely, whether we've minimized the use of inputs for a given level of output. In casual conversation, you might refer to this as getting the biggest bang for the buck.

Consider a nonprofit group that shelters women and children experiencing abuse; suppose it has a staff of five members. When we ask about the program's efficiency, we're asking whether the organization's structure, systems, procedures, and facilities have been set up to allow those five staff to provide the highest possible level of service to its clients. If the answer were no, we would say that inefficiencies exist and would hope that our program evaluation can point us toward operational changes that would improve efficiency (i.e., offer a higher level of service to more clients with the same inputs). Efficiency can also be thought of in inverse terms. Imagine that our shelter serves 250 women and children per year. Now imagine another shelter that also does an equally good job of serving 250 people, but it does so with three staff, rather than five. Getting the same results with fewer resources is another example of increased efficiency.

While a program evaluation asks whether the program is doing things as efficiently as possible, an impact evaluation asks whether the program is doing the right things. In other words, in an impact evaluation, we broaden our scope to include outcomes and impacts and ask *whether the program has been effective at achieving the goals*

---

[3]You may be familiar with fuel efficiency standards for automobiles where the metric of interest is miles-per-gallon and our goal is usually to maximize the number of miles we can drive on one gallon of gasoline. When we assess efficiency in a program evaluation, we're engaged in a conceptually analogous way of thinking.

and objectives that comprise its core purpose. There are no universally acknowledged definitions of the terms efficiency and effectiveness (Productivity Commission, 2013). For me, I think Drucker (2009) got it right when he said that efficiency is "the ability to do things right" while effectiveness is the ability to "get the right things done" (pp. 1, 2). For our hypothetical shelter, we'd ask not how efficiently services are being delivered but rather how effective the program has been in creating a significant positive impact on the lives of the women and children it serves.

Sometimes students wonder which is more important: efficiency or effectiveness. My short answer is that both are important, although effectiveness is more important. Why?, Given that the concept of effectiveness captures the degree to which a program achieves its goals, and that such goals are the motivating driver of the program's existence in the first place, it stands to reason that we care more about a program's effectiveness than its efficiency.

That said, we can't ignore efficiency even in a very effective program. That's the case for at least a couple of reasons. First, since we're talking about public policy, most folks would agree that government has an obligation to make best use of the funds it raises through taxes. If an effective program is being operated in an inefficient manner, there exists a latent opportunity to attain the same policy goals but at a lower cost. Failing to seize that opportunity represents a waste of taxpayer money. Second, some studies have shown that efficient programs are more effective than inefficient programs (Choi & Jung, 2017). When you think about it, this makes sense. An inability to use resources efficiently could be a signal that a program's design has fundamental problems or that its managers don't have the necessary skills and abilities to run it well. In either case, these inefficiencies may make it hard to deliver meaningful results that serve the program's overarching goals and objectives.

On the other hand, efficiency in an ineffective program isn't much better. Linda Langston, President of the National Association of Counties, crystalized the issue when she observed that "you can be really efficient at going 100 mph, but if it's in the wrong direction, what good does it do?" (Luzer, 2013). She goes on to give the example of a city-run health clinic that efficiently sees a large number of patients every day. But if the fast turnaround of patients means that underlying health conditions are not being addressed, then patients may return repeatedly to the clinic for additional treatment, costing the local government more money and leaving the patients in worse health for longer periods of time. In other words, such a clinic would be efficient in its operations but ineffective in achieving its goals and objectives.

Even though both concepts are in fact continua, with gradations of efficiency or effectiveness along a spectrum, you can visualize their relationship by thinking in binary terms and juxtaposing effectiveness and efficiency in a 2×2 matrix (Choi & Jung, 2017), as shown in Exhibit 2-5.

Exhibit 2-5	Impact of Efficiency and Effectiveness on Evaluation	
	Ineffective Program	**Effective Program**
Efficient Program	*3rd Best Situation* Goals Not Being Achieved but Resource Waste Minimized	*Best Situation* Goals Being Achieved and Optimal Resource Use
Inefficient Program	*Worst Situation* Goals Not Being Achieved and Resources Being Wasted	*2nd Best Situation* Goals Being Achieved but with Suboptimal Resource Use

The distinction between a program evaluation and an impact evaluation also has important implications for the data sources, methodology, and types of analysis one uses in the evaluation. For a program evaluation focusing on inputs, activities, and outputs, the objects of study are generally inside the studio and tangibly linked to the program. By talking to people directly involved in the program (both staff and stakeholders) and looking at the associated documentation and administrative data, we should be able to collect most of the data we need.

In contrast, for an impact evaluation, we look outside the studio, beyond the program itself. It may be harder to trace direct, well-documented, lines between the program and its outcomes and impacts. The analytic challenge is exacerbated by the need for a counterfactual that permits us to visualize the world without the program, so that we have something against which to benchmark the program.

The second element of the scope of the evaluation is whether it will focus primarily on making suggestions for improving program operations or on rendering a definitive verdict about the value of the program. The first type of inquiry is usually characterized as a **formative assessment**, the latter as a **summative assessment** (Kellogg Foundation, 2004; NSF, 2010). The difference is cleverly explained by the University of Illinois's Robert Stake who is reported to have said that "when the cook tastes the soup, that's formative; when the guests tastes the soup, that's summative" (NSF, 2010, p. 8).

Formative assessments are best used in the early phases of a program's development. A *formative assessment is an opportunity for learning and program improvement* before a program is fully implemented. In contrast, a *summative assessment aims to discern whether the program is serving its purpose* and is typically applied to a mature program in full operation. A summative assessment can focus on the program itself and investigate whether the program is efficiently creating valuable outputs, or it might address outcomes and impacts and ask whether the program is effective at producing meaningful results.

To recap, at this point in the process, you've defined the scope of your retrospective policy analysis and you've determined whether you are conducting an inside-the-studio program evaluation or an outside-the-studio impact evaluation (or both). And lastly, you've decided whether to do a formative assessment to improve the performance of a developing program or a summative assessment to render a verdict on the performance and value of a mature program. Now, your next task is to come up with specific evaluation questions that will guide the design of your retrospective evaluation project.

2.5 IDENTIFY THE EVALUATION QUESTIONS AND SELECT AN APPROPRIATE RESEARCH DESIGN

Carefully specifying your evaluation questions is a critical step in producing a high-quality analysis. Simply put, an **evaluation question** is one that your retrospective analysis will try to answer. The typical evaluation might pose three to seven primary questions. Your evaluation questions should be tightly linked to your previous decisions about the program's logic model and Theory of Change and the scope of your review (i.e., inside the studio vs. outside the studio and formative vs. summative assessment).

Take a look at Exhibit 2-6 for suggested questions that correspond to the types of analysis we've been talking about. These questions should get you started, but expect to customize them. Your goal is an understanding of how well a program is working, not a set of answers to rote questions in a textbook. As you finalize the questions, retain your curiosity about how the pieces fit together. Remember the Five Whys technique and ask questions to identify causal linkages among program components. Take care to ask questions that tease out both the positive and negative attributes of the program.

The importance of such questions is twofold. First, by answering the full set of evaluation questions, you should be able to get a sufficiently complete picture of the program to allow you to evaluate it. If you leave out an important evaluation question, then your study will have a gap when it comes to generating the evidence you need to reach a judgment about how well the program is performing. To put it bluntly: If you ask the wrong questions, the answers won't be much help in developing a credible understanding of how and why a program is or is not producing meaningful results.

Second, the evaluation questions drive the **research design**. In short, you need to design an approach to the research process that lets you collect and analyze data in ways that yield answers to the questions. Without evaluation questions to guide you, you can't put together a coherent plan for what to study and, perhaps more importantly, what not to study. The result can be a lot of wasted time and effort.

Exhibit 2-6   Common Evaluation Questions Asked in Different Types of Retrospective Evaluation

Step of Logic Model	Purpose of Evaluation	Type of Assessment	Common Evaluation Questions
• Inputs • Activities • Outputs	Program Evaluation to Assess Efficiency	*Formative*: Early phase of program or new activity within program	• Have adequate resources been made available? • Has reasonable progress been made toward implementation? If not, why not? • How well do assumptions made during program design match "real-world" conditions? • Is program being implemented as envisioned? If not, why not? • Have problems emerged? If so, why? • Have corrective actions been taken? If so, how well have they worked? • What, if anything, should be done differently?
		Summative: After full implementation of program	• To what degree was program implemented as envisioned? • Were intended outputs delivered? • Did program have unintended side effects? • Were program resources used to produce outputs as efficiently as possible? If not, why not?
• Outcomes • Impacts	Impact Evaluation to Assess Effectiveness	*Summative*: After full implementation of program	*Outcomes* • Were intended program outcomes attained? If not, why not? • Was there a demonstrable link between outputs and outcomes? • Did program produce unintended side effects? • Did outcomes vary over time or across program components? If so, why? • Were outcomes commensurate with resources invested? *Impacts* • What would the state of the world have been in the absence of program (i.e., counterfactual)? • How has the state of the world changed as a causal consequence of the program? • Did program cause the envisioned impact? If not, why not? • Within program, was any particular approach more effective than another in creating impacts?

Source: Adapted, in part, from GAO (2012)

Exhibit 2-7 illustrates how the appropriate options for your research design are closely linked to the scope of your analysis. Note that Exhibit 2-7 is not exhaustive, but it is meant simply to provide you with an illustrative list of some research designs you might consider. In fact, there are so many options for your research design that it

Exhibit 2-7	Appropriate Research Design Depends on Questions Being Asked and on Type of Evaluation
Type of Assessment	**Illustrative Research Design Options**
Formative Program Evaluation	• Compare program activities to authorizing statute, regulations, or other policymaker decisions • Compare program activities to project plans, schedules • Compare actual allocated financial and human resources to resources expected at program initiation • Investigate state of management systems, fitness for purpose • Interview a diverse range of people with firsthand knowledge of implementation progress • Characterize early outputs of program and assess degree of alignment with expectations • If possible, compare early outputs to provided inputs to develop preliminary assessment of efficiency
Summative Program Evaluation	In addition to the research design options noted above, consider additional options: • Compare program activities and outputs to stakeholder expectations • Compare program performance to quality, cost, or efficiency expectations • Assess variations in program performance across different locations, target groups, or program components • Interview a diverse range of people with firsthand knowledge of program outputs • Conduct in-depth case studies of areas where program performance appears especially strong or especially weak • Assess if and how mediating factors external to the program affected its internal operations
Summative Evaluation of Outcomes	• Compare program outcomes to stakeholder expectations about efficiency and effectiveness • Assess change in outcomes for participants before and after exposure to the program • Characterize causal linkage between program outputs and program outcomes • Assess variations in outcomes across different locations, target groups, or program components • Assess if and how mediating factors external to the program affected its outcomes
Summative Evaluation of Impacts	In addition to a summative evaluation of each outcome (see above), compare outcomes for: • Randomly assigned participating treatment group and nonparticipating control group (assuming random assignment is both ethical and feasible) • Program participants and a comparison group of nonparticipants closely matched on key characteristics • Participants at multiple points in time before and after program participation with statistical analyses

Source: Adapted, in part, from GAO (2012)

would take a textbook to cover all of them in detail. My purpose here is simply to introduce the concept of a research design.

Once you've settled on a general approach, you need to develop a specific research design. The *research design typically comprises three elements: the information you seek, the method by which you collect it, and the techniques you use to analyze it.* You have many options at this point in the process. You can collect qualitative information by interviewing or doing focus groups with people who may have answers to your questions, or you might assemble quantitative data from a survey of potentially hundreds of folks. You'll want to talk to people who work in the program you're studying, people who are served by it, and people who represent key stakeholders who authorize and fund the program. Make a special effort to hear from folks who are targeted by the program but who may find it hard to participate in the evaluative process (e.g., single parents, isolated rural residents, undocumented immigrants, small businesses, to name just a few).

You might do a few deep-dive case studies where you look very closely at specific instances of the program's operation in different locations, among different target groups, or across different program components. Alternatively, you could take a broader approach by investigating the entirety of the program's operations but at a higher level of aggregation. If you're lucky enough to have the time and resources, you could combine individual case studies with a broad characterization of the program.

You will also want to take a look at the administrative records being kept by the program. If the program was set up with an eye toward its future evaluation, data on important metrics regarding inside-the-studio inputs, activities, and outputs should be available to support your program evaluation. If you're lucky, the program may also have tracked some of the types of outside-the-studio outcomes you'll need to measure to conduct an impact evaluation. Even if there was no planning for a future evaluation, you will still likely be able to cobble together important information from a review of program administrative data. With data in hand, you could apply sophisticated statistical techniques, use text processing software, convene a group of experts to review it, or just think deeply about the interpretation of what you found.

2.6 DEFINE THE COUNTERFACTUAL FOR IMPACT EVALUATION

If your retrospective analysis includes an impact evaluation, your evaluation questions and research design must incorporate a sound method for developing *a counterfactual that describes the state of the world in the absence of the program.* Recall that a program's impact is not simply the result we observe after program implementation, but is the difference between the observed outcome and what the outcome would have been had the program not existed.

Why is that the case? When it comes to impact evaluation, we are interested in causal reasoning; we want to figure out if the program 'caused' the outcome we observed, hence the need to conjure a world in which the program didn't exist and then to compare results across the two worlds. Social scientists sometimes refer to the result of this comparison as an estimate of the **treatment effect**. Such vocabulary envisions the evaluated program as a treatment, akin to a therapy that a doctor might administer to her patient. The change in the patient's condition—*caused* by the therapy and not some other factor—is then characterized as the treatment effect.

Imagine we develop a semester-long program to help first-generation college students improve their academic performance. Suppose that we observe that students who complete the program have an average GPA of 3.10 in the semester after the program. Using the terminology of a logic model, students' postprogram GPA is an outcome. Because 3.10 is a very respectable GPA, we might be tempted to tout the beneficial impact of the program, but we shouldn't—at least not yet. We have to first figure out what student GPAs would have been in the absence of the program. There at least four different techniques we might consider (Dye, 2011).

First, we could simply do a **before and after comparison** of GPAs. With this approach, we would calculate the students' GPAs in the semester immediately before they completed the program. If the average preprogram GPA was, say, 2.95, then we would estimate the impact as an increase of 0.15 points in students' GPA (i.e., 3.10 minus 2.95). Unfortunately, this is a pretty weak estimate of the program's impact because a number of factors other than the program itself might have affected students' average GPA. As just one example, the GPAs of many students progressively improve over their college careers as they improve their study habits, become more enthusiastic about their chosen majors, and worry more about getting a job.

The second approach for thinking about the counterfactual explicitly takes account of **underlying trends not attributable to the program** that might affect the reported outcomes of the program. To continue our example from above, we might do some research and discover that the average GPA of the students in the program has been increasing by 0.05 points per semester since they entered college. If we used this approach, we'd take the preprogram GPA of 2.95 and add 0.05 to it (to account for another semester of typical GPA growth) and come up with a counterfactual GPA of 3.00 for the first semester after program completion. The program impact would then be estimated at 0.10 points (i.e., 3.10 minus 3.00). While this is an improvement over our first method, our causal case is still not as strong as it might be. Maybe the factors that have driven gradual increases in GPA are changing over time; in other words, the fact that GPAs went up by 0.05 points per semester in the past doesn't mean that they will continue to do so in the future. As you often hear in ads promoting financial investment opportunities, past performance may not be indicative of future results.

To overcome this concern, a third method uses a different approach to projecting changes in results over time by introducing a comparison group that doesn't participate in the program. (The group that participates in the program is called the treatment group.) The core idea here is that both the treatment and comparison groups would be similarly influenced by any nonprogram factors (such as a mid-semester switch to online classes) that might affect GPAs over time. We then compare the changes in the GPAs of the two groups from one semester to the next using a technique known as a **difference-in-differences** approach. This may make more sense if we continue our example.

We already know that the average GPA of the treatment group increased by 0.15 points in the first semester after the program, relative to their GPA in the prior semester. Suppose we have another group of first-generation students who don't participate in the program. Like the treatment group, their GPA starts at 2.95. Then, in the semester after their classmates complete the program, the comparison group has an average GPA of 3.05, for an increase of 0.10 points. In other words, the treatment group has a GPA increase of 0.15 points while the comparison group shows an increase of 0.10 points. We take the difference in these two differences to arrive at an estimated treatment effect of 0.05 points. Our new estimate is certainly more credible than the first two estimates, but it's still not as strong as it might be. Perhaps there's something unique about the group that has signed up for the program. Maybe they're among the hardest-working, most-motivated students at the college and their apparent increase in GPA has nothing to do with the program but simply reflects their drive and ambition.

A fourth approach—known as a **Randomized Controlled Trial** (RCT)—can overcome such challenges. With an RCT, we would randomly assign first-generation students to either participate in the program or to sit it out. While the first group is still called the treatment group, we now refer to the second group not as the comparison group but as the control group. This vocabulary reflects the increased analytic power of the RCT approach. With random assignment, we can assume that the two groups are identical (in a statistical sense), with all types of students (e.g., hard workers and slackers) having an equal chance of being assigned to each group. In short, the only difference between the two groups (again, in a statistical sense) is whether or not they've completed the program. We can then compare the postprogram GPAs of the two groups and compute the treatment effect as the difference in the two. For example, the treatment group might have a postprogram GPA of 3.10 while the control group has a GPA of 3.08. Because of the random group assignment, we know that the only difference between the two groups—as a whole—is whether they participated in the program. We then characterize the treatment effect of the studied program—its impact—as a 0.02-point increase in GPA. The RCT design is sometimes referred to as the 'gold-standard' of causal inference because of its ability to rule out other competing explanations of the observed changes in a program's outcomes. Exhibit 2-8 recaps these four methods for computing program impacts and works through the numbers associated with our hypothetical program for first-generation college students.

Exhibit 2-8 Methods for Estimating Program Impacts

Method	Group(s)	Observed Program Outcome	Counterfactual Outcome	Program Impact (Treatment Effect)
Before and After Comparison	Treatment Group	Postprogram Treatment Group GPA = 3.10	Preprogram Treatment Group GPA = 2.95	0.15 = [3.10 − 2.95]
Comparison to Projected Outcome	Treatment Group	Postprogram Treatment Group GPA = 3.10	Projected GPA of Treatment Group in Absence of Program = 3.00	0.10 = [3.10 − 3.00]
Difference in Differences	Treatment Group and Comparison Group	Change in Treatment Group GPA = 0.15 = [3.10 − 2.95]	Change in Comparison Group GPA = 0.10 = [3.05 − 2.95]	0.05 = [3.10 − 2.95] − [3.05 − 2.95]
Randomized Controlled Trial	Treatment Group and Control Group	Post-Program Treatment Group GPA = 3.10	Control Group GPA = 3.08	0.02 = [3.10 − 3.08]

The topic of drawing causal inferences from real-world data is the subject of a vast and complex literature, and we'll revisit the topic in Chapter 5. But for now, this brief discussion is meant to underscore the fact that if you want to make a causal claim in your retrospective impact evaluation, then you need to make sure that you are asking the right evaluation questions and that you have created a suitable research design to enable you to credibly characterize a counterfactual world in which the program didn't exist.

2.7 CONDUCT THE EVALUATION, DRAW YOUR CONCLUSIONS, AND COMMUNICATE THE RESULTS

Having identified your evaluation questions and crafted a research design to answer them, your next step is to conduct the evaluation. Given, however, that this is not a textbook on program evaluation and that there are more than twenty possible research designs suggested in Exhibit 2-7, and many more designs not listed, we won't get into the specifics of how to execute each design. For a deep dive, you might want to take a look at texts by Newcomer et al. (*Handbook of Practical Program Evaluation*, 2015),

Weiss (*Evaluation: Methods for Studying Programs and Policies*, 1997), or Davidson (*Evaluation Methodology Basics: The Nuts and Bolts of Sound Evaluation*, 2004). In addition, guidance provided by the Government Accountability Office (*Designing Evaluations*, 2012) is quite good. The remaining chapters of this book also provide an overview of how to combine logic and evidence to reach policy-relevant conclusions in prospective policy analysis and retrospective program and impact evaluation.

After conducting your evaluation—collecting and analyzing the data—you have to think about how you'll go about drawing conclusions and communicating your results. As you do, you may want to bear in mind recent US government guidance on the topic:

> … fundamental principles [for evaluation have] emerge[d] as common themes in established U.S. and international frameworks … These principles include rigor, relevance, independence, transparency, and ethics. Principles and practices for evaluation help to ensure that Federal program evaluations meet scientific standards, are relevant and useful, and are conducted and have results disseminated without bias or inappropriate influence. (OMB, 2018, p. 60)

How do these principles affect the reporting of your retrospective evaluation? For starters, if you conducted a formative assessment—intended to help a developing program improve its operations—be sure to include a set of actionable suggestions about how the program can be enhanced. It may help to think of yourself as a coach and mentor to program managers. Your goal is to help them understand, embrace, and act on your suggestions. But be mindful of program resources and avoid suggesting changes that the program lacks the capability to make.

If your retrospective evaluation was a summative assessment, think about the uses to which it might be put. Will it be used to allocate resources? Hold managers accountable? To inform the design of another program? Think also about who will be the audience for your report—program managers? Their bosses? The program's funders? Make sure your report provides clear responses to the questions you know your audience wants answered. But don't let an enthusiasm for definitive statements cause you to forget that conclusions must be informed by the evidence you collected and guided by sound logical inference. *If—despite your study—you still don't have an answer to a key question, don't be afraid to say so.* Honesty about uncertainty is a defining attribute of a professional policy analyst.

In addition, *don't be surprised if at least some folks seem threatened by your program evaluation.* If they work in the program, have staked their reputations on the program by funding it or authorizing it, or are the beneficiaries of the program's activities and outputs, trepidation on their part is only natural. You might have evaluated a program, the primary purpose of which is symbolic. Such programs:

… do not actually change the conditions of target groups but merely make these groups feel that the government 'cares'. A government agency does not welcome a study that reveals that its efforts have no tangible effects …. (Dye, 2011, p. 333)

If you declare that the program is poorly managed, inefficient, ineffective, or not a good use of taxpayer money, the program might be terminated or downsized. No wonder folks worry about what you might say. There is not much you can do about this phenomenon. Your results are your results and if they paint the program in an unflattering light, professional ethics prevent you from pretending otherwise.

At another level, however, there are many things you can do to avoid the worst of such situations. First, *be scrupulously neutral* in your assessment of the program; your preconceived notions about the program or the people who run it should play no role in your evaluation. Any hint of bias on your part will undermine both your credibility and that of your evaluation. Second, be sure to *report what you learned from the broad and diverse set of stakeholders* who you consulted; that way, readers of your finished report can be confident that all important voices with something to say about the program were heard. Third, when presenting results, *err on the side of transparency*. Share as much of the information that you collected during the study as you can (i.e., without breaking any commitments of confidentiality or exposing private information about individuals). That way, interested readers can dig more deeply to understand the basis of your conclusions. Fourth, while not shying away from sharing negative feedback about the program, you should always *be as constructive as possible* when you present your findings. If you need to be critical, take care to criticize the program's actions, not the people who run it. If a manager has made a poor decision, criticize the decision but not the person. In short, the advice you probably got in elementary school was right: *always try to be nice*.

Finally, keep in mind that there may be *other future audiences for your work beyond the clients of your current project*. For example, your evaluation might become a part of the greater body of knowledge that is available for future prospective policy analysis (as we talked about in Section 2.1). It may end up in an online clearinghouse of program evaluations or on an agency website where folks you've never met discover it and think about replicating the policy or program that you've studied in their own jurisdiction or organization. With a pay-it-forward mentality, try to include as much information in your report as possible to allow others to assess the potential for replicability. By providing background information in your evaluation on, for example, budget and staffing levels, community characteristics, legal authorities and structures, schedules and project plans, problems encountered and solutions found, and other lessons learned, you will make it much easier for others to extrapolate from your findings to conditions in their own situation (Bardach, 2004).

As mentioned in Section 1.6, communicating the results of a policy analysis doesn't differ very much between a prospective and retrospective evaluation. Because strong written and oral communication skills are a prerequisite to success in your career as a policy analyst, this topic deserves a deep dive, which you'll find in Chapter 7.

CHAPTER SUMMARY

This chapter began by describing several rationales for retrospective program and impact evaluation. We next considered a stylized version of the policy cycle as a means of putting both prospective policy analysis and retrospective program and impact evaluation in the same context.

We then reviewed ways to clearly delineate a program's boundaries and purpose, thereby facilitating subsequent analysis. Next up was a review of both Theory of Change thinking and logic modeling. We saw how logic models can be used to comprehensively describe the causal connections among a program's inputs, activities, outputs, outcomes, and impacts. From there, we moved on to the concepts of efficiency, effectiveness, formative assessment, and summative assessment.

We then talked about the development of evaluation questions to guide the design of retrospective research. We closed with a review of some of the common challenges that may affect the communication of the results of a retrospective analysis.

DISCUSSION QUESTIONS

1. Pick an existing program with which you are familiar. If you were to evaluate it, how would you characterize the counterfactual? What would the world look like had the program not been implemented? How do you know?

2. Pick a different existing program. How would you define its boundaries? What is its purpose—its goals and objectives? Do you think everyone sees it the same way as you do? Or are there competing visions of what the program should be doing? How would you reconcile different views about the program's purpose in order to evaluate it?

3. Pick yet another existing program. Is it obvious what the Theory of Change is? Or is it hard to discern? Do you think the Theory of Change—opaque or transparent—makes sense? Could you describe the program with a logic model?

4. What's the difference between efficiency and effectiveness? How would you assess whether a program is efficient and/or effective? Can you think of a specific program that you believe is both efficient and effective? How about an example of an efficient but ineffective program?

5. Just like a taxpayer who might be nervous about an IRS audit, politicians and public administrators may be hesitant to subject programs for which they are responsible to retrospective evaluation. Is this reasonable? Why? Why not? Can you come up with ways to frame such evaluations in a positive light?

6. Is spending money on program evaluation (which can be costly) a good use of public funds? Or should all available funds be used to maximize a program's delivery of services to its beneficiaries?

CHAPTER THREE

OBSTACLES TO USING CLASSICAL POLICY ANALYSIS MODELS IN THE REAL WORLD

Having studied Chapters 1 and 2, you've seen how the classical models tackle prospective and retrospective policy analysis and evaluation. You're in good company; these models have been taught in just about every policy school in the United States over the past few decades and thousands of students have been trained in their use. Unfortunately, there are several features of these models—and the way they're taught—that impede their value. Nonetheless, if used appropriately, the tools of policy analysis have a lot to offer when it comes to understanding and acting on public policy issues.

Accordingly, this chapter explores the obstacles that limit the value and impact of the classical models so that you're better prepared to cope with those impediments in your professional work. We start in Section 3.1 with a quick history of the field of policy analysis. Next up is an examination of the shortcomings of the classical models, split into two sections. The first set of impediments (Section 3.2) are inherent and inescapable limitations of policy-making in a democracy which cannot be overcome, even with hard work, clear thinking, or new paradigms. The second set of impediments (Section 3.3) comprises obstacles which can be mitigated, at least partially, with a rebooted version of policy analysis. Section 3.4 explains why these impediments don't fatally undermine the value of policy analysis and motivates the rebooting of the field proposed later in the book.

Learning Objectives

By studying this chapter, you should be able to:

- Describe the policy sciences movement and its influence on graduate education in policy analysis.

- Characterize postpositive policy analysis and contrast it with the classical models of policy analysis.

- Define the concepts of preference aggregation, collective action, and wicked problems, and explain how each limits the applicability of classical policy analysis.

- Explain why the classical models of policy analysis can't deliver comprehensive rationality or the certainty of the natural sciences.

- Define and differentiate descriptive and normative thinking.

- Define and differentiate analysis as inquiry and analysis as advocacy.

- Explain the characteristics of a good-faith argument and differentiate them from the characteristics of a fight.

- Explain why defining policy analysis as comprising only one or two disciplines severely limits its value and ability to generate meaningful insights.

- Describe the rationale for rebooting the field of policy analysis.

3.1 A BRIEF HISTORY OF POLICY ANALYSIS

Given the adage that 'past is prologue', it's worth your time to understand how this educational enterprise got started. As mentioned before, the field of policy analysis—referred to in its early days as the **policy sciences**—launched itself after World War II with exceedingly high ambitions. As Charles Rothwell (1951), a drafter of the 1945 United Nations Charter and later president of Mills College put it:

> [O]ur power to attain world peace, universal well-being, and individual self-realization will depend in part upon how rapidly the policy sciences develop and how widely they are accepted and used. (p. x)

Harold Lasswell (1951), a political science professor at Yale who is widely regarded as a key architect of the policy sciences, echoed Rothwell's words:

> It is probable that the policy-science orientation in the United States will be directed toward providing the knowledge needed to improve the practice of democracy. In a word, the special emphasis is upon the policy sciences of democracy, in which the ultimate goal is the realization of human dignity in theory and fact. (p. 15)

To be fair, not all early proponents of the new field of policy analysis made such grandiose claims about its potential impacts:

> Policy analysis does not presume to bring about a radical change in policymaking. ... Good policy analysis can at best become an additional component in aggregate policymaking, contributing to that process some better analysis, some novel ideas, some futuristic orientation, and some systematic thought. Policy analyses are one of the bridges between science and politics, but they do not transform the basic characteristics of the 'political' and of organization behavior. ... No metamorphosis of policymaking is aimed at, but improvements of, say, 10 to 15 percent in complex public decision-making and policymaking can be achieved through better integration of knowledge and policymaking with the help of policy analysis—and this is a lot. (Dror, 1967, p. 202)

Whether motivated by the goals of universal well-being and the realization of human dignity, or a marginal improvement of ten to fifteen percent in the quality of policy-making, the emerging field of policy analysis began to attract attention from policymakers. The field got a significant boost in the early 1960s when Defense Secretary

McNamara instituted the Policy Planning Budgeting System (PPBS) to apply cost–benefit analysis to weapons acquisition and warfighting decisions. Impressed with McNamara's innovation, President Johnson ordered government-wide adoption of PPBS, creating a demand for civil servants skilled in quantitative and economic fields. By 1971, at least 10 new graduate programs had been created in policy analysis (Allison, 2006).

Enter the Ford Foundation. Between 1973 and 1978, the Foundation gave $4.15 million (about $17 million in 2021 dollars) to 14 public policy schools. Most, if not all, of these programs had existed before the grants, but the support of the Ford Foundation solidified their standing as individual schools, as well as exemplars of a new national focus on graduate training in public policy analysis. These grants were made in response to a 1972 charge from the Foundation's Board to support "first-class programs of advanced, professional training for young people aimed at public service" (Bell, 1981, p. 1).

So, how have things turned out? On the upside, there's no doubt that policy schools are able to attract "bright and socially motivated" students (Bell, 1981, p. 39). And graduates of these programs appear to be readily employable in government, the nonprofit sector, and consulting (Friedman, 2017). On the downside, there seems to be a disconnect between what's being taught in policy schools and what can be observed in practice. As Hird (2017) put it:

> Ironically, there is little evidence of written classical policy analysis … There are copious opinions, position papers, budget analyses, testimonies, white papers, memos, and reports but little in the way of classical policy analyses. (p. 63)

Moreover, many of the policy analyses that are produced every year that seem to have little discernable impact on real-world policy decisions (Weiss, 1979).

But what about those aspirations of world peace, an improved democracy, and the realization of human dignity? Regrettably, the record is more than a bit spotty. By the 1980s, the idea that rational policy analysis could be used to significantly and continuously improve public-sector policymaking "began to wear a little thin" (Parsons, 1995, p. 434). After comparing a series of policy successes and failures in the United States after World War II, deLeon (2006) concluded that:

> American expectations and achievements have hardly produced universal progress compared to other industrialized nations, with crime, the environment, health care, and public education being only four examples. What motivated the spread of the public policy orientation was the expectation that well trained, professional analysts, appropriately focused, would produce an unbroken succession of policy successes. … the narratives above [suggest] that *the promise of the policy sciences has not been fulfilled.* (p. 47), *emphasis added*

To be sure, a collection of policy mistakes, missed opportunities, dysfunctional programs, and failed leadership is clearly disappointing, if not tragic. What is much less clear, at least to me, is whether the field of policy analysis deserves the blame for these shortcomings.

Nonetheless, a new school of thought known as **postpositive policy analysis** (so named because it represented a break from the ostensibly purely descriptive nature of the positive approach) emerged in the 1980s. Postpositivists generally believe that the classical models are doomed to provide results that do little to improve the quality of public policy (Durning, 1991). In the extreme, some postpositivists see users of the classical models as enablers of exploitive and unequal policies supported by wealthy and privileged interests. Along these lines, most postpositivists would like to see a "more authentic democratization of the policy process" (Dryzek, 2002, p. 32).

In 2012, Fischer and Gottweiss traced the arc of what became known as the argumentative turn in policy analysis:

> At the outset, the approach emphasized practical argumentation, policy judgment, frame analysis, narrative storytelling, and rhetorical analysis, among others. ... [In the intervening years], the argumentative turn expanded to include work on discourse analysis, deliberation, deliberative democracy, citizen juries, governance, expertise, participatory inquiry, local and tacit knowledge, collaborative planning, the uses and role of media, and interpretive methods. (p. 1)

The postpositivist view is not without its critics. Lawrence Lynn at Harvard's Kennedy School, for example, doesn't mince words when he argues that postpositivists are wrong to assert that traditional policy analysis is narrow and technocratic. He characterizes postpositivism as an "esoteric, pedantic irrelevance" and defends policy analysis, saying that contrary to the postpositivists' claims, the classical models do account for ethical and normative considerations, political arguments, and the voices of those who lack political power (Lynn, 1999, p. 421).

Characterizing Lynn's attack on postpositivism as "savage," Dryzek (2002) fires back:

> Even if analysis in the technocratic idiom stands no chance of being acted upon in efficient and unchanged fashion, the mere presence of technocratic policy analysis serves to reinforce a discourse of disempowerment for those who are not part of the technocratic specialization being deployed or are not the targeted 'policymakers' for the analysis in question. (p. 33)

Let me jump into this back and forth and make three quick observations. First, it's clear that both Lynn and Dryzek agree that a narrow, formulaic, and technocratic version of policy analysis doesn't align well with the processes of democratic policy-making. I think they've got that right.

Second, while the postpositivists are correct that the classical models have significant shortcomings, my personal view is that it's unreasonable to hold workaday policy analysts responsible for deconstructing the impact of dominant ideologies on policy choices, ferreting out the sinister influence of powerful but opaque interests, and creating a more genuine version of democracy. On their face, none of these goals is unreasonable. But in the same way that it was wildly unrealistic to expect the policy sciences to achieve the goal of "universal well-being," it seems equally unrealistic to expect postpositive policy analysis to deliver a "more authentic democratization" of policymaking. And, from a purely pragmatic perspective, I suspect that there aren't many employers out there who are willing to pay the salaries of postpositive policy analysts.

Third, no matter how compelling you find the postpositive critique of traditional policy analysis, its glaring weakness is that it doesn't offer a feasible alternative approach for a restructured policy analysis (Durning, 1991). Even Dryzek (2002) admits that:

> Postpositivism does not … connote a well-defined recipe book for doing policy analysis, and in this it is at a disadvantage with more traditional kinds of policy analysis, especially when it comes to curriculum design. It has perhaps done better when it comes to critique of its traditional opponents than in providing such recipes. (p. 32)

Where do we go from here? Yes, many of the early proponents of the policy sciences were quixotic, overpromising on results that couldn't be delivered. On the other hand, the postpositivists seem to miss the mark when they unfairly blame traditional models for the maladies of democratic governance writ large without having a specific and actionable alternative to offer to aspiring policy analysts.

We might be tempted to dismiss both schools of thought, but we need to take care not to throw the baby out with the bath water. Policy analysis can and does make a meaningful, albeit limited, contribution to public-sector problem-solving (Friedman, 2017; Hird, 2017; Lynn, 1999; Shapiro, 2016). Rather than viewing the classical models as the essence of policy analysis, we need to see them for what they really are: simply a point of departure for substantially more thoughtful, realistic, and nuanced ways of contributing to the analysis of public policy issues.

3.2 INESCAPABLE PATHOLOGIES OF THE CLASSICAL MODELS

The first step in my proposed rebooting of policy analysis is therefore to better understand where and why the classical models come up short. In my view, understanding what policy analysis cannot do is a prerequisite to visualizing what it can do. As shown in Exhibit 3-1, there are at least five important things that the classical models of policy analysis can never offer. *These issues are inherent features of democratic governance itself; they don't originate in the field of policy analysis.* These vexations virtually guarantee that the classical models of policy analysis can't provide a definitive recommendation about the socially optimal way of resolving any particular policy problem.

Exhibit 3-1 Classical Policy Analysis Models Don't…

- Solve the preference aggregation problem
- Solve collective action problems
- Solve wicked problems
- Deliver comprehensive rationality
- Offer the certainty of the natural sciences

3.2.1 The Models Don't Solve the Preference Aggregation Problem

As noted in the Introduction to Part I, policy analysis aims to inform public policy decisionmaking. At the time, I glossed over the question of who is doing the deciding. Unless we live in a society with an authoritarian dictator, public policy decisions inevitably reflect the preferences of more than one actor. These actors could be individual citizens casting votes, interest groups advocating different policies, or elected officials debating and deciding which policies to enact.

In a democracy, therefore, we need to **aggregate preferences**. Unfortunately, unless we're only making a binary choice between two options and have adopted majority rule, there is no unambiguously correct way to aggregate everyone's individual preferences into a single set of social preferences. Nobel Laureate Ken Arrow proved as much with his impossibility theorem (1951). Arrow demonstrated that it is impossible to go from multiple individual preferences to one society-wide preference without violating one or more very reasonable assumptions (e.g., all voters' preference should be given equal standing, that voters can express their preferences as a rank ordering of available choices, and that individual voters' preferences be transitive—if A is preferred to B, and B to C, then A should be preferred to C). Stokey and Zeckhauser (1978) summarize the conundrum:

> Philosophers and economists have tried for two centuries to devise unambiguous procedures for measuring and combining the welfares of two

or more individuals to provide a measure of total social welfare. Their quest has been about as successful as the alchemists' attempts to transmute lead into gold. ... Indeed, Kenneth Arrow has virtually demonstrated that we should give up the search. (p. 276)

When Arrow published his mathematical explanation of the situation in the 1950s, the problem of preference aggregation had already been around for a long time. Constitution writers and nation builders have worked for at least the last three centuries to build democratic institutions—like elected legislatures and parliaments, presidents and prime ministers, ballot initiatives and referenda, and federalist systems that share power among national, regional, and local governments—to approximate public preferences on matters of public policy.

So, where does this leave the field of policy analysis? In a democracy, we want citizen preferences to have a strong influence on policy choices, but policy analysts are stuck without an obvious mechanism for aggregating those preferences to inform their advice to policymakers. It's clear that a nationwide direct democracy where citizens vote on every element of every public policy isn't remotely feasible. Moreover, most of the analytic techniques embedded in the classical model of policy analysis sidestep the issue:

[The traditional model assumes a] unitary decision-maker, or a group acting as a unit, and [is] not immediately applicable to situations involving two or more actors with different objectives. ... If a joint decision is required, they will have to resolve their differences through interactive processes like negotiation and persuasion, about which the model is silent. (Majone, 1989, p. 15)

The three techniques described in Section 1.5—cost–benefit analysis, cost-effectiveness analysis, and multiattribute analysis—are all attempts to solve the preference aggregation problem. In some circumstances, they can be helpful, but the process of discerning social—rather than personal—preferences is not formulaic. Instead, it is complex, dynamic, and filled with uncertainty. In this context, it is both unreasonable and unfair to expect policy analysts by themselves to point us to the policy choice that best reflects aggregated citizen preferences. Indeed, *if policy analysis were up to this task, it would somehow have managed to solve a fundamental challenge of democratic governance* that has vexed societies for centuries.

3.2.2 The Models Don't Solve Collective Action Problems

A common role for governments is to provide or manage **public goods**, resources that exhibit two important characteristics. First, they are **nonrivalrous**, meaning that one person's consumption of a good doesn't reduce another person's ability to consume the same good. Second, they are **nonexcludable**, meaning that it is infeasible to prevent somebody from consuming the good. The quintessential example of a public good is national defense. Once the military provides protection, one person's 'consumption' of national defense doesn't diminish the next person's ability to also 'consume' it (nonrivalry). Moreover, everyone benefits from national defense, irrespective of how much they pay in taxes or whether they would choose to be protected in the first place (nonexcludability). A closely related type of good is a **common pool resource** which is rivalrous but from which people can't be excluded. Here, the quintessential example is a fishery where anyone with a boat can go out and take fish, but the more fish they take, the fewer fish that are available for others.

When dealing with a public good or common pool resource, it is often possible to achieve a better, society-wide outcome through mutual cooperation, than is possible when everyone pursues their own narrow self-interest. When it comes to a public good, for example, it is in an individual's self-interest to shirk responsibility for paying for the public good, because he or she knows that once other citizens have provided the good, he or she will benefit from it despite not paying for it. This phenomenon is referred to as **free riding**. Imagine we went around the country and asked everyone how much they were willing to pay for national defense. Most folks would be tempted to free ride, and would report a number lower than their true willingness to pay for defense. We would then add up all the numbers and fund national defense at a lower level than what folks, in the aggregate, were actually willing to pay. This phenomenon is known is the **underprovision of a public good**.

Similarly, with a common pool resource, a self-interested individual may endeavor to maximize his or her use of the resource, despite the fact that if everyone pursues the same strategy, the resource will not be put to best advantage in the aggregate. This phenomenon is sometimes referred to as the **tragedy of the commons**, based on an influential essay by Hardin (1968).[1] Remember, a common pool resource is nonexcludable. Thus, in the case of a fishery, anyone can go fishing. A typical outcome will in turn be an unsustainable level of overfishing as each fisher gets all the benefit of taking more fish while only incurring a portion of the cost (i.e., the destruction of the fishery over time, an impact which is shared among all fishers). The irony is that as each fisher pursues his or her own short-term self-interest, the fishers—as a group—are working against their own long-term interests.

The **collective action problem** gained substantial attention from scholars after publication of Mancur Olson's influential book, *The Logic of Collective Action* (1965). In

---

[1] Nobel Laureate Elinor Ostrom studied community management of common pool resources around the world and concluded that over-use of such resources is not inevitable. Especially in communities with strong social systems, wise use of the resource can become a norm that ensures its sustainable use (Dietz, Ostrom, & Stern, 2003).

it, Olson explored the consequences of a misalignment between individual and group incentives. Such misalignments can arise when the sum of individual (or private) costs and benefits is not equal to collective (or social) costs and benefits. In the case of a fishery, for example, the gains of overfishing accrue to individuals (at least for a while) until resource depletion leads to social costs for all. Olson argued that the *mere existence of a common interest is not enough to motivate individuals to pursue that interest in the face of competing interests at the personal level* (Heckelman, 2015). In other words:

> [Olson] demonstrated that individual rationality is not sufficient to achieve collective rationality. Thus, individuals may pursue self-interested actions that do not further the best interests of the group. (Sandler, 2015, p. 196), internal references omitted

What does the collective action problem have to do with policy analysis? The answer begins with the realization that public policy is the primary mechanism for mitigating collective action problems among large groups of people and organizations. Without a mechanism for policymaking and the use of the coercive power of the state, providing public goods and managing common pool resources would be almost impossible at all but the smallest, and most local, of scales (where private arrangements and legally enforceable contracts might suffice).

For instance, clean air in an urban setting is a public good. If one group of people invests in cars with lower pollutant emissions, but others don't, then the second group gets the benefit of somewhat cleaner air without incurring the cost of emission reductions (i.e., they free ride on the first group's efforts). Knowing this might happen, the first group loses the incentive to take action in the first place. Similarly, in international waters, which is a common pool resource beyond the control of any one country, several fisheries around the world are currently under intense pressure as the result of substantial overfishing (suggesting an inability to solve a collective action problem).

How then can policy analysis inform decisionmaking in such cases? Policy scholars have developed tools for partially addressing these issues by, for example, coming up with clever ways to assess folks' willingness to pay for public goods (as a means of addressing the underprovision of public goods). Similarly, considerable effort has gone into creating mechanisms to allocate the rights to use common pool resources in ways that align personal incentives with social objectives. While such techniques can be useful, they are, however, imperfect and do little to mitigate the underlying drivers of the collective action problem (i.e., the wedge between private and social costs and benefits). Irrespective of public policy, individuals and countries will always have an incentive to free ride on others' provision of public goods; similarly, there will always be an incentive for an individual to overuse a common pool resource. The fact that policy analysis doesn't offer a definitive means of resolving these dilemmas in all situations is not a flaw in policy analysis per se. Rather, these conditions reflect the intrinsic reality in which public policy exists.

3.2.3 The Models Can Only Help Manage, Not Solve, Wicked Problems

Public policies are targeted at issues that vary widely in their complexity and in our ability to fully characterize their true nature. At one end of the spectrum are **well-structured problems**, like road maintenance and library services. The objectives are well-understood and not especially controversial, the available options are readily apparent, and the pros and cons of different approaches are not particularly uncertain. In the middle of the spectrum are **semistructured problems** where there is greater uncertainty and potential disagreement about public goals. Shoring up the finances of the social security retirement system, for example, might fall into this category. To start, we have to look 50 to 75 years in the future. We can make reasonable, but still uncertain, predictions about the number of beneficiaries, the payments they're entitled to, and the likely contributions they'll make over their working lives. What's more, we have to wrestle with normative questions like the degree to which current workers should subsidize retired workers. Sorting out social security is certainly not as easy as figuring out how to pave a road, but it's still an issue we can get our heads around.

The other end of the spectrum is reserved for what scholars call **wicked problems** (Daviter, 2017; Head, 2008; Levin, Cashore, Bernstein, & Auld, 2012; Rittel & Webber, 1973). Not only are they poorly structured, but also that wicked problems have characteristics that make them especially difficult, or even impossible, to definitively resolve. Examples include climate change, global terrorism, human trafficking, and the pernicious effects of money in politics. Wickedness is not, however, a synonym for difficult. Running the air traffic control system, administering the Federal tax system, and operating a national military force are all difficult tasks, but they are not wicked. Instead, problems become wicked when traditional planning methods provide, at best, limited help in figuring out what to do next and, at worst, can actually lead to 'solutions' that exacerbate the problem (Camillus, 2008).

The concept of wickedness was first applied to public policy in a 1973 article by two Berkeley professors who identified ten attributes of wicked problems (Rittel & Webber, pp. 161–166).

1. "There is no definitive formulation of a wicked problem." The complexity of the issues and the intermingling of multiple causes and effects mean that it is virtually impossible to demonstrate that any one definition of a wicked problem is unambiguously correct.

2. "Wicked problems have no stopping rule." There isn't a definitive solution to a wicked problem. We can always investigate further, learn more, and try to improve our analysis. We must address wicked problems with less evidence and analysis than we'd like.

3. "Solutions to wicked problems are not true or false, but good or bad." For wicked problems, there is no single definition of policy success. What would it look like to end systemic racism? To secure the border? To get money out of politics?

4. "There is no immediate and no ultimate test of a solution to a wicked problem." Policies aimed at tackling wicked problems often cause unintended consequences. It can take years, sometimes generations, to see the full effects (good and bad) of policy action.

5. "Every solution to a wicked problem is a 'one-shot' operation; because there is no opportunity to learn by trial and error, every attempt counts significantly." With well- and semistructured problems, we can reverse course if the solution doesn't work. Not so for wicked problems; when we attempt a solution, we change the nature of the problem.

6. "Wicked problems do not have an exhaustively describable set of potential solutions, nor is there a well-described set of permissible operations that may be incorporated into the plan." Because of their complexity and the divergent normative goals embedded in their potential solutions, there are many policy options to consider as solutions to wicked problems.

7. "Every wicked problem is essentially unique." Public problems may look similar over time or across locations, but for a wicked problem, the drivers of the problem and the likely results of potential solutions depend heavily on case-specific facts and circumstances. Experience addressing it in one place or time may be of little value in another context.

8. "Every wicked problem can be considered to be a symptom of another problem." Wicked problems are linked to one another as causes and effects within a system. The classical model looks at each problem in isolation and struggles with multidimensional problems.

9. "The choice of explanation determines the nature of the problem's resolution." Because of the complexity of wicked problems and starkly contrasting value judgments, a wide range of problem definitions are arguably correct. The contest over solutions to wicked problems thus often reverts to a fight about the problem definition.

10. "The planner has no right to be wrong." Depending on a community's tolerance for trial and error on the part of its public servants, a failed attempt to solve a wicked problem can lead to lost elections for policymakers and lost jobs for policy analysts.

These ten criteria can be distilled into a definition of a wicked problem as one that exists at the intersection of three conditions (Head, 2008). The first is the **complexity** of the system in which the problem arises and the number and nature of interdependencies among the elements and subsystems within that system. The second is the level of **uncertainty** about current conditions, about how policy actions might affect outcomes, and about the risk of undesired outcomes. The third is the extent of the **divergence of material interests and value preferences** among key stakeholders. The presence of any one of these three characteristics does not signify wickedness. Instead, it is the confluence of all three within the same situation—great complexity, significant uncertainty, and widely divergent viewpoints—that together render a problem wicked.

So, what happens when we apply the classical models of policy analysis to wicked problems? Given the nature of wicked problems, it has become almost a truism in the policy analysis literature that such problems are rarely solved. At best, they are partially tamed by policy measures that ameliorate the worst of their impacts (Daviter, 2017). Sometimes, however, policy interventions only make wicked problems worse. Short-term and superficial measures can create the appearance of action when, in fact, the situation continues to deteriorate, or the new measures themselves create problematic unintended consequences. Better policy analysis is not the only answer:

> [Wicked public policy problems] are inherently resistant to a clear statement of the problem and resistant to a clear and agreed solution. Science cannot resolve these dilemmas by filling the gaps in empirical knowledge. (Head, 2008, p. 102)

Expecting a policy analyst to dig into a toolkit of methods and skills to solve wicked problems like systemic racism, narcoterrorism, or intergenerational poverty is to put him or her in an impossible situation. In the same way that we don't expect physicians to cure all illnesses and ensure that we all live long into old age, we cannot expect policy analysts—working on their own—to bring an end to wicked problems. In short, *the difficulty here lies not in shortcomings of policy analysis as a discipline but in the way that historical, social, and economic forces intersect with the limitations of democratic governance* to create wicked problems that often defy solution.

3.2.4 The Models Don't Deliver Comprehensively Rational Conclusions

You could be forgiven for looking at the classical models of policy analysis in Chapters 1 and 2 and overestimating their ability to render a definitive judgment about the best way to address a public policy issue. These models seem to promise a clear path from a public problem to a policy 'solution.' Their formulaic specification appears to lead unerringly from problem to solution. We clarify and agree on the ends (the problem to be solved and the criteria by which to judge policy options) and then characterize the means (the set of policy options) by which we might achieve those ends. We project how the options will play out over time and select the option that will best serve society. What could be more logical or rational?

Unfortunately, it's not that simple. Drill down a bit on this model of comprehensive rationality and you quickly discover just how demanding it is. You'll need to:

- Collect abundant *evidence* about the true state of the world and characterize it without distortion or error.

- Discern and reconcile competing *normative value judgments* to guide problem definition, option identification, and the choice of evaluation criteria. Value judgments also need to be operationalized similarly across issues to avoid normatively inconsistent policies.

- Understand fully the *problem* at hand: its causes, effects, and relationship to other problems of concern. The future evolution of the problem also needs to be characterized.

- Develop a complete *set of feasible options* that might mitigate the problem and fully characterize each of their pros and cons.

- Peer into the future, and with 20/20 vision, determine *how each policy option will perform* over time with respect to each evaluation criterion. Any uncertainty must be quantified with an accurate probability estimate for each potential outcome.

- Process all of this information quickly and accurately to *render a definitive recommendation within the timeframe* available for a decision.

Scholars have given this process a variety of different names. Deborah Stone calls it the "rationality project" (2012, p. 9); Giandomenico Majone refers to it as "decisionism" (1989, p. 12); Charles Lindblom labels it the "synoptic" model of rational choice (1977, p. 314); and Herbert Simon says it's the approach taken by "economic man" (1997, p. xxix). Although they give it different names, all four of these scholars agree that comprehensively rational policy analysis is, at best, infeasible, and at worst, leads analysts in the wrong direction, toward results that don't serve the public interest. As Lindblom (1979) puts it:

> No person, committee, or research team, even with all the resources of modern electronic computation, can complete the analysis of a complex problem. Too many interacting values are at stake, too many possible alternatives, too many consequences to be traced through an uncertain future—the best we can do is achieve partial analysis or, Herbert Simon's terms, a 'bounded rationality'. (p. 518)

There are several forces that drive us away from unboundedly optimal decisions and toward boundedly rational decisions:

- Decisionmakers (or policy analysts advising them) *can't pay attention to everything*. Only some stimuli—events, issues, situations, problems, or people—make it onto the agenda.

- For issues that do make the agenda, decisionmakers tend to rely on *what they already know, what has worked in similar situations in the past, or what they can readily glean* from a quick search of the evidence. Doing so is cognitively comforting and a tangible time-saver.

- When it comes to figuring out which policy option to endorse, decisionmakers are *constrained by their computational skills* (i.e., their ability to analyze the available evidence and judge the desirability of the options being considered).

- Rather than systematically evaluating all courses of action, a boundedly rational decisionmaker will *select the first option that appears good enough* for the issue at hand, meaning that the order in which options are considered can affect the decision.

In short, rather than optimizing based on a comprehensive analysis, the decisionmaker opts to **satisfice**, meaning that he or she "accepts alternatives that are merely satisfactory or sufficient" (Fry & Raadschelders, 2008, p. 221).

For Stone (2012), the problem isn't only that comprehensive rationality is methodologically infeasible. She argues that trying to attain comprehensive rationality also leads us in the wrong direction:

> The process of making public policy rational rests on three pillars: a model of reasoning, a model of society, and a model of policymaking. …. The model of reasoning … ignores our emotional feelings and moral intuitions, both powerful parts of human motivation and precious parts of our life experience.

... The model of society underlying the contemporary rationality project is the market [but] the starting point for political analysis must be a political community, not a market. ... The model of policymaking in the rationality project is a production model [that] fails to capture what I see as the essence of policymaking in political communities: the struggle over ideas. (pp. 10–13)

In short, *the effort to identify optimal public policy by applying a comprehensively rational model is almost certain to fail for all but the simplest of decisions.* It is also unlikely to stimulate the necessary conversation about the normative values that ought to inform the analysis.

In highlighting the inherent deficiencies of the comprehensively rational policy analysis model, I am not suggesting that it be removed from the canon of what aspiring policy analysts are expected to master. It belongs in the curriculum if, for no other reason, than it provides an aspirational target against which we can benchmark the types of analyses we are actually able to feasibly conduct. It's also a great way of organizing and thinking through whatever information we do have.

But we need to be cautious. Kidding ourselves that we can ever use the classical models of policy analysis to deliver a definitively optimal recommendation about public policy can lead us astray, especially in the world of the everyday policy analyst facing time, resource, and information constraints. We might misrepresent phenomena about which there is considerable doubt as true facts. We may exhibit hubris about our conclusions when humility would be far more appropriate. And, perhaps most importantly, our advice to policymakers may be deeply flawed when we attempt comprehensively rational analysis only to, perhaps unknowingly, fall short.

3.2.5 The Models Don't Offer the Certainty of the Natural Sciences

Harold Lasswell's choice of vocabulary in 1951—the policy sciences—lies at the heart of a dilemma for policy analysts. If you're like me, the word science conjures up images of chemists, physicists, and biologists working in a lab. We can visualize scientists collecting data, methodically running and rerunning experiments, building and testing theories, and subjecting their work to the marketplace of ideas through peer review. If they're lucky, scientists come up with lawlike generalizations such as Einstein's Theory of Relativity or the Laws of Thermodynamics. It's tough work, but when they succeed, scientists often deliver powerful insights.

Then there are the social sciences, like economics, political science, and, yes, the policy sciences. While the social sciences also yield important insights, science works differently when it comes to the human, rather than the natural, world. For one thing, the role of experimentation is much smaller. For ethical and practical reasons, we can't easily subject folks to different policy regimes to measure their responses. And, unlike a chemistry lab, there is usually so much else going on in people's lives that it can be difficult to isolate the impact of the one thing we're studying (Best, 2008).

But it's not just Laswell's use of the word science that is problematic. It is still common for policy analysis textbooks to talk about policy 'solutions.' Some texts make explicit reference to solution analysis (Weimer & Vining, 2017), while others are not quite so formulaic but nonetheless talk repeatedly about solving public problems (Bardach & Patashnik, 2016). Some authors are more circumspect yet still refer to policy analysis as problem-solving (Meltzer & Schwartz, 2019). Even the accreditation body for schools granting MPA and MPP degrees says that students should be taught to "solve problems" (NASPAA, 2019). Some of this may just be semantics; when folks talk about solving policy problems, they really mean mitigating, reducing, ameliorating, or improving bad situations, rather than fully and finally solving the problem. But, at least for me, the word solution connotes an ambiguously correct outcome, like the answer to a math equation, physics problem, or engineering challenge. Long story short: don't expect policy analysis to solve a policy problem in the same way that mathematicians, scientists, and engineers solve scientific and technical problems.

What's more, the subject of the social scientist's studies is human affairs, which tend toward substantial complexity, dynamic change, and context sensitivity. In contrast, even though the physical world may exhibit similar levels of complexity, its behavior is more predictable and consistent over time (Flyvbjerg, 2001). For example, Newton's laws of motion were established by the time of the American Revolution, and are still an important part of the standard physics curriculum. On the other hand, when it comes to human rights in 1776, only white, male, property owners were presumed to be entitled to such rights; over the next couple of centuries, human rights were redefined to include all humans, irrespective of race, gender, or economic status. As Heineman et al. (1990) put it:

> As long as human dignity and meaning exist as important values, social science cannot achieve the rigor of the physical sciences because it is impossible to separate human beliefs from the context and process of analysis. (p. 37)

Into this complex and dynamic realm of human affairs, we then introduce the classical models of policy analysis, which only make matters more complicated. Even though application of the classical policy analysis models may seem straightforward, perhaps even formulaic, there is considerable ambiguity hidden within. The subject and methods of policy analysis require the analyst to make dozens of choices that will profoundly affect the nature of the analysis and its conclusions. Here are just a few of the many decisions the analyst needs to make when doing a policy analysis:

- Which policy issues are worth worrying about;
- Which potential policy solutions are in-bounds and which are out-of-bounds;

- What constitutes success in addressing a problem;
- What types of evidence and forms of logic should be considered persuasive;
- How uncertainty about current conditions and future outcomes should be characterized;
- How divergent policy preferences and normative values should be accounted for; and
- If asked, what to recommend as an appropriate response to a policy issue.

What is the consequence of all this ambiguity? Because policy analysis requires the analyst to make so many methodological choices and value judgments, it is unlikely that two equally competent (and open-minded) analysts examining the same policy issue would arrive at identical results. Essentially, every policy analysis is unique.

Can you imagine a parallel in a chemistry lab? It would be like having two chemists combine the same chemicals in the same way, creating the same reaction, and yet produce different chemical compounds at the end of the process. We'd immediately know that at least one of the chemists had made a mistake. But, we likely couldn't say the same thing about two policy analysts who reached different conclusions about the same policy issue.

Moreover, policy analysis—unlike policy research—is not an academic exercise. With its focus on informing real world policy decisions, policy analysis is constrained by:

- Limited time, human resources, and budget to conduct the analysis;
- Substantial gaps in knowledge about important policy-relevant social phenomena;
- Institutional rules, statutory and regulatory requirements, and client preferences that limit the content of the analysis; and
- A short-term perspective that values action now over study and more effective action later.

These constraints also change the analytic **stopping rule**. A scientist working in an academic setting studies a research question for as long as it takes to come up with a convincing answer. In contrast, the stopping rule for a policy analyst is driven not by the quality of the research results but by the needs of the decision process. The work stops when the decision it aims to inform must be made.

In short, we need to dispense with the notion that policy analysis can ever be a value-free, purely analytic exercise that will always lead to the same answer irrespective of the identity of the analyst or of the context in which the work is done. What's more, the *social sciences in general and policy analysis in particular can never be 'scientific' in the same way as the natural sciences*. To think otherwise is to set a policy analyst up for failure.

But just because policy analysis differs substantially from both the natural and social sciences does not mean that policy analysts are allowed to abandon all efforts to be systematic, logical, and scientific, and instead opt for a chaotic version of policy analysis where anyone can claim to have studied a topic and produce whatever conclusion they like. Despite the inherent limitations of policy analysis, methods can still be transparently explained, evidence can be presented and critiqued, and reasoning and logic can be carefully reviewed. We'll spend time in Section 5.1.1 talking more specifically about what it means to apply the scientific method in the context of policy analysis. But for now, I will leave you with the words of policy scholar Deborah Stone who, when asked in a 2015 interview how she viewed the future of policy sciences, replied:

> For starters, get rid of the term 'policy sciences' and perhaps use 'policy studies' instead. With all due respect to this journal and its title [Policy Sciences], the term 'science' inevitably connotes the positivist approach to knowledge creation. … [P]ositivism is only one approach to understand the world, and for many purposes, it is limited and even distorting. (van Ostaijen & Jhagroe, 2015, p. 133)

3.3 TYPICAL IMPEDIMENTS TO THE EFFECTIVE USE OF CLASSICAL MODELS

Having described several inescapable limitations on the results of classical policy analysis, let's turn now to some of the other difficulties that impede the use of these models. Unlike concerns raised in the previous section, these impediments are not inherent in the analytic process or in the nature of democratic governance. They can be at least partially mitigated with clear thinking and hard work. Exhibit 3-2 lists these impediments, each of which is discussed in turn in the material that follows.

Exhibit 3-2   Impediments to Policy Analysis

- Commingling descriptive and normative thinking
- Confusing *analysis as inquiry* with *analysis as advocacy*
- Mistaking a fight for a good-faith argument
- Focusing too narrowly on only one or two disciplines

3.3.1 Commingling Descriptive and Normative Thinking

One constraint on the success of the classical policy models is the inevitable intertwining of descriptive and normative thinking in policy debates. The difficulty of integrating these two modes of thinking has important implications for policy analysis.

Sometimes, one of the two modes is simply left out of the analysis, rendering it incomplete. In other instances, policy analyses are formed into arguments that, in the best of cases, leave folks confused about what's true and what's not, and in the worst of cases, can lead to the outright weaponization of policy analysis.

Let's start with the basics. The elements of policy analysis can be characterized in many ways; one of the most important is whether the element in question is descriptive or normative in nature. **Descriptive** statements aim to explain *what is*, while **normative** statements characterize *what ought to be*. The statement, for example, that police officers in the United States shoot disproportionately more persons of color than white persons is a descriptive claim about a factual situation.[2] On the other hand, a call to defund the police is a normative claim—albeit a vague one—about a state of the world that the speaker would prefer over the status quo. Similarly, to say in 2002 that Iraq might possess weapons of mass destruction was to make a descriptive claim—albeit a claim later proven false—while saying that the United States and the United Kingdom should invade the country to topple the Hussein regime was to make a normative claim. Descriptive statements are sometimes called positive statements (based on the philosophical principles of logical positivism) while normative statements are sometimes referred to as prescriptive in nature (similar to your doctor's prescription that tells the pharmacist to give you a particular medicine). Exhibit 3-3 may help you keep the vocabulary straight.

Exhibit 3-3 Other Ways to Think About the Is/Ought Dichotomy

- Positive vs. Normative

- Descriptive vs. Prescriptive

- Way Things Are vs. Way Things Should Be

Bardach and Patashnik liken policy analysis to storytelling and suggest that descriptive statements belong to an analytic plotline while normative statements belong to an evaluative plotline (2016). It's not a stretch to think that neutral, open-minded, and equally skilled analysts could—on the basis of evidence and logic—come to mutual agreement on a descriptive claim (Robert & Zeckhauser, 2011). Because normative claims originate in values, morals, and personal preferences, however, it's easy to see that agreement might be more elusive and that irreconcilable differences of opinion might persist.

Look at Exhibit 3-4. In it, I list the steps of the classical policy analysis models and characterize for each whether the associated analytic task is primarily descriptive or

---

[2] We can debate whether and under which circumstances this claim is valid, but it would remain a descriptive claim.

Exhibit 3-4 Components and Tasks of Policy Analysis: Descriptive vs. Normative Focus[a]

Classical Policy Analysis Models		Primary Focus	
Component	Task	Descriptive	Normative
Prospective Policy Analysis (Chapter 1)			
Set Policy Agenda	Select Issues on Which to Work		✓
Characterize Problem	Identify Which Populations Have Analytic Standing		✓
	Characterize As-Is Condition	✓	
	Characterize To-Be Condition		✓
Specify Policy Alternatives	Choose Options to Consider		✓
	Design Options to Maximize Efficiency/Effectiveness	✓	
Identify Evaluation Criteria	Choose Criteria to Apply		✓
	Weight Each Criterion		✓
Predict Performance and Create Criteria-Alternatives Matrix	Project Option Performance for Each Criterion	✓	
	Characterize Risk and Uncertainty about Each Option	✓	
Analyze Trade-offs	Maximize Commensurability Across Options	✓	
	Determine Tolerance for Risk and Uncertainty		✓
	Recommend an Alternative		✓
Communicate Results	Fully Describe Analysis and Results	✓	
	Argue for Recommended Alternative		✓

Retrospective Program Evaluation (Chapter 2)	Task		
Set Evaluation Agenda	Select Programs to be Evaluated	✓	
Delineate Program and Identify Purpose	Determine Aspects of Program to Evaluate	✓	
	Inventory Potential Program Purposes		✓
	Select Focal Purpose(s) to be Used in Evaluation	✓	
Build Logic Model and Theory of Change	Inventory Potential Theories of Change		✓
	Select Theory of Change to Guide Evaluation	✓	
	Identify Relevant Inputs, Activities, Outputs		✓
	Determine Outcomes, Impacts of Interest	✓	
Set Scope of Evaluation	Opt to Do Program and/or Impact Evaluation	✓	
	Opt to Do Formative and/or Summative Assessment	✓	
Identify Questions and Select Design	Identify Evaluation Questions		✓
	Select Research Design		✓
Design Impact Analysis (if needed)	Characterize Counterfactual		✓
	Adjust Research Design to Include Impact Analysis		✓
Conduct Evaluation, Draw Conclusions, and Communicate Results	Conduct Evaluation		✓
	Draw Conclusions		✓
	Fully Describe Analysis and Results		✓
	Recommend Follow-up Program Actions	✓	

aSome tasks entail a mix of descriptive and normative thinking; the checkmark denotes the primary mode of analysis for that task.

normative in nature. The results are clear: descriptive and normative elements are woven together throughout policy analysis. The two plotlines are inextricably linked; removing one or the other from the story would produce an incomplete result. The only way to confine analysis to a single plotline (i.e., to make the exercise exclusively descriptive or normative) is to focus on only one or a few elements in the analytic process.

And indeed, many policy analysts spend their entire careers focused on the analytic plotline. This phenomenon, by itself, is not a problem; after all, there are plenty of descriptive issues that deserve scrutiny. What is the scope and scale of an issue like homelessness? What has been the impact of policy measures taken around the country to combat homelessness? Multiple analytic tools and statistical techniques—many requiring substantial expertise—exist to tackle such questions. But *unless the analyst ventures into the normative plotline, he or she can't execute all the steps* listed in Exhibit 3-4. As a result, the analyst won't be able to offer a credible opinion on what should be done, if anything, about the problem of homelessness.

The ubiquity of normative thinking throughout the policy analysis process, as shown in Exhibit 3-4, has been evident to scholars since the earliest days of the policy sciences. When deLeon (2006) summarizes the historical roots of the field (roughly covering the late 1940s to late 1960s), he notes that the policy sciences comprise three core elements, one of which is that:

> The policy sciences' approach is consciously and explicitly *value oriented*; in many cases the central theme deals with the democratic ethos and human dignity. This value orientation ... recognizes that no social problem nor methodological approach is value free. As such, to understand a problem one must acknowledge its value components. (p. 41), *emphasis in original*

As many critics see it, however, this original attention to normative values has been lost in the teaching and practice of policy analysis over the ensuing decades. For one thing, while Laswell (1951) explicitly intended that the policy sciences have a normative component in the service of democratic governance, he really didn't provide much guidance on how the analyst should incorporate values into his or her analysis. In 1951, for example, he foreshadows challenges to come with an observation that could just as easily have been made in the summer of 2021:

> When the [policy] scientist is reminded to take note of value objectives, he quickly discovers conflicts within culture and within his own personality.[3]
> ... [For example,] the dominant American tradition affirms the dignity of

---

[3]These conflicts can create what psychologists call cognitive dissonance, a topic we will return to in Chapter 4.

man, not the superiority of one set of men. … A glaring discrepancy between doctrine and practice in the United States is the mistreatment of Negroes and other colored peoples. (p. 10)

The fact that seventy years later America is still grappling with issues of racial justice suggests that having thousands of students trained in the policy sciences is, by itself, not enough to resolve these sorts of deep and profound value-based normative challenges.

Venturing into the normative plotline, however, brings challenges for the analyst. Normative issues have an intrinsically personal component, based on individual ethics, values, morals, and preferences. And in a democracy, each person's preferences ostensibly carry the same weight in matters of public policy. Suppose Ron thinks that homeless people should take responsibility for their own lives and 'pull themselves up by their bootstraps' while Jimmy wants government to extend a helping hand, asking 'am I not my brother's keeper?' Whose values—Ron's or Jimmy's—should be used in the policy analysis? In short, we face the type of preference aggregation problem described in Section 3.2.1.

Beyond the potentially difficult and uncomfortable internal and interpersonal conflicts that often come along with normative value analysis, there are other reasons why normative analysis may fall by the wayside. The seeming precision of micro-economics, quantitative analysis, and simulation modeling often displaces the confusing and messy process of first eliciting the multiple and often conflicting value preferences of relevant actors, and of then figuring out how to integrate those preferences in a meaningful way into policy analysis. In the process, policy analysis also often neglects the influence of powerful economic and political interests that profoundly shape policy outcomes.

3.3.2 Confusing Analysis as Inquiry with Analysis as Advocacy

Some textbooks—when describing classical policy analysis models—seem to assume that we're all working together in good faith to discern the best path forward. I refer to this approach as **analysis as inquiry**. But it doesn't always work this way. Instead, policy analysis may be used to create a deliverable that serves a client's narrow interests or the author's personal viewpoint, an approach we might refer to as **analysis as advocacy**. In such cases, policy analysis is used strategically in an attempt to prevail in a policy debate. Why does this happen?

To understand the answer to the question, it helps to distinguish the types of organizations that sponsor policy analysis. To start, policy analysts are employed throughout government itself and the consulting firms that support public agencies. Because of the government's public service mission, fewer incentives exist for these analysts to intentionally skew their analysis to serve a particular interest or viewpoint.

Nonetheless, efforts to distort analysis sometimes come from within government itself. Elected officials and political appointees might pressure career staff or consultants to conduct an analysis to support a politically motivated conclusion. Perhaps career civil servants are not quite as apolitical or as neutral as we'd like. Maybe bureaucrats, aiming to protect organizational turf, undermine an evaluation that might cast their work in an unfavorable light. Perhaps partisan congressional staff try to manipulate nonpartisan agencies like the Congressional Budget Office or the Government Accountability Office to produce politically favorable analytic results.

Policy analysis is also sponsored and conducted by commercial firms, nonprofit organizations, trade associations, and advocacy groups from across the ideological spectrum. Public policies often affect the economic interests of these sponsors or serve to promote or undermine their political preferences. Someone must pay the analyst's salary, give him or her an office, and so on. The folks who foot the bill are usually not paying to advance good public policy writ large, but to protect their interests or promote their preferences. In turn, self-interest or political and ideological interests are frequently disguised as neutral policy analysis.

Finally, one-sided analysis is not always the intentional result of narrow self-interest on the part of the analyst, or his or her employer. Such folks often believe that they have truly identified the optimal public policy and want to make the case for it. In doing so, the analysis might become unbalanced as the advantages of the preferred option get overemphasized and its drawbacks deemphasized.

Given these motivations for distorting policy analysis, Angela Evans (2015), president of the Association for Public Policy and Management,[4] summarized the situation when she told the group's annual meeting:

> … consultants, 'experts,' and practitioners in organizations, think tanks, and policy shops all compet[e] to have a place at the policy table [and] exploit a broad array of channels, techniques, and settings … through the Internet and the 24/7 news cycle. The rub comes when one looks at what self-proclaimed policy analysts are often really producing: advocative, brief treatments of complex problems that are driven by political or ideological agendas and marketed as objective, nonpartisan analysis. These advocative, self-proclaimed analysts have invaded the policy environment. This invasion is worrisome since many of these sources are skilled at self-promotion and are masters of aggressive marketing. (p. 259)

Evans' invaders certainly sound like dubious characters that we ought to keep an eye on, but let's put a finer point on why you need to determine whether you're

---

[4]APPAM is the primary professional society of public policy scholars.

looking at an analysis based on inquiry or one based on advocacy. There are two simple reasons: one theoretical and one practical.

First, a *well-executed analysis driven by the goal of inquiry can, standing alone, offer a sound basis for policy action*. On the other hand, *analysis motivated by advocacy always provides an incomplete basis for policy action*.[5] Because the advocate wants to win the argument for a particular policy, his or her decisions about what to include and to omit from the analysis will reflect strategic calculations about how to raise the odds of a win. In such cases, you need to fill in the blanks, either with your own analysis or by using the work of other advocates with alternative points of view.

Second, from a practical point of view, *you don't want to get fooled by an analysis you mistakenly think is based on a spirit of neutral inquiry* when in fact it has been crafted by its author—intentionally or not—to steer you to a foregone conclusion. It doesn't matter whether you are motivated by inquiry or advocacy; what matters is the author's motivation. In short, if the material you're looking qualifies as policy *analysis as advocacy*, it needs to be treated with caution.

How can you tell if a policy analysis has been weaponized by folks primarily motivated by narrow and parochial interests or if it's the product of someone with a broader public service perspective? Start by asking yourself whether its core purpose appears to be a neutral exploration of all aspects of an issue or if its purpose is to persuade its audience to undertake a particular course of action (Garvin & Roberto, 2001). In the first case, inquiry is the goal. With an open mind, the author considers multiple points of view and all sources of evidence before drawing conclusions. In the second case, advocacy is the purpose. Here, the author emphasizes only the evidence and arguments that best support their conclusion. Exhibit 3-5 summarizes the most important differences between inquiry and advocacy.[6]

But what if your career ambition is to be an advocate? Am I suggesting that *analysis as inquiry* is superior to *analysis as advocacy*? Not at all! Mastering the techniques of neutral policy analysis will make you a more effective advocate because those techniques help you ground your arguments more firmly in logic and evidence. What's more, private inquiry—among you and your colleagues and clients—is a prerequisite to strong public advocacy. The most effective advocates understand where their case is weak and where concessions can be made without fatally undermining their argument. And an open-minded policymaker, uncertain about which position to advocate, will doubtlessly find it valuable to privately engage in *analysis as inquiry* to better understand the full complexity of the issue and perhaps decide on a policy position to take in public.

---

[5]And, of course, even though motivated by a spirit of inquiry, a neutral analysis may also not provide a sound basis for policy action owing to data gaps, unsound reasoning, a weak methodology, or other analytic flaws.

[6]To simplify the exhibit, I make the distinction between inquiry and advocacy binary; in reality, it's a continuum.

Exhibit 3-5   Alternative Approaches to Policy Analysis

	Advocacy	Inquiry
Starting Point	Preferred policy	Problem of concern
Primary Purpose	*Win* the argument for a specific policy action; attract readers, viewers, or clicks; go viral	*Understand* entirety of issue; clarify nature of problem; alert policymakers to upsides and downsides of policy choices
Consideration of Options	Focus on a single preferred option and offer only unrealistic alternative options	Identify and consider broad range of policy options that take fundamentally different approaches to problem
Approach to Trade-offs Across Options	Highlight strengths, hide weaknesses of preferred option; treat other alternatives as analytic foils to bolster case for preferred option	Display all strengths and weaknesses of all options; identify trade-offs of options relative to each other
Use of Evidence	*Selective*: Use only evidence that best supports the argument being made	*Broad*: Use all evidence even if doing so undermines ability to draw definitive conclusions
Extent of Analysis	Motivated by desire to win, analyst focuses only on best evidence and strongest logic to support the preferred option and attack other options	Motivated to understand *all* aspects of problem and potential responses to it, analyst faces time and resource constraints that limit depth, extent of analysis
Approach to Uncertainty	*Hide* analytic uncertainty that may undermine argument	*Expose* analytic uncertainty so policymakers understand the risks associated with their choices
Nature of Conflict	*Affective*: Rely on intuition, emotion, ideology, symbolism; analyst changes view only if politically expedient	*Cognitive*: Appeal to reason, evidence, and deliberative processes; analyst changes view only if evidence or logic dictate
Attitude Toward External Review	*Avoid*: Reviewers may identify weaknesses in the argument, undermining its persuasiveness	*Welcome*: Reviewers may identify weaknesses in the analysis, so that they can be addressed or acknowledged
Normative Rationale	All stakeholders have effective advocates; all points of view have voice; clash of advocates in the marketplace of ideas uncovers all factors relevant to policy choice	Analyst has responsibility to give voice to all stakeholders and points of view so that policymakers needn't rely only on vocal advocates to identify all factors relevant to policy choice

3.3.3 Mistaking a Fight for a Good-Faith Argument

After looking at Exhibit 3-5, you may think I am being unfair to advocates, calling their work a weapon and perhaps dismissing them as narrow-minded or analytically incompetent. To the contrary, debate and argument, based on sound logic and credible evidence, is essential to wise policymaking. *Democracies are built to accommodate debate across competing points of view, and policy choices that emerge from such debates are legitimated by the process.* In short, inquiry and advocacy can coexist. Think about the statues of a blindfolded Lady Justice that adorn courtrooms around the country. She's usually holding a sword and a set of scales. Her blindfold metaphorically connotes the spirit of impartiality we expect of judges and juries. Lady Justice embodies the attributes listed in the column labeled "Inquiry" in Exhibit 3-5. In those same courtrooms, however, attorneys representing their clients operate in a manner consistent with the principles laid out in the column labeled "Advocacy."

Some scholars even argue that policy analysis should embrace, rather than hold at arm's length, the concept of advocacy. For example, Majone suggests that classical models err by not recognizing the inevitability and the value of argumentation—in and of itself—as a means of policy analysis. He asserts that this is no surprise to politicians who routinely argue about policy issues, but is a point often missed by social scientists. Majone (1989) opines that "[w]hether in written or oral form, argument is central in all stages of the policy process" (p. 1). He goes on to suggest that:

> The job of analysts consists in large part of producing evidence and argument to be used in the course of public debate. … The arguments analysts produce may be more or less technical, more or less sophisticated, but they must persuade if they are to be taken seriously in the forums of public deliberation. (p. 7)

Deborah Stone makes a similar point when she notes that classical models of policy analysis tend to dismiss politics as irrational and analytically intractable when in fact it's a powerful driver of public policy. For Stone, political debate also has the potential to build community as folks learn to see issues from other points of view (2012). Majone and Stone's perspective rings true. Argumentation and debate are cornerstones of the legislative, judicial, and electoral processes in a democracy.

But are all forms of argumentation equally useful as analysis? Probably not. You saw, in the prior section, a distinction between *analysis as inquiry* and *analysis as advocacy* that depends on whether the analysis aims to develop a neutral understanding of an issue or to win the case for a particular point of view. Majone's enthusiasm for argumentation clearly fits into the latter category, but I'm not sure we should stop there. I only have to think of antifa protesters and rightwing activists screaming at and sometimes physically attacking each other over the past few years to convince myself that not all arguments are conducive to a careful exploration of relevant issues and the development of a shared understanding of disagreements. So, are there productive ways to argue about public issues?

The answer is almost certainly yes. For starters, there's a difference between a good-faith argument and a fight (Heinrichs, 2020). Both qualify as advocacy, but in an argument, you aim to persuade your opponent that your point of view is correct while a fight is intended to vanquish your opponent. In both cases, you want to prevail, but in a fight you don't care what your opponent thinks afterward as long as they retreat sufficiently that their opinion is no longer an obstacle to getting your way. Conversely, your goal in an argument—though you may not succeed—is to get your opponent to come around to your point of view. Even if he or she doesn't, you may build some goodwill that makes the next debate with that person more productive. Majone is clearly talking about a good-faith argument rather than a fight. Senator Mitt Romney put it well when describing negotiations about infrastructure legislation that took place between the White House and a bipartisan group of Senators in the summer of 2021:

> You can tell the difference between an adversarial negotiation and a collaborative one. In this case, when one side had a problem, the other side tried to solve the problem, rather than walk away from the table. (Min Kim, August 1, 2021)

Why should you care if you're in an argument or a fight? In an argument, if you have a strong case, your opponent may be willing to change his or her mind. Similarly, if you approach the conversation with an open-mind, you could discover that you've changed your mind when you come to recognize a new perspective or appreciate a new piece of evidence. On the other hand, if the argument is actually a fight, where no one is going to change their closed mind and where evidence is intentionally misrepresented and arguments are advanced and then withdrawn simply as tactical debating maneuvers, you should think very differently about how best to engage the debate. *You don't want to play the dupe where your good intentions are manipulated to the benefit of the other side.*

It's not always easy to tell the difference between a fight and an argument. One way to define a good-faith argument is that it exemplifies what philosopher Jurgen Habermas (1990) called the principles of discourse ethics (pp. 87–89):

- "No speaker may contradict himself.

- Every speaker who applies predicate F to object A must be prepared to apply F to all other objects resembling A in all relevant respects.

- Different speakers may not use the same expression with different meanings.

- Every speaker may assert only what he really believes.

- A person who disputes a proposition or norm not under discussion must provide a reason for wanting to do so.

- Every [person] with the competence to speak and act is allowed to take part in a discourse.

- Everyone is allowed to question any assertion whatever.

- Everyone is allowed to introduce any assertion whatever into the discourse.

- Everyone is allowed to express his attitudes, desires, and needs.

- No speaker may be prevented, by internal or external coercion from exercising his rights as laid down [here]."

Habermas (1990) argued that if these principles are satisfied, then the result will be a "cooperative search for the truth, where nothing coerces anyone except the force of the better argument" (p. 198).

Habermas's principles indeed appear conducive to a robust, good-faith, debate, but I find them a bit naïve by seeming to imply that political power and self-interest can be neutralized. I am not the only one:

> The basic weakness of Habermas's project is its lack of agreement between ideal and reality, between intentions and their implementation. This incongruity … is rooted in an insufficient conception of power. … But discourse about discourse ethics is all Habermas has to offer. This is the fundamental political dilemma in Habermas's thinking: he describes to us the utopia of communicative rationality but not how to get there. (Flyvberg, 1998, p. 215)

Perhaps Flyvberg goes a bit too far by describing discourse ethics as utopian. Surely, there are instances where policymakers and policy analysts open-mindedly engage in constructive debates about how to resolve public issues. But just as surely, there are many, many instances where the exercise of political and economic power significantly distorts the discourse. In such cases, the debate bears little resemblance to a good-faith discussion and becomes nothing more than a fight in which policy arguments are wielded as weapons rather than tools of persuasion. While she doesn't cite Habermas, Deborah Stone (2012) offers a similar conclusion when, after extolling the value of explicitly incorporating politics in policy analysis, she recognizes "the dark self-interested side of political conflict" (p. 10).

So, if it's difficult if not impossible, to satisfy Habermas's principles of ideal speech, are those principles even relevant? Yes, you can use his principles as a checklist to help you assess the nature of the policy debates in which you're participating. The closer a debate come to satisfying Habermas's principles of a noncoercive good-faith debate, the more likely it will resemble Majone's notion of policy analysis as argument. In such cases, you may want to approach it with an open mind, grounded in the spirit of inquiry.

Conversely, if you end up in a debate that doesn't exhibit any of the principles of discourse ethics, and where policy arguments have been weaponized as each party tries to vanquish the other, then:

> You can end up in a 'conga line' of ignorance because—and this is the point—when you are outside your domain of competence and intentionally in unstudied conditions, you can believe anything you want and ignore anything you don't want to hear. (Roe, 2016, p. 358)

A great example of how argumentation can turn into a fight where the facts don't matter are the events of January 6, 2021. On that day, 147 House and Senate members voted to overturn the 2020 Presidential election based on false claims of significant electoral fraud (Yourish, Buchanan, & Denise Lu, 2021). Moreover, the insurrectionists who stormed the Capitol building sure seemed to be looking for a fight rather than a good-faith debate about who won the election. Clearly, Majone's hope of using robust argument in lieu of neutral analysis has its limitations.

3.3.4 Focusing Too Narrowly on Only One or Two Disciplines

Another obstacle that frequently undermines the value of policy analysis is its myopic focus on only a very few academic fields. You may recall from the Introduction to Part I that when Lasswell sketched out his vision of the policy sciences in the early 1950s, he was clear about his belief that public problems shouldn't be looked at only through the lens of a single discipline (deLeon, 2006). Instead, he called for a multidisciplinary approach to policy analysis that incorporated insights from diverse fields such as economics, political science, law, psychology, and the natural sciences. Over the subsequent decades, however, graduate education in public policy has tended to be implemented in a much narrower fashion, with the bulk of the required curriculum focused on three specific fields.

- *Applied Microeconomics:* In many programs (as well as academic societies and government policy offices), policy analysis is often seen as little more than the study of markets, firms, and consumers, with a focus on market failures such as monopolies, an undersupply of public goods, and the impacts of nonmarket externalities like air pollution (Brady, 2019; Stone, 2012). Social welfare is defined in terms of economic efficiency, and students are taught how to measure the impact of policy interventions as changes in aggregate social welfare.

- *Tactical Political Science:* In other academic venues, policy analysis is grounded in a version of political science focused on political action. In such cases, students study theories of the policy process that purport to explain how and when issues come onto the policy agenda, how they get 'sold' to policymakers, and how coalitions of stakeholders can be assembled to support (or oppose) policy change. Students are taught to be policy entrepreneurs who know how to turn policy preferences (their own or their client's) into implemented policy.

- *Quantitative Methods:* Most policy analysis programs emphasize probability, statistics, econometrics, and perhaps simulation modeling, supplemented with a focus on research methods and inferential reasoning. More advanced courses include sophisticated statistical techniques that many graduates rarely use in their subsequent careers. Nonetheless, pushing students to master these topics has the ancillary benefit of sharpening their critical thinking and analytic reasoning skills, independent of the quantitative methods themselves.

Teaching policy analysis from the perspective of only one—or at most three—fields does students a disservice. Laswell is right. The complexity of the world is best understood (and potentially managed) when looked at from a multidisciplinary perspective. As the Dean of UC Berkeley's school of public policy puts it:

> For many years, I have been worried that public policy schools would just become 'schools about market failure and economic efficiency.' ... Schools of public policy should consider the larger architectonic questions of how government can ensure everyone's rights to 'life, liberty, and the pursuit of happiness'. (Brady, 2019)

Combining applied microeconomics, tactical political science, and quantitative methods is certainly an improvement over teaching just one of the three subjects, but there are other topics that deserve a prominent spot in the policy analysis curriculum. Ideally, graduate training would also equip students to:

- Analyze issues of equality, liberty, justice, social stability, and wealth and poverty;

- Integrate citizen perspectives while guarding against undue influence by special interests;

- Think about how institutions affect the processes by which public agencies make and deliver policy across branches and levels of government;

- Understand the connection between policy analysis and the legal system, as influenced by constitutional, statutory, regulatory, and common law, as well as the role of the courts;

- Consider the long-term economic, social, and environmental sustainability of current public policies and of proposed policy changes;

- Recognize the profound effects—positive and negative—of scientific advances and technological innovations;

- Appreciate the dynamic complex systems in which policy issues arise and the dangers of applying simple mental models to such systems;

- Better visualize how future conditions may be driven by policy changes made in the present;

- Incorporate the principles of user-oriented design in the development of new public policies and the revision of existing ones; and

- Work effectively and ethically in the day-to-day roles of a policy analyst.

The takeaway here is that *thinking of policy analysis as nothing more than applied microeconomics, tactical political science, or quantitative methods is to constrain its focus to the point where its potential impact on real-world policymaking is inherently limited.* If, as an aspiring policy analyst, you'd like to maximize your contribution to ongoing policy debates, then I recommend that you invest the time to become at least minimally proficient in these additional fields. Later sections of the book will give you some of the tools for doing so.

3.4 REBOOTING THE CLASSICAL MODELS: KEEPING THE BABY, BUT LOSING THE BATHWATER

Thus far in the book, we've covered a lot of material. Perhaps it's time to step back and get our bearings. For starters, Chapters 1 and 2 laid out the traditional models of policy analysis and program evaluation. Mastering these models will put your career as a policy analyst on a solid foundation, but they're not enough. If the only tools in your toolkit are the two classical models, you'll frequently find yourself in situations where you lack the relevant and appropriate tools you need to tackle the policy issues you're interested in. Why might this happen?

As discussed earlier in this chapter, many of the impediments to the successful use of the traditional models are what I call inescapable pathologies. Some of these pathologies—like the impossibility of unambiguous preference aggregation, the wedge between individual and social incentives that drives collective action problems, and the impossibility of ever solving wicked problems—are inherent to democratic governance in a modern society. Other pathologies—the fact that policy analysis can never be comprehensively rational and its inability to offer conclusions with the certainty of the natural sciences—are intrinsic to the analysis of human behavior in a social context. While these pathologies can never be fully overcome by a policy analyst, the worst of their consequences can be mitigated by an analyst who is aware of their presence and is prepared to acknowledge, rather than dismiss, their impacts.

Still other impediments to the use of traditional policy analysis models are obstacles that arise frequently, but which can be circumvented by a skilled policy analyst. At the root of many of these obstacles is a confusion about the type of discourse within which a particular instance of policy analysis is developed and used. Sometimes analysis is guided by a neutral spirit of inquiry; in other cases, it is fully integrated into an advocate's case for or against a policy measure. Sometimes analysis is part of a good-faith argument in which participants are genuinely trying to persuade their opponent with the power of a good argument, while remaining open-minded about changing their own point of view in the face of a compelling counterargument. Other times, arguments are nothing more than a fight among closed-minded opponents. A failure to recognize the type of debate into which a policy analysis is being introduced often leads to unsatisfactory outcomes, for both the policy analyst and the client. Moreover, looking at a policy issue through only one or two disciplinary lenses creates a myopia that may cause you to miss some of the most important aspects of the policy issue you're analyzing.

As shown in Exhibit 3-6, I propose a rebooting of the field of policy analysis. It's a reboot, rather than a redefinition, because the traditional models have so many valuable features that it would be foolish to abandon them. But the impediments to their use that we've talked about necessitate a reimagining that yields a rebooted version of policy analysis less vulnerable to these impediments. The lower portion of Exhibit 3-6 depicts how the remaining three parts of the book comprise my proposed rebooting of the field:

- *Part II* reviews four competencies that aspiring policy analysts need to master: an understanding of metacognition as a means of minimizing bias, a knowledge of the principles of logic that are needed to tentatively identify policy-relevant truths, the ability to collect and understand evidence about real world conditions, and a mindset that facilitates insightful analysis of almost any situation.

Exhibit 3-6 Rebooting Policy Analysis

Classical Models of Policy Analysis

Prospective Policy Analysis
(Chapter 1)

Retrospective Program Evaluation
(Chapter 2)

Obstacles to Use of the Classical Models
(Chapter 3)

Inescapable Pathologies

The classical models don't:

- *Solve the preference aggregation problem*
- *Solve collective action problems*
- *Solve wicked problems*
- *Deliver comprehensive rationality*
- *Offer the certainty of the natural sciences*

Typical Impediments

- *Commingling descriptive and normative thinking*
- *Confusing analysis as inquiry with analysis as advocacy*
- *Mistaking a fight for a good-faith argument*
- *Focusing too narrowly on only one or two disciplines*

A Rebooted Model of Policy Analysis
(Chapters 4 through 15)

Thinking Clearly
(Part II)

4. *Using <u>metacognition</u> to check your own biases*
5. *Using <u>logic</u> to identify tentative truths*
6. *Collecting and evaluating the quality of <u>evidence</u> in policy claims*
7. *The <u>mindset</u> of an effective policy analyst*

Looking through Different Lenses
(Part III)

8. *The <u>equity</u> lens*
9. *The <u>economics</u> lens*
10. *The <u>political</u> and <u>institutional</u> lenses*
11. *The <u>legal</u>, <u>sustainability</u>, <u>science and technology</u> lenses*

Building Blocks of Policy Analysis
(Part IV)

12. *Incorporating <u>systems</u> thinking in policy analysis*
13. *Using policy analysis to <u>visualize the future</u>*
14. *<u>Designing</u> public policies*
15. *Having an <u>impact</u> while preserving your <u>integrity</u>*

- *Part III* explains the value of a panoptic, or multiperspective, view of policy issues. By intentionally looking at issues through lenses of equity, economics, politics, institutions, the law, sustainability, and science and technology, you can avoid an unnecessarily narrow view of policy analysis.

- *Part IV* turns to the building blocks of a more advanced version of policy analysis, including systems thinking, the visualization of future outcomes, policy design principles, and an approach to daily life for an analyst who wants to have a meaningful impact while preserving his or her integrity.

The skills described in Chapters 4 through 15 are meant to supplement the classical models of policy analysis presented in Chapters 1 and 2 and critiqued here in Chapter 3. The concepts, techniques, and methods described in Parts II, III, and IV will equip you to do high-quality policy analysis even when your work looks nothing like the classical models.

My proposed rebooting of the field of policy analysis is at once both ambitious and modest. It's ambitious because my aim is to enhance your skills as an analyst and make you a more effective contributor to the policymaking process. It's modest because I am under no illusion that even the best, most competent, policy analysis can ever by itself cause a society to remake its public policies for the greater good. Good policy analysis surely matters a great deal (Friedman, 2017), but just as surely, it is only a necessary but not sufficient condition for better public policies. Recall Dror's claim that policy analysis might be capable of creating a ten to fifteen percent improvement in the quality of public policymaking (and his belief that this would be a big improvement).

If the modesty of Dror's (and my) vision of a successful version of policy analysis leaves you underwhelmed, an analogy between policy analysis and medicine may help (Geva-May, 2005). Over the past couple centuries, medicine has gone from blood-letting to robotic brain surgery and genetic medicine; surely, policy analysis can also evolve for the better over time. Analytic failures associated with, say, the War on Poverty, the invasion of Iraq, and the US response to the COVID pandemic don't dictate that policy analysis will always fail. The policy analyst is like a doctor. He or she must help the patient—here and now—with the knowledge, tools, and conditions that exist today. Policy analysts need to give the best advice they can, despite the constraints of time, budget, and knowledge. The doctor can't save every patient, but we probably don't want quacks treating chronic heart disease and COVID patients. Lots of people smoke, don't exercise enough, need to lose weight, or refuse to wear masks in a pandemic, yet we still need doctors to treat sick people and promote good health, rather than giving up and changing professions. Similarly, even if policymakers often ignore sound policy advice, we don't want to revert to a world in which evidence and logic are systematically deemed irrelevant, and policy is made based on hunches and intuition or on who has the loudest and most bombastic voice.

Thomas Piketty (2014) is an economist who has studied global inequality for a long time. He is well aware of the modest role of analysis in the midst of heated and polarized debates. As you tackle the rest of the book, I hope his words give you a sense of optimism that there is a payoff to mastering these skills:

> Given this dialogue of the deaf, in which each camp justifies its own intellectual laziness by pointing to the laziness of the other, there is a role for research that is at least systematic and methodical if not fully scientific. Expert analysis will never put an end to violent political conflict that inequality inevitably instigates. Social scientific research is and always will be tentative and imperfect. It does not claim to transform economic, sociology, and history into exact sciences. But by patiently searching for facts and patterns and calmly analyzing the economic, social, and political mechanisms that might explain them it can inform democratic debate and focus attention on the right questions. It can help redefine the terms of the debate, unmask certain preconceived or fraudulent notions, and subject all positions to constant critical scrutiny. (p. 3)

CHAPTER SUMMARY

This chapter made the argument for creating a rebooted version of policy analysis. We first traced the historical arc of the policy sciences movement and noted the postpositive reaction to it. We next considered five aspects of democratic governance that inherently limit the insights that can be provided by policy analysis. These obstacles include the preference aggregation and collective action problems, the nature of wicked problems, and the inability of the social sciences in general and policy analysis in particular to deliver comprehensive rationality with the certainty of the natural sciences.

We next looked at four considerations that often—but not always—impede the execution of high-quality policy analysis. Such impediments include commingling descriptive and normative thinking, confusing *analysis as inquiry* with *analysis as advocacy*, mistaking a fight for a good-faith argument, and focusing too narrowly on only one or two disciplines.

Finally, we considered the rationale for a proposed rebooting of policy analysis, and looked broadly at the features of a revised version of the field. I argued for building on the existing foundation of policy analysis while simultaneously expanding its scope. I closed with the observation that we need to be modest in our expectations, and not look to policy analysis to solve all of society's ills.

DISCUSSION QUESTIONS

1. Where do you stand in the debate between the traditional policy sciences and the postpositive critique? Can you explain and defend your position?

2. Think of a specific instance of a collective action problem. Where does the gap between private and social costs and benefits arise? Why does it exist? Can you think of ways in which the problem could be mitigated without resorting to public policy?

3. Pick a wicked problem with which you are familiar. In what ways do the ten characteristics of wickedness apply to the problem? How do you think we should address the problem? How likely is it that your preferred solution will significantly improve conditions?

4. Think about a current policy debate and the arguments that folks are making. Do you see signs of analysis as inquiry? Or is it mostly analysis as argument? If you were a policymaker, would you feel like you could use information gleaned from the debate to make a well-informed and sound decision?

5. Think about politics in general these days. Do policy debates seem like good-faith discussions about the best path forward? Or do they seem like fights motivated solely by self-interest and animosity toward the other side? What conditions lead to one or the other? Do you see a difference among debates at the federal, state, and local levels? If so, why do you think that is?

6. Has your education focused on only one or two academic disciplines? Or has it given you a broad multidisciplinary view of policy analysis in a democracy? If there are gaps, what would it take to fill them?

THINKING CLEARLY

A PRE-TAKEOFF CHECKLIST CAN PREVENT PROBLEMS LATER

Rancorous debates about public policy issues are everywhere: climate change, the Iran nuclear deal, voting rights, the Affordable Care Act, racial disparities in policing, tax cuts for the wealthy, and a crisis at the US southern border, to name a few examples. Depending on who you listen to, the 2020 Presidential election was either a massive fraud or one of the most free and fair elections ever. The COVID vaccine might be a sinister government plot or a triumph of modern medicine. The Green New Deal could be a road map for a just and fair society or a socialist takeover of the country.

The Oxford Dictionaries named "post-truth" their 2016 Word of the Year. An adjective, post-truth is defined as "relating to or denoting circumstances in which objective facts are less influential in shaping public opinion than appeals to emotion and personal belief" (Oxford University Press, 2016). We don't have to look very far to

- Are trains carrying coal to power plants really "death trains" as NASA scientist Jim Hansen called them (2009)? Did he intentionally draw a moral equivalence between the Holocaust and using coal to generate electricity—something done globally for more than a century?

- Was Senator Inhofe—who brought a snowball to the Senate floor to prove his point—correct that climate change is a "hoax" (2012) or was it just a melodramatic way of saying it's too expensive to do something about the problem?

- How about dealing with illegal immigrants living in the United States? Ed Krayewski at Reason.com asks "[W]hat's wrong with granting amnesty to hard-working, tax-paying individuals whose only crime is their immigration status?" (2013).

- David Benkof at The Daily Caller disagrees: "Illegal immigrants, in their arrogance, have shown they believe our immigration rules do not apply to them. They have jumped the line—basically stealing a chance at a better life from millions of people. … The idea they would be granted full citizenship … is obscene" (2015).

Who's right? Hansen or Inhofe? Krayewski or Benkof? It's not easy to say, but we *can* say that heated arguments in a democracy are nothing new. Neither are attempts to make sense of the cacophony of claims and counterclaims.

More than two thousand years ago, philosophers in Athens and Syracuse understood the role of argumentation in a democracy and came to appreciate the value of a form of communication called **rhetoric**. Simply put, rhetoric is a collection of concepts and techniques that together represent a means by which one person tries to persuade another, either verbally or in writing. Aristotle, in the fourth century BCE, claimed that rhetoric had value for several reasons (Crider, 2014). For one thing, many audiences are unwilling or unable to master the detailed concepts, evidence, and logic that lead to a particular conclusion.[1] Instead, they must be persuaded through other means that the conclusion is correct. For another, Aristotle believed that hearing the arguments on both sides of a debate is one of the best ways to fully appreciate the strengths and weaknesses of all claims being made about the topic under debate.

For Aristotle, the tools of rhetoric give you three techniques for winning over your audience. The first is **logos** which entails the use of logical reasoning—inductive, deductive, and causal—to convince your listener of the strength and soundness of your

---

[1]This isn't necessarily a sign of apathy or stupidity. We can't be experts in everything. Whether it's medicine, car repair, or the cellphone system, we routinely rely on others to figure out many important elements of our lives.

argument. The second technique is **ethos** by which you aim to gain the trust and respect of the audience by demonstrating your own competence, character, and credibility, or the lack thereof in your opponent. The third technique is **pathos** in which you play on the emotions of the audience to win them over to your point of view. Both ethos and pathos entail evoking an emotional response in the audience. Ethos is generally aimed at creating positive emotions toward the speaker and negative emotions toward his or her opponents. Pathos is more manipulative and plays on folks' fears, greed, and hopes in order to win their support, irrespective of the speaker's credibility (ethos) or the strength of his or her reasoning (logos).

As a quick aside, you can use Aristotle's words to reinterpret the 2016 definition of post-truth. Post-truth simply means that ethos and pathos have achieved a dominant role in political discourse while logos has been relegated to a minor role.

But let's get back to our historical story. The Aristotelian tradition continued a few centuries later in Rome where Cicero, a prominent politician, gifted orator, and prolific writer, devoted most of his career to perfecting the art of persuasion through rhetoric. One writer places him among "the greatest speakers of all time" (May, 2016, p. viii) while another refers to him as the "attack dog of the Roman Forum" (Leith, 2016, p. 107). Either way, he had a profound influence on the field of rhetoric. Well versed in Aristotle's thinking, Cicero was nothing, if not pragmatic, about how to win an argument:

> *We bring people over to our point of view in three ways, either by instructing them (logos) or by winning their good will (ethos) or by stirring their emotions (pathos). Well, one of these methods we should openly display, and we must appear to aim at nothing but giving instruction, while the other two must, just like blood in the body, flow throughout the whole of the speech. (Cicero M., 55BCE / 2016, pp. 42–43)*

In other words, Cicero suggests that we act as if our arguments are based on only logic and reason, but surreptitiously try to manipulate our audience's emotions in order to win them over. In fact, Cicero says, "nothing is more admirable than being able, through speech, to take hold of human minds, to win over their inclinations, to drive them at will in one direction, and to draw them at will from another" (Cicero M., 55BCE / 2016, p. 5). Cicero's observations would probably come as no surprise to a political strategist or an advertising executive.

I don't know about you, but I find Cicero's words vaguely sinister—at least when we're talking about matters of public policy. His delight at the ability of the orator to get in people's heads and then push them in a particular direction reminds us that argument (i.e., rhetorical persuasion) is simply a method for achieving an end, not an end in itself. Winston Churchill and Adolph Hitler were, after all, both superb orators who effectively motivated large populations to, respectively, oppose and support fascism. Cicero clearly understands that rhetoric can be used to more than one end:

[W]hen I consider the injuries done to our Republic, and ... the ancient calamities of prominent communities, I see that no little part of their misfortunes was brought about through the agency of men who were highly skilled in speaking. ... [W]isdom without eloquence does too little for the good of communities, but eloquence without wisdom is, in most instances, extremely harmful and never beneficial ... *the person who arms himself with eloquence in such a way that enables him not to assail the interests of his country, but rather assist them, this man ... will be a citizen most helpful and most devoted both to his own interests and those of the public. (Cicero, 84BCE / 2016, pp. 9–10),* emphasis added

Cicero's words suggest that rhetorical skill is like a superpower, able to transform the thinking and emotions of those at whom it's aimed. The next logical question, it seems to me, is what happens when this superpower is wielded within the context of policy analysis.

Fast forward a couple thousand years. The political rhetoric in the United States—at least at the national level—is at a fevered pitch not seen in decades. We certainly seem to be experiencing the downsides of Cicero's "eloquence without wisdom." Untethered from sound evidence and rigorous logic, policy claims and counterclaims often become weapons where words do not mean what their plain language implies and where strong rhetoric is used to manipulate the emotions of readers and listeners. At best, the path forward is obscured and at worst, we're too confused to do anything. As Rand's CEO Michael Rich put it:

When everyone has their own facts, then nobody really has any facts at all. ... A policy debate featuring different interpretations of the same facts, that's healthy. It promotes compromise and consensus. But a policy debate featuring opinions about opinions? Without an agreed-upon set of facts? That's a recipe for gridlock. (Bauman, 2016)

My aim in this part of the book is to give you the tools you need to dissect such debates and develop your own understanding of issues that matter to you. In turn, you will be better prepared to analyze, design, and implement effective public policies. One thing you will *not* get is definitive answers to tough policy questions. But the next four chapters will help you learn how to:

- Look in the mirror and use the process of metacognition to check your own biases (Chapter 4),

- Apply the principles of logic to help you tentatively identify what is true (Chapter 5),

- Anchor your work in real-world conditions by assessing the quality of the evidence available to support policy claims (Chapter 6), and

- Cope with inevitable constraints on policy analysis by bringing together logic and evidence within a mindset of critical thinking, pragmatism, competence, tough mindedness, and a self-aware service orientation (Chapter 7).

Pathos and ethos are reflected in Chapter 4 while logos is at the heart of Chapters 5 and 6.

Before diving in, I feel obligated to offer a warning. There is *a lot* here—literally dozens of concepts, frameworks, suggestions, and ideas for you to consider. You can think of them as a checklist, much like the checklist used by a pilot before heading down the runway. Addressing them all can take substantial time and effort, even for a single policy issue. From where I sit, however, everything in the book is important; otherwise, I wouldn't have included it.

I am not, however, naïve. In your day-to-day life as a policy analyst, you will rarely be able to apply all this content at the same time in your work. Nonetheless, I am confident that over the course of your career, virtually all of it will be relevant and helpful at some point. What's more, a substantial portion of Chapter 7 is devoted to the process of triage, in which you strategically accommodate time, resource, and information constraints to minimize their adverse impacts on your policy analysis.

CHAPTER FOUR

USING METACOGNITION TO CHECK YOUR OWN BIASES AND THE BIASES OF OTHERS

Remember Aristotle's concept of pathos—the manipulation by a speaker of his or her audience's emotions to win them over to a point of view? The purpose of this chapter is to help you become less vulnerable to such manipulation. For starters, I want you to engage in some self-introspection. Doing so may not be easy. In a CalTech Commencement speech, Nobel Laureate Richard Feynman (1974) crystalized the problem this way:

> … learning how to not fool ourselves—of having utter scientific integrity—is, I'm sorry to say, something that we haven't specifically included in any course that I am aware of. … The first principle is that you must not fool yourself—and you are the easiest person to fool. (p. 12)

You might scoff at the idea that you're vulnerable to fooling yourself without even realizing it. You're probably a student with a solid academic track record, motivated and intellectually curious enough to tackle the intricacies of policy analysis. But the evidence supports Feynman's claim. Several empirical studies document that most of us have a blind spot that causes us to see bias, incompetence, and self-interest in others while remaining oblivious to it in ourselves (Ditto et al., 2019; Pronin & Schmidt, 2013). The idea that we can be blind to our own shortcomings should be a scary one, especially for someone who aspires to earn a living by making sense of competing claims in policy debates.

Deepening your understanding of flawed thinking, learning how to minimize it in your own work and detect it

Learning Objectives

By studying this chapter, you should be able to:

- Define metacognition and explain its relationship to policy analysis.

- Define cognitive dissonance and describe how trying to avoid it may create bias in policy analysis.

- Describe and differentiate fast System 1 thinking and slow System 2 thinking.

- Describe and differentiate accuracy motivated reasoning and directionally motivated reasoning.

- Describe and differentiate hot and cold cognition.

- Explain how the speed of cognition, the nature of an analyst's motivating objective, and the affective content of cognition can have adverse impacts on the quality of policy analysis.

- Characterize the cognitive errors and biases to which policy analysis is most vulnerable and describe mechanisms for overcoming their adverse impacts.

in the work of others, is time well spent.[1] This chapter starts with an overview of cognition—the process of thinking—and contrasts two forms of cognition: fast and slow. Section 4.2 introduces the concept of cognitive dissonance and describes how an aversion to it can undermine the quality of policy analysis. Sections 4.3 and 4.4, respectively, review the concepts of motivated reasoning and of emotion's effect on cognition. Section 4.5 integrates several of these concepts into a framework known as Dual Process Thinking. Finally, there are several specific cognitive traps of which you should be aware, so that you can work to mitigate them. Section 4.6 introduces and briefly describes eleven such traps.

4.1 METACOGNITION: THINKING, FAST AND SLOW

To get a handle on how your thought processes may affect your approach to policy analysis, I suggest you start with the subject of human **cognition**, or more formally, "the mental action or process of acquiring knowledge and understanding through thought, experience, and the senses" (Oxford University Press, 2001, p. 332). When you focus on your own thought processes, it's called **metacognition**. In other words, I'd like you to think about how you think.

Scholars typically distinguish two types of cognition: System 1 (fast) and System 2 (slow) thinking (Frederick, 2005; Kahneman, 2011; Norman et al., 2017; Stanovich & West, 2000). Some folks refer to the processes used in the two systems as, respectively, intuition and reasoning (Balla, Heneghan, Glasziou, Thompson, & Balla, 2009; Haidt, 2012).

Kahneman defines **System 1** thinking as intuitive and reflexive, operating automatically and quickly (2011). System 1 relies on mental shortcuts and simple rules of thumb, called **heuristics**, and doesn't require any conscious thought to go from a stimulus to a reaction. System 1 enables you to quickly read the words on a large billboard or come up with the answer to two plus two. It also helps you hit the brakes when you see an oncoming car in your peripheral vision and allows an emergency room physician to make dozens of medical decisions in a few short minutes.

System 2, on the other hand, is deliberative, requiring cognitive effort, concentration, and careful analysis. System 2 is more systematic, reflective, and complex than System 1. Importantly, it takes more time to reach a conclusion with System 2 than with System 1. Kahneman notes that you need System 2 thinking to pick out a particular voice in a noisy place, compute the square root of 123, or assess the validity

---

[1]For similar reasons, a majority of psychotherapists undergo therapy themselves. Doing so helps them become more aware of their own emotional responses to their clients' situations. In turn, deeper self-awareness may help them better assist those clients (Orlinsky, Schofield, Schroder, & Kazantzis, 2011).

of a complicated logical argument. System 2 helps physicians figure out how to treat patients with complex and severe symptoms of unknown origin (like HIV in the early 1980s or COVID in the spring of 2020); similarly, it helps an architect draw up detailed plans for a new building.

Stop and look at Exhibit 4-1 without reading further. Answer each question and jot down your results.

Exhibit 4-1   A Short Test

1. A bat and ball cost $5.50 in total. The bat costs $5.00 more than the ball. How much does the ball cost?

2. If it takes 10 machines 10 minutes to make 10 widgets, how long does it take 500 machines to make 500 widgets?

3. A lake has a patch of lily pads. Every day, the patch doubles in size. If it takes 24 days for the patch to cover the entire lake, how many days would it take for the patch to cover half of the lake?

This test is a variation of Frederick's (2005) Cognitive Reflection Test (p. 27).[2] Its purpose is to help identify "cognitive misers [who] give the first response that comes to mind" even though that response may not be right (Topiak, West, & Stanovich, 2011, p. 1275). Cognitive misers operate in System 1 by relying on quick, automatic thinking to develop their answers, whereas providing the right answer almost certainly requires you to expend the cognitive effort to apply System 2 thinking.

So, how did you do? Most folks say the ball costs 50 cents, it takes 500 minutes to make all the widgets, and the lake will be half covered by lily pads in 12 days. And most folks are wrong. If the ball costs 50 cents, then the bat costs $5.50, and the total is $6.00, not $5.50. The ball costs 25 cents. Each machine takes ten minutes to make one widget, so it would also take just ten minutes for 500 machines to make 500 widgets, not 500 minutes. Finally, if the lily pad doubles in size every day, then it would cover half the lake only one day before it covers the entire lake, i.e., on day 23, not on day 12.

If you gave the correct answers to all three questions, you very likely relied on System 2 thinking. If you gave the typical wrong answers (50 cents, 500 minutes, and 12 days), you almost certainly applied System 1 thinking. Finally, if you provided a different wrong answer, then you likely attempted to apply System 2 thinking but ran into analytical difficulties.

---

[2]I've modified the numbers, but not the text, so it won't be too easy if you've already seen this test.

If you didn't do very well, don't feel too bad. Among some 3,500 respondents—primarily university students—taking a virtually identical test, the average number of correct answers was 1.24, out of the maximum of 3.0 (Frederick, 2005). Such results don't mean that most people are incapable of careful problem-solving; instead, the evidence suggests that if we don't invest sufficient cognitive resources in figuring things out and instead rely only on fast, heuristic thinking, then we are prone to mistakes.

Most of the time, System 1 thinking works well for our daily lives in which we face dozens of decisions that are familiar to us and for which heuristic thinking provides perfectly acceptable results. Indeed, *it would be exhausting if we tried to apply full-on System 2 thinking to every decision we made every day*. There are at least three reasons why this is the case (Benson, 2019):

- Considering all information before acting is impossible. Our daily world touches on thousands of events, bits of evidence, truth claims, and points of view. We see only a sliver of what's really out there.

- Interpreting the information we *do* have is not easy. To act on that information, we need to understand what it means, how it fits together, and what its implications are. Doing so is often not straightforward; it takes cognitive effort.

- Our ability to put forth cognitive effort is constrained. We don't have the time, mental or emotional energy, or cognitive skills to thoroughly analyze all of the decisions we need to make every day. We can't help but act on partial information in almost every situation.

Although there are similarities, *System 1 thinking is not synonymous with the notion of bounded rationality* that we discussed in Chapter 3 (Stoker, Hay, & Barr, 2016). As you may recall, bounded rationality is an inability to consider all aspects of all possible paths forward before reaching a decision. Yes, the same constraints that lead to bounded rationality can also lead to fast System 1 thinking and the associated risks of flawed reasoning. But bounded rationality can also create problems for System 2 thinking when, even though we're willing to reason slowly and deliberatively, time, resource, and information constraints in the larger decision environment prevent us from doing so. Moreover, there are cases when System 1 thinking works very well (consider, for example, a veteran public servant well versed in the workings of government who can quickly discern where a new initiative may encounter problems); dismissing such cases as examples of bounded rationality seems a mistake.

Research suggests that System 1 thinking has a basis in evolutionary biology (Wilkinson & Klaes, 2012; Zak, 2011). Tetlock uses a vivid example to explain:

> In the Paleolithic world in which our brains evolved, [System 1 was] not a bad way of making decisions. Gathering all evidence and mulling it over may be the best way to produce accurate answers, but a hunter-gatherer who consults statistics on lions before deciding whether to worry about the shadow moving in the grass isn't likely to live long enough to bequeath his accuracy—maximizing genes to the next generation. Snap judgements are sometimes essential. (Tetlock & Gardner, 2015, pp. 34–35)

In the complex world of public policy, however, System 1 often—though not always—comes up short. Under many conditions, System 1 thinking allows a variety of biases to flourish.

The lesson for policy analysis is clear: to understand complicated policy issues and assess alternative ways of addressing them, then the role of System 1 thinking in policy analysis needs to be carefully circumscribed. Unfortunately, System 1 is an omnipresent force in our thinking and cannot be turned off without considerable effort (Kahneman, 2011). Accordingly, if you want to do high-quality analysis that makes a meaningful contribution to a policy debate, you have to first slow down and think about which preconceptions, assumptions, and heuristic shortcuts that you're bringing to the task. Your starting points may be perfectly valid, but you need to verify them before jumping into your policy analysis.

Here are a few questions you might ask yourself to figure out whether you've jumped too quickly to the (wrong) conclusion:

- Did it take me only a few minutes (or seconds) to reach this conclusion? If so, might I reach a different result if I contemplated the topic for a day or two?

- Did I have all the relevant information at hand when I quickly reached a conclusion? Might taking more time bring to light additional evidence that would change the answer?

- I may be pretty smart, but am I really expert enough on this particular topic to instinctively know the right answer?

- What are the consequences of getting it wrong? If the stakes are high, should I take more time to think things through to ensure that I've got the right answer?[3]

---

[3]In an urgent situation, we may not have time to do a full analysis. In such cases, we have no choice but take our best shot with System 1 and hope for a good outcome.

4.2 TOLERATING COGNITIVE DISSONANCE

How can you avoid inadvertently drifting into System 1 thinking while doing a policy analysis? It can be difficult, but one suggestion is to be on the lookout for the discomfort of cognitive dissonance. First described by Leon Festinger several decades ago (1957), **cognitive dissonance** is an internal intellectual and emotional dilemma we experience in our mind when there is a discrepancy (or tension or inconsistency) between an idea, concept, or belief that we hold as true or valid, and:

- Another idea, concept, or belief we also hold as true or valid,
- Actions we have previously taken or decisions we've made,
- The views of an admired public person or party,
- An ideology, political platform, or worldview to which we subscribe,
- The views of our social reference group, such as our friends, family, and colleagues,
- The way we earn our living, or
- Our sense of self-esteem, identity, and of who we are.

Theories of cognitive dissonance and its effect on our thinking have evolved considerably since Festinger's original work but the concept continues to drive new research and insights (Cooper, 2007).

When confronted with dissonance, we may feel hypocritical and experience guilt, shame, or embarrassment. In turn, *we are motivated to find ways to reduce the dissonance and avoid unwelcome emotions* (Wilkinson & Klaes, 2012). Doing so often entails rejecting the new idea or evidence (or the person providing it), something that is usually easier than devaluing our sense of self, reversing a prior decision, disavowing people and institutions we admire, or contradicting friends, family, or an employer. As Upton Sinclair (1935) put it after an unsuccessful run in 1930 for Governor of California: "It is difficult to get a man to understand something, when his salary depends on him not understanding it" (p. 109).

Elliot Aronson—one of Festinger's protégés—described an example of cognitive dissonance created by the 2020 COVID pandemic:

> … a great many Americans now see the life-and-death decisions of the coronavirus as political choices rather than medical ones. … The cognition *I want to go back to work* or *I want to go to my favorite bar to hang out with my friends* is dissonant with any information that suggests these actions might be dangerous. … How to resolve this dissonance? People could avoid the

crowds, parties, and bars and wear a mask. Or they could jump back into their former ways. But to preserve their belief that they are smart and competent and would never do anything foolish to risk their lives, they will need some self-justifications: Claim that masks impair their breathing, deny that the pandemic is serious, or protest that their 'freedom' to do what they want is paramount. (Aronson & Tavris, 2020, p. 3), *emphasis in original*

So cognitive dissonance explains why some of your friends didn't wear masks in the summer of 2020, but how might an aversion to cognitive dissonance undermine your efforts to conduct a sound policy analysis? For starters, the inability to tolerate cognitive dissonance creates internal pressure to find a psychic equilibrium. In turn, psychic equilibrium usually requires that dissonant thoughts be dismissed from the mind, likely taking with them policy-relevant insights. When you think about it, *the dismissal of dissonant thoughts is a form of self-deception*. With only a part of the picture in mind, it's hard to do a complete and comprehensive policy analysis.

For example, are you for or against an increase in the Federal minimum wage? If you're in favor, chances are that you think it will improve the standard of living for the working poor; if you're against an increase, you probably believe that it will increase unemployment among low-skilled workers and cause higher prices for goods and services. Debates about the minimum wage typically focus on one argument or the other; to admit that both points of view are valid creates cognitive dissonance for most folks. After all, how can a higher minimum wage be simultaneously both a good thing and a bad thing?

Resolving the seeming contradiction is easy if we dismiss one argument as wrong and accept the other as right. But when it comes to policy analysis, doing so is a mistake. The reality is that an increase in the minimum wage would almost certainly have multiple effects. If someone is lucky enough to keep their job, they're unambiguously better off because they get paid more for the same work, although their employer will likely need to raise prices to cover the additional labor cost. On the other hand, if a worker's contribution to their employer's business is of limited economic value, they will probably lose their job (or not be able to find a job in the first place).

The nonpartisan Congressional Budget Office studied the issue carefully and concluded that an increase in the Federal minimum wage to $15.00 per hour would likely have the following effects by the year 2025 (CBO, 2019, p. 13):

- 17 million workers would see an increase in their average weekly earnings,
- 1.3 million fewer workers would be employed,

- Families with income less than three times the poverty threshold would see an effective aggregate increase in annual income of $21.9 billion,
- Families with incomes more than three times the poverty threshold would see an effective aggregate decrease in annual income of $30.5 billion, and
- The number of people in poverty would be reduced by 1.3 million.[4]

In short, raising the minimum wage would cause some good things to happen *and* some bad things to happen. In turn, if you aim to have a complete understanding of the impacts of raising the minimum wage, you must be prepared to hold dissonant thoughts in your head at the same time.

When evaluating multiple policy options, the potential for cognitive dissonance is inescapable because virtually all proposed policies entail trade-offs. After all, if a recommended policy offers nothing but upsides, it begs the question of why it hasn't already been implemented. In short, trade-off-free policy proposals (all pros and no cons) are as common as unicorns.[5] Accordingly, I suggest you embrace F. Scott Fitzgerald's (1936) observation that "the test of a first-rate intelligence is the ability to hold two opposed ideas in the mind at the same time, and still retain the ability to function" (p. 1).

You can test your ability to withstand cognitive dissonance by assessing how hard it is for you to answer "yes" to questions like these:

- Can you separate your feelings about a public figure from your beliefs about the policy claims that he or she is making? Are you ready to believe that a person whom you trust and respect could be wrong? Or that someone you intensely dislike might be right?

- Are you ready to acknowledge that a policy you personally support almost certainly has at least some downsides, disadvantages, or costs?

- If you encounter a credible policy claim, only to realize that accepting it would put you at odds with friends, family, or your boss, would you advocate for it despite their disapproval?

- If you recognize the severity of a problem but oppose the logical policy response to it, can you resist the temptation to claim that the problem isn't a big deal after all?

---

[4] It's only a coincidence that both the change in employment and in the number of people in poverty is 1.3 million.

[5] I once had a student who insisted that unicorns were real, so too the Loch Ness monster (my backup metaphor). Suffice it to say that trade-off free policies don't exist.

4.3 REASONING: WHAT'S YOUR MOTIVATION?

One way to avoid cognitive dissonance is to use motivated reasoning to rationalize the dismissal of dissonant evidence, thoughts, and feelings. When we reason, we draw linkages from intellectual inputs—principles, goals, events, and observations—to intellectual outputs—conclusions, beliefs, inferences, and recommendations. These *acts of reasoning don't happen in a vacuum; motivation is omnipresent* (Taber & Lodge, 2012). When we analyze the world, we are typically motivated by a "wish, desire, or preference that concerns the outcome of a given reasoning task" (Kunda, 1990, p. 480). When motivated reasoning is at work in our minds, these preferences play an important role as we reason our way through issues and sort out what we believe (Bolsen & Palm, 2019; Jost, Hennes, & Lavine, 2013).

As shown in Exhibit 4-2, scholars separate motivated reasoning into two categories depending on the goal being pursued (Flynn, Nyhan, & Reifler, 2017; Kunda, 1990; Taber & Lodge, 2012). The first is called **accuracy motivated reasoning**, meaning that a neutral evaluator aspires to provide the best approximation of true conditions, irrespective of any prior preferences he or she might hold. The second category is referred to as **directionally motivated reasoning** because the goal is to reach a particular conclusion identified at the outset. This distinction should remind you of some of the differences between *analysis as inquiry* and *analysis as advocacy* that we talked about in Chapter 3. In the first case, we start with the analysis and reason toward the conclusion; in the second, we start with the conclusion and construct an analysis to support it.[6]

As an anecdotal example of accuracy motivated reasoning, I once heard the director of the policy office at a big Federal agency tell a roomful of policy professionals that you can't do a high-quality policy analysis unless "you just don't care what answer you come up with." His attitude was that you have to take your best shot at a neutral analysis without worrying about the consequences. As an anecdotal example of directionally motivated reasoning, I once had a colleague who explained why he had turned down a lucrative consulting contract he'd been offered by a commercial client. As he described it, he had been asked to "start with unfounded assumptions and work toward foregone conclusions"—an extreme example of directionally motivated reasoning.

When it comes to less sinister examples of directionally motivated reasoning, consider an attorney preparing to present a case. Given the way the legal system works, he or she will not tell both sides of the story but instead strategically select evidence and witnesses to weave a narrative that motivates the jury to find in favor of the client.

---

[6]In common parlance, when we 'rationalize' our behavior, we retroactively use directionally motivated reasoning to construct a plausible rationale for why we acted as we did.

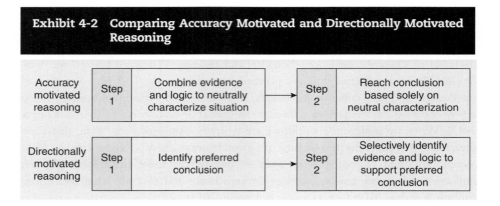

Exhibit 4-2   Comparing Accuracy Motivated and Directionally Motivated Reasoning

Accuracy motivated reasoning	Step 1	Combine evidence and logic to neutrally characterize situation	Step 2	Reach conclusion based solely on neutral characterization
Directionally motivated reasoning	Step 1	Identify preferred conclusion	Step 2	Selectively identify evidence and logic to support preferred conclusion

Similarly, a policy analyst working for an elected official may be pointed toward a policy problem and a particular policy option and be told to use the available evidence and logic to make the case for that option. Finally, I recall the 2002 Senate debate on the authorization of military force in Iraq, as Senators took the floor to make their case for or against the resolution. Each speech was an instance of directionally motivated reasoning as Senators sought to explain and justify their vote.

You might think that these examples of directionally motivated reasoning aren't cause for significant concern; after all, they simply demonstrate how our legal, political, and legislative systems are meant to work. And I wouldn't disagree with you. But *it's when directionally motivated reasoning goes undetected that we have a problem.* Kunda (1990) explains how things can get off track:

> The objectivity of this justification construction process is [however] illusory because people do not realize that the process is biased by their goals, that they are accessing only a subset of their relevant knowledge, that they would probably access different beliefs and rules in the presence of different directional goals, and they might even be capable of justifying opposite conclusions on different occasions. (pp. 482–483)

The difference between directionally and accuracy motivated reasoning is not just theoretical. Empirical studies have found that folks' existing opinions and principles often motivate them to rely on only some of the information and arguments available to them when drawing conclusions (Baekgaard, Christensen, Dahlman, Mathiasen, & Petersen, 2017).

In one study, for example, subjects were given numeric data about the ability of an intervention to produce an outcome (Kahan, Peters, Dawson, & Slovic, 2017). The data were identical, but one group was told that the intervention was a skin cream intended to treat a rash while the other group was told that the intervention was a gun control policy intended to reduce crime. In the case of the skin cream, subjects' ideological preferences (characterized on a continuum from conservative Republican to liberal Democrat) had little impact on how the data were interpreted. Both sides judged the effectiveness of the skin cream in similar ways. But when the identical data were described as measuring the impact of gun control on crime, the impact of ideology became clear as liberals were more apt to incorrectly claim that the data supported gun control while conservatives made similar reasoning errors but in the other direction (i.e., to support an antigun control position).

The results of this study aren't unusual. **Partisan bias**, the propensity to consider otherwise identical evidence more persuasive when it reinforces our political identification and preferences than when it refutes them, has been documented repeatedly in multiple studies using a variety of methodologies. Moreover, partisan basis appears to be symmetric. It affects both liberals and conservatives alike, with liberals apt to dismiss evidence supporting conservative positions, and vice versa (Ditto et al., 2019).

Another example of how of directionally motivated reasoning can affect policy analysis is known as **solution aversion**. In such cases, when we deny the existence of a problem, it's not always because we really believe the situation is not problematic. Rather, it may be that we find the obvious solution to the problem unacceptable. In other words, acknowledging the severity of a problem while simultaneously endorsing a solution we find objectionable creates cognitive dissonance. Faced with the internal discomfort of that contradiction, we may decide that the problem is not so bad after all.

It shouldn't be hard to see the downside of solution aversion for policy analysis. When it occurs, we find ourselves arguing with others about something on which we actually agree—that there is a problem. It's the desirability of potential policy responses where the disagreement lies, but we'll never get to a discussion of how to move forward because we're stuck in a fight over the problem definition.

We might dismiss motivated reasoning as irrelevant to policy analysis if it were confined solely to the general public, i.e., to those whose daily work doesn't entail evaluating and making policy decisions. If you devote your professional life to policy analysis, might you be immune to these cognitive maladies? Probably not. Before you get trained for a career in policy analysis, you are certainly a member of the general public, so these phenomena are likely already present in your thinking about policy issues.

There is also growing evidence that it's not just the public in general, but policymakers and policy advisors, who are affected by motivated reasoning and other cognitive biases (Hallsworth, Egan, Rutter, & McCrae, 2018; Liu, Stoutenborough, & Vedlitz, 2016; Sheffer, Loewen, Soroka, Walgrave, & Sheafer, 2018). For example, a survey of about 3,000 staff at the World Bank and the United Kingdom's Department for International Development demonstrated that policy professionals can also fall prey to multiple cognitive decisionmaking traps, despite their duty to provide neutral, evidence-based, policy analysis (Banuri, Dercon, & Guari, 2017). Similar cognitive errors were found in a study of 600 Italian public sector officials (Belle, Belardinelli, & Cantarelli, 2018) and among local politicians from across the partisan spectrum in Denmark (Baekgaard et al., 2017).

But what about your own motivations in the context of your own career? Recal the distinction between *policy analysis as inquiry* and *policy analysis as advocacy*.. If you want to make your living as an advocate, then motivated reasoning may not be a significant concern for you. If you aspire to practice policy analysis as inquiry, then you should worry about it.

Moreover, *aspiring to reach only accurate results rather than preferred conclusions doesn't guarantee that you'll succeed* (Bolsen & Palm, 2019; Pietryka, 2016). You could fall prey to cognitive mistakes originating in your fast System 1 thinking. On the other hand, your System 2 reasoning—while slow and deliberate—could still get it wrong. You might collect seemingly strong evidence but fail to detect bias within it; you may spend so much time collecting this evidence that you give the analysis short shrift or make an unnoticed error in logical and inferential reasoning. Moreover, in an effort to listen to all points of view, you might give undue weight to a disreputable fringe theory:

> … it is not always the case that more elaborate and complex thought will lead to improved judgment. There are situations in which the harder we think, the more likely we are to resort to faulty reasoning strategies. In such situations accuracy goals can, ironically, increase error and enhance bias. (Kunda, 1999, p. 239)

In short, an accuracy motivation does not, by itself, ensure that you will reach a sound conclusion. On the other hand, *if you don't even try to come up with an accurate result, the odds of doing so are small*. You can get a sense of your vulnerability to directionally motivated reasoning by asking yourself questions like these:

- Can you honestly say you don't care what answer you come up with, as long as you do a careful job of sifting available evidence and applying sound logic to it?

- Are you ready to look at all potentially relevant evidence and points of view, irrespective of where they originate?

- Are you ready to embrace an analytic result that contradicts what you or your client previously believed about the topic at hand?

- Are you ready to take the heat that may come from generating an unpopular or unconventional answer to the policy question you're asking?

4.4 COGNITION: HOT AND COLD

Motivated reasoning originates in cognition, the process by which we come to know or understand something based on thought, experience, and the senses. Sometimes **cognition is hot** when we experience an affective response (one based in feeling and emotion), typically at a subconscious level, to the stimulus we've encountered (Bolsen & Palm, 2019). If so, we say the stimulus carries a **valence**. Kraft, Lodge, and Taber (2015) claim that:

> [A]ll concepts that have been evaluated in the past are affectively charged (i.e., they arouse positive or negative valence), and this affect response springs spontaneously to mind on mere exposure to the name or image of a person, group, or idea to influence all subsequent processing, is unintentional, and is difficult to control. Almost immediately, the decision stream becomes affectively charged, viscerally "hot" … All subsequent considerations and deliberations are necessarily influenced by this spontaneously activated affect. (p. 127)

Cold cognition, on the other hand, occurs when the stimulus doesn't carry an affective valence. In the study cited above, for example, whether the skin cream cured the rash was not an affectively charged question and ideology didn't affect the subjects' cognition of the evidence presented to them. Or, put another way, evaluating the effectiveness of skin cream posed little risk of cognitive dissonance, thus liberating the study subjects to evaluate the data as best they could, using cold cognition.

The concepts of hot and cold cognition have an analogy in Aristotle's framework of argumentation that we discussed in the introduction to Part III. Devoid of emotional reasoning, his concept of logos is akin to cold cognition. But because ethos is intended to provoke an emotional response from the audience toward the speaker/writer and pathos aims provoke an emotional response to the topic under discussion, both ethos and pathos are forms of hot cognition.

Although they're related, hot and cold cognition are not quite the same concepts as fast and slow thinking. For instance, *cold cognition can be as instantaneous as hot cognition*. A decision to stop at a red light or to pick up something we've dropped comes from System 1 but isn't emotionally charged. Like the emergency room physician cited previously, subject matter experts exist in all areas of public policy. Their experience and training allow them to use System 1 thinking to ascertain—in a neutral and unemotional (i.e., cold) way—the likely validity of new evidence, the feasibility of novel ideas, or the relevance of existing institutional arrangements to new situations far more quickly and accurately than a novice in the same policy field.

Near-instantaneous, affectively charged, *hot cognition often can't be avoided, especially when it comes to controversial or personally sensitive matters*. It can, however, be modulated by subsequent effortful System 2 thinking (Kraft et al., 2015). Or, more pragmatically, some of the emotional intensity may simply abate as things 'cool down.' Moreover, responding emotionally to an important policy issue isn't a problem per se. After all, as we talked about in Chapter 3, the typical policy analysis includes multiple normative elements that depend heavily on values and preferences; it's no surprise that such elements can trigger an emotional response. In fact, your emotional response can help you sort out your normative beliefs and to make value judgments across disparate topics (Peters, Vastfjall, Garlin, & Slovic, 2006).[7] What's most important, however, is that you recognize your emotional response and clearly understand its role in your analysis.

There are two important take-aways from this discussion of hot and cold cognition and its link to motivated reasoning. The first has to do with a broad threat posed to democratic governance and the second has to do with a specific threat posed to your ability to succeed as a professional policy analyst.

The *broad threat posed by directionally motivated reasoning arises when such reasoning dominates political and policy conversations.* When hot cognition is the norm and accuracy-motivating reasoning goes missing, productive policy debates become less and less possible:

> Normatively, the conjuring up of facts and reasons in a policy dispute should be independent of one's hopes for which way the evidence will point. In particular, scientific debates should be independent of partisan considerations. The results of many empirical studies find significant deviations from this ideal, however. Partisans in these studies systematically denigrate, depreciate, and counterargue evidence that is contrary to their political views but accept uncritically the supportive evidence. (Kraft et al., 2015, pp. 121–122)

Systematically denigrate contrary evidence? *Uncritically* accept supportive evidence? Wow, directionally motivated reasoning certainly sounds antithetical to the definition of policy analysis that I offered in the early pages of this book: the consideration of available evidence, coupled with well-reasoned inferences, to illuminate trade-offs among available choices for exercising government power to modify existing programs or to enact new policies. Kahan, Peters, Dawson, and Slovic (2017) put a finer point on the problem:

> Collective welfare demands *empirically informed* collective action. To be sure, decision-relevant science rarely generates a unique solution to any policy dispute:

---

[7]We'll take a deep dive into the connection between emotional intuition and moral reasoning in Section 5.4.

even after the basic facts have been established, *what to do* will involve judgments of value that will vary across citizens who hold competing understandings of the public good. But unless citizens and their representatives possess empirically sound understandings of the dangers they face and the likely effects of policies to abate them, they will not even be able to identify, much less secure enactment of, policies that advance their ends. (p. 55), *emphasis in original*

The second threat posed by directionally motivated reasoning occurs at the personal, rather than societal, level. The threat manifests itself when you, as a policy analyst, fall prey to hot cognition and the unwise use of System 1 thinking. If you rely primarily on instinctive, emotionally driven ways of thinking about policy issues, you will probably be a less effective policy analyst than you otherwise might be. Part of becoming a successful policy analyst, especially at the outset of your career, is the assiduous application of System 2 thinking to your work. As you gain more experience, you will find it increasingly easier to apply quick, instinctive System 1 thinking to your work. Until then, try asking questions like these to figure out if hot cognition has crept into your policy analysis:

- As you work through the analysis, what emotions are you feeling? Anger or pleasure? Confidence or self-doubt? Is a finding at odds with your prior belief upsetting or exciting?

- If you are experiencing an emotional response during a debate, can you detect whether it's directed at a particular person or group, or at their ideas and statements? Reacting to specific content, rather than to the speaker or writer, may help you manage hot cognition.

- Do you get the sense that the person you're talking to is approaching the conversation using hot cognition? Are they offering insults or empty claims? If you make a strong claim, do they dismiss it out of hand, or do they offer a reasoned response? It's tempting to respond to someone else's hot cognition with your own hot cognition, but it's also probably counterproductive.

4.5 PUTTING IT ALL TOGETHER: DUAL PROCESS THEORY

So far in this chapter, we've covered a lot of terrain, much of it interrelated. I created Exhibit 4-3 to summarize the three cognitive constructs that we just discussed: speed of cognition, motivated reasoning, and the emotional aspect of cognition. Each construct comprises a pair of elements that have both positive and negative implications for policy analysis.

Exhibit 4-3　Three Dichotomous Constructs Relevant to Cognition and Policy Analysis

Construct	Element 1	Element 2	Implications for Policy Analysis
Speed of Cognition	**System 1 Thinking** • Fast • Intuitive • Cognitively easier	**System 2 Thinking** • Slow • Deliberative • Cognitively harder	• System 1 thinking prone to bias and cognitive error • Used by analyst with relevant expertise, however, System 1 may yield high-quality results quickly • System 2 thinking usually offers high-quality results, but may be infeasible given time, resource, and information constraints of real-world policymaking
Motivating Objective	**Accuracy Motivated Reasoning** • Analyst endeavors to best approximate true conditions, irrespective of personal preferences • Starts with analysis and reasons toward conclusion	**Directionally Motivated Reasoning** • Analyst endeavors to make strongest case for a preferred conclusion • Preferred conclusion comes from analyst, client, or prior analysis • Starts with conclusion and constructs analysis to support it	• Accuracy motivated reasoning aligns with *policy analysis as inquiry* • Accuracy motivated reasoning (behind closed doors) can be used as part of *policy analysis as advocacy* to anticipate counterarguments • Directionally motivated reasoning aligns with *policy analysis as advocacy* • Unrecognized directionally motivated reasoning undermines policy discourse when one-sided analysis mistakenly viewed as neutral
Affective (Emotional) Content of Cognition	**Hot Cognition** • Stimulus creates affective response based on emotion and feeling • Affect often arises nearly instantaneously but may evolve over time • Affect may be positive or negative	**Cold Cognition** • Stimulus creates response that lacks emotional content • May be present from point when stimulus first encountered or may appear over time (as things 'cool off')	• Affect an important driver of values and normative preferences • Hot cognition may lead to unwise use of System 1 fast thinking or directionally motivated reasoning • Hot cognition used simultaneously by multiple analysts and policymakers may lead to polarization and unproductive policy arguments

One framework for pulling all these pieces together is referred to as **Dual Process Theory (DPT)**. The word 'dual' in the name refers to the two systems we've been discussing—the quick intuitive System 1 and the slower deliberative System 2. The DPT framework first emerged in the field of cognitive psychology in the 1990s

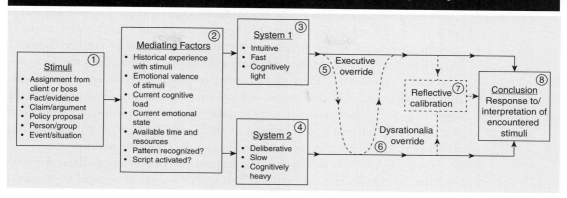

Source: Adapted, in part, from Crosskerry and Nimmo (2011)

(Epstein, 1994; Shafir & LeBoeuf, 2002) and has since been applied in a number of fields. A prominent recent application has been in medical clinical reasoning in an effort to help nurses and physicians come to more accurate diagnoses and more helpful therapeutic decisions (Crosskerry & Nimmo, 2011; Marcum, 2012; Norman et al., 2017). Take a look at Exhibit 4-4, which provides a graphic depiction of how Dual Process Theory might be applied to policy analysis.

In medicine, it's a clinician's encounter with the patient that starts the process. To draw the analogy to policy analysis, it may help to work with an example. Perhaps we're talking about air pollution policy. For starters, there are several **stimuli** (1) that might initiate your cognitive process. Your client might point you to air quality in a particular urban area. You might come across evidence about pollution's effects on people's health. You might be handed a specific policy proposal with a program for cleaning up the air. Alternatively, you might hear from an advocacy group or a politician about the problem and/or what should be done about it.

The stimuli you encounter will evoke a cognitive response on your part—your brain's attempt to comprehend the situation. Several **mediating factors** (2) may quickly come into play and shape your cognitive response. Perhaps you already know a lot about air quality issues. You might also have strong feelings about the topic; maybe you despise the company that owns the polluting factory (or conversely, you work there). You might be having a bad day and feel like you have only a minute or two to contemplate the situation, or you might be a retiree in a great mood with ample free time. You might have the experience or technical expertise to quickly recognize the pattern of pollution you're seeing. You might even have encountered similar situations before and intuitively have a script of questions to ask and information to seek as you start to think about the problem. Bear in mind that the stimuli (1) and the mediating factors (2) can interact in a few seconds (sometimes, in milliseconds) to push you into a particular cognitive reaction—**fast** (3) or **slow** (4).

In some instances, once you're in a particular mode of cognition, you don't stray from it. On the other hand, instead of staying the course with a single mode of thinking, you might change modes mid-stream. For example, if you start in System 1 but realize that the situation demands a more thoughtful and measured response, you may switch to System 2 thinking with what is called an **executive override** (5). Alternatively, you might have started out in System 2, fully intending to process the situation in a deliberate and calculating manner, but something (e.g., an inconvenient fact, a competing demand on your time, or an emotional trigger) might cause a shift into System 1 thinking in what is referred to as a **dysrationalia override** (6).

Finally, before fully concluding your thought process, you might pause for what could be called **reflective calibration** (7). If you do so, you're engaged in metacognition, or thinking about how you're thinking. The calibration step gives you the chance to double check your thought processes before drawing a final conclusion. Reflectively calibrated or not, the process ends when you finish cognitively processing, at least for the time being, your reaction to the stimuli and reach a conclusion (8).

While some scholars believe that all cognitive errors originate in System 1 and manifest themselves only when System 2 thinking fails to correct them, other scholars argue that errors can arise in both systems (Norman et al., 2017). I'm pretty sure that the latter group has it right. Yes, mistakes occur in System 1 when fast heuristic thinking is highjacked by hot cognition and flawed reasoning that is never corrected by System 2 thinking. But keep in mind that if we're talking about a highly skilled individual working in his or her area of expertise, fast System 1 thinking can also deliver excellent results (Yaakobi, 2017). What's more, as we discussed previously in the context of accuracy motivated reasoning, there are plenty of mistakes that can occur solely within System 2. In addition, as our review of the DPT suggests, you might start down the path of System 2, only to be derailed by something that triggers a dysrationalia override.

Another common, and often inescapable, limitation of System 2 thinking originates in time and resource constraints. Many important decisions are on the clock—the emergency room patient who dies before doctors figure out what's wrong with him or an attempt at a complex policy analysis that can't be finished before the politician client has to cast her vote in the legislature. The title of Kahneman's book points directly at the problem: System 1 is fast and System 2 is slow. But, in many cases, we don't have the luxury of being slow.

To summarize, it would be a *mistake to treat System 1 as the problem and System 2 as the solution*. I use the 2×2 matrix in Exhibit 4-5 to perform a simple thought experiment. In it, I try to identify what success and failure look like in the context of Systems 1 and 2. In short, both systems of cognition can each result in a positive or a negative outcome.

Exhibit 4-5   Possible Outcomes of System 1 and 2 Processes

		Outcome	
		Positive	**Negative**
Cognitive process applied	**System 1**	Quick, accurate, useful result	Quick, but flawed, erroneous result
	System 2	Time consuming but accurate and useful result	Failed attempt to execute complex analysis within time, information, and resource constraints

We'll talk more in Chapter 7 about the process of integrating both systems in your work as a policy analyst. For now, here are a few questions to consider as you think about applying DPT to policy analysis:

- If you find yourself thinking fast, are you working on a topic for which you have sufficient expertise to be confident that your intuitions are sound? If not, do you have the time and resources to shift to slow thinking?

- Is your System 1 thinking driven primarily by an emotional (or hot) response to the stimuli at hand and has cognitive deliberation been neglected? If so, it may be time for an executive override and a transition to System 2.

- If you find yourself thinking slow, do you have the time, resources, and expertise to reach a sound conclusion, or will you come up short and reach a flawed result? Would you be better off thinking fast, doing the best you can with the information and intuitions you have at the ready?

- If you started out in System 2, did an emotional trigger cause a dysrationalia override that pushed you into System 1 thinking? If so, can you get back to a System 2 approach?

- Irrespective of your mode of cognition—System 1 or 2—did you pause for a moment of reflective calibration before reaching a final conclusion?

4.6 WATCH OUT FOR THESE COGNITIVE TRAPS

As shown in Exhibit 4-6, this section summarizes several cognitive errors and biases that can infect our thinking.[8] Some authors have identified close to 200 cognitive biases (Benson, 2019). Rather than overwhelm you with information, I've focused on the biases most relevant to policy analysis.

Exhibit 4-6   Potential Cognitive Traps

- Downsides of Defending Against Dissonance
  - Selective Exposure and Compartmentalization
  - Confirmation and Disconfirmation Bias
  - Group Bias: The Halo and Horns Effect
  - Aversion to Uncertainty and Risk

- Mood-Driven Mistakes
  - Priming
  - Backfire Effect
  - Overconfidence Trap

- Mental Missteps
  - Framing
  - Anchoring
  - Availability and Mirror Imaging
  - Coherence and the WYSIATI Phenomenon

Why is it so easy—even for veteran analysts—to fall into these traps? Recall from Section 4.1 that we tend to be cognitive misers. Cognition takes time, and time spent in deliberative thinking has an opportunity cost. It's time that we can't spend on something else, hence the lure of System 1 thinking. Add in the emotional appeal of hot cognition, the temptation to engage in directionally motivated reasoning, and the fact that System 1 thinking can kick in within milliseconds of encountering a stimulus, and it's not hard to see how cognitive mistakes can happen.

Several studies of medical education suggest that students and residents can be taught to recognize cognitive biases, although it's not clear that doing so always

---

[8]The material in this section represents an amalgam of ideas that originate in multiple sources. Specific factual claims and studies are cited in the usual fashion. The remainder of the material is based primarily on my personal experience but also reflects an integrated reading of less formal commentary offered by these websites, news reports, and blog posts: (Bensen, 2017; Dwyer, 2018; Dwyer, 2017; Richardson, 2018; Richardson, 2017).

improves diagnostic accuracy (Norman et al., 2017). Accordingly, we need to be realistic here. As the first five sections of this chapter emphasized, the drivers of flawed reasoning are all deeply embedded in our cognitive processes. As Benson (2019) puts it: "Biases are here to stay because they're fundamental to how we think" (p. 91).

Fully eliminating them is virtually impossible, but at a minimum, you'll want to familiarize yourself with common errors that result from faulty cognitive processes. Doing so will not only give you a foundation for avoiding them in your own work, but may also help you detect them in others' work. What's more, the impediments to clear thinking described in this chapter represent tendencies—not iron laws—that affect human thinking. While many study participants fall prey to cognitive bias, not all participants do so, especially if the evidence is clear and unambiguous (Anglin, 2019).

For ease of presentation, each of the potential failures of cognitive reasoning has been sorted into one of three categories. The first category of problems originates in our discomfort with cognitive dissonance. The second category stems from the connection between our emotional mood and our thinking processes. A third category reflects errors of reasoning that can occur without our realizing it.

4.6.1 The Downsides of Defending Against Dissonance

As we previously discussed in Section 4.2, the psychic discomfort of cognitive dissonance can be a powerful motivator that drives us to find ways to avoid it. Below are four responses to cognitive dissonance that can threaten the quality of your policy analysis.

Selective Exposure and Compartmentalization

It may seem obvious, but if you're not exposed to dissonant ideas, evidence, or people, then you're unlikely to experience cognitive dissonance. Because dissonance is profoundly uncomfortable, it's understandable that we often arrange our lives to **selectively minimize exposure** to things that might trigger dissonance. Think about whom you choose to spend time with and where you spend that time, what social media sources you follow, what news media and advocacy groups you pay attention to, and which politicians you listen to. *Odds are that your exposure is tilted toward ideas and people that you find agreeable.*

A related phenomenon is cognitive **compartmentalization**, which occurs when, with a cognitive sleight of hand, we "manage—at least temporarily—simply to avoid thinking about one side of the inconsistency in our beliefs and behavior … dissonance is thus avoided rather than defeated" (Bardon, 2020, p. 9). Whether compartmentalization can be a successful long-term strategy for dealing with dissonance is unclear; lodged in the subconscious mind, the underlying tension may surface at inconvenient times or may affect our emotional and cognitive states in unpredictable ways.

Confirmation and Disconfirmation Bias

Another tactic to protect against cognitive dissonance can spontaneously arise when we're looking for and evaluating new information. If new material confirms something we think we already know, **confirmation bias** may weaken our analytic filters to the point where we uncritically accept the new information as valid. Or, conversely, **disconfirmation bias** comes into play when we dismiss new information simply because it challenges our existing beliefs. Haidt (2012) explains the power of such biases:

> People are quite good at challenging statements made by *other* people, but if it's *your* belief, then it's your possession—your child, almost—and you want to protect it, not challenge it and risk losing it. (p. 91), *emphasis in original*

The information age has made it incredibly easy to succumb to confirmation and disconfirmation biases. No matter the topic—police reform, gun rights, immigration, you name it—Google searches and Twitter feeds take only a few seconds to deliver the studies, opinions, or evidence you need to reassure yourself that your beliefs are valid (Haidt, 2012). By selectively dismissing contradictory evidence and embracing supportive evidence, you may tame your cognitive dissonance, but *your existing beliefs and ideas can take on a self-reinforcing character that makes them powerful distortions of reality*.

If you're still not convinced about the downsides of confirmation bias, consider the fact that trying to validate a belief by seeking confirmatory evidence is at odds with the scientific method. Most scientists test a hypothesis by trying to refute it and then infer its validity if they can't falsify it (Kahneman, 2011). To take a famous example, if you're pretty sure all swans are white, then finding more examples of white swans doesn't give you any new information. Instead, you ought to specifically look for black swans; if you can't find any, that's better evidence that all swans are white than yet one more picture of another white swan (Bardon, 2020).

Group Bias: The Halo and Horns Effect

Halos and horns are clever turns of phrase often used to describe biases associated with the **group identification** process. When we think about the groups—political, racial, socioeconomic, religious, gender, cultural—that we identify with, we often look at them in positive terms (i.e., wearing metaphoric halos). Conversely, when it comes to groups with which we don't identify, our emotions are typically more negative; in the extreme, we may be tempted to demonize the other (hence the metaphor of a devil's horns). This phenomenon is called in-group favoritism (Benson, 2019).

In-group favoritism occurs because group membership is important to our sense of self-identity. Threats to these groups can provoke an emotional reaction that's almost the same as if we were personally threatened (Bardon, 2020). Moreover, the halo and horns effect help our psyches resolve cognitive dissonance. If someone is a member of a group that we respect and admire, we are predisposed to take their statements more seriously, while if someone is aligned with a group we dislike or distrust, we tend to discount what they say. Finally, using System 1 to decide whether new people and ideas are benign or malign is a more efficient use of cognitive resources than a deliberative, potentially time-consuming and dissonance-inducing evaluation of each new person or situation (Kahneman, 2011).

So, what do horns and halos have to do with policy analysis? Policy is made amid debates among multiple groups at multiple times and places. Accordingly, most policy analyses require that you identify and understand several points of view at the same time. Doing so is much harder if you allow both positive and negative emotions to distort your understanding of those points of view. We need to remember that *people and groups whose values we share can and do say foolish things and that folks with whom we disagree may have good insights worth listening to.*

I am not suggesting that all points of view are equally valid, that you need to listen to folks who don't know what they're talking about, or that closed-minded people who deny the authenticity of your grievances deserve a seat at your table. Nonetheless, I am suggesting that it is a good idea to familiarize yourself with alternative points of view.

Aversion to Uncertainty and Risk

The human mind often struggles with uncertain futures, especially those with negative outcomes. Unsurprisingly, we don't like losing income, wealth, or life's amenities. In fact, losses can be so psychically unpleasant that we're often willing to pay more to keep things we already have than we would have paid for them in the first place (Benson, 2019). The phenomena of **risk and loss aversion** almost certainly have at least some basis in evolutionary biology:

> Any species that is fearless and does not take into account the prospect of a loss is destined to be extinct. … in most policy debates, fear moves us in a profound way. (Gupta, 2011, p. 14)

But potential losses are often tempered by potential gains. To chase a gain, we usually must risk a negative outcome. We take a new job because it pays well and looks exciting, but it may turn out that we're miserable in the new job. Governments adopt new policies, hoping they'll work, but sometimes they don't. There are few decisions of any consequence that don't have at least some downside risk. In short, policy analysts must recognize the existence of risk and uncertainty without over-reacting to it.

While the terms risk and uncertainty both get at the unobservable nature of the future, the word **uncertainty** is typically interpreted as a broad lack of knowledge about the future, while **risk** suggests an ability to both identify possible outcomes and attach a probability to each outcome. Buying a lottery ticket embodies risk, because all the payoffs and likelihoods are specified with mathematical precision. Conversely, which of the dozens of movies currently in production will be next summer's blockbuster hit is a matter of uncertainty.

Attitudes toward future gains and losses, their magnitude and probability, and their uncertain and ambiguous nature have been studied for decades. Most issues fit into a framework called Prospect Theory, for which Kahneman won the 2002 Nobel Prize.[9] We don't have space for a full discussion of Prospect Theory, so we'll concentrate on three topics relevant to policy analysis.

First, when doing policy analysis, be sure to isolate your own feelings about risk and uncertainty. For example, the possibility that you could be held responsible for a motor vehicle accident, and your sense of risk aversion, might reasonably prompt you to buy auto insurance for your own car (even if doing so isn't legally required). But if you're a public servant thinking about risks across large numbers of cases, your approach should differ. For example, as a city manager responsible for a fleet of 15,000 vehicles, you may want to skip auto insurance. Odds are that only a few city vehicles will be in an accident each year and that the cost of repairing them will be less than that of an insurance policy for all 15,000 vehicles. Those few accidents will not bankrupt the city. In short, *attitudes about risk and uncertainty that make sense for your own life are almost certainly irrelevant to your work as a policy analyst.*

Second, the consequences of a **rare event** can, paradoxically, be either overemphasized or ignored by the typical person. Overemphasis happens when we conjure vivid images of something like a terrorist attack or natural disaster and give it more weight than it statistically deserves. On the other hand, low probability events may instead be ignored by folks who lack experience with the rare event; this can provide them a sense of internal equanimity, but it may be less than ideal when we're thinking about long-term, slowly evolving events like climate change (Kahneman, 2011) or the deteriorating state of the social security trust fund. *When working with low probability but high consequence outcomes, take care that your (or your community's) emotional reaction to the consequence isn't biasing your estimate of its likelihood or magnitude.*

Third, a cognitive trap known as **ambiguity aversion** can arise when a decisionmaker is choosing between two options, both with uncertain outcomes. The probabilities of possible outcomes under the first option might be well defined and confidently characterized while the probabilities for the outcomes under the second option are unknown or ill-defined. Evidence suggests that "even if the best estimates of

---

[9]His collaborator, Amos Tversky, died in the late 1990s; the Nobel Prize is not awarded posthumously.

the latter have the same value as the former" (Weber, 2013, p. 385), decisionmakers often favor the first option. Typically framed as a choice between a risky outcome and an uncertain outcome, this phenomenon is referred to as ambiguity aversion. Yes, *ambiguity can be psychically unpleasant but it's typically not a good reason to dismiss a choice that has a reasonable prospect of success.*

4.6.2 Mood-Driven Mistakes

As noted when we were discussing hot and cold cognition, sometimes our emotional state of mind affects our reaction to a stimulus. Below are three mood-driven mistakes that may adversely impact your work as a policy analyst.

Priming

Given that affect influences our interpretation of the ideas we encounter, it's not surprising that others may, intentionally or not, manipulate our emotions when making a policy claim. This process—known as **priming**—means that our emotional state when we encounter an analytic claim affects how we interpret that claim. The way I see it, *priming is today's version of Aristotle's pathos.*

Contrast two openings for a claim about climate change. In the first, the author describes an emaciated polar bear perched atop a shrinking Arctic ice floe, and then goes on to argue for prompt action on climate change. In the second, the author opens with a blighted Appalachian town where hopeless unemployed coal miners have succumbed to opioid addiction; the author then argues that policies to limit coal use are ill-advised. In both cases, you've been primed.

There's nothing wrong with appealing to your sense of environmental steward-ship nor to your sense of obligation to fellow citizens. The trick is to recognize that such appeals to emotion may color your reaction to the policy claim and, moreover, that the author has focused your emotions in a specific direction rather than letting you decide for yourself which aspects of the problem are most important.

The Backfire Effect

When someone challenges our beliefs and understanding of the world—even if they're calm and respectful, but especially if they're rude and offensive—we can feel emotionally threatened. After all, our beliefs and opinions are part of our self-identify. Recall that Haidt referred to them as our children. What's more, when someone tries to change our mind, we may see it as an attempt to limit our freedom of belief (Benson, 2019). If we perceive that it's not just our ideas that are being challenged but instead feel that we ourselves or our right to think freely is under attack, we may react defensively and double-down on our point of view. Doing so is called the **backfire**, or boomerang, effect.

The backfire effect has been observed in studies where additional evidence and arguments were provided to folks holding fringe beliefs about, for example, the presence of weapons of mass destruction in Iraq, the impacts of the Affordable Care Act, and the consequences of climate change. Not only did the new information not generally change minds, it often led a strengthening of the misconception (Bardon, 2020). The backfire effect is not, however, a universal one (Wood & Porter, 2019); it appears most prevalent for affect-laden and controversial issues (Flynn, Nyhan, & Reifler, 2017). Given our discussion of hot cognition and directionally motivated reasoning, this should come as no surprise.

When it comes to policy analysis, *clinging more tightly to your beliefs in the face of contradictory information is almost certainly a mistake*. No matter how hostile and rude the other person is being or how dissonant their new information feels, they might still be right about the subject of the debate.

The Overconfidence Trap

The **overconfidence** trap ensnares folks who believe that they are smarter or more knowledgeable than they really are. It's been documented in many fields and is typically confirmed by administering tests on various subjects and then asking test-takers how they did. Folks routinely overestimate their expertise, scoring worse than they thought they had. Known as the Dunning-Kruger effect, it's named after two scholars who first identified it (Kruger & Dunning, 1999). When it occurs, the overconfidence trap typically comprises two parts:

- The affected person has little expertise on a topic about which they claim competence.

- The affected person is unaware of their lack of expertise.

In short, their lack of self-awareness blinds them to their own shortcomings. If you come across someone who fits this pattern, caution is in order, especially if that person is you!

Overconfidence in yourself is a form of self-deception. Even though your undergraduate education, life experience, native intelligence, and graduate training have prepared you for a career as a policy analyst, it would behoove you, at least at the start of your career, to remember your status as a novice. Yes, you may have good insights about a subject, but take care not to overestimate the depth of your knowledge, especially if you find yourself working quickly, without time for reflection on what you really do and don't know. Over time, you will gain knowledge and expertise, and your intuitions and instincts will become more reliable and trustworthy. And one more suggestion: as you move through your career, and your expertise grows, don't lose sight of the specific field to which your expertise is relevant. Just because you're an expert in one field, as Dunning and Kruger remind us, it doesn't mean you're an expert in other fields.

At the same time, of course, you don't want to be so cautious that you never speak up or challenge a weak point of view, especially when your qualifications and competence are solid. You've probably heard of the **imposter syndrome** in which talented but self-doubting folks consistently underestimate their talents and fail to live up to their professional potential. Like many things in life, it's a balancing act; aim for the sweet spot where you operate fully within your zone of competence, but not beyond it.

The second thing to watch out for is overconfidence in other folks (i.e., when they have fallen prey to the Dunning-Kruger effect). This occurs frequently in the political world, as issue advocates attempt to defend a policy position by making confident assertions that are not based on sound evidence and logic. They may not even be aware of their lack of expertise. For example, think about the award-winning actor who takes a position on a policy issue about which he or she knows little. Or a scientist—whose expertise is in atmospheric chemistry, not environmental economics—who opines on the correct level for a carbon tax to address climate change.

4.6.3 Mental Missteps

Not all the mistakes we make in System 1 are directly linked to emotional precursors. By moving fast, we may simply overlook some key elements of basic reasoning. Below are four examples.

Framing

In the context of policy analysis, a **frame** reflects choices made by an author about how to structure and present an analysis or policy claim. There is nothing wrong with framing; we can't (easily) discuss a concept without framing it. The problem arises when we uncritically accept a frame and forget to think about its implications for the conclusions we draw. Problems with framing can be broad or narrow in scope; we'll look at both cases below.

For starters, the economic, political, and cultural systems in which policy issues arise are complex, dynamic, and uncertain. Faced with an array of potentially relevant considerations, someone making a policy claim must develop a framework within which to present the claim. In turn, the frame dictates which goals, evidence, methodologies, and forms of reasoning will be included and how to organize and present them. The alternative—an uncensored flow of all relevant information—would be an overwhelming mess.

Consider two analyses of global warming that both call for policy action: a UK government review by Nicholas Stern (2007) and Pope Frances's Papal Encyclical (Bergoglio, 2015). The Stern Review is framed as a cost–benefit analysis that monetizes the impacts of climate change and of actions to mitigate it. The Papal Encyclical frames the issue in religious and moral terms, with an emphasis on damage to an earth to which humanity owes a duty of stewardship, and on impacts unjustly suffered by the poor and vulnerable. Neither frame—cost–benefit analysis or religious-ethical argument—is unambiguously right; both add valuable insight.

As another example, consider how framing affects policy debates about health care. If we frame it as an issue of health insurance, we are led into a discussion of the mechanics of insurance policies and insurance markets (like individual mandates and coverage of preexisting conditions) and, in turn, an analysis of rules for subsidizing and regulating insurance companies. If instead health care is framed as a form of human protection, akin to food safety and police services, the conversation goes in another direction. We end up treating the issue as a moral concern and considering how best to guarantee universal health care for everyone (Lakoff, 2009). Whether it's climate change, health care, or some other policy issue, you should recognize that if you accept a single framing of an issue, then you have limited the discussion substantially.

Problems with framing can also be narrower, when word choice and selective emphasis is used to present the same information in one way rather than another. For example, the rate of violent crime in the United States has generally trended downward in the past three decades (Morgan & Oudekerk, 2019).[10] Below are two ways we might frame these data:

- *Frame 1*: Crime is near its lowest level in 26 years with only 12 violent crimes per 1,000 people in 2018.

- *Frame 2*: Even though crime has fallen over the past 26 years, there were still 12 victims of violent crime for every 1,000 people in 2018.

You probably think the second statement makes it seem like violent crime is a bigger problem than does the first.[11] The factual content is identical, but the framing differs. The word 'only' in the first statement implies that we should be pleased that the rate is so low, while the words 'even though,' 'still,' and 'victim' in the second suggest that the rate is too high.

Alternative approaches to framing may stem not only from honest differences of opinion (e.g., the Papal Encyclical versus the cost–benefit study of climate policy). Sometimes, framing is used strategically by political advocates whose goal is to manipulate your thinking in ways that makes their argument seem more persuasive than it would be with another frame. Lakoff (2009) puts it this way:

---

[10]The most recent data indicate an increase in such crimes in 2020 and 2021, at least in large cities (Acevedo, 2021).

[11]This example is a modified version of a scenario described by Chatfield (2018, p. 208).

When a PR firm sells a [public] policy honestly, the visual and linguistic framing of its ads should fit the moral framing of the policy. When the ads are deceptive, the deception is that the ads are linked to a supposed moral framing inconsistent with the one the policy is really based on. (p. 68)

In short, framing is an inescapable part of talking about policy issues, but *given its impact on the conclusions you draw, you don't want to unquestioningly accept an author's framing of an issue.*

Anchoring

Psychological experiments have repeatedly demonstrated that if we have a number in mind before we undertake an analytic task, then that the number can influence our approach to a subsequent task. The phenomenon of **anchoring**, in which our mind overemphasizes something to which we've been previously exposed, has been called "one of the most reliable results of experimental psychology," observed both in laboratory and real-word settings and among novices and experts (Teovanovic, 2019).

In one experiment, respondents were asked to spin a random wheel rigged to land on one of only two numbers: 10 and 65. They were then asked how many African countries were in the United Nations. The average answer for those who saw a 10 on the wheel was 25 countries while those who saw a 65 averaged a guess of 45 countries, despite the fact that the result of the wheel spin has no plausible connection to the number of African UN countries (Tversky & Kahneman, 1974).

If you've ever been in a price negotiation, the following example of anchoring may seem familiar: the seller tosses out a ridiculously high price or the buyer offers an absurdly low price. Both parties know that the transaction will not occur at their initial price, but those prices create an anchor which makes all subsequent offers seem more reasonable (even if they're not).

So, what does anchoring have to do with your work as a policy analyst? With anchoring, we can easily overestimate the typicality of the first instance we encounter. Suppose we are trying to figure out if tutoring programs cause more kids to graduate high school. We look at the local high school and see virtually no change in graduation rates. We then anchor on an effectiveness rate of zero percent improvement, and as a result, tend to discount the importance of other, more effective, programs we encounter later.

In short, using a particular value of an unknown parameter as the 'right' point of departure during policy analysis is usually a mistake and can easily taint the results of the analysis (Pherson & Huer, 2021). *Because anchoring puts extra emphasis on the information we first encounter, as policy analyst, you'll want to pay special attention to the sequence in which you receive new information*; just because a piece of evidence shows up first doesn't mean that it's typical of what you would find with a longer and more extensive search for evidence.

Availability and Mirror Imaging

Refer to Exhibit 4-3, which applies Dual Process Theory to policy analysis. It starts with your initial encounter with a stimulus—an event, claim, or proposal. In this encounter, you are immediately challenged to think about its magnitude and likelihood. For starters, is the stimulus even a real thing or just an illusory issue? Are we talking about a widespread problem? How serious is it? As you ponder these questions, answers probably spring to mind—almost instantaneously, thanks to System 1—using the **availability heuristic**, or as some call it, the bias of relative retrievability (Gupta, 2011). The first idea to pop into your head is not, however, necessarily the right answer. And therein lies the problem: the ease with which particular information comes to mind is not always a reliable indication of its relevance, veracity, or validity. In turn, the availability heuristic can quickly lead us in the wrong direction (Chatfield, 2018).

How does the heuristic work? By substituting one question for another. You really need to answer the hard questions of what's true or relevant in a specific situation. But, if you have recent, vivid, or personal examples ready to go in your mind, you may end up using those examples to answer a different question: What information can you easily recollect that's vaguely related to the initial question? As Kahneman (2011) puts it: "Substitutions of questions inevitably produces systematic errors" (p. 130).

The *availability heuristic puts a premium on vivid events*, even if they're atypical. Terrorist incidents, for example, get a lot of media attention and incite fear among the general public, but it is instructive to note that in the decade ending in 2003, the average death rate from road crashes across 23 developed countries was 390 times that of international terrorism (Wilson & Thomson, 2005), yet most of us don't think twice about hopping into a car to get somewhere. The availability heuristic also boosts the importance of things we've encountered recently to the disadvantage of things we've seen in the past; it also favors sensational and extreme information over bland and boring evidence.

The flip side of the availability heuristic is that folks who lack firsthand experience with a particular situation may ignore the chance of it affecting them in the future. Even if future events are very likely or highly consequential, an 'out of sight, out of mind' response may lead to a sense of internal equanimity. Inattention to looming threats can be problematic when we're thinking about long-term, slowly evolving events like climate change (Kahneman, 2011) or the deteriorating state of the social security trust fund.

A special case of the availability heuristic is a phenomenon known as **mirror imaging**. Its origins lie in the fact that the most readily available set of thought processes and belief systems are the ones that reside in your own mind. When you encounter another person or group about which you have only limited information, *it's tempting to (wrongly) assume that their thoughts and beliefs mirror your own.* Western intelligence analysts, for example, struggled to understand Iraq's motives for invading Kuwait in 1990 and for equivocating about weapons of mass destruction a decade later. As one such analyst observed, "just because something seems like the logical conclusion or course of action to you does not mean that the person or group you are analyzing will see it that way" (Watanabe, 2008, p. 1).

Mirror imaging can also strike close to home when we talk about social issues. In this case, consider the relationship between US police departments and communities of color. I am a middle-aged, middle-class, white male. My encounters with police officers—a suspicious car on a neighborhood street, a stolen laptop, or a minor traffic incident—have generally been professional and respectful. But it would be a mistake for me to mirror *my* positive impression of the police in *my* community as a universal situation for *all residents of the United States.* In short, *while each of us has his or her own lived experience, we need to recognize that our experience almost certainly isn't universal.* If we assume that it is when doing policy analysis, we can make significant mistakes.

A Need for Coherence and the WYSIATI Phenomenon

The clunky acronym WYSIATI stands for **What You See Is All There Is**. WYSIATI has been called "the mother of all cognitive illusions, the egocentric worldview that prevents us from seeing any world beyond the one visible from the tips of our noses" (Tetlock & Gardner, 2015, p. 233). This cognitive trap originates in our natural inclination to continuously try to make sense of the world around us. Most of us typically encounter a daily avalanche of stimuli, events, and information. And, as I mentioned at the outset of this chapter, figuring out how to interpret this information is no easy task. If we want to live our daily lives with some semblance of order, it helps to be confident that we've figured out what's going on. As Kahneman puts it, "confidence in our judgements depends on the coherence—internal consistency—of the story, not on its completeness" (Kahneman, 2011, p. 87). Your internal alarm bell should be ringing: The idea that we readily accept incomplete stories of how the world works is antithetical to sound policy analysis.

You've probably heard the metaphor of 'connecting the dots' as a way of making sense the world. These dots are at the heart of the WYSIATI phenomenon. The dots represent your observations of the world, and it's only the dots that you see; your brain comes up with the conceptual connections (i.e., the lines) between them. And when it does, *your mind—abhorring incoherence and ignorance—often doesn't connect them based only on real-world conditions, but instead taps your existing beliefs, assumptions, and stereotypes to fill in missing information.* WYSIATI is more than just a theoretical concern:

> Research studies and real-world events have repeatedly demonstrated that individuals consistently fail to appreciate the limits of the data and information available to them. What is unknown, what is out of sight, is out of mind. (Bruce & Bennett, 2008, p. 129)

The world of public policy can be chaotic, dynamic, confusing, filled with paradoxes, and not fully knowable. These are conditions under which the WYSIATI phenomenon thrives. If you see patterns in random events, leap to unfounded conclusions based on what you incorrectly perceive as similar prior experiences, pay attention only to the evidence right in front of you, and oversimplify complex logical problems, your brain—in its quest for order and sensemaking—can make a mistake. In fact, the *less* you know about something, the *easier* it is to come up with a coherent explanation of what's going on (Kahneman, 2011). Thoughtful and rigorous policy analysis can mitigate the WYSIATI trap by bringing some order and insight to the chaos (at least for a while).

CHAPTER SUMMARY

As Aristotle recognized millennia ago, there is a connection between our logical reasoning skills (logos) and the emotional frameworks (ethos and pathos) within which we apply those skills. Accordingly, this chapter aimed to give you a foundation in the emotional aspects of cognition, as it relates to policy analysis.

We first considered metacognition, which is the process by which we think about how we think. We then moved on to three pairs of concepts—fast System 1 thinking and slow System 2 thinking, accuracy motivated reasoning and directionally motivated reasoning, and hot and cold cognition—to explore how each can affect policy analysis.

We then looked at how Dual Process Theory can serve as a mechanism for integrating these concepts into a single framework. We closed the chapter with a review of several cognitive errors and biases that can adversely affect the quality of policy analysis.

DISCUSSION QUESTIONS

1. Can you come up with examples in your own life when fast and intuitive System 1 thinking has served you well and when it's led you to make significant mistakes? How about slow and deliberate System 2 thinking? When has it helped you uncover new insights and when have you run out of time and failed to come up with a helpful conclusion?

2. Why do you think cognitive dissonance creates such discomfort for most folks? Can you think of examples in public policy where efforts to avoid cognitive dissonance impede our ability to come up with workable and effective policy measures?

3. What are the pros and cons of accuracy motivated reasoning versus directionally motivated reasoning? Can you identify where each type of reasoning might appropriately be applied in the process of public policymaking?

4. How good are you at spotting directionally motivated reasoning in others? How good are you at spotting it in your own thinking? Why is it so hard to recognize our own biases?

5. Under what circumstances does a strong emotional reaction help policy analysis? When does it hinder analysis?

6. Select one type of a cognitive bias from each subsection of Section 4.6. Can you come up with an example of each from current policy debates? Why does it occur? What could be done to overcome its impact?

CHAPTER FIVE

USING LOGIC TO IDENTIFY TENTATIVE TRUTHS

In Chapter 3, I argued that the intellectual enterprise of the social sciences in general and of policy analysis in particular is fundamentally different from that of natural sciences like biology and physics. Given the difficulty of social and policy experimentation, the complex and variable nature of human behavior, and the inevitable time and resource constraints on policy analysis, we can't simply transplant the scientific method from the physicist's lab to the policy analyst's office. But because of its ability to generate powerful insights, we shouldn't discard the method entirely. Instead, we need to identify and retain those parts of the scientific method that *are* useful for policy analysis.

The scientific method sits at the intersection of logic and evidence. Evidence—our observations about the world around us—is the raw material of science, both as something we're trying to theoretically explain and as something we use to test our theories. Logic, on the other hand, is our tool for making sense of our observations and stitching evidence together into consistent and coherent theories. When it comes to the scientific method, logic and evidence are two sides of the same coin, and are the subjects of, respectively, Chapters 5 and 6. Indeed, there are so many connections between logic and evidence that some topics in these two chapters could easily fit in the other chapter. It's, thus, best to think of Chapters 5 and 6 as paired elements in a single holistic framework. And, in contrast to Chapter 4, which focused on the quick and intuitive nature of System 1 thinking, these next two chapters are anchored primarily in the analytic and deliberative nature of System 2 thinking. And in Aristotelian terms, Chapter 4 focused on ethos and pathos, while Chapters 5 and 6 focus on logos.

Learning Objectives

By studying this chapter, you should be able to:

- Explain the basics of the scientific method.

- Define 'truth' in the context of policy analysis.

- Describe the role of the baseline in policy analysis.

- Characterize and differentiate deductive, inductive, and abductive reasoning.

- Explain the principles of causation and the use of causal reasoning in policy analysis.

- Use reasoning by classification to make sense of large collections of disparate information.

- Use both quantitative estimates and words of estimative probability to characterize the uncertainties associated with policy analysis.

- Describe the principles of Bayes' theorem and explain the importance of the base rate in reaching valid conclusions.

- Identify the errors of logic and reasoning, and of rhetoric and debate, to which policy analysis is most vulnerable and describe ways of overcoming their adverse impacts.

In this chapter, our discussion of logic starts in Section 5.1 with four basic points of departure, none of which is particularly complicated but all of which are important to the discussion that follows. Next up are five different types of logical reasoning often deployed in the service of policy analysis:

- Deductive and causal reasoning (Section 5.2),
- Inductive reasoning (Section 5.3),
- Abductive reasoning (Section 5.4),
- Reasoning by classification (Section 5.5), and
- Probabilistic reasoning and Bayes' theorem (Section 5.6).

The chapter closes out with a review in Section 5.7 of a few logical errors and rhetorical tricks that you'll want to avoid.

5.1 STARTERS: POINTS OF DEPARTURE FOR THINKING ABOUT LOGIC

Before diving into the use of logic in policy analysis, I'd like to cover four topics that provide a foundation for the material that follows:

- The scientific method,
- The concept of 'truth' in policy analysis,
- The need to define the terminology used in a particular policy analysis, and
- The importance of articulating an analytic baseline or counterfactual.

5.1.1 The Scientific Method in the Context of Policy Analysis

You can think of the **scientific method** as a standard procedure for conducting research. In broad strokes, researchers start with a theory or hypothesis that explains how some aspect of the world works. Their hypothesis could come from a hunch or might reflect their interpretation of evidence they've already seen. Or it could be an extension of an existing theory, either their own or someone else's.[1] Scholars then predict what careful observation of real-world conditions would show if their hypothesis were correct. Next, they gather relevant evidence and compare their predictions against the collected data. In doing so, a researcher evaluates his or her theory

---

[1] We'll talk more about where hypotheses come from in Section 5.4 when we review abductive reasoning.

by deciding whether the hypothesis is supported by the evidence and answers the question 'does my theory explain my observations?' Next up is a written summary of the research that provides detail sufficient to allow an interested reader to replicate the research if he or she wanted to. Researchers—at least in the academic world—typically submit their work to a peer-reviewed journal. A journal editor then asks two or three scholars to review the manuscript and advise whether it's worthy of publication and, if so, whether revisions are needed. The process is typically anonymous in that the author doesn't know identity of the reviewers.

Once a study passes peer review and is published, its results become part of the scholarly 'conversation.' *A single study, however, is almost never considered definitive.* Instead, it usually takes a collection of studies reaching similar conclusions before consensus emerges among scholars that the results are trustworthy (McNutt, 2018). Even if multiple studies are in alignment, the consensus is still often treated as provisional. Why provisional? If too many subsequent studies come along and refute it, the consensus view may change in what Thomas Kuhn refers to as a paradigm shift (1996).

> Together, transparency and updating are the cleansing mechanism that gradually sweeps away scientific misunderstandings and errors—a sine qua non for scientific advancement. (CRS, 2013)

This "cleansing" process of figuring out what is and is not true sounds great. But the mechanism doesn't always work smoothly; sometimes, there is a stickiness to it. Kuhn pointed out that the scientists working in a field comprise a social community operating within an intellectual paradigm which sets boundaries on what types of new theory and evidence are allowed to change the conversation. It's only when the accumulating weight of new information outweighs the comforting conventional wisdom of the community that the paradigm shifts, sometimes abruptly.

This description of the scientific method is based on how academic researchers—not policy analysts—approach the process. Policy research and policy analysis, while related, are different. The former takes place primarily in academic settings and is typically motivated by questions of the scholar's choosing. He or she also sets the schedule, deciding when the study has reached a satisfactory conclusion. In contrast, policy analysis is almost always time and resource constrained in its efforts to support specific policy debates and decisions.

So, can policy analysis meet the standards of the scientific method? Yes and no. First, some of the impediments: While a seasoned policy analyst always tries to get someone to check his or her work, formal peer review is rare. What's more, there is rarely time for original data collection, so analysts routinely synthesize the work of others. Finally, a thorough policy analysis may require insights from multiple academic disciplines and political perspectives; it's unlikely to fit neatly within the bounds of any one scholarly conversation or paradigm, or find a home in the pages of an academic journal.

On the other hand, the scientific method has a lot to offer the aspiring policy analyst. The method demands rigorous critical thinking. It insists that conclusions be informed by sound evidence. It reminds the analyst to recognize the provisional nature of research. And it places a premium on transparency. As such, the scientific method is not just a recipe for conducting research. It's also a mindset, a way of thinking about how to understand the world. Heineman, Bluhm, Peterson, and Kearny (1990) put it succinctly:

> Essentially, when science is applied as a label to the pursuit of policy analysis, what is being described is the careful accumulation of data, rigorous study of possible interpretations and alternatives, and the articulation of reasons for the recommended course of action. (p. 37)

For another example of what it means to apply the scientific method, we turn again to Nobel laureate Richard Feynman (1974) who urged CalTech graduates to bring to their work:

> … scientific integrity, a principle of scientific thought that corresponds to a kind of utter honesty—a kind of leaning over backwards. … If you make a theory, for example, and advertise it, or put it out, then you must also put down all the facts that disagree with it, as well as those that agree with it. … In summary, the idea is to try to give all of the information to help others to judge the value of your contribution; not just the information that leads to judgment in one particular direction or another. (p. 11)

Whether you're a policy analyst or an academic researcher, if you wanted to explain the scientific method in just a couple sentences, it would be hard to do better than Feynman's words.

5.1.2 What Is the 'Truth' That Policy Analysts Are Supposed to Speak to Power?

Aaron Wildavsky (1979) used the title of his textbook to give policy students their ultimate assignment: *speak truth to power*. His book is filled with helpful observations and provocative questions, but he never directly defines the word truth. Wildavsky comes closest when he observes that "[t]here is always more than one version of the truth and we can be most certain the latest statement isn't it" (p. 404). James Mitchell (2007), a senior Canadian civil servant, put a finer point on the matter when he encouraged Canadian public servants to speak truth to power, admonishing them:

> Not to tell [policymakers] what they want to hear, but rather what they need to hear; not hide the facts but bring them forward, even if the facts run counter to received wisdom, or someone's preferred course of action. ... Speaking truth to power is about the facts, and it can be about ideas, but it's not about you and your ideas. (p. 4)

So, speaking fact-based truth to power is your job, even though the truth is ephemeral and elusive? Sounds tricky. Perhaps we need to take a closer look at what it means for something to be factually true.

As noted in Chapter 3, the positivists of the mid-twentieth century were confident that the scientific method could be used to accurately characterize real-world conditions and correctly predict the impacts of policy interventions (Trochim, 2007). But postpositivist critics have made a strong case that existing paradigms, worldviews, and cultural forces drive the interpretation of observed data:

> The rational ideal [of policy analysis] presupposes the existence of neutral facts—neutral in the sense that they accurately describe the world, but don't serve anybody's interest, promote any value judgments, or exert persuasive force beyond the weight of their correctness. Yet, facts do not exist independent of interpretive lenses. (Stone, 2012, p. 314)

Especially when it comes to the social sciences and the often-freighted topics of public policy, it is frequently inevitable that we each construct our own understanding of reality. But that doesn't mean that everything is relative and that you can claim whatever you want as true. Scientific inquiry and policy discourse are not the activities of a single person. (Note Mitchell's warning that truth is not about what the individual analyst believes.) Instead, policy analysts are engaged in a social enterprise as folks work collectively—cooperatively or competitively, intentionally or accidentally, together or separately—on related topics. Reality is, thus, a matter of social construction. Trochim (2007) describes a path forward:

> Because perception and observation are fallible, all constructions must be imperfect. ... Everyone is biased, and all observations are affected (theory-laden). The best hope for achieving objectivity is to triangulate across multiple fallible perspectives. Thus, *objectivity is not the characteristic of an individual; it is inherently a social phenomenon.* ... Objectivity is never achieved, but it can be approached. (p. 20), *emphasis added*

The social, or collective, nature of figuring out what it means for something to be factually true is also apparent in the work of biologist Stephen Jay Gould (1994) who, in an influential essay on evolution, distinguished theory from fact. **Theories** are "proposed" while **facts** are "established." The verb choice here is telling. He argues that theory is used to structure ideas in ways that arrange and make sense of facts while facts themselves:

> … are the world's data. Facts do not go away when scientists debate rival theories to explain them. … Moreover, 'fact' does not mean 'absolute certainty.' In science, 'fact' can only mean 'confirmed to such a degree that it would be perverse to withhold provisional assent'. (pp. 254–255)

Focus here on the word 'perverse,' the dictionary definition of which is "contrary to the accepted or expected standard or practice" (Oxford University Press, 2001). The dictionary doesn't describe who is doing the accepting or expecting, but it seems clear that we're talking about other people. If a fact has been confirmed to the point where denying it would be a perverse act, then we're really saying that *the truth depends on facts that are broadly confirmable by knowledgeable folks*.

Bear in mind, however, that just because a claim is broadly acknowledged as credible, it may still not be a universal truth. Physicians spent a very long time believing that stomach ulcers were caused by persistent stress, only to later realize that the culprit was actually a bacterial infection. Similarly, it was once thought that the position of the continents on the earth's surface was fixed, until the science of plate tectonics demonstrated that the continents are always on the move.

In short, when you speak truth to power, you don't need (and can't have) absolute certainty. You do, however, need to be on solid ground, relying on confirmed claims that reflect more than just your own idiosyncratic views of the world. You also need to be particularly careful with fringe points of view for which there is little support and with theories that are still being actively and seriously debated.

5.1.3 What Do the Words Mean?

If you don't speak Arabic, it's impossible to have an intelligent conversation with someone who speaks only Arabic. You wouldn't use the same words to describe the same thing. A similar problem can crop up when you try to apply logical reasoning to public policy issues. Language—the written and spoken word—is the currency of policy discourse. *Without a shared understanding of what the words mean, unambiguous dialogue is impossible.* Imprecise concepts like poverty, crime, pollution, a good education—the list is virtually endless—mean different things to different people.

Take, for example, frequent calls for 'border security' on the United States' southern border. Depending on who you talk to, you will hear very different explanations of what these two words are all about. For some, secure borders are a way to deny international terrorists easy access to potential targets or to minimize the flow of illicit drugs into the country. For others, secure borders provide a mechanism for ensuring an orderly and reliable flow of immigrant workers to US industries like food processing, agriculture, and high tech. Still others look at the issue through a normative lens, either as nativists with deep hostility toward foreigners or as multi-culturalists ready to welcome almost all comers. Finally, in some cases, border security may not even be about movements from south to north, but instead about things going in the other direction, such as illegal guns and large quantities of illicit cash from the United States contributing to economic and social instability in Central American countries.

You may have in your own mind a crystal clear definition of what it means to ensure border security, but here's the thing. If you talk about the issue with someone whose definition differs from yours, and you don't first synchronize your definitions, you will talk past one another, using the same words but meaning different things. In turn, the odds of finding common ground will diminish accordingly.

And, as you'll see in Section 5.7, some folks intentionally use ambiguous language to prevent you from clearly understanding what they're saying. You might end up agreeing with them, only to find out later that what you agreed to was not what you thought it was. Similarly, a speaker may use the dog whistle effect—where a phrase is at the same time hot and emotionally charged for some people and benign and unremarkable for others—to trigger the emotions of one group without offending another.

What does all this have to do with the topic of logic? Words are the raw material of reasoning. If they are vague, subject to multiple interpretations, or intentionally manipulative, there's no way for you to structure a meaningful logical argument of your own or to unambiguously interpret someone else's logic. In short, you need to think about the most important terms and phrases being used in a policy debate and ask whether everyone in the debate is defining them in the same way.

5.1.4 Without a Baseline, It's Easy to Get Lost

Often overlooked in policy reasoning is the need for a consistent **analytic baseline**. When someone tells you that a policy proposal is the best way to tackle a problem, your first question should be: compared to what? Policy analysis informs decisions about which path forward to take. The wisdom of taking one path over another depends on the attributes of both paths, not just the path taken. If we select Option A rather than B, we get all the positives (pros) and all the negatives (cons) of A. We also forfeit all the pros and cons of B. To focus only on a single option (i.e., the **factual**) is to omit consideration of the equally important **counterfactual** baseline. It's the difference between Options A and B that should drive our decision, not the attributes of either option in isolation.

Two to three times a year, for example, the Congressional Budget Office (CBO) issues what is commonly referred to as its baseline report. Ranging from 50 to 150 pages, these reports detail projected Federal revenues and spending across all areas of the federal budget for the next ten years (CBO, 2018). Such projections provide a neutral and consistent baseline against which to assess the impacts of proposed legislation. CBO uses its baseline report to estimate, or 'score,' the budgetary impact of about 650 legislative proposals annually (CBO, 2018). It would be impossible to provide Congress with intellectually consistent cost estimates if CBO did not have a baseline from which to work.

Consider, for example, how a new climate regulation might affect the coal industry. An analyst could forecast that, under such a regulation, there will be tens of thousands fewer jobs in coal country by 2030 than there are today. But without more information, we can't attribute the decline in coal jobs to the regulation. We need to know what the employment situation without the regulation will likely be—not today—but in 2030. Perhaps coal jobs will decline because of automation that allows coal to be mined with fewer workers or because many power plants switch from coal to natural gas. If the decrease in employment is likely to occur even if the regulation is not implemented, then it doesn't make sense to argue that the regulation is the cause of the job loss. On the other hand, if a careful comparison between the likely state of the world in 2030 with the regulation and the state of the world without it indicates that employment will drop in the first case but not the second, then it would be reasonable to attribute the impact to the regulation. In short, baselines can make a big difference. Analysts who forget to set a baseline tend to get lost in their analysis.

A related issue has to do with the **"shifting baseline syndrome,"** a term coined by biologist Daniel Pauly (1995, p. 430). His focus was on figuring out the target size of the fish stock that should be used when fishery managers set annual catch limits for fishing boat operators. Should these policymakers aim to reach and sustain the fish stocks observed in 1980 or 1880? Picking one answer over the other has profound implications for how aggressive the catch policy should be. Pauly was particularly concerned that over time, fishery managers had become inured to declining stock levels. In turn, based on a shifting baseline, they set progressively less restrictive fishing policies than were appropriate.

5.2 DEDUCTIVE AND CAUSAL REASONING

Having defined the scientific method, described what it means to speak truth to power, advised you to define your terminology, and reiterated the importance of the baseline,

I'd now like to pivot to the topic of logic itself. In particular, if you want to think logically about policy analysis, you need to master at least five distinct types of reasoning, the first of which is deductive and causal reasoning.

5.2.1 Deductive Reasoning

Deduction is a form of multistep reasoning that starts with a broad principle, adds a specific situation, and reaches (i.e., deduces) a conclusion. The broad principle could be descriptive (e.g., all persons must eat food to survive) or normative (e.g., all persons must be treated equally by the judicial system). A situation is then described (e.g., Grace is a person), and in the final step, a conclusion is reached (e.g., Grace must eat food to survive; Grace must be treated equally by the judicial system). A common form of deductive reasoning is a **syllogism** that has a three-part structure comprising two **premises** and the **conclusion**. The premises are the statements that come before the conclusion (i.e., the broad principle and the specific situation).

The power of deductive reasoning is that, if we do it right, we can be confident that our conclusion is correct. Moreover, any competent analyst looking at the same set of premises will reach an identical conclusion. But what does it mean to do it right? In short, deductive reasoning is sound if it satisfies two conditions: its premises must be *true* and its logic must be *valid* (Chatfield, 2018).

When it comes to testing the truth of the premises, if any of them are false (e.g., if some people can survive without food or if Grace is not a person but is a stuffed animal), then the reasoning is unsound because it is based on untrue premises, and we shouldn't accept the conclusion. Sometimes, assessing the truth of the premises is straightforward (e.g., confirming that food is necessary for survival or that Grace is a person). But in other cases, testing the truth of the premises—especially the broad principle of the first premise—isn't always easy. How do we 'prove' the truth of the claim that all persons must be treated equally? We'll revisit the issue in our discussion of normative issues in Chapter 8 but, for now, keep in mind that sound deductive reasoning requires that all of the premises must be convincingly true.

Things can also be tricky when it comes to assessing the validity of the logic in a deductive claim. To be valid, the premises in the syllogism must be stated and arranged in a particular way, and the conclusion must be correctly framed in terms of the premises. This might be easier with an example. Suppose the town where I live has a local ordinance requiring all tattoo artists to have a license for the shop in which they work. Otherwise, they will be fined $1,000.[2] My friend, Janice, is a tattoo artist.

---

[2]To keep the logic clear in this simple example, I am assuming the local government exercises its authority flawlessly, always fining unlicensed shops and never mistakenly fining a licensed shop.

Let's use deductive reasoning to figure out what we can conclude about the situation. Consider Exhibit 5-1. We start with the broad principle, framed as an if-then statement, as Premise 1. The first part of the premise (operating an unlicensed tattoo shop) is the **antecedent** while the second part (getting fined) is called the **consequent**. In other words, *if* someone operates without a license, *then* they will be fined. Accordingly, if Janice doesn't bother with a license and starts inking customers (i.e., if we affirm the antecedent), then she will have to pay the fine. Our deductive syllogism is valid.

Exhibit 5-1   Valid Syllogism: Affirming the Antecedent

Premise 1: If you operate a tattoo shop without a license, you will be fined $1,000.
Premise 2: Janice operated a tattoo shop without a license.
Conclusion: Janice will be fined $1,000.

What if we get mixed up, and accidently affirm the consequent, rather than its antecedent? Exhibit 5-2 shows what happens. Note that Premise 1 (the if-then statement) is identical to the prior example, but Premise 2 has changed to reflect the fact that Janice was fined $1,000. This change to the syllogism's structure invalidates it. Can you see why?

Exhibit 5-2   Invalid Syllogism: Affirming the Consequent

Premise 1: If you operate a tattoo shop in Town X without a license, you will be fined $1,000.
Premise 2: Janice was fined $1,000.
Conclusion: Janice operated a tattoo shop in Town X without a license.

Yes, Janice was fined, but we can't be sure why. It might not have been for operating without a license, but another reason. Perhaps she repeatedly violated the town's noise ordinance with live music on Saturday nights at the tattoo shop. Our mistake would be taking the fact that Janice was fined as evidence that she's operating her shop without a license when nothing in the premises indicates that she has done so. In doing so, we have rendered the reasoning invalid and the conclusion untrustworthy.

So, does switching up the contents of a syllogism always invalidate it? No. Instead of affirming the antecedent in the if-then statement, we could use deductive reasoning to figure out what happens if the consequent didn't occur. This is called denying the consequent and is illustrated in Exhibit 5-3. Again, Premise 1 stays the same, but in this case we consider the possibility that Janice has not been fined. If Janice isn't fined, then it must be the case that she is not operating a shop without a license; otherwise, she would have been fined. Accordingly, the reasoning in our syllogism is valid.

Exhibit 5-3 Valid Syllogism: Denying the Consequent

Premise 1: If you operate a tattoo shop in Town X without a license, you will be fined $1,000.
Premise 2: Janice was not fined $1,000.
Conclusion: Janice did not operate a tattoo shop in Town X without a license.

As before, however, there is still a way to get things mixed up. As seen in Exhibit 5-4, rather than denying the consequent, we could deny the antecedent by claiming that Janice didn't operate an unlicensed tattoo shop. In that case, can we be sure that she hasn't been fined? No. As we saw before, there may be other reasons that Janice could be fined. Just because she obeys one local ordinance doesn't mean that she obeys all local ordinances.

Exhibit 5-4 Invalid Syllogism: Denying the Antecedent

Premise 1: If you operate a tattoo shop in Town X without a license, you will be fined $1,000.
Premise 2: Janice did not operate a tattoo shop in Town X without a license.
Conclusion: Janice was not fined $1,000.

If a deductive claim (like our first and third examples in Exhibits 5-2 and 5-4) is valid, does that mean it's true? Nope. *In context of formal logic, validity and truth are two separate concepts.* Even though the reasoning in both cases is valid, if Janice is not a tattoo artist or the town doesn't regulate tattoo artists, then neither conclusion is true even though the reasoning is valid. To reach a sound conclusion, the structure of deductive reasoning must be valid, *and* its premises must be true. Another interesting feature of deductive reasoning is that our conclusion never reveals new information that isn't already apparent from the premises. (You'll see later that this is not the case with inductive reasoning.)

These four examples represent variations on the simplest form of deductive reasoning. We can make things more complex by linking, or chaining, multiple if-then statements together to form a new if-then statement. Perhaps Janice is on the verge of bankruptcy. Then we might have something like:

Premise: If Janice operates her tattoo shop without a license, she will be fined $1,000.
Premise: If Janice is fined $1,000, then she will go bankrupt.
Conclusion: If Janice operates her tattoo shop without a license, she will go bankrupt.

Another type of syllogism is the disjunctive syllogism where the first premise (i.e., the broad principle) specifies mutually exclusive conditions. Here's an example:

Premise: Janice needs at least ten customers per day in the coming year to earn enough revenue to keep her business going or she will have to declare bankruptcy.
Premise: Janice will have six customers per day in the coming year.
Conclusion: Janice will declare bankruptcy.

These two examples hint at an important aspect of if-then reasoning. You need to think carefully about the necessity and sufficiency of the conditions that form the antecedent. If only one condition must be true for a conclusion to hold, we refer to it as necessary *and* sufficient.

For example, we might reason that if we increase the number of teachers at a school while holding the student body constant (i.e., the conditions that form the antecedent), then we can decrease class sizes (i.e., the consequent). This statement is only true if we have classrooms in which to hold additional, smaller, classes. In other words, if and only if we have spare space will increasing the number of teachers reduce class size. Suppose we don't have spare space, just like we don't have extra teachers. We need to be clear that having more teachers is necessary, but not by itself sufficient, to ensure that the conclusion holds. One without the other does not allow us to decrease class size. We can rework these considerations into a new statement: To decrease class size, we must both deploy more teachers and obtain additional space.

5.2.2 Causal Reasoning

If-then statements rely on causal reasoning to claim that an underlying mechanism links the antecedent to the consequent. In other words, the antecedent—if it is true—activates a real-world causal force that in turn leads to the occurrence of the consequent. Causal reasoning is an important part of policy analysis. We've already talked about it a couple of times. In Chapter 1, for example, we discussed the Five Whys technique to relate the causes of a policy problem to its consequences. The logic model described in Chapter 2 also prominently features causal reasoning when it connects inputs, activities, outputs, outcomes, and impacts with if-then statements. What's more, at the heart of every policy proposal are causal assertions about its impacts after implementation. In such cases, the proposed policy is the cause and the claimed benefits are its effects.

Because causal reasoning is integral to a great many policy analyses, deepening your understanding of it is a good use of your time. Given your prior schoolwork and your life experience, you undoubtedly already have a good intuition about what it means for one thing to cause another. Philosophers of science have generally agreed that for us to believe that A causes B, three (or maybe four) things have to be true.

First, *A has to occur prior to B.* This is referred to as temporal precedence and simply means that effects follow causes, not precede them. My coffee mug breaks after I drop it on the floor. It doesn't spontaneously break and then jump to the floor.

Second, *changes in A and B have to be correlated.* This is usually referred to as covariance, meaning that if A goes up, then B goes up, and vice versa. When I turn up the heat on my stove, the water boils more quickly; when I turn it down, the water takes longer to boil. It's not always the case that both A and B move in the same direction. When I turn on the furnace, my apartment gets warmer, but when I turn on the air conditioning, it gets cooler. For causal reasoning, we only need to see a consistent pattern in the covariance of A and B. If variations in the extent of B do not follow a pattern with respect to variations in the extent of A, then it would be hard to conclude that A is having a causal impact on B.

Third, even if changes in A and B are correlated, we need to *rule out competing explanations of the covariance.* Perhaps A and B are not causally connected, but are both effects of a third factor C which, when it fluctuates, creates the illusion of a relationship between A and B. You've undoubtedly heard the adage that correlation does not prove causation. A favorite example of stats professors is the correlation between ice cream sales and the murder rate in many cities. Evidence demonstrates that both move together in a similar pattern (i.e., they covary). Does this mean that eating ice cream induces homicidal tendencies? Hardly. It's a function of the weather. On hot summer days, ice cream sales go up, so too does the murder rate as more folks spend time outdoors. There's no causal connection between A and B; instead, there is a causal connection between C and A, and between C and B.

The fourth characteristic of a causal relationship isn't, strictly speaking, a requirement, but more of a 'nice to have.' Ideally, *to be as confident as possible that A and B are causally related, we will have a theoretical explanation of that relationship.* A higher setting on my stove releases more heat energy into the pot, more quickly exciting the water molecules and reducing the time it takes for them to boil. Of course, the water will still boil more quickly even if I am clueless about the underlying physics. And it's also true that, even if we have a causal theory, it could be wrong. (Folks used to believe that blood-letting cured illness.) Nonetheless, if we can't explain why a causal relationship exists between A and B, we need to be more cautious about a claim built on that relationship.

Sometimes, things are more complicated than a bivariate causal relationship between cause A and effect B. Perhaps effect B requires the presence of other causes before it occurs, or maybe we won't see effect B, unless other factors are absent. Such situations are referred to as **multivariate relationships**. For example, I might be riding my bike. My attention wanders (cause #1) and a dog darts across my path (cause #2). I notice at the last second and slam on the brakes, saving the dog but launching myself over the handlebars. Because I am wearing a helmet (cause #3), however, it's all fine. So, if we want a multivariate causal explanation of whether I'm injured (i.e., the effect), we could say there are three causal factors at work—inattention, a dog, and the presence of a helmet. Even though multivariate reasoning is more complicated than bivariate reasoning, the same basic causal logic applies.

What does all this have to do with good policy analysis? It's pretty straightforward. If a policy claim incorrectly reasons that a particular problem is the causal consequence of a specific driver, and then argues for a policy to address that driver, we shouldn't be surprised later when the policy doesn't mitigate the problem. Similarly, we might also be wrong in thinking that the policy will induce a change in that underlying driver. If implementing the policy has no causal effect on the underlying driver, then there will be no change in the problem itself.

5.3 INDUCTIVE REASONING

In many ways, **inductive reasoning** is the opposite of deductive reasoning. Instead of going from broad principles to specific situations, we work from observations of specific situations and attempt to infer (i.e., induce) the principles, patterns, and theoretical mechanisms that explain those observations. Drawing inferences about the future is a special form of inductive reasoning and is referred to as **projective inference**. We'll consider it more detail in Chapter 13 when we discuss the process of visualizing outcomes under different policy alternatives. After a short overview, we will take a look at two common forms of inductive logic: reasoning by example and reasoning by analogy.

While deductive reasoning has a comforting certainty to its conclusions,[3] inductive reasoning can't offer the same certainty. With induction, we're looking for explanations of the available evidence. But no matter how thorough our investigation of specific situations, the possibility always exists that some contradictory evidence will emerge in an unexpected way that undercuts our inferred conclusions. Accordingly, unlike deductive reasoning, we can never be 100% sure that the results of inductive reasoning are true. In turn, two equally competent analysts might apply inductive reasoning to the same situation and reach different conclusions; if so, we cannot say definitively who is right.

For a quick example, let's go back to Janice, the tattoo shop owner. Suppose that despite the ordinance being on the books for years, the town has never fined someone for operating a shop without a license; further suppose Janice operates her shop without a license. Based on these facts, we could reasonably infer that Janice will probably not be fined for violating the licensure requirement. But a new district attorney may get elected

---

[3]If the premises are true and the logic is valid, then the results are definitively correct.

who wants to prosecute scofflaws like Janice. Maybe neighbors upset by the rowdy music use the licensure requirement as a pretext to shut her shop.

The chance (even a small one) of getting it wrong is inherent in inductive reasoning. Why? We aren't omniscient. We can never occupy a lofty enough vantage point to see all the relevant evidence—especially if it's in the future—and thus cannot be sure we haven't missed something important. And, unlike deductive reasoning, inductive reasoning lets us go beyond the evidence that's directly in front of us when we infer broader principles, theories, and conclusions that we've not observed directly.

Consider a real-world example: the safety of genetically modified organisms (GMOs). There is generally a consensus among scientists that, despite significant political opposition, GMOs[4] do not pose a significant risk to human health or the environment (Achenbach, 2015). But is that proof that GMOs are safe? No, it's still possible that counterexamples could emerge and falsify a claim of no GMO risk. The act of balancing costs, benefits, and risk is a topic for a later chapter, but for now, keep in mind that policy controversies often originate in the inherent limitations of inductive reasoning.

As mentioned earlier, a deductive argument is considered sound when its logic is valid and its premises true. The soundness of an inductive argument is assessed in a different, but parallel, manner. An inductive argument is said to be sound when it is both *cogent* and *inductively forceful* (Chatfield, 2018). An argument is cogent if its structure is clear, methodical, and convincing. Inductive force describes the likelihood that its premises are true. Putting the two concepts together, if we have strong evidence that the premises of an inductive argument are likely to be true, and if it is organized in a cogent manner, then we have a solid basis for accepting it as provisionally true.

The word **provisional** is very important here. With inductive reasoning, *we never definitively prove our conclusion true, we only fail to falsify it*. In turn, because inductive reasoning never offers complete certainty about the accuracy of its conclusion, we always need to qualify it. Provisional confidence is not, however, a binary concept. We can think of it as a continuum that captures the degree of confidence we have in our conclusion. A key element in inductive reasoning is, thus, figuring out how to characterize this uncertainty. We'll talk in a more technical way in Section 5.6 about probabilistic reasoning, but for now, we'll just use everyday language. Depending on the cogency and the inductive force of our reasoning, we can use a continuum of words such as very likely, likely, as likely as not, unlikely, and very unlikely, to describe how certain we are about the inductive conclusion we've reached.

When we engage in **inductive reasoning by example**, we do two things. We examine evidence and draw inferences from it. Evidence comprises examples gleaned

---

[4]At least those developed so far.

from observation of the real world.[5] We can focus on just about anything: people, nations, markets, biological and ecological systems—the list is literally endless. Observations can entail one case, several cases, surveys of dozens or thousands of people, transactional data with millions of records ('big data'), experiments that manipulate natural or social phenomena to observe consequences, and just about everything in between. In general, having more examples (e.g., a bigger sample and more experimental results) will strengthen the inferences we make. In short, the first part of inductive reasoning by example is *observing what's going on in the world* around us. The second part of inductive reasoning by example entails *drawing inferences from these observations*. In doing so, we try to create explanations of what we've observed.

Sometimes the explanations are descriptive. We might, for example, want to understand poverty in our community, or we might want to characterize a hostile nation whose military threatens ours. We look at the evidence and come up with (i.e., infer) an organizing principle, a theoretical construct, or a consistent pattern that renders the evidence coherent and understandable.

In addition to descriptive inference, inductive reasoning can also be used in causal inference when we assess theoretical explanations of causal relationships. For example, we might look at programs that provide a stipend to all residents (i.e., a universal basic income) and try to infer the changes it causes in folks' standard of living, or we might look at a history of encounters with hostile nations in an attempt to infer which diplomatic and military strategies lead to better outcomes and which do not.

Whether our inductive reasoning is descriptive or causal, our goal is to figure out which principles, patterns, and theories best fit, or explain, our observed examples. We might use advanced statistics or simple logic. We might apply qualitative or quantitative techniques, but the inductive task is the same:

- Collect evidence about examples of interest,
- Develop hypothetical principles, patterns, and theoretical mechanisms to explain observations,
- Use critical reasoning techniques to assess the alignment between hypotheses and observations, and
- Use evidence and reasoning to infer the strength of the hypothesis.

Let's talk about another form of induction: **reasoning by analogy**. When we draw an analogy between two situations, we use inductive reasoning to infer that the characteristics of one situation can be applied to another situation. For example,

---

[5]As I mentioned before, evidence and logic are tightly linked within the scientific method. Evidence is the focus of Chapter 6. We touch on it only briefly here to illustrate key points about the logical reasoning process.

suppose you're the city manager of a town called Smithtown struggling with an increase in opioid deaths. You hear about Jamestown, a nearby city, that had a similar problem but brought it under control with changes in emergency services, a new addiction treatment program, and a clampdown on local drug dealers. You are considering duplicating the program in your city and trying to reason by analogy to decide if doing so is a good idea.[6]

You have to decide how similar Smithtown and Jamestown really are. You might compare social, demographic, and economic characteristics, consider whether the nature of the problem is similar in both places, and look at the health, human service, and police capabilities of the two governments. There will be differences; after all, they're two different cities. But if the difference between them is sufficiently small or not otherwise relevant, then reasoning by analogy, you might infer that replicating the Jamestown program will work out well. On the other hand, there could be a key difference—maybe Jamestown has a community of mental health professionals, but Smithtown doesn't—that invalidates the analogy. If so, you cannot implement the Jamestown program in Smithtown and expect the same results. *Reasoning by analogy only works when both situations are truly analogous.*

Reasoning by analogy is also often applied to normative issues. For example, an argument in support of the 19th Amendment (women's suffrage) was that men already been given the right to vote. Thus, reasoning by analogy, justice, and fairness required that women be given the right to vote. To summarize the process of inductive reasoning by analogy, we need to:

- Review observable similarities and dissimilarities of two situations and satisfy ourselves that the situations are indeed comparable,
- Observe characteristics of the first situation not seen in the second, because it either hasn't been fully characterized or reflects future events (e.g., it is a yet-to-be implemented policy), and
- Reason by analogy that even though we've not seen the characteristics of interest in the second situation, we think that they do or will exist because of the similarity of the situations.

5.4 ABDUCTIVE REASONING

Abductive reasoning lacks the long tradition of inductive and deductive reasoning, both of which originated with the Greek and Roman philosophers of antiquity. Abduction emerged during the pragmatist movement of the early 20th century. It embraces an

---

[6]In Chapter 14, we'll take a deep dive into this process of looking to other jurisdictions for policy ideas.

iterative process a bit like continued questioning and answering. Its methods are more informal than induction and deduction, and some folks even refer to abduction as a form of argumentation rather than a form of reasoning (Chatfield, 2018). Either way, it can come in handy as part of policy analysis and belongs in your analytic toolbox.

Abduction is similar to inference in that it only offers provisional conclusions that can't be proven definitively correct. But while inference reasons in one direction—from the specific to the general—abduction is iterative. It starts with a careful review of available evidence, uses inference to make educated guesses about hypotheses that could explain the evidence, uses deductive reasoning to predict the types of evidence that would be observed if each of the hypotheses were true, compares predicted to observed evidence, and then focuses on the hypothesis that appears to best explain the available evidence. In an iterative process, that hypothesis may get revised more than once as the analyst tries to align his or her explanation with the evidence, or gathers new evidence to test the hypotheses. As with inductive reasoning, conclusions reached with abductive reasoning should be qualified with an indicator of the analyst's confidence in the conclusion.

Abduction requires both creativity and discipline. There is usually more than one potential explanation of what we see in our evidence. The *creative* part in this exercise is thus the process of conjuring up alternative hypotheses that might explain the evidence. The *disciplined* part of the process entails careful application of the scientific method (as described in Section 5.1.1) to figure out which of the hypotheses offers the most convincing explanation of the evidence. The principles of abduction also suggest that, all else equal, simpler explanations are preferred to more complex explanations. Abduction has been described variously as the "logic of what could be" (Hermus, van Buuren, & Bekkers, 2020, p. 23), the result of "informed judgment" (Dunn, 2018, p. 126), and "inference to the best explanation" (Chatfield, 2018, p. 103).

A good example of abductive reasoning is the **Analysis of Competing Hypotheses** (ACH) (George & Bruce, 2008). The idea is to come up with several different explanations of the evidence and then let them 'compete' with each other to select the most convincing:

> The component parts of ACH are evidence and arguments on the one hand and hypotheses on the other. ... The analyst then evaluates the consistency or inconsistency of each item of evidence or argument with each hypothesis. ... Like the scientific method, ACH proceeds by trying to refute hypotheses rather than confirm them. ... The most likely hypothesis is the one with the least evidence against it, not the one with the most evidence for it. (Pherson & Huer, 2021, pp. 252–253, 257)

As an example, suppose you work for a local government and are trying to understand why vehicle/pedestrian accidents have increased sharply in the past year. You come up with three possible explanations. It might be that, with everyone working at home due to a pandemic, there are a lot more people walking the streets and, because of social distancing, many of them are actually walking *in* the street. An alternative explanation is the end of a police campaign targeted at both drivers and pedestrians to make sure everyone is being as safe as possible. Finally, you suspect that perhaps major construction in the Central Business District (CBD) has forced drivers and pedestrians into unfamiliar and potentially dangerous routes. Having come up with three alternative hypotheses, you lay out all the evidence you think might be relevant. You have information on the location and timing of the changes in accident patterns; you also notice that dog bites reported to the police are also up, suggesting that people and dogs are coming into more frequent contact. Exhibit 5-5 juxtaposes the hypotheses against the evidence.

Exhibit 5-5 Analysis of Alternative Hypotheses: An Illustrative Example

	Hypotheses to explain increase in vehicle/pedestrian accidents		
Evidence	Number of pedestrians greatly increased due to folks working at home during pandemic starting in March	Police department ended its long-running Pedestrian Safe Campaign in January	Major construction in the CBD began last year and continued this year, disrupting vehicle and pedestrian routes
Accidents are up in Central Business District (CBD)	Unclear	Consistent	Consistent
Accidents are up in neighborhoods	Consistent	Consistent	Inconsistent
Accidents are up across the state	Consistent	Inconsistent	Inconsistent
The increase in accidents began last year	Inconsistent	Inconsistent	Consistent
The number of dog bites has increased this year	Consistent	Inconsistent	Inconsistent

For each cell in the matrix, you make a note of whether or not the hypothesis is consistent with the evidence. Once you're done, you may be able to get a better sense of the best explanation of the situation. In this case, it looks like the pandemic is the most likely cause of the increase in accidents. It's probably not the end of the police safety campaign because if it were, the accident rate would only be up locally, not statewide. Moreover, the road safety campaign probably didn't affect the number of dog bites. In addition, the CBD construction is also not the likely cause because accidents are up in both the CBD and the neighborhoods, whereas the construction probably wouldn't have affected pedestrian and vehicle routes outside the CBD. The only anomaly with the pandemic hypothesis is that the accident rate was trending up before the pandemic began. Abductive reasoning is iterative, so we wouldn't stop here; we would look more closely at the anomaly. As with all policy analysis, we need a counterfactual; in this case, we would want to estimate what the accident rate would have been in the absence of the pandemic. We might take the trend from last year and extrapolate it to this year and then ask whether the accident rate is higher than expected. If it is, then we have more evidence in favor of the pandemic hypothesis.

As with inductive reasoning, we can't reach a definitive conclusion with abductive reasoning, but we may gain considerable insight. Exhibit 5-6 compares the processes of induction, deduction, and abduction.

Exhibit 5-6 Comparison of Deductive, Inductive, and Abductive Reasoning

Type of Reasoning	Deduction	Induction	Abduction
Method	Apply broad principles to specific situations	Infer broad principles from specific situations	Explain available evidence through iterative hypothesis generation, deductive reasoning, and inductive reasoning
Offers definitively true conclusions?	Yes, if reasoning is sound	No, conclusions always provisional	No, conclusions always provisional
Yields more information than contained in premises?	Never	Always	Always
Equally competent analysts reach the same conclusion?	Yes	Not necessarily	Not necessarily
Definition of sound reasoning	• Logic is valid • Premises are true	• Structure is coherent • Premises are likely true, thereby generating inductive force • Provisional conclusion qualified by characterization of uncertainty	• Adheres to scientific method • Offers convincing explanation of available evidence • Offers simplest possible explanation of evidence • Provisional conclusion qualified by characterization of uncertainty

5.5 REASONING BY CLASSIFICATION

Have you ever heard someone say that they're trying to take a drink from a fire hose? If so, the speaker is telling you that he or she is overwhelmed by the amount of information coming their way and is struggling to make sense of it all. One of the best ways to deal with situations like these is to apply a special type of logic—**reasoning by classification**.[7] Rather than dealing with each new piece of information as a separate and distinct item, you *group like things in categories*, where each item in the category is similar to other items in the category. These items could be just about anything: people, events, conditions, policies, causes, effects, the list is nearly endless. This process is sometimes referred to as binning, or bucketing, because you're metaphorically sorting your information into bins or buckets.

Doing so saves you from the hassle of trying to separately keep track of every item and its characteristics. Instead, you focus on the characteristics of the buckets, not the things in them.

For an example of how this might be useful in the context of policy analysis, look at Exhibit 5-7, which reports the results of a study of people using homeless shelters in Philadelphia in the early 1990s (Gladwell, 2006). Rather than describing the characteristics of each shelter user, we can sort them into three buckets: short-term users, episodic users, and chronic users. Each type of user is then described in terms of the frequency of shelter use, length of stay, and typical circumstance. Finally, the relative size of each category is captured by the fraction of all shelter users who fall into that category.

Exhibit 5-7 Classification of Homeless Shelter Users in Philadelphia

Category	Typically return to Shelter?	Typical Stay	Typical Circumstance	Share of All Shelter Users (%)
Short-term Users	No	1–2 days	Temporary loss of accommodation	80
Episodic Users	Periodically, especially in winter	3 weeks	Heavy drug user	10
Chronic Users	Frequently	Long-term, sometimes years	Mentally ill/ Physically disabled	10

Source: Gladwell (2006), Summarizing the work of Culhane, D

---

[7]Reasoning by classification is a form of inductive logic.

When it comes to policy analysis, a categorization scheme like this can be very helpful. One might, for example, use it to figure out which social services would be most useful for each group. Perhaps the first group would benefit from rental assistance, the second from substance abuse treatment, and third from long-term mental health services or improved means of coping with physical disability. We might also decide that shelter users would be better served by three types of shelters, each matched to the needs of a specific user group. Finally, knowing the relative size of each group makes it easier to estimate the cost of the shelter system and changes we might make to it.

So, how can you systematically apply reasoning by classification? There are a few rules to keep in mind. First, when you develop your categories, they must cover all the possibilities. *Every item you're classifying must find a home in a category*; orphan items are not allowed.[8] This principle requires that the categories be **collectively exhaustive**.

Second, *each item must fit into only one category*. Consider our example—it wouldn't make sense to think of a shelter user as simultaneously a short-term user and a chronic user. Doing so would defeat the purpose of the classification. This principle requires that the categories be **mutually exclusive**. Together, the first two principles require that each item belong to one, and only one, category.

Third, in developing your classification scheme, the goal is a *manageable number of categories*. This principle can get a bit tricky because you're balancing competing objectives. On the one hand, while the items in a category are unlikely to be identical, you do want them to be as similar (i.e., homogeneous) as possible. If there are too many differences among them, you won't be able to draw conclusions that are broadly applicable to all members of the category. On the other hand, you also want as few categories as possible in order to lighten your cognitive load in understanding the information. Fewer categories, however, mean that you may be forcing too many dissimilar (i.e., heterogeneous) items into the same bucket; in turn, you won't be able to characterize each bucket succinctly and accurately.

To visualize the tension between the two goals, consider the extremes. At one extreme is a classification scheme with a single bucket to which every item has been assigned. This won't help much because everything ends up in the same bucket. Alternatively, you could have a bucket for every item. Doing so ensures the homogeneity of each bucket, but you're simply recreating the fire hose problem.

Fourth, the process of reasoning by classification is context specific. *The right number and correct definition of the categories depends on how you will use the classification scheme*. Consider, for example, categorizing people based on age. If your interest is

---

[8]If you get stuck with an item that just won't fit into any of your categories, a work-around is to create a miscellaneous, or not-elsewhere-classified, category.

employment, you might have categories such as too young to work (0–16 years), early career workers (17–40), late career workers (41–65), and retirees (over 65). If your focus were demand for health care, you might have the pediatric years (0–18 years), early adulthood (19–40), middle age (41–65), seniors (66–75), and the geriatric years (over 75). Bear in mind that a classification scheme that works well in one case may be inadequate in another. And some phenomena may be too complex or poorly understood to sort into buckets.

An often-helpful extension of reasoning by classification is the **2×2 Table**. Sometimes, when you're trying to cope with a lot of complicated information, you suspect that the classification is about more than one thing. You can handle such situations by identifying two dimensions to the information (rather than just one) and then, for each dimension, figuring out at least two different values that the dimension might take on. For example, if you work on programs to encourage economic development in a state, you could split the state into urban and nonurban areas, and differentiate areas where the local economy is growing or shrinking.[9] The result is a 2×2 table with four cells that represents the whole state: urban/growing, urban/shrinking, nonurban/growing, and nonurban/shrinking.

There's a lot you can do with your table. Start by sorting all areas in the state into one of the four cells. Then, assess how similar (homogeneous) all of areas within each cell are. If you're happy with the homogeneity, then you can start thinking about which policies make sense for each type of area. If you're uncomfortable with the degree of dissimilarity (heterogeneity) within one or more of the cells, consider increasing the number of categories for either or both of the dimensions. Maybe it's an oversimplification to use a binary differentiator for urban versus nonurban. Perhaps you need the additional nuance that would come from having, say, four categories: urban, suburban, exurban, and rural. Perhaps it's not just a matter of whether the area is growing or shrinking. Perhaps growing areas need to be differentiated between those growing slowly and those growing rapidly. We've now turned our 2×2 table into a 4×3 table, with twelve cells instead of four, but the same analytic principles apply.[10]

---

[9]Sharp-eyed readers will note that I should have a category for a static economy that is neither growing nor shrinking. To keep things simple, we'll assume that no area of the state has a perfectly static economy.

[10]You might also include more than two dimensions in your classification scheme. If you add, for example, a third dimension to capture whether the area is in the northern, middle, or southern part of the state, you'd have a three-dimensional classification scheme for sorting items. It would have 36 buckets (4×3×3). You can add more dimensions, but the number of buckets will grow quickly!

5.6 PROBABILISTIC REASONING AND BAYES' THEOREM

This section discusses two related, but distinct, topics. The first is probabilistic reasoning writ large and the second is a specific application of probabilistic reasoning known as Bayes' theorem.

5.6.1 Probabilistic Reasoning

The basics of probabilistic reasoning are pretty intuitive. When you flip a fair coin, there's a 50% chance of heads and a 50% chance of tails (i.e., the odds of a particular side turning up are one in two; one divided by two is 0.50, hence, 50%). Or when you roll a single unloaded die, there's 16.7% chance of getting any particular number (i.e., each face of the die has a one in six chance of ending up on top). In short, the probability of something is the likelihood that it will happen.

From there, things diverge depending on whether you're a **frequentist** or a **subjectivist**. You're a frequentist if you believe that probabilities make sense only for real-world events that are repeated, and where we can observe the outcome of each repetition. Measuring human longevity based on birth and death records for millions of people and computing the payoff of thousands of plays of a Las Vegas slot machine are both situations where a frequentist would be comfortable estimating numeric probabilities. A frequentist would, however, be unwilling to put a probability number on a one-off event such as the chance that the District of Columbia will become a state before 2023.

Subjectivists take a more expansive view of probability. They start in the same place as the frequentists: probabilities represent the likelihood that particular events will occur. But a subjectivist extends the concept to events that will occur only once. For example, a subjectivist might characterize a candidate's chance of winning an election at 70%.[11] Of course, the candidate will either win or lose; there's no such thing as winning 70% of an elective office nor is there an opportunity to rerun the election 100 times to see if the candidate wins 70 of the contests and loses the other 30.

Nonetheless, using probabilities to express our degree of subjective confidence in a prediction is intuitively appealing. For example, if I thought someone had a 95% chance of winning an election but ended up losing, I'd be really surprised. On the other hand, if I thought their chance was only 51% and they lost, I probably wouldn't think twice about it. What's more, subjective probabilities also have an important role

---

[11]This is not the same as the candidate getting 70% of the votes. Instead, the subjectivist is saying there's a 70% chance that the candidate will get more than 50% of the votes (assuming a two-person race).

not just in the prediction of future events, but also in qualifying conclusions reached through inductive reasoning.

You will recall from our discussion in Section 5.3 that inductive reasoning never yields definitive truths, but only provisional truths with varying degrees of inductive force. *Subjective probabilities provide a handy tool for characterizing inductive force.* Whether you're a weather forecaster helping people decide if they should carry an umbrella, an intelligence analyst assessing the likelihood of geopolitical events, or a climate scientist describing the consequences of future climate change, your intellectual challenge is the same. Having inductively reasoned your way to a provisional conclusion, you need to find a way to effectively convey the provisionality of that conclusion to others. So, what's next?

You could use narrative language, rather than numeric percentages, to express your sense of the inductive force of your conclusion. Narrative language, however, can be imprecise. I glossed over the issue earlier when I suggested that you use a continuum of words ranging from very likely to very unlikely to describe your confidence in an inductive conclusion. Doing so begs the question of what these words mean. If something is 'likely' to happen, does that mean there's better than a 50–50 chance of it happening, more than a 90% chance, or something in between?

I don't have an unambiguous answer for you. *Relying on words alone is not ideal;* several studies have revealed a wide divergence in the numeric probability that people attach to words such as 'likely' and 'unlikely,' or 'could' and 'might' (Mauboussin & Mauboussin, 2018; Tetlock & Gardner, 2015). If this terminology—sometimes referred to as **words of estimative probability**—is understood differently by analysts and their clients, then clear communication about uncertainty is impossible. This problem is not lost on folks responsible for characterizing uncertainty. As shown in Exhibit 5-8, more than one organization has attempted to address the situation by explicitly matching narrative descriptors of uncertainty to specific numeric probabilities. The first two scales are from the US Office of the Director of National Intelligence (ODNI, 2015, p. 3),[12] the third scale is from the US Global Change Research Program (GCRP, 2017, p. 7), and the fourth scale is from the International Panel on Climate Change (IPCC, 2010, p. 3). Also included in Exhibit 5-8 is a 'crosswalk' from numeric probabilities to various standards used in the US legal system (Weiss, 2008). Most of these probabilities aren't codified in law but simply reflect Weiss's attempt to think rigorously about the meaning of these legal standards.

As you can see from the examples in Exhibit 5-8, such efforts haven't produced universal agreement. As just one example of the misalignment, consider that an

---

[12]The Office of the Director of National Intelligence (ODNI) lets analysts use either of the two scales but requires that only one scale be used in any single work product. In other words, analysts may not intermingle terminology from the two scales in the same document.

Exhibit 5-8   Words of Estimative Probability[a]

Probability	ODNI #1	ODNI #2	USGCRP	IPCC	U.S. Legal Standard
0%	Not on scale 0	Not on scale 0	Exceptionally unlikely 0–1	Exceptionally unlikely 0–1	Insufficient even to support hunch 0
	Almost no chance 1–5	Remote 1–5	Extremely unlikely 1–5	Very unlikely 1–10	No reasonable grounds for suspicion, fanciful conjecture 1
5%			Very unlikely 5–10		Reasonable, articulable grounds for suspicion (stop and frisk for weapons) 1–10
10%	Very unlikely 5–20	Highly improbable 5–20	Unlikely 10–33	Unlikely 10–33	Reasonable indication (initiate FBI investigation or trade inquiry) 10–20
20%					Probable cause or reasonable belief (field arrest, search warrant, arraignment or indictment) 20–33
33%	Unlikely 20–45	Improbable 20–45			
45%			About as likely as not 33–66	About as likely as not 33–66	Clear indication (proposed criterion for nighttime, x-ray, or body cavity search) 33–50
50%	Roughly even chance 45–55	Roughly even odds 45–55			Preponderance of the evidence (standard for most civil cases) 50–66
55%					
66%	Likely 55-80	Probable 55-80	Likely 66–90	Likely 66–90	Substantial and credible evidence (referring evidence for impeachment) 66–80
80%					Clear showing (granting of temporary injunction) 80–90
90%	Very likely 80–95	Highly probable 80–95	Very likely 90–95	Very likely 90–99	Clear and convincing evidence (quasi-penal civil actions, such as termination of parental rights) 90–99
95%	Almost certain 95–99	Nearly certain 95–99	Extremely likely 95–99		
	Not on scale 100	Not on scale 100	Virtually certain 99–100	Virtually certain 99–100	Beyond reasonable doubt (criminal conviction) 99
100%					Virtually certain (exceeds criminal standard) 100

[a]See text for source citations.

outcome characterized as 'very likely' has a probability between 80% and 95% on the ODNI scale, a probability between 90% and 95% on the USGCRP scale, and a probability between 90% and 99% on IPCC scale.[13]

---

[13]To be fair, there is no reason to expect (or institutional mechanism for) these organizations to align their work.

The difficulties of calibrating descriptions of uncertainty reach a peak at the intersection of the analyst's work and the interpretation of that work by a client. The *Washington Post* quotes an unnamed senior Central Intelligence Agency officer:

> Intelligence analysts 'would rather use words than numbers to describe how confident we are in our analysis.' Moreover, 'most consumers of intelligence aren't particularly sophisticated when it comes to probabilistic analysis. They like words and pictures, too. My experience is that [they] prefer briefings that don't center on numerical calculation. That's not to say we can't do it, but there's really not much demand for it'. (Schrage, 2005)

There's no obvious solution to this dilemma, other than to say that, given the client-oriented nature of policy analysis, your job is to convey the provisional nature of your findings to your audience in whatever way makes the most sense to that audience.

5.6.2 Reasoning From Evidence to Conclusions With Bayes' Theorem

Statistics and probability theory are important tools in your analytic toolbox. But our focus here is the broader field of policy analysis, so I'll leave it to other books and classes to give you most of those tools. But one concept from the field of probability is so important that we need to review it here. Developed by Thomas Bayes in the eighteenth century, it can guide us through the process of reasoning from evidence to conclusions. Bayes' theorem, and extensions of it, now comprise a major subfield of probability theory and play a major role in data analytics and artificial intelligence. The math can get complicated, but you can grasp the essentials in an intuitive fashion. We'll first describe Bayes' theorem in general terms and then take a closer look at the importance of something called the base rate.

Two concepts are at the heart of Bayesian thinking: the evidence we have in front of us and the conclusions we infer from it. The direction of our reasoning is very important. We want to make sure we go from our evidence (e.g., the result of a blood test for a virus) to our conclusion (e.g., whether a patient actually has the virus), not the other direction. What do I mean by going the other direction? If I told you that 90% of sick people test positive and 90% of healthy people test negative for this virus, I haven't given you the information you need to interpret a test result. Why? Because what I've given you entails reasoning from the conclusion (the health of person) to the evidence (their test result). That's backward thinking, and we need to use Bayes' theorem to get turned around.

Let's use a fictitious example to illustrate Bayes' theorem. Imagine a government agency tasked with screening applicants who want to immigrate to the United States.

The agency uses a standardized protocol to evaluate applicants—a combination of a background check, personal interview, and review of job skills—that yields one of two results: the person passes the test and is deemed a genuine immigrant with benign intent, or the person fails the test and is deemed a bad actor with malign intent. People who pass the test are allowed entry; those who fail are turned away. The screening protocol result (pass or fail) is analogous to a lab test for a specific disease; the true status (benign or malign) of the traveler is akin to a person being healthy or sick. The test is imperfect, but it is the only evidence to work with. Of course, *what the agency really cares about is not the test result, but the true character of the person* being evaluated. The agency asks for our help to figure out how accurate the screening protocol is.

To assess the protocol's accuracy, we commission a retrospective program evaluation that studies a random sample of several hundred applicants. The evaluation tells us that 90% of true bad actors fail the test while 75% of the genuine immigrants pass the test. Ninety percent sounds great, and 75% seems pretty good too. So, the agency is on solid ground with its protocol, right?

Not so fast. We're reasoning in the wrong direction. We have the accuracy of the test results for each of the two groups of people (i.e., the likelihood of the test result depending on which group they're truly in). But here's the thing, we don't actually know which group each person truly belongs in; we only know their test result. We need to flip the information around and ask two related questions:

- If they pass the screening test, what's the probability that they're a genuine immigrant? This outcome is known as a True Positive. (Hint: It's not 75%.)

- If they fail the screening test, what's the probability that they're a bad actor? This outcome is known as a True Negative. (Hint: It's not 90%.)

And, this is where we need the third bit of information, something called the **base rate** which is just a fancy way of specifying what percentage of the applicant pool are truly bad actors. Let's suppose that our retrospective program evaluation established that it's five percent. We can now use Bayes' theorem to solve algebraically for the answer to our two questions, but I promised you an intuitive approach, so let's skip the algebra and look at the graphic in Exhibit 5-9. In it is an image with 1,000 squares, sometimes called a pictograph, with each color-coded square representing one traveler.

Given the base rate of five percent, we infer that 50 of 1,000 applicants are bad actors. Ninety percent of them (or 45 applicants, shown as light gray squares) will fail the test and be turned away, but ten percent of them (or five applicants, shown in white squares) will be admitted. The other 950 applicants are genuine immigrants; 75% (713, in dark gray) will be admitted but 25% (238, in very dark gray) will be turned away. With this information, we can now work out the answers we

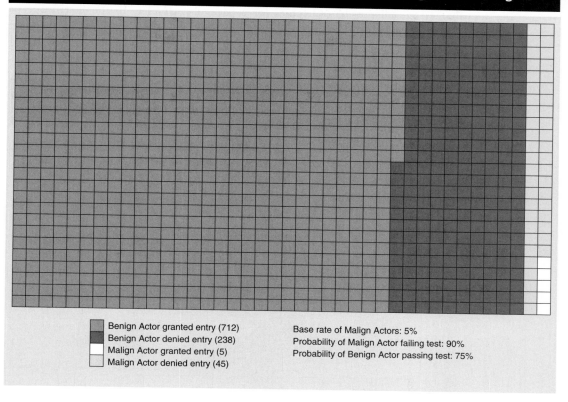

▨ Benign Actor granted entry (712)	Base rate of Malign Actors: 5%
▨ Benign Actor denied entry (238)	Probability of Malign Actor failing test: 90%
☐ Malign Actor granted entry (5)	Probability of Benign Actor passing test: 75%
☐ Malign Actor denied entry (45)	

need. A total of 718 folks pass the test; 713 (or just over 99%) of them are genuine immigrants while five (or a bit less than 1%) are bad actors. As for the 283 folks who fail the test, 45 (or about 16%) are bad actors while 238 (or 84%) are genuine immigrants.

Notice what we did here. At the start, all we had was our program evaluation with information about how each group (malign or benign) did on the test. At that point, the only thing we could do was reason *from* the person's true character *to* their test result. But, since the agency doesn't know each person's true character, we needed to work in the other direction. We needed to go *from* the evidence we do have (i.e., the test result) *to* a probabilistic statement about their true character. We combined the two groups who pass the test (one benign and one malign), and then figured out what fraction of all test-passers fell into each of the two groups. We did the same thing for the two groups who fail the test.

Another way to graphically depict what's going on with Bayes' theorem is to use a **probability tree** to show the successive application of multiple probabilities to characterize all possible outcomes for a particular traveler. In the first image of Exhibit 5-10, we have a probability tree that uses the original information we had about the immigrant screening protocol. It starts with the true character of the

Exhibit 5-10 Flipping the Tree: Using a Probability Tree to Apply Bayes' Theorem to Immigrant Screening

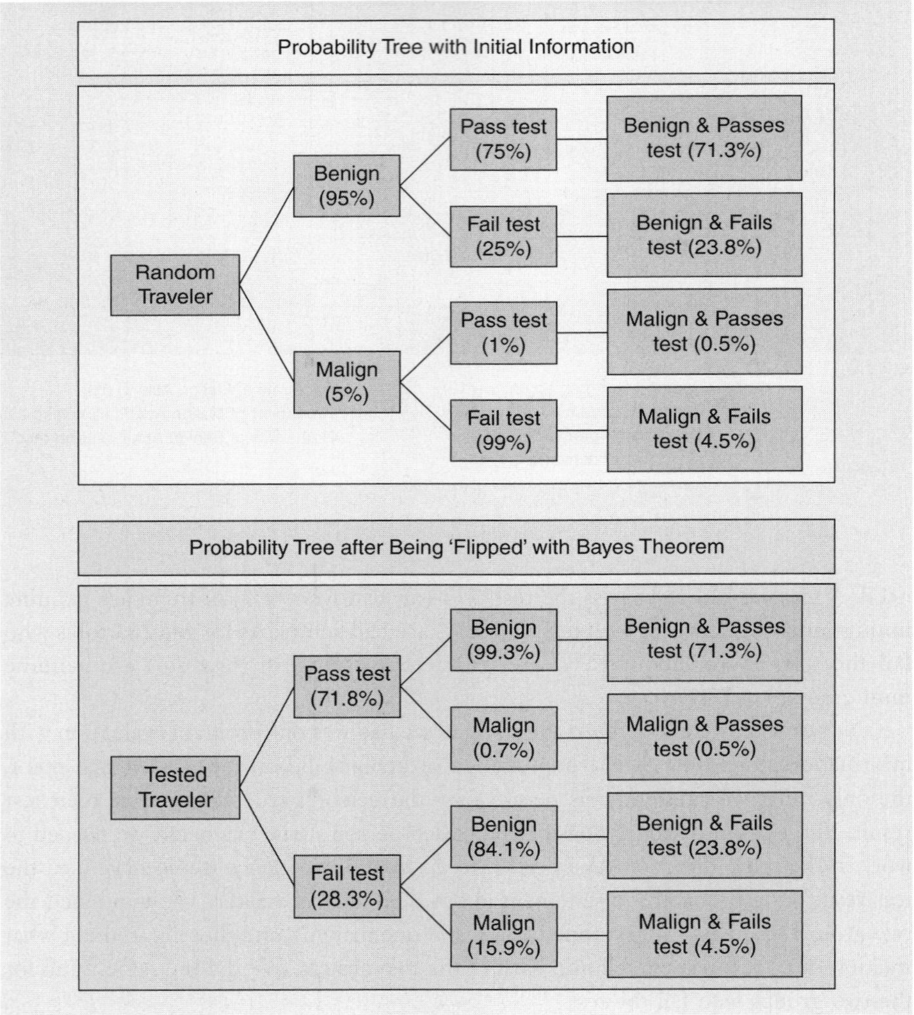

Probability Tree with Initial Information

Random Traveler

Benign (95%)
- Pass test (75%) → Benign & Passes test (71.3%)
- Fail test (25%) → Benign & Fails test (23.8%)

Malign (5%)
- Pass test (1%) → Malign & Passes test (0.5%)
- Fail test (99%) → Malign & Fails test (4.5%)

Probability Tree after Being 'Flipped' with Bayes Theorem

Tested Traveler

Pass test (71.8%)
- Benign (99.3%) → Benign & Passes test (71.3%)
- Malign (0.7%) → Malign & Passes test (0.5%)

Fail test (28.3%)
- Benign (84.1%) → Benign & Fails test (23.8%)
- Malign (15.9%) → Malign & Fails test (4.5%)

traveler and, moving to the right, applies the information we have from the program evaluation about the accuracy of the test. The end points of the four branches of the tree represent the combined probabilities that come before it (e.g., the probability of a traveler having benign intent and passing the test is simply 95% times 75%, or 71.3%). Following the approach outlined above, we then 'flip the tree' so that we start with the test result and reason our way to a probabilistic statement about the true nature of the traveler. The flipped probability tree is shown as the second image of Exhibit 5-10. The probability estimates in each of the four end points are the same as the first tree, but we've rearranged them and then worked backward to complete the restructured tree. We'll come back to it later in this section, but I need to point out now that the base rate of the phenomenon of interest (in this case, that five percent of travelers have malign intent) is an important driver of the results we derive with Bayes' theorem. For now, hold the thought until we revisit it later.

Using either the pictograph or the flipped probability tree, we can now answer the questions posed a few paragraphs ago:

- If a traveler passes, what's the probability that they're a benign immigrant? 99.3% (or 713/718)

- If a traveler fails the test, what's the probability that they're a bad actor? 15.9% (or 45/238)

In short, a positive test should leave us quite confident that we've identified a benign actor, but a negative test is a really lousy indicator that the traveler is a malign actor.

We can take one more step here that is often very important in policy analysis by taking a look at the rate of **true and false positives and negatives**. Our Bayesian analysis yielded a true negative rate of 15.9% and true positive rate of 99.3%. By subtraction, we can discern that the false negative rate is, thus, 84.1% and the false positive rate is 0.7%. Exhibit 5-11 summarizes the results. The test is quite good at detecting bad actors and quite poor at detecting good actors. About 84% of those who fail the test and are turned away are actually true immigrants with benign intent.

One thing to note about our example: the *impact of false positives and false negatives often play out in entirely different policy domains.* To wax poetic for a second: A false positive denies a benign applicant the chance to participate in the US immigrant experience described in the welcoming words inscribed on the tablet held by the Statue of Liberty while a false negative allows a bad actor into the country, putting ourselves, our families, and our communities at the risk of grave harm. Making the trade-off between endangering the homeland and manifesting the American dream is a choice for policymakers, but as a policy analyst, your use of Bayes' theorem will go a

Exhibit 5-11   A Fictitious Example of an Immigrant Screening Protocol

		Result of Screening Protocol	
		Traveler Not a Threat (Passes Test)	**Traveler Is a Threat (Fails Test)**
True Nature of Traveler	Malign	False Positive *Danger to the Homeland* 0.7%	True Negative *Homeland Secured* 15.9%
	Benign	True Positive *Manifest the American Dream* 99.3%	False Negative *Fail to Live Up to Lady Liberty's Words* 84.1%

long way toward clarifying the consequences—positive and negative—of using this particular screening protocol.

5.6.3 The Base Rate

We skimmed over the topic of base rates earlier in this section. It is important to note, however, that *base rates affect the likelihood of false positives and negatives* when we're sorting people (or things) into categories. Exhibit 5-12 shows what happens in our immigrant screening example when the base rate of malign actors (as a share of all applicants) is varied from 0% to 100%. If we compare, say, a base rate of 80% to a rate of 20%, the probability of a false positive jumps from 3% to 35% while the chance of a false negative drops from 53% to 7%.

In sum, when you draw a probabilistic conclusion, it's not just the likelihoods of the evidence in front of you that matters. You also need to set the context by considering the underlying chance of something being true or false in the first place (i.e., the base rate), before you then apply the evidence you do have. Failing to do so is called **base rate neglect**, and it threatens the validity of your conclusions.

What would have happened if we had ignored the base rate entirely? For starters, we wouldn't have had the information needed to apply Bayes' theorem. Perhaps more importantly, we would risk reaching the wrong conclusion from the evidence we do have. To make sure you understand the importance of the base rate to the conclusions you draw, let's think about a simple story.

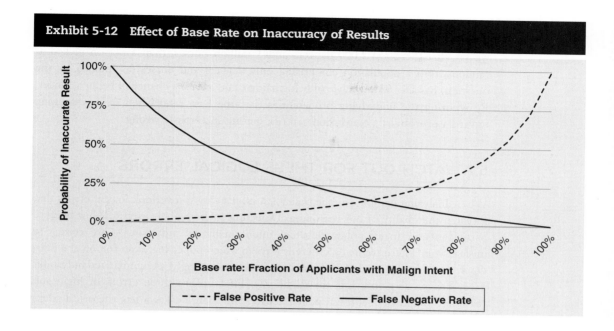

Exhibit 5-12   Effect of Base Rate on Inaccuracy of Results

Hannah loved dance. She started lessons as a child and went to a high school that had an award-winning ballet group in which she was an avid participant. She danced the lead in three university ballet productions and had small roles in two ballets at a professional company. She was a good student and graduated from college with honors. Take a minute and think about which of the following two scenarios seems more likely to describe her situation ten years after graduation:

- Hannah is a lead dancer for a professional ballet company.

- Hannah is a registered nurse.

If you're like most folks, you probably think it more likely that Hannah is a dancer rather than a nurse. Yes, you're just guessing based on a four-sentence vignette, but given her personal history, it sure seems likely that she was destined for a career as a dancer.

For a reality check, however, think about how many professional ballet companies there are in the United States. I couldn't find a definitive source, but Wikipedia lists 157 such companies (Wikipedia, 2020). Even if each designates several lead dancers, there are probably no more than a couple thousand people dancing lead roles at professional companies. On the other hand, there are about 3 million registered nurses in the United States (BLS, 2019). Given the numbers, it's unlikely that Hannah made it as a professional ballerina and far more likely she became a nurse.

To use the language of Bayes' theorem, the base rate for the probability that she's a dancer is very small and the probability that she's a nurse is much higher. In fact, if we say that there are 2,000 dancers and 3 million nurses, then a person picked at random from a population comprising only dancers and nurses (as implied by the question) has a 99.93% chance of being a nurse and a 0.07% chance of being a dancer. By ignoring the underlying probabilities (i.e., the base rate) when we're reasoning toward a probabilistic conclusion, we risk getting it seriously wrong.

5.7 WATCH OUT FOR THESE LOGICAL ERRORS

When analyzing complex public policy issues, it's easy to overlook logical errors that threaten the quality of our reasoning. Detecting such errors is even tougher because participants in many policy debates—intentionally or otherwise[14]—are trying to mislead you. There are many different ways in which policy logic can run off the rails; describing them all would be a book unto itself. Accordingly, as summarized in Exhibit 5-13, this section only hits the highlights. First up are three errors of logic and reasoning found frequently in policy debates; we then look at a few rhetorical tricks often used to hide flawed logic.[15]

Exhibit 5-13   Potential Logical Errors in Policy Analysis

- Errors of logic and reasoning
  - Falling into the is/ought trap
  - Using sloppy inductive reasoning
  - Failing to qualify an inductively reached conclusion

- Rhetorical tricks and traps
  - Wily word choice
  - Argument by appeal
  - Structure, rules, and conduct of the debate
  - Intentional illogic

---

[14]Recall the distinction in Chapter 3 between *analysis as inquiry* and *analysis as advocacy* and the discussion in Chapter 4 about the risks of fast System 1 thinking.

[15]The material in this section represents an amalgam of ideas that originate in multiple sources. Specific factual claims and studies are cited in the usual fashion. The remainder of the material is based primarily on my personal experience but also reflects an integrated reading of less formal commentary offered by these websites, news reports, and blog posts: (Bensen, 2017; Dwyer, 2018; Dwyer, 2017; Richardson, 2018; Richardson, 2017).

5.7.1 Errors of Logic and Reasoning

Sometimes, the misuse of logic is unintentional. Rather than an attempt at deception, such mistakes result from working too quickly or not thinking deeply enough.

Falling Into the Is/Ought Trap

We talked about the is/ought dichotomy in Chapter 3 when we considered how descriptive and normative ways of thinking are intertwined in classical policy analysis models. Here we drill down on a related rhetorical mistake that deserves special mention. It's easy to get tripped up by a claim that carelessly mixes descriptive statements about how the world actually works with normative statements about how the world ought to work. The trap—and its subtle nature—was apparent to philosopher David Hume (1739/1888) 280 years ago when he observed that:

> In every system of morality ... I have always [remarked] that the author proceeds for some time in the ordinary way of reasoning, and establishes the being of a God, or makes observations concerning human affairs; when [all] of a sudden I am [surprised] to find, that instead of the usual copulations of propositions, is, and is not, I meet with no proposition that is not connected with an ought, or an ought not. This change is imperceptible; but is, however, of the last consequence. (pp. 469–470)

Here's my example of what Hume is talking about: 'Global warming will melt Artic ice to the point where polar bears are threatened with extinction, therefore, the world ought to dramatically reduce its use of fossil fuels.' The first clause in the sentence is descriptive; we can examine the evidence and reasoning about whether and how warming may lead to the demise of the polar bear. But the second clause is a normative claim about what ought to be done; despite appearances, it does not follow logically from the descriptive claim. Deciding what to do about warming depends both on a thorough analysis of the pros and cons of alternative ways to respond to the descriptive claim and on the normative value we attach to both polar bears and the potential disruptions of strong climate policy.

Using Sloppy Inductive Reasoning

Applying inductive reasoning to policy analysis can be hard work. When we're looking at a complex policy world driven by multiple forces that seem to change constantly, it's easy to lose sight of the core principles of sound logic and slip into sloppy reasoning, especially when it comes to the inductive reasoning that lies at the heart of most policy debates. You've heard the adage: garbage in, garbage out. It applies here too. So, where might you go astray? Below are a few quick examples:

- *Reasoning by Analogy* entails inferring that what is known to be true of one case is likely to be true of a second similar case. For such inferences to be valid, the two cases must indeed be similar in all relevant respects. Don't let superficial similarities lull you into treating two cases as analogous if they differ in important ways. You may want to adopt the default position that the cases are *not* similar until you've done enough research to convince yourself otherwise.

- *Reasoning by Generalization* entails inferring from a few studied cases to a larger universe of unstudied cases. A persistent threat to the validity of such generalizations is that the sample of cases may be too small to permit valid extrapolation, thereby creating significant uncertainty about your conclusions. Alternatively, the cases you've examined may not be a representative sample of the population to which you wish to infer, thereby biasing your conclusion.

- *Reasoning by Classification* entails sorting items (e.g., people, events) into groups and characterizing each group separately. If you have too few classifications, you may end up with too much heterogeneity in each group. When you then draw conclusions about the group, you may mischaracterize many members of the group.

- *You Can't Have It Both Ways:* Imagine a governor who proposes to give every student a laptop. The state fiscal agency estimates the cost at $15 million—a political kiss of death. The governor picks up the phone to yell at the poor budget analyst, saying that the schools are already moving in this direction, and the cost will be negligible. There's a contradiction here. If we're on track to give the kids laptops, then we don't need the bill. But if a lot of kids need the legislation to avoid being left on the wrong side of the digital divide, then we should expect a big price tag. The governor can't have it both ways: either the proposal will have a low cost and little impact, or a high cost and a big impact. You may not be able to tell which view is correct, but you can be sure there's a flaw in the governor's thinking.

There are other ways you go wrong with inductive reasoning, but these four errors are both prevalent and pernicious in their potential threat to high-quality policy analysis.

Failing to Qualify an Inductively Reached Conclusion

Even if your inductive reasoning is strong and you avoid logical errors, there is another way to go astray. As explained in Section 5.3, when we're characterizing the real-world conditions that create a policy problem or assessing the outcomes of a policy option, we can never achieve complete certainty. We're not omniscient. If we are talking about the present, the possibility always exist that there may be a counterexample, lurking out there somewhere, that would falsify our conclusion, and if we're talking about what will happen later in time, the intrinsic uncertainty of the future can never be fully mitigated.

So, unless you're dealing with a value-oriented, normative claim based on only received wisdom (e.g., all persons are born with inalienable rights) or a specific, noncontroversial factual claim (e.g., in 2020, there were three fatal automobile accidents in Smithtown), you need to qualify the provisionality of your inductively reached conclusions. To do so, you can use the words of estimative probability like those shown in Exhibit 5-8; alternatively, you can use numeric probabilities to qualify your conclusion.

But what if you just don't have the evidence or a logical basis to narrow your uncertainty? You still need to acknowledge its existence with words like 'best guess,' 'highly uncertain,' or 'speculative.' Yes, such words might make you feel like a less competent analyst, but the truth is actually the opposite. By being honest about uncertainty, you come closer to speaking truth to power than by pretending to be more confident than you really are. And, of course, if you're not the author, but instead are on the receiving end of an inductively reached conclusion the provisionality of which has not been qualified, you should immediately suspect its validity and subject it to more scrutiny than you ordinarily would.

5.7.2 Watch Out for These Rhetorical Tricks and Traps

There is another collection of logical errors that happen by design rather than by mistake. This section reviews a few analytic tricks used to disguise weak logic.[16]

Wily Word Choice

- Using ambiguous terminology to impede a coherent critique. If your opponent can't understand what your point is, it's hard for him or her to refute it.

- Making statements that are true but irrelevant. Tossing out true statements enhances a speaker's credibility, even if they don't have much to do with his or her argument.

- Failing to own the argument. Phrases like 'People tell me …' or 'Everyone knows that …' are ways to make a point, while keeping open the option to disown it if a strong counterargument arises.

---

[16]Several of these examples are inspired by Freeley & Steinberg (2014) (pp. 86–102).

- Using bombast to silence counterarguments. Speaking loudly and dramatically, interrupting others, and flooding social media discourages opponents and drowns out their perspectives.

- Including incongruous qualifiers. Some speakers make outlandish claims, but sneak in words that the audience might miss like 'could' or 'may' to ensure that technically they're not lying.

Argument by Appeal

- Appealing to popularity, also known as the bandwagon effect. Just because an idea is popular, or because a popular person has endorsed it, that does not mean that it is necessarily valid.

- Appealing to authority, claiming that because someone in a position of power said something, it is true. Sometimes valid, sometimes not; if a person is an expert, their opinion may deserve deference.

- Appealing to nature, claiming that things observed in the natural world are desirable. The subordination in some species of females to males (and vice versa) doesn't mean that human affairs should be the same.

- Appealing to tradition, claiming that a long history of a practice validates its desirability. But norms evolve over time; hence, tradition can't definitively validate such practices.

- Appealing to emotion by citing dramatic examples in order to provoke an emotional audience response that affects its view of the speaker's arguments (using pathos and ethos rather than logos).

The Structure, Rules, and Conduct of the Debate

- Going first to get an advantage. The party that initiates a debate often benefits by getting the first chance to define terms, identify topics in dispute, frame problems, and propose solutions.

- Shifting the burden of proof. Do you have to prove your proposal is a good idea or does the other side have to prove it's a bad idea? Advocates typically opt for whichever approach makes it easier to get the win.

- Exploiting the advantage of the status quo. Change is difficult, and the status quo typically enjoys an advantage because of the benefits it confers on incumbent interests. Arguing to a stalemate usually leaves the status quo intact; advocates of change need stronger logic and better evidence to prevail.

- Using standard debate tactics. Whether it's high school or collegiate debate, Model United Nations (UN), or law schools' mock trial programs, students are routinely schooled to be on guard against a number of tactics. Alas, such tactics aren't confined to educational settings, but also pop up in policy debates:

  o Attacking individuals rather than their ideas.

  o Refusing to engage a meaningful argument by answering an analytic critique not with a thoughtful and logical response to the point at hand, but with an attack on some other issue.

  o Offering multiple arguments on every point, to waste your opponent's time and sap their cognitive energy.

  o Offering a response with a sliver of truth or logic, in order to force an opponent to make a limited concession to the speaker, thus seeming to vindicate the speaker and weaken the opponent.

  o Using a single flaw in an argument to incorrectly argue that the entire argument is invalid.

  o Raising immaterial objections to others' claims to distract from the weakness of one's own argument.

  o Mischaracterizing someone's argument and then attacking the mischaracterization rather than the original argument.

  o Changing the subject by responding to a point not being made, also known as a non sequitur.

  o Evading the point. When a proposed solution to a problem is attacked, folks sometimes decline to defend the solution but instead make an even more vigorous defense of the problem.

- Changing the argument mid-debate. An advocate might start with a specific problem definition and policy proposal, but if his or her opponent has a strong counterargument, the advocate switches to a different problem or solution to make the counterarguments irrelevant.

Intentional Illogic

- Abusing a false dichotomy. An advocate may create a false choice by claiming that only two alternatives are available (e.g., socialized medicine or fully private free-market health care) when in fact many are.[17]

---

[17]Recall the advice of the classical model (Chapter 1) to consider a reasonable set of at least three policy options.

- Asking a loaded question with an embedded character attack. If you ask someone whether he or she has stopped abusing their partner, both answers—yes and no—make the person look like a criminal. For a policy analogy, consider a question that might be put to a political candidate: 'Do you prefer very harsh punishment for all criminals or a lawless society?'

- Unleashing a zombie argument. An advocate may disingenuously put forth evidence, claims, problem definitions, or policy proposals that he or she doesn't truly support and doesn't intend to defend. Doing so is meant solely to confuse and distract the opponent and complicate the debate.

- Committing the fallacy fallacy. An argument may have a logical flaw or be put forth by an unskilled advocate, but that doesn't make it an invalid claim. Against a weak opponent, you might win the debate, even though your conclusion is wrong.

CHAPTER SUMMARY

We set the stage for this chapter's review of logic with an initial discussion of four starting points: the scientific method, what it means to speak truth to power, the necessity of defining your terminology, and the importance of the baseline. From there, we pivoted to multiple forms of logical reasoning that are central to policy analysis, including deductive and causal reasoning, inductive reasoning, abductive reasoning, reasoning by classification, and probabilistic reasoning. We then explored how Bayes' theorem can help us reason from evidence to conclusions.

Along the way, several key themes emerged—the difference between the generally unbounded nature of academic policy research and the highly constrained nature of policy analysis, the collective and social nature of the 'truth,' the intrinsic uncertainty and provisionality of almost all policy-relevant conclusions, and the trade-off between false positives and false negatives. Finally, we reviewed a menu of logical errors that can confuse and complicate policy analysis. Such errors may be accidental or may be used intentionally to gain strategic advantage in a policy debate.

DISCUSSION QUESTIONS

1. Former President Trump claims that the 2020 presidential election was a massive fraud; others have argued that it was one of the fairest elections in recent years. How might you apply the scientific method to the question? How could you decide who is most likely telling the truth?

2. Which policy issues are amenable to analysis with deductive reasoning? Where might deductive reasoning come up short? What role can inductive or abductive reasoning play in policy analysis?

3. What types of reasoning would you apply if you were asked to assess the pros and cons of a new after-school tutoring program for elementary school kids?

4. Pick a policy problem with which you are familiar. Can you identify at least three distinctly different hypotheses about why the problem exists? What kinds of evidence would support or undermine each hypothesis?

5. What role does probabilistic reasoning play in thinking about if and how to address the prospect of global climate change? What do you think are the biggest uncertainties associated with climate policy? Could you describe those uncertainties with quantitative estimates or with words of estimative probability?

6. Take a look at the latest edition of *The New York Times* or *The Wall Street Journal*. Find the lead editorial and read it carefully. Can you identify any of the logical errors that we discussed in Section 5.7?

CHAPTER SIX

COLLECTING AND EVALUATING EVIDENCE FOR USE IN POLICY ANALYSIS

Having reviewed the types of reasoning that constitute the foundation of policy analysis, we turn now to the evidence to which such reasoning is applied. Why spend an entire chapter on the seemingly generic topic of evidence? To start, you can thank the brain's System 1 mode of fast thinking. When operating in System 1, there's no time to stop and consider the quality of the evidence; the brain simply relies on whatever evidence is readily available, without questioning its value or relevance to the matter at hand (Tetlock & Gardner, 2015). That's fine if you're trying to decide whether to hit the brakes when it looks like a car on a cross-street might run a red light, but in the context of policy analysis, you want to be more discerning about which evidence you rely on.

If mitigating System 1 mistakes isn't enough to motivate you to learn more about collecting and analyzing evidence, consider the context in which policy analysis takes place. It's intertwined with policymaking, surrounded by political disputes, competing claims, and differences over ethics and values. Evidence can be misinterpreted, inadvertently overlooked, intentionally neglected, and even fabricated. After studying 75 major initiatives between 1944 and 2007, Eggers and O'Leary (2009) concluded:

> Too often policymakers begin with a theory, and then seek the facts that support the theory while discounting any evidence that does not support that theory. It's the opposite of the scientific method, which requires looking at all the data, not just some of it. (p. 30)

Learning Objectives

By studying this chapter, you should be able to:

- Develop a research puzzle and set of research questions to guide the evidence collection process within an individual policy analysis.

- Describe several types of evidence that are often relevant to policy analysis and how such evidence can be collected.

- Characterize the pros and cons of each type of evidence when it comes to policy analysis.

- Define four types of validity and, for each, describe threats to valid inference.

- Explain how an analyst can determine which specific pieces of evidence are credible and which should be discounted or ignored.

- Describe and apply an integrated framework for collecting and assessing evidence with the potential to answer relevant research questions.

- Differentiate confidence and uncertainty when it comes to assessing and using policy-relevant evidence.

- Characterize potential errors in the collection and interpretation of evidence that can undermine the validity of conclusions reached with policy analysis.

A final reason for taking a deep dive into evidence is an increased bipartisan interest in the topic in recent years. Yes, even in polarized Washington, there is consensus across party lines on this issue. In 2015, Republican House Speaker Paul Ryan and Democratic Senator Patty Murray teamed up to push for a commission to develop recommendations for facilitating the rigorous use of evidence in policy-making. The result was the Foundations for Evidence-Based Policymaking Act of 2018 (5 USC 311-315) which requires agencies to strategically collect and use data to assess the effectiveness and efficiency of their programs, policies, and organizations. Referred to as the Evidence Act, it passed the House with overwhelming bipartisan support (356 to 17) and was passed by unanimous consent in the Senate. President Trump signed it into law on January 14, 2019.

President Biden's administration has moved aggressively to implement the Evidence Act. In June 2021, the Office of Management and Budget (OMB, 2021) issued strong and detailed guidance directing federal agencies to:

> … use evidence … to further both mission and operations, and to commit to build evidence where it is lacking. … [H]eads of agencies … should engage in creating a culture of evidence in their agencies … This effort demands a comprehensive approach, and implementing this vision will require resources and prioritization from leaders. At the same time, this commitment to an evidence-based government cannot happen solely at the top or in isolated analytical offices, but rather must be embedded throughout each agency … OMB strongly believes that implementing the Evidence Act is not a compliance exercise … Agencies should not simply produce the required documents and then turn their attention elsewhere; success requires that agencies develop processes and practices that establish habitual and routine reliance on evidence across agency functions and demand new or better evidence when it is needed. (pp. 2–3)

In short, for the three reasons noted above, developing your skills in collecting and analyzing data is time well spent. In this chapter, we'll first discuss how you can decide what evidence to look for and where to look for it. We'll then explore the validity and trustworthiness of different types of evidence. Next up is an integrated framework for thinking about how much confidence to have in your evidence. The final section alerts you to some evidence traps that might ensnare you if you're not careful.

6.1 WHAT EVIDENCE DO YOU NEED?

If you want your policy analysis to reflect the reality of the situation, you need to look around to see what evidence is out there. How can you organize the process of collecting the relevant evidence? Exhibit 6-1 gives an overview of that process.

There are three critical initial steps; skipping any of them is a prescription for problems later. First, figure out your *deadline*. Do you have to be done a week from now, or a month from now? It may seem like a no-brainer, but I have seen plenty of talented policy analysts enthusiastically jump into a new project and forget to ask this basic question. The answer is critical to the process of collecting evidence. If you're too ambitious and come up empty-handed at the deadline, that's not good. But neither is settling for weak or incomplete evidence when you had, but didn't use, the time to gather more information.

Second, figure out what *resources* are available to help you. Do you have a team of colleagues ready to go or are you working solo? Are you lucky enough to have research assistants, consultants, or other support that you can rely on? With help, you can launch a bigger effort to collect evidence than if you're doing everything yourself.

Finally, make sure you have a crystal clear understanding of the *context*. What does your boss or client need from your work? Don't necessarily take his or her first suggestion. If you can, engage your boss or client in a conversation about why they're concerned about the topic, what kinds of questions they want answered, and what they hope to do with your work. This background context will be critical in structuring a policy analysis to yield a result that is as helpful as possible.

With these first three steps taken care of, you next want to define your **research puzzle**. The puzzle metaphor is intentional; it often helps to think of policy analysis as a puzzle solving exercise in which you're trying to develop a complete and coherent understanding of the relevant issues (Winship, 2006). Typically, research puzzles are defined in the form of a broad, overarching question that you're trying to answer. Exhibit 6-2 contains four examples of research puzzles used by some of my students over the past few years to develop policy analysis projects.[1] The text in italicized bold face is the research puzzle that shaped each project. By solving the puzzle, the students were then able to give their client valuable insight about the policy issue of interest.

---

[1] They come from a capstone class I teach for masters students in environmental policy, hence, the focus on environmental topics. Small teams of students work with an external client on a semester-long policy project.

Exhibit 6-1　Organizing the Search for Evidence in a Policy Analysis

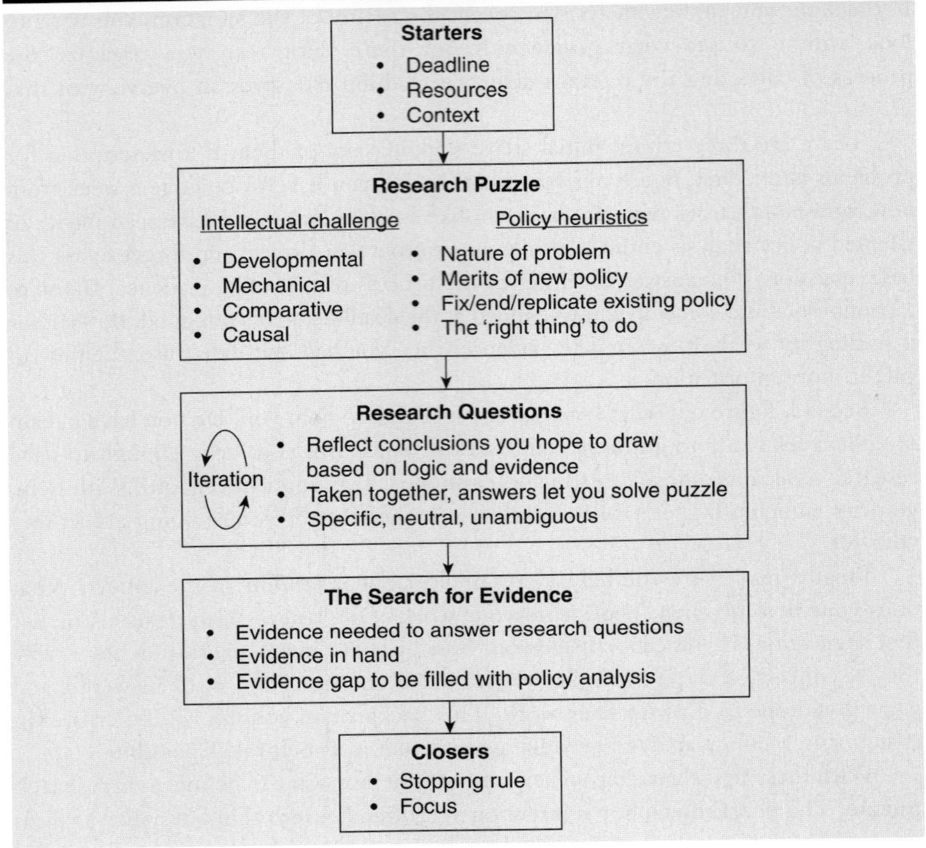

Starters
- Deadline
- Resources
- Context

Research Puzzle

Intellectual challenge
- Developmental
- Mechanical
- Comparative
- Causal

Policy heuristics
- Nature of problem
- Merits of new policy
- Fix/end/replicate existing policy
- The 'right thing' to do

Research Questions

Iteration
- Reflect conclusions you hope to draw based on logic and evidence
- Taken together, answers let you solve puzzle
- Specific, neutral, unambiguous

The Search for Evidence
- Evidence needed to answer research questions
- Evidence in hand
- Evidence gap to be filled with policy analysis

Closers
- Stopping rule
- Focus

If you're having trouble coming up with the research puzzle for your policy analysis, one way to think about it is to decide what kind of intellectual challenge you're facing (Mason, 2002, p. 18):

- *Developmental Puzzles:* How and why did the phenomenon of interest come to exist? Examples include traffic congestion in a metro area, systemic racism in a school district, or the relationship between Israel and Iran.

- *Mechanical Puzzles:* How does the phenomenon of interest work? Examples include how the elements of mass incarceration fit together, or how

Exhibit 6-2   Research Puzzles and Research Questions: Four Examples

To what degree do animal feeding operations (AFOs) threaten surface water quality in Delta County, Colorado?

- What is the AFO situation in Delta County?
- How might AFOs threaten surface water quality?
- How have Western communities similar to Delta County dealt with AFOs and surface water quality issues through policy?
- What policies, if any, in regard to AFOs would be appropriate for Delta County?

Source: Adapted from Schultz, Shattuck, and Streight (2018).

What would it take to have successful urban farming in Baltimore?

- What obstacles have impeded the efforts of Baltimore's urban farmers to establish successful operations?
- Which cities, with socioeconomic conditions similar to Baltimore's, have established successful urban farming sectors?
- Of the obstacles observed in Baltimore, how have other similar cities overcome them with policy and/or programmatic solutions?
- What factors explain the success of programs in other cities?

Source: Adapted from Bartels, Gottschalk, Hopp, and Nozaki (2017).

Is there potential for the yellow lance—a freshwater mussel—to sustain healthy populations in the Hawlings River?

- What are the attributes of suitable habitat?
  - To what degree do portions of the Hawlings have these attributes?
  - Where is there suitable habitat?
- What are the biggest threats (habitat conditions, humans, policies) to the survival of the yellow lance in the Hawlings?
  - Are there point or nonpoint pollutant sources that threaten water quality in the Hawlings?
  - What are the primary land uses in the watershed and how could these uses be affecting the water quality of the river?
- Are there any planned restoration projects in the watershed and, if so, how might they affect yellow lance habitat?

Source: Adapted from Brierre, Ross-Dyjak, Martin, Sivulka, and Woolford (2019).

How can the conservation and restoration of mangroves reduce coastal vulnerability to climate change in the Philippines?

- Which areas are most vulnerable to coastal hazards in the Philippines?
  - What are the main constituents of vulnerability?
  - What is the most appropriate method for integrating all constituents into one metric?
- What are the most appropriate sites for mangrove conservation and restoration among those areas identified as vulnerable?
  - Where are the most vulnerable sites in those areas?
  - What are the effects of existing mangroves in reducing coastal vulnerability?
  - Where would ecosystem services provided by restoring and conserving mangroves benefit the most people?

Source: Adapted from Cogswell, Veiga, and Li (2015).

multilateral institutions like the World Bank and United Nations agencies interact in countries around the world.

- *Comparative Puzzles:* In what ways and why are two situations similar or dissimilar? Examples could include a comparison of two or more local jurisdictions with respect to public transit policy or a comparison of two countries' responses to a global pandemic.

- *Causal Puzzles:* What are the causal drivers of the phenomenon of interest? We might, for example, look at what causes variations in student outcomes, life expectancy, or economic development and at the causal connections between policy and changes in such outcomes.

There are other heuristics unique to policy analysis that can help you define your research puzzle. They're directly linked to the classical models of prospective and retrospective policy analysis:

- *Problems:* What is the size and nature of the policy problem? What are its drivers and downstream consequences?

- *Proposed Policies:* What are the merits of alternative ways of addressing the problem? What would it take to implement each successfully? Should we adopt a particular policy?

- *Existing Policies:* How can we improve, terminate, or replicate an existing public sector program? Are there exemplars of success (or failure) we can look to?

- *Matters of Equity and Fairness:* What is the right thing, ethically oriented and value-driven, to do in a particular situation?

Yes, these are broad, arguably vague, questions. To fine-tune your work, it may help to think about how you would go about solving the research puzzle. Do you plan to reason by deduction, induction, or abduction? Is your focus on normative and moral reasoning, or on descriptive forms of reasoning such as causal and probabilistic reasoning? What kind of conclusions do you hope to draw? To stimulate your thinking, here are six types of analytic conclusion you might try to reach and a fictitious example of each:

- *Descriptive-Retrospective-Unconditional:* The world has warmed by 0.80 °C since 1850.

- *Descriptive-Retrospective-Conditional:* If the 1997 Kyoto Protocol had been adopted by all countries, the world would have warmed by 0.75 °C since 1850.

- *Descriptive-Prospective-Unconditional:* The average temperature in New York City will be hotter in the summer of 2025 than it was in the winter of 2010.

- *Descriptive-Prospective-Conditional:* The world will warm by more than 2.0 °C if the world doesn't cut greenhouse emissions 80% by 2050.

- *Normative Value Judgments* (matters of morality, or of right and wrong): All humans have a sacred duty of stewardship of the earth's natural resources.

- *Normative Policy Judgments* (matters of public policy that ought, or ought not, be addressed): All countries should agree to binding caps on greenhouse gas emissions.

Developing a broad research puzzle is not formulaic. Think holistically about the suggestions I've made, and revisit your starting points (i.e., the deadline, resources, and context for your work). After finalizing the puzzle, the next step is to develop a set of specific **research questions**. Think about how evidence can be logically pieced together to solve the puzzle. Then, create questions to guide your search for evidence. Think of it this way: Answering each research question gives you at least one bit of information to help solve the puzzle.

You'll see, in Exhibit 6-2, a series of questions for each illustrative research puzzle. Note that many of the questions are sequential; often, before you can answer one question, you need to answer another that logically precedes it. Doing so is known as **recursive reasoning**, meaning that you start with the puzzle writ large, or an individual question, and ask what upstream questions must be answered first, before you can answer the downstream questions or solve the entire puzzle.

Brainstorm several research questions before settling on a few about which you will gather relevant evidence. Develop a tentative list of questions and then step back and ponder what results you would have if you manage to successfully answer each. Would you be able to convincingly solve the research puzzle? If not, go back and think again. Treat the set of research questions as a blueprint for your policy analysis; if you don't get it right, then you'll have problems later, as would a carpenter who tried to build a house using a flawed blueprint.

Good research questions are specific, neutral, and don't embed an answer (GAO, 2012). They should be clear and unambiguous (Mason, 2002). Taken together, your research questions—when answered—should add up to a sensible body of evidence that meaningfully addresses the research puzzle. As shown in Exhibit 6-2, sometimes there is a hierarchical structure where subquestions are clustered under higher-level questions. In other cases, all questions are of equal priority. Take care not to omit a research question, which if left unanswered, makes it impossible to generate a complete and coherent solution to your research puzzle.

Your next step is to figure out what is already known about the relevant topics. This is where an evidence search comes into the picture. Don't reinvent the wheel; if evidence already exists to (even partially) answer your research questions, find it rather than take the time to recreate it (Section 6.2 describes several sources of information you might look at). Finally, identify the gap between the evidence you have in hand

and what you'd like to know. This gap, and efforts to narrow it, will become the foundation of your efforts to collect evidence for your policy analysis.

Keep in mind that you only need to narrow the gap to the point where you have usable evidence. You don't need to take the time or expend the resources to narrow the gap further than that. In short, you need a **stopping rule**. Pawson, Wang, and Owen (2011) give us a good example of a stopping rule:

> We simply stop when we are satisfied that explanations are firm enough to carry the policy decision, at least for the time being. (p. 543)

In other words, would gathering more evidence materially change your conclusion about, for example, which proposed policy is optimal or whether an existing program ought to continue or be terminated? If gathering more information wouldn't change the key findings of your work, forget about it, and move on. On the other hand, if you really need more information, keep going with the evidence collection effort.

But what happens if, after doing your analysis (or running out of time), your findings aren't "firm enough to carry the policy decision"? It's an unfortunate, but not infrequent, situation in policy analysis. If you don't have the time or resources to keep going, then stop and develop a clear and concise explanation of why the research questions couldn't be answered with the available evidence. Remember: *your goal is to speak truth to power, not to pretend that you have the truth when you don't.*

One last suggestion for your evidence collection process: stay *focused*. You might get excited about a new database with a great user interface, even though the data themselves aren't particularly relevant to your work, or you could come across a kindly scholar who's happy to spend hours talking to you, even though his or her expertise is applicable to only a sliver of your project. Readily available evidence may be helpful, but it just might be irrelevant, or worse, lead you astray (especially when thrust upon you by issue advocates). In short, look only for the evidence needed to answer your research questions and don't get distracted along the way.

6.2 WHERE CAN YOU FIND NEEDED EVIDENCE?

This section describes seven types of evidence that you might use to conduct a policy analysis:

- Public preferences,
- Stakeholder preferences,
- Expert opinion,
- Academic literature,
- Gray literature,

- Transactional, or 'big,' data, and
- Traditional journalism and social media.

Not all sources of evidence will be relevant or available in every case, but you'll always want to consider whether you can glean useful evidence from each source.

6.2.1 Public Preferences

In a democracy, we aspire for government policy to reflect the views of the people. Public opinion is, thus, a primary source of evidence for policy analysis. But 'the people' don't speak with a single voice. You'll undoubtedly encounter divergent points of view, passion and apathy, bias and bigotry, well-informed opinions, and ignorant opinions. Your goal is not to discern a single, unified public preference (or to substitute your preferences for those of the public). But if you are committed to integrating democratic values into policy analysis, you need to understand the full range of public preferences relevant to the issue on which you're working:

> It may not be possible to get everyone to agree on the same interpretation [of abstract goals and values], but the first task of the political analyst is to reveal and clarify the underlying value disputes so that people can see where they differ and move toward some reconciliation. (Stone, 2012, p. 14)

It's hard to disagree with Stone's (2012) sentiment here, but things get tricky when she aspires to give "every citizen an equal voice in policymaking" (p. 313). The problem is partly logistical. Ensuring that all voices are heard directly is virtually impossible, except in jurisdictions small enough to accommodate direct democracy. Stone (2012) acknowledges as much when she notes that citizen voices must be heard "indirectly through elected officials" (p. 313). So, how can we discern public opinion on specific policy issues? There are several choices:

- *Elections* provide some alignment between citizens' and their representative's views. But elections aren't an especially precise mechanism for discerning public opinion on specific policy issues, particularly for citizens who voted for the losing candidate or didn't vote.

- *Lobbyists* bring preferences and evidence to elected officials' attention. But I once heard a Senate aide say that even though his office was relentlessly lobbied, he never heard the whole story because, as he put it, poor people don't have lobbyists.

- *Community input*, such as meetings, conversations with local organizations, and systematic tracking of constituent comments are ways to understand the views of the citizens. But such techniques must be carefully managed to ensure they're not highjacked by special interests or serve to give a forum only to those with the loudest voices.

- *Opinion polling* offers another means of ascertaining folks' views, although it may provide only broad context rather than the detailed insights needed for policy analysis. Moreover, most surveys capture off-the-top-of-the-head opinions that may not reflect deliberative thought on the part of the respondent.

- *Citizen deliberation* processes can yield insight when, under the management of a neutral nongovernmental institution, a representative group of citizens is recruited to debate a policy issue. Results of the deliberation are summarized and made public (Chhetri, Ghimire, Wagner, & Wang, 2020). These deliberative processes have no formal authority but are sometimes influential in shaping policy debates. Their lack of formal authority and one-off nature, however, may limit their impact (Dryzek et al., 2020).

Having done your best to collect information about the public preferences most relevant to your policy analysis, you have one last task: metaphorically *hearing the voices of those who can't be heard*. As before, I am not suggesting you insert your own personal preferences in lieu of theirs; instead, I am challenging you to figure out first who these folks are and second what they feel and believe so that you can reflect it as appropriate in your policy analysis. Doing so entails asking questions like:

- Who are the voiceless? Where can they be found?

- Why haven't their voices been heard thus far in the process? Do they not care about a particular issue, or have they been systematically excluded?

- Who might be experiencing the consequences of the problem of concern? How and why are they experiencing it?

- Whose lives will be changed if new policies are adopted? How would those changes impact people, families, and communities?

Answering such questions may be a lot tougher than it sounds because *the unheard may have profoundly different worldviews than you do*. Approaching the task with empathy and open-mindedness will help; nonetheless, be prepared for some cognitive dissonance along the way.

I've emphasized citizen preferences and discussed them first because this book is about policy analysis in a democracy. But I am not naïve. You will frequently encounter *clients who aren't interested in the preferences of the general public.* They may be politicians interested in only one slice of the electorate. They could be advocacy groups or government policymakers who already know what policies they support. Or they may be driven to take policy positions that reflect the political and economic power held by their patrons and donors, irrespective of the broader public interest.

6.2.2 Stakeholder Preferences

Stakeholders are folks who have a direct and tangible connection to the policy problems and policy options you're analyzing. Stakeholders may currently be experiencing the cost and downside of a policy problem, or they may be beneficiaries of the status quo with an interest in seeing things remain as they are. Looking to the future, stakeholders' fortunes and well-being could improve, or deteriorate, in different ways under the different policy alternatives you're considering.

Stakeholders can be individuals, firms, nonprofit organizations, communities, governments (e.g., cities or states, or other nations), or agencies within a government, and may be relevant in different ways at different stages in the process of developing and implementing policy. Some stakeholders are important because they can champion a new policy; others are important because they are able to thwart policy change. Stakeholders can also tell you things about a policy issue that you would never have thought of on your own.

When it comes to gathering evidence about stakeholder preferences, you have two tasks: identify specific stakeholders and figure out what they think. Both tasks are much easier when it comes to **self-identified stakeholders**. Such folks lobby policymakers, sign petitions, write op-eds, are visible on social media, or run TV, radio, and online ads. Sometimes, they march in the streets or turn up en masse at public meetings. In short, self-identified stakeholders and their opinions aren't hard to find.

It's harder to characterize the interests of what might be called **invisible stakeholders**. These folks may not even realize there is a debate going on about policy issues that could affect them, directly or indirectly. A school kid and his or her parents, for example, could be *directly affected* if a school board redraws elementary school boundaries and the student ends up assigned to a new school. *Indirect effects* occur when a policy targeted at one group changes their behavior in ways that affect another group. For example, a city's regulation of ride-sharing companies (like Uber and Lyft) might not even mention traditional taxi services. But because they compete for the same customers, regulating ride sharing will probably affect taxi drivers. If the city makes it harder for ride-sharing services to operate, then the taxi industry benefits, and vice versa. In short, when trying to identify stakeholders, don't overlook invisible stakeholders who may be directly or indirectly affected by the policies being debated.

6.2.3 Expert Opinion

Google has made it so simple to find information online that it's easy to forget how much we can learn by talking to a real person. There are plenty of smart people who know a lot about policy issues, but who stay out of the public eye and don't share their expertise online. My advice is to find the time to push back from your keyboard, pick up the phone, and talk to some knowledgeable folks. The nature of human interaction means that you can often uncover a lot of information very quickly in a person-to-person conversation. Even a 15-minute call with a well-informed source will help you climb the learning curve.[2] But don't rely on one person to get the whole picture. He or she may not share your passion for neutral analysis and might inadvertently—or intentionally—give you only one side of the story. Chat with several folks to get insights from different perspectives.

So, who should you talk to? You're looking for folks so deeply familiar with the issue you're working on that their 'off-the-top' comments will be valuable. Before you pick up the phone, however, do your homework. Make sure you know the basics of an issue; don't waste precious time on the phone asking questions that you could answer for yourself with a few seconds on the web. Create a loose list of questions or topics to guide the conversation, but leave ample time for follow-up questions that are prompted by the discussion itself.[3] Toward the end of the conversation, be sure to ask whether there are any questions that you haven't asked but you should have. (You'd be surprised at how often this one question yields valuable nuggets of information that you might otherwise not have found.)

Finally, you may be lucky enough to work for an organization that has access to on-call expertise. If you work for the US Congress, for example, you can call on agencies like the Congressional Research Service. If you work in an executive branch agency, there is almost certainly a policy office, program evaluation group, or research and development function that employs folks with relevant expertise.

6.2.4 Academic Literature

Academic literature, which we touched on in Section 5.1.1, is peer reviewed and published in a scholarly journal or by a university press. While imperfect, peer review often ferrets out unfounded assumptions, incomplete data, and weak conclusions. The strongest policy claims, thus, rely on evidence from the peer-reviewed literature.

One difficulty with academic literature is that the intended audience is almost always other scholars rather than practicing policy analysts. In most journals, authors

---

[2] If the expert is a busy person, you might have to settle for an email exchange, but the concept is the same.

[3] Academics call these conversations semistructured interviews.

assume that readers have deep subject matter expertise and strong technical skills. Extracting actionable, policy-relevant insights from such literature can be tough for a policy analyst. Rather than trying to plow through an academic article from start to finish, study the abstract carefully, then read the introduction, scan the section and subsection headings, and read the conclusion (Keshav, 2007).

Depending on the topic, you may find a great deal of relevant literature. I just searched Google Scholar (which indexes only academic literature) for 'best practices for policy reform' and got 1.4 million hits. In other words, you almost certainly can't find and read all the relevant academic literature. Even if you have two or three months to do an analysis, you probably can't scan more than a few dozen academic studies. And if you have a tight timeline, you may have to be content to read a few abstracts. If you can find the right person, an academic expert may be able to help you navigate the literature.

Another way to narrow your search of the academic literature is to investigate the contents of What Works Clearinghouses maintained by both independent researchers and by government agencies. These sites collect retrospective evaluations of existing policies and programs. The Cochrane US Network (us.cochrane.org), for example, compiles a wide range of systematic evidence on various health-care programs while the Campbell Collaboration (campbellcollaboration.org) offers similar content focused on criminal justice, disability, education, international development, nutrition, and social welfare. The Pew and MacArthur Foundations manage the Results First Clearinghouse Database which links to nine clearinghouses with information about programs in fields like criminal justice, child welfare, education, and health (www.pewtrusts.org/en/projects/pew-macarthur-results-first-initiative).

Clearinghouses typically include studies from the academic literature about how well the evaluated programs actually worked in the real world and whether they created significant impacts. Such material can be helpful in two ways. First, evidence about whether a particular program has a track record of success can help you decide whether to include an analogous policy option in your analysis. Second, if you do decide to include it, historical evidence about its prior performance can then be used in the later parts of your analysis when you are weighing the pros and cons of the options under consideration.

You may recall from our discussion of the scientific method that the scholarly community doesn't consider a single study definitive. Instead, it takes several studies, tackling a topic in different ways, to reach similar conclusions before a finding is accepted as provisionally true. Therein lies another problem for a policy analyst trying to rely on the academic literature. The typical journal article won't give you a good handle on the degree of scholarly consensus on all the issues you care about. As a rough rule of thumb, however, the more times an article has been cited in other research, the bigger its impact on the scholarly conversation. Accordingly, it often makes sense to focus on widely cited academic studies.

There are two other types of academic literature that may be more useful to you. The first is a **systematic review** which synthesizes the literature on a particular topic. It will typically trace the arc of thinking on the topic, note broad themes within the literature, identify areas of consensus, and characterize ongoing academic debates. A related form of synthetic study is a **meta-analysis**, which collects studies that focus on measuring the same phenomenon. The term of art here is **effect size**, meaning a quantitative measure of the result of an intervention. A meta-analysis looks at the underlying data in each study and aggregates them. The result is an estimate of the effect size based not just on one study, but on a collection of studies.

6.2.5 Gray Literature

While the academic literature offers the strongest and most credible evidence, you may have a hard time finding directly relevant material. You can, however, often find an abundance of **gray literature**, which tends to be issue-specific and more up to date than academic literature. Gray literature refers to:

> … a wide variety of unpublished or informally published information from different groups such as professional associations, research institutes, government agencies, and non-profit organizations. (University of Vermont Libraries, 2017)

Gray literature relevant to public policy issues comes primarily from two sources: government agencies and nongovernmental organizations (NGOs). As for government agencies in the United States, gray literature is produced by:

- Executive branch departments and independent agencies (like the Department of Defense or the Environmental Protection Agency);
- Units within the executive branch that have a specific data collection mission (like the Agency for Healthcare Research and Quality or the Bureau of Labor Statistics);
- Congressional agencies (like the Congressional Budget Office, the Congressional Research Service, and the Government Accountability Office); and
- State and local agencies (like the California Legislative Analyst's Office and the New York City Office of Management and Budget).

In addition, the Federal Reserve Board—not part of the executive or legislative branches—compiles statistics and does analyses of a wide range of topics related to the nation's economy.

Some of the gray literature produced by government agencies is of very high quality. Programs in the Federal Statistical System, for example, operate under Statistical Policy Directives that dictate best practices and quality control measures (OMB, 2017). And more than twenty agencies have adopted formal scientific integrity policies to guide their work (CRS, 2021).

In other cases, government agencies have broad latitude to undertake analyses that result in publication of gray literature, such as program evaluations, agency reports, white papers, legislative testimony, budget justifications, and rulemaking documents. These analyses may originate in a request from Congress or may be initiated at the behest of political appointees in the Executive Branch. Such analyses are often a neutral and reliable source of evidence. But sometimes their ultimate purpose is to support a politically derived policy position. A case-by-case evaluation is needed to assess the quality and objectivity of the evidence in this type of governmental gray literature.

Nongovernmental gray literature is very diverse, ranging from neutral studies of specific issues to materials plainly advocating a particular point of view. When it comes to NGOs, gray literature is produced by think tanks, foundations, the National Academies of Science, multilateral institutions (like the World Bank), and advocacy groups from across the ideological and economic spectrum.

Gray literature is sometimes so flawed that it offers a weak foundation for a policy claim. Shoddy work by an inept analyst can be relatively easy to detect, but given the frequent weaponization of policy analysis, you should be cautious when looking at work published by advocacy groups. These groups intentionally abandon the goal of neutrality, often without acknowledging that they have done so. Strong writing, lots of facts and figures, a polished presentation, and an impressive website may camouflage a one-sided analysis intended only to achieve a political win.

Finally, there's Wikipedia. Some people think of it as gray literature, others as social media. Either way, remember that all information on Wikipedia is crowd-sourced, meaning that almost anyone can change the content of the site at any time. It's ok to check Wikipedia to stimulate your thinking on a topic and to find links to other sources you may want to check out, but serious scholars don't consider Wikipedia definitive, and neither should you.

6.2.6 Transactional, or 'Big,' Data

Thanks to a revolution in information and communication technology, the types of data available to policy analysts are profoundly different from what were available even a decade ago. As transactions between citizens and government (like benefit transfers, issuance of drivers' licenses, provision of health care, collection of road tolls, standardized testing of students … the list is long) have become increasingly automated, a by-product has been vast amounts of data. What's more, new technologies like smart vehicle and road technologies, real-time air pollution measurements, and police bodycams, to name just a few, disgorge enormous quantities of data. Coupled with an internet capable of quickly transferring gigabytes of information, 'big' data are everywhere.

This is not a data science textbook, so I won't talk about how to use transactional data for policy analysis, but I do want to make two quick observations. First, it's important to be aware of the deeper insight you might be able to gain from the work of data scientists mining policy-relevant data. Second, be on the lookout for opportunities to combine datasets of administrative records in novel ways. Perhaps, for example, you can link income tax records to participant records from social welfare programs to study the causal impact of the program on participant earnings. Of course, privacy protection is an important concern, but researchers continue to develop methods to link and anonymize administrative data to protect privacy while still giving researchers what they need.

6.2.7 Traditional Journalism and Social Media

Traditional **journalism** comes from organizations that aspire to "seek truth and report it, minimize harm, act independently, and be accountable and transparent" (SPJ, 2014, p. 1). Examples include national and regional newspapers, newsmagazines, news services, and radio and television news. Often referred to as the first draft of history, traditional journalism can be a source of evidence to help you understand the context of an issue and point you to the stakeholders who are affected by an issue. But because it is deadline-driven, time- and space-constrained, and focused on newsworthy stories that hold its audience's attention, traditional media is not a source of definitive evidence for your policy analysis.

One exception to this rule may be investigative, or long-form, journalism. Pulitzer Prize winning examples include *The Boston Globe's* investigation of sexual abuse in the Catholic Church, the *Anchorage Daily News* and ProPublica's series on the lack of police services in Alaskan villages, and *The Wall Street Journal's* probe of fraudulent stock options for business executives (Pulitzer Prize Board, 2020).

The definition of traditional *journalism does not extend to the free-form punditry* of charismatic people on talk radio, cable news, or online. Even though such folks may address issues of public policy and sometimes sound like journalists, they are offering opinion and occasionally entertainment. You might tune in, but only to hear what folks are saying, not to gather reliable evidence.

Finally, remember that traditional journalism comes in three forms: **reporting, analysis**, and **editorial opinion**. *The New York Times* and *The Wall Street Journal*, for example, take a very similar approach to news reporting, but have multiple columnists whose analysis reflects different points of view. The two papers also offer radically different editorial opinions. Make sure you know what kind of journalism you're looking at.

A tidal wave of information flows through **social media** every day. In general, it is a bad idea to rely on social media when doing policy analysis. During the 2020 US elections, for example, dozens of falsehoods circulated on social media. But given its ubiquity and the fact that researchers, think tanks, advocacy groups, and government agencies all take to social media to tout their latest findings and policy pronouncements, you can't ignore it. So, how should you think about policy-relevant claims found on social media?

First, never forget that virtually all social media outlets are in the advertising business. Facebook, Twitter, and Instagram are free, not because of the high-mindedness of their shareholders, but because advertisers pay for access to you and your attention. The more time you spend looking at your feed, the more links you click, and the more items you like and share, the more money they make. Think about what this business model does to the motives of the social media companies. They don't want to lose your eyeballs; instead, the algorithms that create your newsfeed try to keep you in an affectively charged state (interested, outraged, validated). Exposing you to both sides of an issue, pushing inconvenient truths to the top of your feed, and causing you cognitive dissonance might be great for policy analysis, but it is antithetical to the social media business model.

Second, look at the set of folks you follow on social media. Ask yourself whether you're *using social media for information or for affirmation* of your worldview. If your newsfeed is composed primarily of influencers, pundits, and activists who share your ideological point of view, then it's not a reliable source of news about public policy.[4] There is no harm in using social media to broaden your thinking, but always click through to the source and subject that source—not the tweets about it nor the comments when it is shared—to critical review.

If the original source is a blog, proceed with caution. Blog posts can be timely and insightful; several brilliant analysts maintain blogs. So do a lot of folks with fringe opinions. Blogs are easy to churn out and are not peer reviewed. They can be idiosyncratic and dependent on the attitudes, research skills, and whims of their authors. If you're suspicious about a claim, visit websites like factcheck.org, snopes.com, politifact.com, or *The Washington Post* fact-checker to see if you can learn more.

---

[4]One assignment I give my policy students is to follow at least a couple dozen politicians, activists, and advocacy group whose views they disagree with. It is often an eye-opening experience for students.

6.3 ASSESSING THE VALIDITY OF INFERENCES FROM EVIDENCE

You've sifted through all the potential sources of information—from public and stakeholder preferences to expert option and big data to the academic and gray literature—to uncover evidence relevant to your policy analysis. But not all evidence is equally relevant; some of it is really important and some of it can be safely ignored. So, how can you sort the useful stuff from the not-so-useful stuff? For me, the most intuitive place to start is with the concept of **validity**.

Scientists use the word validity to capture the *degree to which relevant evidence demonstrates that an inference, knowledge claim, or proposition is the best available approximation of the truth* (Shadish, Cook, & Campbell, 2002; Trochim, 2007). Put another way, validity captures the quality of the fit, or degree of alignment, between:

- Our mind's internal understanding of the external world, and

- The nature of the evidence we glean from that external world.

If the inferences you draw from your evidence don't satisfy the tests of validity because they're not the best approximation of the truth, then practically speaking, the evidence isn't of much use. In this section, we'll talk about construct validity, conclusion validity, internal validity, and external validity.

6.3.1 Construct Validity

A **construct** is our internal, or mental, representation of some aspect of the external world. In policy analysis, constructs typically capture the ways in which we think about public problems, their causes, their effects, and efforts to address them. You might remember from Chapter 1 our mock policy analysis of affordable housing in Arlington; that example was full of constructs including quality of life, affordability, development incentives, administrability, public housing, and about a dozen more. Each of these topics is a mental, or conceptual, representation of a particular phenomenon of interest.

Of course, if we just let constructs bounce around in our heads without testing them against reality, they wouldn't be much use to us when it comes to policy analysis. So, from the real-world side of things, we use observation to collect *evidence* about phenomena of interest. *Constructs* are then linked to evidence in a process usually referred to as *operationalization*, in which we try to align our internal ideas and theories with our external observations and collected data. The better the fit between our construct and our evidence, the higher the construct validity. Exhibit 6-3 summarizes the process.

Exhibit 6-3   The Elements of Construct Validity

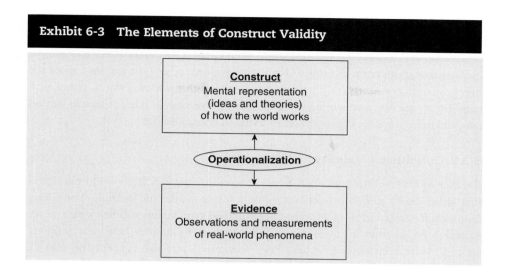

Operationalization can go both ways. Sometimes, we look at evidence (collections of tents beneath freeway overpasses throughout a city) and attach to it a construct (perhaps, in this case, pervasive homelessness). In other cases, we go in the opposite direction, when we already have in mind a construct and then develop measures for which we'll collect data to characterize the state of that construct in the external, real world. For example, we might be interested in the construct of a high-quality secondary education. To operationalize our construct, we need to identify measures that capture its essence and connect them to our internal mental representation. We might, for example, decide that the quality of secondary education can be operationalized by looking at metrics like test scores, graduation rates, or equality of postgraduation employment outcomes across socioeconomic lines.

Construct validity also comes into play when we engage in causal reasoning. We might have a theory that Cause A produces Effect B. In this context, both A and B are mental constructs; to test our theory, we need to find a way to operationalize both constructs with a collection of observations about each of them. To continue our example from above, we might have a theory about how to improve the quality of secondary education using, say, curriculum reform, smaller class sizes, and after-school tutoring. These three policy measures, each of which is its own construct, would then be viewed as potential causal drivers in changing educational quality; accordingly, we need to operationalize all three. What, specifically, would be changed in the curriculum? How much smaller would classes be? What would be the nature and extent of the tutoring? Once we've operationalized all our cause constructs and our effect constructs, we can then collect the evidence we need to assess the causal relationships among them. We'll talk more about this in Section 6.3.3.

Before leaving the topic of construct validity, we need to look more closely at the lower portion of Exhibit 6-3, which depicts the collection of evidence through the observation and measurement of real-world phenomena. Observational evidence can be qualitative or quantitative in nature. **Qualitative** evidence relies on a narrative about the things we're interested in and the connections among them. It uses words, rather than numbers, to describe what's being studied. **Quantitative** analysis relies at least in part on numbers to measure the constructs we're trying to operationalize.

6.3.2 Conclusion Validity

Another test of validity captures the degree to which the conclusions and inferences that we've drawn from our evidence are sound, reasonable, and credible. For a long time, scholars referred to this concept as **statistical conclusion validity** with a heavy emphasis on whether all quantitative and statistical techniques had been properly applied. More recently, researchers have recognized that the concept can also be applied to qualitative research by simply asking whether "a reasonable conclusion" has been "inferred from the observations" (Trochim, 2007, p. 258). Let's take a look at conclusion validity in three contexts: univariate quantitative, multivariate quantitative, and qualitative applications.

Univariate quantitative measures capture the behavior of a single variable. The average temperature in July, the percentage of voters who approve of the President's performance, and the rate of violent crime in a city are all examples of phenomena that can be described with univariate statistics, such as their mean, median, and standard deviation. To ensure that inferences drawn from univariate measures exhibit conclusion validity, we need to check for the correct application of the appropriate statistical techniques. This isn't a stats textbook, so I'll just mention two key points:

- First, in most cases, we don't study the entire population of interest, but instead analyze only a sample of cases. The thing to remember is that we want our sample to be as representative as possible, meaning that each member of the population is equally likely to be sampled.

- Second, samples need to be big enough to deliver the desired level of precision. If we're looking at the percentage of folks who approve of the President's performance, the margin of error for a sample of 100 people is about plus or minus ten percentage points.[5] If the sample size is 1,000 people, the margin of error shrinks to about three percentage points. Though more difficult to obtain, when it comes to samples, bigger is better.

---

[5]Meaning that 95 out of 100 random samples of the population would yield an approval rating within this range.

Multivariate quantitative analysis focuses on the association between two or more variables. Crosstabulation, correlation and covariance, and multiple regression are all multivariate statistical techniques. Each technique carries with it assumptions that must be satisfied and methods that must be followed for the result to be considered valid. As with univariate statistics, multivariate analyses exhibit the highest levels of conclusion validity when the data to which they are applied are most representative of the population. Similarly, sample size is also important for multivariate analysis, with larger samples allowing for more precise inferences.

Statisticians use probability theory to determine how likely it is that the observed relationship between two variables might have occurred by random chance within the sample, rather than because of a true association in the population. The statistical likelihood of a particular finding depends on both the true effect size and the sample size. If two variables are, in fact, highly correlated, a small sample may still allow you to distinguish that relationship from random variation, while a more modest effect may go undetected in a small sample. With a larger sample, you can detect smaller effect sizes and, if they exist, confirm that they are unlikely to have occurred by random chance.

But just because a relationship is unlikely to have occurred because of random sampling error, that doesn't mean it's substantively significant. Suppose a vocational education program raises average participant income by a miniscule amount, say, $10 per year. If your sample is big enough, you will be able to detect this effect and distinguish it from random chance, but in a real-world context, it hardly matters. In short, conclusion validity depends not only on the quality of your statistical analysis but also on how reasonable your interpretation of those statistics is.

Qualitative analysis doesn't typically entail mathematical computation; nonetheless, conclusion validity is still important. Even if there isn't a number anywhere to be found in an analysis, we can still assess conclusion validity. Recall the basic test of conclusion validity: are the inferences about a particular phenomenon that we've drawn from our evidence sound reasonable and credible? If so, those inferences can be said to exhibit conclusion validity.

This might make more sense with an example. Suppose we read a series of narrative case studies done by a researcher who visits several rural counties to investigate opioid abuse. She observes repeated patterns of conditions related to employment, health care, and education that systematically differ between counties severely affected by opioid abuse and those that are not. If she has selected the counties to study in an unbiased way, proceeded in a consistent and methodical way, and carefully and logically drawn her conclusions from the evidence she has observed (rather than from preconceived notions), we can feel comfortable ascribing conclusion validity to her findings.

6.3.3 Internal Validity and Causality

Internal validity focuses on the degree to which the inferred relationship between two constructs is a causal one. To confirm the internal validity of inferences related to causality, we need to do two things. First, we need to verify that the tenets of causal reasoning are met. As you may remember from Section 5.2.2, there are three mandatory and one optional test for assessing causality:

- Check for temporal precedence to ensure that the cause takes place prior to the effect.

- Confirm that there is covariation between the cause and the effect. Such covariation needn't be linear, but it must be consistent and predictable.

- Rule out competing explanations that, if true, could have produced the observed pattern of covariation. Doing so leaves the posited causal relationship as the only plausible explanation of the observed relationship.

- Try to come up with a theoretical explanation of how and why variations in the cause are producing variations in the effect. With a theory in hand, you can be more confident about the inferred causal relationship than if you don't know why the cause is producing the effect.

The second task is to incorporate the two forms of validity we just discussed, construct and conclusion validity, in your assessment of internal validity. This should make intuitive sense. If we haven't convincingly operationalized both the cause constructs and the effect constructs, then inferences about their relationship are inherently suspect, no matter what observed evidence we have at hand. Similarly, if we can't confirm the validity of the conclusions drawn about the nature and magnitude of the relationship between cause and effect (e.g., by checking that appropriate statistical techniques have been correctly applied and that any qualitative reasoning is logically sound), then we can't make a valid causal claim.

The most powerful means of validating internal causality is the **randomized experiment**, which is often called the "gold standard" of research (Shadish, Cook, & Campbell, 2002, p. 13). As explained in Section 2.6, random assignment of participants between treatment and control groups ensures that, in a statistical sense, the two groups are identical save for the first group's exposure to the treatment (examples of a treatment might include a new drug or medical procedure, a revised educational curriculum, or a program for former prisoners returning to their community). Any subsequent differences between the outcomes (i.e., effects) observed in the treatment and control groups can then be attributed to the treatment (i.e., the cause).

If a randomized experiment is infeasible, scholars often turn to **multivariate quantitative analysis** of whatever data are available, and endeavor to statistically control for factors (beyond the treatment itself) that might vary between folks who receive a treatment and those who do not. In this way, it may be possible to rule out competing explanations of the observed relationship between the cause and effect constructs, thereby satisfying the third test of causality. Of course, if a multivariate quantitative analysis can't confirm a statistically significant relationship between cause and effect, after controlling for other variables that might distort our understanding of the causal relationship, then conclusion validity is absent and so too is internal validity.

6.3.4 External Validity and Generalizability

External validity refers to the degree to which findings from one study can be generalized to other situations. For starters, we can only meaningfully consider the topic of external validity after we've convinced ourselves that the inferences drawn from our evidence satisfy the tests of construct, conclusion, and internal validity. If they don't, then we needn't bother with external validity because these other tests provide the foundation upon which external validity rests.

If those tests *are* met, however, we can investigate whether it's possible to generalize—in a valid way—from the study we have in hand to other situations where we might apply its findings. Other situations are traditionally characterized along four dimensions (Shadish, Cook, & Campbell, 2002):

- *Units* are the objects of study. They are the entities that are exposed to causes and that may consequently experience causal effects. Examples of units include people, groups, events, governments, institutions, relationships, or communities.

- *The Treatment* can include policies, programs, actions, events, or therapies to which units are exposed. The goal is to figure out whether treatment induces changes among treated units and whether lack of treatment is associated with the absence of such changes.

- *Observations* are the measured outcomes that researchers suspect are affected by treatment. In a well-designed study, observations credibly operationalize all the constructs being analyzed.

- *The Setting* is the location and conditions under which treatment is studied. It might refer to a school or workplace, or perhaps a geographical location. Conditions like the time of day, or the sense of safety felt by people in the study, might be relevant attributes of the setting.

When we assess external validity, we aspire to figure out if a causal relationship that has been credibly confirmed in one situation (i.e., a unique and specific combination of units, a treatment, a collection of observations, and a particular setting) can be reasonably generalized to other units, treatments, observations, and settings.

Doing so is not easy. Having passed the tests of construct, conclusion, and internal validity, you can be confident that the program or policy you're looking at did work at a particular point in time and in a given context. But the fact that the policy *worked* (then and there) is not proof that the policy *works* (in general) or that the policy will *work* (here and now). These changes of verb tense are not trivial differences; they are at the heart of the issue of external validity (Cartwright & Hardie, 2012). We'll spend more time on this topic in Chapter 14, when we talk about generalizing from existing policies when designing new policies. For now, just bear in mind that it's a long path, with respect to causal reasoning, relevant evidence, and real-world implementation, to get from a successful policy in one place to a successful policy in another. And, unfortunately, sometimes that path leads to a dead end.

6.4 CAN YOU TRUST THE EVIDENCE YOU'VE FOUND?

Section 6.2 identified seven different information sources you might check to find evidence relevant to your policy analysis, and Section 6.3 laid out four tests of validity that if satisfied increase the likelihood that inferences drawn from your evidence are tentatively true. But even if you meticulously follow the advice in these two sections, you may still not be where you need to be with respect to your evidence. You will probably have uncovered contradictory evidence or evidence that, despite your best efforts, you don't have the right technical skills to fully comprehend. After all, sophisticated policy analysis can get complicated. Few of us have the right experience and training to critically evaluate all the evidence. Just like we might consult a physician when dealing with a health issue, we are often forced to rely on the expertise of others when we analyze a policy issue.

Your approach to assessing expertise needs to be calibrated to which source of evidence you're looking at. The easiest case is social media, where you should not presume the expertise of anyone who posts anything. If you click through to the original source, then you're likely to find one another form of evidence and you can evaluate its analytical value accordingly. But if you don't dig deeper, then social media content by itself does not deserve a place in your policy analysis.

When it comes to citizen preferences, my advice is to take them at face value. Whether you agree or disagree with those preferences, or whether they seem well founded or completely irrational, they are—by definition in a democracy—a source of evidence that must be considered. Stakeholder preferences are similar in that they reflect points of view that are undoubtedly relevant to your analysis, but you'll want to cast a critical eye on any evidence proffered by those stakeholders. As the saying goes, people are entitled to their opinions, but not their own facts. Accordingly, you need to assess stakeholder-provided evidence in the same manner as you would the evidence you've collected yourself from experts, the academic and gray literature, traditional journalism, and the analysis of transactional data. The remainder of this section focuses on these sources of evidence.

How can you decide who to believe when you can't be an expert in everything? As far as I know, you can't check Yelp for ratings of scholars, pundits, and policy wonks. Philip Tetlock, a political scientist who has been studying the issue for close to 40 years, gives us a modern take on the risks you face when you rely on the expertise of others:

> ... every day, all of us—leaders of nations, corporate executives, investors, and voters—make critical decision on the basis of forecasts whose quality is unknown. Baseball managers wouldn't dream of getting out the checkbook to hire a player without consulting performance statistics. ... And yet when it comes to the forecasters who help us make decisions that matter far more than any baseball game, we're content to be ignorant. ... It is as though we have collectively concluded that sizing up the starting lineup for the Yankees deserves greater care than sizing up the risk of genocide in South Sudan. (Tetlock & Gardner, 2015, pp. 3, 291)

This section aims to help you avoid the risks that Tetlock eloquently points out by figuring out who to trust. As a point of departure, let's consider how the US judicial system defines expertise. Witnesses in court may offer an opinion only on things about which they have firsthand knowledge. But, if the witness is formally designated as an expert, then she may offer an opinion that goes beyond firsthand observation. The Federal Rules of Evidence specify that someone who is qualified:

> ... as an expert by knowledge, skill, experience, training, or education may testify in the form of an opinion ... if (a) the expert's scientific, technical, or other specialized knowledge will help the trier of fact to understand the evidence or to determine a fact in issue; (b) the testimony is based on sufficient facts or data; (c) the testimony is the product of reliable principles and methods; and (d) the expert has reliably applied the principles and methods to the facts of the case. (U.S. Supreme Court, 2019)

If we parse this language, we observe a couple of things. Although expertise depends in part on a person's background and capability, it also must fit the current situation appropriately. What's more, the expertise must be relevant to the matter at hand, and it must be applied in an expert manner.

The expert whose evidence you rely on for your policy analysis might not clear the high bar set for an expert witness in a federal court, but you still want them to be as trustworthy as possible. As management guru Stephen M. R. Covey is fond of saying, **trustworthiness** depends on competence and character (2017). I think of competence as expertise and of character as the author's propensity to use that expertise in appropriate ways. Below are three suggestions for figuring out whether someone's statements are worth your trust.

First, consider the author's **competence**. When it comes to competence, the Federal Rules of Evidence point us in the right direction. An author with the relevant skills and knowledge, and a well-earned reputation for successfully applying their talents to difficult problems, deserves more deference than an author who does not. Assessing competence—without personally knowing the author—can be difficult, but it's worth a try.

- Google the author to figure out what credentials and work experience they have. Try to get a handle on their reputation—good, bad, or indifferent.

- Look for reviews of their earlier work and its strengths and weaknesses. Folks may find it difficult to repudiate earlier work even if new evidence suggests doing so would be wise.

- Even if you decide the author is an expert in one area, confirm that his or her expertise matches the subject at hand, and they haven't fallen prey to the Dunning–Kruger effect.[6]

If you decide the author isn't particularly competent, or that he or she is operating outside their areas of expertise, you really don't have a choice. You need to discount (perhaps considerably) what they say.

Next, apply the second element in Covey's definition of trustworthiness and assess the author's **character**. It can be hard to get a handle on character from a distance but if you can satisfy yourself that the author consistently tends toward open-mindedness, integrity, and transparency, then they deserve a higher level of your trust. You're looking for indications that the expert is offering advice untainted by close-mindedness, conflict of interest, or an intent to mislead. These forms of bias, if undetected, can lead you to uncritically accept a policy claim that is, in fact, flawed.

---

[6]See Chapter 4 for a refresher on the Dunning–Kruger effect as a source of cognitive error.

There are several questions you can ask about a particular piece of analysis that may tip you off to the presence of bias.

- Does the author's job depend on supporting the interests of his or her employer? If so, it may be difficult to stake out positions contradictory to the employer's.

- Is the funder of the work active in partisan politics? If so, the sponsor might endeavor to influence the analyst.

- Does the author work in an institutional environment with a single ideological perspective? If so, his or her work may not capture the full range of issues relevant to your analysis.

- Does the author have a personal interest in the outcome of the debate? If he or she is potentially a winner or loser under the policies being considered, it may be hard to set aside their economic interest and deliver an unbiased analysis.

- Does the author have a motive to be overly dramatic in their presentation? Driven by a desire for viewers, readers, likes, or upvotes, some authors focus on telling an exciting and sensational story rather than on conveying the subtleties and nuances of a complex issue.

If you detect bias, does that mean you need to disregard the evidence entirely? No. Despite the bias, it may contain useful information that you are able to independently validate. Your goal is to become a critical consumer of policy analysis, rather than someone who accepts all claims at face value.

Finally, look for **humility about uncertainty**. Our insight into past events and current conditions is often limited. Data can be incomplete, and key phenomena may be subject to debate. What's more, visualizing the future under different policy scenarios is even tougher. But that doesn't stop many folks from offering a forceful opinion about what will happen if a particular policy is, or is not, adopted. Ironically, rather than increasing your confidence in an author's conclusions, bold statements that admit no uncertainty about current or future conditions should cause you to question his or her credibility. The following questions may help you figure out if the person behind the evidence meets this test.

- Does the claim display appropriate humility when characterizing the uncertainties associated with current conditions?

- Does the claim recognize uncertainty about the future? Are projected outcomes qualified with explanations about how and why events might turn out differently?

- Does the author mistakenly extrapolate from a single example to conclude that inherently uncertain events are in fact certain?

- Instead of providing quantitative forecasts only as point estimates, does the claim suggest a range of outcomes (e.g., a best case and a worst case) to capture future uncertainties?

- When describing uncertainty, is the claim clear about the meaning of the vocabulary it uses? For example, is the probability of a 'likely' outcome 51% or 90%? Phrases such as probably will, might not, extremely unlikely, and almost certain mean different things to different people.[7]

The author of a policy claim that displays absolute, unchecked confidence in their own conclusions does not deserve your full trust, and their evidence should be discounted accordingly.

6.5 AN INTEGRATED VIEW OF COLLECTING AND ASSESSING EVIDENCE FOR POLICY ANALYSIS

We've covered several topics related to evidence: figuring out what to look for, identifying where to look, and assessing the validity and trustworthiness of what you find. Now, let's think about *putting everything together*. I've sketched an overview of the process in Exhibit 6-4 to guide this discussion. Like all stylized representations of a policy analysis process, it should be taken with a grain of salt. I've given the process a linear and algorithmic structure to help you follow its logic. Doing so is an over-simplification; in the real world, you would likely jump around within (and outside) the process. But the holistic view described here should get you on your way toward a well-reasoned, credible, and defensible evaluation of your evidence.

If you look at Exhibit 6-4, it may seem overwhelming. For now, just try to get the gist of it and save it for later reference. This process has three main parts. The first reviews the process of collecting and evaluating evidence—both on a piece-by-piece basis and in the aggregate. The second describes how to decide how much confidence in the evidence you've collected is warranted. And the third describes how probabilistic reasoning can be used to characterize the likelihood of uncertain outcomes or the degree of confidence in your conclusion.

In this context, it's easy to mix up the words **confidence** and **likelihood**. Both are measured on a continuum and address similar concepts, but they have different

---

[7]Revisit Section 5.6 if you want a refresher on probabilistic reasoning and words of estimative probability.

Exhibit 6-4   Evaluating the Available Evidence to Answer Your Research Questions

Evidence Search
Based on Research Puzzle & Questions (Section 6.1)

Available Evidence (Section 6.2)

Sources
- Public Preferences
- Stakeholder Preferences
- Expert Opinion
- Academic Literature
- Gray Literature
- Transactional Data
- Traditional Journalism

Techniques
- Quantitative: Statistical & Experimental
- Qualitative: Narrative & Interpretative

Evaluation of Each Piece of Evidence (Sections 6.3 & 6.4)
- Extent & Rigor of Data Collection
- Validity of Reasoning
- Potential for Bias
- Strength of Conclusion
- Trust in Author's Expertise
- Relevance to Research Questions

Evaluation of Body of Evidence
- Quantity & Quality of Evidence
- Degree of Agreement Across Evidence

Sufficient Evidence & Agreement to Characterize Confidence?
- Yes
- No

Describe nature of evidence and level of agreement, noting **inability to assess confidence**

Describe level of **confidence in evidence** related to each research question

Level of Confidence		Extent of Evidence		
		Limited	Moderate	Robust
Level of Agreement Across Sources	High	Medium	High	Very High
	Medium	Low	Medium	High
	Low	Very Low	Low	Medium

Very High Confidence	Strong Evidence: Established theory, multiple sources, consistent results, well documented & accepted methods, high consensus
High Confidence	Moderate Evidence: Several sources, some consistency, methods vary and/or documentation limited, medium consensus
Medium Confidence	Suggestive Evidence: A few sources, limited consistency, models incomplete, methods emerging, competing schools of thought
Low Confidence	Inconclusive Evidence: Limited sources, inconsistent findings, poor documentation, untested methods, negligible expert opinion
Very Low Confidence	Little to No Evidence: Very few sources, unconvincing findings, no documentation, opaque methods, no expert opinion

Sufficient Confidence in Evidence to Permit Probabilistic Reasoning?
- Yes
- No

Describe level of confidence in evidence, noting **inability to reason probabilistically**

Characterize **likelihood of uncertain outcome or or degree of confidence** in validity of answer to each research question

Words of Estimative Probability	Numeric Probability	
Virtually certain	>99%	> 99 in 100
Very likely	90%-99%	> 9 in 10
Likely	66%-90%	> 2 in 3
About as likely as not	33%-66%	~ 1 in 2
Unlikely	10%-33%	< 1 in 3
Very unlikely	1%-10%	< 1 in 10
Exceptionally unlikely	<1%	< 1 in 100

Present likelihood of uncertain **outcome or or degree of confidence** in validity of knowledge claim, using numeric probabilities and/or words of estimative probability for each research question

Create **traceable account** to capture & make transparent your use of evidence

Source: Adapted from EFSA Scientific Committee (2017), Janzwood (2020), Mach, Mastrandrea, Freeman, and Field (2017), and USGCRP (2018)

meanings here. Confidence reflects the degree to which we believe our evidence provides a sound and credible basis for drawing a conclusion. Or, as the US Intelligence Community puts it, "confidence levels ... reflect the scope and quality of the information supporting its judgments" (ODNI, 2011, p. 60). On the other hand, the word likelihood has a meaning akin to statistical chance. The ODNI explains: "Statements that address the subject of likelihood are intended to reflect the ... probability of a development or an event occurring" (ODNI, 2011, p. 59).

For example, a robust body of qualitative evidence on childhood development might give us high confidence that we understand how such development occurs, but might not be sufficiently detailed to permit quantified, probabilistic statements about various aspects of the development process. On the other hand, we might have a robust collection of evidence on a different topic (e.g., the relationship of national debt to economic growth) in which we have high confidence *and* that allows probabilistic reasoning (e.g., that a 20% increase in debt leads to a 2% decrease in growth).

The process in Exhibit 6-4 is sequential. Let's look at each major element in the exhibit. The ultimate goal of this process is to come up with the evidence you need to solve your research puzzle and answer the associated research questions, so that's where we start. Section 6.1 described how to come up with the puzzle and questions to guide your search, while Section 6.2 suggested seven types of evidence to consider. When you finish this step of the process, you will have a collection of evidence that needs to be reviewed on a piece-by-piece basis.

As described in Sections 6.3 and 6.4, for each piece of evidence, you want to think about the quality of its data, the validity of its reasoning, the potential for bias, the strength of its conclusion, its relevance to your research question, and how much you trust its source. If an individual piece of evidence doesn't pass muster, meaning that it's just not credible, you need to disregard it. After doing so, you then look at the remaining collection of credible evidence related to each research question and ask whether—given the quantity, quality, and level of agreement in the evidence—sound conclusions can be drawn. If the answer is no, then you're done. The available evidence is simply insufficient to serve as a basis for further analysis. But if the answer is yes, you can then move to the next part of the evaluation.

The goal in this step is to figure out how much confidence you have in the evidence you've collected. At this point, you're no longer characterizing individual pieces of evidence but instead are focused on the body of evidence relevant to each research question. Given the academic tradition of not relying on just one study to support a definitive conclusion, we assess confidence based on two underlying characteristics of the collection of evidence: the **extent of the evidence** (do we have only one or two data sources, or do we have many?) and the **level of agreement** within the evidence (do the studies and data point in the same direction, or are they all over the place?). As shown in the table labeled Level of Confidence, we intersect these two considerations to form a continuum of confidence from very high to very low. If you have low, or very low, confidence in the evidence, you're almost certainly done. Further analysis of such evidence would likely strain credulity. If you have medium confidence in the evidence, you'll have to make a case-specific judgment call about whether to move on to the next step or refrain from further analysis.

On the other hand, if you have high or very high confidence in your evidence, you need to figure out if you can apply probabilistic reasoning to your evidence. Does the evidence allow you to attach a credible probability estimate to the likelihood that something will occur in the future or to the likelihood that some description of current conditions is true? If the answer is yes, you would move to the next part of Exhibit 6-4, but if the answer is no, then you would stop and write up the results.

Let's assume you've decided that you can reason probabilistically with the evidence you have. As shown in the exhibit, you would then capture the result of your probabilistic reasoning in a narrative form with words of estimative probability or in a numeric form with a specific probability (either a range or a point estimate) of the type we talked about in Section 5.6. You may recall that a frequentist will generally be comfortable attaching numeric probabilities only to repeatable events for which the outcome can be measured, while a subjectivist believes that probabilities are also meaningful for one-off events and for capturing the likelihood that a particular conclusion is true.

Finally, note that all paths in the algorithm end up in the same place—the creation of a **traceable account**. What exactly is a traceable account? It's a written record that links your answer to each research question to the evidence base upon which it rests. The traceable account might be just a few notes for your own use, or it could be more expansive, suitable for sharing with others.

The rationale for creating a traceable account is twofold. First, the need to document how you reasoned your way from the evidence to the answers to your research questions creates a useful *discipline for your thinking process*. If you know you're going to have to put down in writing is how you got from one to the other, you'll be more inclined to follow a logical and consistent approach. Second, depending on the uses to which your analysis will be put, there may be a *normative obligation to be transparent* about your work. If your use of evidence will end up playing an important role in the policymaking process, then arguably you have an ethical obligation to be as clear as possible about the evidence upon which you relied and how you synthesized it to reach your conclusions.

6.6 WATCH OUT FOR THESE EVIDENCE TRAPS

As shown in Exhibit 6-5, when it comes to the use of evidence within a specific policy analysis, there are several ways to go wrong. This section describes a few of the traps you'll want to watch out for, either as you do your own policy analysis or as you review the work of others.[8]

Exhibit 6-5   Potential Errors in the Use of Evidence

- Evidence based on flawed generalizations
  - Cherry picking unrepresentative examples
  - Conclusions from unrepresentative samples
  - The small-n problem
  - Changing your mind is OK

- Strategic misuse of evidence
  - Playing with evidence
  - Who needs evidence?
  - Valid evidence doesn't change someone's mind
  - Neglecting to collect evidence to stall debate

- Statistical mishaps
  - The flaw of averages
  - Absolute vs. percentage change
  - Playing with arbitrary end points
  - Playing with the baseline

6.6.1 Evidence Based on Flawed Generalizations

In Section 5.3, we talked about inductive reasoning, which entails looking at specific situations or examples and drawing inferences about broader principles based on those examples. This mode of thinking is, for example, at the heart of survey research in which we look closely at a sample drawn from a population and then generalize our findings from the sample to the population. It turns out that many of the statistical mistakes we might make in survey analysis have analogs in qualitative analysis.

---

[8]The material in this section represents an amalgam of ideas that originate in multiple sources. Specific factual claims and studies are cited in the usual fashion. The remainder of the material is based primarily on my personal experience but also reflects an integrated reading of less formal commentary offered by these websites, news reports, and blog posts: Bensen (2017), Dwyer (2018), Dwyer (2017), Richardson (2018), and Richardson (2017).

Cherry-Picking Unrepresentative Examples

Sometimes, a speaker uses Aristotle's concept of pathos to provoke an emotional response from an audience. He or she might elect to focus only on sensational examples of something—say alcohol-related accidents by teen drivers—to make a point. But a random sample is one in which every member of the population has the same chance of being selected. By cherry-picking dramatic cases, he or she *can* describe their tragic nature, but without a representative sample of teens (e.g., those who do and don't drink, and those who do and don't drive), *cannot* draw broad inferences about the problem.

Drawing Conclusions from an Unrepresentative Sample

Unlike cherry-picking, the mistake here is unintentional. Imagine you work for a Member of Congress and are in charge of tallying comments from residents who write, call, or email the office. Suppose contacts are running 80/20 against a particular policy. Does that mean a large majority of the district opposes the policy? Not necessarily. Remember, you only have information from the folks who bothered to contact the office. Those people are self-selected; they're not necessarily a representative cross section of the residents in the district.

The Small-n Problem

Statisticians traditionally use the letter 'n' to denote the size of a sample. Beyond the need to have a broadly representative collection of individual cases, we also need to recognize the link between sample size and the precision of our estimates. There's no definitive rule, but if you have fewer than several dozen cases, you won't be able to draw very precise inferences about the population. A statistician can help you put a number on the precision of your estimate as a function of the size of the sample.

Changing Your Mind Is OK

For scientists, finding new evidence is typically a mechanism for greater insight and discovery. In the political world, however, if new evidence suggests a policy change is warranted, you may have a problem. Changing your mind is often seen as a sign of incompetence or weakness (Al-Khalili, 2020). As a policy analyst, it can be tough to come out and admit that a conclusion you'd reached previously is no longer valid. But in the long run, doing so typically enhances your reputation as an honest and transparent analyst. What's more, if you heeded my suggestion about not overselling your conclusion in the first place, your humility then will be make it easier to change your stance now.

6.6.2 Strategic Misuse of Evidence

As noted in Chapter 3, when policy analysis is used for advocacy rather than inquiry, there are incentives for selective use of evidence. Indeed, emphasizing supportive evidence, and dismissing or ignoring contradictory evidence, are hallmarks of advocacy. Below are a few things to look out for.

Playing with Evidence

Sometimes, someone will assert that a particular piece of evidence proves a point. They might be right, but don't take their word for it; instead, examine the evidence closely and the conclusion it purportedly proves. Decide for yourself. Similarly, you might encounter an assertion early in a debate that, at the time, no one objects to. The assertion then takes on a life of its own as it is repeated multiple times. Eventually, it can get accepted as valid evidence, even though it is not. In short, repetition does not strengthen weak evidence.

Who Needs Evidence?

Given the political processes that surround policy analysis, advocates sometimes come to policy debates with little to no evidence. The absence of evidence might suggest that the only available evidence would undercut the advocate's case. As essayist Christopher Hitchens put it: "what can be asserted without evidence can also be dismissed without evidence" (Knowles, 2014). While this is simply a heuristic and can't be proven valid in all cases, it reminds us that, in the absence of evidence, most claims are considerably weakened.

Valid Evidence that Doesn't Change Someone's Mind

An advocate may profess to be open-minded (a way to use Aristotle's concept of ethos to engender positive feeling in an audience), but when confronted with sound and strong evidence, doesn't adjust his or her position. This is a tip-off that you're dealing with a close-minded person. You might be tempted to work harder to present better evidence, but if you don't have such evidence, you be stuck. Better to call them out for their close-mindedness than get tangled up in an unwinnable argument over evidence.

Neglecting to Collect Evidence to Stall Debate

The case for new policy measures logically rests on the demonstration of a problem in need of attention. Opponents of policy action may thus oppose collection of information about the scope and magnitude of a potential problem to deny advocates the evidence upon which to make a case. There have long been, for example, heated debates about collecting information on the environmental impacts of concentrated animal feeding operations (Stecker, 2015). Environmental activists hope to use collected data as evidence to argue for increased regulation while the agriculture industry has generally resisted data collection efforts. Similarly, opponents of gun control were instrumental in the 1996 enactment of the Dickey Amendment prohibiting the Centers for Disease Control (CDC) from conducting public health research on the causes and impacts of gun violence because of what Representative Dickey called CDC's "emotional antigun agenda" (CRS, 2019, p. 1).

6.6.3 Statistical Mishaps

Probability and statistics are core components of almost all graduate programs in policy analysis. There are plenty of ways to go wrong with statistical evidence. Don't worry, I won't try to summarize them all here. I do, however, want to address four that seem to come up frequently.

The Flaw of Averages

While the mean value of a collection of numbers is often a great way to summarize them, it can also be highly misleading (Savage, 2012). For example, even if the average income in a city goes up 5% in one year, that doesn't mean everyone's better off. Lots of folks could have lower incomes, but their losses may be more than offset by the great fortune of a few people in the town. In short, in policy analysis, you always want to investigate the full range of values rather than relying on a single point estimate.

Absolute vs. Percentage Change

When we compare the change in an important measure, we have two options. We can report the absolute numeric change, or we can report the percentage change. Look at Exhibit 6-6. Depending on how we present the data, we can tell two very different stories:

- Crime in State A has soared this year; it's up by 43% compared to an increase of only 17% in State B. The increase in State A is 2.6 times the increase in State B.

- Crime in State B has soared this year; it's up by 250 victims per 100,000 persons, compared to an increase of only 97 victims in State B. The increase in State B is 2.6 times the increase in State A.

Both stories correctly interpret the data but appear to reach different conclusions. Neither is right and neither is wrong. The bottom line is that you need to pay close

Exhibit 6-6 Violent Crime per 100,000 Persons		
	State A	State B
Last Year	228	1,500
This Year	325	1,750
Change (#)	97	250
Change (%)	43%	17%

attention to the difference between an absolute change and a percentage change, both when you're doing policy analysis and when you're analyzing someone else's work.

Playing with Arbitrary End Points

When you have a series of data that fluctuates over time, you can distort its interpretation by modifying the end points of your analysis. For example, Exhibit 6-7 provides annual average global temperatures (NASA, 2020). The trend is generally upward over time, but I could honestly report that the temperature in 2019 was either down by 3% (compared to 2016), or up by 10% (compared to 2015). In short, changing the starting point by just one year radically changes the conclusion.

Playing with the Baseline

On a Thursday morning in October 2020, the Federal government released its regular quarterly report on gross domestic product (GDP) (BEA, 2020). The news quickly spread across the web:

- US economic growth shatters record at 33.1% (Fox Business, 2020)

- GDP rose by a record 7.4% in the third quarter (Washington Post, 2020)

That's a big difference: 33.1 vs. 7.4%! What's going on? Turns out that the two headlines—based on the same government report—used different baselines. Third quarter GDP *was* 7.4% larger than second quarter GDP. But, if you annualize that rate (by assuming 7.4% growth continues for four quarters), you get 33.1% growth. So both headlines are right, but you couldn't blame a person for getting confused. What's more, if you compare the third quarter of 2020 to the same quarter in 2019, you get a *decrease* of 2.9%. The economy may have done great over the prior three months, but it's still smaller than it was a year earlier, something you'd never know from the headlines.

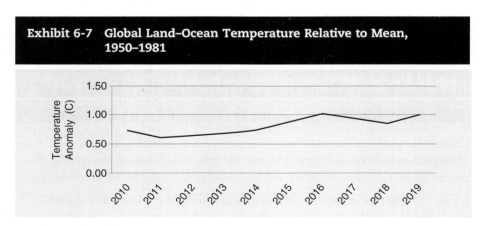

Exhibit 6-7 Global Land–Ocean Temperature Relative to Mean, 1950–1981

Data from NASA, 2020

CHAPTER SUMMARY

When it comes to policy analysis, logic (the subject of the prior chapter) and evidence (the subject of this chapter) are two sides of the same coin. You can't do high-quality policy analysis without using both. In this chapter, we began with the idea of using a research puzzle and a set of associated research questions to figure out what evidence to collect. We then moved on to seven types of evidence often important in policy analysis. We took a theoretical detour to consider four types of validity—construct, conclusion, internal, and external—to understand what it means to draw credible and defensible inferences from evidence.

Because none of us can be an expert on every topic, we also looked at the conditions under which we can trust evidence from others, observing that trustworthiness often depends on a combination of competence and character. Noting that academics rightly prefer a body of evidence to the conclusions of a single study, we looked at ways to consider the magnitude of evidence and the extent of agreement within it before deciding how confident to be in the evidence. We also distinguished the degree of confidence in the evidence from the degree of uncertainty in predictions from that evidence. Finally, we identified a few practical traps to avoid when it comes to collecting and using evidence in policy analysis.

DISCUSSION QUESTIONS

1. Think about a public policy issue with which you are familiar. If you were to undertake a policy analysis of the issue, how would you define the research puzzle? What three to five research questions would you endeavor to answer with your analysis?

2. In the 2020 Presidential Election, 81 million people voted for Joe Biden, 74 million voted for Donald Trump, and 80 million eligible citizens didn't vote. How would you use these results to discern public preferences on matters related to federal public policy? How important are the preferences of those who voted for Trump relative to those who voted for Biden? How about the preference of those who didn't vote?

3. Suppose your client tells you that she's just heard about a successful after-school program in another city. She's excited about the idea of introducing the program in your town. How would you go about deciding whether that's a good idea? How would you use the principles of validity to assess whether the program actually works and whether it might work in your town?

4. Pick a specific policy-related topic and express it in a phrase of three or four words. Enter that phrase in Google Scholar. How many hits did you get? How would you decide which of the search results deserve closer scrutiny?

5. Pick the top three results from your search of Google Scholar and scan the original articles. How easy is it to understand the findings of those studies? Do you think any of the studies would be useful in doing a policy analysis of the topic? Why? Why not? Do you think the author(s) of each article qualify as 'experts'? Do you trust the validity and truth of the articles' conclusions? Why? Why not?

6. Look at the latest edition of *The New York Times* or *The Wall Street Journal*. Pick one of the op-eds (i.e., an opinion piece written by someone other than the paper's editorial board). Can you identify any invalid uses of evidence of the type that we discussed in Section 6.6?

CHAPTER SEVEN

THE MINDSET OF AN EFFECTIVE POLICY ANALYST

We now turn our attention in this chapter to a view of policy analysis that integrates the processes of cognition from Chapter 4 with the themes of logic and evidence from the last two chapters. We'll focus on the real-world constraints that can get in a policy analyst's way and consider some suggestions for overcoming those constraints.

Section 7.1 presents a framework for integrating evidence and logic that will allow you to formulate a specific policy-relevant claim while Section 7.2 focuses on how you can critically evaluate—or deconstruct—policy claims made by others. We turn in Section 7.3 to strategies for coping with the real-world time and resource constraints that often prevent the classical models of policy analysis from being applied in their entirety. This section focuses on how you can still use policy analysis to make valuable contributions to policy debates. Section 7.4 takes a deep dive into one technique—decomposition—that is particularly helpful when doing policy analysis in a constrained world. Section 7.5 reviews the process of effectively communicating the results of your policy analysis. Finally, Section 7.6 describes the foundational mindset of a successful policy analyst: a framework for viewing the world of public policy in general and the role of the policy analyst in particular.

7.1 FRAMEWORKS FOR POLICY REASONING

In Chapter 5, we talked about the forms of logic most relevant to policy analysis: deductive, inductive, causal, abductive, and probabilistic reasoning, as well as reasoning by classification. Then, in Chapter 6, we focused on evidence: where to look

Learning Objectives

By studying this chapter, you should be able to:

- Develop a sound, well-reasoned, evidence-based policy claim.

- Deconstruct policy claims made by others to assess their validity and potential value in policy debates.

- Describe an input-output framework for policy analysis.

- Explain how narrowing the scope, setting priorities through triage, applying Dual Process Theory, and increasing efficiency can overcome constraints that often limit policy analysis.

- Use back-of-the-envelope and Fermi-izing techniques to decompose tough analytic problems with limited data.

- Effectively communicate the results of policy in writing and verbally.

- Bring together the key characteristics of effective policy analysis to describe the mindset of a successful policy analyst.

for it, how to collect it, how to draw valid inferences from it, and how to evaluate our confidence in a body of evidence. Let's talk now about how logic and evidence can be integrated into a broader framework for policy reasoning.

The purpose of policy reasoning is to substantiate a claim, i.e., *make the case that a particular conclusion is, at least provisionally, true*.[1] For starters, it's important to distinguish policy reasoning from other methods of trying to convince a reader or listener that a claim is true. If a policy-relevant claim is made without any rationale or explanation, or is supported only by empirical claims we can't test (e.g., that magical forces, not viral transmission, explain the progression of a pandemic illness), or contains claims that are obviously flawed (e.g., that a public health program implemented in October improved health outcomes the previous March), then I would refer to it as an unsubstantiated assertion. Such assertions do not provide a sound basis for designing, analyzing, or implementing public policies.

Turning to policy-relevant claims that *are* based on logic and evidence, Exhibit 7-1 depicts the content of a generic policy-relevant claim. The claim itself—the conclusion based on **logic** and **evidence**—provides the overarching context. Integral to the claim is the **qualifier** that reflects the provisional nature of the claim. The collection of reasons (#1 through #N), each based on some combination of evidence and logic, provides the foundation for the claim. Some reasons may themselves rest on other subordinate reasons to validate their veracity. In this example, Reason #1 depends on the strength of Subreasons A, B, and C. Finally, the strongest of claims anticipates potential objections to the claim and embeds a **rebuttal** to the objection in the claim itself.

You may recall from Chapter 3 that claims generally fit into one of two categories: descriptive or prescriptive. The content of a policy claim differs somewhat between the two categories, so to help illustrate the distinction, I developed the two illustrative policy claims, one descriptive and the other prescriptive, shown in Exhibit 7-2.

We can use these sample policy claims to make a couple of observations. First, while all aspects of the claim need to be backed by compelling reasons, *not all reasons are equally important*. If, in the first case, suburban construction of homes turns out to be unrelated to congestion, the increase in the number of cars and the increase in commute times are still strong indicators that the problem is getting worse, and the claim would likely survive the loss of this piece of evidence. On the other hand, in the second example, if a well-designed public opinion survey finds a majority of citizens are unwilling to raise taxes to fund the project, that's a pretty strong indication that the counterargument about affordability is correct, and that the claim is flawed.

Second, *we evaluate the strength of descriptive and prescriptive claims in different ways*. For example, there is little normative reasoning in the first case. There is an implicit value judgment that waiting in traffic (i.e., the extra 15 minutes) is a bad

---

[1]In this context, I use the terms claim and conclusion interchangeably.

Exhibit 7-1   Content of Policy-Relevant Claim

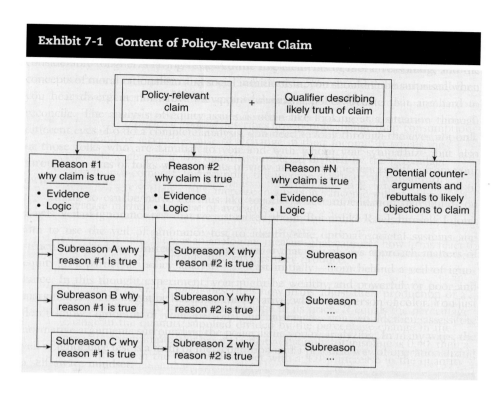

thing, but that doesn't seem controversial. Equally competent, open-minded analysts with access to the same data would thus likely judge the strength of the first claim similarly. On the other hand, the second case incorporates normative value judgments related to, for example, the desirability of increased mobility, the importance of meeting the needs of the poor and seniors, the desirability of lower taxes, and the social value of providing new jobs. Because these reasons offered in support of the claim originate in normative thinking, it may not be possible to reach agreement on them, even among well-intentioned and open-minded citizens, policy analysts, and policymakers. Structuring normative policy claims in a clear, logical, and transparent manner can make it easier to identify areas of agreement and disagreement and move more effectively toward resolving policy disputes (Robert & Zeckhauser, 2011; Stone, 2012).

To close out our discussion of frameworks for policy reasoning, let's talk about the process of developing a policy-relevant claim. Exhibit 7-3 lays out one approach that may help you stay organized.[2] You start by creating a preliminary

---

[2]This approach is loosely based on the work of Toulmin, Ricke, and Janik (1979).

Exhibit 7-2   Fictitious Examples of Two Policy-Relevant Claims

Descriptive	Prescriptive
Claim: Traffic congestion on the local highway has almost certainly gotten worse over the past year.	*Claim:* Our city should construct a light rail system to better connect residential areas to commercial districts.
Reason 1: More drivers are using the road at the same time.	*Reason 1:* It will be easier to travel from home to work and from home to shopping areas.
Evidence: Rush hour traffic volume has grown from 1,000 to 3,000 cars per hour in the past year.	*Evidence:* Citizens have told elected officials they want faster and cheaper ways of getting around town than using their car.
Reason 2: Drivers spend a great deal of time sitting in traffic; drivers can't do anything productive while stuck in traffic.	*Reason 2:* A light rail system is the best way to help the poor and the elderly to participate more fully in community life.
Evidence: The average commute time has gone from 30 to 45 minutes.	*Evidence:* A policy analysis looked at options for better integrating the poor and elderly in the community, and light rail was identified as optimal.
Reason 3: Suburban development has put additional pressure on the road system.	*Reason 3:* Construction of the light rail system will provide desperately needed jobs for unemployed residents.
Evidence: 5,000 new homes have been built in the outer suburbs over the past 10 years.	*Evidence:* The 3-year construction project will employ 500 workers at good wages.
Likely counterargument: Traffic is worse because of ongoing construction that will end soon.	*Likely counterargument:* Light rail is very expensive, and our city can't afford it.
Rebuttal: The problem was getting worse before the construction; it is likely to continue doing so even after the project is finished.	*Rebuttal:* Our city has a large tax base that can be tapped to raise extra money, and a cost–benefit study has shown the project to have net benefits.

version of the claim. Look at your evidence and ask what it shows. Think about how that evidence can be stitched together with logical reasoning to infer broader conclusions. Then, flip the process on its head and start over with the conclusions you think you can draw, and see if you can logically support them with the

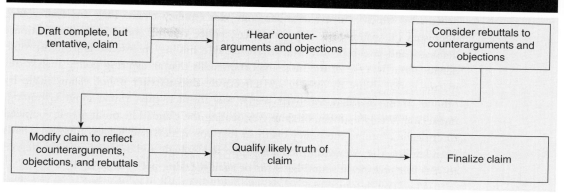

Exhibit 7-3 The Process of Developing a Sound, Well-Reasoned, Evidence-Informed, Policy-Relevant Claim

```
Draft complete, but   →   'Hear' counter-       →   Consider rebuttals to
tentative, claim          arguments and             counterarguments and
                          objections                objections
                                                            ↓
Modify claim to reflect  →  Qualify likely truth  →   Finalize claim
counterarguments,           of claim
objections, and rebuttals
```

evidence you have. After you've iterated a couple times between available evidence and the potential claims it might support, you should have a draft of your tentative claim.

Turn now to 'hearing' the counterarguments and objections to the claim. This can happen in two ways. You might show your draft to colleagues and ask them to spot the weaknesses in your evidence and thinking. Alternatively, you might do some personal role playing, and shift from being the author of the claim to be its fiercest opponent. Either way, the goal is to spot flawed logic, figure out if evidence is invalid or unreliable, determine whether any relevant evidence has been overlooked, identify any valid reasoning that you neglected to apply, and decide whether the qualifier is either too strong or too weak.

With these counterarguments and objections in hand, step back and think about how you might rebut them. Do you need to modify the claim? You could add or drop evidence, add or drop logical arguments, or rewrite the claim itself. If you think the counterarguments are unpersuasive, you could also stand pat and change nothing.

Once all that's done, being mindful of the quality of the evidence and any counterarguments, objections, and rebuttals, you need to settle on the level of confidence you believe is appropriate for the qualifier. (Revisit Exhibit 6-4 if you want a refresher on this process.) Remember, there are few if any definitive truths to be found in policy analysis. Indeed, *a properly qualified conclusion is often far closer to the truth than is a bold confident claim that admits no uncertainty*. After taking care of all these steps, the result should be a sound, well-reasoned, evidence-informed policy claim.

7.2 DECONSTRUCTING POLICY CLAIMS MADE BY OTHERS

Let's pivot from the process by which you develop your own policy claim to the process by which you evaluate someone else's policy claim. Pick an issue you're interested in—pandemics, climate change, police reform, social inequality, national defense—and you probably won't have trouble finding an intense and high-profile debate about it. One of the most important skills that an aspiring policy analyst can master is the ability to quickly and effectively **deconstruct** policy claims made by others.[3] If the word deconstruct seems too abstract, then think about critiquing, unpacking, breaking down, or simply evaluating the claim. The point is that you need to critically examine the policy claim so that you understand what's in it and what's been left out, the extent to which it is supported by logic and evidence, and the degree to which it provides a sound basis for or against taking policy action.

When you deconstruct a policy claim, you first need to *decide whether you're looking at inquiry or advocacy*. As we saw in Chapter 3, in the first case, the analyst aims for a neutral exploration of the issue while in the latter case, the analyst aims to win the argument in support of a specific policy action. Why is it important to decide which sort of analysis underlies the policy claim you're deconstructing? If the claim's author is motivated primarily by advocacy, then the claim won't give you the whole story. You'll need to hear other, competing, claims on the same issue and calibrate them with each other to figure out what's really going on. On the other hand, if the author's motive is inquiry, you will likely see a broader and more complete presentation of the issue.

Neither type of analysis is immune to problems. In both cases, the author may have relied on weak evidence or applied flawed reasoning or run out of time to do a more thorough job. Therein lies another important distinction between the two types of policy analysis. With an advocacy-based claim, analytic shortcomings may be either intentional or accidental. With an inquiry-based claim, such shortcomings are usually accidental.

When you're deconstructing a policy claim, a second question to *ask is whether the claim is complete*. There are only two cases in which you don't have to worry about whether the claim is complete. First, if an author maintains that there is no problem in the first place (rather than arguing for or against a particular policy option), then you only need to assess the strength of the evidence and logic being offered to demonstrate the absence of a policy problem. Second, and conversely, if an author claims that a particular policy problem demands action but doesn't provide a policy solution, then you can limit your inquiry to the nature of the problem and of its causes and consequences.

---

[3] I use 'deconstruction' colloquially to describe the process of critiquing a policy claim. I am not referring to deconstruction as characterized by postmodern philosophers, like Derrida, who use it to examine philosophical and literary texts.

But if the author is trying to make a convincing case for or against policy action, then—apropos of the classical model of policy analysis described in Chapter 1—he or she needs to deliver the five items listed in Exhibit 7-4. Of course, the simple fact that all five of these elements are present doesn't mean you should accept the claim as valid since it can suffer other weaknesses. But if any of these elements *is* missing, then the policy claim does not—by itself—provide a sound basis for policy action.

Exhibit 7-4   Elements of a Complete Policy Claim

1. Compelling problem definition
2. Diverse set of viable policy options
3. Criteria that surface all pros and cons of all options
4. Sound approach to projecting the likely outcomes of each option
5. Clear articulation of trade-offs across options

Another means of deconstructing a policy claim is to *search for cognitive mistakes, invalid logic,* and *weak evidence*:

- *Cognitive errors*: Look for mistakes that seem to result from flawed System 1 thinking, motivated reasoning, or hot cognition. As we saw in Section 4.6, there are multiple ways to go wrong here.

- *Unsound reasoning*: Evaluate the logic used in the claim and ask whether the author's reasoning is sound. If you detect weak reasoning or rhetorical trickery, based on the suggestions in Section 5.7, you should discount the claim accordingly.

- *Weak evidence*: Check the evidence in the claim. You might not have time to fact-check all the data or to figure out if key evidence has been missed, but assessing whether the author has fallen into any of the traps mentioned in Section 6.6 will help you evaluate the evidence in the claim.

- *Obvious flaws*: Internal contradictions, tables that don't add up, missing citations, grammar errors, and typos can be symptoms of deeper problems. If you can't trust the author to sweat the details, you ought not trust him or her to competently execute the analysis itself.

Finally, *watch out for heroic assumptions about implementation.* Many claims propose a particular solution to a specific problem and confidently tout the benefits that will accrue from implementation of the proposed policy change. Reality is a bit more complicated. Even if enacted into law, words on a piece of paper—the new policy—have no effect; only the implementation of the policy generates tangible changes in real-world conditions. But that doesn't stop many advocates from making the often-unrealistic assumption that implementation will be smooth, fully effective, and immediate. To discern whether this is the case with the claim you are deconstructing, consider several questions.

- *Institutions*: How many governmental actors must come into alignment to ensure effective implementation? To what degree do they share common interests? Or are they likely to work at cross-purposes?

- *Complexity*: How complex is the proposed policy? Is it a modest change from the status quo? Or is it radically new and different? The latter will face more daunting implementation challenges.

- *Resources*: Will the policy have sufficient human, financial, legal, and technological resources to allow implementation as anticipated by the advocate? Might its opponents starve it of resources?

- *Unintended consequences*: How might the policy incentivize unexpected behavior by firms, individuals, and institutions that undermines implementation?

- *Winners, losers, and politics*: Who wins and who loses under the policy? How powerful are winners and losers? How might winners facilitate implementation? How might losers impede implementation?

In short, because we get only the costs and benefits—not of the words on paper—but of the policy as actually implemented, you always need to think critically about implementation when you're deconstructing a policy claim. If the claim ignores implementation or makes heroic assumptions about the timing or likelihood of successful implementation, then its conclusions may merit skepticism.

7.3 POLICY ANALYSIS IN A CONSTRAINED WORLD

Because policy analysis is client-driven, you rarely get to set the schedule. *Your work invariably takes place under time and resource constraints that impede your ability to fully execute the classical models* of policy analysis presented in Chapters 1 and 2. Accordingly, this section (and the next) gives you some suggestions for mitigating constraints while still generating useful results.

7.3.1 An Input-Output Framework for Policy Analysis

For starters, *think of policy analysis as a production process*, with inputs and outputs.[4] **Inputs** are the time, cognitive effort, and human and data resources you invest in a policy analysis project. **Outputs** might be measured by the project's ability to create insight that enhances the policymaking process. At the extremes, the value to the client of your final deliverable could range from useless to very helpful.

Exhibit 7-5 illustrates the relationship between analytic effort (measured on the horizontal axis) and the value of the analytic result (measured on the vertical axis). The upwardly sloped line simply demonstrates that the more effort you expend, the more value you can create for your client. Imagine the maximum effort you can devote to the project. Maybe you only have a couple days to spare; perhaps the client must take a public position on an issue by Friday. Either way, your analytic inputs are capped at the level denoted on the horizontal axis by Point M. In turn, based on the relationship between inputs and outputs, the value of the best deliverable you can feasibly produce is capped on the vertical axis at V.

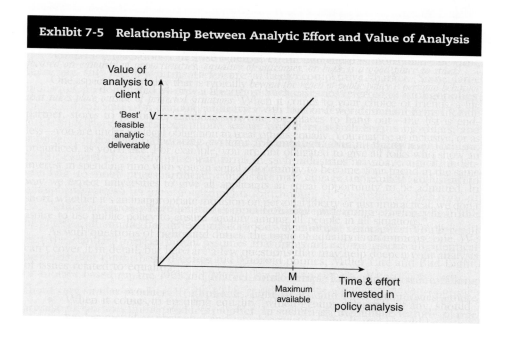

Exhibit 7-5   Relationship Between Analytic Effort and Value of Analysis

[4]My focus here is a single project: a discrete, time-limited analysis of an issue in response to a specific client assignment.

The relationship between inputs and outputs is, however, rarely linear. Each hour you invest in your policy analysis doesn't create the same incremental increase in value for your client. Look at Exhibit 7-6. In it, I illustrate two possible relationships between the input effort and the output value. In Case A, you're able to generate a lot of valuable insight quickly with your initial investment of effort. Perhaps you're already an expert in the topic, or the analysis is simple and straightforward. In Case B, it takes a lot of work before your analytic productivity improves significantly. Maybe you know nothing about the policy topic you've been asked to look at or you lack the technical skills to execute the analysis. Perhaps the policy issue is an intractable mess (e.g., a wicked problem). Either way, you invest significant upfront effort before you start to see the pay off. When we overlay constraint M on your time and effort, you can see that you're in good shape if you can operate within Case A. On the other hand, if you're stuck in Case B, you won't have much of a deliverable when the deadline rolls around.

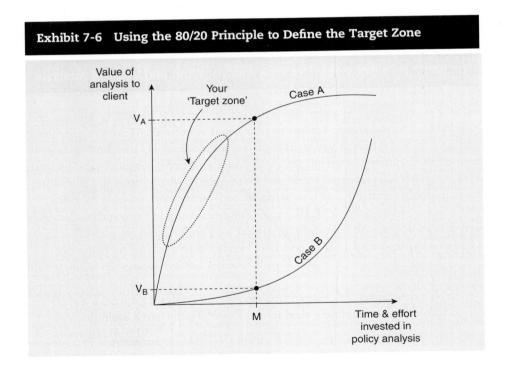

Exhibit 7-6   Using the 80/20 Principle to Define the Target Zone

The steep incline at the start of Case A (which I've labeled as the 'Target Zone') reflects what is colloquially known as the **80/20 principle**, which posits that in many cases, 80% of the result is attained with the first 20% of the effort. While it's only a heuristic that shouldn't be taken as a universal principle, the 80/20 principle does provide an aspiring policy analyst with hope that a valuable contribution to the policy process can still be made, even in a time-constrained and resource-constrained environment. The remainder of this section offers you a few suggestions for how to get closer to the Target Zone.

7.3.2 Narrowing the Scope of the Analysis

One way to meet a deadline is to downsize the task so that you can do a good job within the available time. Your output will be more modest than if you took more time. But, here's the thing: you often don't have more time. The choice is not between more or less time, but is between a complete, coherent deliverable, and a half-finished deliverable. In short, you need to adjust the scope of the analysis to allow you to hit the deadline with a product that doesn't embarrass you.

One way to downsize a policy analysis is to *reduce the size of your Criteria–Alternatives Matrix* (CAM) (Carrigan & Shapiro, 2017; Patton, Sawicki, & Clark, 2013).[5] The CAM arrays a full set of policy options against a complete collection of evaluation criteria. Because filling in each cell of the CAM requires evidence and analysis, each extra option or criterion increases your workload.

If time is short, you might analyze only one or two policy options (presumably, the options most likely to be adopted). Similarly, you might consider only the evaluation criteria that are most important to your client. For instance, a client might ask you to estimate the governmental cost of a new legislative proposal. In that case, you're filling in only one cell of the matrix. If your client doesn't narrow the analysis for you, you may be able to do so on your own. Think about which criteria will probably surface the most important pros and cons of the options being debated (or, if you're doing a cost–benefit analysis, the highest benefits and costs), and focus on only those criteria (Carrigan & Shapiro, 2017).

Another way to downsize your policy analysis is to *opt for a "quick analysis" rather than a "researched analysis"* (Patton, Sawicki, & Clark, 2013, p. 150). The difference is the extent of research and evidence collection. A **quick analysis** doesn't entail any original data collection; instead, you synthesize only information that's readily available, from colleagues, reference materials, or online, to conduct your analysis.[6] By contrast, as its name implies, **researched analysis** entails a more extensive search for evidence to inform your policy analysis and comes closer to the classical policy analysis models described in Chapters 1 and 2.

Again, there's a trade-off here. A quick analysis will yield a less precise, less robust, analytic result, with a higher likelihood of overlooking something important, than

---

[5]Revisit Chapter 1 if you need a refresher on how to set up and use a CAM.
[6]If you opt for quick analysis, pay careful attention to the risks of relying on online sources, described in Chapter 6.

would a researched analysis. In an unconstrained world, we'd obviously prefer the latter over the former. But if you're working under a tight time constraint, it's again a false choice; you're not choosing between a quick analysis and a researched analysis. You're choosing between a quick analysis and no analysis (e.g., relying only on hunch or intuition). If so, quick analysis is the better choice.

Over the course of my career, I'd guess that at least half of the policy analyses I've been involved with would qualify as quick analyses, with the rest characterized as researched analyses. My experience is not unique. In looking at empirical studies of public service, Abrams (2016) reported that "quick analysis is pervasive in public agencies" (p. 532). Getting good at quick analysis is thus an important element in your professional toolbox.

7.3.3 Speeding Up the Process of Analysis

Within the confines of a downsized analysis, there are several techniques you can use to speed up the analysis while minimizing the adverse impact on the value of your final analytic deliverable. You can think of these techniques as a form of **triage**, a concept drawn from the field of medicine. When a hospital, for example, receives a large number of patients in a short period of time, emergency room personnel will triage the patients, sorting them in priority order, based on the urgency of their conditions. A similar process can be used to prioritize the specific tasks within your policy analysis.

For starters, *stay focused on evidence and analysis that has the potential to change the answer* in a material way. If your client asks you which option, Policy A or Policy B, is best, you only need to study factors that might tip the balance from one policy to the other. You don't need to collect a lot of 'nice to know' information that won't change your answer to your client's question.

Don't take the time to come up with a precise estimate when an approximation will suffice. When a policymaker is deciding whether to support a particular policy option, for instance, it may be enough to know the rough magnitude of its cost. You might need only to offer a conclusion about whether the cost will be closer to $1 million or to $10 million. Perhaps your agency has been appropriated $25 million by the state legislature. The only relevant question may then be whether a policy will cost less than $25 million. Time spent coming up with a more exact estimate could very well be time wasted.

Don't let the perfect become the enemy of the good. Sure, you can imagine a deliverable that surveys all the evidence, probes innovative policy choices, applies sophisticated analysis, and offers profound insights. Unfortunately, in a time-constrained and resource-constrained environment, a quest for such a result can impede your ability to deliver the most value possible for your client in a timely deliverable. With a deadline looming, time spent pursuing analytic ambitions you can't achieve creates an opportunity cost: time not available for a modest, but still useful, analysis, or for other important work on another project. As tech entrepreneur and Amazon founder Jeff Bezos (2017) puts it:

> Most decisions should probably be made with somewhere around 70 percent of the information you wish you had. If you wait for 90 percent, in most cases, you're probably being slow.

Apply principles of metacognition to tap both System 1 and System 2 thinking. Even though it carries significant risks of cognitive bias and error, System 1 thinking has one very compelling advantage: it's fast! If you're on a tight schedule for a policy analysis, for example, System 1 may help you quickly focus on the concerns of key stakeholders, weed out infeasible policy options, and identify workarounds to political and institutional obstacles. Most importantly, it may help you figure out what kinds of analysis are possible given time and resource constraints.

The more subject matter expertise and professional experience you have, the more likely it is that your System 1 intuition will be reliable. But to be clear here: I am not giving you license to rely solely on your gut instincts while doing a policy analysis! Don't forget that Section 4.6 identified 11 major failures of System 1 thinking that can cause even the smartest and most capable analysts to go wrong with fast thinking. And some policy issues are so complex and novel that there is no way to make sense of them without the careful, deliberative, analytic approach of System 2 thinking. In such cases, if you're time-constrained, you need to be honest with the client, telling her or him that they've asked a policy question that you can't answer on their time schedule.

To mitigate the risks of System 1 thinking, look back at Exhibit 4-4 which illustrated the principles of Dual Process Theory (DPT). It's the integration of Systems 1 and 2 that seems to offer the most promise for better decisionmaking:

> Popular books often draw a dichotomy between intuition and analysis—blink versus think—and pick one or the other as the way to go. … [But this] is another false dichotomy. The choice isn't either/or, it is how to blend them in evolving situations. That conclusion is not as inspiring as a simple exhortation to take one path or the other, but it has the advantage of being true. (Tetlock & Gardner, 2015, p. 41)

In short, you need to maintain a metacognitive monitor on your work, and stay ready to apply an executive override from System 2 if needed to keep your System 1 thinking on track (Marrin & Torres, 2017). And don't forget that the final element of DPT—reflective calibration—gives you the chance to self-inspect your work to help you figure out if you should trust it.

Finding patterns in available evidence may help speed your analysis. Champion grandmaster chess players can quickly recognize the details and consequences of upwards of 100,000 different chess positions (Amidzic, Riehle, Fehr, Wienbruch, & Elbert, 2001). In a chess game, there isn't time to analyze each of several thousand positions; instead, grandmasters rely on pattern recognition as the source of their intuition about good and bad moves. Herbert Simon (1992) linked intuition to the process of cognition:

> In everyday speech, we use the word *intuition* to describe a problem-solving or question-answering performance that is speedy and for which the expert is unable to describe in detail the reasoning or other processes that produced the answer. The situation has provided a cue; this cue has given the expert access to information stored in memory, and the information provides the answer. Intuition is nothing more and nothing less than recognition. (p. 155), *emphasis in original*

Kahneman and Klein (2009) build on Simon's insights by noting our tendency to see intuition as inscrutable, perhaps even mystical. They welcome Simon's definition of intuition as recognition because it

> … demystifies intuition. … The recognition model implies two conditions that must be satisfied for an intuitive judgement (recognition) to be genuinely skilled. First, the environment must provide adequately valid cues to the nature of the situation. Second, people must have an opportunity to learn the relevant cues. (p. 520)

So, what does all this have to do with speeding up your policy analysis to meet a tight deadline? Pattern recognition can be a powerful technique to quickly deepen your understanding of a situation. This might make more sense with a quick policy example. You may remember from studying economics that when we see only two or three firms dominating a market, the conditions for an oligopoly might exist. If an oligopoly does arise, then firms might be tempted to behave collusively and charge higher prices than they otherwise would. The characteristics of an oligopoly represent a pattern that we can recognize and use to quickly organize a policy analysis of the situation. In short, our intuition that an oligopoly might exist will help us to decide what evidence to look for and guide us toward a range of possible policy options to address the situation.

But the pattern recognition technique comes with caveats. First, you must have mastered and committed to memory the characteristics of the patterns you aspire to reliably recognize. Doing so takes time and effort; you aren't born with dependable intuitions about complex public policy issues. Second, when you apply your intuition in the form of pattern recognition, there must be appropriate signals from the situation to ensure that the pattern you have in mind actually aligns well with the facts and circumstances on the ground. Conceptually, this test of pattern recognition is the same test we used to assess construct validity (see Section 6.3.1). The pattern you think you recognize is the mental construct. The signals from the environment represent the evidence you have at hand. And the operationalization is the link between the two. As with construct validity, we want to confirm that the pattern we mentally see in the evidence is actually the pattern that's guiding real-world events.

7.3.4 Improve the Efficiency of Your Policy Analysis Work

When we talked about retrospective evaluation in Chapter 2, we touched on efficiency, a concept that reflects the degree to which the maximum output is obtained from a fixed set of inputs, or conversely, the degree to which the inputs used to attain an output are minimized. Moreover, at the beginning of this section, I suggested that policy analysis should be set in the context of an input-output framework. Putting these two concepts together, it seems clear that *if you undertake a policy analysis in a time-constrained and resource-constrained world, then you need to be as efficient as possible.*

Chapter 15 includes a deep dive into the art and science of managing a policy analysis project. For now, I just want to make a few suggestions to enhance the efficiency of your policy analysis. First, make sure you know what your client is looking for—your work can't add much value if it doesn't meet the client's expressed needs and will cost you precious time if the client sends you back to start over. Think carefully about the components of your planned analysis and how long each will take. Do you have time to get it all done before the deadline? If not, better to realize it at the outset than midway through the analysis when it's too late to shift to another approach. Don't shortchange planning; time spent upfront may save you time wasted later in the project. Finally, things inevitably go wrong; data turn out to be unavailable, people cancel meetings, and mistakes creep into spreadsheets. Be sure to build spare time into your schedule to fix glitches and still deliver a quality product on time. In short, the better you are at project management, the more efficient you will be at turning analytical inputs into a valuable deliverable for your client.

Many policy analysis projects are done by more than one person. Accordingly, your (and others') ability to be effective team players can have a big impact on the efficiency of a policy project. Identify your own strengths and weaknesses; play to your strengths while managing your weaknesses to minimize their impact. Recognize when to lead and when to follow. Contribute the best of your thinking to the team but make room for new ideas from others. As a group, you don't want to endlessly debate each issue, but you also don't want to rush to closure on a topic before it's been thoroughly examined, especially if someone is pushing their own ideas a bit too hard. Learn how to have constructive conversations about the analysis where you, as the adage says, disagree without being disagreeable.

Some of the things you can do to more efficiently manage a policy analysis project have to happen before you launch the project. I recommend that you pay attention to your professional development. Higher education gives you a good start, but successful policy analysts engage in lifelong learning. For one thing, the policy world is constantly changing. Issues come and go. New policies get tried; sometimes they work, sometimes they don't. Science and technology profoundly shape (and reshape) the policy environment. New analytic techniques get developed (think big data science).

In short, keep up with developments in your field, so that when you're in the middle of a policy analysis project, you're not frantically trying to figure out what's going on. The same is true of your technical skills. Do you, for example, find yourself using spreadsheets frequently, based on what you've taught yourself by trial and error? Maybe it's time to take a class. Similarly, when I was back in grad school, behavioral economics didn't seem to be on anyone's radar screen; now it's a mainstay of the curriculum. Investing in your own professional development isn't just fun and exciting, it also has the more utilitarian impact of making you more efficient at your job. And efficiency is one of the best ways to cope with the inevitable constraints on policy analysis while still delivering high-quality work.

7.4 DECOMPOSING TOUGH PROBLEMS

The previous section gave you a broad overview of how to streamline your policy analysis to accommodate time, resource, and information constraints. This section now looks specifically at one technique—**decomposition**—that can be an especially effective way to streamline your analytic work.

Nobel Laureate Enrico Fermi was a brilliant physicist. He had a reputation for tackling complex and seemingly impossible problems by breaking down, or decomposing, them into smaller, more manageable, problems that could be solved individually. He would then take these individual answers and combine them into a solution of the original problem (Abrams, 2011). It turns out that individual estimates don't have to be especially precise to generate a reasonable answer to the big question because errors in the estimates often offset one another (Epstein, 2019). The process of decomposing big problems into little pieces is known as **Fermi-izing** a problem. Sometimes, it's called a back of the envelope calculation, or **BOTEC**.

Not just physics problems can be Fermi-ized. The technique also works well for many of the questions that we often encounter in policy analysis. For instance, under the sponsorship of the Intelligence Advanced Research Programs Activity (IARPA), Phillip Tetlock and several colleagues directed a study between 2011 and 2015 in which about 2,800 volunteers regularly made probabilistic forecasts about specific geopolitical questions, such as "Who will win the January 2012 Taiwan Presidential election? Tsai Ing-wen, Ma Ying-jeou, or neither" (Mellers et al., 2015). Tetlock then identified the best of the forecasters in his sample by looking for high levels of accuracy in answering such questions over extended periods of time. Based on his work for IARPA, and empirical analysis of hundreds of forecasters and thousands of forecasts, Tetlock (2015) noted how well the Fermi-izing process can work:

> The surprise is how often remarkably good probability estimates arise from a remarkably crude series of assumptions and guesstimates. (p. 278)

For an example of the Fermi-izing process, let's try an exercise I use with students in my policy analysis class. It focuses on problem-solving by decomposition, with a back of the envelope calculation.

In class, I give students 20 minutes to Fermi-ize an answer to the following question: If Congress levied a one cent tax on Starbucks' cardboard coffee cup sleeves, how much revenue would the Feds net annually? Students can't check online sources; instead, they're asked to rely only on intuition as they use a BOTEC process to decompose the problem. I have no idea what the right answer is, but that's not the point. The goal is to practice the method. Below is a typical approach taken by my students:

- For starters, Congress can't levy a tax on just one company. We need to assume all cup sleeves get taxed.

- There are about 325 million people in America; a quarter are probably kids who rarely drink coffee. Let's assume there are 245 million adults. Not all of them drink coffee. Let's guess that 60%, or 130 million, drink coffee daily.

- A lot of coffee drinkers probably brew it at home or use a workplace coffee pot, rather than buying it. Let's say 25% are in this category, giving us about 110 million buyers.

- Most folks probably buy one cup per day, but some caffeine fiends buy more. Let's assume an average of 1.5 cups per day.

- Folks likely don't buy coffee every day; so, let's limit ourselves to the working week. Five days times roughly 50 weeks in the year, gives us 250 working days.

- Our first approximation would be that about 41 billion cups of coffee (110 million buyers times 1.5 cups per day times 250 days) are sold each year.

- As good policy analysts, we know to expect a behavioral response to the tax. Folks might not want to pay the extra penny or folks might switch to reusable cup sleeves. Let's suppose demand for cup sleeves drops by 10%. So, we cut our estimate to 37 billion cups.

- Lots of my students then multiply by a penny and declare an answer. But policy implementation is rarely perfect. Some coffee merchants will flout the law and not collect the tax. It's a guess, but perhaps 5% of the cup sleeves will slip through the system, bringing the total down to 35 billion sleeves that actually get taxed.

- Finally, tax administration is not free. Remember, we're interested in the net revenue, so we'll need to cover the government cost of running the system. Let's deduct another 10% for the cost of administration.

- So, a reasonable estimate might reflect 35 billion cup sleeves, times a penny per sleeve, minus 10% in administrative costs, or about $317 million per year in net revenue. Not chump change, but a small share of a $4.4 billion federal budget.

So, is $317 million the right answer? Almost certainly not, but it's a much better answer than we'd get if we just guessed at the number without first thinking through all the pieces of the puzzle.

When you decompose a problem like this, there are several techniques to use. Try to deal in round numbers to make the math easier. Pay attention to decimal places; if you mistakenly assume the tax is $.10 rather than $.01, your answer will be off by a factor of 10. Take care not to mix up the units by, example, conflating the number of coffee drinkers with the number of cups of coffee.

I don't want to oversell the Fermi process here. Yes, errors in the answers to individual questions tend to offset one another, thereby usually improving the accuracy of the final result. But if each subquestion is answered based only on intuition, the results will be less accurate than if each answer is carefully researched before being aggregated into a final estimate. If you have the time and resources, of course, the latter approach is preferred to the former. But, if your work falls into the first category, you owe it to your client to clearly qualify the provisionality of your findings with words like 'rough estimate' or 'first approximation.'

To get better at the Fermi process, it helps to *identify and commit to memory benchmarks that you can subsequently use to calibrate your numeric estimates.* Statistician Joel Best (2008) puts it this way:

Having a small store of factual knowledge prepares us to think critically about statistics. … When interpreting social statistics, it helps to have a rough sense of scale. Just a few benchmark numbers can give us a mental context for assessing other figures we encounter. (p. 7)

As a practical exercise, I suggest you identify a policy issue that you're interested in (e.g., housing policy in Detroit, criminal justice in urban areas, or international refugee migration) and put together what I call a Fermi Cheat Sheet. It's a one-pager with the most important facts and figures relevant to your policy issue. One of my areas of interest is American research and development. Accordingly, I created the Fermi Cheat Sheet on R&D activity in the United States shown in Exhibit 7-7.

In it, I assembled the basic, big-picture data, on the topic. I can then use it as a benchmark as I encounter various policy matters. If someone suggests that the federal government spend an extra $100 million on R&D for renewable energy, I can quickly see that, even though that's a big number, it pales in comparison to the total spending of $121 billion. Similarly, someone might hold up Israel as an exemplar and argue that the United States should also spend 5% of GDP on R&D. My cheat sheet quickly reveals the shakiness of the comparison, with the United States spending over 35 times as much per year as Israel does ($548 billion versus $15 billion).

Over a career spent analyzing issues in a particular policy domain, you will certainly develop an expertise in these kinds of benchmarks. But rather than accruing those data on an ad hoc basis over time, you can jumpstart the process by developing a few Fermi Cheat Sheets on the topics you're most interested in. The process of Fermi-izing problems may feel a bit alien at first, but as one scholar put it:

The ability to think and calculate rapidly can be learned. The key words are practice, practice, and more practice. (Abrams, 2011, p. 8)

7.5 SHARE YOUR RESULTS

Analytic competence and the ability to master a policy issue are prerequisites to doing your job well, but they're not the only things that matter. At the end of the day, *it's what your audience understands, after looking at your work, that counts*. Some aspiring analysts have trouble with this concept. Having worked hard on their policy analysis, they may dismiss a client who doesn't understand their analysis as incompetent, closed-minded, or overly political. These criticisms might be valid, but they don't negate the fact that the work won't inform the decisionmaking process if the decisionmaker can't follow its reasoning or grasp its conclusions. Like a doctor whose patient doesn't understand the diagnosis or can't follow a treatment plan, the analyst should focus on how to communicate more clearly and effectively. Doing so is likely a better use of time than blaming the client for the problem.

Funding for U.S. R&D in 2017 ($B)				
	Basic research	Applied research	Experimental development	Total
Business	$26	$59	$296	$381
Federal govt	$39	$38	$45	$121
Nonfederal govt	$2	$2	$1	$5
Higher Education and Non-profits	$24	$11	$6	$41
Total	$91	$109	$348	$548

Country	R&D spending ($B)	R&D as % of GDP
United States	$548	3%
China	$496	2%
European Union	$430	2%
Japan	$171	3%
South Korea	$91	5%
India	$50	1%
Russia	$42	1%
Taiwan	$39	3%
Australia	$21	2%
Israel	$15	5%

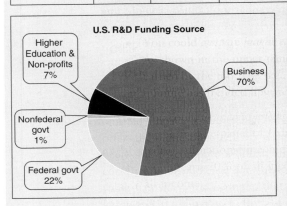

U.S. R&D Funding Source

Higher Education & Non-profits 7%
Business 70%
Nonfederal govt 1%
Federal govt 22%

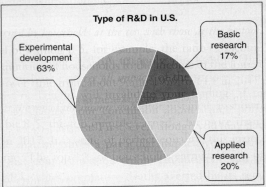

Type of R&D in U.S.

Experimental development 63%
Basic research 17%
Applied research 20%

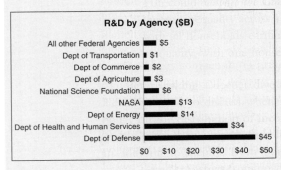

R&D by Agency ($B)

All other Federal Agencies $5
Dept of Transportation $1
Dept of Commerce $2
Dept of Agriculture $3
National Science Foundation $6
NASA $13
Dept of Energy $14
Dept of Health and Human Services $34
Dept of Defense $45

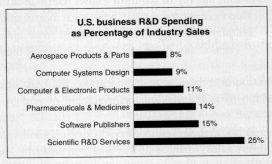

U.S. business R&D Spending as Percentage of Industry Sales

Aerospace Products & Parts 8%
Computer Systems Design 9%
Computer & Electronic Products 11%
Pharmaceuticals & Medicines 14%
Software Publishers 15%
Scientific R&D Services 25%

Benchmarks

- Basic research: Work to acquire new knowledge without any particular application or use in view
- Applied research: Work to acquire new knowledge directed toward a specific, practical objective
- Experimental development: Work, drawing on knowledge gained from research and practical experience, directed to producing new or improving existing products or processes
- U.S. GDP ($B): $21.4 trillion (2019)
- U.S. Federal spending ($B): $4.4 trillion (2019)

Source: NSF (2020)

Exhibit 7-8 Sharing the Results of Policy Analysis

1. You need a good understanding of the audience
2. You can't explain what you don't understand
3. Written communication is as important as substance
4. You need to master the art of verbal communication
5. Watch out for the slippery slope of storytelling
6. Check your personal agenda before communicating

Listed in Exhibit 7-8, and described in more detail later in this section, are a few things to keep in mind when it's time to share the results of your policy analysis. First, if you want to ensure that your analytic work finds its way into the minds of your audience with nothing lost in translation, you need a *good understanding of the audience's skills, background, interests, and level of expertise*. If your reader has been working on an issue for years, you should produce a different deliverable than if you are advising a newly elected politician with scant knowledge of the topic. In short, you need to have a specific audience in mind and speak clearly to that audience. Or, as billionaire investor Warren Buffet put it:

> When writing Berkshire Hathaway's annual report, I pretend that I'm talking to my sisters. I have no trouble picturing them: Though highly intelligent, they are not experts in accounting or finance. They will understand plain English, but jargon may puzzle them. My goal is simply to give them the information I would wish them to supply me if our positions were reversed. To succeed, *I don't need to be Shakespeare; I must, though, have a sincere desire to inform.* (OIEA, 1998) *emphasis added*

In addition, recall from Chapter 4 the problem of mirror imaging. Think about the degree to which you share an intellectual and cultural connection to your audience. *Don't assume that your audience's lived experience is the same as yours.* Assumptions you take as fixed may be in fact be up for grabs in the minds of your audience. Finally, don't be tone-deaf to the emotional content of your work. On topics like equality, justice, and personal rights, your readers and listeners may have an emotional reaction—positive or negative—to your work. I am not suggesting that you modify your conclusions to avoid offending audience sensibilities. But I am suggesting that you choose your words carefully to not *needlessly* trigger a negative affective response from your audience.

Second, though it may seem a no-brainer, *you can't explain what you don't understand*. A well-crafted policy analysis can be complex, blending incomplete evidence with careful inference to reach provisionally qualified conclusions. Seemingly minor points and nuances can be important to the conclusion. You need to have a crystal-clear understanding of how the work was done, what aspects of it drive the key results, and what makes it important. Anticipate questions that a reasonable person might ask (before they're asked) and recraft your prose to avoid the need for the question in the first place. If you find that you don't quite understand the analysis itself, suspend your writing and get the answers, before resuming the process of explaining the analysis.

My third suggestion is that you *focus just as intently on the style and presentation of your written work as you do on the substantive and analytic components of the work itself*. Let's assume that, like Warren Buffet, you are motivated by "a sincere desire to inform." How do you deliver on that desire? The Federal Plain Language Initiative points us in a useful direction:

> The first time that members of your audience encounter your work, they should be able to find what they need, understand what they find, and use what they find to meet their needs. (PLAIN, 2011, p. i)

In short, being able to render complex, uncertain, and incomplete policy analysis in plain language is not just a 'nice-to-have' skill in your professional toolbox. To be a successful policy analyst, you need to be an effective communicator. For starters, the format, structure, length, and style of policy writing *are not at all* like a research paper, essay, short story, or article in an academic journal.

- Policy writing is brief, to-the-point, and clear.

- The most important conclusions are upfront, in the first paragraph, rather than buried at the end of the document.

- Five pages is long for a policy brief (two to three pages is the norm). If you need to cover more content, prepare a separate report to give additional detail and technical material.[7]

- Forget the vocabulary that you learned for standardized tests like the SATs and GREs; instead, use words that your least educated reader will understand.

Exhibit 7-9, which extracts and extends key themes from the Plain Language Guidelines, illustrates some of the techniques you'll need to master. Practice your writing skills as often as you can. Ask for feedback from others. Your goal is to improve your writing, not protect yourself from criticism!

---

[7]Policy reports, issued in conjunction with a policy brief, are often in the range of 30–40 pages. The writing style of these longer reports remains the same: succinct, to-the-point, and crystal-clear.

Exhibit 7-9 Plain Language Guidelines for Policy Writing

- The Audience
  - Identify the specific audience for your work
  - Think about the information they need to extract from your work
  - Write in a way that allows the audience to easily get the information they need
  - Address separate audiences separately, but maintain a consistent message
- Cultural Competence
  - Recognize that different communities may use language differently
  - Recognize that the audience will interpret text based on its lived experience and educational background, not yours
  - If English is audience's second language, consider translation
- Word Choice
  - Use short, simple words
  - Omit unnecessary words
  - Give common words common meaning
  - Use same term consistently for a specific thought or object
  - Avoid legal, foreign, technical jargon
  - Minimize abbreviations and acronyms
- Organization of the Text
  - Organize text to meet readers' needs
  - Organize text in a logical way
    - Chronological organization
    - General to specific
    - Most to least important
  - Provide definitions, abbreviations, and acronyms near the start of the text
- Headings
  - Use headings to show document structure
  - Try to limit headings to three sublevels
  - Use helpful headings
    - Question headings
    - Statement headings
    - Topic headings
  - Avoid long headings that take two lines
- Style
  - Highlight key points in bold or italics, but don't overdo it
  - Use bullets for lists of things

- Word Use
  - Verbs
    - Maximize active voice
    - Minimize passive voice
    - Use simplest form of a verb
  - Nouns and pronouns
    - Don't turn verbs into nouns
    - Don't turn nouns into verbs
    - Do speak directly to audience with pronouns
    - Avoid gendered language
- Strength of statement
  - *Must* indicates a requirement
  - *May* suggests choices
  - *Should* and *ought* denote a normative stance
  - *Could* and *might* denote uncertainty
- Use contractions as appropriate
- Sentences
  - Write short sentences
  - Include only one idea in each sentence
  - Keep subject, verb, object close
  - Avoid double negatives
  - Avoid exceptions to exceptions
  - Put main idea before exceptions, qualifiers
- Paragraphs
  - Write short paragraphs
  - Cover only one topic in each paragraph
  - Use a topic sentence, usually the first
  - Use transition words to link paragraphs
- Other Aids to Clarity
  - Use examples and lists
  - Use tables, rather than text, to make complex material easier to understand
  - Highlight important concepts
  - Minimize cross-references
  - Design text layout for easy reading
- Edit for Clarity
  - Read, edit, and rewrite
  - Read text out loud; edit until text 'sounds' clear

Adapted from PLAIN (2011, pp. iii–v).

Fourth, *master the art of verbal communication*. Sometimes, a client is too busy to even read your policy memo or prefers to engage in a back-and-forth conversation about your work. In such cases, analysts are often called on to deliver a verbal briefing that conveys their analysis and its results. Typically, such briefings include a 'slide deck' created with a software package like PowerPoint or Google Slides. Exhibit 7-10 provides some pointers on the creation and delivery of a verbal presentation.

And, of course, not all verbal communication takes place in formal briefings. Instead, you may be called on to extemporaneously explain your policy analysis to your client or others, and answer questions about your work. You may have heard of an **elevator speech**, which is a metaphor for your ability to convey an important point in the time it would take someone to ride the elevator to or from their office (i.e., a minute or two). If you're asked for an off-the-cuff verbal description of your work, focus on the most important aspect of your work. Decide what your client cares about and speak to those issues. Hit the highlights and leave out all the details; you can explain the details if and when you're asked. The ability to deliver a good elevator speech takes practice. Think about what you'd say, well before you're put on the spot with an unexpected request to explain your work.

Fifth, *watch out for the slippery slope of storytelling*. Public policy students are routinely advised that the final step in policy analysis is telling the story.[8] In the context of public policy, a story grabs an audience's attention and engages them in a narrative that weaves together settings, characters, a plot, and often a moral (Cairney, 2020). But bear in mind that stories can be fiction or nonfiction. Giving analysts a green light to tell stories may lead to narratives that overemphasize some elements of a policy analysis while neglecting others, all for the sake of a better tale. *The result can be a story that is closer to fiction than nonfiction*:

> Open any newspaper, watch any TV news show, and you find experts who forecast what's coming. ... With few exceptions, they are not in front of the cameras because they possess any proven skills at forecasting. ... The one undeniable talent that talking heads have is their skill at telling a *compelling story with conviction, and that is enough.* (Tetlock & Gardner, 2015, p. 5), *emphasis added*

A great story with little substance behind it might satisfy the need of a media outlet to attract viewers, readers, and listeners, but it's antithetical to the norms of high-quality policy analysis. In short, it's fine to think of communicating with your audience as storytelling, but take care to stay in the realm of nonfiction and tell the whole story, not just the part that appeals to your audience's emotions.

---

[8]See, for example, Bardach and Patashnik (2016).

Exhibit 7-10   Suggestions for Verbal Briefings

When you create a set of slides, be mindful that they are only an aid to the presentation, *not* a textual presentation that you read to the audience.

- Use graphics and images to get your points across, but take care not to get too cartoonish in your style.

- Words are fine, but don't get carried away. Use key words and phrases only, rather than complete sentences.

- Don't put more than four or five main bullet points on a single slide.

- Ensure that all bullet points on the page have parallel grammar (e.g., they all start with a verb or are all noun phrases).

- Make sure the font size is big enough to read from the back of the room, and that the text color contrasts well with the background color of the slide.

- Be sure to proofread your slides! It's really disconcerting to be at the front of the room, with no idea why everyone in the room is giggling.

When it comes to delivery of the presentation, aim for a natural and engaging style. Think of yourself as a travel guide giving your audience a tour of your work.

- Vary your style, tone, and speed from time to time to keep your audience engaged.

- Highlight the parts of your work that are most relevant to your audience, rather than slogging through every detail of your analysis.

- Try to connect to your audience; don't turn your back on the audience by staring up at your slides. Instead, use a monitor or laptop in front of you to keep track of your slides.

- Smile, make eye contact, and assume a relaxed, but confident, posture.

- Figure out how much time you have and watch the clock; losing track of time and racing through the last part of your presentation is a rookie mistake.

- Practice your presentation at least once, and probably more.

- People can't read and listen at the same time. If possible, reveal one bullet at a time.

- When you pull up a content-heavy slide, give the audience a few seconds to absorb it before starting to speak.

- Always number your slides to facilitate conversation with the audience (so that they can ask questions like, "What did you mean, back on slide 6, when you said …?").

- Don't finish by saying "the end." Instead, use the last slide and the last couple minutes to drive home three to five important takeaways that you want your audience to remember.

Sixth, *check your personal agenda before communicating your findings*. It can be tempting, after completing a policy analysis, to come on too strong when sharing the results. Particularly if you are passionate about the issue and enthusiastic about a policy alternative that shows well in your analysis, it's easy to slip into the role of an advocate. There's nothing wrong with advocacy. It's part of the democratic tradition. But if your passion leads you to shade your results, overemphasizing the positives of your preferred option and minimizing its downsides, you do your client a disservice by failing to expose her to all aspects of the policy issue at hand.

In addition, if you don't check your personal agenda, you might unintentionally use overly provocative language when presenting your findings. You might even question the competence or motives of those who disagree with you. Such language may make you feel good and get you a round of applause. But to an audience that doesn't share your agenda, over-the-top language will be a turn off or maybe an insult, closing their minds to the information you have to share. Moreover, your credibility is one of your most important assets; don't risk it by letting your personal agenda skew the presentation of your work.

7.6 THE POLICY ANALYST'S MINDSET

Mastering the art of policy analysis is a heavy lift. You need a toolbox full of analytic techniques, along with subject matter expertise in the policy domains in which you work. You need the ability to look at issues from multiple perspectives and to communicate effectively with diverse audiences. Along the way, you're expected to guard against biases, make effective use of evidence, and wisely apply logic and reasoning to messy issues. What's more, you need to deliver high-quality work, even though there is rarely as much time, information, or other resources as you'd like. And, if you're in an advocacy role, you need to be skilled at strategic political thinking while preserving your personal integrity.

As important as all these skills and capabilities are, *your work—and your career—won't reach its full potential unless you're grounded in the right mindset*. By mindset, I mean the collection of attitudes and behaviors that you bring to your professional work. Prior chapters have previewed many of these themes. My goal here is to distil that material down into the essential characteristics of effective policy analysts. You can think of the six elements shown in Exhibit 7-11 as a job description of sorts. The remainder of this section discusses each element in turn.

7.6.1 Critical Thinker

Critical thinking is the number one characteristic of an effective policy analyst and **skepticism** is the cornerstone of critical thinking. What does it mean to be skeptical?

Exhibit 7-11   The Policy Analyst's Mindset: A Job Description

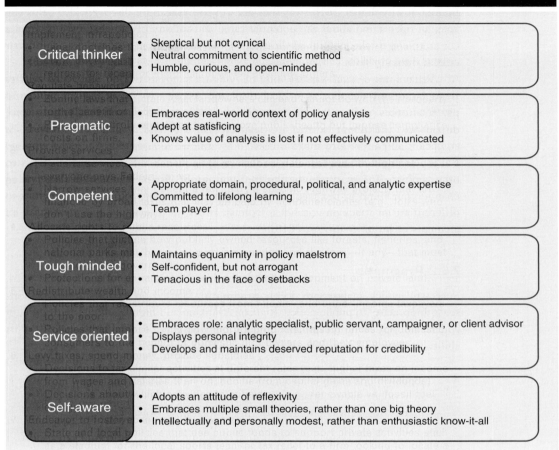

Critical thinker	• Skeptical but not cynical • Neutral commitment to scientific method • Humble, curious, and open-minded
Pragmatic	• Embraces real-world context of policy analysis • Adept at satisficing • Knows value of analysis is lost if not effectively communicated
Competent	• Appropriate domain, procedural, political, and analytic expertise • Committed to lifelong learning • Team player
Tough minded	• Maintains equanimity in policy maelstrom • Self-confident, but not arrogant • Tenacious in the face of setbacks
Service oriented	• Embraces role: analytic specialist, public servant, campaigner, or client advisor • Displays personal integrity • Develops and maintains deserved reputation for credibility
Self-aware	• Adopts an attitude of reflexivity • Embraces multiple small theories, rather than one big theory • Intellectually and personally modest, rather than enthusiastic know-it-all

All the evidence, theories, and claims upon which you might build your policy analysis need to be scrutinized before you accept them as valid. Your opening position should be that the material you're looking at is potentially flawed, and that the author needs to convince you otherwise. Yes, it can be a lot of work to critically filter and validate all the information that comes your way. But a suspicion that an author has overlooked something, made a mistake, is biased, or is manipulating your emotions can protect you from inadvertently accepting weak evidence or unsound reasoning.

If taken to an extreme, however, uncontrolled skepticism can make you **cynical**, instinctively and deeply distrusting all claims, people, and institutions. Cynicism impedes clear thinking. Skepticism needs to be paired with a spirit of inquiry that motivates you to proactively seek out new information, rather than waiting for it to arrive in your inbox. In a word, you need to be curious, excited to learn new things and figure out why things are the way they are. An enthusiasm for discovery also helps you keep an open mind about the potential value and validity of new information. And a commitment to the neutral application of the scientific method will enhance your critical thinking skills.

What's more, a substantial body of evidence suggests that intellectual **humility** is an important element of critical thinking. As we saw in Chapter 4, powerful psychic forces push us toward *uncritical* thinking: the discomfort of cognitive dissonance, the temptation of motivated reasoning, and a proclivity toward hot cognition all combine to make it easy to assume we're right and others are wrong. But if you think you know it all, you almost certainly don't! Listening respectfully to other points of view, remembering that you might just be wrong, a willingness to change your mind in the face of new evidence and strong logic, and the ability to differentiate an attack on your ideas from an attack on your worth as a person, are all elements of humility (Snow, 2018).

7.6.2 Pragmatic

Successful policy analysts are deeply **pragmatic**, focused on practical and common-sense approaches to public policy. Rigorous thinking and high-quality evidence are, of course, the goal, but a pragmatist pursues knowledge not for its own sake but for its ability to improve the quality of real-world policy decisions. In other words:

> Pragmatism encourages us to orient ourselves to the concrete situations in which policy issues arise, focusing in particular on the opportunities or demands for action entailed by these situations. (Ansell & Geyer, 2017, p. 152)

Likewise, *a pragmatic attitude can help you see time, resource, and knowledge constraints not as annoying impediments to your work, but as the defining characteristics of all policy analysis.* Similarly, successful analysts recognize and acknowledge the legitimacy of political, budgetary, legal, and institutional constraints on the policymaking process. In short, they aspire to make the most valuable contribution to policymaking that is possible given the constraints.

In Chapter 3, we considered how the concepts of bounded rationality and satisficing often better explain policymaking than do the comprehensively rational perspectives embedded in classical policy analysis models. For example, both Lindblom and Simon argue that you can never collect and thoroughly analyze all evidence, and remove all uncertainty about the future, before a decision must be made. Instead, they tell us that we need to content ourselves with boundedly rational conclusions that are *good enough* for the matter hand. But pragmatic policy analysts don't use these boundaries as an excuse for timid, narrow, or superficial analysis. Instead, they constantly push against the boundaries, always looking for ways to do the best possible work within these constraints. Accordingly, if you want to get good at the craft of policy analysis, aspire to become a 'super-satisficer.'

A pragmatic analyst also realizes that if the analytic work stays stuck insider his or her head because of poor communication, then it becomes irrelevant. As we saw in Section 7.5, it doesn't matter how amazing your work is. If you can't explain it clearly, in a way that moves all that insight from your mind to the mind(s) of your audience, then in a word, you've failed.

7.6.3 Competent

An essential ingredient in the policy analytic mindset is a deep affinity for and lifelong pursuit of **competence**, defined here as the knowledge, skills, and abilities needed to do the analyst's job well. The nature of the required competence, of course, varies tremendously across career paths, job types, and personal interests. There are at least four competencies that may be relevant to your career:

- *Domain* expertise in, for example, health care, criminal justice, or foreign affairs,
- *Procedural* expertise in, for example, specific institutional rules, budgetary processes, and statutory and regulatory requirements applicable to the jurisdiction in which you work,
- *Political* expertise as regards the relevant stakeholders, political norms, and decision processes that affect your work, and
- *Analytic* expertise in the application of tools like cost–benefit analysis, program evaluation, systems analysis, policy design, or forecasting.

Beyond expertise in domains, procedures, politics, and tools, *competence also requires intellectual agility*. Effective analysts move easily from the micro level to the macro level, and back again. For instance, you may need to validate specific data in a spreadsheet one minute, and in the next, think broadly about the statistical techniques you'll use to draw reasonable inferences from those data. Or you could spend the morning talking one on one with the clients of a social welfare program about their personal experience and the afternoon working with government accountants to understand nuances of the program's budget. In short, you need to be able to see the forest and the trees at the same time.

Similarly, you need to be *adept at looking at issues from more than one perspective or discipline*. When, for instance, you're designing a new policy option, you may need to think not only about how to make it optimal from a microeconomic perspective but also consider whether it complies with relevant statutory provisions or falls unequally across socioeconomic lines. It's not easy to bounce around from discipline to discipline during a policy analysis, but the ability to do so is a skill worth mastering.

And given the ever-evolving environment in which policy analysis takes place, a *commitment to lifelong learning* is also important. If you don't make the effort to stay current, your competence will grow stale and progressively less valuable over time.

Another element of professional competence depends on *strong interpersonal skills*. Successful policy analysts are usually team players, who can collaborate effectively with others and, in doing so, maximize their personal productivity. We touched briefly on teamwork in Section 7.3.4 and we'll talk more about maximizing your interpersonal effectiveness in Section 15.2. For now, it's important to recognize that the ability to work with others can be just as important to your professional career as your ability to execute a complex analysis or craft a winning political strategy.

The final aspect of competence in policy analysis is, somewhat ironically, the ability to *recognize your own incompetence*, or more specifically, the limits of your competence. Remember the Dunning-Kruger effect from Section 4.6? It crops up when subject matter expertise in one area tricks you into thinking you're an expert in other areas. The problem isn't particularly severe for novice analysts, who are usually acutely aware that they don't yet know everything they need to. But, over the course of your career, as your competence grows, overconfidence can become more of a threat. The antidote? Always stay within your zone of competence; be humble when your work takes you outside that zone.

7.6.4 Tough-Minded

Effective policy analysts have a *mental resilience that helps them maintain their equanimity amid dynamic, often ill-defined, sometimes chaotic, policymaking processes*. Time can be short, resources limited, and expectations high. In a politicized situation, folks aren't always kind and respectful; sometimes, they're rude and dishonest. What's more, I've encouraged you to live with cognitive dissonance, avoid hot cognition, and stay away from motivated reasoning. Doing so is likely to create at least some psychic disequilibrium for you. An ability to take it all in stride, without losing your cool, is an important professional skill.

For starters, you need to be sufficiently self-aware to realize that a criticism of your idea or of your analytic work isn't necessarily a criticism of you. It can be hard, but try to avoid being self-defensive and instead welcome feedback on your work. For one thing, critical input from others can improve the quality of a specific deliverable. And, if taken as a learning experience, openness to feedback can improve your long-term career prospects as you learn to avoid mistakes and teach yourself more effective ways of working.

Another aspect of tough-mindedness is the ability to recover from inevitable setbacks. You're human; you *will* make mistakes during your career (though hopefully not too many). Mistakes can be of your own creation: you might get too busy to meet all your commitments or think you're more capable than you are. In turn, you miss a deadline or deliver a shoddy work product. Moreover, because policy analyses are produced under time and resource constraints, with incomplete information, you are always vulnerable to being proven wrong as time passes and hindsight makes clear where you were mistaken. Sometimes, setbacks originate from others who, in one way or another, undermine your work. It could be a political opponent who succeeds in making you and your analysis look incompetent or flawed, even when it is not. You might even have an incompetent boss, or a jealous colleague, who gets between you and a successful result. *Stuff happens, even to the best analysts.*

Accordingly, policy analysts who enjoy long run success tend to be tenacious and willing to persevere in the face of setbacks. Remember that you're a smart, well-trained analyst, capable of making a difference. If you work hard, stay within your zone of competence, and protect your credibility, you deserve to be taken seriously. Self-confidence helps in this regard, but *you don't want to edge over into arrogance or cockiness.* (Arrogant analysts often make mistakes that others don't; they're also not likely to be team players.) Finally, it pays to recognize that policy change often takes a long time—sometimes years or decades—and usually depends on a lot more than just your policy analysis. Don't get discouraged if your work doesn't immediately change the world.

7.6.5 Service Oriented

Policy analysis doesn't take place in a vacuum. Clients, funders, and practitioners engage the process with particular objectives in mind. To be a successful analyst, *you need a clear sense of the purpose of your work and of the role you personally serve in the policy analysis process.* Roles can be differentiated based on the balance in your work between normative and descriptive issues, and by the primary purpose of your work: *analysis as inquiry* or *analysis as advocacy*.[9] Exhibit 7-12 juxtaposes these two dimensions to identify four roles that policy analysts may play, each implying a different definition of what it means to be service-oriented.[10] You'll note that there is no role identified for advocates engaged solely in descriptive work. When you think about it, this should make sense.

---

[9]Exhibit 3-4 categorized each task in classical policy analysis based on whether its focus is primarily normative or primarily descriptive, while Exhibit 3-5 distinguished *analysis as inquiry* from *analysis as advocacy*.

[10]My characterizations of the Analytic Specialist, the Campaigner, and the Client Advisor are very loosely based on the work of three scholars (Jenkins-Smith, 1982; Weimer & Vining, 2017). The description of the Public Servant is inspired by the work of Stone (2012) and Denhardt and Denhardt (2007).

Exhibit 7-12   The Roles Played by Policy Analysts

		Type of Issues Addressed	
		Only Descriptive	Descriptive and Normative
Primary analytic approach	Analysis as inquiry	The Analytic Specialist	The Public Servant
	Analysis as advocacy	Not applicable	The Campaigner The Client Advisor

The act of advocacy is itself intrinsically normative as you argue that we should or should not take action on a policy issue.

- The *Analytic Specialist* is motivated by the goal of inquiry but focuses on only the descriptive elements of policy analysis, deferring the inclusion of normative preferences and political considerations to other actors. His or her expertise focuses on domain and procedural matters or on the application of analytic tools. Service entails delivering the most technically sophisticated analysis possible. Exhibit 7-13 provides an example of this approach applied to the work of the US intelligence community.

- The *Public Servant*, like the Analytic Specialist, is motivated by inquiry but goes farther and considers normative as well as descriptive issues. But these normative values are neither the analyst's own nor are they those of a client. Instead, Public Servants aim to reflect the values of the public writ large (conflicting though they may be) in their analysis. Service requires that voices across the political, ideological, and socioeconomic spectrum be (at least metaphorically) heard throughout the analysis, without sacrificing rigorous analysis of descriptive issues.

- The *Campaigner* is motivated not by the goal of inquiry but by the goal of advocacy. As such, both descriptive and normative considerations are selectively and strategically reflected in the analysis. The source of normative beliefs lies in the analyst's personal preferences. He or she will typically seek employment with an interest group whose political agenda aligns with his or her own. For the Campaigner, service entails the use of analytic and political skills to effectively advance policies that comport with the analyst's personal agenda.

- The *Client Advisor*, like the Campaigner, is also not motivated by the goal of inquiry but by the goal of advocacy. In turn, descriptive and normative elements

The IC Analytic Standards are the core principles of intelligence analysis and are to be applied across the IC. ... The Standards also promote a common ethic for achieving analytic rigor and excellence and for personal integrity in analytic practice. ... All IC analytic products shall be consistent with the following five Analytic Standards, including the nine Analytic Tradecraft Standards.

A. Objective: Analysts must perform their functions with objectivity and with awareness of their own assumptions and reasoning. They must employ reasoning techniques and practical mechanisms that reveal and mitigate bias....

B. Independent of political consideration: Analytic assessments must not be distorted by, nor shaped for, advocacy of a particular audience, agenda, or policy viewpoint. Analytic judgments must not be influenced by the force of preference for a particular policy.

C. Timely: Analysis must be disseminated in time for it to be actionable by customers. Analytic elements have the responsibility to be continually aware of events of intelligence interest, of customer activities and schedules, and of intelligence requirements and priorities, in order to provide useful analysis at the right time.

D. Based on all available sources of intelligence information: Analysis should be informed by all relevant information available....

E. Implements and exhibits Analytic Tradecraft Standards, specifically:
   1. Properly describes quality and credibility of underlying sources, data, and methodologies ...
   2. Properly expresses and explains uncertainties associated with major analytic judgments ...
   3. Properly distinguishes between underlying intelligence information and analysts' assumptions and judgments ...
   4. Incorporates analysis of alternatives ...
   5. Demonstrates customer relevance and addresses implications ...
   6. Uses clear and logical argumentation ...
   7. Explains change to or consistency of analytic judgments ...
   8. Makes accurate judgments and assessments ...
   9. Incorporates effective visual information where appropriate ...

Source: ODNI (2015)

are strategically included in the analysis. The client is a policymaker, likely a politician, and it is the client rather than the analyst, who determines which normative value preferences belong in the analysis. Client Advisors typically opt to work for clients with shared values, but in the case of a conflict, the client's perspective prevails. Service thus entails the use of analytic and political skills to advance the client's political agenda.

The service orientation may test an analyst's personal integrity. Demanding clients and polarized debates can tempt an analyst to lose touch with the truth, misrepresent an analysis, or breach the ethical or legal constraints that apply to public service. We'll revisit professional ethics in Section 15.1, but for now, keep in mind the words of a former colleague of mine: never do anything you'd be embarrassed to have your family or friends read about in the newspaper or see in their social media newsfeeds. In short, *if you think something is ethical only if no one hears about it, then it probably isn't.*

Finally, it's important to recognize the value of a *deserved reputation for integrity and credibility*. Being honest about what you do and don't know to be true, routinely meeting the commitments you make to others, and honestly pursuing a mission of service are all elements of your reputation. Protecting that reputation has two benefits: it makes you a more credible and trusted analysts. It also helps you sleep at night.

7.6.6 Self-Aware

At the beginning of Chapter 4, I recommended that you embrace the principle of meta-cognition—thinking about how you think—as a means of improving your analytic skills. Here I'd like to go further and recommend that you work diligently to bring a broad sense of self-awareness to your work as a policy analyst. Regardless of whether we're talking about gender, age, race, ethnicity, income, education, political party, ideology, or myriad other personal characteristics, it's inevitable that *who we are* is intertwined with *how we work*:

> A researcher's background and position will affect what they choose to investigate, the angle of investigation, the methods judged most adequate for this purpose, the findings considered most appropriate, and the framing and communication of conclusions. (Malterud, 2001, pp. 483–484)

While you can't (and don't need to) sever the connection between who you are and how you work, you can manage that connection in productive ways by adopting an attitude of **reflexivity** (RWJF, 2006). The first step in doing so is to engage in some self-reflection to better understand how your identity and your preconceived notions about how the world works are affecting the ways in which you approach your professional life. The second step is to continuously monitor your own work, being alert to how the analytic choices you make, the normative positions you take, and the nature of your relationships with others are all potentially affected by internal psychic processes of which you are only vaguely aware.

For a demonstration of the value of reflexivity, let's revisit the work of Philip Tetlock. After studying hundreds of forecasters, pundits, and public intellectuals and the quality of their commentary on domestic and international affairs, Tetlock identified two distinct analytic approaches at work (2005). Based on an essay by Isaiah Berlin, he dubbed these two mindsets of the fox and the hedgehog.

The intellectually aggressive hedgehogs knew one big thing and sought, under the banner of parsimony, to expand the explanatory power of that big thing to 'cover' new cases; the more eclectic foxes knew many little things and were content to improvise ad hoc solutions to keep pace with a rapidly changing world. (pp. 20–21)

Foxes also tend to be comfortable with ambiguity and contradiction while hedgehogs often force their existing theories onto new evidence without worrying about how good the fit is.

Tetlock noted that foxes were more likely to make accurate predictions, and that ironically, hedgehogs were not especially self-aware about their limited forecasting skills. Despite their superior predictive skills, foxes tend to be more self-critical and tentative about their conclusions. Hedgehogs, on the other hand, can be very self-assured and passionate about their opinions. Not surprisingly then, the more modest fox readily admits previous mistakes of reasoning and inference, while, when challenged, the enthusiastic hedgehog tends to double down and defend or rationalize his or her previous pronouncements.

You may be thinking that some of the characteristics of foxes and hedgehogs are reminiscent of concepts we've already discussed earlier in this section. You're right about that. The reason I'm highlighting Tetlock's work here is that the metaphors of the fox and the hedgehog neatly collect our earlier discussion into two distinct clusters, or mindsets—one useful for policy analysts and the other not. In short, the self-aware mindset of the fox provides a solid foundation for your career as a policy analyst and a fitting conclusion to this section.

CHAPTER SUMMARY

This chapter brought together the themes of Part II of the book—cognition, logic, and evidence—to offer an integrated view of policy analysis aimed at building on and rebooting the classical models described in Chapters 1 and 2. We started by reviewing the essential ingredients of a strong, policy-relevant claim and examined methods for building your own policy claim. We next turned to the deconstruction of policy claims made by others to help you decide when to accept such claims as valid and when to discount or ignore them.

We also looked at several techniques for streamlining the analytic process to live within real-world constraints while still delivering valuable analytic insight to your client. In particular, we looked at one technique—decomposition or Fermi-izing of tough questions—when solid data are not available. Next up was a review of the principles of effective communication that all policy analysts should master. Finally, we wrapped all the material in Part II into a broad mindset that offers an enduring, adaptable, and lifelong professional development paradigm for a policy analyst.

DISCUSSION QUESTIONS

1. Pick a policy issue with which you are familiar and, in one sentence, make a policy claim (either a problem in need of action or a particular policy you support). What reasons would you offer in support of the claim? What logic and evidence is needed to substantiate each of those reasons? What counterarguments would you expect to hear in response to your claim? How would you respond to those counterarguments?

2. Find an op-ed or editorial in *The New York Times* or *The Wall Street Journal* that advocates a change in public policy. Can you identify weaknesses in the logic or evidence used to support the claim? What changes would you make to the claim, while still reaching the *same* conclusion?

3. If your client asks for an analysis of a complex policy topic, but only gives you a day to complete it, how would you respond? What steps could you take to ensure a useful result in the available time?

4. Suppose the federal government decides to replace all diesel school buses in the United States with electric buses. Your client asks how much this will cost. Assume you don't have time for anything other than a quick decomposition using Fermi's method. Can you list all the elements that would go into your calculation?

5. Pick a public policy measure you would like to see enacted. If you only had 60 seconds (the length of your client's elevator ride) to verbally make the case for the new policy, how would you make the most coherent and persuasive case possible in the time available?

6. Section 7.6.5 defined four roles that a policy analyst may play: the Analytic Specialist, the Public Servant, the Campaigner, and the Client Advisor. Which role do you think you'll play in your first job after graduation? Do you expect to stay in that role for most of your career? How do you see the pros and cons of each role when it comes to your own career?

LOOKING AT POLICY ISSUES THROUGH DIFFERENT LENSES

YOU CAN'T FIGURE OUT A PUZZLE IF YOU DON'T HAVE ALL THE PIECES

Policy debates can be a chaotic mix of disparate parts—ideas, arguments, bits of evidence, moral claims—that have little to do with one another. The urge to simplify, to fit things into tidy boxes, can be powerful. One of the easiest ways to do so is to narrow your focus and interpret the world from a single perspective or discipline. For instance, if you're a lawyer, your first instinct is probably to look at policy issues as legal matters. If you're an economist, sizing up costs and benefits might seem like the way to go. If you work for a legislator or an advocacy group, you probably see things through a political lens.

The core theme of this third part of the book is that, while it might be tempting and perhaps even comforting to stay within one perspective,[1] doing so is usually not a good idea. Recall, for example, our discussion in Section 4.6.3 about the framing of the climate change issue. The 2007 Stern Review used a cost–benefit analysis to look at the topic through the lens of microeconomics while the 2015 Papal Encyclical framed the issue in religious and moral terms. Both documents are thoughtful, coherent analyses that yield valuable insights about the topic of climate change. There is no obvious way to decide which one has the right perspective. In short, climate change has both an economic *and* an ethical and religious component. Dismissing one in favor of the other will almost certainly cause you to overlook important considerations that are relevant to your policy analysis:

> … *reliance on disciplinary socialization means that, even in complex interdisciplinary problem arenas, professionals tend to make assumptions about other people's goals, pay too little attention to what has occurred outside of their own specialty, and choose alternatives that are familiar to them. (Wallace & Clark, 2018, p. 111)*

It doesn't have to be this way. Fortunately, when it comes to developing a deep appreciation of a policy issue, you don't need to settle on one 'correct' perspective. As scholar Floyd Matson (1966) put it:

> *The point is rather that the two alternative perspectives or frames of reference are complementary, i.e., mutually exclusive if applied simultaneously but mutually 'tolerant' if considered as opposite sides of the same coin—differing faces of the same reality. (p. 136)*

The process of looking at an issue through multiple lenses can be referred to as a panoptic approach. A **lens** is a particular discipline or technique for investigating a topic. And a **panoptic** approach invites us to look simultaneously at the same policy issue from multiple vantage points (i.e., lenses) while using different techniques of observation. Harold Lasswell said as much when he identified multidisciplinarity as a key component of the policy sciences (deLeon, 2006).[2]

A great example of multiperspective thinking can be found in Graham Allison's classic text, *Essence of Decision* (1971). In it, he used three alternative lenses to evaluate the behavior of the Soviet Union in the context of the 1962 Cuban Missile Crisis. The rational actor lens treats the Soviets as a single entity systematically pursuing its strategic objectives through military action. The governmental politics lens instead looks at Soviet

---

[1]Applying multiple perspectives simultaneously may induce cognitive dissonance, a phenomenon that you'll recall from Chapter 4 most of us try to avoid whenever possible.

[2]'Multidisciplinary' suggests the use of multiple disciplines without implying their integration. By contrast, 'interdisciplinary' implies a synthetic blending of the insights of disciplines to reach a conclusion (Clark & Wallace, 2015).

policymakers as a collection of competing political interests, each enjoying differing degrees of success and failure during the crisis. Finally, the organizational process lens treats the Soviet government as a bureaucracy, the behavior of which is guided primarily by standard operating processes and governmental systems. No one lens is unambiguously right; all three help to explain Soviet behavior during the crisis.

A more recent example of a panoptic policy analysis model comes from Cohen who, after citing Allison, offers a multilens framework for analyzing environmental policy issues such as fracking, e-waste, and climate change (2014). He recommends looking at such issues through five lenses: values, politics, science and technology, economics and policy design, and sustainability management. While focused on environmental issues, Cohen's commentary is broadly relevant to policy analysis in general:

> The power of this approach is that the same facts are reinterpreted from several perspectives and different facts are brought to light by the different dimensions of the framework. One purpose of this framework is to counter analytic bias deep within the way we understand environmental problems. ... Lip service to the notion that environmental problems are inherently interdisciplinary does little to amend the tendency to assume that one's own discipline is the central one. When analyzing an environmental issue, ignoring other fields is an obstacle to improved solutions. (pp. 13–14)

Beyond the ability of a panoptic approach to illuminate previously invisible aspects of a policy issue, a panoptic approach also has the practical virtue of relieving the analyst of the need to select and defend a single perspective or frame:

> In an American political and social system often defined by polar politics and overwhelming complexity that result in a general lack of consensus, reaching agreements on how best to frame policy issues could be tantamount to impossible .... (deLeon, 2006, p. 49)

Another reason to ensure that you've considered multiple perspectives, or frames, in your policy analysis is that political advocates will often select a frame that displays their policy claim in the most favorable way possible. If you accept someone else's framing of an issue, you may unknowingly be manipulated into reaching a foregone conclusion (Lakoff, 2014).

Building on Allison's and Cohen's work, I offer below seven lenses through which policy issues can be productively viewed. In my experience, almost all policy debates revolve around one or more of these ways of looking at the world.[3] The lenses are not ends in themselves; you don't need to slog through a detailed analysis of a lens that's

---

[3]This approach reflects a core tenet of the book: Policy analysts must adjust their work to reflect the way that policy discourse happens in the 'real world,' not the other way around.

not relevant to a particular policy issue. Instead, you can think of these suggestions more as a checklist to ensure you don't miss anything rather than as a list of required elements for all policy analyses.

- The **equity lens** helps you better understand issues like equality, liberty, justice, stability and security, and wealth and poverty.

- The **economics lens** helps you appreciate how the behavior of firms, consumers, and markets relates to policy analysis and the conditions under which markets may fail to deliver efficient outcomes.

- The **political lens** helps you characterize and understand the role played by politics in policymaking and the motives of folks who participate in policy debates.

- The **institutional lens** helps you recognize how the behavior of governmental institutions, and the people who work in them, shapes policy.

- The **legal lens** helps you recognize constraints on policy created by constitutional, statutory, administrative, and common law.

- The **sustainability lens** helps you understand the tensions between the needs of current generations and those of future generations, as well as the balance between human needs and natural resources.

- The **science and technology lens** helps you understand how the natural sciences and engineered technologies intersect with policy analysis, and how the accelerating pace of technological change can lead to major social disruptions.

The process of incorporating these seven lenses into a policy analysis to yield a synthetic panoptic view of a particular policy issue is depicted in Exhibit III-1.[4] As you examine a policy issue through these lenses, you might be wondering what you're supposed to look for. At the broadest level, you're *hoping to be surprised when the panoptic approach triggers unanticipated insights* that you might otherwise have missed. At a more granular level, you can think about the classical model of policy analysis and its focus on problems and potential policy responses. When you panoptically consider a policy issue, therefore, your goal is to do two things.

---

[4]The equity and economic lenses are each reviewed in a chapter of their own (Chapters 8 and 9). The political and institutional lenses, which are closely related, are presented in Chapter 10. The legal, sustainability, and science and technology lenses are described in Chapter 11. These final three lenses are not directly related to each other, but are presented together in order to keep all four chapters of Part III at about the same length.

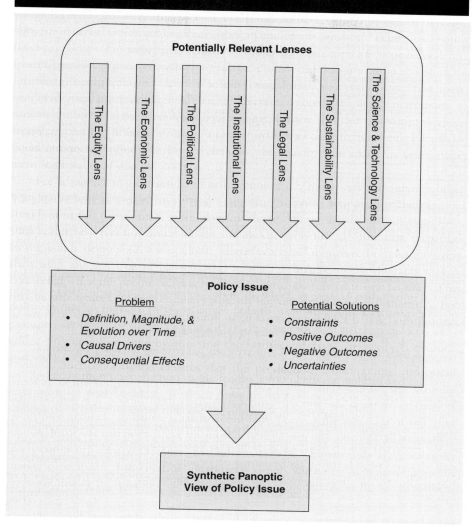

First, you want to *deepen your understanding of the policy problem* by clearly defining it, identifying its constituent parts, characterizing its magnitude, and tracing its evolution over time (both in the past and as it might play out in the future). You may remember the Five Whys and Five So-Whats techniques from our discussion of the problem definition process in Chapter 1. We use these techniques to probe for the underlying causal drivers of the problem, as well as to better understand the full array of its downstream consequences. The multilens approach can be especially helpful in identifying causes and effects of the problem that you hadn't previously appreciated. Try asking the Five Whys and Five So-Whats from within each lens. Depending on which lens you're applying, the policy problem may look quite different from your initial assessment, or from the view gleaned through other lenses.

The second use of the seven lenses is to *sharpen your understanding of potential policy responses* to the problem. In some cases, one or more lenses may expose an insurmountable constraint (e.g., budgetary, legal, or technological) that makes a particular policy option infeasible. Alternatively, the panoptic approach might reveal a flaw in a potential policy solution that you can overcome with a change to its design. More expansively, the use of multiple lenses to examine each available policy option helps you minimize the chance of overlooking an important outcome—good or bad—that the option might create. Finally, a panoptic analysis can identify uncertainties in your analysis that, in turn, may help you qualify the provisional nature of your findings.

Recall the definition of the word 'analysis' from Part I. It means to break something apart into its constituent components to reveal intrinsic and potentially hidden characteristics that you might otherwise have missed. A panoptic approach will help considerably in this regard. Of course, after having broken a policy issue into smaller pieces, the final step is to reassemble those pieces into an integrated and holistic view of the issue, a task which is described in Part IV. But first, we'll spend the remainder of Part III taking a closer look at each of the seven lenses.

CHAPTER EIGHT

THE EQUITY LENS

One way to view a policy issue is through the lens of **equity**. In this context, the word equity refers to value-oriented normative concepts like human rights and duties, equality, liberty and freedom, security and privacy, and justice and fairness.[1] As we'll see in this chapter, opinions on normative issues can be intensely personal, with such opinions—and the ways by which folks arrive at them—varying widely across society. Universally agreed and definitive constructions of right and wrong have eluded philosophers—and people in general—for centuries. Despite the intangible, ephemeral, and freighted nature of moral issues, policy analysis has an important role to play here.

This chapter offers a few guidelines for tackling normative issues in your work. We start in Section 8.1 with a quick review of how the topic of moral reasoning has been approached by a small group of philosophers over the last couple centuries. In Section 8.2, we focus on one particular approach, a thought experiment known as the veil of ignorance. Section 8.3 then summarizes seven dimensions of equity that appear frequently in policy debates. Each of the next two sections focuses on a specific mechanism for thinking about inequity in the context of policy analysis. Section 8.4 explores how the passage of time can affect perceptions of equity, while Section 8.5 addresses the differences between an equitable process and an equitable result. Section 8.6 considers the impact of

---

[1] In Section 6.1, I divided the types of conclusions you might draw from evidence into six categories, two of which were normative in nature. The first comprised normative *value* judgments (matters of right and wrong) and the second comprised normative *policy* judgments (which public policies ought to be adopted). This chapter focuses on the former, while Section 1.5 addressed the latter.

Learning Objectives

By studying this chapter, you should be able to:

- Characterize the five elements of moral reasoning, and explain and differentiate two forms of moral reasoning: rationalism and social intuitionism.

- Use the 'veil of ignorance' test to limit the impact of your personal views on your assessment of moral reasoning used by others.

- Understand and apply the concepts of rights, duties, equality, liberty, justice, stability, safety, and security to specific public policy issues.

- Understand the elements of income inequality and poverty and their potential connection to matters of inequity.

- Evaluate the degree of alignment between the costs and benefits of specific public policies as a means of identifying potential inequities.

- Locate a present-day inequity in an historical arc that reflects both the past experience of key stakeholders and their anticipation of future events.

- Distinguish inequities that are the result of systemic processes from inequities that originate in the facts and circumstances of a particular case.

- Explain the nature of cumulative and systemic inequity.

- Understand the limitations of public analysis when it comes to reaching definitive conclusions about normative issues.

cumulative inequities experienced by a particular group, community, or segment of society. Finally, Section 8.7 addresses some of the limitations of policy analysis when it comes to offering definitive insight into normative issues.

8.1 MORAL REASONING

It should come as no surprise that most public policy debates entail at least some discussion of normative values. Take a look back at Exhibit 3-4 where each of the elements of the classical policy analysis models is characterized as either descriptive or normative. You'll see about twenty instances in which normative considerations play the dominant role. A policy problem, for example, constitutes a gap between a descriptive as-is condition and a *normative* to-be condition. Similarly, the decision about which evaluation criteria warrant inclusion in a policy analysis is, intrinsically, one of *normative* values. As Deborah Stone (2012) puts it: "Sure, policy disputes entail some disputes over facts, but the deeper and more important conflicts are over values" (p. 312).

Integrating normative value-centric issues into policy analysis requires an understanding of moral reasoning—which incorporates concepts like ethics, values, principles, and religious tenets—as a means of deciding how, as a matter of public policy, people should treat one another. After a brief overview that describes one framework (there are many) for thinking about issues of morality and ethics, we'll look at two schools of thought when it comes to moral reasoning.

8.1.1 A Framework for Moral Reasoning

Moral reasoning can cover a lot of ground, but almost always addresses one or more of the following five foundational topics (Haidt, 2007; Haidt & Graham, 2007):

- *Harm and Care*: Feelings of altruism toward others and their implications for the protection of vulnerable people

- *Fairness and Reciprocity*: Rights to resources or to just treatment by others and by institutions

- *Ingroup Loyalty*: Values of patriotism and cooperation with one's own group and distrust of and reticence to engage other groups

- *Authority and Respect*: Importance of deference, duty, obedience to legitimate holders of power

- *Purity and Sanctity*: Living in a virtuous and sanctified, rather than a corrupt and profane, way

There is wide variation when it comes to specific viewpoints on these five topics, the importance of each topic relative to the others, and whether all five or only some are relevant to moral reasoning. Positions on these topics may cluster along ideological lines with liberals tending to put more emphasis on the first two and conservatives often emphasizing the latter three. Accordingly, this set of five topics does not, by itself, give you any guidance about how to resolve normative issues. Rather, you should *view it as an organizing framework for deepening your understanding* of how the parties in a policy debate may be thinking about the normative aspects of policy issues. Why is this important? Because the more thoroughly you appreciate the rationale behind folks' moral reasoning, the better equipped you will be to characterize the nature and source of agreements and disagreements among the parties.

Two broad schools of thought exist about how we should approach the development of moral principles. The first, referred to as **rationalism**, uses logic to discern guidelines for moral and ethical behavior. By contrast, the second school of thought, known as **social intuitionism**, locates moral principles not in reasoning but in the reflexive domains of intuition, emotion, and perception.

8.1.2 Rationalism as a Form of Moral Reasoning

To illustrate how moral principles can be derived from a logical and deliberative reasoning process, let's consider three examples from the field of political philosophy: utilitarianism, the categorical imperative, and the veil of ignorance (Lovett, 2011). Each is an attempt to *derive a framework for ethics and moral philosophy based solely on the principles of rationality* (Haidt, 2001). But, first a quick warning: these three approaches have generated probably tens of thousands of pages of review, enhancement, and critique over, in some cases, centuries; it's impossible to provide even a summary in just a few paragraphs. My aim is not to describe the specific thinking embedded in each approach but instead to illustrate—in broad strokes—what it looks like when we attempt to derive normative conclusions solely from within a logic-based perspective.

The first example of a rationalist approach to moral reasoning is **utilitarianism**, developed in the late eighteenth century by Jeremy Bentham and advanced by John Stuart Mill in the mid-nineteenth century. In a nutshell, utilitarianism holds that a person's behavior or a government's action can be judged by the degree to which it maximizes the total utility (or happiness) of all people, weighting each person equally. At the time, utilitarianism was a radical break from prevailing norms because it weighted the happiness of a commoner, a French person, and a woman equal to the happiness of, respectively, a king or queen, an English person, or a man.[2]

---

[2]Utilitarianism is also one of the logical foundations of cost benefit analysis (CBA) and motivates the summation of all costs and all benefits across all members of society in order to arrive at an estimate of the net benefits of a proposed policy, with the understanding that the policy option with the highest net benefits is optimal. CBA was introduced in Section 1.5 and we'll examine it in more detail in Chapter 9.

Utilitarianism can, however, lead to some uncomfortable conclusions. For instance, it could be used to justify the public punishment of an innocent person to deter others predisposed to commit a crime. The utilitarian rationale for doing so might be that the averted pain and suffering of multiple potential victims outweighs the pain and suffering inflicted on the one innocent person. In short, "utilitarianism can diverge significantly from common sense morality" (Lovett, 2011, p. 6).

A second example of the rationalist approach comes from Immanuel Kant. Writing in 1785, he used a systematic approach, based on his version of rationality, to define moral behavior. One of his conclusions was the **categorical imperative**: that a person should behave only in accordance with principles that he or she believe can be appropriately universalized to all people (Bucciarelli, Khemlani, & Johnson-Laird, 2008). If you would not be satisfied by a world where everyone applied your moral reasoning to their actions, then your action cannot be morally justified. For example, I have a moral duty not to lie because I would not want to live in a world where no one felt compelled to tell the truth.

There is, however, a "serious loophole" in Kant's framework (Lovett, 2011, p. 11). The problem with a universal imperative is that it needn't treat everyone equally. For example, a bigot who discriminates against one social group could argue that doing so is morally acceptable because—believing in the legitimacy of bigotry—he or she would be content to see such behavior deemed universally permissible.

The third example of a moral framework built on a foundation of logic comes from John Rawls whose work spanned the last half of the twentieth century. Acknowledging an intellectual debt to Kant (and others), Rawls developed a theory of justice that he argued could be used to structure the institutions of a society, specify the rights and duties of its citizens, and define the mechanisms of societal cooperation. In particular, Rawls aspired to close the loophole in Kant's universal imperative with a clever thought experiment intended to remove self-interest from moral reasoning.

Rawls asked us to imagine ourselves cloaked by a **veil of ignorance** that blinds us to our position in society. For example, we might be a wealthy, privileged member of the majority or we might be a poor, disadvantaged member of the minority; behind the veil, we simply don't know. We are asked about the society in which we'd like to live, and our answer is then used to logically derive the structures and processes of a fair and just society. Worried that we might end up among the less fortunate, we would likely opt for a more equal society where the disadvantages for such folks are mitigated and institutional processes are in place to ensure their equitable treatment.

8.1.3 Social Intuitionism as a Form of Moral Reasoning

In the three examples we've just looked at—Bentham and Mill, Kant, and Rawls—moral reasoning is a philosophical exercise in which logical thinking is used to derive principled guidelines for differentiating right and wrong. In contrast, **social intuitionism** views the process of making moral decisions in a fundamentally different way. Rather than relying on reason and logic, this school of thought focuses on instinctive judgments of the type often seen in System 1 thinking. A prominent example of moral intuitionism is Thomas Jefferson's list of *self-evident* 'truths' at the start of the Declaration of Independence. There was no need in 1776 America for a logical, reasoned defense of the principle that all men are created equal and possess unalienable rights to life, liberty, and the pursuit of happiness. These principles were perceived to stand on their own as intrinsically true.[3] As two more examples, let's take a closer look at the work of David Hume and Jonathan Haidt.

Writing in 1739—a half-century before Kant—Hume argued that detailed logical explications and proofs were not the way that people actually decide which moral rules to live by. Instead, the *rules of morality originate in human sentiments, perceptions, passions, and aesthetics*. Hume writes that:

> Reason of itself is utterly impotent in this particular. The rules of morality, therefore, are not conclusions of our reason … 'tis vain to pretend, that morality is discover'd only by a deduction of reason. (Bucciarelli et al., 2008, pp. 121–122)

Hume's framework doesn't eliminate the reasoned use of evidence and logic when we're trying to figure out the right thing to do. We still need to consider the consequences of our choices prior to taking action by, for example, determining who might be helped and who might be harmed by each of the choices open to us. But, according to Hume, it's not until we attach an emotional value to each of those consequences that we have a moral basis for taking action (Haidt, 2001).

Fast forward about 250 years, and we find another social intuitionist, Jonathan Haidt, explicitly building on Hume's thinking, albeit informed by a modern understanding of social and cognitive psychology (Bucciarelli et al., 2008). Drawing an analogy to dual process theory, he defines moral intuition as the:

> sudden appearance in consciousness of a moral judgment, including an affective valence (good-bad, like-dislike), without any conscious awareness of having gone through steps of searching, weighting evidence, or inferring a conclusion. (Haidt, 2001, p. 818)

---

[3]The fact that most folks today would not limit these rights to white, property-owning, men demonstrates the fluidity of conclusions reached through moral intuitionism.

Moreover, he argues that personal moral intuitions have a strong social component rooted in cultural, religious, ethical, political, and civic norms, rather than in methodical reasoning processes (Haidt, 2001).

Accordingly, for proponents of the social intuitionist school of thought, moral reasoning does not lead to moral judgment; instead, the process usually runs in the other direction. *Moral judgments are reached intuitively and quickly, and then after-the-fact reasoning is used to support the judgment.*[4] Haidt (2007) underscores the point with a clever analogy:

> Moral reasoning is often like the press secretary for a secretive administration—constantly generating the most persuasive arguments it can muster for policies whose true origins and goals are unknown. (p. 1000)

Social intuitionists recognize that moral reasoning is not always subservient to intuitive instinct. Like the executive override of System 1 by System 2 in dual process theory, intuition can also be countermanded in the realm of moral reasoning. Such overrides are, however, the exception rather than the rule.

So, where does all this leave us? For starters, normative issues are pervasive in policy analysis, popping up in just about every step of the process. And even though they may not be framed as such, these issues are usually rooted in one or more of the foundational elements of moral reasoning: harm and care, fairness and reciprocity, ingroup loyalty, authority and respect, and purity and sanctity. In turn, if you aspire to address the entirety of an issue in your policy analysis, you'll need to be ready to tackle normative issues. You might do so as an intentional consequence of rational thought of the type applied by Bentham, Mill, Kant, and Rawls. Alternatively, as suggested by Hume and Haidt, moral positions may be the by-product of quick and intuitive responses to particular situations based on cultural, religious, ethical, political, and civic instincts. I can't tell you who has it right; my experience tells me that both perspectives are relevant to policy analysis and that as a policy analyst, you will often need to recognize how and why folks—including yourself—come to hold their moral positions.

8.2 DONNING A VEIL OF IGNORANCE IN POLICY ANALYSIS

Back in Chapter 1, when we talked about which evaluation criteria belong in your policy analysis, I included equity as an 'on-off-the-shelf' criterion that ought to be

---

[4]This thesis is consistent with the impact of hot cognition on normative thinking discussed in Section 4.4.

routinely considered for inclusion in every policy analysis. But *deciding* to include matters of equity in your policy analysis is easy; *figuring out how* to analyze equity is considerably tougher. Having reviewed the five elements of moral reasoning, and the concepts of moral rationalism and social intuitionism, you shouldn't be surprised when you hear divergent normative viewpoints during a policy debate that are hard to reconcile. The analysis of equity issues is often like looking at a situation through different eyes. To do a complete analysis, you need to look through the eyes not only of those folks who are familiar to you and with whom you sympathize, but also through the eyes of folks whose points of view and lived experiences differ from your own.

Doing so can be hard. I'd thus like to offer a recommendation that builds on Rawls' veil of ignorance test that we just talked about. But unlike Rawls himself, I don't aim to use the veil of ignorance test to identify the optimal societal systems and structures writ large. Instead, my suggestion is that you always approach matters of equity in a particular policy analysis—at least initially—from behind a veil of ignorance. In this thought experiment, you might be wealthy and powerful, or poor and marginalized. You might be liberal or conservative, white or a person of color. You just don't know. Ignorant of your personal circumstances, you would then assess the normative arguments surrounding the policy issue you're analyzing. In many ways, the veil of ignorance test is a form of metacognition and a practical way of operationalizing a self-aware mindset.

As a simple example, consider a state legislature redrawing its Congressional district boundaries. You're trying to decide if it is doing so fairly. The veil of ignorance means that you don't know which party you belong to, and thus that your assessment of the redistricting process is untainted by self-interest. In general, we don a veil of ignorance in the hopes of reaching a conclusion not influenced by our personal stake in the outcome, our cultural background, or our ideological or political preferences.

But things can get more complicated than this simple example suggests when, behind your veil, you're trying to imagine the circumstances you might face under different public policies. The veil of ignorance test works best when it's based on an accurate understanding of the situations faced by different folks in society. That's why, back in Section 6.2, when we talked about collecting evidence regarding public preferences, I suggested that you go out of your way to metaphorically hear the voices of those in society who can't be heard and to figure out the concerns of invisible stakeholders.

I recognize that it's virtually impossible to fully ignore your personal situation; after all, the veil of ignorance test is just a thought experiment. But while you may have a great deal of confidence in *your own* sense of how public policy should reflect normative considerations, don't forget that *your personal opinion is just one among many*. Because policy analysis aims to inform the public policymaking process, you need your veil of ignorance to help you to think more expansively than just your own views. My

> **Exhibit 8-1   Dimensions of Equity**
>
> - Rights and Duties
> - Equality
> - Liberty
> - Justice
> - Stability, Safety, and Security
> - Wealth and Poverty
> - Alignment of Benefits and Costs

goal in this chapter is therefore to help you ask the right equity-relevant questions in your policy analysis. You will find lots of questions, but not many answers. *In a democracy, after all, the answers don't come primarily from you (or from me) but from the community you serve* (Denhardt & Denhardt, 2007).

8.3 DIMENSIONS OF EQUITY

When it comes to policy debates, most normative issues revolve around the concepts in Exhibit 8-1.[5] To keep things simple, each category is presented separately; in policy debates, however, these issues are often commingled. My focus in this section is on diagnosing and understanding inequities; potential remedies for these inequities are reviewed in Section 8.7.

8.3.1 Rights and Duties

When it comes to debating the equities associated with public policy, the conversation often turns to a discussion of **rights**. Rights occupy a special place in policy discourse. If a normative principle is deemed to be a right, it becomes an entitlement, a promise that society is obligated to deliver on. You can think of a right as a legitimate claim by one person on the behavior of others. The right to a public education, for example, obligates a community to provide schools for its children. A right to free speech prohibits others from impeding one's ability to speak freely.

---

[5]This section is inspired by Deborah Stone's *The Policy Paradox* (2012). I have, however, added to, taken away from, and reinterpreted much of her work. Accordingly, she bears no responsibility for what follows.

The real-world impact of a right varies widely. For starters, *many asserted rights are not codified as a matter of public policy*. In turn, no one is mandated to deliver on the right. For example, the UN Universal Declaration of Human Rights—which is not fully reflected in US federal law—includes a positive right to medical care. In the United States, however, universal access to medical care does not exist. Accordingly, if a US resident can't afford health insurance and is ineligible for government support, their notional human right to health care under the UN declaration isn't much help. Because it hasn't been enacted into law, it doesn't impose an enforceable duty on someone else to provide health care. The lack of a codified right, however, doesn't usually stop advocates of government health care spending from asserting a moral or ethical duty to enact public policies to provide such care.

At the other extreme, *some rights are both codified and enforceable*. Thanks to the Fourth Amendment to the US Constitution, for instance, if the police search your home without a warrant and find incriminating evidence, you have the right to have the evidence tossed out of court. Even for codified rights, however, enforcement mechanisms vary. For example, the US Civil Rights Act prohibits discrimination based on race, color, or national origin in any program or activity that receives Federal financial assistance. If you think your rights have been improperly denied under the Act, you can take the offending Federal agency to court, but only if you can prove intentional discrimination. If there are disparities across the lines of race, color, or national origin, but no evidence of discriminatory intent, you can't go to court; instead, you must complain to the agency and hope it resolves the matter.

We can divide rights into two categories: A **positive right** is one in which others are obligated to do something for the right holder. A **negative right** is one where others are obligated to refrain from doing something that affects the right holder. Notice that every right possessed by an individual implies **a duty** on the part of another individual, or of society, to respect or satisfy that right. You can think of rights and duties as two parts of the same whole. Whenever a right is claimed, there is always a corresponding duty being asserted, either explicitly or implicitly. Exhibit 8-2 may help you keep the vocabulary straight.

Policy debates that focus on rights and duties can be very complex. In the short space we have here, there's no way to provide a full overview of all the relevant material. But there are several questions you can ask as part of a policy analysis to organize your thinking about rights and duties:

- *Who holds the right?* Some rights are restricted to certain people. For instance, in several states, ex-felons do not have the right to vote; in other states, they do. In addition, not all rights are held by humans. For example, the US Supreme Court has decided that corporations—as nonhuman persons—have free speech rights.

Exhibit 8-2	Examples of Rights and Duties	
	Right	**Duty**
Negative Rights	I have a right to free speech.	Others have a duty not to impede my speech; I may not impede others' speech.
Positive Rights	I have a right to the satisfaction of my basic human needs (e.g., food, shelter, health care).	Others have a duty to assist me in meeting my basic human needs; I must assist others in meeting their basic human needs.

- *Has the right under debate been codified?* While there may be little moral difference in your mind between a codified right and an asserted right, there is a practical difference. With an asserted right, advocates must rely on the power of persuasion to ensure the right is observed; if it has been codified, legal recourse may be available to enforce the right.

- *Who has a duty to satisfy a negative right?* Because negative rights obligate folks to refrain from doing something, it is the duty of people, firms, and governments to respect such rights (e.g., even if I find your remarks distasteful, I may not restrict your speech).

- *Who has a duty to satisfy a positive right?* A positive right obligates someone to provide a thing of value that is rarely free (e.g., education, health care) to the right holder. If the right has been codified, it often but not always falls to government to satisfy the right, and the cost to taxpayers becomes part of the debate about whether and how to observe that right.

- *Does one right conflict with another?* Protecting one person's right may hinder the protection of another's. As a simple example, consider a prohibition on employment discrimination based on disability. What happens when one employee's service dog triggers a severe allergic response in another employee? Whose right should prevail?

8.3.2 Equality

Equality has become so embedded in our understanding of right and wrong that even a suggestion that people have been treated *unequally* is often taken to mean they have been treated *unfairly*. But what exactly do we mean by equality? In its narrowest reading, the word 'equal' means that two things are the same; 1/4 and 2/8 measure the same value. But human affairs are not as tidy as mathematics.

If you think about it, you'll realize that *while equality is a core value of modern democracies, we don't actually want to treat all people equally all the time*. If you need to go to the hospital, you want to see a professional who knows what they're doing. In turn, you're probably fine with the idea that the hospital can discriminate in its hiring between those who have medical credentials and those who don't. You're also probably ok with the idea that a local store can discriminate between those willing to pay for merchandise and those who would steal it. Similarly, if you support accommodations for people with disabilities, you are likely willing to endorse their differential treatment when it comes to, say, preferential parking, admission of service animals, or extra test-taking time in a classroom. In other words, the *unequal treatment of folks—discrimination if you will—is often a routine, and normatively acceptable, fact of everyday life.*

But we can't stop here. If we did, we'd open the door to many kinds of inequality—racism, sexism, homophobia, and the like—we find morally offensive. When it comes to public policy, we thus need a more nuanced definition of equality: *equality implies that people who are or should be similarly situated are to be treated similarly.* To continue our examples from above, the physician and the quack are not similarly situated, nor are the customer and the shoplifter. It's only when similarly situated folks (e.g., two well-qualified MDs, one a woman and one a man) are treated unequally that policy-relevant normative concerns may become important.

Such concerns usually arise when two factors come into play at the same time. First, there must be unequal treatment of specific types of people. The term **protected class** is often used to define groups to be shielded from unequal treatment. A good example of a policy intended to ensure equality is the Human Rights Code of Ontario, which prohibits discrimination based on:

> … citizenship, race, place of origin, ethnic origin, colour, ancestry, disability, age, creed, sex/pregnancy, family status, marital status, sexual orientation, gender identity, gender expression, receipt of public assistance … and record of offences. (OHRC, 2012)

In most jurisdictions, being poor, uneducated, a criminal, or an undocumented immigrant doesn't put one in a protected class; hence, some discrimination against such groups is typically permissible, at least as far as the law is concerned.[6]

---

[6]President Biden has directed federal agencies to ensure that their hiring practices do not discriminate against a broader set of protected classes than is used in Ontario including, for example, parents, caregivers, first-generation professionals, rural residents, veterans, non-English speakers, and military spouses (2021).

The second factor that gives rise to unacceptable inequality is the existence of a **protected situation**. For example, in Ontario, discrimination based on membership in one of the 17 protected classes is prohibited only in certain situations: when residents receive goods or services, buy or rent housing, enter contracts, seek or hold a job, or join a union or professional association (OHRC, 2012). Note that by defining protected situations to which antidiscrimination policies apply, we are also implicitly defining unprotected situations to which such policies do not apply. If Ontario had omitted housing from its list of protected situations, for example, then race-based inequality in housing would be legal.

Virtually all disputes about matters of equality revolve around the definitions of protected classes and protected situations. Such definitions are often contested, with some advocates arguing for more classes (e.g., transgender persons) to be protected from unequal treatment in additional situations (e.g., accessing social services from government-funded, faith-based groups). Conversely, other advocates assert that policy measures to promote equality can go too far, impeding citizens' rights and liberties to choose when and how to interact with other members of society.

Another important aspect of equality which figures prominently in policy analysis arises from the difference between **equality of opportunity** and **equality of results**. Let's start with opportunity. You might believe that everyone should have an equal opportunity to attend college. But not everyone takes advantage of the opportunities offered to them. For example, you might not be bothered when a hard-working, talented high schooler is given a spot at a prestigious university while the class clown who ditched school every other day is not. After all, a meritocracy in which everyone has the same opportunity to have their individual accomplishments fairly and equally rewarded seems reasonable.

In fact, the prospect of earning personal recognition or rewards that are not offered to everyone may incentivize hard work toward socially beneficial outcomes. In this case, however, the slacker failed to take advantage of the opportunity that was available.[7] But if you were told that women or persons of color (i.e., members of a potentially protected class) were denied spots at the university, you probably would feel differently. If that's your stance, you're essentially saying that it's ok to offer unequal opportunities based on merit, but not based on race or gender.

Now let's pivot to the equality of results. Consider two equally talented students from similar backgrounds who put forth equal effort at the same college. Both have identical opportunities, but one enters the world of corporate finance and earns a six-figure salary; the other chooses a career as an artist, and while talented, struggles to earn

---

[7]You might also think that an 18-year-old slacker deserves a second chance to get back on track. Most of us wouldn't disagree, but would you go so far as giving the talented student's spot at the university to the slacker?

a living wage. Over the course of their careers, they accumulate highly unequal levels of wealth. Later, the financier's child attends an elite private university while the artist's child goes to the local community college. Even this simple vignette raises important questions about the link between equality of opportunities and equality of results:

- Does the inequality in wealth suggest an inequity? Maybe not. Our two graduates had the same opportunities. The inequality of results stems only from freely made personal choices.

- But were the opportunities truly identical? Perhaps it's only in an unequal society that financiers earn so much more than artists.

- Even if our two graduates were treated equally, what about the kids? Given the inequality in parental wealth, has the artist's child been denied an equal opportunity for success?

- Would it matter if the financier is a white male and the artist is a woman of color? Could racism and sexism possibly mean that life's opportunities haven't been offered equally?

Inequality can indeed be a vexing subject to analyze, but *deciding whether you're focused on equality of opportunities, equality of outcomes, or both is a good place to start.*

One aspect of inequality that is typically *beyond the reach of public policy is personal behavior that takes place outside of protected situations.* When it comes to your choice of friends, a life partner, stores to patronize, candidates to vote for, places to hang out—the list is end-less—you are under no legal obligation to treat others equally. You may be as inclusive, or as prejudiced, as you'd like. For example, you are not obligated to give all folks who show an interest in spending time with you an equal opportunity to become your friend in the same way we expect universities to give all applicants an equal opportunity to be admitted. In short, whether it's an inappropriate intrusion on personal liberty or just impractical, we don't aspire to use public policy to ensure equality among all people in all situations.[8]

As with questions of rights and duties, the topic of equality is an immense one. We can't cover it in detail, but here are a few questions that may help deepen your analysis of issues related to equality:

- When it comes to ensuring equality, which groups of people, if any, should be designated as protected and which aspects of life, if any, should be designated as protected situations?

---

[8]We'll talk briefly in Section 8.7 about how public policy might be used to remedy some forms of inequity.

- Do people have equal opportunities to obtain and enjoy life's amenities?

- Do we observe equality of results when it comes to obtaining and enjoying life's amenities?

- Does the principle of meritocracy mean that observed disparities can be satisfactorily explained as the result of talent, hard work, personal choices, or other 'acceptable' causes?

- Are inequalities only isolated cases or do they result from widespread discrimination or bias against groups or individuals who deserve to have been treated equally?

- Why do inequalities exist? Are they the result of intentional bias, unintentional discrimination, or simply the choices freely made by those involved?

- Might the prospect of future rewards—even if unequal in their ultimate allocation—motivate beneficial and salutary behavior in the present?

8.3.3 Liberty

The concept of **liberty** is central to the American ethos of democracy. It's in the opening line of the Declaration of Independence and the closing line of the Pledge of Allegiance. And, in 1775, as the colonies edged their way toward war with England, Patrick Henry famously uttered the words 'Give me liberty or give me death.' Strong stuff surely, but what exactly do we mean by the word liberty?

Liberty comes in two forms—one **negative** and one **positive**—that represent potentially competing visions of freedom (Stone, 2012).[9] *In the negative version, liberty allows you to do as you please*, to use your talents, property, and time as you choose, free of interference or coercion from others. John Stuart Mill, an ardent proponent of liberty, made the case in 1859 as follows:

> [When a person's conduct] merely concerns himself, his independence is, of right, absolute. Over himself, over his own body and mind, the individual is sovereign. (p. 13)

This is almost certainly the version of liberty that Henry had in mind back in 1775. By contrast, the positive notion of liberty—also rooted in the concept of

---

[9]In this lexicon, the words positive and negative do not connote a judgment of better or worse.

freedom—goes on to suggest that *liberty can only be realized when one is free to choose his or her own life path*. Deprivation of material necessities like housing, education, and health care impedes one's ability to live freely and attain their own version of liberty. In turn, liberty for all means that all must be free of the coercion of deprivation. Even Mill (1859/2001) argues that the right to liberty is not absolute. In doing so, he lends credence to the positive version of liberty:

> There are also many positive acts for the benefit of others, which [one] may rightfully be compelled to perform; such as … to perform certain acts of individual beneficence, such as saving a fellow creature's life, or interposing to protect the defenseless against ill-usage, things which whenever it is obviously a man's duty to do, he may rightfully be made responsible to society for not doing. A person may cause evil to others not only by his actions but by his inaction, and in either case he is justly accountable to them for the injury. (pp. 14–15)

To be fair to Mill, he was writing before the emergence of the modern welfare state. While he implicitly endorses the use of public policy to promote the benefit of others, it's not clear how far he'd be willing to go in supporting programs to redistribute wealth and income.

These two versions of liberty are often at the heart of ideological differences of opinion about the role of government. Conservatives tend to support the negative version of liberty and argue that government ought to minimize restrictions on individuals' liberties, thereby ensuring the highest level of freedom possible. On the other hand, liberals tend to believe that to deliver on the positive version of liberty for all residents, it's necessary for government to undertake programs to relieve the burdens of material deprivation (thereby enhancing the liberty of the beneficiaries). Because such programs aren't free, proponents of the positive view are more willing to impose taxes to fund them or to use other public policies to protect poor and vulnerable communities, while those attuned to the negative view of liberty are likely to see such taxes and policies as infringements on liberty. Differences are also observed cross-nationally, with the negative definition of liberty having a more powerful political impact in the United States than in Europe, where the positive version is more evident in policy (Stone, 2012).

These competing visions of liberty set the stage for a perennial conflict in policymaking: how to balance a desire to liberate disadvantaged groups from poverty and deprivation with the desire to protect the liberty of others whose behaviors may need to be regulated or whose resources may need to be taxed to deliver on the positive version of liberty. This tension isn't new:

... the practical question, where to place the limit—how to make the fitting adjustment between individual independence and social control—is a subject on which nearly everything remains to be done. (Mill, 1859/2001, p. 9)

Your policy analysis probably can't render a definitive verdict on how and where to strike the balance between the two versions of liberty, but by answering the following sorts of questions, you should be able to generate insights that will help your client make better informed policy choices:

- To what degree does public policy constrain liberty and limit folks' freedom to choose how to live their lives or to use their property, time, and resources as they see fit?

- Are there alternative ways to achieve the sought-after policy objectives with less coercive measures that constrain individual liberties to a lesser degree?

- To what degree do firms and other nongovernmental institutions exercise coercive power in ways that constrain individuals' liberties?

- Do disadvantaged groups experience material or other deprivations that undermine their liberty and freedom to enjoy a full life?

8.3.4 Justice

In the context of public policy, **justice** can be defined as the consistent application of all government actions to all residents. Whether we're talking about policing, the courts, elections, welfare programs, schools, drivers' licenses, or building permits, we expect government processes to dependably operate in a fair, predictable, and nondiscriminatory way. If they don't, concerns about injustice may arise.

When it comes to specific cases, the Fifth and Fourteenth Amendments prohibit, respectively, the Federal government and the states from "depriv[ing] any person of life, liberty, or property, without **due process** of law." The specific elements of due process vary across issues and jurisdictions. In death penalty cases, for example, due process is subject to close scrutiny, while in an agency's adjudication of claims about improperly denied welfare benefits, the definition of due process is considerably more relaxed (Szypszak, 2011). Though not codified as law, a still-influential generic definition of due process, depicted in Exhibit 8-3, was offered in 1975 by Federal appellate Judge Henry Friendly. We'll take a deeper dive into legal issues in Chapter 11.

The use of due process to deliver just outcomes applies primarily to the formal adjudication of individual cases. But the purpose of many public policies is to deliver justice at a broader scale to society as a whole. As you think about how to

Exhibit 8-3   Indicators of Due Process

- Unbiased tribunal
- Notice of proposed action and grounds asserted for it
- Opportunity to present reasons why proposed action should not be taken
- Right to present evidence and call witnesses
- Right to know opposing evidence
- Right to cross-examine witnesses
- Decision based exclusively on evidence presented
- Opportunity to be represented by counsel
- Record of evidence prepared by tribunal
- Written findings of fact and reasons for decision prepared by tribunal

Source: Friendly (1975)

incorporate concerns about the topic of justice in your policy analysis, several considerations may be relevant. First, you need to *delineate the boundaries of your analysis of justice.* Are you looking at a single instance of injustice or a pattern of injustice? Are you looking at just one government program or are you looking at all government activities in a geographic area? What time frame are you investigating? The past year, or the past two or three decades (or centuries)? You can't escape the need to bound your work to keep it analytically tractable. But always bear in mind that *the individuals and communities you're studying do not live the whole of their lives within your analytic boundaries.*

You may, for instance, only be studying interactions between the police and the community over the past year. But remember that citizens interact with government not just through police departments, but also through schools, the health-care system, social welfare agencies, and other public services. Moreover, your study may be of the prior year, but members of the community and their families have a lifetime of interactions with both police and other parts of government. Finally, because not all inequities originate in government action and may instead stem from the behavior of individuals, firms, or nongovernmental institutions, a policy analysis focused only on the relationship between the police and the community in a particular locale or at a particular point in time may neglect the totality of a community's lived experience. In short, the community's understanding of justice exists within a **web of concerns**, many of which may go beyond the specific issue you're studying.

Next, figure out if the injustice *results from intentional policy or is the by-product of other factors.* Most forms of intentional, government-approved discrimination have ended in the United States, but there was a time when discrimination and segregation were explicitly embedded in US policy. Moreover, some public policies are intentionally designed to not apply to all persons in the same way. Examples include:

- The denial of voting rights to ex-felons;
- The denial of drivers licenses to undocumented residents;
- Limitations on gender expression in the military;
- The exemption of incarcerated persons who work in prison from most minimum wage and labor standards; and
- The denial of Medicare benefits to noncitizens who aren't permanent residents.

These sorts of cases are referred to as **de jure** (Latin for 'of law') disparities, meaning the differential treatment of individuals is explicitly permitted by public policy. Whether de jure disparities constitute an injustice is a matter of opinion, but they typically merit close attention in your policy analysis.

Even if the disparate treatment of individuals by government systems and processes is not codified as de jure public policy, the day-to-day operation of government policies may still have differential impacts on people. Such impacts are referred to as **de facto** (Latin for 'of fact'), meaning that disparities exist irrespective of codified public policy. Such disparities can arise from the behavior of front-line government personnel (like police officers, social workers, or school administrators) who–without good cause–treat people differently. Such disparate treatment may be random or systematic. For example, a qualified applicant for public assistance might be turned away simply because the case worker is in a bad mood or because the case worker harbors a prejudice against the skin color of the applicant. In either case, an injustice is newly created each time a resident is treated inconsistently without good reason.

In other cases, de facto disparities may exist as the by-product of factors other than overt, and ongoing, discrimination. Consider, for example, elementary schools, the students of which are drawn from nearby neighborhoods. If residents of some neighborhoods are predominantly of one racial or ethnic background, then the schools will end up segregated by race or ethnicity as well. If the schools accept all neighborhood kids equally, irrespective of their background, then we'd say we're seeing de facto rather than de jure segregation in the schools. (De jure segregation of schools was found to be unconstitutional by a unanimous Supreme Court in 1954.)

But *even though observed disparities aren't the result of intentional action in the present, they may still have an historical antecedent in de jure discrimination.* After World War II, for example, Federal, state, and local governments, as well as many developers, lenders, and real estate agents, engaged in a variety of systematic tactics to perpetuate neighborhood segregation (Rothstein, 2017). In turn, even though the segregation of today's schools in the prior example is not the result of current policy, it might stem from neighborhood segregation that was created by prior policy. In other words, you're looking at an injustice that occurred in the past, the legacy of which persists today.

It's also important to recognize that, legacy issues notwithstanding, *even if a policy is neutral on its face, it may still have disparate impacts that cleave along socioeconomic lines.* In the summer of 2021, for example, several state legislatures were considering changes to voting laws that would make it harder to vote by, for example, restricting absentee balloting, instituting strict voter identification rules, or making the voter registration process more complicated. Both the US Constitution and federal statutory law prohibit states from specifically subjecting poor or minority voters to different rules; such de jure discrimination would be impermissible. But because the propensity of citizens to vote varies across socioeconomic lines, making it harder to vote is likely to reduce turnout of certain types of voters. If such voters' political inclinations are in one direction rather than another, then voting restrictions can have partisan implications. I'll leave it to you to decide whether proponents of such restrictions are motivated by a valid fear of electoral fraud, by a calculated political strategy to win more elections, or by racial and social resentment. It's also up to you to decide whether these new restrictions—neutral on their face—would constitute an inequity.

Finally, as you analyze issues of justice, you may find it helpful to focus on **representativeness** (i.e., the degree of alignment between the demographics of a community and that of specific components of government). For example, we typically expect fair representation of the community in the halls of government. As a proxy for procedural justice in the electoral and judicial systems, you could analyze the degree to which the racial, ethnic, age, and gender profile of elected officials, government employees, or judges and juries matches that of the community. A mismatch between the two suggests an area worth deeper investigation. Similarly, there are situations where, if government systems and processes are working in an unbiased and inclusive fashion, you would expect to find that the demographic makeup of those citizens who interact with government matches those of the community. You might thus compare the socioeconomic profile of the community to the profiles of people in the criminal justice system, to citizens who vote, to participants in social welfare programs, and to students and their performance in school. *A perfect match does not preclude the existence of unjust policies, nor does a mismatch prove that injustice has occurred.* Nonetheless, it's often a good idea to investigate the representativeness of government systems and processes.

As you investigate matters of justice and injustice in your policy analysis, asking and answering the following sorts of questions may give you useful insights:

- Are all government policies in the area you're studying consistently and uniformly applied across all residents?

- Are injustices rare and, when they do occur, distributed uniformly across the community? Or are they frequent or concentrated among particular members of the community?

- Does the injustice under study represent a single act of injustice or is it part of a larger pattern of injustice?

- Do potential injustices originate in specific features of codified current public policy or do they result from the unsanctioned action of individual civil servants?

- If injustices don't emanate from current public policy, might they be the result of prior public policy?

- What is the broader context of historical justice (or injustice) that is relevant to the life experiences of those affected by current conditions or public policies?

- Are some individuals or communities subjected to multiple, cumulative injustices?

- Does the demographic profile of government officials and of citizens interacting with government match that of the community?

8.3.5 Social Stability, Safety, and Security

The Preamble to the US Constitution lists several reasons that motivate its adoption, one of which is to "insure domestic tranquility." In using this language, the authors of the Constitution focus on an important goal of many public policies: to provide citizens with **social stability, safety, and security.** Whether it's protection from neighborhood criminals, foreign terrorists, or abusive law enforcement personnel, the Constitution implies that government should take action to keep such actors from destabilizing society. By extension, we also typically look to government to mitigate the dangers of natural disasters (e.g., hurricanes, earthquakes, and pandemics) and of manmade calamities (e.g., oil spills, cyberattacks, and nuclear meltdowns). And, in an increasingly online, networked world, we expect that our privacy will be protected and that online systems will operate reliably.

The constructs of safety and security can, however, be tough ones for policy analysts. For one thing, the *threats being defended against are not round-the-clock certainties*, but happen episodically in ways that can be hard to predict. Policies in the public safety domain thus usually operate by reducing the probability of a bad outcome, rather than assuring its elimination. Effective criminal justice strategies, for example, may reduce crime, but don't drive crime rates to zero. Similarly, design and operating standards for oil and gas companies may reduce the risk of a spill but cannot ensure that a spill never happens. The inability to fully eliminate risk is not intrinsic to public policy. You may conscientiously wear a seatbelt every time you get into a car, but that doesn't guarantee you'll never be hurt in an accident. The probabilistic nature of most things that threaten our wellbeing means that even after taking reasonable precautions, a **residual risk** will remain.

Moreover, *reducing risk is rarely costless*. It takes time, money, and other resources to prepare for disasters, implement measures to reduce their likelihood, forego the benefits that the risky behavior might create, or continuously and vigilantly monitor all potentially risky situations. Sometimes, emphasizing safety and security can even threaten other normative values, like civil liberties. Should, for instance, the military be able to torture a suspect who might have information about an impending terrorist attack? Should local governments invest in supplemental social and community programs in high-crime neighborhoods, even if it means raising taxes or reducing services elsewhere? Balancing, on the one hand, enhanced security and lower risks for individuals against, and on the other, monetary costs and potential threats to civil liberties is an important task for policy analysts.

Another conundrum for policymakers is that it's not just the statistical risk of bad outcomes that affects people's sense of security. *The perception of the risk can be just as important as the reality of the risk*. And, as we saw in the Chapter 4 discussion of cognition, recent and dramatic events can play an outsized role in our internal understanding of a risk. Early in my career, a colleague and I were analyzing an increasing fear of crime among residents in a once thriving, now decaying, Midwest industrial city. I came across data showing that crime rates had actually dropped in the prior year. I remarked, naively, that residents thus needn't be concerned about crime. My colleague quickly pointed out that while crime might be dropping, the fear of crime was increasing and that such fears were antithetical to a safe and secure community. At that point, I began to truly appreciate that *both the reality and the perception of reality are usually important in assessing folks' sense of well-being*.

Another challenge to social stability stems from the rapid pace of change in the information and communication technology arena. Whether it's false information on social media, the loss of privacy when so much of our lives are lived online, or cyberattacks that hobble government and commercial systems, *new technologies often have a destabilizing impact* on our sense of safety and security. I am not arguing against all the wonderful things we can do with new technologies; I am simply noting the emerging, and perhaps poorly understood, nature of the impacts they may have on people's lives.

When it comes to incorporating issues of safety and security in your work, answering the following sorts of questions may help you deepen your analysis:

- To what degree do people experience a sense of stability, safety, and security across all domains of their lives?

- Have risks to public safety been reasonably minimized in a way that is mindful of the cost of doing so and of the potential risk to civil liberties?

- Have policymakers unrealistically promised to eliminate all risk in a particular area? If so, what are the likely consequences if the risk is realized in the form of an adverse event?

- To what degree do calculable, objective measures of safety and risk differ from folks' perceived experience of safety and risk?

- To what degree has personal privacy been appropriately protected, in person, in health-care settings, at school, at work, or at home?

- In what ways are new technologies changing social relationships—either for the better or in ways that disrupt communities?

- Are the critical information technology systems upon which government, business, and social media users rely sufficiently protected against hackers and other forms of disruption?

8.3.6 Wealth, Income, and Poverty

Human well-being is certainly about a lot more than just dollars and cents. But when we're talking about issues like tax policy, access to food, shelter, and health care, or income inequality in society, policy debates often turn on matters of wealth, income, and poverty. Accordingly, this section gives you some ideas to consider as you integrate concepts related to material wellbeing into your policy analysis.

Let's start by distinguishing income and wealth. **Income** is the money someone receives over a period of time while **wealth** is the total value of their financial holdings at a point in time. The median US income in 2019 was $58,600 per household while the median wealth was about twice as high at $121,700 (Federal Reserve Board, 2020). Income can come in the form of wages and salaries paid for working at a job or in the form of returns on investments made in interest-earning accounts, stocks, or bonds. When it comes to wealth, the usual approach is to deduct any liabilities (like the balance on a car loan or credit card debt) from the value of a person's assets to compute their wealth, or net worth.

The distinction between income and wealth is important for at least a couple of reasons. First, *wealth provides a safety cushion in the event of financial distress*. An unexpected and costly illness, the loss of a job, or an eviction from one's home can be disastrous for someone with no savings (i.e., no wealth), but may be much less disruptive for someone with sufficient wealth to tide them over until the event passes. Second, *wealth affords its holder the opportunity to earn a return through investments* that yield interest, dividends, or capital gains that enhance their income in future years. By contrast, if a worker is unable to accumulate wealth, then all their future income will depend only on continued work.

When we think about the equities (or inequities) associated with the distribution of wealth and income, we often consider two distinct perspectives. In the first case, we think about *whether variations across society are equitable*. It might be that all values of wealth or income are clustered in a narrow range, with the richest citizens not that much better off than the poorest citizens; or the distribution could be highly unequal with a few folks who are extraordinarily well off, and a large majority who are barely getting by. In contrast, the second perspective *considers only the degree to which people fall below a threshold* (e.g., an income-based poverty line) and asks whether the number and distribution of such folks across socioeconomic groups pose an inequity.

Let's start with variations in wealth and income. Exhibit 8-4 reports the mean and median of both income and wealth for folks living in the United States. Both income and

Exhibit 8-4 Family Income and Wealth by Education and Race 2019, *Thousands of Dollars*						
	Pretax Income[a]		Wealth		Ratio of Wealth to Income	
	Median	Mean	Median	Mean	Median	Mean
All Persons	58.6	106.5	121.7	748.8	2.08	7.03
By Education						
No HS Diploma	30.8	39.6	20.5	137.8	0.67	3.48
HS Diploma	45.8	63.8	74.0	305.2	1.62	4.78
Some College	51.2	79.0	88.8	376.4	1.73	4.76
College Degree	95.7	176.5	308.2	1,519.9	3.22	8.61
By Race						
White non-Hispanic	69.0	122.8	188.2	983.4	2.73	8.01
Black non-Hispanic	40.3	59.6	24.1	142.5	0.60	2.39
Hispanic	40.7	58.5	36.2	165.5	0.89	2.83
Other	55.7	112.0	74.5	657.2	1.34	5.87

Source: Federal Reserve Board (2020, pp. 7, 11)

[a]Includes social security and pension income, and public assistance such as Temporary Assistance to Needy Families (TANF), Supplemental Nutrition Assistance (Food Stamps), and Supplemental Security Income (SSI).

wealth vary significantly across racial and ethnic lines, as well as among folks with different levels of education. When it comes to certain groups—those without a high school diploma, Hispanics, and non-Hispanic Blacks—the median wealth is less than one year's worth of income. By contrast, among those with a college degree, median wealth exceeds median income by more than threefold. When we look at mean values, the differences are more pronounced, as high-income and high-wealth households pull the mean value well above the median. And, if we look at the ratio of median wealth to median income, we also see significant disparities. The ratio for white non-Hispanics is over 8.0, while it is only about 2.4 for Black non-Hispanics and about 2.8 for Hispanics.

Analyzing the full distribution of wealth or income can get tricky. The mean and median values provide important information, but don't capture variability across levels of income and wealth. Here are three other measures of variability income that you might consider:[10]

- You could *compare income earned by households at the top with those at the bottom*. As shown in the upper panel of Exhibit 8-5, for example, the ratio of income earned by the top 20% (i.e., quintile) of households to the income of the lowest quintile has trended upward over time from about 9.5 in 1979 to 14.5 in 2017.

- You could *focus only on folks at the top of the income scale*. For instance, as shown in the middle panel of Exhibit 8-5, the top quintile earned a bit more than half of all national income in 2017. In a state of perfect equality, this group would earn 20% of all income. The top 1% of households earned 16.7% of all income.

- You could *compute the Gini Index*, which ranges from 0.0 to 1.0 and measures income inequality across a population. A value of 0.0 suggests perfect equality, with all households earning the same income, and 1.0 suggesting complete inequality, with one household accounting for all income in the country.

Before taking a deeper dive into the Gini coefficient, there's another important factor we need to discuss when it comes to income inequality: the effect of public policy on the distribution of income.

In general, two types of public policies directly affect income: transfers and taxes. In addition to income from wages, investments, and pensions, many folks receive means-tested **transfers** from government.[11] On the other hand, **taxes** reduce available income. The net effect is 'annual household income after taxes and transfers.'

---

[10]These examples all focus on income, but analogous measures can be computed for wealth.
[11]These data are for Federal transfers and taxes. Aggregated data on state and local transfers and taxes are sparse.

Exhibit 8-5   Measures of US Income Inequality: 1979–2017

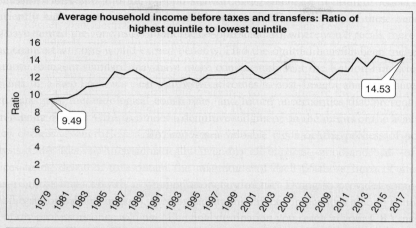

Average household income before taxes and transfers: Ratio of highest quintile to lowest quintile

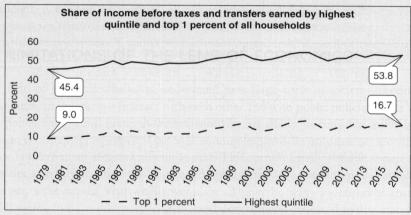

Share of income before taxes and transfers earned by highest quintile and top 1 percent of all households

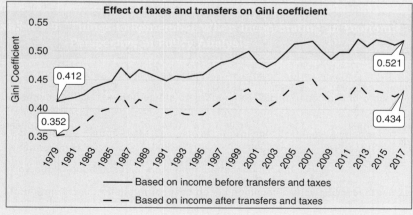

Effect of taxes and transfers on Gini coefficient

Source: CBO (2020)

Exhibit 8-6 shows these calculations for the average household in each income quintile. For folks in the lowest quintile, taxes and transfers raise income by a factor of 1.69 (from $21,300 to $35,900) while, for the highest quintile, the effect runs in the opposite direction as taxes and transfers reduce incomes by a factor of 0.74 (from $309,400 to $229,700). Another way to consider the effect of taxes and transfers is to compare their differential impact on households in the highest and lowest quintiles of income. Before taxes and transfers, the average household in the most affluent group earns 14.53 times as much as the least affluent group; after taxes and transfers, the ratio drops to 6.40. Households in the top quintile receive some transfers, but only about 6% of the amount received by the lowest quintile; on the other hand, households in the top quintile pay about 269 times as much in taxes.

Exhibit 8-6   Effect of Federal Taxes and Transfer Programs (2017)

	Average Household by Quintiles of Income					Ratio of Highest to Lowest Quintile
	Lowest Quintile	Second Quintile	Middle Quintile	Fourth Quintile	Highest Quintile	
Annual market income, Social Security, Medicare, Unemployment Insurance, and Workers' Compensation	$21,300	$46,500	$74,900	$113,400	$309,400	14.53
Plus means-tested transfers, such as TANF, SSI, Food Stamps, and Medicaid	$14,900	$7,100	$3,600	$1,700	$900	0.06
Minus federal taxes paid, such as individual income taxes, payroll taxes, corporate income taxes, and excise taxes	$300	$4,300	$10,500	$20,300	$80,600	268.67
Equals annual income after transfers and taxes	$35,900	$49,300	$68,000	$94,800	$229,700	6.40
Ratio of before and after income due to taxes and transfers	1.69	1.06	0.91	0.84	0.74	Inapplicable

Source: CBO (2020)

Detail may not sum to totals, due to rounding.

Having reviewed the impact of taxes and transfers, we can return to the Gini coefficient. As shown in the bottom panel of Exhibit 8-5, we can compute the coefficient before and after taxes and transfers. In the absence of such policies, the coefficient was 0.521 in 2017, but drops to 0.434 after taking into account taxes and transfers. Countries with a higher Gini index (more inequality) than the United States include South Africa, the Central African Republic, Brazil, and Mexico while countries with lower indexes (less inequality) include China, Japan, France, Germany, and the United Kingdom (World Bank, 2020).

Debates about the normative implications of inequality, and its upward trend in the United States, aren't hard to find. You might believe that high levels of income and wealth are nothing more than appropriate, merit-based rewards for hard work and entrepreneurial talent. Alternatively, you might believe that inequality results primarily from the systemic denial of equal opportunities for success to some groups or individuals. Or, you might not care very much about its origins, but simply believe that inequality ought to be minimized.

As an alternative to thinking about material wellbeing as the difference between rich and poor, you could instead focus only on the extent to which members of a community are in **poverty**. As two economists at the Department of Labor observe, figuring out what it means to be 'poor':

> … has been a challenge since at least the time of Adam Smith, with poverty referring to both one's ability to meet basic needs and also to social exclusion. Thus, regardless of the mechanics of the measure, poverty is a social concept. In the U.S., poverty has been defined in terms of economic deprivation with a comparison of resources to meet particular basic needs of people living in the U.S. (Garner & Gudrais, 2018, p. 3)

The federal government uses two definitions of poverty in its published statistics. By one metric (the Official Poverty Measure), 12.3% of the US population (or 39.5 million people) lived in poverty in 2019. A slightly different metric (the Supplemental Poverty Measure) suggests that 38.2 million people, or 11.7% of the population, were in poverty in 2019. Yes, it's confusing that there are two metrics, but the Census Bureau has spent the past decade trying to sort out the best way to measure poverty (Fox, 2018). Both metrics have pros and cons; together, they nicely illustrate the issue of construct validity that we talked about in Section 6.3.1. Depending on how we operationalize the construct of poverty, about 1.3 million people are either poor, or not poor.

Exhibit 8-7 provides additional detail on how poverty varies across demographic groups, using the Supplemental Poverty Measure. The data make clear that poverty in the United States is not uniformly distributed throughout the population. The problem is appreciably more acute among those without a high school diploma,

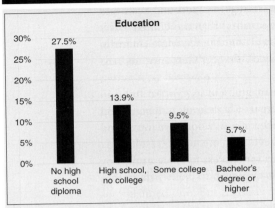

Education

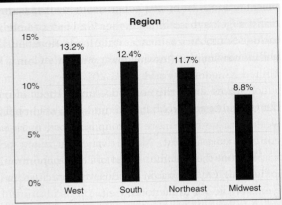

Region

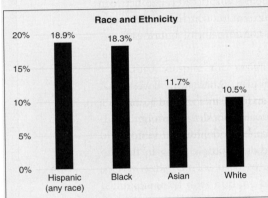

Race and Ethnicity

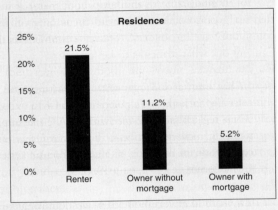

Residence

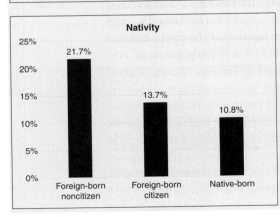

Nativity

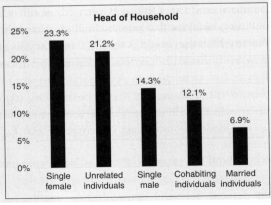

Head of Household

Source: Census Bureau (2020a, p. 22)

Hispanic and Black residents, renters, foreign born noncitizens, and households headed by a single female or by unrelated individuals. Residents of the Midwest are somewhat less likely to live in poverty than residents in other regions of the country.

The COVID pandemic provides a compelling example of the interplay between public policy and poverty levels. In March 2020, near the start of the pandemic, the US poverty rate stood at 11.9%. It peaked at 17.3% in August 2020 and had dropped to 13.8% by May 2021 (CPSP, 2021). In that fifteen-month period, the US government provided over $5 trillion in COVID relief funding (CBO, 2021). The funding went to a wide variety of recipients, but much of it went to programs that directly aided individuals including enhanced weekly unemployment benefits, three rounds of stimulus checks, increases in the Supplemental Nutrition Assistance Program (SNAP), and increases in the Earned Income Tax Credit and the Child Tax Credit. Without COVID relief funding, the poverty rate would have hit 19.9% in May 2020 (in contrast to the observed rate of 14.3%). On a month-to-month basis, the observed poverty rate was, on average, 2.8% points lower than it would have been in the absence of Federal COVID relief (CPSP, 2021). Clearly, there is an important connection between public policy and poverty levels.

Money is, of course, only one aspect of human life, but it is an important one. Wealth and income can act as a shock absorber to help people cope with life's ups and downs; what's more, wealth and money allow folks to enjoy more of life's material amenities today and create future opportunities for family and friends tomorrow. Conversely, living in poverty creates persistent vulnerabilities to shocks like job loss, ill health, or family breakup; for the poorest members of society, hunger and homelessness are persistent threats. And if you conceive of liberty as a positive right, poverty also intrinsically limits one's ability to take advantage of all that life has to offer.

Thinking about how wealth, income, and poverty fit into your analysis will enhance your understanding of the relevant equity implications. You may want to ask the following sorts of questions:

- To what degree is the policy problem you're looking at primarily a consequence of poverty (i.e., of the limited wealth or income) of affected groups of people?

- To what degree is the problem not one of limited resources of one group, but of disparities in income and wealth of one group relative to another?

- Is the distinction between wealth and income relevant to your policy analysis? If so, how?

- What are the underlying drivers of poverty, or of income and wealth inequality, in the situation you're looking at?

- How effective are existing government transfer programs in mitigating the impacts of poverty? Are government tax policies contributing to poverty?

- How effective are existing government tax and transfer programs in mitigating the impacts of inequalities in wealth and income?

8.3.7 Potential Misalignment of a Policy's Benefits and Costs

As we talked about in Chapter 1, one step in the classical model of prospective policy analysis entails making trade-offs across policy options with respect to their pros and cons. Doing so is necessary because all policies have positive and negative impacts, or to use the language of economics, benefits and costs. The degree of **alignment of benefits and costs** across individuals, groups, firms, geographic regions, governments, and industries can affect the relative equity of policies being analyzed.

Consider a simple example: a petroleum refinery that's the source of hazardous air pollutants to which nearby residents are exposed. The refinery produces gasoline that fuels cars driven by folks throughout the region, the vast majority of whom live nowhere near the refinery. In this case, we have a misalignment between the costs of production (exposure to hazardous pollution) and the benefits of consumption (mobility for drivers). If we require pollution controls at the refinery, the price of gasoline (and the cost of driving) will rise for all drivers, but nearby residents' health will also improve. Such trade-offs are a frequent component of policy analysis. To further demonstrate the potential for such misalignments, Exhibit 8-8 lists the eight types of public policies identified back in Part I, and for each, gives examples of how the benefits and costs of policies may fall on different sectors of society.

You should always check for a misalignment between benefits and costs when you're doing a policy analysis. If the benefits and costs—either of an existing policy or of a proposed policy—affect different sectors of society, you'll want to go further and investigate potential inequities because:

> The equity of a policy presumably depends on the distribution of net benefits; it seems implausible that one can determine whether a particular distribution of benefits is equitable without knowing how the costs are allocated. (Hammitt, 2020, p. 3)

To visualize Hammitt's point, look at Exhibit 8-9, which shows the benefits and costs of two illustrative policy options. For simplicity, I have assumed that all impacts can be convincingly monetized. You'll see that Policies A and B are similar in that they both create $1,500 in total benefits, $600 in total costs, and $900 in net benefits. The two policies differ, however, with respect to the alignment of benefits with costs. For

Exhibit 8-8   Illustrative Examples of Public Policies That Create Benefits and Costs for Different Groups[a]

1. Implement infrapolicies
   - Legal doctrines that make it easier or harder for landlords to evict tenants.
   - Legal doctrines that facilitate or impede aggrieved parties' ability to seek legal redress for recent or historical injuries caused by others.
2. Regulate behavior
   - Zoning laws that dictate what landowners can and cannot do with their property to the benefit or detriment of their neighbors.
   - Pollution control regulations that improve public health but impose compliance costs on firms.
3. Provide services
   - Federal services that benefit all (e.g., national defense) even though not everyone pays Federal taxes.
   - Narrow services that benefit a few (e.g., a specific highway project) that are financed by broad taxes that may be paid by nonbeneficiaries (e.g., folks who don't use the highway).
4. Allocate rights to public resources
   - Policies that dictate how publicly owned resources like forests, fisheries, and national parks may be used by private entities and the fees—if any—that must be paid to the government.
   - Protections for endangered species that limit development on private land.
5. Redistribute wealth and income
   - Policies that redistribute resources from middle- and upper-income taxpayers to the poor.
   - Policies that impose tariffs on imported products, raising prices for domestic consumers to the benefit of domestic firm owners and their employees.
6. Levy taxes, spend money, provide subsidies
   - Decisions to tax similar activities at different rates (e.g., higher taxes on income from wages and salaries than on income from capital gains and dividends).
   - Decisions about which activities to subsidize (e.g., renewable vs. fossil fuel energy).
7. Endeavor to foster economic development
   - State and local policies that use public funds to support private activities such as a stadium for the local sports team or tax relief to a firm looking to locate a new facility.
   - Fiscal policies that stimulate the economy during a recession but create debts to be repaid by future taxpayers.
8. Facilitate the flow of information
   - Policies that require plain language disclosures for firms issuing credit cards, perhaps making folks less likely to take on burdensome new financial obligations, to the detriment of lenders.
   - Vehicle mileage information that helps consumers purchase more efficient vehicles, thereby reducing their spending on gasoline to the detriment of oil companies.

[a]See Introduction to Part I for more detail on the eight types of public policy.

Exhibit 8-9 Potential for Misalignment of Benefits and Costs

Benefits of Policies

	Policy choices	
	Option A	Option B
Group 1	$500	$750
Group 2	$500	$500
Group 3	$500	$250
Society	$1,500	$1,500

Costs of Policies

	Policy choices	
	Option A	Option B
Group 1	$200	$100
Group 2	$200	$200
Group 3	$200	$300
Society	$600	$600

Net benefits of Policies

	Policy choices	
	Option A	Option B
Group 1	$300	$650
Group 2	$300	$300
Group 3	$300	–$50
Society	$900	$900

Policy A, all three groups in society experience the same level of benefits and of costs, meaning that net benefits are the same for all three. In contrast, Policy B entails a misalignment of benefits and costs across groups, with Group 1 experiencing net benefits more than twice as large as Group 2, and Group 3 experiencing a net cost. If this were a real-world case, misalignment would deserve a prominent place in your policy analysis.

What's more, if the misalignment falls along racial, ethnic, regional, or other socioeconomic lines, you'll probably want to pay more attention to it than if it falls broadly and randomly across society. Suppose, for example, Group 3 comprises primarily poor rural residents who lack college degrees while Group 1 is mostly affluent city-dwellers with advanced degrees. This isn't proof of an inequity, but certainly deserves further investigation.

To help you think about the extent to which potential misalignments of benefits and costs are important to your policy analysis, consider these questions:

- For existing policies, are there situations where one part of society experiences most of the benefits while another part of society experiences most of the costs?

- Which parts of society will experience the benefits of the proposed policy options being evaluated? How about the costs of the options?

- To what degree are the costs and benefits of each proposed option likely to accrue to the same parts of society?

- To what degree do misalignments of costs and benefits reflect disparities along socioeconomic lines?

8.4 HOW IS THE INEQUITY UNDER STUDY RELATED TO THE PASSAGE OF TIME?

The previous section reviewed seven dimensions of equity that typically deserve attention in policy analysis. Not all seven will be relevant to all analyses; sometimes, there will be considerable overlap among them. Nonetheless, they provide the building blocks for normative policy analysis. We now turn our attention to a couple of equity-related topics that are broader in scope.

Let's first consider how the passage of time relates to policy analysis. If we look at conditions only in the present moment—the degree to which an inequity exists today—we may overlook factors relevant to judging the equity of current policy. *People remember the past and project themselves into the future*. The injury of a prior inequity may still be felt today and fears about what's to come can drive one's assessment about the fairness of today's situation. As you incorporate equity into your policy analysis, contemplate the arc of history: from the past, through today, and into the future.

Consider a quick example of *the impact of the past on the present*: the siting of the Dakota Access Oil Pipeline, which crosses land just to the north of the Standing Rock Sioux Reservation. In the summer of 2016, tribe members objected to the risk to their water supply posed by the pipeline. Ultimately, seeing as how the pipeline did not actually cross Reservation land, the courts allowed the pipeline to be built. But here's the thing: the land underneath the pipeline was granted to the Sioux under the Fort Laramie Treaty of 1868 and improperly repossessed by the Federal government in the late 19th century. In 1980, the US Supreme Court agreed and observed that:

A more ripe and rank case of dishonorable dealings will never, in all probability, be found in our history. (United States vs. Sioux Nation of Indians, 1980, p. 388)

The Supreme Court did not, however, order the land returned to the Sioux, but instead ordered the Federal government to pay the tribe the financial value of the improperly taken land (which the tribe refused to accept). Don your veil of ignorance and put yourself in the position of the Standing Rock Sioux: the pipeline was being built across land that even the Supreme Court agrees was wrongly taken from you. When it comes to assessing the equity of the matter, one cannot look only at the present-day situation. Certainly, more than a century's worth of history is relevant to understanding the grievances of the Sioux.

The passage of time may be equity-relevant not only when we look to the past, but also when we contemplate the future. When it comes to *the impact of the future on today's perceptions* of what is a fair policy, consider the example of autonomous vehicles. Such vehicles currently operate to only a limited degree in just a few cities. But, as technology improves, they are sure to proliferate. In turn, folks who drive vehicles for a living could find themselves out of a job. The fact that autonomous vehicles aren't in widespread use today doesn't mean that professional drivers and their political allies aren't concerned about potential inequities that may occur in the future. As a major trucking union puts it:

Autonomous trucks threaten the livelihoods of millions of truckers across the country. But job losses are expected to hit African American and Latino drivers particularly hard … [O]ne study shows that four million jobs will likely be lost if a rapid transition is made to automate the industry. That would be devastating in this well-paying field … African American … and Latino … workers are overrepresented in trucking, thus any such cuts would hit them particularly hard. (Teamsters Union, 2019)

In short, in the same way that we need to look to the past to better understand present-day inequities, we also need to appreciate how potential future inequities are perceived today.

As you contemplate the relationship between equity and the passage of time, try to *characterize the normative reasoning (if any) that underlies current policy*. Deepen your understanding of an issue by reviewing debates that took place when the current policy was adopted and by checking out any legal rulings that offer commentary on the equity of the status quo. Your goal here is to **learn from the past**. For example, you may think a particular group of people deserves a level of civil rights protection that the law does not provide. Figuring out why policymakers previously neglected to provide protection may clarify the equities of the situation you're studying. Maybe current policy reflects the balancing of multiple inequities of which its designers were aware; in such cases, you might not be able to improve on that balance.

On the other hand, you might look at the normative basis of existing policy and decide that it's no longer persuasive. For example, with the words "all men are created equal," American colonists proclaimed their equality with men of similar standing in England, but were silent about inequalities between themselves and women and enslaved persons in the colonies. In other words, the historical understanding of the concept of equality isn't especially relevant to an assessment of equality today.

Finally, think carefully about *the equity of retroactive policies intended to correct problems that have only recently been recognized*. A pertinent legal principle here is the US Constitution's prohibition on the enactment of ex post facto laws which criminalize past behavior that was legal at the time it occurred.[12] In 1789, the Supreme Court held in Calder vs. Bull that the prohibition applies only to criminal behavior for which a penal sanction is imposed. Accordingly, the government may not fine a chemical company (or imprison its executives) for environmental contamination caused by industrial activities that were legal at the time, but which have since been banned. The government may, however, require such companies to clean up the contamination in order to continue operations. Depending on the circumstances, the companies might also be held civilly liable for damages caused by their actions. This issue is playing out in debates about whether to hold fossil fuel companies accountable for damages caused by climate change given that production and consumption of oil, gas, and coal resources has been and continues to be legal. Some folks believe that these companies are clearly liable. Others argue that such companies should be held responsible only if it can be shown that they knowingly misled policymakers about the dangers of climate change. Still others maintain that it would be wrong to hold them retroactively responsible for legally producing fossil fuel resources that were widely put to beneficial uses throughout society.

8.5 ORIGINS OF INEQUITY: THE PROCESS OR THE RESULT?

Let's turn now to the second equity-related issue that is broader in scope than the seven dimensions of equity delineated in Section 8.3. When we think about inequities that might necessitate a policy response, it's often helpful to clarify whether the normative concern relates to a **general process** or to a **specific case** that has resulted from that process. The distinction is probably easiest to understand with an example from the criminal courts. Imagine a case where the defendant was convicted. Further

---

[12]The prohibition can be found in Article I of the Constitution. Section 9 constrains the Federal government while Section 10 limits the states.

imagine that we have a magic scanner that can tell us whether the verdict was correct or incorrect (i.e., the defendant was, respectively, guilty or innocent). In this case, our scanner tells us that the defendant was innocent, and thus wrongly convicted. We'd probably all agree that the verdict is unfair to the defendant.

But where do we go from there? Ideally, we would figure out if the inequity is confined to only the verdict itself or whether the injustice is a broader systemic one. The difference has important implications for policy analysis. If the system is fundamentally fair, then its breakdown in this case probably doesn't indicate a need for policy reform. Maybe a witness lied in court and, when found out, is sent away for perjury and the defendant is released. Perhaps the verdict can be reversed on appeal. Depending on the circumstances, the wrongly convicted defendant might be entitled to monetary compensation. Or maybe we just have to accept that no system is perfect and occasionally makes mistakes that go unaddressed. Don't get me wrong; I am not suggesting that an inequity hasn't occurred or that we shouldn't try to mitigate it. I am simply saying that in our imaginary case, *the inequity is in the specific result rather than the general process*.

Alternatively, the inequity might lie within the process itself. Such inequities could be *unintentional*. Perhaps the local government is cash strapped and can't afford to fully fund the public defender's office or maybe the system is being haphazardly run by folks oblivious to their own incompetence. On the other hand, the inequity could have an *intentional* origin. If, motivated by bigotry, the criminal justice system consistently treats folks differently, based on race, income, or some other unacceptable criterion, then we're facing a different sort of inequity. Either way, we'd likely conclude that *not only is the result unjust, but that the underlying process is also unjust*.

The criminal justice system provides a vivid example of the difference between an inequitable process and an inequitable result. But this difference is also relevant to a broad swath of public policymaking. In a healthy democracy, where competing points of view and policy proposals are debated prior to a decision, we inevitably end up with some folks who are unhappy with the final result. But if all voices were heard and the decision was made by well-intentioned policymakers trying to balance competing interests, we'd be hard pressed to say that the process was inequitable. What's more, folks whose preferences do not prevail are more likely to acknowledge the legitimacy of the final decision if they feel the process that produced it was an equitable one.

For example, imagine you're a policy analyst asked to help a local government site a new waste incinerator. Nobody wants it in their neighborhood. No matter where it ends up, someone will be unhappy. Suppose the mayor wants you to identify the 'fairest' location for the new facility. If you're honest, you really can't say; doing so would require you to substitute your judgments about the relative equities of different locations for the judgments of the community. Instead, you might tell the mayor that although you can't identify a fair outcome, you can help design a fair process. For example, you might make sure that all feasible sites are considered, that all members of the community have the opportunity to meaningfully engage the process, that all relevant information is widely shared, that decisionmaking processes are transparent, and that impacts on the selected neighborhood will be mitigated to the greatest degree possible.

The idea here is that *if the process is fair and equitable, then its results are probably fair and equitable as well.* Conversely, if special interests dominate policymaking and decisionmakers are beholden to only a small set of patrons, then we might conclude the problem lies in the system itself. Or if some folks in the community are—intentionally or unintentionally—excluded from the decisionmaking process, we might conclude the system is flawed. In turn, all decisions produced by such a system would be suspected of being intrinsically inequitable.

The notion that a policy analyst can't analytically reason his or her way to a definitive conclusion about the equity of a policy proposal is at odds with the classical model of policy analysis discussed in Chapter 1. You may recall that the classical model assumes you can complete your Criteria-Alternatives matrix, assess the trade-offs, and identify the optimal policy choice. The foregoing discussion of process equity suggests otherwise. Majone agrees when he criticizes the classical model for

> … its exclusive preoccupation with outcomes and lack of concern for the process whereby outcomes are produced. A lack of concern for process is justified in some situations. If the correctness or fairness of the outcome can be determined unambiguously, the way the decision is made is often immaterial; only results count. But when the factual or value premises are moot, when there are no generally accepted criteria of rightness, the procedure of decision-making acquires special significance and cannot be treated as purely instrumental. (Majone, 1989, pp. 17–18)

In short, when it comes to public policy, the equity of the policymaking process is often as important as equity of the policy itself.

There's also a pragmatic reason why policy analysts should appreciate the difference between an inequitable result and an inequitable process: the former is harder to analyze than the latter. When it comes to the equities of a specific decision, case, or policy, there are numerous unique facts and circumstances that come into play: Why did the jury not accept the defendant's claim of innocence? Did the county board truly listen to citizens affected by a redevelopment project? Did a lobbyist convince the legislator with the power of a good argument, or with a big campaign contribution? The one-off nature of individual situations and the inability of the analyst to peer inside the minds of all those who were involved can make it difficult to assess the potential inequities of a particular result.

The analyst's job is easier when assessing the equities of a policy process (i.e., a collection of cases) rather than the outcome of a specific case because the *sample size is bigger*. Rather than looking at one case, you can analyze many cases for patterns that suggest an inequity. For example, if you see one racially homogenous jury in the courtroom of a diverse community, it might be the result of random chance. But if you repeatedly see such juries, there may be problems in the jury selection process.

8.6 CUMULATIVE AND SYSTEMIC INEQUITIES

In the preceding sections, we looked at some of the potential origins of policy-relevant inequity. Now, let's pivot to the perspectives of the individuals and groups who may experience such inequities. To start, it may help to distinguish *whether an individual experiences only a single, isolated case of inequity or is subjected to repeated inequities*. Consider, for instance, an election official's one-off and mistaken denial on election day of the chance to vote due to confusion over the voter's home address. If the denied voter happens to be someone whose interactions with government are otherwise consistent, reasonable, and fair, then we are likely looking at a less pressing matter of inequity than if the denied voter is a member of the community who often experiences inconsistent or wrongful treatment by government officials.

Another important consideration is *whether those suffering inequities are spread randomly across the community or are concentrated within a single demographic group*. You may remember the idea of a protected class from our discussion of equality back in Section 8.3.2. Such classes are defined by the characteristics of their members. We saw earlier, for example, that Ontario's Human Rights Code extends protected status to persons of color, the elderly, and ex-offenders, among others. If the folks exposed to inequity are predominantly members of a protected class, then the inequity is arguably more severe than if a person's membership in a protected class has no effect on the likelihood that he or she is exposed to an inequity.

You might also consider *whether multiple types of inequities intersect within one person's life*. Perhaps a child suffers material deprivation as the result of parental poverty and also lives in a high-crime neighborhood that undermines his or her sense of safety and security. The child is thus exposed to two of the inequities we've discussed in this chapter. Or consider wage disparities across socioeconomic lines. In 2019, the median full-time wage of women was 90% of the median wage of all workers, while workers identified as Black earned 80% of the wage of all workers (BLS, 2021). But when we intersect race and gender, the median wage for Black women drops to 77% of the wage for all workers. In other words, the cumulative effect for Black women is greater than it is for either Black or female workers considered in isolation. As you think about the incidence of inequities in society, consider them holistically, rather than on topic-by-topic basis. It can be analytically easier to consider each inequity as a distinct construct, but when multiple inequities come together in one person's life, the impact may be more than the sum of each inequity's impact considered on its own.

Finally, think about *whether the inequities you're looking at rise to the level of being systemic*. Such inequities are pervasive and affect multiple aspects of folks' lives. They originate not in one–off events, but in the operation of multiple public and private systems like education, housing, employment, and the justice system. Systemic inequities may persist over time, as the legacy of conditions and events from the past affect conditions and events in the present. Moreover, as we talked about in Section 8.4, the sense of injury created by inequities experienced in the past (e.g., the mistreatment of the Standing Rock Sioux) can be passed down to descendants of those who experienced the inequity firsthand. Material deprivation may also be passed down in the form of intergenerational poverty. Systemic inequities may originate in public policy, in social norms and customs, or in both. Finally, if the inequity results from intentionally pernicious behavior by many actors, then the systemic inequity is arguably more severe than if it is the unintended result of actions taken by only a few people.

I can't give you a precise definition of cumulative or systemic inequity or a definitive view of the relative importance of each of the factors mentioned above. But I am confident in saying that if you want to think broadly about inequity in the context of public policy, you need to pay special attention to situations in which multiple inequities come together for a single person, group, or community. Moreover, as an empirical matter, folks subjected to repeated inequities have a different relationship to public policy than do folks who rarely experience inequitable situations.

8.7 EQUITY ANALYSIS: PUTTING IT ALL TOGETHER

Recall the elements of moral reasoning that we discussed in Section 8.1: attitudes about altruism, fairness, reciprocity, group loyalty, respect for authority, and a desire for purity and sanctity. Given the deeply personal nature of those sentiments, we shouldn't be surprised when folks find it hard to agree on what constitutes a policy-relevant inequity and what should be done about it.

First, folks can disagree about whether there is even an inequity in need of a policy response. One person, for example, might believe that a national poverty rate of 12% is a profound inequity that demands strong policy action, while another might see it as a normatively acceptable consequence of a meritocracy that rewards education and hard work. Similarly, someone might believe that government is obligated only to ensure the equity of current policies but needn't worry about the legacy effects of prior policies. Proponents of this limited role for government might, for example, agree that public K-12 schools shouldn't engage in de jure racial segregation, sending white kids to one school and students of color to another. But they might not be concerned if neighborhood segregation leads to continuing de facto school segregation.

In the second case, folks can agree that a problem exists but disagree about the best remedy. For most people, the 2020 murder of George Floyd by a Minneapolis police officer was a profound injustice, and was for many folks, also an example of a larger problem of abusive policing tactics targeted at particular groups. Some felt that the jury's guilty verdict and the city's $27 million payment to Mr. Floyd's family ended the matter, while those who sought to 'Defund the Police' didn't want to stop with the verdict and payout. Some advocates agitated for deep budget cuts in police departments around the country while others called for a collection of different police reforms. In short, shared outrage about the murder didn't translate into a shared program of proposed policy changes.

You might be able to resolve certain disagreements with descriptive policy analysis. For example, some police reforms may be more effective than others in reducing police brutality, but may have high costs or significant adverse consequences. In such cases, the classical policy analysis model can serve you well. You would think creatively about opportunities for police reform and build a criteria-alternatives matrix to evaluate them in a consistent fashion. As long as you limit yourself to descriptive analysis of likely effects on police behavior, crime rates, and program costs, doing so will reveal some of the pros and cons of the alternatives and help you identify associated trade-offs.

But sometimes, disagreements are inherently normative, and the classical model of policy analysis won't be much help. Consider, for example, a criminal justice reform that reduces police brutality but arguably also leads to increased crime as the result of less aggressive policing. Although traditional policy analysis will help you estimate the likelihood of the two outcomes, it cannot tell a community how to make a trade-off between reduced brutality and increased crime.

In short, many important normative issues in policy analysis aren't simply a matter of right versus wrong. Sure, it's wrong to cast two votes in the same election, steal books from the local library, or refuse to ride in a Uber because the driver is from another country, but sorting out right and wrong in such cases is a no-brainer. Policy analysis often vexes us with more difficult cases. Their difficulty emanates from the fact that policy choices are often between two options, both of which can be construed as the right thing to do (Badaracco, 1997). The decision is thus not a matter of right or wrong, but instead of calibrating inequities to discern which path is 'least wrong' or 'most right.'

In the deeply personal domain of moral reasoning about public policy, how can policy analysis make a meaningful contribution to the debate? As a first approximation, if you identify a current policy causing an inequity, the obvious answer is to change the policy and bring the problem to a stop. Beyond that, things get trickier, sometimes, a lot trickier. Your initial move is to recognize that, when it comes to normative matters of fairness and equity, policy analysis by itself can't identify the optimal path forward. But that doesn't mean that anything goes; as a well-trained policy analyst, you don't have license to make any normative claim that strikes your fancy. Instead, using the frameworks and vocabulary provided throughout this chapter, your goal is to:

- Transform a destructive and unproductive argument with clear and calm consideration of matters of equity.

- Clarify normative disputes by delineating areas of agreement and disagreement among the participants in a policy debate.

- Work backward from the disagreements to understand the principles and values that motivate divergent points of view.

- Build on areas of agreement among advocates to identify shared beliefs that may temper the intensity of the disagreement.

- Make sure you metaphorically hear the voices of the unheard and consider the interests of invisible stakeholders.

- Use your skills in logical reasoning, careful use of evidence, metacognition, and self-awareness to frame disputes in ways that make them easier, not harder, to resolve.

- Apply your communication skills to help the parties in a policy dispute better understand one another and the positions they've taken.

To be clear, the foregoing suggestions are not a panacea. Thoughtful analysis of normative disputes will often not resolve them. At best, it may make them easier to address. But don't despair if, despite your hard work, the parties in a policy dispute remain diametrically opposed to one another. Such is the nature of democracy.

CHAPTER SUMMARY

This chapter introduced the equity lens as the first of seven lenses through which policy issues should be considered. We observed that differences of opinion on matters of equity often originate in variations in folks' fundamental approach to moral reasoning. I recommended that you don an imaginary veil of ignorance to limit the impact of your personal opinions on the conclusions you draw.

We then explored seven dimensions of equity that routinely appear in public policy debates. In many cases, there are tensions and contradictions embedded in these concepts, meaning that pursuit of one aspect of equity often compromises the ability to attain another aspect of equity.

We also considered how beliefs about the past and the future can influence our understanding of present-day inequities. In addition, an important distinction was made between an inequitable process and an inequitable result. We reviewed situations in which multiple inequities combine to affect particular individuals, groups, and communities. Finally, I recommended that you temper your expectations when it comes to the ability of policy analysis to offer definitive conclusions about normative issues.

DISCUSSION QUESTIONS

1. Think about the murder of George Floyd by a police officer and the Black Lives Matter movement that came to prominence in 2020. What *specific* issues of equity are associated with this case? To what degree did the jury's conviction of the officer resolve the matter?

2. What do you think about the veil of ignorance test? Can you think of examples where you view the equity of a particular situation differently depending on whether or not you're wearing the veil?

3. Think about the community where you grew up. Do you feel that there were significant inequities in public policy that adversely affected folks' lives? If so, how might policy have been changed to mitigate such inequities? Why weren't such changes implemented?

4. To what extent do you think rising inequality of income in the United States is a major problem? Why? Why not? Who bears responsibility for inequality—folks with lower incomes or the system writ large?

5. How much responsibility does government bear for correcting the inequities of the past as opposed to simply ensuring that additional inequities are not created anew by current policy? Why?

6. Think about a policy-related inequity in the place where you now live. Can you identify three distinct options for mitigating it? What are the pros and cons of each option? Can you imagine the counterarguments to your preferred approach? Do those counterarguments have any validity?

CHAPTER NINE

THE ECONOMICS LENS

Another way to look at policy issues is through the lens of economics. Economists study the production and consumption of goods and services, as well as capital investments and labor markets. They also study how prices affect the behavior of individuals and firms, and how transactions among buyers and sellers are aggregated by markets. In addition, the field of economics examines the ways in which trade-offs get made when constrained resources are allocated among competing priorities.

What does economics have to do with public policy? As we'll see in this chapter, there are a number of important connections. First, the field of economics offers us a way of figuring out if and how public policies are enhancing or undermining the efficiency of the economy's operations. Second, with its focus on behavioral responses to market signals, economics is a helpful tool for projecting the outcomes of policies that affect prices or production costs, or change the incentives that motivate the decisions of firms, workers, consumers, and investors. Finally, government itself constitutes a large portion of the US economy. In 2020, spending by localities, states, and the federal government totaled $3.8 trillion, comprising 18.3% of a $21 trillion economy (BEA, 2021). For all three reasons, it's important for aspiring policy analysts to familiarize themselves with basic economic principles.[1]

---

[1]Economics comprises two subfields: microeconomics and macroeconomics. The former focuses on individual firms and consumers and their interactions in the marketplace while the latter studies the economy as a whole. Our focus here is almost exclusively on microeconomics. Thus, I omit the prefix and refer simply to 'economics.'

Learning Objectives

By studying this chapter, you should be able to:

- Understand the characteristics of a competitive market at equilibrium and recognize its potential ability to deliver an economically efficient outcome.

- Use the principles of economics to project the behavior of firms and individuals as they respond to the incentives they face, especially when those incentives are affected by public policy.

- Appreciate how markets organize economywide production and consumption, reward beneficial behaviors, and provide resources for families, communities, and governments.

- Explain how market failures can make it difficult for a market to deliver an economically efficient outcome, and why such failures may justify a public policy intervention.

- Apply the Kaldor–Hicks compensation principle as a means of figuring out whether it's possible for public policy to enhance efficiency in cases of market failure.

- Understand how cost–benefit analysis can be used to operationalize the Kaldor–Hicks principle in an analysis of alternative policy proposals.

- Recognize the limitations inherent in the use of traditional economic analysis when analyzing public policy issues.

Economics is a vast subject, the study of which can be extraordinarily technical and complex. The purpose of this chapter is not to turn you into an economist (or to substitute for a full course in economics), but to convince you that looking at policy issues through the lens of economics can reveal important insights about the drivers of policy problems and about some of the pros and cons of alternative responses to those problems. The description in this chapter is offered in broad strokes, focused on only the conceptual essentials and a few relevant examples.

We start, in Section 9.1, with an overview of freely competitive markets and economic efficiency, and move to a discussion in Section 9.2 of how economics can be used to predict behavioral responses to public policy. The next section is a reminder of the important role played by markets in organizing productive activity in a large, complex economy. Section 9.4 reviews situations in which markets fail to deliver efficient outcomes. The next two sections describe how efficiency might be enhanced through public policy and how cost–benefit analysis can be used to evaluate alternative policies. Section 9.7 concludes the chapter with a summary of the limitations on the use of economics in policy analysis.

9.1 COMPETITIVE MARKETS AND ECONOMIC EFFICIENCY

Economists use the word **market** broadly to describe buyers and sellers as they engage in transactions to exchange one thing (usually money) for another (goods and services, as well as labor and capital investments). The concept can be used narrowly (e.g., the grocery stores serving a city) or broadly (e.g., the world's oil market with a global group of buyers and sellers). If a market is free and competitive (defined below), then most economists argue that it will produce an efficient outcome (also defined below). In this section, we'll define a competitive market and the idea of a market equilibrium. Finally, we'll link the concepts of competitive markets and economic efficiency.

9.1.1 Characteristics of a Competitive Market

The concept of a **competitive market** is a cornerstone of modern economics. Markets are considered freely competitive if they exhibit all of the characteristics described below.

The legal system must *protect property rights* so that people are motivated to trade, rather than steal. If we could go to the grocery store and take what we wanted without paying, the store couldn't stay in business. The legal system must also *enforce contracts*, so that parties to a transaction can be reasonably confident that everyone's behavior will comport with agreed terms. If I buy a house, and stop making payments, the lender can go to court with the mortgage document and get an order to repossess the house. Without the right to enforce its contract, the lender wouldn't make the loan.

Freely competitive markets comprise a sufficiently large number of buyers and sellers so that all are considered **price takers**, meaning that no one buys or sells a large enough quantity of a good or service that their individual behavior affects prices. Put another way, *no market participant holds pricing power*. For example, if there is only one seller in a market, it can set its price higher than it otherwise would because it doesn't need to worry about being undercut by a competitor offering a lower price.

Buyers and sellers must be able to freely enter and exit markets as they choose. This means, for example, that sellers know that if supplying a market becomes too financially lucrative, other sellers may enter the market in an attempt to capture some of those returns. Likewise, *firms and consumers must be free to shift their purchasing from one supplier to another*, thereby creating pressure to offer competitive pricing of similar goods and services. In the aggregate, such mobility ensures that resources flow to their most highly valued uses.

For a market to be considered fully competitive, the goods and services being bought and sold in it *must be very similar in nature*. Commodities like corn, lumber, and steel best fit this definition. Transactions involving differentiated yet similar products, such as different types of family sedans, can also fit the definition. But if the disparities in the goods being sold, for example, motorcycles and minivans, become too great, then we'd say that they're being traded in separate markets. Two markets may be connected when the products being traded are somehow related to one another. They may be **substitutes**, when consumers typically buy one product or the other (e.g., beer or wine) or they may be **complements** when consumers typically buy both products together (e.g., bicycles and bicycle helmets).

Information about the quality and key attributes of goods and services must be readily available. Such information ensures that the production, consumption, and pricing decisions of market participants reflect an accurate understanding of the true costs and benefits that will accrue from each transaction. Because an uninformed person's behavior is unlikely to match what it would have been in the presence of full information, he or she will not achieve the most beneficial outcome possible. In particular, a freely competitive market requires that information be symmetrically available among market participants. **Information asymmetry** occurs when one party to a transaction possesses private information relevant to the transaction that is unavailable to the other party.

The goods and services being traded in a freely competitive market must be *pure private goods*, displaying both **excludability** and **rivalry**. The purchaser of a private good can exclude other parties from extracting value from the good. For example, if I own a car, then I can decide when, where, and by whom it will be used. Private goods are also rivalrous, meaning that if one party consumes a good, then it is no longer available to other consumers. If, for example, I buy wood to build a shed, then that wood is no longer available to other consumers.

9.1.2 Equilibrium in a Freely Competitive Market

If the criteria described in the prior section are satisfied, we define the market as freely **competitive**. The essential features of such a market can be depicted graphically, as in Exhibit 9-1. The vertical axis shows the price of the good (in this case, fictional widgets) while the horizontal axis measures the quantity of the good sold. The preferences of buyers are reflected in the demand curve while the situation of sellers is captured by the supply curve.[2] The demand curve shows how many widgets would be purchased by buyers as a function of the price charged. The curve slopes downward because, as the price increases, consumers will likely buy fewer widgets. The supply curve shows how many widgets would be produced by suppliers as a function of the price. The curve slopes upward because, as the quantity increases, producers typically find it increasingly expensive to produce an additional unit of output.

Exhibit 9-1   Equilibrium in a Competitive Market for Widgets

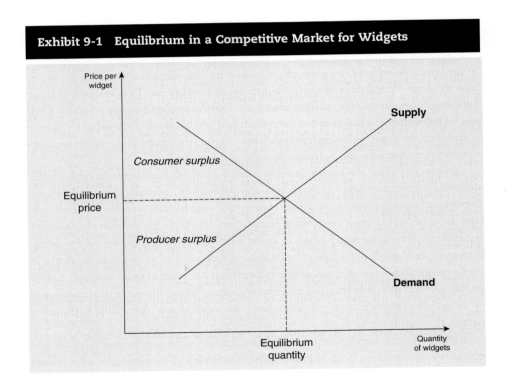

---

[2]For simplicity, the demand and supply 'curves' in Exhibit 9-1 are shown as straight lines.

Freely competitive markets are assumed to come into **equilibrium** at a point where no one has an incentive to change their behavior and all potential producers and consumers have decided if and how to participate in the market. The equilibrium occurs where the supply and demand curves intersect, thereby determining an equilibrium price and quantity. Before going on, however, it's important to note that the idea of *an equilibrium is more of a theoretical construct* that helps us understand how supply, demand, and price interact in the marketplace, rather than a lawlike description of how markets universally operate in the real world (Arrow, 2010; Bryant, 1997).

While markets may tend toward equilibrium over time, we need to recognize that firms face relentless pressure to upset that equilibrium by driving down production costs, creating innovative products that their competitors do not offer, finding ways to make customers dependent on their goods and services, sustaining higher prices by controlling unique resources, and limiting competition (Hamel, 2000). Moreover, markets can be periodically pushed out of equilibrium, as economywide fluctuations in the business cycle (think economic expansions and recessions) sometimes cause capital resources to be underutilized and labor to go unemployed (Arrow, 2010; CBO, 2021a). In short, *markets—even those that are free and open—are sometimes not in equilibrium.* Nonetheless, thinking about the forces that push a market toward, or away from, an equilibrium can yield important insights for policy analysis.

For producers, the market equilibrium represents an optimum, because deviations from it (i.e., producing more or fewer widgets) would reduce producers' financial gains. To understand why this is the case, consider that the supply curve combines the costs of production for all suppliers in the market. Suppliers are not motivated to bring more product to market at equilibrium because additional units have a cost higher than the market price, thereby reducing producer profits (e.g., you wouldn't produce an additional widget only to sell it at a price less than it cost you to make it). Conversely, producers will be motivated to increase quantities up to the point at which cost just equals market price (i.e., to the equilibrium). A failure to do so implies that producers are passing up a ready opportunity to improve their returns by producing widgets at a cost lower than the price. The difference between the market price and the cost of production is referred to as **producer surplus** and in the aggregate (i.e., for all units being produced by all firms serving the market) is maximized at the equilibrium price. Producer surplus is measured by the area above the supply curve and below the equilibrium price.

From the perspective of consumers, the equilibrium is also an optimum. The demand curve reflects the quantity of a good that consumers will purchase at different prices. By subtracting the actual price paid from the **willingness to pay** (or total value received), the residual is a good measure of the net value, or **utility**, enjoyed by consumers. If a consumer is willing to pay $10 for a widget, but the market price is $6, then the net value would be $4 (i.e., he or she gets $10 of value but pays $6). If consumers collectively purchased more than the equilibrium quantity at the market price, they would be reducing their utility since the value received from the last few widgets purchased would be less than the price paid (i.e., you wouldn't pay $6 for a widget if the value you attached to it is $3). Conversely, if consumers buy less than the equilibrium quantity, they are failing to maximize utility (since they can purchase more widgets at a price below the value they would receive). The difference between consumers' willingness to pay and the market price is referred to as **consumer surplus** and in the aggregate (i.e., for all units being bought by all consumers in a market) is maximized at the equilibrium price. Consumer surplus is measured by the area under the demand curve and above the equilibrium price.

The sum of producer and consumer surplus is referred to as **social surplus** or, sometimes, social welfare. Seen graphically, social surplus is the area under the demand curve between the origin (i.e., the intersection of the two axes in the lower left of the graph) and the equilibrium quantity, minus the area under the supply curve over the same range. Movement to either side of the equilibrium reduces social surplus. To the right, production entails wasted resources, because the cost exceeds the value created. Conversely, production to the left of the equilibrium creates an opportunity cost where resources are suboptimally deployed (because of a failure to produce when sellers' production costs are lower than consumers' willingness to pay). In short, in freely competitive markets for purely private goods, the market equilibrium leads to the maximization of social surplus.

The foregoing discussion focuses on the market mechanisms by which the goods and services produced by firms are *allocated to and among consumers*. Economics offers two other helpful frameworks for understanding equilibrium conditions:

- The first framework describes the *optimization of production processes* as firms select a mix of inputs, such as labor from workers, capital from investors, and intermediate goods from other firms, to produce outputs at the lowest possible cost.

- The second framework explains how *markets synchronize production and consumption* to ensure that the mix of goods and services produced by firms aligns with consumer preferences and their willingness to pay for goods and services.

We won't go through the details of these two additional frameworks, but irrespective of whether we're talking about the allocation of goods and services to consumers, the optimization of production processes, or the synchronization of production with consumption, the bottom line is the same: across freely competitive markets, aggregate consumption, production, and pricing decisions of market participants come into an equilibrium from which no one has an incentive to deviate because doing so will only reduce their economic well-being.

9.1.3 Economic Efficiency

Economists define an **efficient allocation** of resources as one where it is not possible to make one person better off without making someone else worse off. An allocation that meets this test is referred to as Pareto efficient, named after the Italian economist who sorted out the concept around the turn of the last century. To better understand the concept of efficiency, it may help to think about its opposite: *inefficiency*. An inefficiency can arise if one or more of three conditions exist.

First, if goods and services are allocated inefficiently, there will exist potential transactions that would leave buyers and sellers better off compared to the status quo. For example, if we see two different prices for the same product, then an inefficiency may exist. Consider a grocery store that charges $2.50 for a gallon of milk, while another charges $3.00. You could buy milk from the first store and sell it to customers of the other store at a price above $2.50 but below $3.00. You and the other folks would be made better off without making anyone worse off, the definition of a Pareto efficient situation.

Second, inefficiencies may arise on the production side of a market. If firms don't optimize their use of labor (i.e., workers) and capital (i.e., investments in plant, equipment, and other productive assets), it would be possible to produce the same quantities of goods and services but at a lower cost, or a greater quantity at the same cost. If, for example, you observe a manufacturer that could upgrade its assembly line to produce more output with fewer inputs, and still recoup the cost of the upgrade through a mix of higher revenue and cost savings, then you're looking at a case of production inefficiency.

Third, if production decisions and consumer preferences aren't aligned, firms will produce a mix of goods and services that doesn't match what consumers want and can afford to buy; in turn, firms could produce a different mix at no additional cost that would better satisfy consumer preferences. The former Soviet Union experienced inefficiencies of this sort when central planners often misjudged the needs of consumers for finished goods and of firms for intermediate inputs. Combined with price controls, the result was frequent shortages, the occasional surplus, and a ubiquitous black market.

The concept of economic efficiency is also tightly linked to the concept of **free trade**. Free trade describes the ability of buyers and sellers to engage in transactions when they like and to refrain from trading when they believe doing so is not in their interest. In turn, we can assume that virtually all voluntary transactions are mutually advantageous for both parties.[3] In other words, both parties must gain from doing

---

[3]Exceptions include coerced transactions (e.g., extortion), consumption as the result of addiction (e.g., drug abuse), or hidden product defects (e.g., health and safety concerns). In international trade, there may be cases where trade restraints give one country a strategic advantage over another (Pindyck & Rubinfeld, 2009).

business with each other; else, they wouldn't bother to trade. Except in markets that have 'failed' (the subject of Section 9.4), free trade typically delivers transactions that are Pareto efficient: both parties are made better off, and no one is made worse off.

Why is efficiency such an important topic in economics and policy analysis? The answer is simple. Resources and budgets—for firms and consumers—are inevitably limited but, across the population as a whole, humans' material wants and needs are essentially unbounded. And you may recall from Chapter 2 that improving the efficiency of a process allows us to produce more output without increasing the quantity of inputs. If we make a process more efficient, the value of the incremental increase in output (after subtracting the cost of improving the process) is essentially 'free.' If resources and budgets are constrained but wants and needs are unbounded, then efficiency is an important goal.

The concepts of market equilibrium and economic efficiency are closely connected. At an equilibrium, no one is motivated to change their situation, implying that no one can be made better off without making someone worse off. Accordingly, the equilibrium in a freely competitive market is also an efficient allocation. Given the traditional assumption in economics that social welfare is simply the sum of the welfare of all individuals in society, an important link can be drawn between the supply and demand framework we reviewed in the prior section and the concept of economic efficiency. If social surplus is at a maximum in a market, then it is not possible to make any market participant better off without making someone else worse off—the definition of Pareto efficiency. Freely competitive markets at equilibrium thus both maximize social surplus and meet the test of economic efficiency.

How does the concept of efficiency relate to policy analysis? For one thing, if a market is operating in a free and competitive fashion, then government intervention in that market cannot be justified as a means of increasing efficiency.[4] In such cases, we expect the market—on its own—to achieve an equilibrium that maximizes efficiency. But *if a market is not free and competitive, and unlikely to achieve an efficient outcome, public policies might be able to increase efficiency.*[5] Because improved efficiency generates more resources for whatever people value (i.e., for themselves, for their families, for their communities, or for the country or the world as a whole), schools of public policy have long given economics a prominent position in their curricula.[6]

---

[4]There may be, however, other rationales for government intervention in the situation.
[5]We'll revisit the topic of how markets may fail to deliver efficient outcomes in Section 9.4.
[6]I argued in Chapter 3 that while economics belongs in the curriculum, care must be taken not to overemphasize it and that its inclusion ought not come at the expense of other disciplines equally important to policy analysis.

9.1.4 Impact of Taxation on Efficiency

The supply and demand framework can also be used to illustrate the efficiency impact of government taxation. Take a look at Exhibit 9-2 which extends our analysis of the market for widgets. Suppose that government levies an excise tax of $T on each widget. The practical effect is to raise the supply curve by a distance equal to T. Whereas the original price and quantity were, respectively, P_1 and Q_1, things change after the tax. As widgets become more expensive, demand drops to Q_2. The price paid by the buyer climbs to P_2 while the price received by the seller drops to P_3. The difference between P_2 and P_3 is equal to the tax T. The revenue to the government is simply the new quantity (Q_2) times the tax T, which is also the same as the rectangle labeled *abde*.

Exhibit 9-2   Impact on Efficiency of Government Taxation

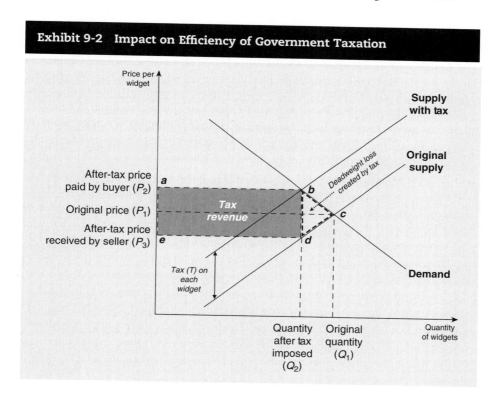

While revenue to the treasury is one readily apparent consequence of the tax, there is another, more subtle, impact that comes in the form of an **opportunity cost**. It occurs because fewer widgets are being bought and sold. When quantity drops from Q_1 to Q_2, buyers and sellers are both worse off. Buyers lose the consumer surplus they would have enjoyed on those extra widgets while sellers lose the producer surplus they would have earned by selling those widgets. Together, the losses constitute what economists call a **deadweight loss** (depicted in Exhibit 9-2 as the triangle *bcd*). Whenever government taxes an activity (such as sales transactions, investment returns, income earned from work, or property ownership), it makes that activity less financially attractive than it otherwise would have been and thereby creates an opportunity cost.[7] In short, taxation creates a burden that goes beyond the tax revenue itself. Of course, thinking holistically, we need to also consider the value created by the uses to which government puts those revenues. While taxation almost always creates a deadweight loss, the loss may be offset by the benefits of the associated government spending.

9.2 PEOPLE AND FIRMS RESPOND TO INCENTIVES: USING ECONOMICS TO PROJECT BEHAVIOR

The fourth step of the classical model of policy analysis (described in Chapter 1) advises you to project the outcomes of the policy options you're analyzing. You may be able to use the model of a competitive market to do so. A foundational concept in economics is that people and firms respond to incentives. Public policies often have a significant effect on the incentives faced by firms and individuals. Accordingly, if we can characterize how folks will alter their behavior as incentives change, economics gives us a powerful tool for policy analysis.

In a freely competitive market, individual consumers, for example, are assumed to buy a mix of goods and services as they aim to maximize their well-being, given their personal preferences, their financial resources, and the prices of goods and services. If prices change or a consumer's income rises (or falls), economists are not surprised when the consumer changes his or her purchasing patterns. Such effects reflect a concept known as the **elasticity** of demand.

- The *price elasticity of demand* describes how people change their consumption of a good or service because of a change in its price. It equals the percentage change in the quantity purchased divided by the percentage change in the price. If, for example, the price elasticity of demand for gasoline is –0.25, then a 10% increase in the price will be met with a 2.5% decrease in demand.

- The *cross-price elasticity of demand* describes how people change their consumption of one good or service because of a change in the price of

---

[7]Different types of taxes create different levels of deadweight loss, but that's a topic for another textbook.

another. It equals the percentage change in the quantity purchased divided by the percentage change in another good or service's price. If, for example, the cross-price elasticity of apples with respect to oranges is 0.50, then a 10% increase in the price of oranges will cause a 5% increase in the demand for apples, as buyers substitute apples for oranges.

- *The income elasticity of demand* describes how people change their consumption of a good or service because of a change in their income. It equals the percentage change in the quantity purchased divided by the percentage change in income. If, for example, the income elasticity of demand for avocados is 1.5, then a 10% increase in a person's income will prompt a 15% increase in their purchase of avocados.

On the supply side, there is an analogous measure that captures how firms react to changes in the price of the goods and services they produce.

- The *price elasticity of supply* describes how firms adjust their production of a good or service in response to a change in its price. It equals the percentage change in the quantity supplied divided by the percentage change in the price. If, for example, the price elasticity of supply for gasoline is 0.40, then a 10% increase in the price will be met with a 4.0% increase in the quantity supplied.

These tools of economics can be useful in sorting out the impacts of government policy on production and consumption decisions. For example, if we're trying to figure out how much money a government tax on cigarettes would raise, and how much it would decrease tobacco consumption, we could combine the market model described in Section 9.1, with the idea of elasticity we just discussed to work out an answer.[8] I won't go through all the calculations, but conceptually the process is straightforward. We start with the current price and the quantity of cigarettes purchased. We treat the tax as an additional cost of production. Using the elasticities of supply and demand, we find the intersection of the revised supply curve and existing demand curve and identify a new, posttax market equilibrium. At this equilibrium, we observe predicted cigarette consumption, the price to consumers, and the price received by producers (with the difference in the two prices being remitted to the government as taxes). Multiplying consumption by the tax rate yields total tax revenue. Dividing the projected change in

---

[8]This example assumes we have valid estimates of current prices and quantities, as well as of the relevant elasticities. Revisit Chapter 6 for a refresher on the definition of valid evidence.

consumption by current consumption yields the tax-induced, proportional reduction in cigarette use.

As another illustration of how economics can be used to project the impact of policy changes, recall the case of the minimum wage increase discussed in Section 4.2. You may remember that CBO projected that if the minimum wage were raised to $15 per hour, 1.3 million fewer workers would be employed. To derive this estimate, CBO relied on multiple empirical studies that estimated the elasticity of employment (i.e., the change in employment caused by a change in the minimum wage). After reviewing the literature, CBO settled on –0.25 as the appropriate estimate of this elasticity, meaning that a 10% increase in the minimum wage would be met with a 2.5% decrease in employment (CBO, 2019, p. 27).

9.3 BENEFICIAL BY-PRODUCTS OF MARKETS

Beyond providing a means for attaining efficiency in consumption and production, markets serve other valuable functions. To start, it's important to appreciate *the role of economics in sorting out a staggeringly complex set of arrangements and relationships for producing goods and services.* Consider the enormity of the task: the US economy has a gross domestic product of over $21 trillion, the equivalent of more than 140 million full-time workers, and almost 6 million commercial firms operating 7.9 million business establishments, woven together in millions of daily transactions (USCB, 2020).

To help you visualize the magnitude and complexity of this enterprise, Exhibit 9-3 shows an 'input–output' table for the US economy. In it, the economy is divided into 15 sectors (e.g., agriculture, mining, etc.). Each sector appears twice, once as a supplier of inputs (row headings) and again as a user of inputs (column headings). The easiest way to read the table is to look across the rows. The finance, insurance, and real estate sector, for example, provides $34 billion of inputs to agriculture, $43 billion to mining, $14 billion to utilities, and so on. Its total contribution to the economy is about $3.4 trillion (far right column). If you read down a column, you can identify which other sectors supply the sector in that column. Across the bottom are the number of full-time equivalent workers, firms, and establishments within each sector. This is just a high-level aggregation. The detailed version of the input–output table for the US economy is broken into 405 specific industries and is too big to reproduce here.[9]

You don't need to master the details of the table. The point here is simply that the table makes tangible the processes described in the prior section—consumers' purchase decisions, firms' production decisions, and the synchronization of the two. While government policies in the United States certainly influence daily economic

---

[9]You can look at it online at https://apps.bea.gov/iTable/index_industry_io.cfm.

Exhibit 9-3 Inputs and Outputs Among US Industries in 2019

Producing industry	Value of Inputs Used by Industry ($ billion)															
	Ag, forestry, fishing	Mining	Utilities	Construction	Manufacturing	Wholesale trade	Retail trade	Transport and warehousing	Information	Finance, insurance, real estate	Professional and business svcs	Educ, health, social assistance	Arts and rec, food svcs, accomodation	Other svcs, except govt	Government	Total
Ag, forestry, fishing	114.8	0.2	0.0	3.4	322.7	1.8	5.3	0.2	0.0	0.0	5.4	0.3	10.1	0.3	9.0	473.4
Mining	2.5	59.0	40.9	27.9	371.5	0.0	0.0	0.2	0.9	0.1	2.0	0.4	1.6	0.7	39.2	547.1
Utilities	4.4	9.1	22.6	4.8	55.7	15.1	33.2	12.2	5.4	108.6	16.4	18.9	28.7	4.0	26.8	365.8
Construction	1.7	3.5	6.8	0.2	14.2	2.0	4.5	5.9	2.5	160.5	1.8	1.7	2.9	3.5	95.8	307.4
Manufacturing	110.8	87.2	24.5	592.2	2,458.6	92.6	93.6	144.8	120.4	114.2	210.9	265.2	147.8	78.4	523.9	5,065.2
Wholesale trade	1.5	0.2	1.1	0.1	25.1	44.6	19.2	0.2	2.2	7.4	0.2	0.4	0.1	0.0	0.0	102.4
Retail trade	0.0	0.0	0.0	0.0	0.0	0.0	2.2	0.0	0.0	0.0	0.0	0.0	0.0	0.0	0.0	2.2
Transport and warehousing	0.7	3.0	10.5	1.2	54.4	81.7	76.3	149.1	21.6	43.6	64.8	22.7	10.3	5.3	49.5	594.7
Information	0.6	2.2	2.8	8.6	22.7	25.3	29.6	13.9	237.0	73.6	121.2	42.4	23.0	18.9	104.5	726.2
Finance, insurance, real estate	33.7	42.8	13.5	56.7	108.3	189.8	234.5	138.5	89.1	1,420.1	301.0	335.1	160.7	86.9	193.7	3,404.4
Professional and business svcs	3.8	59.5	29.4	87.1	373.7	313.0	243.5	102.9	264.0	629.8	703.4	311.2	203.0	59.7	286.7	3,670.6
Educ, health, social assistance	0.0	0.0	0.2	0.0	0.1	2.8	8.6	0.3	0.4	0.0	1.7	43.7	2.5	4.8	35.8	101.0
Arts and rec, food svcs, accomodation	0.6	0.7	2.3	1.1	12.1	10.6	9.9	21.6	48.0	89.0	84.3	60.0	41.7	8.7	26.8	417.3
Other svcs, except govt	0.7	0.9	0.5	8.3	21.6	29.3	19.2	19.6	8.7	39.1	34.9	27.9	18.0	10.2	33.4	272.3
Government	0.0	0.0	2.9	0.0	4.7	14.6	7.1	12.2	2.9	18.0	9.5	8.8	6.5	2.5	9.7	99.4
Scrap, used and secondhand goods	0.2	0.2	9.0	3.5	48.1	0.0	0.5	13.1	0.3	0.0	0.2	3.9	1.0	12.0	0.0	91.7
Total Production	277.1	270.5	168.0	797.3	3,913.4	829.4	792.2	656.4	813.7	2,751.4	1,566.1	1,143.5	661.4	296.4	1,447.1	16,383.8

Industry Characteristics in 2017

Number of Employees (1000s)	1,254	663	544	7,412	12,515	5,722	13,706	5,408	2,645	8,467	20,142	21,984	13,614	6,319	20,523	140,918
Number of Firms	22,641	19,080	5,957	701,477	248,039	298,127	647,927	185,028	79,662	547,777	1,186,105	748,569	669,993	696,668	Not applicable	5,996,900
Number of Establishments	23,363	25,732	18,965	715,641	290,936	409,656	1,064,449	237,308	153,934	884,792	1,390,925	1,002,808	869,563	764,840	Not applicable	7,860,674

Sources: Input-Output Data (BEA, 2019); Industry Characteristics (USCB, 2020)

decisions, there is no central planning authority to orchestrate the workings of the economy. Moreover, efforts at central planning often fail, as in the Soviet Union and Mao's China. In market economies, instead of central planning, there often seems to be what Adam Smith calls an **invisible hand** that brings order to economic activity. The driver of this invisible hand is not an overarching concern for social good, but rather an individual focus on self-interest. In Smith's (1784) words:

> [M]an has almost constant occasion for the help of his brethren, and it is in vain for him to expect it from their benevolence only. He will be more likely to prevail if he can interest their self-love in his favour, and show them that it is for their own advantage to do for him what he requires of them. ... It is not from benevolence of the butcher, the brewer, or the baker, that we expect our dinner, but from their regard to their own interests. ... He generally, indeed, neither intends to promote the public interest, nor knows how much he is promoting it. ... [B]y directing [his] industry in such a manner as its produce may be of the greatest value, he intends only his own gain, and he is ... *led by an invisible hand to promote an end which was no part of his intention.* (pp. 21–22, Vol I, & p. 181, Vol II), *emphasis added*

The operation of the invisible hand depends, in large measure, on the concept of free trade that I mentioned back in Section 9.1.3. In other words, *as folks freely engage in transactions that make them individually better off, they simultaneously generate the forces that animate Smith's invisible hand.*

The *rapid pace of innovation* in information and communication technologies is just one example of how profit-motivated behavior by entrepreneurs produces a great many goods and services that society values highly. When it comes to individuals, the prospect of a higher income or a more secure livelihood for themselves and their families may motivate them to pursue additional education or seek employment that most highly rewards their specific skills and talents.[10] In doing so, they *may be able to make a more valuable contribution to society* than they otherwise would.

Economic activity also provides a *tax base to governments.* Most of the revenues that finance government services and redistributive policies come from income, sales, and property taxes. Even though virtually all taxes create at least some deadweight loss, without the underlying economic activities upon which to levy taxes, there would be no tax revenue to fund government operations. In addition, as an employer, a firm

---

[10]I am not suggesting that freely competitive markets ensure success and prosperity for everyone, but rather, only that such markets often create salutary incentives for individuals. For reasons beyond the scope of this section, hard work and talent are not always rewarded with increased income, wealth, and economic security.

offers its workers a way to earn the financial resources to help *meet their family's material needs.* Moreover, as we've seen in the 2009 and 2020 recessions, *employment is a cornerstone of community stability and well-being.*

In short, when we look through the economic lens, we see how markets deliver a broad and diverse array of material goods and services that consumers willingly buy. Markets also provide a decentralized and dynamic mechanism for organizing the millions of transactions that take place every day in a complex, modern society. In addition, the prospect for market rewards motivates producers to develop new and innovative goods and services. Finally, markets are the foundation of the tax base and the source of jobs on which individuals, families, communities, and governments depend.

9.4 MARKET FAILURES MAY UNDERMINE EFFICIENCY

Markets are not always freely competitive. In such cases, the market is said to have failed. In the presence of **market failure**, privately motivated behavior is unlikely to maximize the sum of consumer and producer surplus and the market won't efficiently allocate resources. Another way to think about market failure is that supply and demand curves—based on the private situations of buyers and sellers—no longer capture all the benefits and costs that accrue from market transactions. In turn, inefficiencies are likely and social welfare at the equilibrium will be lower than it could be.

Why is the idea of a market failure so important in policy analysis? If markets—on their own—are not freely competitive and thus not generating efficient outcomes, then as described in the next section, it *may be possible to use public policy to enhance efficiency.* Moreover, different types of market failures may point us toward different types of policy interventions. As an aspiring policy analyst, you should develop a basic understanding of at least four important types of market failures: public goods, limited competition, externalities, and imperfect information.

9.4.1 Public Goods

In Chapter 3, when we discussed the collective action problem, we previewed the topic of **public goods**. Public goods are nonrivalrous or nonexclusive, or both. As noted earlier in this chapter, *rivalry* exists when one person's consumption of a good eliminates another's opportunity to consume the same good; *exclusivity* captures the degree to which people can be prevented from consuming a good. To illustrate the potential inefficiencies associated with public goods, let's consider three permutations.

Goods that are rivalrous, but nonexclusive may be overconsumed if demand exceeds available supply. Such goods are called common pool resources. Overconsumption occurs because of a divergence between individual and collective interests. One example is a congested highway where each additional driver slows everyone else down. Suppose you're potentially one of those extra drivers, and you're deciding whether to get on the road. Even though traffic is very heavy, taking the highway will still save you a few minutes over the next best route you could take. But because the road is congested when you join in, you slow everyone else down. Even if you cause only a small slowdown, when aggregated over all the other drivers, their collective extra wasted time may far exceed your modest individual time saving. If the flow of traffic could be managed (e.g., by controlling the onramps or by charging a toll), it would be possible to minimize the aggregate time spent commuting by all drivers. The inefficiency arises because, without such management, as drivers choose what's in their individual best interest, they collectively create a situation in which everyone is worse off than they otherwise would be. This wedge between individual and collective interests is sometimes called the Tragedy of the Commons, a name taken from an influential article by Garrett Hardin (1968).

Goods that are nonexclusive and nonrivalrous are very unlikely to be supplied by private entities because there's no way to charge consumers a price for consuming the good. The inability to exclude consumers allows *free-riding*, a phenomenon in which people consume a good without paying for it. The classic example is a national military defense that protects all residents of a country. Another example is a citywide rodent control program. If rats are eliminated, everyone benefits irrespective of whether they helped fund the program (nonexclusivity); moreover, the fact that one person's property is rat-free doesn't diminish the benefit to another person whose property is also rat-free (nonrivalry). An inefficiency arises when a nonexclusive, nonrivalrous public good has benefits in excess of costs, but private markets do not supply it.[11]

Goods that are exclusive, but nonrivalrous are sometimes supplied by private providers, but priced inefficiently. Because serving more consumers imposes no additional costs on a producer, the efficient price is zero. But producers won't supply the good if they can't get paid. An example is an existing private toll road that has ample capacity and is not congested. The inefficiency arises because, when the road owner does charge a toll, some folks will be deterred from using the road, even though they would benefit from doing so while not creating additional costs for other drivers or the road owner.

9.4.2 Limited Competition

The standard model of a free market assumes that many firms are ready and able to compete vigorously to produce and sell products that satisfy consumer preferences. In the absence of such competition, markets often fail to deliver an efficient outcome. In

---

[11]Private markets do supply pest control services to individual property owners seeking to rid their own property of pests. But because rodents are mobile, such services are unlikely to rid the entire community of the problem.

some cases, there is only one supplier in a market, a situation referred to as a **monopoly**. Natural monopolies exist when high upfront costs and low operating costs give one firm an enduring cost advantage over potential competitors, thereby creating a barrier to market entry for other firms. For example, after a gas, electric, or water utility has built the infrastructure to deliver its product to customers, it can serve those customers at a lower price than could a potential competitor that would have to charge higher prices to cover not only its operating costs (like the incumbent firm), but also the cost of building a second set of infrastructure.

In addition to natural monopolies, a monopoly may also be the eventual result of persistent efforts by one firm to continuously improve its market position. For example, one firm could buy up other firms in its industry, thereby reducing competition, taking advantage of economies of scale, and growing larger in the process. In addition, if an industry is capital-intensive (i.e., it takes a lot of money to get an enterprise up and running), it can be hard for new firms to enter the market and compete with incumbent firms. Moreover, if a large firm has sufficient financial resources, it can engage in predatory pricing by charging below-cost prices that its smaller rivals can't match, forcing them out of business. Eventually, there may be only one firm left in the market. If so, it can then charge customers a higher price than if it had to worry about those customers defecting to its competitors.[12]

Similar complications can arise when, even though there is more than one firm, there are still too few firms to ensure a freely competitive market. Some large industries are dominated by only a few firms. Such cases are referred to as **oligopolies**. In the United States, for example, industries with four or fewer dominant firms include airlines, delivery services, cell phone service providers, search engine providers, and suppliers of computer operating systems (Shambaugh, Nunn, Breitwieser, & Liu, 2018). Fearful of a costly price war, firms in such industries may have a tacit understanding to hold prices artificially high or may engage in explicit collusion to manipulate prices.

A final situation where limited competition may undermine efficiency is in the production of similar but differentiated goods by multiple companies. You'll recall that the standard market model assumes that firms are selling essentially identical products. But think about iPhones and Android phones, Miller Lite and Bud Light, or movies based on the DC and Marvel comic series. Even though we're talking about very similar products—cell phones, light lagers, and superhero movies—there are also differences in the products on offer. In such cases, the unique features of one product may entice consumers to pay somewhat more to obtain those features, but ultimately, if the price rises too high, then the customer can shift to the other

---

[12]This narrative explains how things could unfold in the absence of public policy. In many countries, antitrust policy aims to limit these sorts of anticompetitive practices.

provider's product. In short, producers face some competitive pressure—more than they would in a monopoly, but less than in a competitive market for identical goods and services.

If there is no competition because of a single monopoly supplier, or insufficient competition because of a handful of dominant firms in a particular market or because of similar but differentiated goods, then economic inefficiencies will likely result. The core concern with less-than-competitive markets is that firms can set prices at a level higher than they would if they feared being undercut by a competitor with a lower price. With limited competition, prices are not driven by production costs (as they are in efficient markets) but by the strategic pricing decisions of firms with market power. In turn, customers pay more, and fewer purchases are made, than would be the case in a freely competitive market.

9.4.3 Externalities

Externalities exist when the *behavior of one party affects (or 'spills over' to) other parties who did not consent through a voluntary market transaction to experience that effect.* For example, unregulated wastewater discharges from a factory may damage a downstream fishery. If so, the fishers are external to the transactions between the factory and its customers, and the cost of damages to the fishery is not reflected in the prices of the goods produced by the factory. In turn, the production of those goods is inefficiently higher than it would otherwise be.

Exhibit 9-4 depicts such a situation by extending the supply and demand framework we considered earlier in this chapter. Recall that the supply curve represents the cost of production. With a supply curve not corrected for the externality, we expect a price of P_1 and a quantity of Q_1 at the equilibrium. But with the externality in our example, production costs are understated because they don't reflect the cost of the damages done to the fishery. Imagine that each widget produced by the factory causes $1 of environmental damage. To capture the full, society-wide cost of production (i.e., private costs incurred by the factory owner, plus the social cost of the environmental damage), we need to adjust the supply curve upward by $1 per widget to reflect the externality. After doing so, we can observe that the price would climb to P_2, thereby causing the quantity to drop to Q_2. From a society-wide perspective, the efficient level of production is Q_2 rather than Q_1. The extent of the inefficiency can be measured by multiplying the number of extra widgets produced (Q_2-Q_1) by the value of the externality ($1 per widget), and then subtracting the lost social surplus (producer and consumer surplus) that would result from the lower production of widgets after correcting for the externality. This impact is shown graphically in Exhibit 9-4 as the triangle outlined in heavy dashes. In other words, addressing the externality would yield the benefit of reducing the environmental damage but incur the social welfare cost of reduced widget production and consumption.

Exhibit 9-4   Market for Widgets With Externality

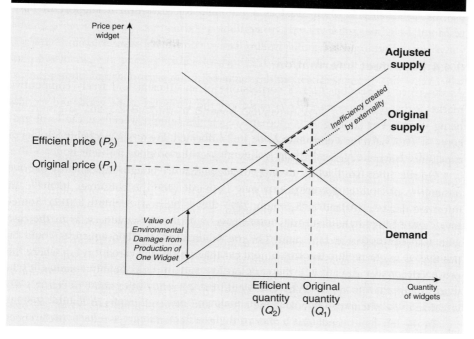

An important consequence of taking an economic perspective on externalities is that, *even in a state of efficiency, some spillover from one party to another may occur.* To continue our example from above, where the production of each widget causes $1.00 worth of environmental damage, if our goal is to achieve an efficient allocation, then we ought to aspire only to clean up to the point where the cost of control is just equal to the value of the damage done. If, for example, the cost of the pollution control technology is $1.50 per widget, then it is inefficient to install the technology. To see why this is the case, consider that we'd be spending $1.50 to avoid $1.00 of damage, thereby 'wasting' $0.50 per widget, a losing proposition. In short, from the perspective of efficiency, we want to reduce the wastewater discharge only when the cost of doing so is less than $1.00 per widget. In other words, within this framework, *the optimal level of pollution is often not zero.*

Externalities are not always negative. Positive externalities arise when the spillover from a transaction has a beneficial impact on a third party. One example is basic science research, where newly created knowledge cannot easily be kept secret by the entity that paid for the research. Knowing that some of the value will spill over to others, private firms are thus likely to invest less in such research than they otherwise would. This underinvestment in research in turn creates an inefficiency because additional investments in research could yield benefits in excess of their cost. This positive externality is often cited as a rationale for government support of basic research.

9.4.4 Imperfect Information

As described in Section 9.1.1, a cornerstone of an efficient and freely competitive market is that *consumers are well informed* about the attributes of the goods and services being traded. For some goods—perhaps vegetables bought weekly at the local grocery—it's not hard for a consumer to be well-informed. He or she probably has lots of experience buying veggies and can readily inspect the produce for defects.

On the other hand, when it comes to goods that are bought infrequently or have difficult-to-observe characteristics, it may be harder for the consumer to make an informed decision (Allcott & Sunstein, 2015; Levy, Norton, & Smith, 2017). Sometimes those hidden characteristics might have negative consequences, as in the case with lead-contaminated tap water. On the other hand, the consequences could be positive, as might be the case with a used car that's been well cared for, but where the prospective buyer can't verify the car's quality and thus reasonably assumes it's in worse shape than it looks. (Why else would the current owner want to sell it?) To visualize these phenomena, look at the supply and demand graphs in Exhibit 9-5.

In the left-hand panel, the higher of the two demand curves reflects preferences when consumers are unaware of the hidden undesirable attribute of the good. If consumers were aware of the product's risks, there would be another demand curve, this one informed. It would be beneath the first curve. In turn, the equilibrium price would be lower (P_2 instead of P_1), as would the quantity (Q_2 instead of Q_1). The inefficiency arises because consumers, in their uninformed state, buy a quantity of the good, at a higher price, than they otherwise would, even though their extra consumption yields no benefit to them. The triangle outlined in heavy dashes measures the efficiency loss created by the extra product (Q_2–Q_1) bought by uninformed consumers at the higher price of P_1.

In the right-hand panel, the higher of the two demand curves depicts the increased demand for a good with hidden desirable attributes that would result if consumers were better informed. The quantity sold would move from Q_1 to Q_3, while the price would climb from P_1 to P_3. In this case, the efficiency loss associated with uninformed consumption, again outlined in heavy dashes, reflects the lost opportunity for both producers and consumers to enjoy the welfare gains created by greater production.

The problem of imperfect information can be magnified when there is an **asymmetry of information** between buyers and sellers. The phrase **adverse selection** describes situations where either the buyer or seller is in possession of information unknown to the other and acts on that information in a way that disadvantages

Exhibit 9-5 Consequences of Incomplete Information

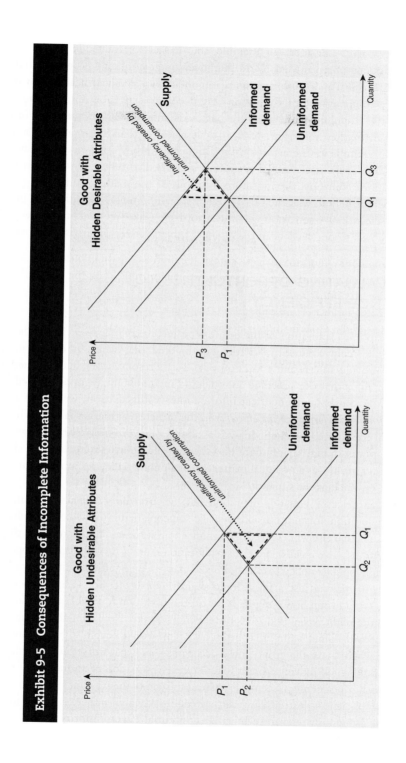

the other party. Consider, for example, the market for individual health insurance (i.e., insurance not provided by an employer or government program). Individuals have a great deal more information about their own personal health than does the insurance company. A healthy person may decide to skip the insurance and save the cost of the premium while a sickly person is more likely to purchase insurance, meaning that policy holders are likely to be less healthy than the population as a whole. In turn, premiums for the insured will be higher than they otherwise would be. A self-perpetuating cycle may result if premiums are raised to reflect the additional cost to the insurance company, driving more folks out of the market, and leaving only the sickest people behind who then face even higher premiums. Mitigating this process of adverse selection is one reason why the Affordable Care Act contained a mandate for all individuals to purchase health insurance if they weren't otherwise insured.

9.5 EVALUATING OPPORTUNITIES TO ENHANCE EFFICIENCY

Let's recap our exploration of the economics lens thus far. We reviewed the characteristics of freely competitive markets and noted that when at equilibrium, such markets provide an efficient allocation of society's resources. We next looked at four market failures that can preclude an efficient outcome: public goods, limited competition, externalities, and imperfect information. In this section, we'll look at a conceptual *framework for enhancing efficiency* in the presence of market failures while in the next we'll consider cost–benefit analysis as a *tool for implementing the framework*. Bear in mind that even though there might be a theoretical opportunity to enhance efficiency, that doesn't mean—as a practical matter—that a public policy response can necessarily improve on the current situation.

To start, let's revisit our definition of efficiency (i.e., with an efficient, Pareto-optimal allocation, it is not possible to make someone better off without simultaneously making someone else worse off). If you think about it for a minute, you'll see that this is *a strong test*. It is also an absolute test; an allocation is efficient, or it is not. Suppose we're considering a public policy that would make many people substantially better off, but at the price of making just a few people slightly worse off. For example, perhaps the occupants of a group house regularly sit on the back porch and blast their loud music late into the night, keeping dozens of neighbors awake. Even though enacting a noise ordinance with 'quiet hours' that begin at 9 p.m. would benefit a great many people, doing so would make the group house occupants somewhat worse off. Accordingly, the policy would entail moving from a Pareto efficient situation to an inefficient situation.

At first glance, it might seem like we're at the end of the story (at least with respect to economic efficiency). Instead, however, we could ask whether there is a path to a better outcome. Economists refer to such paths as **potential Pareto improvements** that could enhance relative efficiency. Imagine each sleepless neighbor would willingly contribute $1 for a good night's sleep, and that those contributions when pooled, sum to $50. Offered $50, the music lovers might happily go inside and shut the door. Another potential Pareto improvement could run in the other direction, with folks in the group house paying every neighbor some amount as compensation for enduring the ruckus. In other words, even though the initial situation was Pareto efficient, we might still be able to improve on it.

This approach is called the **Kaldor–Hicks compensation principle**: a change to the status quo increases efficiency if those made better off by it could compensate those who lose out, and still have a bit left over. As another example of the Kaldor–Hicks principle in action, recall the widget factory with wastewater discharges that reduce the yield of a downstream fishery (i.e., the factory creates an externality). Suppose the installation of a fully effective pollution control technology would cost the factory owner $1 million. If the value of the lost fish is less than $1 million, then a public policy to require the equipment would be inefficient because its costs would exceed its benefits. Applying the Kaldor–Hicks principle wouldn't change anything.

But, on the other hand, if the value of the lost fish was $2 million, then a public policy intervention might potentially enhance efficiency because the winners could compensate the losers and still come out ahead. How? In one scenario, the fishers could pay the factory an amount over $1 million but below $2 million in return for the factory's installation of the pollution control device. The factory comes out ahead because, even after installing the equipment, it has more money and the fishers come out ahead because, even after paying the factory, the increased fish yield more than compensates them for the payment to the factory. In another hypothetical scenario, where the factory is liable for the loss incurred by the fishers, the factory could install the technology for $1 million, thereby avoiding a $2 million payment to the fishers. Again, the Kaldor–Hicks calculation is a theoretical one; no money ever needs to change hands for us to claim that a new policy mandating installation of the pollution controls is relatively more efficient than the status quo.

> It is critically important to understand that the compensations are not in fact made. If they were, the change would then indeed be Pareto-superior. Thus the [Kaldor-Hicks] compensation principle is a test for potential Pareto superiority. Think of the gains from a change as its benefits and the losses from a change as its costs. Define net benefits as the sum of all benefits minus the sum of all costs. … *Trying to maximize net benefits is thus the same as trying to maximize relative efficiency.* (Friedman, 2002, p. 173), *emphasis added*

Essentially, the Kaldor–Hicks principle treats the economy as a single unitary entity. If gains from a policy change exceed losses, regardless of where in the economy the gains and losses occur, then the economy—as a whole—is presumed to be better off.

9.6 COST–BENEFIT ANALYSIS

A rigorous application of the Kaldor–Hicks compensation principle requires that we enumerate all the costs and benefits of the policy options being studied. As previewed in Section 1.5 and alluded to above by Friedman, the process of **cost–benefit analysis** (CBA) is conceptually simple: monetize all the costs and benefits of each proposed policy change and select the one with the highest net benefits. The apparent simplicity of this framework, however, obscures substantial complexity (and at least some controversy) when it comes to performing the calculations. A thorough review of CBA is not feasible in the space we have here. Indeed, there are entire textbooks, and semester-long courses, devoted to the topic. This section will, accordingly, only preview some of the most important highlights of the method, as illustrated by a 'real-world' CBA of an environmental regulation.

The starting point for a cost–benefit analysis is the Criteria-Alternatives Matrix (CAM) which, as we saw in Chapter 1, arrays all policy options under consideration against all evaluation criteria relevant to the policy decision. Each cell of the matrix contains the projected outcome of one option with respect to one criterion. To convert the contents of the CAM into a CBA, we need to attach a monetary value to each outcome in the CAM. This may make more sense with an example.

In 2015, the Environmental Protection Agency (EPA) revised its regulations related to ground-level ozone, an air pollutant with adverse respiratory and cardiovascular health effects (EPA, 2015). The prior standard was 75 parts per billion (ppb), and EPA was considering whether to lower it to 70- or 65-ppb. Ultimately, EPA settled on the 70-ppb standard and changed its regulations accordingly. Exhibit 9-6 shows some of the projected benefits of changes to EPA's ozone standard, taken from the CBA of the regulatory revisions. Each of the avoided health impacts (e.g., 80 fewer cardiovascular hospital admissions) is akin to the content of a single cell in a standard CAM.

EPA estimated the benefits of improvements in public health. More specifically, for each type of health impact, EPA first combined toxicology models with demographic data to predict the number of cases under each standard (i.e., 75-, 70-, and 65-ppb). Then, because the CBA estimated the incremental impact of the regulatory changes, the projected numbers of cases in the 70-ppb and 65-ppb scenarios were subtracted from the number of cases in the 75-ppb scenario to compute the avoided health impacts of each scenario. The Agency next estimated the economic benefit of avoiding a single instance of that impact. For example, avoiding one pollution-related premature death is assumed to have a value of $10 million while avoiding the exacerbation of someone's asthma (not requiring medical treatment) is valued at $60 per case. The right-hand column of the exhibit describes the basis of the valuation.

With these estimates in hand, the final three steps were straightforward. First, EPA multiplied the number of cases avoided for each health impact by the monetary

Exhibit 9-6   Examples of Annual Benefits (in 2025) of EPA's (2015) Revision of Ozone Air Quality Standard (49 States, Excluding California)

Avoided Health Impacts	Revised Standard		Estimated Unit Benefit	Basis of Estimated Unit Benefit
	70-ppb	65-ppb		
Premature deaths	316–660	1,590–3,320	$10,000,000 (value of a statistical life)	Contingent valuation surveys and labor market studies
Nonfatal heart attacks	28–260	140–1,300	$100,000–$210,000, depending on age	Lost earnings, plus medical costs
Cardiovascular hospital admissions	80	400	$42,000–$44,000, depending on age	Lost earnings, plus medical costs
Emergency room visits for asthma	630	3,300	$440	Cost of treatment
Lost workdays	28,000	140,000	Varies geographically, US median = $150	County-specific median wage
Asthma exacerbations	11,000	53,000	$60	Willingness to pay based on survey information
Lost school days	160,000	790,000	$98	Probability that parent misses work times lost productivity

Source: EPA (2015)

benefit of avoiding one case of that impact. If the number of cases was expressed as a range (e.g., 316–660 premature deaths), this process produced a range for the value of the associated impact. Second, the Agency used a process known as discounting to adjust the result in cases where the benefits were expected to occur over time rather than in a single year.[13] Third, EPA added up the benefits across all types of health

---

[13]To discount a cost or benefit that occurs n years in the future, we divide it by $(1+r)^n$, where r is the discount rate. In policy analysis, r is typically between 0.02 and 0.10. This calculation converts a future cost or benefit into its present value. The process is akin to earning interest on an account balance, where next year's balance is higher than this year's. In short, it's more valuable to have $1 in hand today that the promise of $1 in the future.

impact, including impacts expressed as a range, to compute a total (e.g., total benefits of $2.9–$5.9 billion).

When it comes to the cost side of the ledger, EPA first identified which entities (primarily power plants, factories, and other industrial processes) would be required to modify their practices and then identified which technological changes would be needed. Finally, it used engineering cost estimation techniques to put a price tag on compliance costs. The Agency didn't identify uncertainties in the cost estimates, so the result is a point estimate rather than a range of values. The 70-ppb standard was estimated to have an annual cost of $1.4 billion in 2025 while the more stringent 65-ppb standard would cost $16.0 billion. Exhibit 9-7 presents the results of EPA's CBA of the two policy options.

Exhibit 9-7	Annual Costs and Benefits (in 2025) of EPA's (2015) Revision of Ozone Air Quality Standard (49 States)		
	Revised Standard		
	70-ppb		**65-ppb**
Total Costs	$1.4 billion		$16.0 billion
Total Health Benefits	$2.9 to $5.9 billion		$15.0 to $30.0 billion
Net Benefits	$1.5 to $4.5 billion		$1.0 to $14.0 billion

Source: EPA (2015)

For the 70-ppb standard, total benefits are predicted to exceed total costs by at least $1.5 billion, and perhaps by as much as $4.5 billion. The 70-ppb standard thus unambiguously satisfies the Kaldor–Hicks principle, thereby enhancing efficiency relative to the status quo. Results are not as clear for the 65-ppb standard, where net benefits could range as high as $14 billion per year, but also might be negative (i.e., that costs exceed benefits by $1.0 billion). Given uncertainty in the economic value of the health benefits, EPA's analysis suggests that the 65-ppb standard could impose costs greater than benefits; in other words, it might not satisfy the Kaldor–Hicks principle.

Having reviewed EPA's ozone analysis, let's think more broadly about what it takes to use CBA to apply the Kaldor–Hicks principle to a policy analysis. There are at least three important factors you need to consider. First, you need to decide who has **standing**, i.e., whose costs and benefits will be included in your tally. Doing so might be straightforward, as in the case of a local road project where you decide that road users and folks living near the road comprise the universe of people potentially affected by the project and who should thus be given standing in your CBA. Thinking about the concept of standing in this way may also help you identify affected parties who might otherwise have been neglected. For example, costs and benefits experienced by marginalized communities will be reflected in a well-executed CBA, even though such folks usually don't have lobbyists to represent their interests to policymakers.

On the other hand, the issue of standing can be controversial. Consider the US government's estimate of the social cost of carbon (SCC). The SCC monetizes the adverse climate impacts of emitting one additional ton of carbon dioxide at a particular point in time. In its final year, the Obama administration estimated the SCC for the year 2030 at $60 per ton. Three years later, using the same models and the same discount rate, the Trump administration concluded that the 2030 SCC was $8 per ton (GAO, 2020), but early in the Biden administration, the SCC was pegged at $62 (IWG, 2021).

What accounts for these wide variations in the SCC? Standing. When the Obama team tallied up the adverse impacts of climate change, it considered global impacts. The Trump team limited itself to impacts experienced within the United States. In other words, the former granted standing to the world's 7+ billion residents while the latter granted it to only the 325 million or so people living in the United States. The difference is more than an academic technicality. Using the higher estimate of the social cost of carbon means that application of the Kaldor–Hicks principle would justify much more aggressive (i.e., up to seven times more costly) policy measures to reduce emissions. Within a month of coming into office, however, the Biden Administration reversed course and again extended standing to all global residents (and updated the figures for inflation), yielding an SCC for 2030 of $62.

The second factor to consider when conducting a CBA is how to **monetize the impacts** of the policies being considered. Sometimes, measuring costs and benefits is conceptually straightforward. If, for example, we need to put a price tag on a pollution control technology or on medical care, we can almost certainly find the data we need by looking at 'real-world' market transactions to observe the typical price paid for these goods and services. Such valuations reflect what economists call **revealed preferences**, meaning that they reflect not what people say they value, but instead reflect what people actually value as demonstrated by their willingness to spend their own money on the good or service.

But for things not traded in markets, like clean air or folks' aversion to suffering an illness, there often isn't any market data to rely on. In some cases, however, it may be possible to infer a revealed preference indirectly from available market-based data. For example, we might be able to put a price on air pollution by comparing housing prices in polluted and unpolluted neighborhoods. Such valuations have the advantage that they are based on observed spending patterns (i.e., they are revealed preferences), but their accuracy depends on the quality of the statistical analyses that underlie them.

When market data are not available to compute, directly or indirectly, a revealed preference, CBA practitioners often rely on **stated preferences**. Doing so entails use of what are referred to as **contingent valuation** methods that rely on surveys or behavioral experiments to estimate how much people would be willing to pay to secure a positive outcome or to avoid a negative one (i.e., as if those harms and benefits were being freely traded in a marketplace). Such techniques have their limitations, chief among them that it's easy for folks to say they value something when they know they don't actually have to spend any money on it. Exhibit 9-8 summarizes the three approaches for monetizing impacts in a CBA.

Exhibit 9-8 Methods for Monetizing Impacts

- Revealed Preferences
  - Direct: Observation of market transactions
  - Indirect: Statistical analysis of related transactions

- Stated Preferences
  - Contingent valuation based on surveys and experiments

The third factor to consider when using a CBA to apply the Kaldor–Hicks principle is how to ensure that your analysis *captures all impacts* of the proposed policy changes. The omission of a cost or benefit will invalidate your findings if the omitted impact is sufficiently large to change your conclusion about which policy offers the highest net benefits. This is a two-part test. First, even though you may have been able to compute a dollar value that measures a particular impact, you need to convince your audience (or client) that your estimation technique and its result are valid. Consider, for example, that EPA values premature deaths averted by its regulation at $10 million each. But not everyone believes that putting a price tag on human life—even if only in a statistical sense—is ethically acceptable. If the monetary benefit of avoided premature deaths is excluded from the calculations, it won't be possible to draw a valid conclusion about whether revision to the ozone standard would satisfy the Kaldor–Hicks compensation principle.

Assuming you succeed in coming up with convincing monetary estimates of the impacts you've identified, your second challenge is to ensure that you haven't overlooked anything. If you haven't been able to monetize *all* impacts of a policy, you need to be cautious in your use of CBA. For example, EPA's regulation to control ozone pollution was expected to also reduce other pollutants like oxides of nitrogen. But EPA lacked the data needed to quantify and monetize the benefits of reductions in these pollutants, and thus left them out of the CBA. In turn, total benefits were underestimated. Similarly, EPA valued each averted case of many health impacts (e.g., a hospital admission for asthma) as the cost of medical care plus the lost wages that resulted from being unable to work for a period of time. No monetary value was assigned to the inconvenience, discomfort, and distress of going into the hospital. If such impacts were monetized, then the benefits of the policy change would be higher.

You might think these are minor details, and they could be, depending on their effect on aggregate costs and benefits. Leaving out a few benefits doesn't affect the conclusion with respect to the 70-ppb standard, for which the measured benefits are sufficiently high to satisfy the Kaldor–Hicks principle. But omission of these benefits may have tainted the conclusion about the 65-ppb standard, where you'll recall, there was some chance that costs would exceed benefits. Had the omitted benefits been included, the more stringent standard may have more convincingly met the Kaldor–Hicks test.

Taking a step back, it's clear that when it comes to cost–benefit analysis, there are often data gaps, methodological constraints, and future uncertainties that prevent you from relying on your CBA to render a definitive judgment on the merits of the available policy choices. Nonetheless, CBA imposes a valuable rigor on the process of policy analysis. CBA asks you to systematically inventory all impacts—good and bad—of the choices being debated, to estimate the magnitude of each of those impacts, and to measure those impacts with a common monetary metric. Doing so provides commensurability among policy options, thereby facilitating direct comparisons among them. As one of my professors once told us: "The final destination you reach in your CBA may be an imperfect one, but the journey will certainly be an enlightening one."

9.7 LIMITATIONS OF THE LENS OF ECONOMICS

The field of economics helps us understand how large parts of society—producers, consumers, and markets—interact with each other and with public policies. Your work as a policy analyst will certainly be enhanced by an ability to consider policy issues from an economic perspective. That said, economics provides only one perspective on policy issues, and an incomplete one at that. This section briefly reviews some of the limitations on the view that can be gleaned through the lens of economics. Exhibit 9-9 gives you a preview of what we'll cover.

Exhibit 9-9 Things to Remember When Incorporating an Economic Perspective in Policy Analysis

- Markets don't always ensure an efficiency-maximizing outcome.
- Economic efficiency ignores the distribution of wealth, income, and other resources.
- CBA and the Kaldor–Hicks compensation principle both have important shortcomings.
- The public good is about more than just economic efficiency.
- Policymakers are often not focused on economic efficiency.

First, it's important to remember that *in the presence of a market failure, we shouldn't expect an efficiency-maximizing outcome.* As we reviewed in Section 9.4, there are a variety of situations in which markets will almost certainly not deliver an efficient outcome including the provision of public goods, limited competition, externalities, and imperfect information. Some of these situations, such as a single supplier in a market or pollution that causes an externality, may be easy to detect. In other cases, like subtle efforts to limit competition, for example, or imperfect information among market participants, it may be harder to recognize and verify the market failure. Why is this important? As a policy analyst, you can't assume that a seemingly free market satisfies all the conditions under which we expect it to reach equilibrium and deliver an efficient outcome. You need to analyze the evidence before reaching such a conclusion. This can be especially important in policy debates when the beneficiaries of market failure defend the status quo by making appeals to the value of a freely competitive market, even though the market in which they are operating doesn't meet the definition of an efficient market.

Even if you don't see major failures in the market you're studying, you can't assume it's delivering a Pareto efficient equilibrium. As discussed in Section 9.1.2, most firms work assiduously to avoid getting stuck at the intersection of the supply and demand curves where the price they receive barely covers their production costs. Instead, the most profitable firms are those who can "lock in customers" and "lock out competitors" (Hamel, 2000, p. 102). Or as a typical management strategy textbook advises:

> [A company must] search for and develop the strategic control points in its industry. The purpose of a strategic control point is to protect the profit stream that the business design has created against the corrosive effects of competition and customer power. (Slywotzky, Morrison, & Andelman, 1997, p. 52)

Consider, however, that the "corrosive effects of competition and customer power" to which the authors refer are the same forces that push markets toward equilibrium. The consequence, in the words of the UK Minister of Science and Innovation, is that:

> [T]he assumption that the market economy is one of perfect competition … is a completely unrealistic view of the world, as can be seen by a quick trip to any shopping center or car showroom. (Sainsbury, 2020, p. 82)

In other words, if firms can block competition to the detriment of customers, we can't expect an efficiency-maximizing market outcome.

Other indicators of inefficiency include price discrimination and underutilized labor and capital resources. Consider a grocery store that charges its club members a lower price for bread and other staples. Known as price discrimination, this tactic helps maximize profits, but the presence of two prices for the same good is a hallmark of an inefficient allocation. Moreover, as we saw earlier, the effect of economywide business cycles, especially contractions and recessions, can disturb a market's equilibrium and may lead to inefficiencies like unemployed labor and underutilized capital assets. In short, markets with failures, and those not at equilibrium, don't maximize efficiency.

Second, it's important to recognize that the concept of *economic efficiency ignores the distribution of wealth, income, and other resources*. If all we care about is maximizing social surplus (i.e., the sum of consumer and producer surplus), it's clear that moving from an inefficient situation to a more efficient one is a good idea. But even if we've corrected all market failures and reached an efficient market equilibrium, an excessive focus on efficiency can blind us to another important feature of market economies. To understand it, let's work backward for a second. Look at Exhibit 9-10. In a freely competitive market, an equilibrium is an endpoint (3) that reflects an efficient allocation of all resources. Equilibrium is reached via a process where market participants (consumers, workers, firms, and investors) in a freely competitive market trade their way (2) to the best outcome given their circumstances. The result is efficiency both in consumption and in production, and in the alignment of the two. But what comes before all this trading? We start with what economists refer to as endowments (1), which reflect the initial distribution of wealth, income, and other resources (like education, talent, and opportunities for advancement) across market participants.

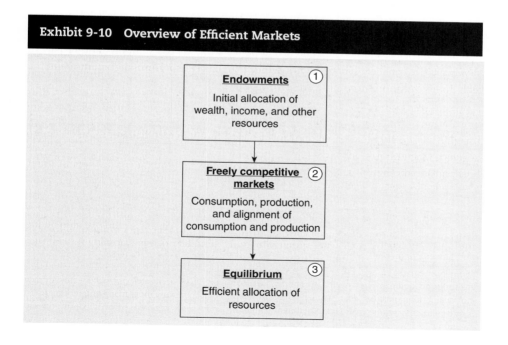

Exhibit 9-10   Overview of Efficient Markets

Endowments ①
Initial allocation of wealth, income, and other resources

Freely competitive markets ②
Consumption, production, and alignment of consumption and production

Equilibrium ③
Efficient allocation of resources

And here's the thing: the test of efficiency is silent about endowments. We could have vast inequalities in wealth and income, yet a freely competitive market would still deliver an efficient result. If folks are poor, then an efficient market helps them allocate their meager resources to best meet their needs, but it doesn't alleviate their poverty. In short, while we need to appreciate the advantages of an efficient, rather than inefficient, allocation of resources, we also need to recognize that *efficiency by itself provides no assurance that the final allocation of resources will be normatively desirable*.

Interestingly, according to economist Gabriel Zucman, the focus on economic efficiency that anchors the curriculum of many economics departments (and, I would argue, policy schools) is somewhat of an historical anomaly:

> During the postwar decades, economics was almost entirely about questions of efficiency, of demonstrating that a market economy worked better than a planned one. But this was a historical parenthesis, economics in a Cold War context. Historically, economics was about questions of distribution [of wealth and income] … Now, in the 21st century, we're rediscovering the importance of distributional issues. (Meyerson, 2021, p. 7)

Third, despite the insights they can yield, both *cost–benefit analysis and the Kaldor–Hicks compensation principle have important shortcomings*. For starters, CBA treats a dollar of benefit equally, irrespective of where in society it is experienced, meaning that it ignores distributional consequences.[14] And, as we saw in Chapter 8, a key source of inequity in public policies is the misalignment of costs and benefits. In such cases, one part of society enjoys the benefit of a policy while its costs fall on another part of society. CBA can be used to identify and characterize such misalignments, but the technique itself does nothing to resolve them.

Moreover, CBA typically gives more emphasis to the preferences of those who are more affluent.[15] To understand why this is the case, consider a fictitious example. Imagine a large city that, based on prior projects, has budgeted half a million dollars to develop a neighborhood park. City officials want to use CBA to select the neighborhood for the new park. The cost side of the ledger is straightforward; the cost is

---

[14]Some scholars suggest the use of "distributionally weighted CBA" in which costs and benefits experienced by different socioeconomic groups are weighted to reflect normative considerations (Boardman, Greenberg, Vining, & Weimer, 2011). There is, however, no consensus on how such weights should be developed.

[15]Sometimes, data limitations eliminate this potential problem when only a single value for willingness to pay is applied to all persons. For example, in EPA's ozone RIA, rich and poor alike were assumed to value the avoidance of an asthma exacerbation at $60, and every life (from a newborn to an octogenarian, irrespective of race, ethnicity, wealth, or income) was valued at a consistent $10 million.

$500K. But neighborhood parks are not bought and sold in markets, so things get trickier when it comes to benefits. To measure benefits, the city needs to discern the neighborhood's willingness to pay for the park's amenities.[16] Using a contingent valuation survey, the city discovers that a wealthy neighborhood values the park at $1 million, but that a poor neighborhood with twice as many residents (who struggle to make ends meet) is only willing to pay $100K. Clearly, putting the park in the rich neighborhood maximizes net benefits ($500K); indeed, within a CBA framework, putting the park in the poor neighborhood creates net costs of $400K. But in a democracy, where a principle of one person/one vote is observed, if the matter were put to a vote, the park would end up in the poor neighborhood, a result at odds with the CBA. In short, to the degree that a CBA relies on willingness to pay in order to value impacts, it will amplify the preferences of the wealthy relative to those of less affluent folks.

Another concern about the use of CBA to select an optimal public policy stems from its reliance on the Kaldor–Hicks compensation principle. As described in Section 9.5, this principle treats the economy as an entity unto itself. If the aggregate benefits of a proposed policy are greater than its aggregate costs, then the policy is deemed to make the economy—as a whole—better off. Gains and losses, however, are experienced not by an intangible entity called 'the economy,' but by real people (workers, consumers, and investors). And while the Kaldor–Hicks compensation principle helps us think about ways we might use policy to improve efficiency, it's important to remember that the principle does not require that winners from a policy change actually compensate losers, only that they could do so. Because winners don't compensate losers, the Kaldor–Hicks principle opens the door to adoption of policies that create or exacerbate inequities without actually satisfying the Pareto test of efficiency that at least one person is made better off without making anyone worse off.

Fourth, *the public good is about more than just economic efficiency*. If we look at policy issues *solely* through the lens of economics, we are left with the idea that aggregate social welfare is nothing more than the sum of everyone's individual welfare, and that the source of an individual's welfare is nothing more than the collection of goods and services they buy in markets. But because, as we saw in Chapter 8, normative considerations are an intrinsic part of policy debates, a policy analysis based only on economic efficiency is almost certainly incomplete. If you listen to debates about the typical policy issue, you'll hear arguments about what's best for society that go far beyond economic efficiency and which are instead rooted in politics, ideology, and morality. Philosopher Michael Sandel (2020) puts it this way:

---

[16]Assuming that the park's benefits are limited to one neighborhood and don't spill over to other parts of the city.

The technocratic conception of politics is bound up with a ... belief that market mechanisms are the primary instruments for achieving the public good. This way of thinking about politics is technocratic in the sense that it drains public discourse of substantive moral argument and treats ideologically contestable questions as if they were matters of economic efficiency, the province of experts. (pp. 19–20)

As one quick example, consider that most economists would view the offshoring of a factory to a country with lower labor costs and more lenient environmental laws as an efficiency-enhancing change. Why? Because consumers will enjoy lower prices, shareholders will enjoy increased returns, local residents will enjoy cleaner air and water, and unemployed workers will find new jobs as labor markets re-equilibrate. Moreover, adverse impacts in the second country would be outside the scope of the typical CBA. Missing from the analysis, however, would be the disruption of personal, family, and community lives caused by the offshoring, as well as the ethical dilemma of letting a country 'export' pollution by moving production to a country with lax environmental controls. Economics doesn't do especially well when it comes to measuring the dignity of work, the value to a community of a stable economy, or the morality of adverse impacts on individuals who lack standing for purposes of a CBA.

Fifth, *policymakers are often not focused on economic efficiency*. Politicians, in particular, spend a good deal of time looking after their constituents' interests. While spending taxpayer resources on a public project may look like a cost from within a CBA, the recipients of that spending will experience it as a benefit. And politicians get reelected, at least in part, by delivering benefits to voters. Based on an empirical study of Congressional decisionmaking, John Kingdon concluded that:

Efficiency does not always carry the day, particularly as an issue moves from the community of specialists ... into a larger political arena. Some respondents even argued that political processes systematically favor inefficiency. [One respondent] spoke of large-scale, expensive subway systems: "... they take so much money, they are so inefficient, that there is a great deal of support for them." Then he added, in an absolute masterpiece of pithy summary, "*For a politician, the costs are the benefits*". (p. 137), *emphasis in original*

If policymakers often aspire to implement policies without regard to economic efficiency, does it make sense to anchor policy analysis in an economic framework that puts a premium on efficiency? That's a tough question and it lacks a definitive answer. You might answer yes on the grounds that analysts should guide policies toward greater efficiency because doing so will make best use of society's limited resources.

You might answer no on the grounds that, in a democracy, analysts are obligated to help properly elected policymakers implement their own decisionmaking rubrics, irrespective of economic efficiency. Either way, you're taking a normative stance about the appropriate role of a policy analyst. It's up to you; I can't answer the question for you.

Having reviewed these five reasons why a policy analysis focused only on economics will come up short, you might think I am arguing against the inclusion of economic analysis in policy analysis. Far from it. Not only does economic analysis force a logical and methodical approach to understanding real-world conditions, it can also reveal lots of policy-relevant insights. It just won't reveal everything you need to consider when it comes to public policy. You can think of it this way: a policy analysis comprised exclusively of economic analysis is almost certainly incomplete, so too is a policy analysis that ignores the economic interactions of prices and markets with consumers, workers, producers, and investors.

CHAPTER SUMMARY

This chapter introduced the economics lens as the second of seven lenses through which policy issues should be considered. We looked at the role played by market prices in pushing buyers and sellers toward an equilibrium and observed that under certain conditions, the equilibrium represents an efficient outcome. We noted the value of efficiency in generating the most value from society's resources. Because firms and people typically respond to incentives, economic analysis can be a key part of policy analysis. Markets also play an important role in organizing economywide production and consumption decisions, creating rewards for entrepreneurial innovation and other salutary behavior, and providing resources for individuals, families, communities, and governments.

We then examined cases where markets may fail to deliver efficient outcomes. Examples include the failure of markets to supply public goods, the inefficiencies that result from limited competition, the propensity of externalities to create adverse consequences for entities not a party to a market transaction, and the inefficiencies that result when market participants are not fully informed about the attributes of goods and services.

I characterized CBA and the Kaldor–Hicks compensation principle as flawed, but useful, tools to analyze policies that aspire to address such market failures. The chapter closed with a review of the limitations of economic analysis and noted that policymakers often don't pay much attention to the scholarly definition of economic efficiency and instead routinely make policy decisions based on other, noneconomic considerations.

DISCUSSION QUESTIONS

1. Why is efficiency so important in policy analysis? Do you think that policymakers should make enhancing the efficiency of markets a high priority? Why? Why not?

2. Do you think that most markets in the United States meet the test of being freely competitive? Why? Why not? What are the implications for public policy?

3. Can you think of companies with too much market power? If so, would a change in public policy be appropriate? What are the pros and cons of taking policy action to address such situations?

4. Do you see CBA as an appropriate way of making policy decisions? What are the pros and cons of using CBA in policy analysis?

5. How comfortable are you with the idea of attaching a monetary value to all impacts of policy options being analyzed? Are there some impacts more or less suitable for monetization?

6. In what ways are equity and efficiency connected? How should policymakers reconcile tensions between the two concepts?

CHAPTER TEN

THE POLITICAL AND INSTITUTIONAL LENSES

This chapter describes two closely related lenses through which you might look to better understand a policy issue. Both lenses focus on the day-to-day workings of government itself. We'll start in Section 10.1 with the political processes that drive policymaking and then in Section 10.2, review the institutions of government and consider the roles they play in shaping and delivering public policies.

10.1 THE POLITICAL LENS

It's hard to ignore politics when you think about public policy. The media, with its 24/7 news cycle, covers politics like a spectator sport, tracking who's up and who's down, which agenda is winning, and which is losing. I don't know about you, but my newsfeed is full of opinions, post-truth claims, and fragmentary facts from pundits and influencers trying to shape political debates. I'd like to offer a less febrile way of thinking about politics and the exercise of political power in the context of policy analysis.

Section 10.1 starts with a few definitions and Section 10.1.2 presents the Multiple Streams Framework, which is one framework—among several—that scholars have developed to describe the political drivers of policy change. Section 10.1.3 explores how the substantive content of policies affects political debates while Section 10.1.4 introduces the concept of political economy and notes some of the connections between money and politics.

10.1.1 Getting Started

Politics vs. Policy

Politics and policy are distinct constructs but are bound together. Think of **politics** as a production process

Learning Objectives

By studying this chapter, you should be able to:

- Explain connections between politics and policy, recognizing that politics can be the unapologetic pursuit of self-interest, a means of realizing shared societal goals, and sometimes, a theatrical performance.

- Recognize the political conditions that make policy change more likely and those that make it less likely.

- Make educated guesses about how the politics of a particular situation will play out, based on the policy options being considered.

- Understand feedback loops that connect the accumulation of wealth in the marketplace to the exercise of political power in the formulation of public policy.

- Assess the degree to which governmental institutions can be trusted to effectively implement public policy and deliver expected outcomes.

- Characterize differences between commercial and governmental institutions, and assess the impact of those differences on the ability of government to successfully implement policy.

- Define the principal–agent problem and explain how it may lead to suboptimization in the performance of governmental institutions.

- Explain the principles of federalism and describe how the interplay among federal, state, tribal, and local governments can affect public policy.

- Incorporate issues related to taxation and governmental spending into a policy analysis.

comprising structural mechanisms, institutional rules, and human behavior that produces public **policy** as its output. Or think of them as two sides of the same coin. Mead (2013) uses the term 'statecraft' to describe how politicians try to reconcile policy and politics by devising policies that will be effective *and* politically acceptable (p. 390). Policies that don't attract sufficient political support don't get enacted. On the other hand, if too many politically motivated changes are made to an otherwise sound policy, it may become so distorted that it doesn't mitigate the original problem, or worse, creates new ones (Eggers & O'Leary, 2009). Political processes are hardly formulaic:

> Decisions made in the public sector are the result of efforts to balance competing societal interests, resolve power conflicts, and appease groups with widely divergent values, not the end-point of a linear, rational, instrumental exercise. (Newman, 2017, p. 1)

But this book is meant for policy analysts, not politicians. It's also not an instruction manual for political operatives. We thus won't take a deep dive into politics, but the discussion would be incomplete if we didn't spend at least some time on the links between politics and policy analysis.

We first touched on the topic of politics in Chapter 1 when I advised against the use of political feasibility as a criterion in a criteria-alternatives analysis. Exhibit 10-1 recaps the highlights of that discussion; the remainder of this section explores key links between policy analysis and politics.

Exhibit 10-1   The Basics of Policy Analysis and Politics

- Doing a good job of political analysis inside a policy analysis is almost impossible.
- Political bargaining among policymakers doesn't follow a predictable pattern.
- The political feasibility of a policy option can change quickly and without warning.
- A politically popular policy may be a bad idea and a politically unpopular policy may be a good idea.

Source: Chapter 1

Politics is the animating driver of the processes by which public policies are proposed, debated, modified, and sometimes enacted by government. Politics also explains why some issues are kept off the agenda, rather than considered and debated. The substance of political action and the exercise of political power within these processes are in turn shaped by the motivations, intentions, and tactics of the participants.

Targets of Political Attention

Politics refers to both the behavior of people inside government as they engage in the process of creating and implementing public policy, and the behavior of people outside government who try to influence that process. There are generally three phases of policymaking where politics come into play:

- *The Legislative Phase*: During this phase, statutory law is debated and sometimes enacted. Policymakers engage one another in negotiations in attempts to secure passage of proposals they support or defeat proposals they oppose. At the same time, stakeholders outside government often pressure lawmakers to take positions that reflect their preferences.

- *The Regulatory Phase*: At the Federal level, and in most states, executive agencies are often tasked with drafting regulations that turn statutory language into specific requirements. Political efforts to shape this process are aimed at the appointed officials and civil servants developing the regulations. Such efforts usually originate outside government, but sometimes, one agency (or level of government) lobbies another.

- *The Implementation Phase*: After statutory and regulatory language is codified, political processes often continue as stakeholders aim to influence program implementation. Legislators may be pressured to modify budgets to strengthen or weaken a program. Appointed officials may be pushed to enforce regulatory requirements more or less aggressively. And program administrators may be lobbied to adjust a program's operations to benefit a stakeholder.

The tactics used by nongovernmental actors seeking to influence public policy can be split into two types: inside and outside. **Inside tactics** are aimed directly at policymakers. The most fundamental tactic for influencing policymakers is to vote them into or out of office. Other examples include lobbying a government official, working for, or donating to a political campaign, speaking at a public hearing, or submitting comments on a proposed regulation. **Outside tactics** are meant to indirectly pressure policymakers through the media and public opinion. Examples include advertising and social media campaigns, having advocates appear on news and entertainment programs, petitions and letter writing initiatives, and public protests and demonstrations. Political advocates often combine inside and outside tactics to enhance their impact; coalition building—where like-minded individuals, interest groups, and industries join forces—offers another mechanism for amplifying political power.

The Inescapable Nature of Politics

Before going on, it's important to remind ourselves why *politics is intrinsic to policymaking*. Recall Chapter 3's discussion of the collective action and preference aggregation problems. Collective action problems arise when we need to decide if and how to act as a group, rather than individuals, while sharing the costs and benefits of doing so. Preference aggregation problems exist because philosophers and social scientists still haven't come up with a formula for fairly and unambiguously integrating the diverse preferences of multiple people into a single point of view that can serve as the basis of new public policies. Back in Chapter 3, I argued that because these are inherent features of democracy, policy analysis can never—by itself—be used to derive *the* optimal path forward.

Instead, we are forced to look to institutional and political mechanisms—democratic elections, the separation of powers among branches and levels of government, and an independent judiciary—to help to modulate the conflicts and bargaining that inevitably accompany efforts to act collectively while respecting the preferences of citizens. In short, *when you combine a commitment to democracy with the inescapability of the collective action and preference aggregation problems, the push and pull of politics in policymaking becomes inevitable.*

The Origins of Political Opinions

Positions taken by folks in the policymaking process may reflect one or more considerations. First, positions may reflect participants' **material concerns**—tangible costs and specific benefits—about the policies being debated. An individual, for example, might pay more in taxes or receive more generous services because of a change in public policy while a firm might be advantaged or disadvantaged by a regulatory change or by new international trade policies.

Second, **ideological principles** may drive political positions. If someone is a liberal or a conservative, or a free-marketeer or a democratic socialist, for example, then ideology will often drive his or her policy preferences. Ideology and morality often go hand in hand. As discussed in Chapter 8, moral reasoning lies at the heart of how folks identify right and wrong. Morality-driven politics influences issues like the death penalty, abortion rights, assisted suicide, prayer in schools, and rights for transgender persons.

Third, **social identity**—the interwoven nature of a person's intrinsic sense of self and his or her membership in various social groups—often drives political preferences. Identities can emerge along virtually any dimension of the human experience, such as race, gender, ethnicity, sexual orientation, education, wealth and income, religion, or geographic region. Allegiance to a political leader, party, or movement, or antagonism toward another leader, party, or movement may also be a source of social identity.

Empirical evidence suggests that, for many people, social identity plays a powerful role in determining political opinions and beliefs:

> ... voters, even the most informed voters, typically make choices not on the basis of policy preferences or ideology, but on the basis of who they are—their social identities. In turn, those social identities shape how they think, what they think, and where they belong in the party system. (Achen & Bartels, 2017, p. 4)

Fourth, **political sectarianism**—an extreme form of social identification—appears to explain the beliefs and behavior of at least some folks in the United States (Finkel et al., 2020). Having reviewed cognitive processes in Chapter 4, these tendencies should sound familiar to you. Sectarianism takes these tendencies to extreme and intense levels:

- *Othering*: Seeing those with competing views as alien and fundamentally different from oneself

- *Aversion*: Holding a deep-seated suspicion and distrust of those with different opinions

- *Moralization*: Ascribing evil and malevolent intentions to folks who hold dissenting views

Some scholars have argued that political sectarianism is on the rise in the United States and, moreover, that it has important implications for policymaking:

> When politics becomes an identity-based struggle against depraved opponents—when ideals and policies matter less than dominating foes—government becomes dysfunctional. ... Insofar as politicians are pursuing unpopular policies, they are incentivized to destroy the idea of objectivity altogether .... (Finkel et al., 2020, p. 536)

Political sectarianism is likely to have motivated many of the individuals who attacked the US Capitol on January 6, 2021 in a failed attempt to stop certification of the 2020 Presidential election. Moreover, political sectarianism—rather than careful consideration of the evidence or a principled stand based on a coherent world view—often seems to drive opinions about issues like the origins of COVID, the nature and purpose of the US southern border, how to address the legacy of slavery, the wisdom of vaccines and facemasks, and the threat posed by climate change. I'm not sure about the best antidote for political sectarianism. For now, I suggest simply that you be aware of the phenomenon and think of it as one more element to observe as you look through a political lens in policy analysis.

To recap, depending on whose behavior you're analyzing, and the context of a specific policy decision, the relative political importance of citizens' and stakeholders' material concerns, ideological principles, social identity, and politically sectarian beliefs will vary. Of course, it's not just individual citizens who participate in politics, and politics is about more than just elections. Politics is also about how politicians both shape and react to the preferences and behavior of citizens. Moreover, it's about the efforts of firms, trade associations, unions, advocacy groups, nonprofit institutions, and government agencies to influence all phases of the policymaking process.

Politics as a Simultaneously Mercenary, Noble, and Theatrical Process

Political analysis can be tough, in part, because there are at least three versions of politics and it's often hard to tell which you're looking at. Sometimes, politics is **mercenary**, entailing unapologetic attempts to protect or expand the interests of one group, often at the expense of another. But politics can also take on a more **noble** character as folks engage in good-faith discussions with a shared sense of purpose about finding the best course of action. Stone contrasts these first two aspects of politics when she compares the "dark self-interested side of political conflict" with a second vision of politics as a "valuable creative process for social harmony" (2012, p. 10). In my experience, however, there is also a third version of political discourse that is **theatrical** in nature. In such cases, the positions espoused and the rhetoric offered have little to do with governance and public policy but instead are more like a performance in which the speaker—usually a politician or media pundit—plays to the audience to evoke an emotion-laden response of solidarity and affinity.

In short, sometimes politics is a fight in which participants seek only to vanquish the other. Politics can also be a benevolent mechanism for realizing our collective aspirations for a well-governed society. And sometimes, politics is nothing more than a series of performances from politicians who seem more interested in reelection than in governing and news personalities looking to increase their ratings. Given its complex and dynamic nature, the politics of policymaking can certainly appear chaotic. Compared to the precision of microeconomics and quantitative methods, political and social affairs are undeniably more difficult to analyze and evaluate. Stone juxtaposes politics and traditional policy analysis (which she refers to as the rationality project):

> From inside the rationality project, politics looks messy, foolish, erratic, and inexplicable. Political events seem to leap outside the categories that logic and rationality offer. (2012, p. 10)

While it may induce cognitive dissonance, I suggest that you always keep all three aspects of politics—mercenary, noble, and theatrical—in mind. But rather than writing off politics as inscrutable and impervious to useful analysis, I also suggest that you familiarize yourself with a few basic concepts.

10.1.2 Policy Streams, Windows, and the Roles of the Policy Analyst

You may have heard the expression that politics is like 'herding cats,' or keeping a bunch of independently minded folks heading in the same direction. Former Los Angeles Deputy mayor Michael Keeley has a better metaphor:

> Think of city government as a big bus … divided into different sections with different constituencies: labor, the City Council, the mayor, interest groups, and contractors. Every seat is equipped with a brake, so lots of people can stop the bus anytime. The problem is that this makes the bus undrivable. (Eggers & O'Leary, 2009, p. 138)

Herding cats and driving crowded buses are great metaphors, but let's see if we can go a bit deeper.

The Multiple Streams Framework of Policymaking

As I mentioned in Chapter 2, policy scholars have been working for years to develop a theoretical explanation of how issues come to be on the political agenda and of the forces that shape the likelihood of policy action. I noted that there are at least seven prominent theories of the policy process, none of which is universally recognized as correct. Our focus here is not political science, so I've selected one of these theories simply as a way to organize the discussion that follows.

In 1984, John Kingdon developed what is referred to as the **multiple streams framework**.[1] While his framework isn't a perfect fit for all policymaking situations, it has enjoyed widespread application in academic literature (Herweg, Zahariadis, & Zohlnhofer, 2018) and, at least to me, provides an intuitive way of thinking about politics and policy. Kingdom's approach starts with the idea of three streams—problems, policies, and politics—that constantly flow through public debates about societal issues.

---

[1]Kingdon's empirical work focused on major policy initiatives (like health-care reform in the Clinton and Obama administrations and deregulation of the airline, rail, and trucking industries in the Carter administration). His framework may be less relevant to smaller scale policy decisions made during daily government operations, particularly those made by public servants without the involvement of politicians and within existing authorities.

First, the **problem stream** describes the dynamic ways in which issues come to be viewed as problems in need of a public policy response. Recall from Chapter 1 that a policy problem is a gap between a descriptive as-is condition and a normative to-be condition. Accordingly, problems rise and fall in importance in the problem stream when public and stakeholder perceptions of the current as-is conditions change or when normative to-be goals in a particular area evolve. These forces can push in both directions: problems can become more prominent if current conditions appear to deteriorate or if our aspirations grow more ambitious; conversely, problems may become less salient—or drop off the agenda entirely—if conditions improve or if we become inured to defects of the status quo.

Second, the **policy stream** describes the work of folks who develop, analyze, and debate policy options to address problems in a particular policy domain.[2] Often referred to as "**policy wonks**," they can be found in government, think tanks, advocacy groups, academia, or consultancies (Wheelen, 2011, p. 519). They spend their time working out the details of how new public policies might be designed and implemented, paying attention to both efficacy and political desirability. Within the policy stream, which Kingdon described as a "primeval soup," you may see fully specified policy proposals, as well as fragments of policy ideas that have yet to form into coherent whole policies (Kingdon, 2011, p. 116).

Third, the **political stream** describes the evolving and interacting flow of public opinion, interest group advocacy, media coverage, electoral results, and the fortunes of politicians and their parties. Sometimes, conditions in the political stream are conducive to significant change (e.g., in the aftermath of a decisive election) and sometimes they are not (e.g., during a stalemate between two equally matched political parties). Political coalitions among advocacy groups with similar—though not necessarily identical—interests may also form and splinter as the political stream rolls along. Such coalitions can either impede or enhance the prospects for policy action.

If the problem, policy, and political streams flow together for some period of time, then a **policy window** may open. An open window represents a confluence of forces that facilitate policy action, while a closed window suggests that policy change is exceedingly unlikely. More specifically, an open policy window occurs when there exists broad recognition of a problem in need of attention, a sufficiently popular policy option able to address the problem, and a suitably strong political coalition to enact the option into law. If any one of these three elements is missing, then the window won't open.

But just because a policy option is popular, as we saw earlier, that doesn't make it a good idea. In many cases, policymakers feel compelled to take action—any action— when dealing with a crisis or unexpected turn of events with broad consequences such

---

[2]A policy domain is a specific substantive area like criminal justice, education policy, or environmental protection.

as the attacks of September 11, the 2008-2009 housing crisis, or the repeated energy supply shocks of the 1970s and 1980s. Such events can lead to an open policy window even though the best course of action is highly uncertain. In turn, policymakers often face intense pressure to 'do something' and frequently worry more about being blamed for inaction than taking the time to come up with an effective policy response to the crisis (Grossman, 2018).

The final element in Kingdon's framework is the role played by **policy entrepreneurs** who connect the streams, find ways to open policy windows, and push policy initiatives through those windows. They work in the executive or legislative branches of government, think tanks, interest groups, private firms, or as lobbyists. Many are what Wheelan calls **"political hacks,"** a term *not* meant to be pejorative:

> [H]acks have a deep understanding of the political process and a keen appreciation of what is politically feasible at any given time. (Wheelen, 2011, p. 520)

In addition to being political hacks, policy entrepreneurs have several other talents. They know how to frame and reframe policy problems to enhance the case for action. They know how to adjust the design of a policy option to mollify its critics without undermining its efficacy (or the support of its proponents). And they are skilled in political deal making. Kingdon describes their work:

> They hook solutions to problems, proposals to political momentum, and political events to policy problems. ... Without the presence of an entrepreneur, the linking of the streams may not take place. (Kingdon, 2011, p. 182)

To recap, while Kingdon's multiple streams framework might not fit every situation, it reminds us that policy action is most likely when a salient problem has a popular (though not necessarily effective) policy solution that can engender sufficient political support to permit its enactment. If the problem, policy, and political streams never come near each other, policy action is unlikely.

The Role of a Policy Entrepreneur vs. the Four Roles of the Policy Analyst

Is the role of a policy entrepreneur the same as that of a policy analyst? It depends. Bardach and Patashnik seem to answer in the affirmative when, in their book on policy analysis, they tell readers:

> All policy is political, whether the politics takes place in a backroom or within a legislature, an organization, or a community. You must build support and

neutralize opponents. To do this, at the interpersonal level, you must make arguments, frame and reframe 'the facts,' call in favors, and imply threats. At the organizational and institutional levels, you must mobilize allies, manipulate arenas and calendars, offer (and extract) concessions, and negotiate side payments. (Bardach & Patashnik, 2016, p. 165)

Bardach and Patashnik's repeated use of the pronoun "you" implies that they'd prefer that policy analysts also be skilled political operators. I think that's going too far. While I wouldn't recommend that aspiring policy analysts ignore politics, there are many policy-analytic roles where politics has little to do with an analyst's daily work. In Chapter 7, I identified four types of policy analysts:

- The Analytic Specialist
- The Public Servant
- The Campaigner
- The Client Advisor

How can we square this typology of policy analysts with Kingdon's definition of a Policy Entrepreneur? For starters, the balance between working as a political hack or as a policy wonk varies across the four types of analysts. Because both the Campaigner and the Client Advisor are hacks who embrace the ethos of *policy analysis as advocacy*, their work readily aligns with that of the Policy Entrepreneur. Depending on the person and the job he or she holds, the alignment might be complete or only partial.

When it comes to the Analytic Specialist and the Public Servant, however, neither of them typically functions as a Policy Entrepreneur. Both roles are closer to that of the policy wonk and both embrace the ethos of *policy analysis as inquiry*. The Analytic Specialist doesn't typically consider politics, and political analysis is rarely a part of his or her work. On the other hand, the Public Servant does aim to incorporate normative and political considerations in his or her work but only as a mirror of public sentiment rather than as something to be shaped or manipulated by the analyst. Accordingly, the Analytic Specialist and the Public Servant are more likely to study policy problems from a neutral perspective and to design policies independently of their client's or their own political preferences.

10.1.3 Policy as a Driver of Politics

Arguments heard in political debates usually reflect the specifics of the policies being considered. This section describes two techniques for thinking about how policy may drive political debates.

Making an Educated Guess About How the Politics Will Play Out

The political agendas of those affected by public policy are not always transparent; lobbying and the calling in of political debts usually happens behind closed doors. Moreover, the political power of key players may remain unknown until policy debates move to the point where the players feel compelled to exercise their power. Nonetheless, you may be able to make an educated guess as to how the politics will unfold on an issue by investigating the issues described below and summarized in Exhibit 10-2.

Exhibit 10-2   Connections Between Policy and Politics

- How do the politics of the status quo affect the policy problem you're studying?

- Who will be directly affected by the policy changes you're analyzing? Who will be indirectly affected?

- If policy action is taken, will costs occur right away, with benefits deferred until later?

- Who will be made better off by the policy changes being analyzed? Who will be worse off?

- How big will their wins and losses be?

- Are the wins or losses concentrated among a small group or are they broadly spread across society?

- How politically powerful are the winners? How about the losers?

Start by thinking about the *politics of the status quo* as it relates to the policy problem you're analyzing. Current conditions tend to occupy a politically privileged position, in part because existing programs create stakeholders who resist change and because institutional inertia usually makes it easier to block change than to champion it. Next, figure out *who will be directly affected* by the policies you're analyzing. Section 6.2 provided some suggestions about how to do so. Bear in mind that politically relevant effects may be material, ideological, or identity based. Then think about *who will be indirectly affected*. Policy impacts don't always stay where they are first experienced; sometimes, they diffuse across society. An excise tax on one type of firm may, for example, reduce profits for upstream suppliers and increase costs for downstream consumers. Even though these folks wouldn't directly pay the tax, they may still politically oppose its adoption.

Is there a *mismatch in the timing of costs and benefits*? As we saw in our discussion of both equity and economics in the prior two chapters, the costs and benefits of government action often fall on different parts of society. We can extend this thinking to contrast folks who experience current conditions with those who will experience future conditions. Politicians' time horizons often don't extend beyond the next election. While this phenomenon makes government attentive to current citizen needs, it can cause a problem if measures are needed now to avoid problems later. Consider policies to combat climate change: today's politicians may not be in office when the benefits of such policies are realized.

Look at your completed criteria-alternatives matrix and ask *which stakeholders will do better, and which will fare worse*, under each of the policy options you are considering. As a first approximation, expect winners to be political supporters and losers to be opponents. Ask *how big the wins and losses are* for each of the stakeholders. All else equal, you can expect big winners to be stronger proponents of a policy than stakeholders with smaller wins. Similarly, expect opposition to grow as the size of a stakeholder's loss increases.

Consider *whether wins and losses are concentrated among a few stakeholders or diffused across many stakeholders*. A small group of stakeholders who incur big wins or losses may be motivated to exert concerted pressure on policymakers. But if small wins or losses are spread across a large group, it may be costly and logistically challenging to build a coalition to take political action. Finally, think about *how politically powerful the winners and losers are*. If the affected parties are already influential, well-connected, or members of an existing coalition, their potential wins and losses may have a bigger political impact on policymaking than similar wins and losses among disadvantaged, disorganized, or disenfranchised stakeholders.

As you contemplate all these factors, you can't be sure you'll uncover everything relevant to the politics of the particular policy issue you're analyzing. In many cases, you'll need to watch unfolding policy debates closely to figure out who is participating and to assess their motives for doing so.

Policy Bundling as a Driver of Politics

You will also want to evaluate whether the politics of the issue you're studying might be affected by a phenomenon known variously as log rolling, horse trading, or **policy bundling**. I know it doesn't sound very scientific or systematic, but bundling refers to a process in which disparate policy measures—even those that have little to do with each other—with divergent stakeholders are melded into a single piece of legislation, thereby creating support to pass the full package when its individual components might not attract sufficient support to permit enactment. Conventional wisdom in Washington DC, for example, is that bundling explains why the Supplemental Nutrition Assistance Program (SNAP, or food stamps)—a social welfare program—is under the auspices of the Agriculture Department rather than the Department of Health and Human Services. SNAP has 33.1 million urban beneficiaries and only 6.8 million rural beneficiaries (Cunnyngham, 2018, p. 16). This imbalance might hinder support for the program among politicians representing rural areas, but combining a social welfare program with farm support programs creates a winning political coalition.

Another example of policy bundling at the Federal level is often seen in high priority, so-called 'must-pass' legislation. Examples include spending bills without which large portions of government would shut down, increases in the debt limit without which the government could not pay its bills, and the annual Defense authorization bill which sets policy for ongoing military operations. When it comes to the waning days (and sometimes hours) of debates about must-pass bills, legislative text from virtually any policy domain may get attached to the bill under consideration. In other words, a specific proposal which, on its own, stands no chance of enactment can suddenly become politically feasible if its sponsors can convince legislative leaders to include it in a must-pass bill (often in exchange for the votes of those sponsors). As Congressman Frank said, "anything can be the basis of a deal" (Binder & Lee, 2015, p. 246), or as novelist Charles Dudley Warner observed in 1850, "politics makes strange bedfellows" (Safire, 2008, p. 707).

10.1.4 Political Economy: The Link Between Money and Politics

An ideologically diverse group of political economists like Adam Smith, Karl Marx, and Friedrich Hayek, among many others, have pondered the link between politics and markets. These scholars investigate how political power is used to influence public policies that affect markets in ways that favor some groups and disadvantage others. They also study feedback loops in which wealth accumulation confers political power that in turn enhances wealth accumulation. Governments, for example, set many of the rules that dictate the operation of markets, as well as tax and spending policy, thereby affecting the fortunes of firms, investors, consumers, and workers.

One common phenomenon in the feedback loop between politics and markets is referred to as **rent-seeking**, in which firms try to persuade policymakers to restrict competition or market-entry to boost the profits of industry incumbents (a violation of the conditions for a freely competitive market and an efficient, social-welfare maximizing equilibrium) at the expense of consumers and excluded firms (Krueger, 1974).

In this context, it should come as no surprise that political power may be used to advance and protect economic interests. MIT economist Daron Acemoglu puts it this way:

[S]tates throughout history and even today serve the interests of the political elite and are part of their economic problems, not their solution. But this is not because the state is unnecessary or evil, but because of who controls it and what capacities it has invested in and developed. … We cannot benefit from so many things we take for granted without a powerful state, but then civil society and our institutions need to be even more powerful in order to be able to control the state …. (2016, p. 7)

We don't have space to explore the field of political economy in detail here. Nonetheless, I suggest you always consider how the symbiotic relationship between wealth and power may affect policymaking.

Money and Politics

In the United States, in particular, money and politics are tightly linked. The Supreme Court has held that spending money to promote political opinions is a form of speech protected by the First Amendment, that corporations have rights to free speech, and that the ability of corporations and unions to make political contributions should not be limited. In turn, large sums of money now routinely flow into both the electoral and lobbying processes. Let's look at each process in turn.

When it comes to *spending on election campaigns*, the 2020 Federal election was very expensive. A total of $13.9 billion was spent, comprising $7.3 billion for Congressional races and $6.6 billion for the Presidential race (Center for Responsive Politics, 2021d).[3] About 4.5 million donors (about 1.4 percent of the population) gave more than $200, about 91,200 folks donated more than $10,000, about 5,100 donors contributed over $100,000, and 64 donors gave more than $5 million (Center for Responsible Politics, 2021b). Casino magnate Sheldon Adelson donated $218 million and former New York City Mayor Michael Bloomberg donated $152 million (Center for Responsive Politics, 2021a).

Firms, unions, trade groups, and advocacy groups also try to influence the content of public policy by *lobbying legislators and executive branch agencies.*[4] Sometimes these entities hire lobbyists who work for multiple clients; in other cases, lobbyists are full-time employees of the firm or interest group they represent. In 2020, about 11,500 active, registered lobbyists represented clients before the Federal government. One view of lobbying is that it's nothing more than an effort to make the specialized and subject-specific expertise of lobbyists available to supplement the generalized expertise of policymakers and their staffs. Another view of lobbying is that it's a mechanism by which special interests undermine the public interest.

Either way, a lot of money goes into lobbying. Annual spending on lobbying (not including campaign contributions) is about $3.5 billion (Center for Responsive Politics, 2021c). To get a sense of this process, look at Exhibit 10-3 which lists the ten biggest spenders on lobbying. Similar patterns, albeit smaller in scale, exist at the state and local levels.

---

[3]These figures include all money spent by presidential candidates, Senate and House candidates, political parties, and independent interest groups trying to influence federal elections during the 2019 to 2020 cycle.

[4]Their right to do so is guaranteed by the First Amendment which protects the right to "petition the government for a redress of grievances."

Exhibit 10-3 Spending on Lobbying

Rank	Entity	Total Spent on Lobbying in 2020
1	National Association of Realtors	$84,113,368
2	US Chamber of Commerce	$81,910,000
3	Pharmaceutical Research and Manufacturers	$25,946,000
4	American Hospital Association	$23,648,466
5	Blue Cross/Blue Shield	$22,662,720
6	Facebook Inc	$19,680,000
7	American Medical Association	$19,575,000
8	Amazon.com	$18,725,000
9	Business Roundtable	$16,970,000
10	NCTA The Internet and Television Association	$15,460,000

Source: (Center for Responsive Politics, 2021c).

The Impact of Money in Politics

What does all this money—for campaign contributions and lobbying—get for the folks who spend it? Most US residents believe that money buys political influence (Pew Research Center, 2018), but social scientists have had a tough time proving the case. Recall our Chapter 5 discussion of the inference process: it can be hard to establish causality when multiple factors are at play and we can't run experiments. In this case, we have lots of spenders—whose preferences may vary widely—supporting politicians with differing degrees of power and influence over policy. What's more, drawing a causal link between a specific donation and a politician's vote on a particular matter requires that we get inside the politician's head to understand his or her motivation: was it the donation or a genuine sense of what's best for society that motivated the vote? Finally, to protect reputations and avoid hints of corruption, politicians and lobbyists rarely publicize their relationships. As a result, despite decades of research, scholars have only limited direct evidence that money affects public policy (Koerth, 2019; McKay, 2020).

Nonetheless, a few studies provide strongly suggestive evidence. Firms, for example, adjust their contributions to specific politicians as those politicians join or leave Congressional committees with jurisdiction over the company's affairs (Neff

Powel & Grimmer, 2016). In another study, corporate spending on lobbying (not campaign contributions) was shown to lead to tax breaks for the lobbying firm in subsequent years (Kelleher Richter, Samphantharak, & Timmons, 2009). Finally, lobbyists' campaign contributions were statistically linked to changes in particular legislative provisions during debates in the Senate Finance Committee during enactment of the Affordable Care Act (McKay, 2020).

It seems very unlikely that corporations, unions, and advocacy groups would spend billions of dollars a year lobbying public officials and contributing to election campaigns if doing so didn't yield tangible benefits in the form of more favorable public policies. What's more, anecdotal evidence suggests a continuing link between money and politics. Barney Frank, a member of Congress who served sixteen terms in the House of Representatives, puts it this way:

> [Some legislators] say 'Oh, [contributions don't] have any effect on me.' Look, if that were the case, we would be the only human beings in the history of the world who, on a regular basis, took significant amounts of money from perfect strangers and made sure that it had no effect on our behavior. That is not human nature (2012).

Frank goes on, however, to note that money is not the only driver of policy positions taken by politicians. He stressed the importance of public opinion within a Member's District:

> … if the voters have a position, the votes will kick money's rear end any time. I've never met a politician … who, choosing between a significant opinion in his or her district and a number of campaign contributors, doesn't go with the district (2012).

What's the bottom line here? Lobbying and contributions from donors, be they corporations, advocacy groups, unions, or wealthy individuals almost certainly influence the policymaking process. But, to the extent that Representative Frank has it right, engaged, vocal citizens can still have a significant impact.

What Happens When the System Itself Is the Problem?

I'd like to make one last point before leaving the topic of politics and policy. Every year, I encounter a few students who are getting a degree in public policy or public administration not because of an interest in advising policymakers on specific public policy decisions or in serving in government, but instead because they have larger aspirations to fundamentally revamp the country's political and economic systems and to redistribute wealth and power in society. These students often *see the system itself as the problem* and are interested in overhauling the infrapolicies driving societal outcomes.[5] They also often embrace a strong version of political economy: that money and politics are tightly linked in a powerful reinforcing feedback loop that strengthens the wealth and power of those at the top and excludes the rest of us. They may attribute such cleavages to systemic racism, hostility toward immigrants, or disrespect for once prosperous communities that have suffered job losses and economic dislocation.

These students often aspire to completely rethink society's approach to issues like criminal justice, property rights, political corruption, bias in the media or higher education, and wealth and poverty, along with pretty much everything in between. In my experience, their preferences range from progressive democratic socialism to small-state libertarianism to a strong law-and-order state. But policy analysis has limits when it comes to sorting out the pros and cons of fundamentally different ways of organizing government, the economy, or society as a whole.

In short, the classical model of policy analysis isn't a good fit if your goal is a radical restructuring of the social order. Imagine, for example, building a criteria-alternatives matrix where the policy options were democratic socialism, free-market capitalism, social-welfare capitalism, or small-state libertarianism. Such labels are so generic that any form of rigorous policy analysis would require you to add dozens, maybe hundreds, of specific details about how each of these political-economic systems would work. What's more, you'd also have to add countless (likely controversial and contradictory) criteria to measure the degree to which each system would deliver a free, just, and prosperous society. Finally, you would need to project how each form of governance would perform with respect to each of the numerous evaluation criteria. There's nothing wrong with thinking through the pros and cons of particular paths forward, but it would strain credulity to think we could settle on the optimal forms of society, the economy, and the political system, using only the methods of classical policy analysis.

If you're one of these students, don't worry, the field of policy analysis still has a lot to offer you. Its analytic tools are, for example, needed to analyze the individual policy changes that would accompany such sweeping reforms. Metacognition, critical thinking, evidence-informed analysis, and the ability to apply panoptic analysis will also stand you in good stead as you pursue your vision of a better society.

To *recap our discussion of the political lens*, there are several key takeaways. Politics and policy should be seen as two sides of the same coin; we rarely see one without the

---

[5]Refer back to the Introduction to Part I for an explanation of the concept of an infrapolicy.

other in both policymaking and implementation. Because people form political opinions based on a mix of material interests, ideology, and identities, politics can be simultaneously a means of unabashedly promoting self-interest and a sincere pursuit of mutual cooperation to achieve collective goals. Politics may also be little more than a theatrical means of expressing one's social identity and may sometimes edge over into political sectarianism. Even though policy theorists are still debating the mechanisms by which issues do and don't command the attention of policymakers, I suggested that you might find Kingdon's framework helpful. In it, the merging of the problem, policy, and political streams opens the window for policy change. We next considered how politics is often, but not always, driven by the types of policies being debated. We wrapped up with a review of the connection between politics and markets, and of the role of money in politics.

10.2 THE INSTITUTIONAL LENS

Governmental institutions—the departments, agencies, and military services that employ government workers, procure goods and services, give grants, and execute government functions—are the primary mechanism by which public policies are delivered in society. In turn, the behavior of these institutions can have profound effects—positive or negative—on the consequences of public policies. Accordingly, it's important to consider the role of institutions when you're analyzing a new policy proposal, or trying to evaluate an existing policy. As a case in point, a prominent environmental economist attributes the failure of policymakers to implement market-based climate policies to an "institutional blindspot" in economics:

> Why then are economic methods not the central tools for implementation of environmental policy? One reason may be that these tools have been developed in an intellectual laboratory that, for the most part, is free from consideration of institutions that influence how they will be used. These institutions include the agencies that implement regulations, the broader legal structure of business and government, and existing regulations. (Burtraw, 2013, p. 110)

Looking through an institutional lens can thus add valuable insight to your policy analysis.[6] This section reviews a few institutional issues relevant to policy analysis. The first section addresses public trust in government institutions while the second considers some of the differences between government and commercial institutions. The

---

[6]We'll address the legal and regulatory issues that Burtraw mentions in Chapter 11.

third section introduces the concept of a principal–agent problem and discusses implications for public sector agencies. The fourth section addresses federalism and intergovernmental relations while the fifth focuses on the financing of government institutions.

10.2.1 Can Government Institutions Be Trusted to Address the Problem?

Before we even get to the question of which government institution should implement a particular policy, you should first *ask yourself why the issue you're analyzing is ultimately a matter of public policy.* As noted in the Chapter 8 discussion of equity, many things happen every day throughout society that are in some way unsatisfactory. It does not follow, however, that a public policy response is always the best way to deal with the situation. Because the appropriate role of government in society is a contentious issue, I can't give you definitive guidance on this point. A libertarian, for example, would typically argue in favor of the smallest possible role for government while a democratic socialist is likely to be comfortable with a much greater role for government. In short, while I can't say where you should end up on the question of the appropriate role of government, I can say you should start your policy analysis by asking and answering the question of why the problem you're looking at should be the responsibility of a government institution, rather than being left to private actors to address.

Once you've convinced yourself that a policy response is needed, your next move is to figure out whether an existing agency, or perhaps a new agency, can be counted on to successfully implement the selected policy option. Bear in mind that successful implementation is not ensured and is often elusive. Maybe we are looking at a wicked problem—like human trafficking or global terrorism—for which there is no easy solution. Perhaps the obvious policy response is too expensive or exceeds the capability of government to deliver it. In the policy analysis literature, these concerns fall under the heading of **government failure**, a concept akin to the idea of a market failure that we discussed in Chapter 9, where governments predictably struggle to deliver effective public policies. As much as you might like to use public policy to tackle a problem, you need to be realistic about what government can and can't do.

I won't go into detail, but you should also recognize that over the past 40 years in the United States, there has been a substantial debate about the intrinsic ability of government—especially the Federal government—to competently address many policy issues. In his first Inaugural Address, President Ronald Reagan famously claimed that "government is not the solution to our problem; government is the problem" (1981, p. 2). To a large degree, this is political rhetoric. A moment's reflection yields dozens of examples where government institutions have profoundly improved US residents' quality of life. Local governments educate our children, police our streets, and provide water and sewer services. States operate colleges and universities, build roads and public transit systems, and administer public welfare programs. And the Federal government's Social Security and Medicare systems protect seniors, the military maintains national security, and regulatory agencies facilitate food safety, environmental quality, and consumer financial protection. But multiple successes don't mean that government institutions routinely handle all policy issues successfully:

> Federal employees still make miracles every day, but many do so against the odds created by poorly designed policy, antiquated administrative systems, uncertain funding, widening skill gaps, and uncertain political leadership. ... [M]any Americans have come to believe the worst about the federal government. Some of these doubts are rooted in partisan conflict and a drum beat of antigovernment rhetoric, but some reflect the escalation of government failures. (Light, 2020, p. 14)

Scholar Donald Kettl argues that both liberal and conservative policymakers bear responsibility for the current situation:

> [T]he twin ideals of [governmental] competence and responsiveness have faded because of neglect from the left and assault from the right. Liberals have developed a disconcerting habit of launching big ideas without paying much attention to how to make them work. ... But conservatives have been complicit as well. Instead of repealing policies they disagreed with, they have savaged the bureaucracies charged with administering them. Through hiring freezes, political attack, and ultimately 'starving the beast,' they have undermined the agencies charged with responsibility for administering the law. In the process both liberals and conservatives have eroded confidence in government's ability to work. (2017, p. 639)

The issue of public trust in government is an important one when it comes to designing and implementing policy. The Directorate for Public Governance at the OECD[7] recently concluded that:

> Lack of trust compromises the willingness of citizens and business to respond to public policies and contribute to a sustainable economic recovery. Trust is the foundation upon which the legitimacy of public institutions is built and is

---

[7]The OECD is the Organization for Economic Cooperation and Development, a multilateral group of 37 democracies established in 1961. It functions like a global think tank on matters of governance.

crucial for maintaining social cohesion. Trust is important for the success of a wide range of public policies that depend on behavioural responses from the public. (OECD, 2020)

If you're still not sure about the importance of trust in government, think about the public response to mask mandates and vaccination campaigns during the COVID pandemic. Whether folks took the advice of public health officials seemed to depend, in large measure, on whether they trusted the government to be acting in their best interest.

For an historical perspective on the issue of trust, look at Exhibit 10-4. You will see that public confidence in the federal government has deteriorated over the past 20 years to the point where barely more than 40 percent of all US residents have a great deal or fair amount of trust and confidence in it. Note, however, that, save for a dip around the time of the 2009 Great Recession, confidence in state government is typically about 20 percentage points higher than it is in the federal government. And local governments enjoy an even higher level of public trust, consistently hovering around 70 percent. In other words, declining public trust in government is primarily a problem for the federal government, with states and especially localities enjoying appreciably higher levels of support.

Exhibit 10-4   Trust in Government, by Level of Government

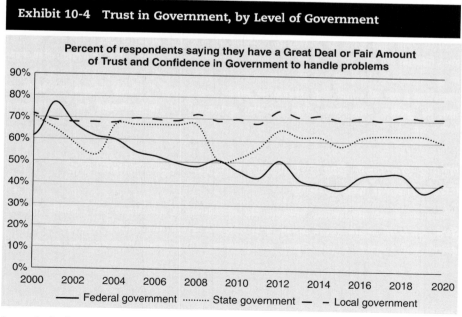

Source: Author's analysis of data from Gallup (2020).

Exhibit 10-5   OECD's Framework for Enhancing Citizen Trust in Public Institutions

Drivers of Trust	Public Policy Objective	Institutional Behavior
Competence: Ability of government to deliver to citizens the services they need, at a quality level they expect	Responsiveness	Provide public services
	Reliability	Anticipate change, protect citizens
Values: Principles that inform and guide government action	Integrity	Use power and public resources ethically
	Openness	Inform, consult, and listen to citizens
	Fairness	Improve socioeconomic conditions for all

Source: Adapted from OECD (2017, p. 24).

A policy analysis textbook isn't the best place for a deep dive into the complex issues of citizen trust in government. My reason for introducing these issues is simply to alert you to the fact that they exist, and to provide context to your work. Nonetheless, you may want to glance at Exhibit 10-5 which summarizes OECD's recommendations for enhancing trust in public institutions. In brief, OECD argues that trust in government depends on its *competence* in delivering services and in its ability to manifest a set of *values* that engender public confidence.[8] These drivers are built on specific policy objectives that can be enhanced or undermined by institutional behavior.

10.2.2 Context: The Difference Between Commercial and Government Institutions

There are many similarities between the operations of a business and a public agency. Both types of organization invest in productive assets and employ workers to deliver goods and services to customers and citizens. They create bureaucratic governance

---

[8]You might note a parallel here to our discussion in Section 6.4 when we defined the trustworthiness of an individual expert as a function of his or her competence *and* character.

structures to implement rules and procedures that ensure consistency in their operations. They execute similar internal functions like personnel management, accounting, procurement, and facilities management. These similarities notwithstanding, applying an institutional lens to your policy analysis will reveal profound differences between commercial enterprises and government institutions. This section briefly describes five such differences.

The first difference is that *the public sector often lacks a singular overriding objective* for the enterprise. Executives and managers in the private sector can focus uniquely on maximizing shareholder value. Of course, doing so requires that they meet their customers' needs at the right price, provide a work environment acceptable to their employees, and maintain their reputation among relevant stakeholders, but ultimately, every business decision can be calibrated against a single objective: its contribution to the financial health of the company. On the other hand, managers in the public sector are often expected to attain multiple, sometimes competing, objectives that may change over time.[9]

Most of us would probably agree that the purpose of government is not to turn a profit, but beyond that, agreement among those within and outside government may be elusive. For example, when an agency's stakeholders have different views on the appropriate role of government in a particular policy domain or on the relative importance of one aspect of an agency's mission vis-à-vis another, a public institution may lack a single guiding principle upon which to base decisions. Instead, it must balance competing objectives in ways that its private sector counterpart need not.

A second *difference between private and public institutions lies in their origin stories.* Think of a private firm as a group of owners, managers, and workers who voluntarily come together to pursue their own economic interests. By contrast, public policies come into existence when an 'enacting coalition' of politicians and interest groups legislatively enact a particular institutional response to a social concern (Moe, 2005, p. 220). The success of the enacting coalition comes at the expense of factions that didn't support creation of the new institution. Moreover, the general public is compelled to deal with the new institution and pay for it with their taxes, even if they don't support its mission. Yes, private firms face competition, but they can usually rely on their owners and executives to back their efforts to deliver profits. Moreover, firms deal with customers who usually voluntarily choose to pay for goods and service rather than being compelled, as taxpayers are, to hand over their money.

---

[9]We saw this phenomenon in our Chapter 2 discussion of retrospective analysis, when I noted that deciding on a program's goals and objectives is the first step in conducting a program evaluation.

Third, public institutions are expected to be *prudent stewards of taxpayer resources, while delivering goods and services not typically sold* in a marketplace. In a private firm, it's easy to tell if production at a particular level is a good idea: if revenue exceeds cost, thereby generating profit, then production is beneficial for the firm. But when it comes to services like national defense, safe communities, or educated students, we lack clear price signals about the value of these government outputs, making it difficult to decide how much of each to produce. Often, to value a government service, we have to envision a counterfactual in which the program did not exist and then view the benefit of the program as the adverse consequences that are avoided by the existence of the program.[10] Doing so is hardly a precise process. Government institutions may thus produce goods and services even if the cost of doing so exceeds the social value created (Edwards, 2015).

Fourth, *government agencies face little, if any, competition* for most of the goods and services they supply. If a public works department doesn't fill potholes or the department of motor vehicles treats customers poorly, citizens can't take their business elsewhere. Even when alternatives are available, they aren't free. Parents can send their kids to private school but must pay the tuition. Why is this lack of competition important? As we saw in Chapter 9, economic market forces create relentless pressure on private firms to keep customers happy and production processes efficient. Limited competition to provide government services may lead agencies to deliver suboptimal service because doing so doesn't pose an existential risk in the same way it might for a private business. I'm not saying that government agencies don't typically do the best they can with the resources they have. But I am saying that, when you look through an institutional lens, you'll see that the lack of competition alters the environment in which public institutions operate.

Fifth, *government institutions typically work under personnel and procurement rules which, while well-intentioned, may impede mission execution* (Linquiti, 2015). Employment, for example, in federal agencies, and in most states and localities, is governed by civil service rules. Established to reduce political intrusion into the government workplace, the rules can be rigid, limiting public sector managers' ability to hire, promote, transfer, and dismiss employees. In turn, it may be hard to deploy the right person to the right job at the right time. The system by which the federal government procures goods and services is also highly regulated. Its goal is to minimize fraud and abuse, provide fair access to government contracts, and ensure the government pays a reasonable price, but the system is so complex that it often discourages firms—including those with new and innovative approaches—from participating. Private firms also have personnel and procurement systems, but rarely are they as inflexible as those found in the public sector.

---

[10]I am indebted to an anonymous reviewer of an earlier draft for this insight.

10.2.3 The Principal–Agent Problem: Suboptimization within Organizations

As you look through an institutional lens at the behavior of institutions, you may notice that they don't always operate at an optimal level of performance—delivering the highest level of service given the available resources. Instead, you may see examples of suboptimization. In the public sector, such examples can originate in the five factors described above. But there is another, ubiquitous, phenomenon that can undermine institutional performance of any institution: **the principal–agent problem**. After a quick definition, we'll talk about four key implications specific to public sector institutions.

A **principal** is someone who has the ultimate responsibility and authority to control an organization's operation.[11] Because such a person can personally undertake only a limited set of activities and is rarely expert in all aspects of the work to be done, other folks referred to as **agents** are routinely enlisted to support the principal's work. In a business setting, a firm's owners are its principals, and its employees, managers, and contractors are its agents. When it comes to government, we could view the public in general as the principal, or we could think of elected politicians as principals. But either way, government employees are agents in a role distinct from that of their principal's. The *divergence between principals and agents when it comes to incentives, expertise, and the ability to monitor behavior is referred to as the principal–agent problem.*

A discrepancy between the incentives of principals and agents is one driver of the problem. A principal wants his or her agents to diligently pursue his or her objectives (as if the principal were performing the work personally), but usually lacks the time, capacity, or expertise to continuously monitor the agents' behavior. Agents, on the other hand, have different motives. They may not be interested in working as hard as the principal might like (a phenomenon referred to as shirking) or they may have personal career ambitions that take them in directions inconsistent with their principal's preferences. Think, for example, of police officers, social workers, and health department inspectors whose daily activities are not usually observed firsthand by their bosses. Such agents may have their own notions about how to do their jobs, irrespective of the principal's wishes. Subject to limited oversight, such agents have frequent opportunities to prioritize their own objectives over those of their principal. Moreover, agents who supervise other agents can amplify their personal preferences by directing subordinates to advance their own, rather than the principal's, agenda. In

---

[11]For simplicity, I refer to a single principal. In some cases, the principal is actually a group of individuals, such as multiple shareholders in a private firm or a city council comprised of equally empowered members.

this environment, where both parties understand the incentive structure and information is not shared equally, principals have reason to distrust their agents and even those agents who do embrace the principal's agenda may not put forth their best effort, if they think their work may go unrecognized (Moe, 2005).[12]

Such problems exist in both the public and private sectors but have unique characteristics when it comes to public institutions. Four implications of the principal–agent problem in the public sector are described below in broad terms. It's important to recognize that these aren't lawlike descriptions about how all bureaucracies behave. Think of them as vulnerabilities you might see when you look through an institutional lens at an agency unable to align the motives and incentives of its principals and agents.

The first manifestation of the principal–agent problem in the public sector stems from routine *changes in political leadership brought on by electoral cycles*. Most public agencies are staffed by civil servants with a limited number of political appointees in senior roles. Civil servants tend to spend long portions of their careers in public service while political appointees may serve for only two or three years. Civil servants are also apt to have more expertise in their agency's workings than do the political appointees they serve. Moreover, government workers tend to be protected by personnel rules that limit the ability of political executives to fire or reassign them. Finally, the personal political preferences of career staff may, or may not, align with the agenda of the political administration they serve.

A second manifestation of the principal–agent problem is a phenomenon known as **turfism**, *or empire-building*, in which some government managers aspire to accumulate greater budgetary and human resources, as well as power and authority, for their own agency or unit within it (i.e., their own 'turf'). Such accumulation often comes at the expense of other government agencies and units, even when those other entities might be able to better use the resources and authorities to serve the public. Turf-oriented bureaucrats may also avoid cooperation with other governmental organizations, so as to not undermine their own power and that of their agency, even if cooperation among agencies would lead to better outcomes.[13]

The motives of such managers may vary. They may want to enlarge their domain of operation and enjoy the sense of power that comes with supervising more employees and commanding more financial resources. They may have close

---

[12]I once had a boss often given the unenviable task of trying to coax subordinates to embrace the latest, but typically unpopular, corporate initiative. They'd nod in agreement but go back to their desks and resume business as usual. He referred to this as the "Say yes. Do no." phenomenon, a perfect example of a principal–agent problem!

[13]They may also believe that the burden of cooperating with other agencies (often referred to as transaction costs) exceed the benefits of cooperation. We'll return to this topic in the context of the complexity of joint action.

relationships with legislators, interest groups, and regulated entities that would be threatened if another agency encroached on their turf.[14] Or they may hope to be viewed as a more important 'player' on issues that capture media and public attention. And, of course, they may truly believe that their agency is the best equipped to serve the public interest and that therefore that their actions are not a form of self-aggrandizement but of public service.

A third manifestation of the principal–agent problem is its *impact on government spending patterns*. In a private firm, if a manager finds a way to reduce costs, there will usually be a corresponding increase in profitability. In most organizations, this manager will earn accolades for his or her contribution to the bottom line. By contrast, in a public institution, if a manager doesn't spend his or her full budget in a particular year, he or she may find that next year's budget has been cut. In turn, there will be fewer staff and less money to cope with whatever demands arise in the subsequent year. This phenomenon creates a perverse incentive, sometimes referred to as 'use it or lose it,' in which public agencies are tempted to spend their full budgets every year, even if the funds aren't put to especially beneficial uses or if another agency could put the resources to better use. A converse problem arises when an agency needs more budgetary resources to accomplish its mission than are available but is unable to convince senior executives or lawmakers of the need for extra funding.

A fourth manifestation of the principal–agent problem can be an *excess of rules, procedures, and paperwork, often referred to as* **red tape**. As noted above, agents like police officers, social workers, or health inspectors often have wide latitude in the exercise of their duties and their behavior can be hard to monitor. In turn, principals may try to control agents' behavior with detailed prescriptions about how jobs are to be done and extensive reporting requirements intended to document compliance with these prescriptions. Excessive red tape is not limited to the internal workings of a single agency. A state may, for example, delegate a public health program to its local governments, but hoping to constrain the behavior of the localities, may also impose burdensome recordkeeping and reporting rules. The local government (the agent) may fail to see value in the red tape while the state government (the principal) may see it as an important mechanism for aligning the agent behavior's with the principal's objectives.

Red tape thus represents a quintessential example of a policy trade-off. For starters, even the word itself is loaded; for most listeners, it's pejorative. But the origins of red tape lie in the reasonable desires of principals seeking consistent implementation of government programs, greater efficiency by streamlining routine

---

[14]A close relationship between an agency and the entities it regulates can lead to regulatory capture, defined as "insider domination of the policymaking process resulting in regulation for the benefit of the industry rather than the public" (Lindsey, Teles, Wilkinson, & Hammond, 2018, p. 11).

operations, and protection against agents operating at cross purposes with institutional objectives. On the other hand, red tape can stifle innovation, limit agents' ability to deal with unique situations, and sap agent morale. Striking the right balance—enough but not too much red tape—is not an easy task and depends on case-specific details.

These four principal–agent problems tend to be bigger concerns in the public sector than in the private sector. The primary reason for the difference lies in the loose links between principals and agents. Citizens can always complain to elected representatives, legislators might hold oversight hearings, or a program evaluation might identify problems, but these approaches all entail a circuitous path for synchronizing the behavior of public sector agents with the objectives of the relevant principals. In this context, it's not surprising that principal–agent problems are common in public sector institutions.

10.2.4 Federalism: Intergovernmental Governance

Responsibility for public policy in the United States is distributed among Federal, state, tribal, and local governments. This system of governance is referred to as *federalism* and entails shared power, authority, and monetary transfers across levels of government. Based on the amount of money being spent (see Exhibit 10-6), it's clear that all levels of government play a major role in policy delivery.

Exhibit 10-6 Total Government Spending: 2018 ($trillion)[a]		
Level	Spending	Share
Federal	$4.11	48.3%
State	$2.41	28.4%
Local	$1.98	23.3%
Total	$8.50	100.0%

[a]Excluding transfers among governments; does not include spending by tribal governments.
Sources: (OMB, 2020; USCB, 2018).

In 2018, total government spending in the United States was about $8.5 trillion. The Federal government spent about half of the total, while states and localities together spent the other half.[15] (Of course, Federal spending comes from a single

---

[15]These data predate the COVID-19 pandemic when government spending rose dramatically.

government, while the states represent 50 jurisdictions and localities represent tens of thousands of governments.)

Policy analysts need to understand federalism because it affects the causes and effects of many policy problems, in addition to the feasibility and desirability of potential policy choices. Intergovernmental policymaking is a big topic, so we'll only hit a few highlights, starting with a descriptive review of the most important elements of the system, and then tease out a few practical implications.

Elements of the US System of Shared Governance

Federal–State Relationships: Article VI of the Constitution specifies that it, along with Federal statutes, comprises the supreme law of the land. While establishing the supremacy of Federal policy, this language is not an unqualified grant of power to the Federal government. States are also considered sovereign authorities within the Constitutional framework. The Tenth Amendment specifies that "the powers not delegated to the United States by the Constitution, nor prohibited by it to the States, are reserved to the States respectively, or to the people."[16] The national government, for example, has the sole authority to engage in international diplomacy, to declare war and maintain a military, and to set immigration policy. On the other hand, states may not deny due process and equal rights to their citizens, enter foreign treaties, or mint money. Similarly, states may not regulate interstate commerce while the Federal government may not regulate exclusively intrastate commerce.

Tribal–Federal–State Relationships: There are over 570 Federally recognized American, Indian, and Alaskan Native tribes and villages, about half of which occupy designated areas of land. There are about 326 such Federal reservations, for which the Federal government holds the land title in trust for the tribe(s) who live there (BIA, n.d.). The Supreme Court held in *Worcester v. Georgia* (1832) that tribes have a status akin to nationhood and possess an inherent right to self-government. The tribes and the Federal government have a government-to-government relationship. In February 2021, President Biden issued a Presidential Memorandum reiterating a federal commitment to respect tribal sovereignty, comply with treaty obligations, and engage in meaningful consultation with tribes (CRS, 2021c).

But because the Constitution gives the Federal government ultimate authority over 'Indian tribes' in the United States, tribal political sovereignty is not absolute. It can be limited by Congress, the Federal courts, or as the residual impact of treaties signed between tribes and the Federal government. Native Americans are US citizens and are entitled to all the rights and protections extended to all other Americans. With

---

[16]This language always confuses me! 'United States' refers to the national government while 'States' refers to individual states.

few exceptions, states do not have jurisdiction over tribal lands that lie within their borders. Tribes are free to enact civil and criminal laws that differ from those of the surrounding states. They may also establish taxes and exclude others from tribal lands. At the same time, states and tribes can establish relationships and share authorities with each other on a sovereign-to-sovereign basis. Codified agreements between states and tribes often cover topics such as law enforcement, environmental protection, and casino gambling on Native American land (BIA, n.d.).

State–Local Relationships: The US Constitution is silent when it comes to the existence and authority of local governments. Instead, localities are creations of the state in which they exist, and their power depends on the states' delegations of authority to them. States generally use one of two approaches. In the first group of states, known as Dillon Rule states, local governments have only the authority explicitly delegated to them by their state. If there is no such delegation, power remains at the state level. The second group of states is called Home Rule states. There is variation across states, but in a Home Rule state, localities are free to enact any public policy except in cases where the state has specifically pro-hibited local authority.[17] The way I think about it is as a matter of defaults. In a Dillon Rule state, in the absence of a specific grant of authority to localities, jurisdiction defaults to the state while in a Home Rule state, in the absence of a prohibition on local action, it defaults to the local government. If you work at the state or local level, make sure you understand the division of authority between the state and its local governments (as well as any authorities shared with Tribal governments).

State-to-State Relationships: Article 1 of the Constitution allows states to voluntarily enter into enforceable contracts with other states; these arrangements are known as interstate compacts. There are about 200 interstate compacts (NCIC, 2006). They typically address issues like apportionment of water rights for rivers that flow through multiple states, the resolution of boundary demarcation disputes, mutual assistance agreements to share police and fire services during emergencies, transit systems that operate across state lines like the New York-New Jersey Port Authority, and agree-ments to address transborder air and water pollution.

National-International Relationships: While the United States is a sovereign country over which other nations have no formal power, the country has entered into a number of global relationships that are relevant to domestic public policy. The United Nations is the primary example, but other examples include the United States-Mexico-Canada Agreement (the trade agreement that is the successor to the NAFTA Treaty) and the Montreal Protocol (a global agreement to phase out the production and consumption

---

[17]The variations reflect differences in the types of local actions that are subject to home rule and whether the concept of home rule is codified in a state's constitution or in an act of its legislature.

of substances that deplete stratospheric ozone). Depending on the nature of the international agreement, Federal and state policymakers often take action to bring US law into alignment with international commitments.

The Operation of Shared Governance

Having described the key players in the system of shared governance—the Federal government, states, localities, tribes, and international bodies—and considered the relationships among them, we turn now to the pragmatic implications of these relationships.

We saw in the previous section that the Constitution simultaneously grants and denies powers and authorities both to the states and to the federal government. But there are many policy areas where both levels of government are constitutionally permitted to act, and neither is prohibited from acting. Accordingly, the demarcation between Federal and state public policy is anything but sharp. In many policy domains, the federal government, states, and localities are all active. As Exhibit 10-7 illustrates, the three levels of government often spend considerable sums of money in the same general policy area. If you begin working in a policy domain with substantial participation from multiple levels of government, one of your first To Do's is to make sure you understand the relationships among levels of government in the area in which you're working.

Exhibit 10-7 Shared Spending for Selected Public Services: 2018 ($billion)			
	Federal	State	Local
Law Enforcement and Corrections	$38.2	$66.8	$133.3
Higher Education	$24.6	$258.4	$43.4
Transportation (all modes)	$92.8	$116.4	$107.6

Sources: (OMB, 2020; USCB, 2018).

These intergovernmental relationships can take on many different forms. Sometimes, individual programs explicitly involve multiple levels of government. For example, most Federal environmental laws, the Medicaid low-income health-care program, and the national guard's reserve military units are all programs *jointly administered* by the Federal government and the states. In such programs, however, it's important to recognize that considerable interstate variability may be the result. As Burtraw points out in the context of climate policy, these variations can be important:

Most economic analysis focuses on national policy within a uniform model of governance and implicitly assumes the harmonization of climate policies at the subnational level. However, harmonization is not guaranteed; the design and implementation of policy in a federal union will diverge in important ways from policy in a unitary government. Economic advice built on the assumption of a unitary model of governance may not achieve the expected outcome in a federal system because of interactions with policy choices made at the subnational level …. (2013, p. 112)

In some cases, programs operated at one level of government must meet *mandatory obligations* imposed by higher levels of government (e.g., under Federal law, local schools must ensure disabled public-school students are given opportunities for academic success). In other cases, *conditional grant funding* is used to incentivize, but not require, states to act (e.g., to raise their minimum drinking age to 21 or lose Federal highway grant funds).

In other situations, *Congress decides a nationwide approach is appropriate and preempts state action that would complicate a national program.* For example, in 2019, Congress reauthorized the Terrorism Risk Insurance Program Act, which provides a Federal framework for privately issued insurance against terrorist incidents. It also prohibits states from regulating terrorism insurance. Federal preemption of state law often reflects pressure from firms that operate across state lines because it relieves them of the challenges of complying with a patchwork of potentially inconsistent state laws. According to the Congressional Budget Office, 37 Federal bills were enacted between 2015 and 2020 that explicitly preempted state action in one or more policy domains (CBO, n.d.).

The relationships among levels of government are also characterized by the intergovernmental flow of substantial financial resources. Exhibit 10-8 traces the flow

Exhibit 10-8 Intergovernmental Revenue Flows: 2018 ($billion)

| | | To | | | |
		Federal	State	Local	Total
From	Federal	*	$670.6	$69.1	$739.7
	State	$0.0	*	$543.0	$543.0
	Local	$0.0	$17.6	*	$17.6
	Total	$0.0	$688.2	$612.1	*

Source: (USCB, 2018).

of money among levels of government. The Federal government transfers about $740 billion per year to states and localities, with most going to the states. The states also support their local governments; in the aggregate, localities receive over $600 billion from higher levels of government. And in some cases, localities transfer money to their states.

In policy areas where states *are* free to set public policy independently of the Federal government, you will find considerable variability in state-level policies—even on some high-profile issues:

- There are 28 states that have a death penalty while 22 do not (DPIC, 2020).

- Fourteen states have legalized adult recreational use of marijuana, 36 have established comprehensive medical marijuana programs, and the remaining states either prohibit marijuana or have only limited medical programs (NCSL, 2021).

- Thirty states have used Federal funding under the Affordable Care Act to expand Medicaid coverage to more people than the original program, 12 states declined to expand Medicaid, and 8 states have opted for other mechanisms to expand Medicaid (NASHP, 2020).

- Five states do not impose a statewide sales tax; among those states that do, five levy a tax of seven percent or more and six impose a tax at or below four percent (Cammenega, 2021).

- Five states do not have a minimum wage, two have a minimum below the Federal standard of $7.25 per hour, 14 states have a minimum equal to the federal level, and 29 states have a minimum above the federal level (USA Facts, 2021).

A discussion of Federalism would be incomplete without mentioning the long and contentious history of states' rights. Arguments about the proper balance of power and authority between the federal government and the individual states have been around since the country's inception (Newbold, 2008). The topic was central to debates about the adoption of the Constitution in the 1780s, at the core of the Civil War over slavery in the 1860s, and integral to disputes about the role of the Federal government in reducing segregation and enhancing civil rights in the 1960s. In the words of one scholar, federalism is America's "endless argument" (Donahue, 1997, p. 16). It seems likely to remain so for the foreseeable future.

As you think about whether a policy issue would be best addressed at the Federal, state, or local level (or some combination thereof), here are a few things to consider:

- *Local officials may better understand their communities* and be able to devise policies that more effectively meet constituents' needs than policymakers in a state capital or in Washington, DC. (And as we saw above, citizens have more trust in local government than in other governments.)

- Policy *variability across states and localities gives residents the freedom*—albeit assuming their willingness to relocate—to best align their personal preferences with the taxation, spending, and other policies of the jurisdiction in which they reside.

- If a policy issue in one jurisdiction is connected to the same issue in a nearby jurisdiction, *coordination among jurisdictions* may be advisable. If, for example, water pollution crosses jurisdictional boundaries, it may make sense to address the problem through agreements between the affected governments or by elevating the issue to a higher level of government.

- If you think a mix of Federal, state, and/or local jurisdictions should respond to a policy issue, expect to experience the *complexity of joint action*. The more agencies and levels of government that are involved in designing and implementing a policy, the greater the opportunities for inefficiencies, administrative difficulties, and unintended consequences.

- If you're thinking about using more than one institution to implement a policy, be sure to weigh *transaction costs against the benefits of a multiagency approach*. Institutions can synchronize their work with careful coordination, shared systems, and an alignment of incentives. But these arrangements don't just appear; they require active, intentional effort. If the transaction costs get too high, the result may be a dysfunctional program or suboptimal outcome.

- Sometimes *lower levels of government lack the capacity to handle calamities* like natural disasters, public health crises, or economic upheaval. Higher levels of government typically have larger tax bases, bigger workforces, and a greater ability to borrow money and mobilize other resources.

- In some cases, it makes sense to *handle a policy issue at a higher level of government simply to enhance coordination*. The design of interstate highways, the operation of the air traffic control system, and research into the health risks of industrial chemicals are three examples of activities that can be done more efficiently if coordinated at the highest level possible.

- *A nationwide policy may reduce undesirable competition among states* (i.e., a race to the bottom). States typically aim to maximize business activity to protect jobs and tax revenue. They may thus be tempted to reduce tax rates and regulatory burdens to entice firms to locate in the state. Once one state pursues this strategy, others may feel compelled to keep pace. As each state acts in its narrow self-interest, all states may become worse off. Nationwide policies may be nationally uniform, or may allow individual states to set stronger, but not weaker, policies.

- There may be some issues about which you feel so strongly that there is *no room for variability among states or, if you're working at the state level, among localities.* Perhaps you believe the issue is a matter of fundamental human or civil rights, or that the problem is so severe that only a response at the highest possible level of government is acceptable.

Finally, there's one last point to keep in mind when it comes to the topic of states' rights. In my experience, normative *arguments about states' rights in a federalist system are sometimes politically highjacked* to support a foregone conclusion, rather than reached as the result of a coherent and rigorous application of the principles of federalism to a specific set of facts and circumstances.

Consider a fictitious example. Suppose you believe that automobiles ought not be painted red. If you thought you had strong political support, you might argue for a Federal ban on red cars and a preemption of states' authority to regulate the color of cars, knowing that if you succeed, you'll have achieved universal policy success. On the other hand, if you test the political winds and conclude that a national policy is not in the offing, you might rethink your claim that the issue is a matter of national prerogative and instead become a proponent of states' rights. After all, you might persuade at least a few states to prohibit red cars, thereby attaining partial success.

Another way in which debates about federalism become politicized reflects variations in the intensity or enthusiasm with which states approach their assigned role in the federal system. States vary widely, for example, in how aggressively they enforce Federal environmental standards (EPA/OIG, 2011). Policymakers interested in a de facto weakening of environmental protection may thus argue for more devolution of authority to states, knowing that enforcement is weaker in some jurisdictions. At times, the politics cut in the other direction when a state takes a more aggressive approach than preferred by Federal authorities. For example, the Trump administration moved in 2019 to curtail California's longstanding Clean Air Act authority to set vehicle tailpipe emission standards more stringent than in other states (Joselow, 2019).

It may seem cynical, but in my experience, political advocates often become proponents of states' rights only after realizing that they're unable to attain a political win at the national level and fall back to seeking enactment of their preferred action in whichever states are most hospitable to their point of view. On the other hand, if states begin to adopt policies to which advocates object, Federal action to limit states' rights may become the preferred strategy. In short, whenever you hear an argument about states' rights, *ask yourself whether it reflects a nuanced and principled understanding of federalism or if it's an argument of convenience aimed at maximizing the chance of a political win.*

10.2.5 Financing the Institutions of Government

Virtually all public programs create costs, most of which are borne by today's taxpayers. But when borrowed money (e.g., Federal deficit spending, or state or local bond proceeds) is used to fund a program, future taxpayers are on the hook to cover the costs.[18] In this section, we'll start with a quick review of the types of costs associated with government programs and then look at different sources of revenue for financing them. Finally, we'll consider how government might raise the money for the policies you're considering. This material is not intended to make you an expert in government finance; rather, the idea is to illustrate the types of issues that may come up as you look specifically at financial matters through an institutional lens of policy analysis.

In all but the most affluent jurisdictions, there isn't enough revenue to accommodate all potentially valuable uses of public monies, making trade-offs inevitable. Policymakers must trade off stakeholder demands for government benefits and services, with a general aversion to higher taxes. Enacted policies thus reflect political and normative judgments about which problems and stakeholders merit attention. There's an adage in the public budgeting world: 'Don't tell me what you value; show me your budget and I will tell you what you value.' If policymakers opt to spend little or nothing on a particular issue, they are signaling that they value it less than they value issues for which they do provide funding.

In virtually every policy analysis, you'll want to think about the kinds of costs that each policy option might create for government. You don't want to overlook items with a big price tag, so be expansive in your thinking. The list below can get you started; of course, given your specific policy option, there may be other taxpayer costs not mentioned on the list. Note that the examples aren't mutually exclusive. Take care not to double count (e.g., when debt service costs are incurred to pay a contractor to build a new toll road).

- Government worker salaries, health and pension benefits, work facilities

- Information and communication technology

- Construction of infrastructure

- Ongoing operation and maintenance of government facilities and equipment

- Utilities such as water, power, natural gas

- Consumable supplies that must be replenished

- Grants to states, localities, and the nonprofit sector

---

[18]In this discussion, I am focused on costs to the government, not the broader construct of cost that we covered in Chapter 9 that reflects the effect of a policy on overall economic social surplus.

- Contracts used to procure goods and services

- Subsidies for firms and transfer programs for individuals

- Debt service (interest and principal repayments) on borrowed funds

Two types of government spending deserve special attention. First, when it comes to the number of people who 'work' for the government, be sure to think beyond direct government workers. There are, for example, about 3.9 million Federal civilian employees, military personnel, and postal workers (Light, 2019). But if you're trying to tote up personnel costs, it's important to recognize the Federal government executes much of its work by hiring contractors (firms and individuals) and by giving grants to organizations that execute government-like functions. Even though their paychecks bear the name of a contractor or grantee, the money to cover those checks comes directly from the Federal government. Light estimates that there are about 4.1 million people employed by Federal contractors and another 1.2 million working for Federal grantees, bringing the size of what Light calls the blended workforce to about 9.2 million workers.[19] About 39 percent are directly employed by the Federal government and the other 61 percent are employed by contractors and grantees (Light, 2019).[20]

Second, when it comes to grant funding, it's important to recognize that government funding is an important source of support for nonprofit organizations in the United States. Nearly a third of all revenue for such organizations comes from federal, state, or local governments. In 2012, governments paid nonprofits of all types about $137 billion; non-profits specializing in human services received about $81 billion from government. About a third of all health and human service nonprofits receive more than 60 percent of their revenue from government sources and about three-quarters receive at least 10 percent (Pettijohn & Boris, 2013). In other words, without government support, the nonprofit human services sector in the United States would almost certainly be appreciably smaller.

Let's move from the spending side of the ledger to the revenue side. Different levels of government rely on different sorts of taxes to finance their operations. There is considerable variation across state and local jurisdictions, but as Exhibit 10-9 shows, in the aggregate the Federal government primarily relies on income taxes and on Social Security and Medicare taxes (which are also levied on income) while the states rely on a mix of income taxes and sales and excise taxes. Finally, the predominant source of tax revenue for local governments is the property tax.[21]

---

[19] Light's analysis includes subcontractors and subgrantees, in addition to prime contractors and grantees.

[20] Data on government contractor and grant-supported workers at the state and local level are not readily available.

[21] Recall that localities derive all their powers from the states in which they are located. State level policies can thus constrain the set of tax revenue options that a local government is permitted to adopt.

Exhibit 10-9 Source of Tax Revenues by Level of Government: 2018

	Level of Government		
	Federal	State	Local
Individual Income Tax	50.6%	38.1%	4.8%
Corporate Income Tax	6.1%	4.7%	1.1%
Social Security and Medicare Tax	35.2%	0.0%	0.0%
Excise and Sales Taxes	2.9%	47.0%	17.7%
Property Tax	0.0%	1.7%	71.7%
Motor Vehicle Licensing	a	2.7%	0.3%
Other	5.3%	5.8%	4.3%
Total	100.0%	100.0%	100.0%

aIncluded in 'other' category.
Detail may not sum to total due to rounding; as explained in the text, state and local totals exclude revenues from non-tax sources.
Sources: (OMB, 2020; USCB, 2018).

In addition to tax revenues, governments collect funds from other sources. Examples include revenue from government-run businesses like water, electricity, natural gas, and sewerage utilities; services like trash collection, park entry fees, road tolls, and public transit systems; retail sales of alcoholic beverages; and tuition for higher education; as well as interest earned on monies held in the public treasury.

What does this discussion of institutional financing have to do with policy analysis? It depends. If you're trying to revise school district boundaries, realign transit routes, or identify the best location for the new city library, financing may not matter much. On the other hand, if you're devising a new policy that will cost a significant sum, you may need to consider its financing. Having worked out the likely government cost of each option you're analyzing, you can then take one of four approaches.

- You might *decide that the specific financing mechanism is not germane to the policy decision.* Either you're confident that sufficient funding is already available, or your client prefers to treat the funding choice as a secondary question to be answered later, perhaps during the next budget cycle when all spending priorities are considered.

- You might *identify a funding source for each policy option*, perhaps a dedicated tax or a user fee. The funding source would then be seen as integral to the option itself, and its pros and cons evaluated accordingly. One characteristic of a dedicated funding source is that it ensures that funds designated for the associated program cannot be diverted to other uses.

- Rather than identifying a new revenue source for each new policy being considered, you might instead *identify an existing program to cut when the new policy is enacted.* The expenditures no longer needed for the existing program would thus 'pay-for' the cost of the new program. This approach makes the new policy revenue-neutral, but obligates you to compare the pros and cons of eliminating the existing program to those of creating the new policy.

- You might *specify that costs will be debt financed.* States and localities are generally prohibited from running budget deficits but can issue bonds to cover capital investments in long-lived assets. Debt financing at the Federal level occurs when a new program is funded by a mix of tax revenues and general borrowing.

There is no one correct way to reflect financing considerations in your policy analysis. Regardless of the approach you take, be sure to apply it consistently. It will distort your conclusions if you consider financing for only some, but not all, of the policies being compared.

To recap our discussion of the institutional lens, which focused on the behavior of governmental agencies tasked with implementing public policies, there are several key takeaways. I first suggested that you always consider the questions of why a particular problem is the government's to address and whether its institutions are up to the task or might instead exhibit government failure. Along the way, we observed that the public seems to have the most trust in local government, followed by the states and then the federal government.

I suggested that there are five key differences between public institutions and commercial enterprises that often hinder the performance of government institutions. Next, we examined how the principal–agent problem—the potential misalignment of incentives between the person(s) ultimately responsible for an institution's performance and those delegated the responsibility for executing its functions on a daily basis—may lead to suboptimization within government institutions. We then moved on to the topic of federalism and noted how the interplay among federal, state, tribal, and local governments can have significant impacts on public policy. Finally, we briefly considered how issues of taxation and spending can be reflected in policy analysis.

CHAPTER SUMMARY

This chapter presented two lenses through which you can examine policy issues: the political lens and the institutional lens. A summary of the material relevant to each lens appears as the final paragraphs of Sections 10.1 and 10.2.

DISCUSSION QUESTIONS

1. Pick a policy issue in which you're interested and think about the politics that drive debates about it. To what degree are these debates motivated by unabashed self-interest, good faith attempts at problem-solving, expressions of social identity, or political sectarianism?

2. How can the multiple streams framework be used to explain political debates about immigration, climate policy, or a national minimum wage?

3. To what degree do you think money inappropriately influence politics? Do you think systemic reform is needed? If so, what types of policies do you think would be appropriate?

4. Does government deserve the trust of citizens? Why? Why not? What would you do to enhance trust in government?

5. Think of an amusement park operated by a commercial entity and a wilderness area operated by the National Park Service. What principles should guide the operation of each? How are they different? How are they the same?

6. Suppose you're designing a new policy to enact reforms in policing in communities of color. What roles would you expect federal, state, tribal, and local governments to play? What revenue sources would you tap to cover the cost of such reforms?

CHAPTER ELEVEN

THE LEGAL, SUSTAINABILITY, AND SCIENCE AND TECHNOLOGY LENSES

Having introduced you to the lenses of equity, economics, politics, and institutions, this chapter looks at three more lenses—the legal, sustainability, and science and technology lenses—that may be relevant to your work as a policy analyst.[1] Together, these seven lenses should help you see policy issues in a more holistic and comprehensive fashion than if you only considered one or two.

11.1 THE LEGAL LENS

As you consider the legal lens, you'll see connections to the four lenses we've already discussed. We often look to the legal system to ensure justice and to remedy societal *inequities*. The legal system also has a profound influence on the business environment in which the *economy* operates. Similarly, at the core of many *political* disputes are questions about what the law should and shouldn't allow. Finally, the legal system is both a product of and a profound influence on the *institutions* of government.

As we'll discuss in this section, however, unless you pause to also view policy issues through a *legal* lens, you're at risk of overlooking an important part of public policy. Multiple legal constraints—constitutional, statutory, regulatory, and procedural—limit the nature

Learning Objectives

By studying this chapter, you should be able to:

- Explain how the rule of law and the operation of the legal system affect the nature and scope of permissible public policies.

- Distinguish legal reasoning from policy reasoning.

- Characterize the four types of law relevant to policy analysis and the role played by the three branches of government in crafting public policy.

- Describe how and why sustainability is a contested concept that, despite its contested nature, typically reflects five basic themes.

- Portray sustainability in terms of capital stocks, benefit flows, consumption and investment decisions, and society's ability to meet the needs of present and future generations.

- Characterize the United Nations Sustainable Development Goals and describe their historical development.

- Describe the mechanisms that link research and development to scientific and technological change.

- Anticipate the circumstances under which scientific and technological advances will be disruptive, with the potential to create broad, persistent, and adverse societal changes.

- Pose appropriate research questions to organize a policy analysis that effectively integrates scientific and technological considerations into its methodology and findings.

---

[1]As mentioned in the introduction to Part III, these three lenses are not directly related to one another, but are grouped together in one chapter simply to ensure that all four chapters of Part III are roughly the same length.

and scope of permissible public policies, as well as the processes by which they are implemented. Accordingly, by incorporating a legal perspective into your policy analysis, you may uncover insights that you might have otherwise missed. The first section below motivates the discussion by linking the legal foundations of democratic governance to the practice of policy analysis. The next section describes the different types of law that give public policy its tangible legal form. The final three sections consider the specific role played by each of the three branches of government—legislative, executive, and judicial—in lawmaking.

11.1.1 How Does the Legal Lens Relate to Policy Analysis?

The classical models of policy analysis typically focus on figuring out the most cost-effective or the fairest and most equitable means of addressing a public issue, often at the expense of legal analysis. To a degree, this is understandable; policy analysts are taught to broadly imagine new public policies as alternative paths forward and to think expansively about the pros and cons of each path. The focus is on figuring out which policies will work and, in particular, which will work best. In doing so, it's easy to mistakenly assume that any existing laws and regulations that contribute to the problem can be swept away and that any that remain can simply be made to conform with the preferred policy option. But such an approach is too simplistic. Legal issues pervade the policymaking and implementation processes; analysts ignore them at their peril. There are at least three reasons why you should apply a legal lens to policy analysis.

Public Servants as Good Shepherds of Governance

Not all policy analysts are public servants who work for government, but many are; moreover, analysts who work outside of government frequently interact with those who are public servants. It thus behooves all policy professionals to understand the legal context of government service. As Kettl puts it:

> Public organizations exist to administer the law and every element of their design—their structure, staffing, budget, and purpose—is the product of legal authority (2015, p. 55).

The centrality of legal authority in public service has important normative implications. Heller coined the term "good shepherd" to describe the idea that public servants have multiple duties (2018, p. 73). They must respect and promote:

- The rule of law;
- The separation of powers among the executive, legislative, and judicial branches of government;

- Shared governance among federal, state, tribal, and local government; and
- The rights and freedoms afforded to citizens by the constitution.

The Rule of Law: When Chief Justice John Marshall wrote in 1803 that the "government of the United States has been emphatically termed a government of laws, and not of men," he was describing the constitutional foundation for the rule of law (Marbury v. Madison, 5 U.S. 137). Adherence to the rule of law requires that elected officials, government employees, judges, and law enforcement personnel predictably comply with the written laws, policies, and principles that legitimate the exercise of their powers. It also prohibits arbitrary, capricious, and nontransparent acts by public servants (Hill & Lynn, 2016). Moreover, the rule of law means that disputes among citizens, institutions, and governments can be resolved in a consistent and predictable manner through channels open to all citizens. Meeting such challenges can be a tall order for public servants from whom we expect consistency and predictability even when their government positions afford them considerable discretion in ambiguous situations (Hill & Lynn, 2016). Stephanie Newbold puts it this way:

> Without being educated in the legal environment of public administration, it becomes increasingly challenging for future civil servants to understand how they will use their discretionary authority in responsibly sound, legal manners (2011, p. 473).

When relevant policies and principles are precise and unambiguous, observing the rule of law may not be too difficult. But in a system of separate powers and shared governance, things can get murkier.

Separation of Powers: In the federal government, the states, and many localities, government authority is distributed among executive, legislative, and judicial branches of government, in a system referred to as **checks and balances**. The constitutional rationale for such an approach is that by spreading governmental power across multiple institutions, no one institution (or person) can garner excessive power that leads to authoritarian abuses (Hill & Lynn, 2016). Shared power may be a great antidote for tyranny, but it complicates things for public servants when they must answer to three branches of government while working within the bureaucratic and institutional constraints of public agencies (Newbold, 2011). Doing so often necessitates a balancing act:

> [P]ublic administrators … should learn to think like judges as well as legislators and executives, because they are all three of these. In a regime of separated powers, administrators must do the work of statesmen. (Rohr, 1990, p. 83)

It's important to recognize that this struggle among the branches of government for legal control of public policies is not an unintended quirk but an intrinsic feature of US government (Newbold, 2008). Or, as an app developer might put it: *it's a feature, not a bug, of the system.*

Intergovernmental Relations: In the last chapter, we explored shared governance among federal, state, tribal, and local actors in the context of the institutional lens. Here, when we look through the legal lens, we focus more narrowly on constitutional and statutory requirements that shape these relationships. The idea may be clearer with an example. As mentioned in Chapter 10, the federal government sometimes attaches conditions to grants given to states, incentivizing but not requiring them to adopt specific policies. By doing so, the federal government avoids running afoul of the constitutionally protected sovereignty of the states. But use of this strategy faces constitutional limitations. In 2010, for example, the Affordable Care Act offered states generous financial aid to expand their Medicaid programs to cover more uninsured people. States that declined to expand Medicaid not only wouldn't get this new support; they would also have to forfeit all federal funding for their existing Medicaid programs. But likening the arrangement to a "gun to the head," the Supreme Court held that:

> Congress may offer the States grants and require the States to comply with accompanying conditions, but the States must have a genuine choice whether to accept the offer. The States are given no such choice in this case: They must either accept a basic change in the nature of Medicaid, or risk losing all Medicaid funding. The remedy for that constitutional violation is to preclude the Federal Government from imposing such a sanction. (National Federation of Independent Business v. Sebelius, 567 U.S. 519, 2012)

In short, when we're talking about shared governance among levels of government, the federal government doesn't have carte blanch to impose requirements on the states. Moreover, this is just one example. The language of federal and state constitutions, statutory law, and treaties with Native American tribes together have a profound effect on the nature of intergovernmental relationships in the United States.

Rights of Citizens: Government plays a key role in protecting the rights of citizens. Indeed, many of the most important rights are protections from improper government behavior (e.g., restrictions on free speech or on illegal search and seizure). In other cases, government enforces rights threatened by private institutions (e.g., discriminatory employment practices). Finally, when citizens interact with government—whether it's dealing with the police, getting a driver's license, or seeking a welfare benefit—they are entitled to due process. (You may want to revisit Exhibit 8-4 for a refresh on the elements of due process). The existence of citizens' rights thus creates a duty for public servants to, at a minimum, respect these rights, and at best, to promote them. As Newbold puts it:

> [T]he legal approach to public administration ... emphasizes procedural due process, substantive rights like those found in the Bill of Rights and the Fourteenth Amendment; and values associated with equity and fairness (2011, p. 466) *internal citations omitted.*

Accordingly, when you look through a legal lens, you'll want to think about whether the problem you're analyzing or the policies you're considering promote or hinder the protection of citizen rights.

What does being a good shepherd have to do with the legal elements of policy analysis? To start, when you're investigating the causes of a policy problem, ask yourself whether the rule of law is being threatened by public agencies acting in an arbitrary, capricious, or non-transparent fashion or failing to respect citizen rights. If you see a dysfunctional public policy, ask whether the implementing agency is being pulled in different directions by the executive, legislative, and judicial branches or is being forced to work across federal, state, tribal, or local levels when doing so doesn't make sense. And, when you think about new public policies, be sure to consider whether your planned approach truly respects the rule of law and the rights of citizens. Finally, think about whether a new policy can engender sufficiently aligned support from the legislature and executive to ensure success.

Law Is Often the Raw Material from Which Policy Is Made Tangible

In addition to helping public servants be good shepherds of governance, a second rationale for applying the legal lens is that it reminds us that new public policies are typically operationalized in the form of law.[2] As a policy analyst, you need to think not only in conceptual terms about the policy options you're analyzing but also about how those options can be described in writing as sensible, coherent, and internally consistent legislation. If enacted legislation doesn't match the thinking implicit in your analysis, you can't expect it to yield the outcomes that you've projected for it. Moreover, you also want your enacted policy option to survive judicial review. If it is struck down over constitutional concerns or because it doesn't comport with relevant statutory authority, or is interpreted by courts in unexpected ways owing to vague or contradictory language, then you won't have accomplished much.

---

[2] Public policy may also come in the form of new policies and procedures applied by government agencies in their daily operations, but that are not codified in law.

Where should you focus your legal lens? Typically, two types of law are relevant to policy analysis: **substantive** law and **procedural** law. In my work on environmental issues, for example, domain-specific substantive legal requirements originate in statutes like the Clean Air Act and the Safe Drinking Water Act, as well as in the regulations that the Environmental Protection Agency and other agencies issue as a means of implementing statutory law. Relevant procedural law includes the Administrative Procedure Act (APA), which prescribes the processes for promulgating regulations, and the National Environmental Policy Act (NEPA), which dictates how the environmental impacts of federal actions are to be studied. Both APA and NEPA are silent about policy outcomes; they only define process requirements. In short, to stay abreast of relevant legal issues, you need to pay attention to both substantive and procedural law, often across multiple branches and levels of government.

What does the idea that law is the raw material of policy have to do with policy analysis? For one thing, when you project the outcomes of policy proposals, you need to do so with an eye toward their legal interpretation. Think about how your generalized description of a policy option will be rendered into formal legal language and subsequently interpreted by the courts. That's the version of the policy you want to use for your analysis, not a vague idea of what the policy is all about. Moreover, unless you're analyzing a policy that will change underlying statutory law, remember that all new policies must comport with existing substantive law and be put in place in accordance with relevant procedural law.

Legal Thinking and Policy Thinking Are Not the Same Thing

The third motive for applying a legal lens to policy analysis is that legal logic and policy logic can sometimes lead to different conclusions. Nowhere is this more apparent that at the US Supreme Court. Split decisions often grab the headlines, but the Justices agree more often than you might realize. Between 2005 (when John Roberts became Chief Justice) and 2019, the Supreme Court decided 1,160 cases (Spaeth et al., 2020). The vote was unanimous in almost half of the cases, and in two-thirds of the cases, the margin was four or more votes (e.g., 8 to 1 or 7 to 2). It was only in the remaining one-third of cases that the court split sharply (e.g., in a 6-3 or 5-4 vote).

The unanimous (and near unanimous) cases nicely illustrate the distinction between policy and legal thinking. To draw a policy conclusion, you consider alternative ways to address an issue and figure out how to best move forward. Legal reasoning isn't the same. Drawing a legal conclusion entails identifying the legal requirements applicable to a case and making a decision based on the combination of the law and case-specific facts. Whether the outcome constitutes good policy or matches public sentiments is not often the focus of legal logic (Szypszak, 2011). When seven or more Justices from across the ideological spectrum see a case the same way, it's a safe bet that the legal logic is straightforward.

Consider, for example, a 2021 dispute between Noah Duguid and Facebook. Duguid never had a Facebook account but kept getting texts saying that someone was trying to log in to his account. Despite being asked to stop, Facebook kept texting him.[3] He sued Facebook for violating the Telephone Consumer Protection Act (TCPA) of 1991, but lost. For a unanimous Court, Justice Sotomayor wrote:

> TCPA proscribes abusive telemarketing practices by … imposing restrictions on making calls with an automatic telephone dialing system [which] is a piece of equipment with the capacity … to produce telephone numbers to be called, using a random or sequential number generator … The question before the Court is whether that definition encompasses equipment that does not use a random or sequential number generator. It does not. … Duguid's quarrel is with Congress, which did not define an autodialer as malleably as he would have liked. … This Court must interpret what Congress wrote. (Facebook, Inc. v. Duguid, 592 U.S., 2021, opinion, pp. 1, 12), *internal citations omitted*

In other words, from a legal point of view, it didn't matter what Congress intended when it enacted TCPA 30 years earlier. What mattered was what the law said. Nor did it matter whether the Court's opinion was smart policy for today's world which, according to the L.A. Times, it most certainly wasn't:

> Few things unite Americans like our shared hatred of robocalls, which have become a daily affliction for far too many of us. … [The] ruling undermining the main federal law against robocalls was a slap to the face. … [T]he justices laid out a roadmap for telemarketers, scammers and the rest of the robocall fraternity to ping your phone with impunity. … Now would be the time to open a window and scream. (Healey, 2021)

The takeaway here is that courts don't—or at least aren't supposed to—apply policy considerations in support of decisions that can't be justified by the law itself (Heller, 2018).

But things aren't always so straightforward. Recall that about a third of the Supreme Court's decisions are closely split. In such cases, there is more than one way to apply legal principles to the matter at hand and, in turn, legal reasoning doesn't lead to a single unambiguous conclusion. Instead, the Justices engage in a form of legal reasoning that looks a lot like policy reasoning.

---

[3] Apparently, the person who used to have Duguid's phone number did have a Facebook account, hence the texts.

Consider, for example, a voting rights case from Arizona that made headlines when it was decided in July 2021. By a six to three margin, the Court ruled that Arizona could prohibit anyone other than a family or household member from collecting absentee ballots and that the state could discard ballots received at the wrong location. Writing for the majority, Justice Alito opined:

> [The] mere inconvenience [of voting] cannot be enough to demonstrate a violation of the [Voting Rights Act]. ... [T]he mere fact there is some disparity in impact does not necessarily mean that a system is not equally open or that it does not give everyone an equal opportunity to vote. ... Every voting rule imposes a burden of some sort, and therefore in determining ... whether a rule goes too far, it is important to consider the reason for the rule [and o]ne strong and entirely legitimate state interest is the prevention of fraud. (Brnovich v. Democratic National Committee, 594 U.S., 2021, opinion, pp. 17–19)

Writing in dissent, Justice Kagan vehemently disagreed:

> [T]he Court ... fears that the statute Congress wrote is too 'radical'—that it will invalidate too many state voting laws. So the majority writes its own set of rules ... Wherever it can, the majority gives a cramped reading to broad language. And then it uses that reading to uphold two election laws from Arizona that discriminate against minority voters. ... [T]his is not how the Court is supposed to interpret and apply statutes. ... What is tragic here is that the Court has (yet again) rewritten—in order to weaken—a statute that stands as a monument to America's greatness ... The majority's opinion mostly inhabits a law-free zone. (Brnovich v. Democratic National Committee, 594 U.S., 2021, dissent, pp. 2–3, 20), *internal citations omitted*

What does the difference between legal thinking and policy thinking have to do with policy analysis? As the Facebook case makes clear, when it comes to legal reasoning, it often doesn't matter what policymakers originally intended or whether the current state of affairs reflects sound policy. What matters is what the written law says. But as the Arizona voting rights case makes equally clear, legal reasoning is hardly a formulaic process akin to linear algebra. Instead, legal reasoning can lead to starkly different conclusions, often aligned with the ideological or political preferences of the jurists. Accordingly, when developing a new policy proposal, be sure to think like an appellate judge and ask whether what you've written will lead to a legal interpretation that matches your intent. If it doesn't, take the time to go back and redraft the proposal to ensure that legal reasoning leads to the same conclusion as your policy reasoning.

11.1.2 Types of Law

There are four types of law relevant to policy analysis: constitutional law, statutory law, administrative law, and common law. This section briefly describes each type of law. To start, **constitutional law** is the supreme law within a jurisdiction. In addition to the US Constitution, each state has its own constitution. Article VI of the US Constitution, in what is often referred to as the Supremacy Clause, makes state law subordinate to the US Constitution. It's important to remember, however, that this supremacy is not absolute or unconditional. As we discussed in Chapter 10, the constitution explicitly gives the states several sovereign powers and also, by virtue of the Tenth Amendment, reserves to the states powers that aren't otherwise prohibited to them.

If you were educated in the United States, you are probably familiar with the US Constitution. One thing that may be less familiar to you is the diverse content of state constitutions. If you're working at the state, tribal, or local level, you'll want to familiarize yourself with the relevant state constitution:

> One cannot make sense of American state government or state politics without understanding state constitutions. After all, it is the state constitution—and not the federal Constitution—that creates the state government, largely determines the scope of its powers, and distributes those powers among the branches of the state government and between state and locality. It is likewise the state constitution that structures political conflict within the state and provides mechanisms for its resolution. (Tarr, 2000, p. 3)

The second type of law relevant to policy analysis is **statutory law**, which is likely the first thing that comes to mind when someone mentions 'the law.' Statutory law is any form of binding public policy enacted by a legislature at the federal, state, or local levels. Published statutes are typically available in two formats: as a chronological record of enacted legislation and as a code organized by topic. The former may be of historical interest, but it's not much help when you're trying to figure out which statutory laws are relevant to a particular issue. For example, a law may have been passed in 1990, amended in 1995, and amended again in 2000. Sorting through a multiyear chronological history to integrate multiple legislative actions can be an overwhelming—and error-prone—task. The second format, which is known at the federal level as the United States Code, is typically the go-to source for understanding the current state of statutory law. It captures in one place the cumulative effect of all enacted legislation in a topic area.

The third type of law is **administrative** or **regulatory** law. Administrative law—discussed in more detail in Section 11.1.3—originates in the executive, rather than legislative, branch of government. Administrative law is subordinate to statutory law, meaning that the executive branch may only promulgate[4] regulations as authorized by the legislature. Most, but not all, states develop, promulgate, and implement regulations using processes similar to that of the federal government (Justia, 2018).[5] As with statutory law, administrative law is typically published in two ways: chronologically (at the federal level, in the daily Federal Register) and topically (at the federal level, in the Code of Federal Regulations).

The final type of law is **common law**, comprising the collection of judicial decisions relevant and applicable to a topic. Common law does not originate in the prospective enactment or promulgation of a statute or regulation, but is instead created retrospectively as courts resolve cases brought before them. The power of courts to establish common law was affirmed by the Supreme Court in Marbury vs. Madison (5 U.S. 137, 1803). Common law—discussed in more detail in Section 11.1.4—is built on the notion of **precedent** that like cases should be decided in a like manner. Figuring out which common law is germane to a specific policy topic, however, can be a lot more work than finding the relevant statutes and regulations. You'll need to find, read, and understand all relevant court decisions—which may have been rendered over many years in multiple jurisdictions—and then extract the key legal conclusions before you can characterize pertinent common law. You'll likely need the help of an attorney.

In short, *all three branches of government make law*. The legislative branch enacts statutory law, the executive branch promulgates administrative law, and the judicial branch creates common law. Let's take a closer look at the lawmaking activities of each branch.

11.1.3 Law Originating in the Legislative Branch

The legislative branch plays a central role in creating public policy. As long as their actions comport with the US Constitution, or the relevant state constitution if we're talking about a state legislature, lawmakers have broad authority to enact, modify, or repeal public policies across a wide range of issues. They must also obtain Presidential or gubernatorial approval of legislation or muster a supermajority if it is vetoed. Moreover, enacted legislation is always subject to judicial review.

---

[4]In legal parlance, legislation is 'enacted' while regulations are 'promulgated.'
[5]If state-level administrative law is especially relevant to your policy analysis, be sure to take a deep dive into the requirements of the state you're interested in. State-to-state variations may be important (Saiger, 2014).

Legislatures also shape the legal environment of public policy in other ways. They typically hold the *power of the purse*, meaning that they authorize spending for government programs. A fully funded program is likely to have a much bigger impact than a similar program starved for resources. For example, even if a particular policy is codified as binding law, but little or no funding is available to support its programmatic activities or enforce compliance with its requirements, then its practical impact may be negligible. In most jurisdictions, the legislature also exercises *oversight* of the executive branch and can hold hearings at which senior administration officials are expected to explain, defend, and answer criticisms about policy issues and existing programs. Such oversight can have a significant impact on how policies are implemented. Finally, the legislature must *confirm* many Presidential or gubernatorial *nominees* for positions in the executive branch and the judiciary. The US Senate's refusal to consider President Obama's nomination of Merrick Garland to the Supreme Court in 2016, thus opening the door to confirmation of a more conservative justice in 2017 nominated by President Trump, is testimony to the ability of the Senate to shape the US legal landscape.

11.1.4 Law Originating in the Executive Branch

In describing executive branch law, I'll focus on the federal government. There are some variations across states, but in general, the states operate in a similar fashion. The President and the rest of the executive branch play a key role in creating and enforcing the legal authorities of the US government. Along the way, they are bound by numerous legal constraints. When looking through a legal lens at the work of the executive branch, two phenomena are particularly prominent: the power of the President to shape policy writ large and the role of administrative law as a source of public policy. We'll consider each in turn.

Presidential Authority

The President's authority originates in Article II of the Constitution, but has been expanded considerably over the years by delegations of authority from Congress, decisions of the federal courts, and the sheer complexity of managing an enterprise as big as the federal government. To start, congressionally passed legislation doesn't become binding law until the President signs it. If he or she elects not to sign or to veto a bill, it doesn't become law unless two-thirds of the House and Senate vote to override the President's action.

Moreover, each President selects about 4,000 individuals for positions in the federal government. More than 1,200, including Cabinet secretaries, agency heads, and other senior executives, require Senate confirmation (Partnership for Public Service, 2021). These officials play a critical role in policymaking: they initiate and negotiate legislation in Congress, oversee the process of designing and implementing regulation, and set agency policy agendas and funding priorities. In doing so, they are essentially creating public policy. In addition, 94 of the Senate-confirmed appointments made by the President are of US attorneys who represent the federal government in both criminal and civil matters (DOJ, 2021). US attorneys have immense discretion over which criminal cases to initiate and how to settle civil cases involving the federal government (Nelson & Ostrander, 2016).

In addition to naming several thousand senior members of his or her administration, the President exerts legal control over the executive branch by issuing **Presidential directives** such as Executive Orders and other proclamations. Depending on the administration, such directives may be called memoranda, decisions, notices, or findings. Directives must be within the President's constitutional and statutory authorities, but if they are, they constitute binding constraints on the behavior of federal officials and their oversight of federal agencies. For example, even though President Trump was unsuccessful in overturning the Affordable Care Act, he was able to use executive authority to direct federal agencies to constrain its implementation and to give states more control over the program.

Presidential directives remain in effect across changes in administration, but can always be revoked or modified by subsequent Presidents. The norm in recent years has been for Presidents to issue a flurry of directives in their first few days in office, setting priorities for their new administration and often reversing the policies of their predecessor. When it comes specifically to Executive Orders, for example, President Biden issued 37 in his first 70 days in office, while President Trump issued 23 over the same time period (Federal Register, 2021).

Finally, the President's authority extends into the judicial branch through the authority to appoint trial and appellate judges (including Supreme Court justices). There are 870 federal judges subject to Presidential appointment and Senate confirmation (U.S. Courts, 2021). Other federal judges—like magistrates and bankruptcy judges—are selected by these Presidentially appointed judges.

Administrative Law

The belief that Congress writes federal law, while not incorrect, is incomplete. A substantial portion of Federal law actually comes from the executive branch as **administrative law**. New policy analysts often find it surprising to learn just how prevalent administrative, or regulatory, law is in the United States. As Susan Yackee (2019) puts it: "Given the pervasiveness of rulemaking, U.S. public policy may be better conceived of as chiefly regulatory rather than chiefly legislative" (p. 39).

Within this system, Congress doesn't forfeit its constitutional authority to legislate but instead delegates it to an executive branch agency. Such delegations typically occur when Congress wants to set a broad policy but then take advantage of an agency's technical expertise to identify the best particular way to implement that policy

(CRS, 2021b). For example, when Congress enacted the 1990 Amendments to the Clean Air Act, it set out a broad legal framework for addressing multiple air pollution issues, but also tasked the Environmental Protection Agency with issuing dozens of regulations to fill in the details. Just because a requirement is imposed by an executive branch agency rather than enacted as legislation doesn't make it any less binding. The D.C. Circuit Court of Appeals has made it clear that noncompliance with an agency regulation is like breaking a law passed by Congress (National Latino Media Coalition v. FCC, 816 F.2d 785, 1987).

At the federal level, agency rulemaking is conducted pursuant to the Administrative Procedure Act. The APA generally requires that an agency develop a draft of its proposed regulation and publish it in the Federal Register for 'public' comment. While many comments are indeed received from the general public, proposed regulations often attract detailed submissions from trade groups, unions, and other advocacy groups. This isn't surprising. Most citizens don't have time to monitor and comment on complex regulatory proposals, particularly because there are usually dozens of federal rulemakings underway at the same time. Instead, those with the most at stake—potential members of a regulated community or the probable beneficiaries of a new program—are likely to pay close attention to proposed rules. Moreover, some empirical evidence suggests that business groups tend to provide more technical and sophisticated comments during the rulemaking process and that in turn agency officials may be more responsive to such comments than to those raised by the general public (Yackee, 2019).

After reviewing the comments, and incorporating any that it finds persuasive, the agency will then revise its proposed rule and issue a final regulation. After publication, the final rule is codified in the Code of Federal Regulations, which comprises 50 titles, 200 volumes, and about 185,000 pages of material (GW/RSC, 2021). Many of these pages are informational, rather than prescriptive law. So, for another perspective on the extent of Administrative lawmaking, consider statistics on the number of "major" final regulations issued every year.[6] On average, under both the Obama and Trump administrations, about 86 such regulations were issued annually, while in the George W. Bush administration, the number was about 62 per year (GW/RSC, 2021). Prior to publication of both proposed and final rules, agencies must get approval from an office within the White House (led by a political appointee) that ensures the regulation rests on sound policy analysis, is consistent with its statutory authorization, and reflects the policy priorities of the incumbent Administration.

Once issued in final form, regulations are subject to review by both Congress and the courts. Congress can nullify a regulation within 60 legislative days of its

---

[6]Major rules are defined as those likely to result in an annual economic effect over $100 million, a major increase in costs or prices, or significant adverse effects on competition, employment, investment, productivity, innovation, or trade.

promulgation under the Congressional Review Act (CRA), but such action requires the signature of the President, an unlikely outcome if it was the President's administration that issued the regulation in the first place. A federal court can also invalidate all or part of a regulation if it finds that the executive branch agency exceeded its statutory authority, violated the constitution, acted in an arbitrary or capricious manner, or failed to observe procedures required by the APA. The courts can also compel an agency to act if it fails to take specific action when it is legally obligated to do so (CRS, 2020c).

In addition to the legislative function (of rulemaking) within administrative agencies, there is often also a judicial function. Many agencies grant permits, issue compliance orders, and award financial benefits to individuals (e.g., disability payments or unemployment insurance). In the event of a dispute about an agency action, the aggrieved party's first recourse is typically to appeal the action within the agency itself. Such proceedings are often overseen by independent agency officials known as administrative law judges. If a person is dissatisfied with the outcome of an agency's adjudication process, he or she may appeal the decision to the courts but only after having exhausted all of the available administrative remedies offered by the agency in question (Honigsberg & Ho, 2019).

11.1.5 Law Originating in the Judicial Branch

The judicial branch makes law as it decides cases brought before it. As noted above, the cumulative collection of court decisions comprises common law. This section first provides context with a brief overview of how the US legal system operates and then moves to the mechanisms by which courts create common law.

Overview of the Legal System

To understand the judicial origins of law, you need a basic understanding of the legal system. To start, there are important differences between criminal and civil cases. In **criminal cases**, the defendant is alleged to have committed an offense against the people writ large or society in general. The government initiates criminal cases and the result can be imprisonment or monetary fines for a defendant found guilty. Conviction must be based on proof beyond a reasonable doubt.

On the other hand, **civil cases** are disputes between parties: individuals or groups of individuals, firms, or institutions. The party bringing a civil case is the 'plaintiff' while the party from whom action is sought is the 'defendant.' The government may also be a party to a civil suit—either initiating the case as the plaintiff or being named as a defendant. With few exceptions, no one can be jailed as a consequence of a civil case. Instead, the successful party is awarded monetary damages, or the losing party may be compelled to change its behavior. The threshold of proof in a civil case is lower than it is in a criminal case. To prevail, a party must only demonstrate by a preponderance of evidence that their position is correct.

At the federal level and in most states, there is a three-tiered court system.[7] The first tier comprises courts of original jurisdiction. Legal cases start (and often end) with such courts, which sort out the facts based on evidence offered at trial and then apply relevant law to render a decision. Juries may be used to ascertain the facts and then apply the law—as instructed by the judge—to reach a verdict. In other situations, there is no jury and the judge decides on the facts before applying the law.

In general, if the defendant in a criminal case (or either party in a civil case) is dissatisfied with the outcome, they may appeal to the next higher court. But here's the thing: In most situations, you can appeal only on the basis of an error in the application of the law to a case, not because you think the 'fact-finder' (i.e., the jury or the judge in a judge-only case) got the facts wrong. You can also appeal if you think a procedural error occurred during the trial (e.g., that the judge mishandled jury selection). Moreover, the higher court, while it must receive your appeal, is not obligated to hear your case if it doesn't believe that the lower court made a procedural mistake or that it erred in applying the law. If a party objects to the decision of an appellate court, it may appeal to the Supreme Court in the jurisdiction (except in states with only one level of appellate court).

In civil cases, access to the court system is not automatic. In order to pursue a case, the plaintiff must establish its 'standing.' Doing so entails demonstrating that the plaintiff has suffered an actual injury that is not hypothetical, that there is a causal link between the defendant's behavior and the injury, and that the injury could be redressed by a favorable court decision (Kim, 2021). The plaintiff must also establish that the court receiving the complaint has jurisdiction over the matter, that statutory law doesn't preclude the case, and that other procedural tests (e.g., timeliness) have been satisfied. Finally, a plaintiff cannot ask a court to decide matters of public policy when such issues ought to be the purview of the executive or legislative branch. The Supreme Court puts it this way:

> [We are reticent] to invalidate the acts of the Nation's elected leaders. … Members of this Court are vested with the authority to interpret the law; we possess neither the expertise nor the prerogative to make policy judgments. Those decisions are entrusted to our Nation's elected leaders, who can be thrown out of office if the people disagree with them. It is not our job to protect the people from the consequences of their political choices. (National Federation of Independent Business v. Sebelius, 567 U.S. 519, 2012)

---

[7]Some states have only a two-tier court system.

The Creation of Common Law

Common law is built on the principle of **stare decisis** (Latin for let the decision stand) which aspires to create predictability and consistency about what public policy does and does not require of citizens, firms, and institutions (Honigsberg & Ho, 2019). Common law originates in courts' decisions about individual cases. The outcome of a case reflects three elements. First, the facts are established through the presentation and evaluation of evidence (or, in the case of an appeals court, by review of the lower court's fact-finding). Second, the applicable law, which may include constitutional, statutory, administrative, or common law, is characterized. Third, the established facts are evaluated in light of the applicable law to reach a decision (i.e., the guilt or innocence of a criminal defendant, the successful party in a civil case, or at the appellate level, whether to sustain or overturn a lower court's judgment).

Appellate courts, which typically have three or more members, decide cases based on majority rule. When an appellate court reaches its decision, it publishes an **opinion**, which is a narrative explanation of how the decision was reached. Each judge may publish his or her own opinion to explain their position on the case, but often there is one opinion written on behalf of the majority and another on behalf of the dissenting judges. Common law grows out of a compilation of these court opinions. If you want to develop an intuitive feel for the nature of judicial policymaking, I suggest you identify three or four recent Supreme Court cases related to a policy topic you care about. Reading the opinions in these cases will help you understand the subtleties and nuances of legal reasoning, and appreciate at least some of the legal principles relevant to your area of interest.

The content of legal opinions can be separated into two categories: the **holding** and **dicta**. The holding in a case specifically defines the case-relevant law, explains how that law fits with the established facts in the case at hand, and presents a reasoned connection between the facts and the law to yield a case-specific decision. The remainder of the published material—which may include commentary on arguments made by the parties, a review of tangentially related legal principles, and dissenting opinion(s)—comprise dicta. The distinction between the holding and dicta is a crucial one because only the holding—and not dicta—creates binding precedent to be followed in future decisions (Honigsberg & Ho, 2019). While nonbinding, however, dicta is not irrelevant. It may be cited in future cases to support a legal argument, but will not be treated by other courts as definitive.

So, what does this whole process have to do with the idea that the courts make public policy through common law? It's pretty straightforward. If courts have the authority to interpret and apply both statutory and administrative law and to assess whether such law meets constitutional requirements, and if courts' decisions are viewed as precedents that bind all branches of government, then the judiciary is clearly an important actor in the policymaking process.

As we saw before, courts have a strong preference for avoiding policy questions that they believe ought to be answered by the legislative and executive branches of government. But judicial deference to the other branches is not unlimited. In the same case cited earlier, the Supreme Court noted:

> Our deference in matters of policy cannot, however, become abdication in matters of law. ...Our respect for Congress's policy judgments thus can never extend so far as to disavow restraints on federal power that the Constitution carefully constructed. And there can be no question that it is the responsibility of this Court to enforce the limits on federal power by striking down acts of Congress that transgress those limits. (National Federation of Independent Business v. Sebelius, 567 U.S. 519, 2012)

The relevance of the judiciary to public policy is also made plain by the behavior of advocacy groups from across the ideological spectrum. Such groups not only lobby Congress and the executive branch; they often also engage in legal advocacy. They may, for example, bring a suit aimed at invalidating a new regulation or, conversely, at compelling an agency to issue a regulation that it might not otherwise issue. Particularly in an era of partisan Congressional gridlock, where advocates can't achieve their goals through legislation, they often feel compelled to turn to the courts to advance their cause.

To recap our discussion of the legal lens, there are several key takeaways. For starters, without an appreciation of how law and the legal system work, you risk misunderstanding the causes of a policy problem or the legal feasibility of alternative policy solutions to it. Moreover, public servants derive their authority from the law and, in turn, have a legal duty to comply with it, irrespective of whether or not it reflects optimal public policy. In addition, if you hope to predict how a court might rule on a particular issue, you need to apply narrow legal reasoning rather than more expansive policy or normative reasoning. When doing so, bear in mind that there are four types of law in the United States. Statutory law originates in the legislative branch, administrative law in the executive branch, and common law in the judicial branch. These three forms of law are subordinate to the fourth: the US and relevant state constitutions. Not all policy issues depend heavily on legal issues, but many do. If you neglect to look at your analysis through a legal lens, you can miss important aspects of the situation.

11.2 THE SUSTAINABILITY LENS

As you investigate policy problems and ponder policy options, you can often gain valuable insight by looking through the lens of sustainability. As we'll see below, despite a prominent place in policy discourse in recent decades, the word sustainability means different things to different people. But irrespective of its precise definition, the concept can be helpful to a policy analyst. In this section, we'll start with a working definition of sustainability and then move to a framework that incorporates capital stocks and benefit flows as a way of thinking about whether a particular policy, strategy, or behavior is sustainable. We'll close with a review of the United Nations' Sustainable Development Goals.

11.2.1 Sustainability as a Contested Concept

The idea of sustainability has been around for centuries. In Western culture, it emerged in Germany in the 1700s as foresters recognized that harvesting more wood in a season than naturally regrows over the same period would eventually decimate a forest and was thus unsustainable. The topic emerged again in the early 1900s as folks like John Muir and Gifford Pinchot argued about whether Western lands should be left in a pristine and untouched condition or managed to maximize production of timber, fish and game, minerals, and other natural resources. In the 1960s and 1970s, the popular environmental movement led to new federal legislation to protect land, air, water, and endangered species.

A pivotal shift in thinking about sustainability took place in 1987 when, under the auspices of the United Nations, the Brundtland Commission issued a reported entitled *Our Common Future*. It led to the creation of the UN Commission on Sustainable Development at the 1992 Earth Summit in Rio de Janeiro. In the report, Norway's Prime Minister Gro Brundtland pushed beyond a strictly environmental view of sustainability to instead put human needs at the forefront of the issue and to introduce matters of poverty, technology, and governance of the relationship between today's society and that of the future:

> Sustainable development is development that meets the needs of the present without compromising the ability of future generations to meet their own needs. It contains within it two key concepts: the concept of 'needs,' in particular the essential needs of the world's poor, to which overriding priority should be given; and the idea of limitations imposed by the state of technology and social organization on the environment's ability to meet present and future needs. (UN/WCED, 1987, p. 54)

While the Brundtland Commission defined sustainable development, it did so in very broad strokes. To translate the concept into practical policy choices, many details need to be worked out. But, as with all definitions, there is no way to 'prove' that a particular definition is the right one. After all, the definition of a word is nothing more than a shared understanding among people about what the word means. If you and I use a word like sustainability to mean two different things, there's no objective standard to which we can appeal to resolve the matter.[8]

---

[8]As mentioned in Section 5.1.3, one of a policy analyst's first tasks is to clarify the terms of the discussion.

This definitional problem is particularly acute here. The word 'sustainability' conveys an aura of positivity, beneficence, and desirability that comes not from a careful analysis of its implications, but because in popular speech, 'unsustainability' is universally seen as a pejorative, *always* a bad thing. Admitting that you're engaged in an unsustainable practice is akin to admitting you're behaving in a foolish or reckless fashion. In turn, this phenomenon creates a strong incentive to label actions you support as sustainable and actions you oppose as unsustainable. Politicians, advocates, and corporate advertisers are all fond of attaching the modifier 'sustainable' to concepts they endorse.

Scholar Lisa Pettibone searched the literature for a clear definition of the word sustainability but eventually concluded that sustainability is a 'contested concept' about which there are likely to remain residual differences of opinion (2014, p. 10). She ultimately concluded that "Sustainability is not a concrete policy programme; it is a world view, or dare I say, a political ideology" (p. 12).

Pettibone does, however, identify five principles of sustainability that are ubiquitous in policy and academic discourse and also generally agreed upon by most participants in these debates:

- *Ecological limits*: Sustainability takes as given that natural resources are limited, and that human consumption and production of these resources has the potential to exceed natural limits.

- *Long-term outlook*: Sustainability encourages us to look beyond the next few years and the needs of today's population to consider the needs of future generations in light of population growth and evolving societal and natural conditions.

- *Complex systems view*: Sustainability resists simplistic formulations of how the world works and emphasizes the interconnectedness of disparate elements in both the human and natural worlds, geospatially and dynamically over time.

- *Deliberative, collective, purposive*: Sustainability emphasizes thoughtful and intentional governance of both natural resources and the human world, with a focus on collective and inclusive decisionmaking.

- *Reflexive management*: Sustainability acknowledges the complexity of human and natural systems and the difficulty of making good choices. It asks us to pay attention to unfolding events, learn from mistakes, and adjust our approach to reflect experience.[9]

---

[9]In Chapter 7, I suggested that reflexivity is part of self-awareness and an important characteristic of the mindset of an effective policy analyst.

Although these five considerations seem reasonable, I am mindful of what Pettibone calls the contested and ideological nature of sustainability. So, I'll stop short of recommending that you structure all your policy analysis work to incorporate these elements of sustainability. On the other hand, I'm confident that by at least considering them, you may see aspects of an issue you may have otherwise overlooked.

11.2.2 Sustainability as Capital Stocks and Benefit Flows

If you want to go beyond Pettibone's five elements of sustainability, you may find it useful to think about sustainability in terms of **capital stocks** and **benefit flows**. Doing so requires that we begin with a basic framework and then link it to sustainability. To start, a capital stock is a long-lived asset capable of producing a flow of benefits over time.[10] For example, a government bond produces a flow of interest payments to the bondholder and a factory produces a flow of products to be sold by the factory owner. The concept originates in the business world where capital assets (along with human labor) are an integral part of a firm's ability to turn inputs into outputs. When applied to the concept of sustainability, this framework comprises four types of capital stocks: natural, manufactured, human, and social. Exhibit 11-1 depicts several examples of each type of capital stock.

The next element in the framework reflects the uses to which benefit flows are put. We can do one of two things with a benefit flow: **consume** it today or **invest** it for tomorrow. The difference is easiest to see with a simple example of an interest-bearing savings account. In January, you deposit $100 (the capital stock) and a year later you get, say, $5 in interest (a benefit flow). You can either reinvest the earnings and start the new year with a balance of $105, or spend it on your favorite coffee drink and start the new year with a balance of $100. Spending it today meets your desire for current consumption while reinvesting makes it available for future consumption.

For a real-world example, consider the discovery of substantial oil reserves in the North Sea in the late 1960s (Solow, 2019). Two countries stood to benefit: Great Britain and Norway, and both pumped roughly similar quantities of oil from beneath the North Sea in the ensuing decades. The two countries, however, took very different approaches to public policy. Norway used the proceeds to establish a Sovereign Wealth Fund to invest its oil revenues. The fund now has a balance of over $1 trillion (Smith, 2021). Norway uses earnings from the fund to supplement its annual budget, but doesn't draw more from the fund than it has earned, meaning the value of the fund will be preserved indefinitely. Great Britain, on the other hand, used oil revenues to cover then-current government spending and to finance tax cuts (Elliot, 2012).

---

[10]In Chapter 8, we defined wealth as a person's net worth at a point in time and his or her income as earnings over a period of time. In other words, wealth is a stock and income is a flow.

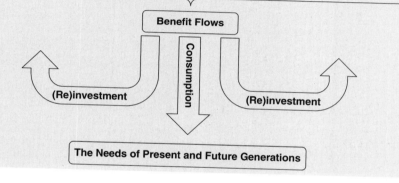

Exhibit 11-1 Sustainability as Capital Stocks and Benefit Flows

Natural Capital (N)
- Energy and mineral resources
- Agricultural land
- Food and water
- Ecosystem services: storm protection, pollution sinks, nutrient cycles, biodiversity

Manufactured Capital (M)
- Homes
- Factories and commercial buildings
- Infrastructure: roads, bridges, schools, airports, hospitals
- Cars, trains, ships

Human Capital (H)
- Physical labor
- Skills, capabilities
- Intellectual property
- Number of people
- Health, longevity

Social Capital (S)
- Government institutions
- Civil society
- Rule of law
- Trust and reciprocity among people
- Social stability

Benefit Flows

(Re)investment

Consumption

(Re)investment

The Needs of Present and Future Generations

Norway's strategy converted a nonrenewable natural resource (oil) into another form of capital asset (investments in stocks, bonds, and real estate) that continues to generate a benefit flow. Having used revenues to finance current consumption, Great Britain doesn't have this option.

Nobel Laureate Robert Solow uses this framework to help us think about how certain policies might be seen as sustainable or unsustainable. He starts by observing that:

> If 'sustainability' is anything more than just a slogan or expression of emotion, it must amount to an injunction to preserve productive capacity for the indefinite future. (1992, p. 7)

If we assume that productive natural, manufactured, human, and social capital assets are measurable quantities denoted, respectively, as N, M, H, and S in Exhibit 11-1, then we can think of a society's total productive capital (K) as equal to N + M + H + S.

Preserving productive capacity for future generations means that—on an ongoing basis—we divert enough of today's benefit flows away from current consumption toward reinvestment for the future to ensure that K (total productive capital) doesn't diminish, thereby preserving its ability to generate benefits in the future. If we were to let K decline over time, then our behavior would be considered unsustainable because, once K reaches zero, society's productive assets would have lost their ability to generate benefits.

Holding K constant is considered **weak sustainability**. Doing so is viewed as sustainable because society's total productive asset base is not being allowed to depreciate. But it's a weak form of sustainability for a couple of reasons. First, if population grows while K remains constant, then per-capita productive capital will decline, and individual members of future generations will have access to less productive capital than members of today's generation. Second, holding K constant without worrying about the mix among the four types of capital implies they are perfect substitutes when, in many cases, they are not.

In order to avoid the problem, we might instead embrace the concept of **strong sustainability**, in which none of the individual elements of productive capital (N, M, H, or S) are allowed to depreciate and where policymakers endeavor to increase total productive capital (K) over time to accommodate population growth. The trouble with this version of sustainability is that it assumes zero substitutability among asset types. Strong sustainability would, for example, prohibit Norway (and Great Britain) from extracting North Sea oil because doing so would result in a decrease in natural capital.

To steer a middle course between weak and strong sustainability, Serageldin and Steer propose a concept they dub **sensible sustainability** (1993). They embrace the premise of weak sustainability that total capital assets (K) must not depreciate. But their approach allows for carefully considered substitutions among asset types that reflect a deep understanding of thresholds below which an asset becomes unproductive, of the need to jointly deploy capital from multiple categories (e.g., trees from a forest (N), a pulp and paper mill (M), and mill workers (H)) to produce a product (e.g., paper), and of where geographic boundaries should be set (e.g., must a single forest be preserved or are we concerned only about the total amount of forest land in a country?).

The topic of sustainability can quickly get very complex. In addition to the vexing decision of whether to pursue strong, weak, or sensible sustainability, you'll quickly discover that efforts to attach a specific number to the value of each type of productive asset poses extraordinarily difficult analytic challenges. Indeed, unlike national statistics generated for gross domestic product, unemployment, interest rates, and the like, no national entity regularly collects, analyzes, or reports data on the value of natural, human, or social capital (Boyd et al., 2018). And the data for manufactured capital are incomplete (Solow, 1992). But, for the purposes of policy analysis, the framework of capital stocks and benefit flows suggests a few simple questions, the answers to which can generate substantial insight:

- To what degree are current practices sustainable over the long run? To what degree are policy options under consideration likely to create solutions that lead to sustained positive changes that persist over time?

- Does the policy issue entail depreciation of a productive asset, such as irreversible damage to the natural environment, the neglect of deteriorating public infrastructure, or inattention to increasingly irrelevant skills and abilities of workers whose jobs are being displaced by automation?

- If so, what measures can be taken to maintain the benefit flows from such assets? If the specific depreciating assets cannot be restored, what other types of productive assets are being established to create a benefit flow to replace the lost benefits of the depreciating asset?

- To what degree does population growth or increasing affluence imply that productive assets must generate greater flows of benefits in the future than they do today? If so, what steps are being taken to enhance the size and productivity of those assets?

- To what degree are renewable assets like forests, fisheries, agricultural land, and natural landscapes and habitat being used in sustainable ways (rather than being overexploited), thereby ensuring their availability to future generations?

- The indefinite use of nonrenewable resources like oil, gas, and coal is, by definition, unsustainable because only a finite quantity of the resource exists. Accordingly, are these resources being used in the most efficient manner possible, and perhaps more importantly, are the associated benefit streams being reinvested to increase the stock of other forms of productive capital for the future or are the benefits being diverted to current consumption?

While economists, development specialists, and statisticians have been grappling with the best way to measure and model multiple types of productive assets, the benefit streams from each, and the consumption and reinvestment of those benefits, policymakers working internationally through multilateral institutions like the United Nations have simultaneously developed another framework for thinking about sustainability. We turn to it in the next section.

11.2.3 The United Nations Sustainable Development Goals

The United Nations' approach to sustainable development has evolved over the three decades between the 1987 Brundtland Commission report and the 2015 UN adoption of the 2030 Agenda for Sustainable Development (UN/DESA, n.d.). At the Agenda's core are seventeen specific goals:

> The Sustainable Development Goals (SDGs) provide a blueprint for the transition to a healthier planet and a more just world—for present and future generations. With concrete targets, the Goals aim to end poverty and hunger, expand access to health, education, justice and jobs, promote inclusive and sustained economic growth, while protecting our planet from environmental degradation. (UN/DESA, 2019)

Exhibit 11-2 lists and gives a brief definition of each SDG. As you look at the goals, they may strike you as a description of a utopian society where all policies and social activities are aligned and moving in a positive direction. It may also seem naive to think that all the SDGs can be achieved in a real-world context. I suggest you view the goals as aspirational and recognize that their highest value is in reminding policymakers about the *trade-offs between human needs and environmental constraints and between the needs of current generations and those of future generations.*

The UN and other multilateral development organizations like the World Bank and International Finance Corporation, along with many national, regional, and local governments, are working to infuse the Sustainable Development Goals throughout their operations and to mobilize financial and technical assistance to support the pursuit of the SDGs. Adopted toward the end of the Obama presidency, the SDGs were not a high priority for the Trump administration. As of early 2021, information on the federal government's SDG website is sparse, with multiple data gaps and outdated information. Despite Federal inaction, however, many other US-based entities have used the SDGs as an important guide to policy development and program implementation:

> … American leadership is not absent. Cities, states, universities, philanthropies, corporations, and NGOs have embraced the SDGs to advance social, economic, and environmental progress in communities across the United States, providing a platform for American local and global engagement on sustainable development. (Pipa & Brown, 2019)

As you consider how, if at all, to incorporate the SDGs into your policy analysis work, there a few things to keep in mind.

- The SDGs don't have the force of law. Unless codified by federal, state, or local governments, the SDGs don't create binding obligations for individuals, firms, or governments.

Exhibit 11-2   Sustainable Development Goals

Indicators should be disaggregated, where relevant, by income, sex, age, race, ethnicity, migratory status, disability and geographic location, or other characteristics.

1. **No poverty**: End poverty in all its forms everywhere

2. **Zero hunger**: End hunger, achieve food security and improved nutrition and promote sustainable agriculture

3. **Good health and well-being**: Ensure healthy lives and promote well-being for all at all ages

4. **Quality education**: Ensure inclusive and equitable quality education and promote lifelong learning opportunities for all

5. **Gender equality**: Achieve gender equality and empower all women and girls

6. **Clean water and sanitation**: Ensure availability and sustainable management of water and sanitation for all

7. **Affordable and clean energy**: Ensure access to affordable, reliable, sustainable, and modern energy for all

8. **Decent work and economic growth**: Promote sustained, inclusive, and sustainable economic growth, full and productive employment, and decent work for all

9. **Industry, innovation, and infrastructure**: Build resilient infrastructure, promote inclusive and sustainable industrialization, and foster innovation

10. **Reduced inequalities**: Reduce inequality within and among countries

11. **Sustainable cities and communities**: Make cities and human settlements inclusive, safe, resilient, and sustainable

12. **Responsible consumption and production**: Ensure sustainable consumption and production patterns

13. **Climate action**: Take urgent action to combat climate change and its impacts

14. **Life below water**: Conserve and sustainably use the oceans, seas, and marine resources for sustainable development

15. **Life on land**: Protect, restore, and promote sustainable use of terrestrial ecosystems, sustainably manage forests, combat desertification, and halt and reverse land degradation and halt biodiversity loss

16. **Peace, justice, and strong institutions**: Promote peaceful and inclusive societies for sustainable development, provide access to justice for all, and build effective, accountable, and inclusive institutions at all levels

17. **Partnerships for the goals**: Strengthen the means of implementation and revitalize the Global Partnership for Sustainable Development

Source: (UNGA, 2020)

- Pursuit of all 17 SDGs implies the need to make trade-offs among individual goals. For example, faster economic growth (SDG#8) may lead to more pollution from production (SDG#12); similarly, construction of new infrastructure (SDG#9) may threaten terrestrial ecosystems (SDG#15). The SDGs have little to say about how to make such trade-offs.

- Each SDG is an aspirational goal, not a tangible public policy proposal. Operationalizing each goal requires that specific policies be developed to reflect the circumstances of the jurisdiction for which they're being considered. In turn, achievement of the SDGs depends largely on the successful implementation of well-designed policies.

- The SDGs leave unanswered many policy-relevant questions including, for example, the appropriate role of government in achieving them, the best means of avoiding market and government failures when pursuing them, and how to work across jurisdictions when coordinated action is needed.

Given these limitations, you may wonder why I am bothering to take the time to present the SDGs. One practical reason is that sustainability in general and the SDGs in particular have entered the US policy discourse over the past several years. Being familiar with at least the basic concepts will help you be a more effective participant in such conversations.

Moreover, when you look at policy issues through the lens of sustainability, the SDGs can serve as a checklist of things to look for. It may turn out that a policy you've developed may support progress toward more than one goal, perhaps giving you additional ideas about how to improve its design to maximize its positive impact. Conversely, you may realize that despite your best intentions, a policy that you're working on may have adverse impacts on the pursuit of one or more of the goals (i.e., an unintended consequence). At a minimum, you'll want to stop and think about whether the potential upsides of the policy justify its potential downsides. Alternatively, you may go back to the drawing board to develop an improved version of the policy to avoid undermining the SDGs.

To recap our discussion of the sustainability lens, we first noted the contested nature of the word itself. We then considered three possible ways of interpreting the concept of sustainability. We looked at Pettibone's five-part framework comprising ecological limits, a long-term outlook, a complex-systems view, deliberative and collective decisionmaking, and a reflexive approach that embraces continual learning. We then defined sustainability in terms of natural, manufactured, human, and social capital stocks and their associated benefit flows. Doing so allows us to conceptualize the process of preserving productive capacity to meet the needs of future generations. Finally, we looked at sustainability as the pursuit of the 17 sustainable development goals that grew out of the 1987 Brundtland Commission report. While extraordinarily ambitious, the SDGs provide policy analysts with an aspirational checklist by which to examine both current conditions and potential new public policies.

11.3 THE SCIENCE AND TECHNOLOGY LENS

Looking through the lens of science and technology is especially important at a time when the pace of change is accelerating. Consider the smartphone. The iPhone was introduced in 2007 and smartphones reached near universal market penetration in little more than a decade. There are about 270 million smartphone users in the United States (Newzoo, 2020). The impacts of smartphone technology on society have been profound. Many people spend hours a day focused on their phones. Twitter and Facebook were launched a couple years before the iPhone, but smartphones were like steroids for social media platforms, which in turn reshaped politics, celebrity, and journalism. Mobile technology has radically altered how we shop, bank, socialize, and get from Point A to Point B. It has also facilitated political action and street protest, on both the left and the right. The ubiquity of smartphones has given rise to the scourge of distracted driving, disputes over siting of cell towers, and concerns about privacy and identity theft. Moreover, the ability to film law enforcement officers as they interact with the community has changed society's understanding of policing. These changes are all the more remarkable (and disruptive) because of the speed with which they happened.

But smartphones are just one of many scientific discoveries and technological advances rapidly reshaping society. These changes have important implications for public policy. Policy may, for example, hinder or facilitate disruptive scientific and technological progress which, depending on your perspective, could be a good thing or a not-so-good thing. And emerging concerns, like the ethics of genetic engineering, the consequences of global warming, or illegal behavior on the 'dark web,' may force policymakers to address issues they've not encountered before. Technological progress also has large impacts on the economy, as startup ventures eager to become the next Google, Amazon, or Facebook work tirelessly to render existing business models obsolete. As startups displace incumbent firms, the demise of once prosperous industries and the loss of jobs often take a political turn, with policymakers stuck in the middle. Finally, as you think about how policy proposals might play out in the future, you can't take the current state of science and technology as a given; instead, you must be alert to the potential impact of future disruptive technological and scientific changes on the performance of new public policies.

This section offers a few suggestions for thinking about science and technology in the context of policy analysis. We start with a quick review of the relationships among research, development, science, and technology and then turn to the mechanisms of disruptive changes. Finally, we'll take a look at some ways in which you can incorporate scientific and technological change into policy analysis.

11.3.1 The Nature of Scientific and Technological Change

We first need to clarify a few terms. Let's start with *science*. We encountered the term earlier when I defined the scientific method as operating at the intersection of logic (Chapter 5) and evidence (Chapter 6). In this context, we go beyond policy analysis itself and consider the implications of science for society writ large. In short, the scientific method refers broadly to efforts to understand how the world works. It aims to characterize the behavior of and causal connections among phenomena of interest, in fields like chemistry, physics, biology, ecology, psychology, and economics.

On the other hand, *technology* necessitates more than a purely scientific understanding of these phenomena and includes intentional efforts to manipulate them to useful ends. For example, think of tangible manufactured products. Both the product itself and the process by which it is made are instances of technology. Suppose you're an engineer designing the brake system for an automobile. The movements of the car will reflect the laws of physics related to mass, force, and thermodynamics, but the performance of your brake system will also depend on how you design and manufacture it. The former is science; the latter is technology. Technologies are not confined to tangible objects. They may also be intangible, like the supply chain algorithms used by Amazon, the techniques used by a skilled craftsman to make furniture, or the systems used to administer the nationwide banking system.

In short, science is about understanding how the world works, and technology is about applying that understanding to create useful outcomes. Though distinct, the two concepts are linked. Sometimes, science precedes technology; other times, it's the reverse. Technology development, for example, often begins with scientific understanding and progresses to a technical solution (e.g., based on their understanding of electromagnetism and the properties of materials, engineers design new methods of producing batteries for electric vehicles). Sometimes, newly emerging scientific phenomena stimulate technology development (e.g., the COVID pandemic set off a race to develop new vaccines and therapeutics, and climate change has intensified work on renewable technologies).

In other cases, efforts to solve technical problems are the driving force behind scientific research. For example, developers may be in the midst of a technology development project when an unexpected problem forces them back to their labs to answer a scientific question (e.g., during deployment of commercial nuclear power in the 1950s, theoretical physicists were called in more than once to do additional basic scientific research in order to resolve technological problems that were impeding progress (Stoneham, 2010)). We also sometimes look to science to help us understand the effects of technologies, particularly as regards their environmental, health, and safety impacts (e.g., the climate effects of fossil fuel combustion, the health effects of smoking, or the efficacy of vaccines).

Advances in both scientific knowledge and technical knowhow typically result from **research and development** (R&D). R&D is the systematic and creative process of accumulating new knowledge and developing new applications of that knowledge. R&D comprises three activities. **Basic research** increases the stock of fundamental knowledge about phenomena of interest without regard to its specific application. **Applied research** also aims to increase the stock of knowledge but is targeted at practical knowledge needed to facilitate or support a specific application or end use. Finally, **experimental development** takes basic and applied research and combines it with newly developed practical and experiential knowledge to create new products or processes or to enhance existing products and processes (OMB, 2021). In general, basic research focuses on science, experimental development focuses on technology, and applied research focuses on both.

The results of R&D are usually new technologies, a deeper scientific understanding, or a combination of the two. But when it comes to applying a science and technology lens to policy analysis, we can't stop there. We need to go further and think about how innovations generated by R&D spread widely (or only narrowly) throughout everyday life. In short, we need to think about the move from technology development to technology deployment. After studying two centuries of technological progress, Joseph Schumpeter used the phrase **"creative destruction"** to describe how successful technologies come to permeate society (1943, p. 83). Schumpeter's critical insight is that two events must happen before innovation affects society in a meaningful way. First, researchers and entrepreneurs must *create* new ways of doing things that offer firms and consumers tangible benefits that exceed those of the status quo. Second, users of the new technology must decide that its lower costs, increased productivity, or other benefits are sufficiently valuable that they are willing to abandon or, in Schumpeter's words, *destroy* business as usual and embrace the new technology (Linquiti, 2015).

When considering whether to adopt a new technology, a firm or consumer typically considers three factors: cost, performance, and uncertainty (Tassey, 1997). If a new technology is more expensive than an existing technology (e.g., electric vehicles relative to gas-powered vehicles), then the motivation to adopt it will be weaker, especially if its performance improvement over the status quo is modest. On the other hand, if the new technology offers substantial benefits relative to the current approach (e.g., a mobile phone versus a landline), then its adoption may be quick even if it carries a higher price. In addition, uncertainty may impede the diffusion of new technology. If there are questions about the performance or reliability of the new technology or about the ease of integrating it with existing ways of doing business (e.g., a car buyer's concern that there won't be sufficient charging capacity to make an electric vehicle practical), then its adoption will likely lag.

The final characteristic of scientific and technological innovation worth noting reflects the cumulative or aggregated effect of individual choices about technology adoption. Both the extent and speed of technology adoption matter. If only a few firms and consumers move to the new technology, its social impact will likely be modest. And even if large numbers of firms and consumers make the change, but do so slowly, over a long period of time, then adaptation to it may not be especially difficult. But if, as with smartphones, large numbers of firms and consumers rapidly move to the new technology, then the consequences can be much more disruptive, a topic to which we turn in the next section.

11.3.2 The Potentially Disruptive Consequences of Scientific and Technological Change

The story of technological disruption is as old as civilization itself. The printing press displaced scribes. Automobiles displaced horse and buggy transportation. Broadband streaming services have (largely) displaced over-the-air TV broadcasts. With a moment's reflection, you can probably come up with your own examples of Schumpeter's creative destruction. The future looks no different:

> Groundbreaking emerging technologies—in fields such as artificial intelligence, quantum computing, gene editing, hypersonics, autonomy, and nanotechnology—are widely anticipated to have substantial economic and social impacts, affecting the ways people work, travel, learn, live, and engage with others and the surrounding world. The impacts are likely to be felt by people of all ages, across most industries, and by government. (CRS, 2020, p. 1)

To further illustrate the types of scientific and technological changes that may have significant societal effects, Exhibit 11-3 provides the titles of analyses done by the science and technology support agencies of the US Congress and the UK Parliament in recent years. As you can see, the list is long and diverse.

Slow and incremental changes in science and technology usually pose less of a challenge for policymakers (and thus policy analysts) than do disruptive changes. **Disruption** is not a precise concept, but it's clear that there are several important drivers of the phenomenon.

- *Rapid* change gives firms and individuals less time to adapt to new ways of doing things, potentially causing a misalignment between their preferred approach and the approach necessitated by the new technology.

Exhibit 11-3 Illustrative Examples of Policy-Relevant Science and Technology Topics[a]

US GAO Technology Assessments

50 to 200 pages, issued 2015 to 2020

- 5G wireless: capabilities and challenges for an evolving network
- Artificial intelligence: benefits and challenges of technologies to augment patient care
- Artificial intelligence: benefits and challenges of machine learning in drug development
- Artificial intelligence: emerging opportunities, challenges, and implications
- Chemical innovation: technologies to make processes and products more sustainable
- COVID-19: data quality and considerations for modeling and analysis
- Critical infrastructure protection: protecting the electric grid from geomagnetic disturbances
- Forensic technology: algorithms used in federal law enforcement
- Internet of things: status and implications of an increasingly connected world
- Irrigated agriculture: technologies, practices, and implications for water scarcity
- Medical devices: capabilities and challenges of technologies to enable rapid diagnoses
- Municipal freshwater scarcity: using technology to improve distribution system efficiency
- Nuclear reactors: status and challenges in development and deployment
- Reducing freshwater use in hydraulic fracturing and thermoelectric power plant cooling

US GAO Science and Tech Spotlights

2 to 4 pages, issued September 2019 to March 2021

- 5G wireless
- Agile software development
- Air quality sensors
- Blockchain and distributed ledger technologies
- Consumer electronics recycling
- Contact tracing apps
- Coronaviruses
- COVID-19 modeling
- COVID-19 testing
- COVID-19 vaccine development

US GAO Science and Tech Spotlights, continued

- CRISPR gene editing
- Deepfakes
- E-cigarettes
- Genomic sequencing of infectious pathogens
- Herd immunity for COVID-19
- Hypersonic weapons
- Nuclear microreactors
- Opioid vaccines
- Probabilistic genotyping software
- Quantum technologies
- Social distancing during pandemics
- Tracing the source of chemical weapons
- Vaccine safety

UK POSTNotes

4 pages, issued February 2020 to February 2021

- 3D bioprinting in medicine
- A resilient UK food system
- Artificial Intelligence and health care
- Bioenergy with carbon capture and storage
- Climate change–biodiversity interactions
- Cloud computing
- Digital sequence information
- Edge computing
- Food and drink reformulation to reduce fat, sugar and salt
- Food fraud
- Heat networks
- Infrastructure and climate change
- Interpretable machine learning
- Low-carbon aviation fuels
- Managing land uses for environmental benefits
- Marine renewables
- Mental health impacts of COVID-19 on NHS staff
- Natural mitigation of flood risks
- Online extremism
- Online safety education
- Remote sensing and machine learning
- Screen use and health in young people
- UK insect decline and extinction
- Woodland creation

Sources: (GAO, 2021b; POST, 2021)

[a]US GAO: Government Accountability Office; UK POST: Parliamentary Office of Science and Technology. The GAO "Science and Tech Spotlight" series was initiated in September 2019, the UK POSTnote series in May 1989.

- *Radical* change necessitates more extensive modifications of current practices to accommodate new technologies; such modifications may be costly, difficult, or force the abandonment of existing assets prior to the end of their useful life.

- *Convergent* technologies bring together multiple disparate functions in one application, causing potentially disruptive changes across multiple domains. For example, smartphones offer in one device the functionality of a telephone, camera, address book, calculator, radio, television, and a library of books, among many other features. In turn, this single technology doesn't just disrupt one aspect of current practices, it disrupts several at the same time.

- *Novel technologies* that lack historical analogues are more disruptive than technologies that are simply a new means of achieving an existing function. For example, the shift from horses to automobiles (a novel technology) was far more disruptive than the current shift to hybrids and electric vehicles, which don't fundamentally change the nature of personal mobility.

- *Widespread* change that affects large numbers of firms, consumers, and workers may be more disruptive than changes that are concentrated within small sectors of society. Geographic reach is also important. Changes confined to a single region are apt to be less disruptive than nationwide changes.

Given the often-significant disruption caused by technological change, it's important to recall why such change happens in the first place. New technologies generally diffuse through society only if firms or consumers find value in them. Otherwise, no one would be interested in changing their current practices. If you see new technologies being adopted, then it's a safe bet that at least some folks are being made better off by them. At the same time, the diffusion of new technologies also suggests that firms and individuals with a stake in the status quo may be suffering adverse consequences. You can think about it this way: it's great to be on the innovative side of Schumpeter's creative destruction, but if you're part of the enterprise that's being destroyed, it's a different matter.

In short, technological change routinely produces winners and losers. Sometimes the losses are tangible as firms lose market share and workers lose jobs. In other cases, the losses are intangible, as, for example, once prosperous communities face economic decline or, as we considered in Chapter 8, when technological change disturbs folks' sense of security and personal sense of control over their own lives. With profits at risk for firms, livelihoods at risk for workers, and a sense of stability at risk for folks in general, it's no wonder that disruptive technological changes can be controversial. Such controversies often become politicized as innovators seek changes in public policy to facilitate their success, and beneficiaries of the status quo aspire to use public policy to obstruct change:

> [P]olitics are often neglected by ... researchers, who tend to assume widespread support for progress in science and technology. In [several] cases, the losing interest groups were able to convince politicians to block, slow, or alter government support for scientific and technical progress. ... Exactly who are these 'losers'? Depending on the form it takes and the economic and political environment in which it appears, technological change can threaten labor, corporations, consumers, governments, and so on. ... Resisters can organize and use their financial or electoral clout to influence government to slow technological change via a range of mechanisms: taxes, tariffs, anti-trust legislation, licensing, standards setting and regulations, manipulation of guidelines for research, and so on. (Sapolsky & Taylor, 2011, pp. 33–34)

To better understand and potentially predict these political controversies, it may be helpful to recall some of the questions we introduced in Chapter 10 in the context of the political lens:

- Who wins and who loses as a consequence of the technological change?

- How big are their wins and losses?

- How politically powerful are winners and losers?

- Are the wins and losses concentrated among a small group or broadly spread across society?

Having looked through the science and technology lens to consider the potential societal disruption and subsequent political disputes caused by advances in scientific knowledge and technical knowhow, it's time to consider how such issues may affect your policy analysis.

11.3.3 Incorporating Scientific and Technological Change in Policy Analysis

The links among science, technology, and public policy have been evident for decades. For example, the Technology Assessment Act of 1972, which established the Congressional Office of Technology Assessment (OTA), noted that:

> As technology continues to change and expand rapidly, its applications are large and growing in scale; and increasingly extensive, pervasive, and critical

in their impact, beneficial and adverse, on the natural and social environment. Therefore, it is essential that, to the fullest extent possible, the consequences of technological applications be anticipated, understood, and considered in determination of public policy on existing and emerging national problems. (2 USC 472(2)(a,b))

Alas, OTA no longer exists. In 1995, amid sporadic accusations of liberal bias and a desire to cut Congressional spending, OTA became a target for then House Speaker Newt Gingrich and OTA was shut down. It operated for more than 20 years, and at its peak, in the early 1990s, OTA had a staff of over 200 and an annual budget of about $20 million (CRS, 2020). OTA's Congressional sister agencies—the Congressional Research Service and the Government Accountability Office—have picked up some of its functions but not at the same scale or level of activity. Even though the institutional capacity to provide advice about science and technology has diminished, according to the National Academy of Public Administration, the need for such advice has not:

Profound scientific and technological changes that are accelerating in this century pose ever greater challenges for the U.S. government to consider how to anticipate issues arising from these advancements, and then fashion a responsive public policy in a timely manner. Congress not only seeks to adequately protect the American people from abuses and downside risks inherent with these changes, but also to consider policies that might harness them in order to enhance safety and prosperity for the Nation's citizens. (Fretwell, Rejeski, Hendler, Peroff, & McCord, 2019, p. 1)

Congress, of course, is just one group of policymakers who need advice about science and technology. Other branches of the federal government, as well as state and local policymakers have similar needs. But the (mostly) unmet need of Congress for such advice illustrates the importance of the topic and motivates my suggestion that you consider it in your policy analysis.

There are different ways in which issues of science and technology might relate to public policy. Exhibit 11-4 describes several ways to characterize such issues. Depending on your approach, different research questions will be relevant.

As you work to answer the research questions posed by Exhibit 11-4, several specific topics merit your consideration. In particular, GAO's Science, Technology Assessment, and Analytics Team has suggested that six aspects of technological change deserve routine consideration by policymakers: economics, ethics, privacy, safety, security, and social stability (GAO, 2018). While there is some overlap among these categories, consideration of all six will reduce the chance of overlooking something important. But be sure to think expansively as you consider these factors, particularly because the impacts of technological change can be far-reaching.

Exhibit 11-4 A Typology of Science and Technology Characterizations

Purpose of Characterization	Sample Research Questions
Describe status of and challenges to the development of a new technology	• What is the current state of efforts to develop the technology? What are the potential applications of the technology? • Does the maturity and readiness of the technology vary across different applications or sectors where it is being developed? • What technical and economic challenges to the development of the technology exist? • How likely is it that such challenges can be overcome by the technology's developers? How quickly might they be overcome?
Identify policy measures to facilitate development and deployment of a new technology	• How does the new technology compare to existing technologies with respect to cost, performance, quality, and uncertainty? • What is the likely market penetration of the technology? • What policy and market barriers might impede development and deployment of the technology? How might such barriers be overcome through public policy? • Are competitive incumbent technologies receiving implicit or explicit support from current public policies? If so, should those policies be modified? • Which potential new technologies merit supportive public policies and which do not?
Understand the scientific implications of a technology	• To what degree might a new or existing technology pose environmental, human health, or occupational safety risks? • How are scientific phenomena (e.g., the global climate or the state of infectious disease) and the associated risks likely to change over time? • To what degree might a new or existing technology mitigate such risks?
Assess opportunities and challenges that may result from the use of a technology	• What are the expected benefits of the technology in its intended application? • What sectors of society and the economy might be directly affected by the technology? • Might there be impacts on sectors other than the ones in which it is deployed? • How disruptive might the effects be, as a consequence of how rapidly and radically the technology changes the status quo, how widely it is deployed, and the types of existing technologies it displaces? • What unintended consequences may arise from deployment of the technology? • How might the direct and indirect impacts of the technology differ across socioeconomic or regional lines, or among industries or other sectors of the economy?
Assess policy options related to a technology	• What are the costs and benefits of new and existing technologies? • To what degree is government intervention to steer the course of technology likely to be beneficial? • If deemed beneficial, which policy tools would be most useful? • What policy options could be used to minimize adverse consequences and maximize positive impacts associated with a transition to the new technology?

Source: Based, in part, on GAO (2021).

Economics: Because technological change is typically associated with creative destruction, it affects firms, industries, workers, consumers, communities, and countries. For example, robotics and automated manufacturing will reshape the workforce, increasing the need for some skills and rendering others obsolete. Jobs will disappear in some sectors while worker shortages may occur in others. Global trade may also be affected, as some countries deal more effectively than others with these changes.

Ethics: Technological change can raise ethical questions that society hasn't previously addressed. For example, genome editing offers the possibility of preventing or treating debilitating diseases but runs the risk of creating unanticipated and undesirable hereditary modifications in the population writ large. The prospect of engineering the essence of life itself also raises profound moral and ethical questions.

Privacy: The right to hold one's personal information confidential is a core value in the US national ethos; technological change has the potential to undermine that right. For example, brain–computer interfaces are systems that connect the brain to external devices as a means of treating hearing or vision loss. Such systems, however, mean that signals from within one's brain are being digitized and manipulated on devices accessible by others.

Safety: Evolving technologies play an important role in safety, ranging from the personal level (e.g., 3-D printable guns) to the community level (e.g., 911 emergency systems) to the global level (e.g., national military capabilities). For example, hypersonic weapons, not yet a reality but currently under development, would reach speeds up to 3,800 mph and be very challenging to defend against. Countries that possess such weapons would enjoy a substantial military advantage over those that don't, potentially upsetting the global balance of power, stimulating an arms race, or leading to armed conflict (GAO, 2019a).

Security: As discussed in Chapter 8, a sense of security and well-being is an important element of healthy community life. But cybercrime, identity theft, and the posting of defamatory content on social media are all made easier by a highly networked world. Moreover, the digital divide—where less prosperous communities don't have ready access to the internet—means that many folks are being increasingly left behind as more and more essential activities move online.

Societal Stability: Some emerging technologies have the potential to fundamentally alter human relationships. Consider, for example, the proliferation of deepfakes, which are videos, photos, or audio clips that appear to authentically represent a real person but are in fact generated using artificial intelligence. The latest animated Hollywood movie might be enjoyable, but the technology can be put to more sinister uses. According to GAO, most current deepfakes are pornographic and often victimize women. And, in a post-truth era, deepfakes have the potential to undermine public confidence in audiovisual material and to sway the electoral process or provoke civil discord (GAO, 2020).

In suggesting that you incorporate the prospect of scientific and technological change in your policy analysis, I am not asking you to predict the future with complete accuracy. The path of technological change is circuitous. Some anticipated changes may never materialize, and others may emerge unexpectedly (CRS, 2019b). But continuous attention to the potential for major scientific and technological change not only minimizes the risk of surprises but also will allow more time for thoughtful and proactive policy responses to changes if and when they do occur.

To recap our discussion of the science and technology lens, we identified several important considerations. We reviewed the ways in which scientific and technological innovations originate in R&D and then diffuse through society. Technological changes may be particularly disruptive when they are rapid, radical, convergent, novel, and widespread. Moreover, because technological change is usually the result of creative destruction, it typically produces both winners and losers who often resort to political action to advance their interests. When thinking about the potential impacts of disruptive scientific and technological change, policy analysts should consider six types of impacts: economic, ethical, privacy, safety, security, and social stability.

CHAPTER SUMMARY

This chapter presented the final three lenses through which you can examine policy issues: the legal lens, the sustainability lens, and the science and technology lens. A summary of the material relevant to each lens appears as the final paragraph of, respectively, Sections 11.1, 11.2, and 11.3.

DISCUSSION QUESTIONS

1. As we saw in this chapter, the executive and judicial branches play prominent roles in policymaking. To what degree do you think this is appropriate? Has the legislative branch delegated too much authority to the executive? Has the role of the judiciary been inappropriately expanded in recent years as the result of vaguely worded or outdated legislation?

2. Think about a recent Supreme Court case that was decided by a closely split court. Which side do you think was right? To what degree is your opinion shaped by legal reasoning or by policy reasoning? Do you think the Court applied the right form of reasoning to the case?

3. How would you define sustainability? Is the concept of sustainability sufficiently precise to permit its inclusion in all policy analyses? Why? Why not?

4. Pick one of the Sustainable Development Goals that interests you. How would you incorporate it in a policy analysis? What aspects of that SDG seem most relevant, least relevant? What aspects are ambiguous? Would pursuit of that SDG compromise the ability to attain other SDGs?

5. Think about driverless autonomous vehicles. As they become more popular, what's sorts of impacts will they have on society? Which of those impacts are a matter of public policy? Which new policies, if any, would you recommend to address a proliferation of autonomous vehicles?

6. Identify a disruptive technological change that you suspect will become widespread in the next decade. How will it affect society? What are its upsides and downsides? What, if any, if a client or important stakeh changes should be made to public policy to increase its positive impacts or to limit its negative impacts?

PART FOUR

THE BUILDING BLOCKS OF POLICY ANALYSIS

WITHOUT THE RIGHT MAP, YOU MAY HAVE TROUBLE REACHING YOUR DESTINATION.

Let's take our bearings. Part I of the book introduced you to the classical models of prospective and retrospective policy analysis. Both are powerful tools for generating insight into important policy issues but also frequently come up short for several inescapable reasons. Accordingly, I argued that we need a new understanding of policy analysis, a rebooted version of the field that strengthens its foundation while also expanding its scope.

Part II focused on the foundation by first stressing the importance of meta-cognition—how we think about thinking—and then describing the integration of logic and evidence to yield the strongest possible conclusions about both current conditions and future outcomes. Part II wrapped up by describing the mindset of an effective policy analyst.

Part III then focused on an expanded understanding of policy analysis that goes beyond the typical subjects of applied microeconomics, political science, and quantitative methods. In Part III, I advocated a panoptic approach that looks at policy issues through multiple lenses at the same time. In particular, I identified seven lenses that almost always deserve consideration when doing policy analysis: equity, economics, politics, institutions, the law, sustainability, and science and technology.

Having broadened the discussion in Part III, I'd now like to narrow our scope here in Part IV. While the first three parts of the book reviewed analytic processes in which we use critical thinking to break phenomena of interest down into their constituent parts, this part of the book focuses on putting the pieces back together to yield a more holistic view of things. The tools you'll find here in Part IV can help you better map out the contexts in which policy issues arise and solutions are attempted. With such a map in hand, your policy analysis can better reflect the reality of the situation that you're dealing with and improve your chances of success. And it may help you avoid the kind of mishaps that await our unsuspecting canoeists in the cartoon. In particular, the four chapters in this part of the book will help you learn how to:

- Use systems thinking to develop a deeper appreciation of the causes and effects of policy problems, to better understand the interrelationships among them, and to appreciate public policy as an intervention in complex and dynamic systems (Chapter 12),

- Recognize that all public policies can be viewed as actions taken today with the potential to change conditions in the future, meaning that the ability to visualize the future is an essential skill for all aspiring policy analysts to master (Chapter 13),

- Apply inclusive, user-focused design principles to revise existing policies and programs, to create new policy options that reflect a coherent theory about how change happens, and to strategically align the components of individual programs and policies (Chapter 14), and

- Complement your analytic and cognitive skills with practical skills that can help you conduct policy analysis in an efficient, ethical, and emotionally intelligent fashion (Chapter 15).

The final section of Chapter 15 comprises an afterword for the book as a whole. It recaps the key takeaways that, at least for me, are the most important. My hope is that, five years from now, even if many of the details of the book have left your mind, you might still be able to recall these takeaways.

CHAPTER TWELVE

INCORPORATING SYSTEMS THINKING IN POLICY ANALYSIS

Unintended consequences frequently undermine the efficacy of new public policies. Whether it's a highway widening project that only leads to more traffic, a national prohibition on alcohol that leads to an increase in organized crime, or a military incursion that destabilizes a country and leads to civil war, new policies can sometimes leave their sponsors regretting their enactment. Such unintended consequences typically have their roots in a narrow focus on a single problem and a single solution. Policymakers often fail to recognize that public policy is only one element in a complex mix of factors that drive the outcomes of policy. Moreover, many policy issues are multifaceted conditions, like crime or income inequality, that have multiple causes and effects.

Unfortunately, the classical model of policy analysis, with its starting point in a single 'problem' and its linear progression toward a recommended policy, can make matters worse. Sometimes, a dysfunctional public program (i.e., a failed prior attempt to solve a problem) causes new and unexpected effects. In short, the world is often much more complicated than suggested by the classical model of policy analysis. Systems thinking can be helpful in such cases because, by looking at the totality of the situation, it may suggest multiple intervention points for public policy and help us anticipate the likely outcomes of such interventions, especially when those outcomes are not directly and immediately connected to the intervention.

This chapter starts in Section 12.1 with a definition of systems thinking and then turns in Section 12.2 to the links between it and policy analysis. Each of the next three sections reviews a specific technique for systems analysis—problem trees, influence diagrams, and causal loop diagrams—while Section 12.6 compares the three techniques by highlighting

Learning Objectives

By studying this chapter, you should be able to:

- Explain systems thinking and characterize its primary components.

- Describe the rationale for incorporating systems thinking into policy analysis.

- Build a problem tree that clarifies the causes and consequences of a public policy problem.

- Build an influence diagram that describes the broader system in which a policy problem arises and that identifies important causal relationships among the elements of the system.

- Build a causal loop diagram that not only describes a system and its constituent elements but also depicts feedback loops and time lags.

- Explain causal polarity, stocks and flows, and balancing and reinforcing feedback loops.

- Explain the trade-offs among the three forms of system maps.

- Identify the limitations of systems thinking when it comes to policy analysis.

their similarities and differences. Finally, Section 12.7 reviews the limitations of systems analysis and the risks of mistaking your understanding of a system for the system itself.

12.1 WHAT IS SYSTEMS THINKING?

For this chapter to make sense, we need to start with a definition of systems thinking. The highlights are listed in Exhibit 12-1. At its core, a systems perspective recognizes that many of the things we care about—policy issues, human behavior, the natural environment, or public health, to name just a few examples—arise not in isolation but occur in a larger context in which multiple factors play an important role in shaping the nature, behavior, and consequences of the thing we care about. A system comprises a set of **elements** whose interconnections determine—at least in part—their behavior.[1] An element can be just about anything: a person, a virus cell, a government institution, a private firm, a car on the highway, an endangered species, or a nation-state.

To constitute a system, the elements must be in **interdependent causal relationships** with one another. In other words, a change in one element leads to changes in other elements, or in the first element itself. For example, a group of buyers and sellers is a system (i.e., a market) because the behavior of each market participant has an effect on other participants. If a new low-cost producer enters the market, buyers benefit when the market equilibrates at a lower price and existing producers suffer by virtue of the additional competition for their customers. By contrast, a bag of potato chips doesn't comprise a system because the elements are not in a causal relationship. Taking one chip from the bag doesn't change the nature of the remaining chips.

Exhibit 12-1   Key Aspects of Systems Thinking

- Interdependent relationships among elements
- Emergent phenomena at the system level
- Dynamic perspective that considers past, present, and future
- Potential time lags between causes and effects
- Delineation of system boundaries
- Differentiation of stocks and flows

---

[1] Another driver of an element's behavior are its intrinsic characteristics, which exist irrespective of the other elements in the system.

Exhibit 12-2 lists some common examples of systems that you might run across in your work as a policy analyst. You'll notice that in some cases, multiple systems are linked such that we care not only about the behavior of each system but also about the nature of the linkages between them.

Exhibit 12-2 Examples of Systems

- **Human Systems**
  - Firms and Markets
  - Politics and Governments
  - Legal Systems
  - Schools and Universities
  - Sports teams
  - Families
  - Neighborhoods

- **Natural Systems**
  - Weather and Climate
  - Tides, Waves, and Currents
  - Plants and Animals
  - Ecosystems
  - Agriculture
  - Human Bodies
  - Epidemics

- **Engineered Systems**
  - Airports
  - Factories
  - Roads and Highways
  - Health-care facilities
  - Housing
  - Telecommunications
  - Military weapons
  - Electric power grids

- **Linked Systems**
  - Human Action and Climate Change
  - Individual Behaviors, Physiological Responses, and Public Health Consequences
  - Transportation Infrastructure, Job & Residence Locations, and Commuting Preferences

---

An important feature of a system is that its behavior can be characterized simultaneously at two levels: the micro and the macro. At the micro level, we study the behavior of a system's individual elements and the nature of their interdependent relationships with the other elements of the system. At the macro level, we take a more holistic perspective and study the behavior of the system as a whole. At the macro level, we're interested primarily in **emergent phenomena** that are not apparent from the individual elements themselves but only emerge when the elements of a system interact. For example, the cars on a highway (and the capacity of the roads on which they're driven) are elements in a system. If too many folks try to go somewhere at the same time (e.g., morning rush hour), new phenomena emerge: congestion, stop and go traffic (with more fender-bender accidents, more air pollution, and lower fuel economy), and longer commute times. In short, a system is more than just the elements that comprise it; it's also an entity unto itself.

In addition to studying the behavior of individual elements at the micro level and emergent system behavior at the macro level, systems analysis also encourages us to take a **dynamic view** of the phenomenon we're studying. In most cases, the current state of affairs doesn't exist in isolation of the prior state of affairs. Past events and conditions typically go a long way toward explaining the current situation. For example, historical practices of redlining (i.e., formal policies that excluded families of color from owning homes in some neighborhoods) go a long way toward explaining current patterns of residential segregation in many US cities (Rothstein, 2017).

Moreover, systems analysis helps us make more educated projections about how the future may unfold as the result of the interaction of a system's elements and its propensity to display emergent behavior. Over the past couple of decades, for example, an increase in the number of women admitted to medical schools has led to an increase in the number of female physicians; seeing med schools and professional practice as a single system allows us to anticipate the changing composition of the physician workforce in the years to come as the result of admission decisions being made today.[2] Doing so can be particularly important in policy analysis when we're thinking about introducing a policy intervention in one part of the system and trying to anticipate how other parts of the system may change as a consequence.

The dynamic nature of systems also alerts us to time delays that create potential **lags** between a change in one element and a subsequent change in another element. A new highway, for example, may initially lead to reduced congestion but later—after a few years—lead to more suburban housing development and a return of congestion. By contrast, a lane closure on an existing highway at rush hour will exacerbate congestion within minutes.

As a practical matter, systems analysis requires us to set **boundaries** on the scope of our analysis, or put another way, on what is inside and outside the system. If we don't find a way to bound our analysis, we can end up with an unmanageably large set of things to consider. Suppose we're looking at a proposed change to the minimum wage. Should we just consider folks who currently have a job? Those who might hold jobs in the future? Should we look only at employment effects or extend the analysis to consumers who might pay higher prices or to business owners who might earn lower profits? Should we consider impacts on workers in foreign countries? There is no 'correct' answer to these questions. In policy analysis, we often take a pragmatic approach to setting the system boundary. If a potential effect of a contemplated policy action would be relevant to the thinking of policymakers as they decide what to do, then we want to set the system boundary expansively enough to capture that effect. Conversely, if the potential effect would have no bearing on the decision, we can set the boundaries more narrowly.

Deciding on the system boundary is not a trivial task; the decision can have a profound effect on the outcome of your analysis. If you define a particular

---

[2] Of course, there are many other factors that could be incorporated into a systems analysis of women in the medical workforce, including pay equity, advancement opportunities, differences across gender lines in fields of specialization, and so on.

phenomenon as beyond the boundary of the system, you're essentially saying that it (and the people affected by it) don't matter to the decision being made. That might be true, but it's best to be intentional in such cases, rather than excluding it simply by accident. As an example, recall from Chapter 9 that the Trump Administration estimated the social cost of carbon at $8 per ton of carbon dioxide while the Biden Administration pegged the number at $62 per ton. The primary driver of the difference between the two estimates is the analytic boundary. In the first, the boundary is a national one, focused only on impacts within the United States, while in the second case, the system is defined more expansively and includes the entire world.

Another feature of systems analysis is the attention paid to the difference between **stocks** and **flows**. A stock is a quantity measured at a point in time while a flow is a quantity measured over time. Continuing the example from above, the number of women graduating each year from medical school is a flow while the number of women who are practicing physicians at a particular point in time is a stock. Similarly, when we talked about sustainability in Chapter 11, we observed that a capital asset such as a factory (a stock that exists today) is capable of generating a stream of benefits (flows that occur in the future). As yet another example, if we want to use systems analysis to understand rush hour congestion on local roads, we need to think not only about how many cars are on the road at one time (a stock) but also about how many cars are entering and exiting the highway (inflows and outflows) over the course of the morning and afternoon commutes. Systems analysis can help us avoid the mistake of mixing up stocks and flows.

12.2 WHY INCORPORATE SYSTEMS THINKING IN POLICY ANALYSIS?

When we identify a policy problem and consider potential policy solutions, we are implicitly applying a **mental map** of how the world works. We need a mental map because the systems we're interested in are largely invisible (Eggers & O'Leary, 2009), comprising intangible behavioral tendencies and emergent phenomena that may exist only in passing. If we've understood the world correctly, then our analysis rests on a solid foundation. Unfortunately, complex systems usually drive the reality of difficult societal challenges while simple or erroneous mental models often drive policy (Sterman, 2000). If the gap between the reality of the system and our mental map of it is too large, then like the unsuspecting canoeists in the cartoon in the Introduction to Part IV, we may be in for a surprise. In such cases, a new policy may not only fail to solve the problem, it may make the problem worse or cause other problems.

In some cases, the classical model of policy analysis is the culprit. In a well-intentioned effort to teach students to find order in the chaos of the real world, policy schools may inadvertently encourage reductionist thinking that focuses narrowly on only one aspect of a situation or, as discussed throughout Part III, applies only a single analytic lens when a panoptic view is needed. And, later in their careers, omnipresent time, resource, and information constraints may tempt analysts to settle for a simple, yet flawed, view of how the world works. As Einstein is reported to have said: "Everything should be made as simple as possible, but not simpler" (Sessions, 1950, p. 89). Systems thinking is a prerequisite to sound policy analysis for at least three reasons:

- Policy problems arise in systems

- Public policies are implemented in systems

- Policy-relevant systems are largely invisible

Given the potential value of systems thinking in policy analysis, it's worth our time to delve a little deeper into the link between the two. Let's start with the concept of **policy resistance**, which refers to the tendency of an intervention (such as a new policy measure) to be undermined at least partially by the system's reaction to the new measure itself (Ghaffarzadegan, Lyneis, & Richardson, 2011; Lane, 2016; Sterman, 2012). For example, when it comes to energy efficiency improvements, we often see what is referred to as the rebound effect. If you buy a high mileage car, you may end up driving more because you can go farther on a dollar's worth of gas. If a policy analyst doesn't take account of the rebound effect when estimating the impact of a vehicle mileage standard, he or she will overestimate its impact in reducing fuel use and vehicle emissions. As another example, consider efforts to fight forest fires which, when successful, preserve trees and other fuel that in turn can lead to more intense and destructive fires in the future (U.S. Forest Service, 2003). Policy resistance often means that only some fraction of the hoped-for improvements are actually achieved by the policy.

Systems analysis can also be helpful in identifying **unintended consequences**. Of course, a system doesn't distinguish intended from unintended consequences. There are only consequences. We introduce a policy measure and the system reacts; it's usually our failure of foresight that leads us to label some outcomes as unintended. Consider the 2003 invasion of Iraq. Two expected outcomes were realized: the removal of Saddam Hussein as the country's leader and an answer to the question of whether Iraq possessed weapons of mass destruction. But there were unintended consequences as well: the collapse of civil society and a failure of hoped-for democratic governance. Many have argued that these consequences could have been anticipated and mitigated with a holistic and long-term view of how events might unfold. The value of systems thinking is that it pushes us to consider the many interdependent relationships in a system and how they play out over time. If we've done a good job of characterizing the system before acting, we have a means of looking at a proposed policy measure and tracing its likely impacts on the other elements of the system. In doing so, we stand a better chance of anticipating its consequences, rather than being surprised by them after policy adoption.

Finally, systems analysis can be particularly helpful when it comes to managing **wicked problems**. Examples of such problems include climate change, global terrorism, human trafficking, and the pernicious effects of money in politics. You'll recall from Chapter 3 that wicked problems have characteristics that make them especially difficult, or even impossible, to definitively resolve, including great complexity, significant uncertainty, and widely divergent societal viewpoints about how to address them. Rather than solving wicked problems, we can realistically hope only to manage them in ways that mitigate their most harmful consequences. A systems perspective gives us an expansive view of such problems and helps us monitor the impacts of efforts to manage them, potentially allowing us to make better policy and management decisions going forward.

The case for applying systems thinking to policy analysis was summarized in a 2012 National Research Council Study which, paraphrasing Sterman (2006), concluded that:

> Perhaps the most important location where systems thinking is called for is in making decisions and crafting policies that help navigate the complex structures that populate the world in which we live. Moreover, because there is a lack of a meaningful systems thinking capability, policies often fail or worsen the problem they are intended to solve. In a world that is interconnected, systems thinking is an iterative learning process in which we replace a reductionist, narrow, short-run, static view of the world with a holistic, broad, long-term dynamic view, reinventing our policies and institutions accordingly. (NRC, 2012, p. 62), *internal quotation marks removed*

12.3 REPRESENTING A SYSTEM WITH A PROBLEM TREE

You can apply systems thinking to policy analysis in one of three ways. Moving from simpler to more complex approaches, you might create a problem tree, an influence diagram, or a causal loop diagram. We'll discuss each in turn below, as well as the similarities and differences among the three approaches.

A problem tree focuses on just one part of a system. Back in Section 1.1, we saw that the classical model of prospective policy analysis uses a problem definition as its point of departure, so let's start there. More specifically, I suggested that a policy problem exists when there is a gap between current circumstances (i.e., a descriptive as-is condition) and our preferred circumstances (i.e., a prescriptive to-be condition). I recommended that you use the Five Whys technique to uncover the causal drivers of the problem and the Five So-Whats technique to identify its consequences. Doing so will certainly deepen your understanding of the problem, but in many cases, we need to go further.

Why is that? Because one limitation of the Five Whys and Five So-Whats technique is that it encourages linear thinking. When we ask why something happened, the technique assumes we get a single answer. In the Toyota Production System example, we asked why the factory machine stopped working and learned that it was because the circuit overloaded and tripped the circuit breaker. We then asked why the circuit overloaded, and so on. The same is true for answers to so what questions, where each consequence is assumed to have one follow-on consequence of its own. The result of this approach is a linear chain of causality with each factor having only one cause and one effect. In the world of public policy, things are usually more complicated.

As we talked about in Chapter 5, many phenomena are multivariate in nature, meaning that several factors combine to produce a result and, in turn, that each result may combine with other factors to yield multiple consequences. Rather than characterizing a policy problem with a linear chain of causes and effects, you can create a **problem tree**. The metaphor of a tree is intentional; the problem is the trunk, the causes are the roots, and the effects are the branches. Arrows denote causal relationships and point from causes to effects. A problem tree can be a helpful heuristic tool when you're faced with "a complex and vaguely defined problem" (Vesely, 2008, p. 69).

This may make more sense with an example. Exhibit 12-3 depicts a problem tree focused on workers over the age of 50 but younger than their official retirement age. The concern is that the level of employment of these workers is lower than we'd like. In probing the causes of the problem, we find some attributable to the individual worker (like their attitude or skillset) and some attributable to employers (like age discrimination or an unwillingness to offer flexible working arrangements). In turn, these drivers can lead to one of two consequences: either the worker gives up and leaves the workforce or the worker persists in seeking a job but remains unemployed. Either choice exacerbates the problem of too few older, preretirement age, workers. The problem tree technique also helps us sort out the consequences of the problem, some of which affect the economy and some of which affect the workers themselves.

Think back to the practice assignment I suggested in Section 1.1 when I asked you to draft a one paragraph problem definition for a policy issue you care about. I suggest that you now try something similar. Take the problem, causes, and consequences that you previously articulated in prose, and convert them into a problem tree like the one shown in Exhibit 12-3. There's no right or wrong approach here. Simply trying your hand at creating the tree will help you understand what the method is all about.

Bear in mind, however, that a problem tree is only a heuristic tool—a rule of thumb—to help you differentiate between the important and unimportant aspects of a policy issue. A colleague could come along and build a different tree, emphasizing alternative causes and effects, perhaps even identifying a different core problem. Moreover, two problem trees representing the same situation but built for separate clients would also likely

Exhibit 12-3 Illustrative Problem Tree: Employment of Older Workers

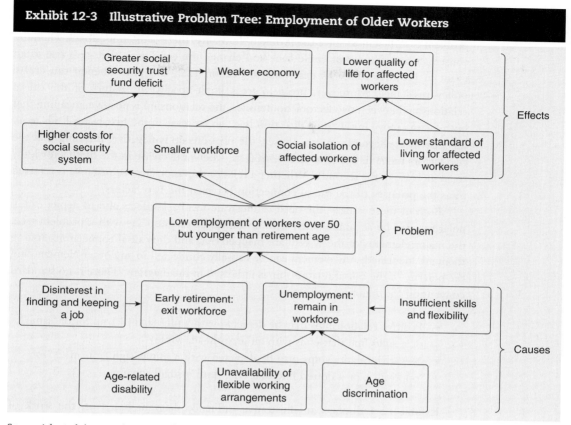

Source: Adapted, in part, from Veselý (2008) which itself is adapted from Doleželová (2007)

vary because of differences in normative assumptions about what constitutes a problem in the first place and which consequences are worth worrying about. The value of building a problem tree is often as much in the discipline it imposes on your thinking process as it is in the final product. Ultimately, the appropriate test of a problem tree isn't whether it's precisely right. Instead, ask whether the tree is helpful in creating insight and a common understanding when it's shared among participants in a policy debate.

12.4 REPRESENTING A SYSTEM WITH AN INFLUENCE DIAGRAM

As useful as a problem tree can be, the method has its limitations. Most importantly, it implicitly assumes that events flow in one direction only—from causes to effects, or in graphic form, from the roots of the tree to its branches. Unless you're careful when looking at a problem tree, you might mistakenly think that addressing the causes of a problem is sufficient to solve the problem. In reality, there is often **feedback** when the consequences of an event circle back and change the conditions that gave rise to an event in the first place. As described in Section 12.2, this phenomenon can create policy resistance. Moreover, problem trees don't specify the nature of the causal relationship between two factors. Sometimes, the relationship is positive, meaning that both factors move in the same direction (e.g., an increase in the first factor leads to an increase in the second); in other cases, the relationship is negative, meaning that the two factors move in opposite directions (e.g., where a decrease in the first factor leads to an increase in the second).[3] Whether a relationship is positive or negative is referred to as the **polarity** of the causal connection between the two factors.

Both of these issues—the need to illustrate feedback effects and to depict causal polarity—can be accommodated with an influence diagram. As with a problem tree, the major elements of the system are mapped out, and the causal connections among them are identified. Any element can be causally connected to any other element, and the polarity of the causal relationship is indicated in the diagram. There is no standard convention for denoting polarity:

- Positive relationships may be depicted with a plus sign (+), an S (for 'same'), or a solid line that ends with an arrowhead, while
- Negative relationships may be depicted with a minus sign (−), an O (for 'opposite'), or a dotted line that ends with a small square.

Exhibit 12-4 displays an illustrative influence diagram based on the work of development specialists interested in fostering microscale agriculture in Ethiopia. Rather than oversimplify the situation, the project managers identified fifteen different factors that play an important role in the food security of households. They next identified 23 causal connections—some positive and some negative—among these factors. With a deeper and more holistic view of the situation, the odds of designing successful policy interventions increase appreciably. A naïve approach might, for example, assume that household well-being can be enhanced by giving each landowner a few goats or cattle. While that might be true, the influence diagram lets us see that doing so could lead to more area being set aside for grazing, with less available for crops. In turn, this may lead to higher cropping intensity, undermining soil fertility and crop production, leading to a decrease in income from crop sales and reducing household grain stocks.

---

[3]Note that the terms positive and negative are given their mathematical meaning and don't connote normative notions of good or bad.

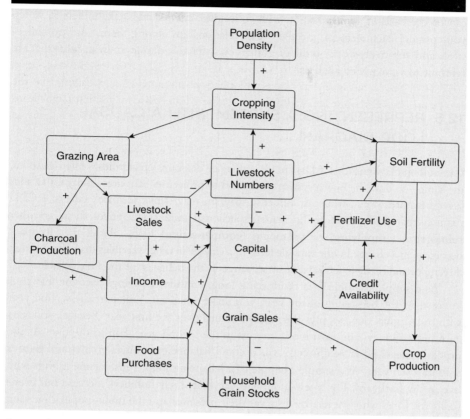

Source: Adapted from Hawkins (2009)

If you took my suggestion in the prior section to mock-up a problem tree, you might now want to try to convert it to an influence diagram. To do so, you would first think more expansively and add any system elements that didn't fit within the narrower, more linear framework of a problem tree. Next, for each causal relationship in the diagram (i.e., each arrow from one box to another), identify its polarity. Finally, identify any additional causal relationships that capture the ways in which consequences from one element may feed back to become causal drivers of another element. Doing so may entail adding arrows that run from top to bottom or left to right (or vice versa), as needed.

As with a problem tree, the primary purpose of an influence diagram is not to yield a formulaic model that precisely characterizes the system you're looking at. Instead, its best use is as a means of ensuring that you're taking a holistic view of the situation and considering how the pieces fit together. Moreover, an influence diagram can be the basis of a conversation with colleagues, clients, and stakeholders in which you consider each element and the causal relationships among them.[4] As you collectively and iteratively work on the diagram, you will likely develop new insights that are relevant to your policy analysis.

12.5 REPRESENTING A SYSTEM WITH A CAUSAL LOOP DIAGRAM

Causal loop diagrams (or CLDs) are like influence diagrams on steroids.[5] Their goals are the same—to describe how a system works and to project its behavior—but a CLD adds several features. First, while an influence diagram may depict feedback effects, a CLD requires that feedback loops be made explicit and then characterizes them as either **reinforcing (amplifying)** or **balancing (compensating)** loops. Recall that feedback occurs when a change in one variable leads to a change in other variables that then—either directly or indirectly—'feeds back' to a change in the behavior of the first variable.

As a simple example of a reinforcing loop, consider a savings account that pays interest. At the beginning of the year, you make a deposit. You start the second year with the original deposit, plus the interest earned over the first year. Because you start with more money, you earn more interest in the second year than in the first. As the process repeats (or is 'reinforced'), the account balance grows by a greater and greater amount each year. As a simple example of a balancing loop, consider the rabbits who live in my backyard. For a few months every year, their numbers increase but eventually the foxes who live nearby discover their presence and the rabbit population soon declines. Later, the then-hungry foxes head elsewhere in search of food and the rabbit population rebounds. In other words, an increase in the number of rabbits provokes an increase in the number of foxes, in turn, reducing (or 'balancing') the number of rabbits, until the cycle repeats again.

A second difference between a CLD and an influence diagram is the former's more rigorous treatment of the **passage of time**. As noted in Section 12.1, effects sometimes quickly follow the events that trigger them; in other cases, effects take a

---

[4]As we'll see later in this chapter, however, there are some circumstances in which the complexity of an influence diagram may hinder communication with folks who don't have the time or inclination to ponder its details.

[5]If you're really adventurous, CLDs can be turned into mathematical models that simulate all aspects of a system over time. More on this later in the chapter.

long time to become apparent. In a sped-up world where information, money, and products move quickly around the world, we can easily overlook the time it takes for public policies to have a meaningful impact on the problems they're intended to address. In a CLD, lags are noted with two small lines perpendicular to the causal arrow to which they apply.[6] By forcing the user to characterize each causal link as working quickly or slowly, a CLD provides a disciplined way to sort out how long it may take to experience the effects of a policy change.

A third feature of a causal loop diagram is the careful delineation of **stocks** and **flows**. As mentioned previously, conflating stocks and flows can lead to serious confusion. If we quantify the stocks and flows in a CLD, we can gain considerable insight into a system's operation. As another simple example, let's consider a young gig worker named John, who drives episodically for Uber and lives in his parent's basement. John decides whether to work on any given day based on the balance in his bank account (the stock). If it's below $500, he puts in four hours of driving and earns $70 (an inflow). Otherwise, he hangs out with friends, going to the movies and eating fast food. His lifestyle costs him $40 per day (an outflow). We can use a CLD to characterize John's situation. If you look at the left portion of Exhibit 12-5, you'll see that his behavior constitutes a balancing feedback loop. As his bank balance goes down, he eventually heads out to earn more money but only after waiting for the balance to drop below his self-imposed threshold of $500. When he does work, he earns $70 which is not quite enough to cover two days of spending. Accordingly, he sometimes needs to work two days in a row, but sometimes, a day of work is enough to top up his bank account. When a balancing feedback loop has a delay, we often see oscillating system

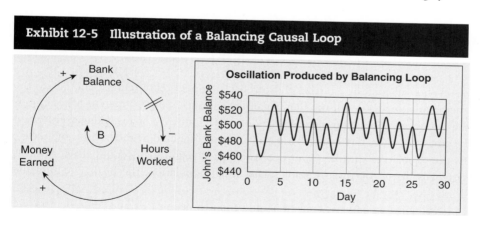

Exhibit 12-5 Illustration of a Balancing Causal Loop

---

[6]In a computerized simulation of a CLD, time lags must be precisely specified (e.g., so many days, months, or years) between the occurrence of a cause and the subsequent occurrence of the effect.

behavior. As shown in the righthand portion of Exhibit 12-5, John's bank balance oscillates between about $460 and $530 over the month, as the result of this balancing feedback loop.

A causal loop diagram can also describe more complex systems with more than one feedback loop. Look at the population model shown in Exhibit 12-6. For starters, note that it contains both stocks and flows. The population is a stock while births and deaths represent, respectively, inflows to and outflows from the population. The population at the end of a year is equal to the population at the start of the year plus births during the year minus deaths during the year. These inflows and outflows are driven by, respectively, the application of the birth and death rates to the overall population.

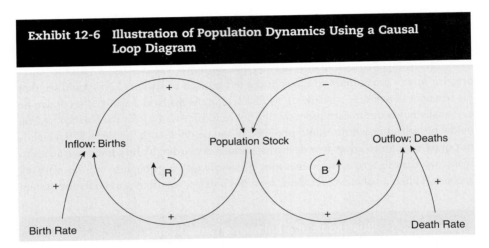

Exhibit 12-6 Illustration of Population Dynamics Using a Causal Loop Diagram

When it comes to births, the feedback loop is reinforcing (denoted by the encircled letter R). With the number of births measured as a fraction of total population, when population increases, so does the number of births. Conversely, when it comes to deaths, the feedback loop is balancing (denoted by the encircled letter B). As the population shrinks, fewer people die each year. The overall behavior of this system is driven by three variables: the initial population, the birth rate, and the death rate.

Assuming an initial population of 1 million people, Exhibit 12-7 depicts the population under two scenarios for the birth and death rates. When the birth rate is higher than the death rate, the population increases and when the reverse is true, the population decreases. As shown by the graphs, the speed and magnitude of population changes depend on the values of the birth and death rates.

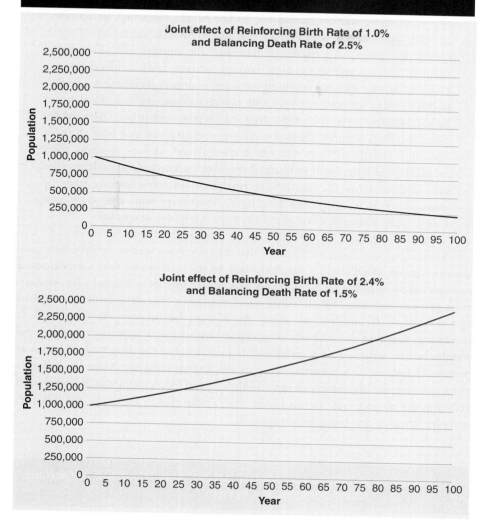

Exhibit 12-7   Population over Time Under Alternative Birth Rates and Death Rates

Joint effect of Reinforcing Birth Rate of 1.0% and Balancing Death Rate of 2.5%

Joint effect of Reinforcing Birth Rate of 2.4% and Balancing Death Rate of 1.5%

As a final example of a complex causal loop diagram, let's build a CLD from scratch based on a narrative description of a system. We'll rely on informal work done by Benson and his colleagues to understand factors driving an increase in Mexico's murder rates in 2017.

From the outside, an obvious factor is that Mexico is a conduit for some of the world's most prominent drug trafficking. Therefore, as a natural result of an industry that is both lucrative and illegal, constant violence between gangs and onto civilians is expected. Nevertheless, although we found through a variety of reports that the murder rate in Mexico was spiking, this simple answer of cartel warfare turned out to not be the full story. In actuality, stronger government enforcement has led to destabilization of Mexican cartels and gangs, and ironically, increased the murder rate. Essentially, captured leaders and other high ranking officers leave a bloody power vacuum, causing massive infighting between members jockeying for higher positions. Also attempting to fill this power vacuum are new, local gangs looking to snag a portion of the drug trade's immense profits. Meanwhile, other members abandon their destabilized organizations and turn to other illicit and violent activities that utilize their illegal skillsets, bringing their criminality into previously untouched neighboring states. As a result, murder rates increase across the board. So in part the murder rate is rising *because of successful efforts to disrupt the drug trade.* Short-term wins can spark new longer-term problems. (Benson, 2019, p. 207) *emphasis in original*

For our purposes here, we'll assume that the system has been accurately described. Benson's group initially had a simplistic view of the system and thus a fundamental misunderstanding of the problem. If you look at the top part of Exhibit 12-8, you can see a graphic depiction of their initial causal reasoning. The drug business is violent and dangerous. If murders are going up, it must be because the drug trade is increasing. Based on this understanding, a policymaker might hope to drive down the murder rate by targeting drug cartel leaders to undermine the drug trade. The lower portion of Exhibit 12-8 presents this approach diagrammatically. More law enforcement will decrease the number of cartel leaders, in turn diminishing the drug trade and reducing the murder rate. But as noted, the murder rate is going up, not down. A complex situation was being oversimplified.

Exhibit 12-8 A Simplistic Mental Model May Overlook Important Characteristics of a System

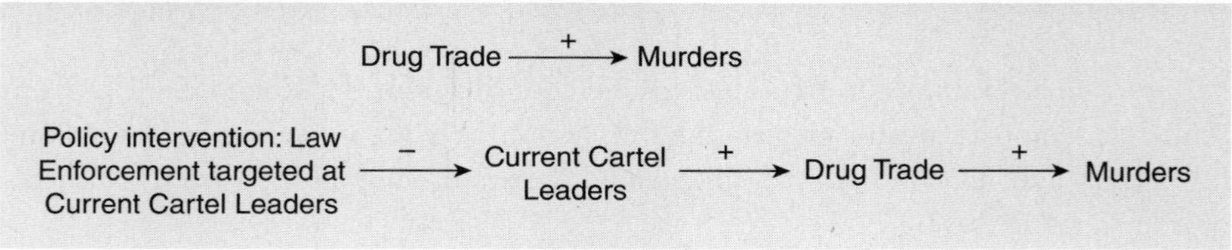

Drug Trade $\xrightarrow{+}$ Murders

Policy intervention: Law Enforcement targeted at Current Cartel Leaders $\xrightarrow{-}$ Current Cartel Leaders $\xrightarrow{+}$ Drug Trade $\xrightarrow{+}$ Murders

---

By converting Benson's narrative prose into the causal loop diagram depicted in Exhibit 12-9, we can more easily see the nature of the system and the causal connections between its elements. As law enforcement officials have arrested and imprisoned current cartel leaders, they have disrupted the drug trade but also set in motion a series of other events that actually increased the number of murders.

There are several feedback loops in this diagram. To keep things simple, I've elected to highlight only two. The first is a balancing loop in which, as the number of current cartel leaders is reduced, the number of violence-prone rivals attempting to seize leadership is increased. The second is a reinforcing loop which captures the totality of the overarching—and initially counterintuitive—phenomenon that Benson describes: as law enforcement pressure is increased, the murder rate climbs. I also incorporated three lags in the causal loop diagram. It's only conjecture on my part, but I suspect there would be a delay before the rival cartel leaders and violence-prone local gangs consolidate their control and restore the drug trade to previous levels. I also added a lag between a change in the number of disaffected cartel members and the point when criminal enterprises outside the drug trade are affected.

Exhibit 12-9 Illustrative Causal Loop Diagram: Relationship between Drug Trade and Murder Rate

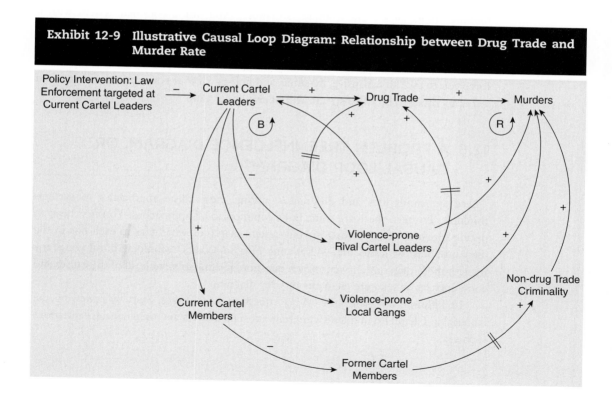

In addition, if we want to visualize what might happen to the drug trade and the murder rate in the future, the causal loop diagram would be a big help. For example, we could consider the degree to which law enforcement sustains the pressure on the cartels (and their new leaders), whether cartel rivalries persist or are resolved, and whether law enforcement prioritizes new nondrug criminal enterprises.

As mentioned earlier, a fully specified causal loop diagram can be converted into a computerized simulation model in which the behavior of each element is predicted and tracked over time.[7] Doing so requires that all causal relationships be specified mathematically, that stocks and flows be measured in commensurable units, and that all time lags are consistently quantified. Doing so can be a tall order. For example, if we eliminate five senior cartel leaders, how many rivals will violently vie for power? Three? Five? Ten? What's the right metric for 'criminality'? The number of murders? The number of assaults? Something else? These are tough analytic issues that defy easy answers. Back in Chapter 5, I mentioned the adage 'garbage in, garbage out' to describe situations where we apply sophisticated analytic tools to inputs that we know to be flawed. In such cases, we can't have much confidence in the results.

Nonetheless, causal loop diagrams can be a powerful tool for clarifying your thinking about messy and complex situations. And, for a confined system with a manageable number of elements (e.g., traffic congestion in a specific location), a computerized system simulation model might very well yield valid results. But even if you never convert your CLD into a simulation model, the process of creating it will force you to take an expansive, dynamic, and holistic view of your subject and give you a way to visualize how the system will operate over time.

12.6 A PROBLEM TREE, INFLUENCE DIAGRAM, OR CAUSAL LOOP DIAGRAM?

There are similarities and differences among these three approaches to systems thinking. To start, there are some tasks common to all approaches. You first need to decide which elements belong in your system map (i.e., what goes in each box in the diagram). Start with the 'Five Whys' and 'Five So-Whats' technique, but if you come up with more than one answer to each question, it's fine to include all of the causes and consequences as separate elements in your diagram.

In addition, try asking the 'Who?' question a few times. Start by reviewing the material in Chapter 6 on identifying relevant stakeholders and then consider questions such as:

---

[7]Simulation software includes Vensim®, AnyLogic, and Stella® Architect.

- If there is a change to public policy, who will be directly obligated to change their behavior? What aspects of their behavior will likely change? In what ways will it change? Might they opt to ignore the new policy?

- Who will be incentivized—though not required—to change their behavior? Would a new policy alter incentives based on changes in prices, taxes, or subsidies? How would firms' opportunities to earn profit or avoid losses, or individuals' opportunity to earn more or less income, change?

- Based on the likely reactions of parties directly affected by public policy, what are the follow-on consequences among those who are indirectly affected?

Whether you're building a problem tree, influence diagram, or CLD, be sure to capture the causes and consequences of the behavior of all relevant stakeholders. By forcing yourself to systematically characterize who is affected by current conditions or who will be impacted by a potential policy change, you will inevitably have to describe the relevant relationships.

When it comes to drawing the arrows that depict causal relationships between the system's elements, keep in mind Chapter 5's definition of **causality**. To claim that one thing causes another, we need to ensure that cause temporally precedes effect, that cause and effect predictably covary, that competing explanations of covariation have been ruled out, and, ideally, that we have a plausible theoretical explanation of why the cause produces the effect.

Systems thinking doesn't require that all elements in the system and the causal relationships among them be quantified. You might think, for example, that social media fosters political sectarianism, or that an increased police presence contributes to a sense of well-being among citizens concerned about crime but a sense of discomfort among those worried about police misconduct, or that a winning local sports team engenders camaraderie and civility among residents. While some parts of these three examples might be amenable to quantification, some are not. Moreover, characterizing in formulaic terms the causal relationship among these elements (e.g., a ten-point increase in the local team's win record leads to a 20 percent increase in civility) would strain credulity. If you think an element, or the relationship between two elements, drives the system's behavior, then the elements and relationships belong in your system map even if they can't be precisely measured or formulaically expressed.

One of the most useful features of a systems analysis is that it helps you identify feedback loops. If you find that you want to draw two arrows—pointing in opposite directions—between the same two elements in your system, be careful. In simple cases, like interest earned on the balance of a bank account, the operation of the system will be clear. But feedback often takes a circuitous route as a change in one element affects other elements before feeding back to produce a change in the first element. Remember John, our gig worker? His bank balance increased when he went out and worked, but not otherwise. That's why, back in Exhibit 12-5, we had to first add the lag to capture his eccentric approach to working and, second, include the act of earning money as a stand-alone element to portray how his episodic labor affects his bank balance. This vignette illustrates an important point: there is no single correct way to diagram a system. The ultimate test of a system map is whether it captures all relevant features of the system and unambiguously conveys how it works.

The final common feature of attempts to capture and describe the operation of a system is that such attempts usually turn out better if approached iteratively and collaboratively. Iteration is needed because the first draft of a system map is invariably incomplete. The act of creating it demands that you think through causes and effects; if you're doing it right, expect to be surprised as new factors come to light and you have to add elements and rearrange the arrows in your system map. Collaboration is also needed because, for most complex policy issues, rarely does a single person (i.e., you) have all the answers to all the relevant questions. You'll probably need help from subject matter experts and from stakeholders affected by policy problems and proposed attempts to remedy them. Getting such help can ensure that you don't overlook important elements of the system. Finally, if you're like me, the simple act of sharing my work and trying to explain it to others often reveals shortcomings in my own thinking.[8]

When it comes to differences among problem trees, influence diagrams, and causal loop diagrams, Exhibit 12-10 contrasts the key features of each approach and notes some important differences. Moreover, as shown in Exhibit 12-11, there is a trade-off between the time and effort needed to prepare the system map and its degree of analytic sophistication and rigor. Problem trees are simplified views of a relatively small portion of the system map. As such, they can usually be developed more quickly than influence diagrams or CLDs. Their narrow focus, however, means that important elements of the system may be overlooked.

If you take a broader and more rigorous view of the system, as you do with an influence diagram or causal loop diagram, you will undoubtedly develop a deeper understanding of how the system works. The price you'll pay, however, is that it takes more research and subject matter expertise to go beyond a basic problem tree. Such trade-offs are common in policy analysis. As discussed in Chapter 7, policy analysts often face a tension between their ability to produce a comprehensive, thoroughly researched deliverable and the constraints created by time, resource, and information limitations. The three variants of systems analysis provide an apt illustration of how this dilemma may play out. You might hope to develop a complete causal loop diagram, but have to settle instead for a problem tree.

---

[8]If you want to make sure you have a solid command of a subject, try teaching it to someone else. You'll quickly find the gaps in your understanding of the subject.

Exhibit 12-10   Comparison of Methods for Visualizing Systems

Method	Depicts Elements of System?	Depicts Causal Relationships Among Elements?	Depicts Lags between Cause and Effect?	Depicts Feedback Loops?	Differentiates Stocks & Flows?	Amenable to Mathematical Modeling?
Problem Tree	Only those closely linked to problem	Yes, but without polarity	No	No	No	No
Influence Diagram	Yes	Yes, with polarity	Sometimes	Implicitly	No	No
Causal Loop Diagram	Yes	Yes, with polarity	Yes	Explicitly	Sometimes	Yes, if all system components are quantified

Exhibit 12-11   Methods of Systems Analysis: Trade-offs

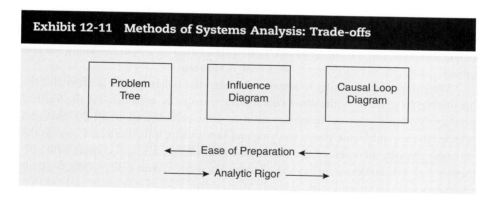

12.7 A CAVEAT: DON'T MISTAKE YOUR SYSTEM MAP FOR THE SYSTEM ITSELF

Systems analysis can be a powerful tool for gaining insight into a policy issue and for thinking through the consequences of potential policy interventions. But no matter how hard you work on your system map, you're always at risk of overlooking something important or misunderstanding a key causal relationship, particularly if, owing to time and resource constraints, you've only been able to prepare a problem tree rather than an influence diagram or causal loop diagram.

On the other hand, don't mistake the complexity of a system map for an indicator of its accuracy. Most folks have a tendency to see detailed descriptions as more credible than those couched in simpler terms (Kahneman, 2011; Tetlock, 2005). The simple fact that your system map contains a large number of elements with many causal connections does not—by itself—make it a better representation of reality than a simpler map. It could be, but only if each piece of the map reflects strong evidence and sound inference. In short, systems analysis is not a panacea. As one scholar put it:

> … businesses do not live in a neat, orderly world where causal relationships are always clearly defined and where causality always works in one direction only. The business environment is much more interactive, full of 'feedbacks' where some 'downstream' development reacts back upon, and alters behavior 'upstream.' Perhaps most important, it is full of unplanned, or accidental developments that then turn out to have an important set of consequences of their own. It is essential to emphasize the unexpected and the unplanned, even if—especially if—it renders serious quantification impossible. (Rosenberg, 1990, p. 168)

So, does that mean that systems analysis is a fool's errand? Not at all. While your system map is not the system itself any more than a map of New York City is an actual city, it still can help you find your way to your destination. The map may leave out some streets and include others that don't exist. It may occasionally send you in the wrong direction, but relying on a map is probably a better idea than randomly walking up and down city streets trying to find your destination.

Moreover, when it comes to systems thinking, the policy analyst is often also the mapmaker. In some ways, the act of creating the map can be as valuable as the finished product. To build a system map, you need to think critically about all the elements relevant to the policy issue you're studying and how they're interconnected, look at the situation through all seven of the lenses described in Part III, and consult with colleagues and stakeholders to help you understand how the system really works. Systems analysis is a lot like planning in general. As President Eisenhower often said:

> In preparing for battle I have always found that plans are useless, but planning is indispensable. (Nixon, 1990, pp. 234–235)

In short, I am making a nuanced argument here. You can never achieve an omniscient, holistic, and perfect understanding of a system. You've heard this point before. Back in Section 3.2.4, we noted Charles Lindblom's argument that achieving a synoptic, or comprehensive, view of a policy-relevant situation is impossible. Moreover, Herbert Simon's boundedly rational decisionmaker who aspires only to satisfice by picking the first option that appears good enough for the situation at hand is unlikely to have any use for a sophisticated systems analysis.

But this is not an argument for ignorance. At a worst, building a system map is likely to be immensely educational. At best, the result will be a solid foundation upon which to build a policy analysis. Either way, Lindblom's and Simon's word provide a cautionary tale. I can assure you—without even having seen it—that your system map is imperfect: I suggest you always keep that thought in mind. As we saw in Chapter 7, the best policy analysts always bring an element of humility to their work.

Another persistent challenge faced by systems analysts is making their work understandable to their clients. In policy analysis, we often aspire to map complex and evolving systems. The social, economic, and political components of such systems may resist simple characterization. The result of trying to capture all relevant factors in one system map can sometimes seem overwhelming. If you have any doubt, take a look at Exhibit 12-12, which was prepared by the United Kingdom's Foresight Programme (UK GOS, 2010).

The purpose of the project was to understand likely land use patterns in the United Kingdom over the coming 50 years with an emphasis on sustainability and on obtaining the highest economic and social benefit from land use decisions. Some readers may find the result—147 elements and 276 causal links among them—a bit intimidating. But, in my opinion, if a policy analyst aspires to think holistically about a complicated issue, he or she has little choice but to embrace the complexity.

But not everyone feels the same way. Influence diagrams have even made the front page of the New York Times, and not in a good way. In an article entitled "We Have Met the Enemy and He is PowerPoint," we learn about a dense, hard-to-read influence diagram of US counterintelligence efforts in Afghanistan. The diagram—with over 100 elements and about 250 causal links among them—was shown to General Stanley McChrystal, leader of American and NATO forces in Afghanistan. His reaction?

> "When we understand that slide, we'll have won the war," General McChrystal dryly remarked, as the room erupted in laughter. (Bumiller, 2010, p. 1)

The article went on to note that influence diagrams are often derisively dismissed by military leaders as "spaghetti charts" that can "hypnotize chickens."

Ultimately, the problem here wasn't necessarily one of a flawed analysis but instead was more likely one of a flawed approach to working with a client. When folks get tested for COVID, they're not looking for an explanation of the genomic structure of the virus. They just want to know if they're sick. Similarly, when you conduct a sophisticated systems analysis as part of a policy analysis, it's typically not a good idea to overwhelm your client with all the details of your work. Instead, think of your system map as a library of information from which you can extract useful insights for

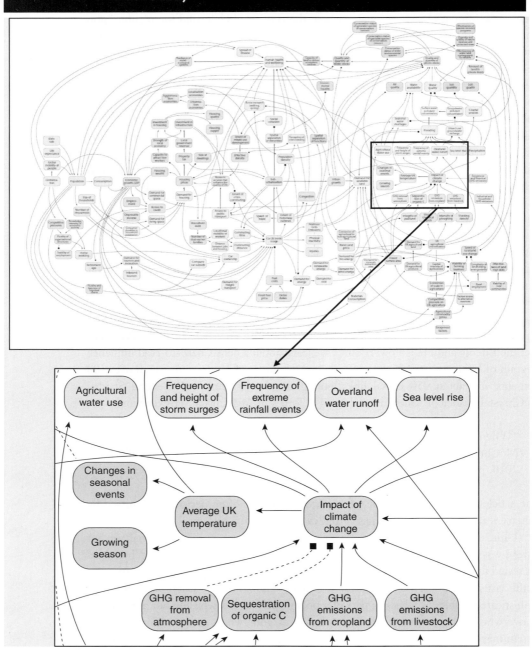

Source: (UK GOS, 2010)

your client. You only need to share those insights, not the minutiae of how they were created. Of course, if asked, you can always share your system map with your client, but my advice is to wait to be asked before showing your "spaghetti chart" to the client.

From time to time, some of my students—frustrated with the complexity of systems analysis and anxious to move quickly to address societal problems they care deeply about—complain that I'm overcomplicating things by asking them to think holistically, panoptically, and systemically about all of the factors related to their issue of concern. I've never come up with a great response to their concerns, other than to point out that the world is a complicated place and to remind them that it's not only public policy that can be exceedingly confusing. Smart phones, robotic surgery, animated feature films, modern automobiles, and jetliners capable of flying halfway around the world are just a few examples of fantastically complex undertakings that take thousands of hours to develop and produce. It seems to me that tackling profound societal challenges is worthy of a similar level of effort.

CHAPTER SUMMARY

This chapter argued that systems thinking is an important skill for aspiring policy analysts to master. I recommended systems thinking as a means of seeing policy issues in a holistic context and for lowering the chances of unintended consequences in the aftermath of a policy's implementation. The value of systems analysis stems from the fact that policy problems arise in systems, that policy interventions take place within systems, and that policy-relevant systems are largely invisible.

We reviewed the defining characteristics of all systems and considered three different ways of mapping the key features of a system: problem trees, influence diagrams, and causal loop diagrams. Problem trees are quick and straightforward to prepare, but are not comprehensive in scope. By contrast, causal loop diagrams are much more expansive but can take considerable time and effort to prepare. Causal loop diagrams can also be hard to understand at a quick glance and are not an optimal means of describing a complex system to a busy policymaker. We closed with a review of the pitfalls of mistaking a system for the system itself and a reminder to always bring an element of humility to your analytic work.

DISCUSSION QUESTIONS

1. Pick a policy issue that you're concerned about. If you were to draw a map to characterize the system in which it arises, what elements would you include? What relationships among the elements are most important? Where would you draw the system's boundaries?

2. Consider the problem of high school dropout rates that differ across socioeconomic lines. Can you think of causal drivers with a positive link to the problem? How about drivers with a negative link?

3. Can you come up with an example of a policy-relevant reinforcing loop? How about a balancing loop?

4. Problem trees are relatively easy to develop, but how useful are they? Does their simplicity undercut their value?

5. Causal loop diagrams can be difficult and time consuming to develop. Are they worth the effort?

6. Is systems analysis a lot of work for little payoff? What are the upsides of incorporating systems thinking in policy analysis? How about the downsides?

CHAPTER THIRTEEN

USING POLICY ANALYSIS TO VISUALIZE THE FUTURE

Since its earliest days, the policy sciences movement has recognized the importance of anticipating how conditions in the future would be affected by policy actions taken in the present (Rothwell, 1951). Seventy years later, Scoblic and Tetlock put a modern spin on the topic:

> Every policy is a prediction. Tax cuts will boost the economy. Sanctions will slow Iran's nuclear program. Travel bans will limit the spread of COVID-19. These claims all posit a causal relationship between means and ends. … This makes every policymaker a forecaster. (2020, p. 10)

To provide policymakers with wise and suitably qualified advice, policy analysts thus need to visualize the future as clearly as possible.[1] This chapter offers you a few tools for doing so. But first a caveat: none of these suggestions will give you a crystal ball that can see the future with 20/20 vision. These tools can only give you *some* insight into the future and help you make better forecasts than you otherwise might.

We start in Section 13.1 with the process of figuring out which aspects of the future need to be characterized in a policy analysis. Section 13.2 explores the process of using projective inference to describe a future that hasn't yet occurred. A key theme is that it's usually a mistake to think

---

[1] In prospective policy analysis, visualizing the future is the central task. There is an analogous process in retrospective program evaluation. Rather than visualizing the future, however, you need to visualize an alternative version of the past in which the program being evaluated didn't exist (i.e., a counterfactual scenario).

Learning Objectives

By studying this chapter, you should be able to:

- Determine which aspects of the future need to be characterized in order to conduct a comprehensive and credible policy analysis.

- Develop succinct and unambiguous evaluation criteria.

- Explain projective inference and distinguish it from descriptive inference.

- Visualize future policy outcomes using disciplined calculation, microeconomic analysis, and extrapolation from evidence and experience.

- Explain the plurality of the future and the role of probabilistic projections in policy analysis.

- Use the expected value approach, sensitivity analysis, and breakeven analysis to make decisions under uncertainty.

- Describe scenario planning and how it can be incorporated in policy analysis.

- Understand and apply specific skills to improve the accuracy of predictions about the future performance of today's policy choices.

about a single future; instead, with multiple possible outcomes, the future is actually plural. Section 13.3 reviews some of the techniques from classical policy analysis for projecting the future while Section 13.4 offers a couple of ideas—systems analysis and scenario planning—as a means of supplementing traditional approaches. Finally, this chapter closes with a few suggestions for honing your predictive skills.

13.1 WHAT ASPECTS OF THE FUTURE DO YOU NEED TO VISUALIZE?

As noted in Section 4.2, trade-off-free policy options don't exist. All policy proposals (including sticking with the status quo) have pros and cons that manifest themselves over time. A key task for policy analysts is thus to identify **trade-offs** among those pros and cons. Comparing policies is much easier when we use a criteria-alternatives matrix to consistently apply a fixed set of **evaluation criteria** to each policy option. In turn, the future you need to visualize is the performance of each option with respect to each criterion.[2]

As explained in Chapter 1, 'off-the-shelf' criteria for evaluating policy proposals include the cost, efficacy, equity, and administrability of the policies being evaluated. But the choice of criteria is always sensitive to the decision context. If a client or important stakeholders are especially interested in a particular attribute of the policies being evaluated, then the analyst should consider converting that attribute to a criterion for the analysis. Moreover, a careful assessment—based on systems thinking—of the potential for unintended consequences will likely point the way to additional criteria that belong in the analysis. Below are a few more suggestions about using criteria to think about the future consequences of policy action.

For starters, when you're defining evaluation criteria, avoid generalities. Instead strive to be specific and succinct in each criterion (Hammond, Keeney, & Raiffa, 1999). Try to express each criterion in a single sentence by trading nuance and detail for brevity and clarity. The discipline imposed by the one-sentence test will force you to focus on the most important idea and leave out the rest, but be careful not to create a two-in-one evaluation criterion. Think about this criterion: 'Reduce delays in airport security queues while minimizing the chance that a potential terrorist is allowed to fly.' Sounds like a laudable goal, right? The trouble comes because delays and threats are two distinct constructs. Yes, they're linked, but combining them into a

---

[2]Not all policy analyses endeavor to visualize the future under all criteria and all policy options. Depending on client needs, you might look at all criteria but only for one option, at all options but only for one criterion, or at the performance of a single option with respect to one criterion. In other words, you could be trying to populate an entire criteria-alternatives matrix, a single row, a single column, or a single cell with projections of the future.

single criterion sets up an intractable analytic problem. Imagine a proposal to end screening at the airport. Delays would vanish, but risks would likely increase. How would you report the performance of this proposal with respect to the two-in-one criterion? Will it perform very well? Or very poorly? In short, we need two separate criteria: 'minimize screening time' and 'maximize the chance of detecting a potential threat.'

In addition, take care not to mix up evaluation criteria with the metrics used to assess them. Imagine you went for a run and a friend asks you how it went. You might answer that it was difficult because the course was hilly, and it was a hot, sunny day. In this case, the difficulty of the run is akin to an evaluation criterion, and you've operationalized your assessment with two metrics: hilliness and weather. Metrics can take different forms depending on how much time and information you have. Suppose you're trying to come up with metrics for a criterion along the lines of 'minimize the health risk associated with air pollution.' If time is short and resources limited, you might have to settle for an expert's subjective judgment whether, for each policy option, air quality would be poor, fair, or good. Conversely, with the right scientific data and appropriate simulation modeling tools, along with enough time and resources, you might be able to predict for each policy option the number and severity of adverse health effects.

Moreover, you need to be intentional as you select metrics to operationalize each criterion. At the end of the day, it doesn't matter what you say your criterion means in an abstract sense. *It's what you measure with your metrics that brings the criterion to life within your analysis.* If your metrics don't capture the full meaning of the criterion you are trying to operationalize, then the results of your policy analysis will have gaps whenever that criterion is used.[3] Recall the example of your hot and hilly, and therefore difficult, run. In that case, weather and hilliness comprised the definition of difficulty. It wouldn't matter if the roads were full of potholes and there was no drinking water. Without metrics for potholes and water, they would have no bearing on an assessment of the difficulty of your run.

You should also ensure that your evaluation criteria are oriented toward outcomes rather than the mechanical steps that might be taken to try to create those outcomes. In other words, when judging policy alternatives, *focus on the ends not the means.* To use the language of logic modeling from Chapter 2, I am suggesting that you focus your evaluation criteria on outcomes and impacts, rather than outputs. For example, in the hope of improving student learning, we may aspire to put more teachers into classrooms in order to reduce class sizes. A means-oriented criterion would look something like 'Minimize the number of pupils per teacher' while an end-oriented criterion might

---

[3]This challenge should sound familiar. It's an example of the issue of construct validity that we talked about in Section 6.3.1.

be 'Maximize student learning outcomes.' The more expansive language of the second phrase better captures our ultimate objective and reminds us not to be satisfied with a policy that reduces the student/teacher ratio but doesn't actually improve learning outcomes.

As a last check before you finalize your evaluation criteria, test them and the associated metrics against the policy alternatives being considered (Hammond et al., 1999). Think about how each alternative performs with respect to each criterion. Which alternatives look good? Which alternatives come up short? Do these results match your intuition? Are you happy with the result? If not, you should revisit the criteria and metrics you plan to use in your analysis. Otherwise, you now have in hand a list of the characteristics of the future that you'll want to visualize.

13.2 PROJECTIVE INFERENCE: CHARACTERIZING A FUTURE THAT HASN'T YET HAPPENED

Now that we have a sense of what aspects of the future we're interested in, let's consider how we might think about a future that hasn't yet taken place. You may recall from Chapter 5 that a key feature of inductive logic (where we reason from specific evidence to general principles) is that we can never prove that an inferred conclusion is definitively true. Instead, we accept its provisional truth after failing to falsify it. This approach—referred to as descriptive inference—makes sense when we're describing current conditions where it is at least conceptually possible to find a counterexample that falsifies our conclusion. But what happens when—in a process referred to as **projective inference**—we want to draw conclusions about the future? How does the principle of falsification apply? Unfortunately, it doesn't. Projective inference is all about the future, so until the future arrives, we can't subject the inference to potential falsification. Because we want to take policy action now, not later, the falsification test won't help us judge the validity of our projected policy outcomes. In short, characterizing the future is intrinsically different from characterizing the present.

So, where does this leave us? In my view, there are at least three means by which we can assess the validity of projective inferences. The first is a conceptual test that focuses on the *soundness of the methods and evidence used to project the future*. We look for careful and systematic data collection, appropriately applied statistical analysis of quantitative evidence, thorough and nuanced exploration of qualitative data, a holistic and sophisticated understanding of the behavior of relevant systems, and high fidelity with the principles of logical inference (including internal and external validity). If any of these elements is missing, then any resulting visualization of the future is inherently suspect.

Second, it's not enough that our approach to visualizing the future is built on solid evidence and sound reasoning. Whenever we can, we need to *test it empirically against real world conditions.* As mentioned above, we can't test a projection against a future that has yet to occur, but we can often find analogous situations in the past or the present to serve as proxies for the future. For example, scientists trying to predict the path of future climate change typically validate their models by going back in time and, using only the evidence that would have been available in the past, test their models' ability to replicate observed conditions. If model outputs match historical observations, that's an indicator that a model's projections of the future are more credible than if it can't replicate prior observations. Similarly, if we build a system map that seems to accurately describe how conditions in one location are causally linked, we might take the map and apply it to another location. If the system map seems to also explain conditions in the second location, that's an indicator that we're on the right track.[4] In short, if your analytic approach is successful in 'projecting' empirical observations based on past evidence or on current evidence from other settings, then you can be more confident in the approach as a reliable means of visualizing the future.

The third test of projective inference depends, somewhat ironically, on how you *qualify the provisional nature of your conclusion.* Remember that we can never prove the truth of an inductively inferred claim. Instead, we can only assess its plausibility. As described in Chapter 6, by using either words of estimative probability or numeric probabilities, we indicate to our audience how likely it is that our conclusion is actually true. The same thinking can be applied to projective inference. Based on the results of the first two tests noted above—the soundness of the evidence and the reasoning and the ability of the projection method to reproduce empirical observations—we can characterize our confidence in the conclusion. Is, for example, there an 80 percent chance that our projection is correct, or is the probability only 40 percent? The point here is that the quality of a projective inference cannot be evaluated in isolation of the qualification you attach to it. Excessive optimism or pessimism in the qualification can invalidate your projective inference irrespective of how well it performs on the first two tests described above.

13.3 VISUALIZING THE FUTURE IN CLASSICAL POLICY ANALYSIS

The classical models of policy analysis don't usually entail systems thinking. Instead, the approach tends to be narrower. A systems analyst might describe the difference as holistic versus reductionist thinking. This section describes three techniques for visualizing the

---

[4]Unfortunately, the converse is not true. If the system map doesn't perform well in the second location, it may have nothing to do with the accuracy of the map but instead result from differences between the two locations.

future frequently associated with classical policy analysis while the next section takes a more expansive approach. When I describe the classical methods as reductionist, I don't mean to denigrate them. Policy analysis is an applied discipline, practiced under time, resource, and information constraints. Reducing problems to manageable dimensions, considering only a few readily available options, or choosing a quick analysis over a deeply researched analysis are all commonsense, pragmatic responses to the realities of policy-making in a complex setting. These methods are often the best we can do.

13.3.1 Completing the Criteria-Alternatives Matrix

The criteria-alternative matrix lies at the core of the classical model of policy analysis. Policy students are traditionally taught to complete the matrix using one of three techniques. The first approach to visualizing the future under different policy options is simply a careful and internally consistent accounting of the factors that drive the likely outcomes of policy changes, using what might be refered to as *disciplined calculation*. Such models do not incorporate formal modeling of human behavior or dynamic changes in outcomes over time. At one extreme, this approach is little more than the disciplined guesswork of the Fermi method. Recall, for example, how, in Section 7.4, we took a 'quick and dirty' approach to projecting the likely future revenue from a tax on coffee cup sleeves.

At the other extreme of disciplined calculation are sophisticated accounting models that incorporate multiple variables and the connections among them. As an example, suppose you're doing a policy analysis of competing proposals for a new program to treat opioid abuse. You might build a model that starts with the number of people in need and then applies the proposed eligibility criteria under each policy option. Your model might next incorporate your estimate of the propensity to participate in order to compute the number who would be served. You might go farther by adding metrics for program success (e.g., the fraction of treated clients expected to be substance-free one year after the program) and for program cost (e.g., the cost per client per year). You would then apply the model to the next policy alternative to predict the number of people who are successfully served by the program and the total program cost. For this form of disciplined calculation, you should build a spreadsheet model that will let you go back and easily change your inputs to reflect new insights, better data, or additional requests from the client. Doing so will save you time and effort compared to doing all your computations on a one-off basis with pen, paper, and a calculator.

Another approach to visualizing the future in classical policy analysis is to apply the *tools of microeconomics* to predict how firms and individuals will behave in response to changes in public policy. As we discussed in Chapter 9, traditional microeconomics historically assumed that firms are profit-maximizers and that consumers allocate their scarce resources to maximize their personal well-being. Modern microeconomics now includes behavioral economics, a subfield that explicitly integrates empirical evidence about firm and individual behavior rather than relying solely on predictions deduced from assumptions about the propensity of firms and consumers to continuously optimize their responses to market conditions.

Microeconomics gives us a set of powerful tools for visualizing the future. As discussed in Section 9.2, we can use supply and demand elasticities for projecting the revenue raised by a tax (or the government outlays associated with providing subsidies), as well as how the prices and quantities of the item being taxed (or subsidized) are likely to change in response to public policy. Economists often calculate both short-run and long-run elasticities which, in turn, permit the calculation of policy impacts that evolve over time. In Chapter 9, we also reviewed how Congressional Budget Office (CBO) studied potential increases in the Federal minimum wage by conducting microeconomic analysis of the ways in which firms and workers would react to an increase in the Federal minimum.

Microeconomics may be less helpful when it comes to visualizing impacts that go beyond goods and services bought and sold in markets (e.g., normative issues of social justice). But it may still be very helpful in understanding some of the origins of such issues (e.g., poverty or income inequality), as well as in providing insight into how firms and individuals will likely respond to policies to address them. For example, a redistributive tax policy may be motivated by normative concerns about income inequality. While microeconomics can't tell us whether one distribution of income is more or less fair than another, it can help us both to identify the market-based drivers of wealth and poverty and to predict how inequality may change as firms, workers, and households respond to new income redistribution policies.

A third approach to visualizing the future relies on *extrapolations from existing evidence and historical experience*. It is depicted in Exhibit 13-1. The basic idea is that we first study real world conditions—which may be from the past in our current location or

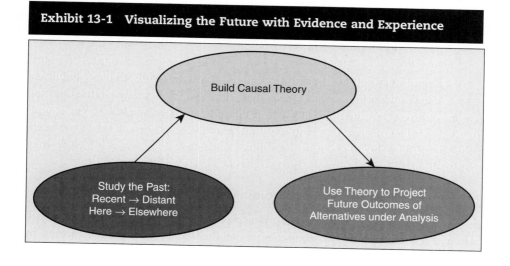

Exhibit 13-1 Visualizing the Future with Evidence and Experience

from the present but in another location—and come up with a causal theory to explain how policy action is linked to policy outcomes. Such studies may reflect purposefully designed policy experiments or may be nonexperimental in nature with statistical techniques used to discern causal relationships in available data. We then apply our theory to project how the future will play out under the policy options we're evaluating. Two forms of reasoning are applied during the process. The first is inductive reasoning where we infer a causal theory that explains our specific observations. With a broad principle established, we then use deductive reasoning to apply our theoretical understanding to the specific facts and circumstances relevant to our policy analysis.

We've discussed different aspects of this process in earlier chapters. Rather than repeat that material, I'll just hit the highlights:

- In Section 1.4, when we discussed the process of projecting outcomes in the classical model of policy analysis, we reviewed how you might *extrapolate* from policy results in one jurisdiction to project likely results in another jurisdiction.

- In Section 2.6, when we discussed how to establish a counterfactual for retrospective impact evaluation, we looked at four methods for *estimating the impacts of a program* including a before and after comparison, a comparison to a projection based on past trends, a difference-in-differences comparison of treatment and comparison groups, and a randomized controlled trial.

- Sections 5.2 and 5.3 discussed the processes of, respectively, *deductive* and *inductive reasoning*. As noted above, both types of reasoning are needed to visualize the future based on extrapolations from existing evidence and historical experience.

- Section 6.3 reviewed the requirements for establishing the *validity of a causal theory* and noted the cumulative nature of construct, conclusion, internal, and external validity. If the test of external validity is not met, then we are unable to extrapolate from one case to another.

I recognize that this is a lot of material to master before you can have confidence in your visualization of the future under alternative policies. But as I said in Chapter 6, it's hard to overstate the importance of establishing external validity and generalizability when you're relying on extrapolation to reach a conclusion. The fact that a policy worked (then and there) is not evidence that the policy works (in general) or that it will work (here and now) (Cartwright & Hardie, 2012).

13.3.2 The Future Is Plural: Avoiding the Flaw of Averages

In many cases, the ultimate impact of a policy depends on how multiple uncertainties play out. It's tempting to give your client a definitive number—a point estimate—of the cost or impact of a policy option. In doing so, however, you are taking a future with many possible outcomes and acting as if there is only one version of the future. As Pherson and Huer put it:

> ... an intuitive trap [is] assuming a single solution, thinking in terms of only one likely (and predictable) outcome instead of acknowledging that "the future is plural" and several possible outcomes should be considered. (2021, p. 25)

Imagine you're in the mountains on a backpacking trip. You need to wade across a stream marked with a sign that says 'Average Depth: 3 Feet.' As a six-footer, you tie your expensive camera equipment to the top of your backpack and start across. You're near the far edge when you step into a deep pool and go completely under. You clamber out, and as you ponder your ruined equipment, you realize that just because the average depth is three feet, that doesn't mean there aren't parts of the stream where the water is much deeper. You've become a victim of the **Flaw of Averages** (Savage, 2012), a concept we first discussed in Chapter 6 as an example of a mistaken use of evidence. Funny story perhaps but what does it have to do with visualizing the future as part of policy analysis?

This might make more sense with a policy analysis example. Suppose you're estimating the cost of an after-school tutoring program where college students help high schoolers with their homework. You're not sure how many students will sign up, how many hours of help each will need, or even how much you'll have to pay the tutors. Think of these three considerations as the input variables to your analysis. The output is your projection of how much the program will cost. You take your best shot and assume 50 students will ask for a tutor, each will need eight hours of help per month, and you'll have to pay the college students $16.50 per hour. Accordingly, you tell your client that the program will cost $6,600 each month.

You've probably done your client a disservice by burying the uncertainty inherent in your analysis. By providing your client a single point estimate, you've implicitly told him or her that there's one version of the future when, in fact, there are many. Suppose that instead of 50 students a month, we get 35 or 65 in the program, and that the number of hours per student might be four or twelve, rather than eight. Finally, imagine that despite our best guess of $16.50 per hour as the cost of a tutor, we might end up paying as little as $15 or as much as $18 per hour. Now, instead of one future, we have 27 versions of the future (each one a combination of the three permutations of each variable.). Assuming all combinations of the three variables are equally likely, we can compute a **cumulative probability distribution** of the type shown in Exhibit 13-2.

The average is still $6,600 per month but we can now generate a lot more information. For example, if your client told you that the budget was $9,000, you could

Exhibit 13-2   The Future Is Plural: 27 Possibilities for Program Cost

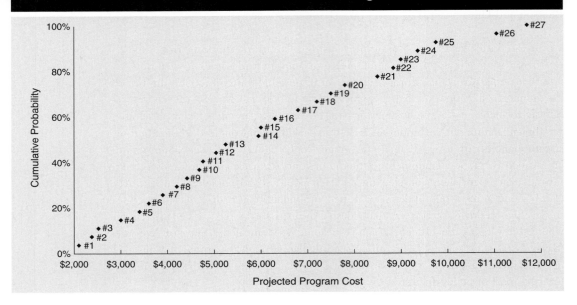

use the graph to discern that there is about an 85 percent chance that the cost will be within budget. (Case #23 lies on the vertical line associated with $9,000 and when we read over to the left axis for Case #23, we get the probability of about 85 percent.) You could also use the information in Exhibit 13-2 to draw other conclusions. There is, for example, a 27 percent chance that the cost will be less than $4,000 and a 63 percent chance that the price will be under $6,800.[5]

And yet even this is an oversimplification. Rather than 27 discrete versions of the future, there is an almost infinite number of possibilities. Instead of having 35 or 50 or 65 students in the program, we could have anywhere between 35 and 65 students. Heck, we could even have more than 65 or less than 35. Similar uncertainty applies to the other two input variables. In more complex situations, where there are multiple input variables that can probabilistically take on a wide range of values and which may interact in complicated ways, policy analysts often resort to a technique known as **Monte Carlo modeling**, or stochastic simulation modeling. This method entails repeated simulations—often several thousand iterations—in which different values are generated for each input variable. The resulting outputs of each simulation are

---

[5]Now might be a good time to glance back at Section 5.6 for a quick review of probabilistic reasoning.

recorded and then used to generate probabilistic forecasts of the range and likelihood of key output variables. Software packages like @Risk and Crystal Ball make it relatively easy to do Monte Carlo modeling within a spreadsheet.

13.3.3 Making Decisions for Uncertain Futures

In this section, we'll review the basics of a method that uses a decision tree to depict how the future may unfold and then applies a technique referred to as **expected value analysis** to identify potentially superior choices. It builds directly on the plural and probabilistic nature of the future that is described in the prior section. There are four basic elements in this type of analysis. We first specify a set of *decision alternatives* that represent the different courses of action we might take. We next identify the relevant *states of nature*, which constitute the uncontrollable and uncertain future events that dictate how well (or poorly) each decision alternative will perform. Third, we need to estimate the *probability of each state* of nature. Finally, we estimate the *payoff of each potential outcome*, where an outcome represents the combination of one decision alternative and one state of nature. To illustrate, let's look at an example.

Suppose you are in charge of firefighting for a county in the western United States prone to wildfires during the summer. A key part of your plan is the use of aerial tankers capable of dropping large quantities of fire retardant from the air. Though very effective, the tankers don't come cheap. Several companies own and lease tankers to localities (like yours), states, and the federal government. You can lease a tanker on an exclusive use (EU) basis, meaning that for the duration of the fire season, yours is the only agency that can use the aircraft. Or, you can lease a tanker on a call-when-needed (CWN) basis, meaning that when a major fire erupts, you contact the company and they send you the plane within 24 hours. The cost differential between an EU and a CWN lease is significant. The cost comprises two elements—one fixed for the season and the other dependent on the number of days of use. In this hypothetical example, an EU tanker costs $1.5 million for the season, plus $10,000 per day of use, while a CWN tanker requires a $200,000 fee for the season but then costs $80,000 per day of use.

Which type of lease should you sign on behalf of your county? Of course, as a prudent steward of taxpayer money, you want to select the least cost option. A problem arises, however, because to figure out which option is cheaper, you need to know how many days during the fire season will require use of an air tanker. To keep things simple, we'll assume that the number of fire days could be 5, 25, or 40. (The method works exactly the same if you want to analyze any number of days; the math just gets more tedious.) Exhibit 13-3 lays out our decision situation.

As you can see, neither option is unambiguously superior to the other. If you need to have the tanker in the air for 40 days of the fire season, the CWN option is much more expensive than the EU option ($3.4 million versus $1.9 million). But, if there are

Exhibit 13-3 Costs of Aerial Firefighting

	Number of Days of Fire		
	40	25	5
Lease an Exclusive Use Aircraft			
Fixed Cost	$1,500,000	$1,500,000	$1,500,000
Variable Cost	$400,000	$250,000	$50,000
Total Cost	$1,900,000	$1,750,000	$1,550,000
Lease a Call-When-Needed Aircraft			
Fixed Cost	$200,000	$200,000	$200,000
Variable Cost	$3,200,000	$2,000,000	$400,000
Total Cost	$3,400,000	$2,200,000	$600,000

only five days when the tanker is used, the situation reverses, and the CWN option becomes a lot less expensive ($600,000 versus $1.55 million). If you're an optimist, you might assume the best case (a five-day fire season) and select the CWN options, thereby saving almost a million dollars. But if you're a pessimist, you might select the EU option, knowing that even though you might spend $1.9 million, you'll be protected against having to spend even more with the CWN option.[6]

But rather than relying on intuition, or pessimistic or optimistic views of risk, can we do better? If we have credible probabilities for the likelihood of each state of nature, then the answer is yes. We can use what is called an **expected value approach**. The basic rule is to calculate the expected cost of each decision alternative by first multiplying the probability of each outcome by the payoff of each outcome under that alternative and then summing the results for each alternative. We then repeat the process for all other decision alternatives.

The decision rule is then to select the alternative with the lowest expected cost. The method also works when there are both costs and benefits to each alternative; in such cases, we first add costs and benefits to yield a net number before multiplying by the relevant probability. Moreover, sometimes we are interested in the option with the

---

[6]If you're committed to the Good Shepard model of public service (see Chapter 11), it's not *your* optimism or pessimism that matters. Instead, your approach should match the risk preferences of the County Board or county residents in general.

Exhibit 13-4   Decision Tree for Aerial Firefighting Decision

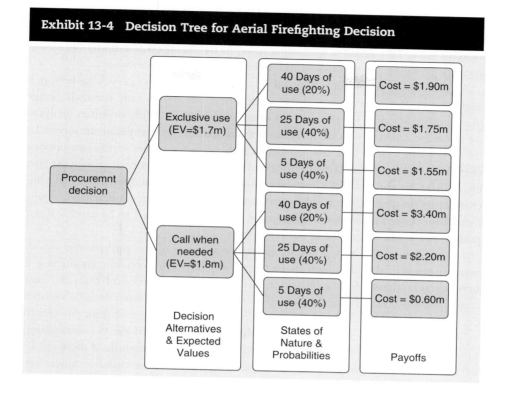

highest benefits, rather than the lowest cost. The method works the same way, but the decision rule is reversed (i.e., select the option with the highest net benefits). All of these calculations can be depicted in a decision-tree format, as shown in Exhibit 13-4.

By looking at the decision tree, we can see that the EU option has an expected value of $1.7 million while the CWN option has an expected value of $1.8 million. According to our decision rule, we should opt for the EU option because, on average, doing so will save $100,000. It's important to recognize that the actual cost that we observe in the future will *not* be $1.7 million. It will be $1.90 million, $1.75 million, or $1.55 million. This method asks us to imagine many, many repeated versions of the future: 20 percent of the time, the cost will be $1.90 million; 40 percent of the time, it will be $1.75 million; and 20 percent of the time, it will be $1.55 million. On *average*, the cost will be $1.7 million (i.e., the expected value). In other words, as we saw in our discussion of the flaw of averages, while an average value conveys important information about an unknown situation, it doesn't convey *all* of the relevant information.

It's also important to recognize that the probabilities used to characterize the future states of nature can affect the outcome significantly. For example, if we decrease the probability of a 40-day fire season from 20 to 10 percent and increase the chance of a 5-day season from 40 to 50 percent, the least cost option switches, with the CWN option having an expected value of $1.52 million while, at $1.665 million, the EU option now has a higher expected value. This should make intuitive sense. As the likelihood of a shorter fire season goes up, paying for the season-long EU option is less likely to save money.

There are a couple of additional analyses you can do once you've set up a decision-tree framework. First, if the results show one option only narrowly better than another, it's time for what we call **sensitivity analysis**. With sensitivity analysis, we assess the extent to which our conclusions are sensitive to changes in our inputs. In this case, we'd look at how the gap between the expected values of the two options changes as we vary the probabilities assumed for the states of nature or change the cost elements of the options. If the least cost option remains the same even as we make big changes in the inputs, we say that our result is robust. On the other hand, if our conclusion is highly sensitive to changes in the inputs, we need to be careful about putting too much confidence in our conclusion.

Second, if you're having doubts about the accuracy of the probabilities you've used to measure the likelihood of each state of the world, consider conducting a **breakeven analysis**. With a breakeven analysis, you work backward from the outcomes of the decision choices and ask yourself what value of the input decision variable (in our example, the number of days with fires) would tip the answer from one choice to the other. Some basic algebra tells us that, given the cost of the two firefighting options, the breakeven point is approximately 19 days. In other words, if there are 19 days of fire, the CWN option and EU option have about the same cost. So, rather than coming up with the probabilities of each of three states of the world (5, 25, or 40 days of fire), we reframe (and simplify) the problem by asking whether it's likely that there will be more than 19 days of fire. If the answer is yes, then the EU option has the lowest cost; otherwise the CWN option is cheaper.

Finally, always bear in mind that the expected value approach can offer meaningful decision guidance *only if all of the important consequences* of the decision choices have been incorporated in the analysis. If, for example, the 24-hour delay in the arrival of the air tanker under the CWN option means that additional land will be burned, with potential property damage or loss of life, then our expected value analysis is incomplete. To address such a shortcoming, we'd need to come up with a way to quantify and monetize the additional consequences.

13.4 VISUALIZING THE FUTURE IN A REBOOTED POLICY ANALYSIS

In this book, I argue that the classical version of policy analysis provides a great foundation for aspiring analysts. But it is not enough. It doesn't provide sufficient guidance about how to tackle many of the tasks typically given to policy analysts;

hence, the proposed 'rebooting' suggested by the book's title. One area where the classical model can come up short is when you're told to fill in the cells of your criteria-alternatives matrix with projections of the future. Yes, the methods described in the prior section can yield significant insight. Such approaches can work well when:

- There is limited uncertainty about current circumstances and about the factors that will drive future conditions

- You have a well-defined problem, a manageable set of well-defined policy options, and a definitive set of evaluation criteria

But these methods can falter in the face of wicked problems, rapidly changing conditions, and an unpredictable future. Below are a couple of suggestions for handling such situations.

13.4.1 Setting Your System Map in Motion

Traditional maps have two primary uses. The first is to provide an accurate depiction of the relevant terrain. The second is as an aid to navigation. The same is true of a policy-oriented system map, irrespective of whether it's a problem tree, influence diagram, or causal loop diagram (CLD). Let's consider how we might use a system map to better visualize the future (i.e., as an aid to navigation). The basic idea is to set your map in motion by introducing a policy intervention that changes one or more of its elements or causal links. You then use the map to trace the likely consequences as those changes spread across the system.

If you look back at the population model in Exhibit 12-6, you'll see a simple example of this process. The middle and lower panels of the exhibit display the impacts of changes in the birth and death rates. Suppose, for example, that the upper panel in Exhibit 12-7 (with a birth rate of 1 percent and a death rate of 2.5 percent) represents the status quo. If we introduce public health measures that reduce infant mortality and extend life expectancy, leading to birth and death rates of 2.4 percent and 1.5 percent respectively, we can expect the system to respond as shown in the lower panel. Instead of declining to about 220,000 people over a hundred years, the population would increase to about 2.4 million.

If you've built a CLD in which all elements are quantified, you can use software tools to simulate the impact of changes to different parts of the system. But even if you're working with a problem tree, influence diagram, or CLD that's not fully quantified, you can still use a system map to visualize the future without specialized software. To do so, you need to take a qualitative but disciplined approach to figuring out how a policy intervention will affect a system. As long as you are methodical, trace causal impacts through the entire system, and keep good notes, your system map will let you see how a policy change in one part of a system will affect the rest of the system.

13.4.2 Scenario Planning

Scenario planning takes the plurality of the future a step further than the probabilistic forecasts described in Section 13.3.2. Rather than predicting the future under each proposed policy option, scenario planning first creates multiple visions of the future—each referred to as a **scenario**—independent of specific policy options.[7] Planners don't worry about the probability of each scenario or whether it satisfies a normative goal about what the future *should* look like. Instead, the test of a good scenario is that it represents a plausible description of what the future might hold (Ramirez, Churchhouse, Palmero, & Hoffman, 2017). Having developed a set of plausible scenarios that capture the range of possible future outcomes, scenario planning then asks what policies might be appropriate and how each policy would fare under each version of the future.

This inverted analytic process goes by different names, including backwards analysis, bottom-up planning, or context-first (Lempert, 2019). Scenario planning can be a complex exercise and is not applied in the same manner by all practitioners, but the basics are straightforward:

> The aim of scenario thinking is to identify important strategic uncertainties surrounding the policy area [of concern] and to explore how they might play out in the future. … Scenarios are not predictions. They are not meant to be 'right' or 'wrong,' 'good' or 'bad,' but to offer interesting (and in some cases challenging, stretching, or controversial) pictures of the future. (UK GOS, 2017, p. 52)

We first establish a timeframe, usually a minimum of five to ten years, sometimes a couple of decades, and occasionally 50 or more years. We next identify the key *drivers most likely to produce major societal change* over the planning horizon. Doing so is not a formulaic process conducted the same way in each case; instead, scenario planning relies heavily on consultation with stakeholders and subject matter experts who are familiar with relevant conditions or who are likely to be affected by changes in those conditions. To jump start the process, we begin by asking whether major change is possible along dimensions such as:[8]

- Political (elections, public opinion, protest movements)

- Economic (cycles of prosperity and recession, patterns of development)

- Social (lifestyle preferences, cultural norms)

---

[7] We got a glimpse of this approach in Chapter 11 when we looked at potentially disruptive scientific and technological changes that could be on the horizon. Exhibit 11-3 listed several examples.
[8] This list is drawn from Stapleton (2020).

- Technological (new products, processes)

- Legal (evolving requirements across levels of government)

- Public health (disease, health-related behaviors, medical therapies)

- Environmental (weather, climate, ecosystems)

- Demographic (population growth and decline; local, regional, and international migration)

You'll note some similarity of these potential drivers of societal change to the seven lenses of panoptic analysis that we talked about in Part III. The key difference is that the lenses are policy-centric, intended to help us understand the nature of specific policy problems and the constraints and opportunities for particular policy actions. On the other hand, the societal drivers considered in scenario planning are much broader. You can think about it this way: With the panoptic use of the lenses, we start with a policy issue and broaden our focus to understand its context. With scenario planning, we work in the opposite direction. We start with drivers of broad societal change and then, having characterized multiple scenarios, narrow our focus to develop and evaluate specific policies in the context of each scenario.

After identifying the potential drivers of societal change, our next task is to decide which to incorporate into our analysis. The selected drivers then become the basis of the scenarios to be analyzed. Our goal is to identify drivers of change that have two characteristics. First, the most relevant drivers will be those about which there is the *greatest uncertainty*; if a particular societal change is all but inevitable, there will be little value in building multiple scenarios to consider alternative paths for that change. Second, we're interested in drivers with the *greatest potential impact on societal conditions*. Drivers potentially responsible for only small changes in conditions don't merit much attention.

Exhibit 13-5 depicts this process graphically. On the vertical axis is the degree of uncertainty and on the horizontal axis is the likely impact. I've divided the plot into four quadrants (based on the compass). For example, drivers of societal change about which there is little uncertainty and only minimal impact (i.e., are not especially relevant to scenario planning) are placed in the southwest quadrant. Moreover, drivers in the northwest and southeast quadrants likely don't merit detailed analysis because they are either, respectively, not particularly impactful or not particularly uncertain.[9] Conversely, as we move to the upper right (i.e., the northeast quadrant), the drivers

---

[9]That doesn't mean you should ignore drivers in the southeast quadrant. Such drivers are likely to have a big impact on society, but because they are virtually certain, there's no need for scenario planning. Instead, you can directly apply the classical model of policy analysis to figure out how to move forward (UK GOS, 2017).

Exhibit 13-5 Analyzing Drivers of Societal Change

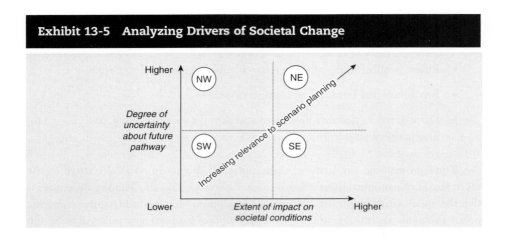

become more relevant to scenario planning since these drivers exhibit high uncertainty and have potentially large impacts on society.

Having identified a handful of relevant drivers of societal change that are both important and uncertain, we move to the next phase of scenario planning where we combine these drivers to form scenarios. An example may help. Assume we're doing regional planning and have identified three drivers—climate, the economy, and social cohesion—for which the future is both very uncertain and especially important in shaping the fate of the region in coming years. In the simplest case, as depicted in Exhibit 13-6, we consider two possible paths for each

Exhibit 13-6 Illustrative Scenario Planning: Key Drivers of Societal Change

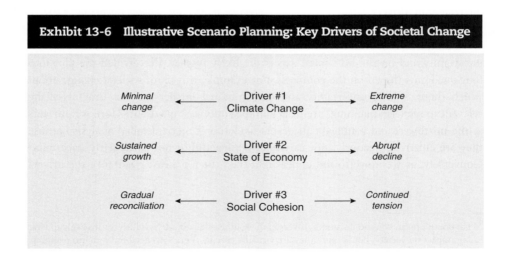

driver, where the future societal changes ultimately turn out to be either major or minor.[10]

We continue the example in Exhibit 13-7 in which we combine the possible pathways for each driver to form scenarios. With two permutations for each of three drivers, we end up with eight potential scenarios. It's possible that you might decide that one or more scenarios is sufficiently unlikely that it can be dropped from further consideration. In this case, for example, we might decide that in the face of extreme climate change and an abrupt economic decline, it's unlikely that gradual reconciliation across socioeconomic lines will happen. Accordingly, we might drop Scenario 7 from further analysis.

The next step is to develop a *narrative description of what the future 'looks like'* in each scenario. Doing so is primarily a qualitative exercise in which policy analysts, subject matter experts, and stakeholders work collaboratively to characterize conditions that would likely result if the drivers embedded in the scenario actually came to pass (Stapleton, 2020). Doing so requires mental discipline. The narrative—which might be a few paragraphs or a few pages—needs to take as given that the societal drivers play out as specified in the scenario. For example, in our illustrative regional planning case, a normally optimistic analyst who believes social reconciliation is likely may encounter cognitive dissonance when working on Scenarios 2, 4, 6, and 8 which presume continued tension across socioeconomic lines. The point of scenario planning is to force ourselves to consider alternate versions of the future. Accordingly, personal predictions need to be set aside when developing scenario narratives.

Finally, scenario analysis is linked back to policy analysis in a process referred to as **policy stress-testing** (UK GOS, 2017). Doing so entails applying the classical paradigm—problem, alternatives, criteria, projections, trade-offs—to each scenario, one scenario at a time. Doing so might reveal that a particular policy option is a great idea under one scenario but could be problematic in another. The key departure from the classical model, however, is that rather than predict a single future and identify the optimal policy, the inverted approach of scenario planning allows for multiple futures and seeks policy options that perform well in a range of plausible futures. Such options are referred to as **robust** (Lempert, 2019).

It's not the norm with scenario planning, but you can combine scenario planning with the type of probabilistic thinking described in the prior section (Scoblic & Tetlock, 2020). To do so, we need to assign a probability to each scenario to capture the likelihood that the scenario would actually come to pass. Across all scenarios, the

---

[10]More sophisticated versions of scenario planning consider many futures for each driver and more than a handful of drivers. Software tools are available to analyze hundreds of possible futures to identify policies most likely to be effective across many scenarios. Doing so makes the work more complex, but the basic idea is the same.

Exhibit 13-7 An Illustration of Scenario Planning at a Regional Level

Scenario	Key Drivers of Societal Change over Planning Horizon					
	Climate Change		State of Economy		Social Cohesion	
	Minimal Change	Extreme Change	Sustained Growth	Abrupt Decline	Gradual Reconciliation	Continued Tension
1: Stable weather patterns, prosperity, improved community relations	✔		✔		✔	
2: Stable weather patterns, prosperity, socioeconomic tension	✔		✔			✔
3: Stable weather patterns, economic disruption, improved community relations	✔			✔	✔	
4: Stable weather patterns, economic disruption, socioeconomic tension	✔			✔		✔
5: Extreme weather, prosperity, improved community relations		✔	✔		✔	
6: Extreme weather, prosperity, socioeconomic tension		✔	✔			✔
7: Extreme weather, economic disruption, improved community relations		✔		✔	✔	
8: Extreme weather, economic disruption, socioeconomic tension		✔		✔		✔

probabilities must sum to 100 percent. Especially in cases where we can't find a policy option that performs well in all scenarios (i.e., a robust policy), it may make sense to focus on options that perform well in the most likely of the scenarios.

13.5 HONING YOUR PREDICTIVE SKILLS

Given the important role played by projective inference in high quality policy analysis, it's worth your time to think about how you can get better at it. For starters, think about the cognitive biases, heuristic traps, and the risks of System 1 thinking, motivated reasoning, and hot cognition that we discussed in Chapter 4. All of these tendencies can impede your ability to develop high quality projections of how policy choices made today will affect conditions in the future. In addition, think back to the distinction I made in Chapter 7 between **foxes** and **hedgehogs**. These labels originate in the work of Philip Tetlock who studied the cognitive styles of pundits who made hundreds of predictions about political and policy matters over several years (2005). Foxes assimilate many points of view and sources of information when they think about the future, while hedgehogs apply a single overarching world view to explain all situations. Foxes are intellectually humble and quick to admit flawed thinking, whereas hedgehogs are highly confident in their predictions and rarely own up to their mistakes. And most relevant to this discussion, foxes are much better at correctly projecting future outcomes than are hedgehogs. Accordingly, as an aspiring policy analyst, I suggest that you adopt the approach of a fox rather than a hedgehog. For a reminder of some of the other differences between the two cognitive styles, you may want to take a look back at Section 7.6 in which I described the mindset of an effective policy analyst.

As mentioned in Section 7.4, Tetlock and his colleagues continued their research into the topic when they undertook a study for the Intelligence Advanced Research Programs Activity (IARPA) between 2011 and 2015. In it, close to 3,000 volunteers made about 150,000 probabilistic forecasts in response to geopolitical and economic questions. Each question was specific and time-limited, so it was possible to assess whether the forecast proved correct or not (i.e., a particular candidate won or lost a foreign election, or military hostilities did or did not occur in a specific location prior to a cutoff date). Tetlock's team then studied the attributes of the most accurate forecasters and the methods they used to make their predictions (2015).

The best of the forecasters scored higher than average on intelligence tests but were typically not at the top end of the scale. In other words, you don't have to be a genius to be a good forecaster. You do, however, have to be thoughtful, curious, and open-minded. It also helps to have domain expertise: a solid understanding of the issues, history, and players relevant to the topic you're studying. But such expertise is not necessarily indicated by academic degrees or professional credentials; instead, it comes from actually putting in the time to study and understand a topic. The best forecasters were also more willing to revise their forecasts. Rather than making an initial forecast and staying with it, the top performers frequently revised their predictions as new information came in.

In addition, the folks who were the best at predicting answers to the study's questions were numerate, at ease with numbers, and able to put them to practical use. They also tended to be adept at probabilistic reasoning. You certainly don't need to be a statistician to be a good forecaster, but you do need an intuitive feel for the difference between odds of 60/40 and odds of 40/60. Moreover, you need to appreciate the logic of Bayesian reasoning (as we discussed in Section 5.6.2) in which the background probability of an outcome *in general* (i.e., the base rate) needs to be combined with case-specific evidence to yield a valid estimate of the probability of the outcome in the *particular* situation at hand.

Tetlock and his colleagues also observed that practice improves the accuracy of predictions. The more predictions a person made, the better they got at the process. But such improvements depend on a feedback loop in which each person learns whether his or her forecast was accurate and knows that others—in this case, the researchers—are paying attention to their accuracy. Accordingly, over the course of your career, you'll want to monitor your predictive skills. Don't be afraid to go back and find your mistakes—you can learn from them!

The same process is also applicable at the institutional level. The Congressional Budget Office (CBO), for example, annually publishes a review of the accuracy of its prior-year projections of government spending and revenue in an effort to improve its future forecasts. CBO also regularly releases comparisons of its economic projections with those of other government agencies and private forecasters (CBO, 2021c). Though it may feel awkward to subject your forecasts to after-the-fact public review, based on Tetlock's work, doing so almost certainly has the benefit of improving the quality of your projections about future conditions.

Working in teams was also shown to improve the quality of forecasts in the IARPA project, as hearing other points of view and explaining your own point of view to teammates can create a kind of scrubbing process in which faulty thinking comes to light, and multiple insights from different people are integrated into a single prediction. When it comes to teamwork, however, there is an important caveat. Yes, teams outperform individuals but only if there is constructive, rather than destructive, confrontation among team members.[11] Open, collaborative debate improves quality of a forecast, but if debate devolves into nothing more than arguments among folks with entrenched points of view, then it doesn't help.

---

[11]You might want to revisit Section 3.3.1 on the difference between a good-faith argument and a fight. And in Chapter 15, we'll revisit the topic of how to enhance your teamwork skills.

CHAPTER SUMMARY

This chapter started by describing how policy action taken in the present is invariably motivated by expectations of its impacts in the future. In turn, visualizing the future under alternative policy measures is an integral part of policy analysis. I noted that the specific aspects of the future that need to be visualized depend on the evaluation criteria that you select for use in your criteria-alternatives matrix. We next reviewed the theoretical basis of projective inference and considered the projection methods typically associated with the classical model of policy analysis.

We discussed the plurality of the future and the role of probabilistic projections in policy analysis. The techniques of expected value analysis, sensitivity analysis, and breakeven analysis were then presented. We next considered other ways of visualizing the future in a rebooted version of policy analysis, including systems analysis and scenario planning. The chapter concluded with a review of empirical evidence about what it takes to make more accurate forecasts of the future.

DISCUSSION QUESTIONS

1. Is it possible that trying to visualize the future is so difficult and error-prone that it's not worth the effort? Why? Why not? If it is worth the effort, how can you judge in the present the quality of projections about the future?

2. Pick a policy reform you would like to see implemented. What impacts do you expect it to have? What unintended consequences might it cause? How sure are you about your predictions of what will (or won't) happen after the policy is implemented?

3. Can you come up with three policies that might be implemented in lieu of the policy you picked in the prior question? What evaluation criteria would you use to capture the pros and cons of each alternative? How would you project future outcomes of each policy with respect to each criterion?

4. What do you think of the expected value approach for probabilistic decision-making? Under what circumstances would it work well? Under which circumstances might it lead a policymaker to the wrong conclusion?

5. Pick a policy reform that you support and the context in which it would be implemented. Can you develop five different scenarios about how that context will have changed a decade from now? How well will your preferred policy perform

under the five different scenarios? Can you imagine a policy that would perform well in all scenarios?

6. Do you like working with colleagues in groups? Or do you usually feel like it's a lot of drama for very little gain? How often do you get new insights from colleagues that you find to be genuinely valuable to your thinking?

CHAPTER FOURTEEN

DESIGNING AND (RE)DESIGNING PUBLIC POLICIES

Take a second and think about this question: If there are three frogs sitting on a log, and two decide to jump off the log and into the swamp, how many frogs are left behind?

Most folks instinctively say that there's one frog left, but they're wrong. There are still three frogs on the log, because deciding to do something is not the same as doing it. When it comes to public policy, good intentions are not enough. If you want to have a meaningful impact on a policy problem, you need to design and implement a sensible, workable, and strategically coherent policy. This chapter addresses the process of designing new, and redesigning existing, public policies. As an aspiring analyst, you'll want to master these skills; if a particular public policy lacks a sound design, the chances that it will mitigate a policy problem are slim.

The chapter opens with a series of questions you need to answer before jumping into the policy design process. The next section looks at how you can take successful policies from one place and adapt them for use in another. We then consider how to develop new policy options from scratch when you don't have other examples to work from. Next up is a review of how to use theory of change thinking and the principles of strategic alignment to improve the quality of a policy design. The final two sections of the chapter focus on working with stakeholders to design policy options. We first consider user-focused design thinking as a means of coming up with policy options and then review a pragmatic technique for keeping track of what it will take to engender support and minimize opposition at each step of the implementation process.

Learning Objectives

By studying this chapter, you should be able to:

- Characterize the differences between design for analysis and design for implementation.

- Find proposed or existing policies and adapt them for use in a different jurisdiction.

- Recognize how public policies affect the choice architecture faced by individuals, firms, and other institutions.

- Explain policy options including mandates, command and control instruments, market-based instruments, nudges, public–private partnerships, outreach campaigns, and information disclosure.

- Recognize the importance of policy sequencing and explain how it can be used to increase the chances of successful policy implementation.

- Develop strategically aligned policy designs that are built on a convincing theory of change, reflect sound logic modeling, facilitate ongoing learning, and provide flexibility to future policymakers.

- Explain and apply the principles of user-focused policy design to remedy an incomplete understanding of a policy issue and minimize the risk of confirmation bias and mirror imaging.

- Explain and differentiate three forms of stakeholder consultation: participation, engagement, and inclusion.

- Use stakeholder mapping and analysis to develop policy designs that engender support and minimize opposition at each step of the implementation process.

14.1 STARTING POINTS

Before thinking about alternative designs for a particular policy, it's important to clarify the context for your efforts. As shown in Exhibit 14-1, you need to answer some basic questions before getting started. If you're using a retrospective program evaluation to redesign an existing policy, the answers to many of the questions may be obvious; nonetheless, it's a good idea to quickly run through them to ensure that you don't overlook opportunities for beneficial changes to the program you're working on. We'll discuss each topic in turn below.

Exhibit 14-1 Starting Points

- Why government?

- Which level of government?

- New or existing agency?

- Build or buy?

- Legal constraints?

- Budgetary constraints?

- One and done?

- Design for analysis (DFA) or design for implementation (DFI)?

- Point of departure: Problem, policy proposal, or existing program?

- Symbolic or instrumental?

Start by asking yourself why the problem at hand is the government's to solve. It may be that markets, civil society,[1] or families and individuals are better able to address the problem than is government. Even if it makes sense to look to government for action, bear in mind that public policy is not a panacea; success is not assured. In Section 10.2, we talked about the concept of government failure in which a number of factors—like electoral cycles, the principal–agent problem, and the absence of a singular overriding objective—may impede government's ability to deliver results

---

[1]Civil society comprises a wide array of nongovernmental organizations such as nonprofit institutions, charities, trade associations, religious groups, colleges and universities, media and journalists, and civic groups.

consistent with a policy's intent. And remember, maintaining current policy is always an option. The status quo may be a lousy situation, but it might be the best we can do (at least with respect to public policy).

Once you've concluded that it makes sense to consider government action to address a particular issue, ask yourself which level of government—federal, state, tribal, or local—offers the best prospect for a successful outcome. Our discussion of federalism in Chapter 10 highlighted the pros and cons of using different levels of government to address policy issues while Chapter 11 reviewed the legal environment in which federal, state, tribal, and local governments operate. Sometimes it makes sense for a particular level of government to act on its own, as in the case of foreign affairs and defense at the national level or water and sewage systems at the local level. In other cases, a federalized response in which different levels of government collaborate to execute policy (e.g., the design and operation of the interstate highway system) may be appropriate. Finally, governments at the same level may find it effective to coordinate policy, such as when local governments in a metropolitan area work together on transportation and air quality issues.

Of course, the answer to the 'which level of government' question depends, at least in part, on context. If you work for a local official, for example, there may be pressure to focus on policies that can be enacted at the local level. Nonetheless, you still need to be ready to answer the question of why, in this example, the local—rather than state or federal—government should take action. Even if your boss doesn't ask the question, opponents of the policy you propose probably will.

Having settled on the appropriate level of government to implement a particular policy, consider whether an existing agency, department, or bureau—or a newly established entity—should be given responsibility for implementation. With an existing agency, you may be able to tap into technical expertise and a network of stakeholder relationships that facilitate a successful result. On the other hand, an existing agency may be trapped in a standard way of doing business that impedes its ability to implement a policy that is a radical departure from the status quo. In such cases, you might elect to establish a new agency that can bring a fresh and innovative perspective to program implementation. Doing so, however, will likely take more time because the agency must be organized and staffed before it can begin implementation.

The final question to ask is whether nongovernmental partners can or should be given a role in program implementation. In the private sector, this is often referred to as the 'build or buy' decision. In the government sector, this decision plays out as a choice between delivering a program using only public employees (i.e., the 'build' option) and using a mix of contractor and grantee resources to support program delivery (i.e., the 'buy' option). Recall from Chapter 10 that only 39% of the federal government's blended workforce of about 9 million workers are directly employed by the government while the other 61% work for the private and nonprofit sectors. You may not be able to definitively answer the build or buy question for a particular policy until after you get farther into your policy analysis, but it's important to bear in mind from the outset that looking to nongovernmental partners to support a program is almost always a possibility.

As you initiate the policy design process, you also need to identify factors that may constrain your choices. While you don't want to be timid about pursuing whatever new and innovative policies seem best suited for the policy problem in front of you, you need to be realistic and avoid spending time and effort on policies that have no chance of enactment. For starters, when you look through a legal lens, it's obvious that your policy design needs to be legal. Policymakers at all levels of government are constrained by their constitutional and statutory authorities. Yes, in some cases, the enactment of new policy alters the legal regime, but policymakers are nonetheless bound by court decisions, statutory preemption of their authority by higher levels of government, and by state and federal constitutions.

Another practical reality is that you and your client face budgetary constraints. If there is a fixed budget available to address a particular policy issue, it doesn't make sense to design policies that cost significantly more unless the intent is to use the greater cost as an argument for increasing the budget. Moreover, don't assume that just because the money appears to be available, spending it to address the policy issue at hand is its best use. All spending creates an opportunity cost; money spent on one problem is money not available to be spent on another (or not raised from taxpayers in the first place).

Another constraint arises if you're in a one-and-done situation, meaning that there's only a single opportunity—at least for the foreseeable future—to tackle a problem, rather than a chance to create an evolving policy design that will be part of an ongoing effort to address the problem. Recall our discussion of Kingdon's theory of the policy process in which change typically occurs only when the problem, policy, and political streams align, and a policy window opens. If you think the window will remain open for a long time, you can consider policy designs that incorporate experimentation, learning, and improvement over time, because the open window affords you and your client the opportunity to adjust the policy's original design. If you expect the window to close soon, you'll be forced to design the best policy you can based on available information, knowing that you probably won't be able to come back later and fix problems that are only discovered after implementation begins.

Policy design is often an evolutionary process (Eggers & O'Leary, 2009). It starts with an idea or a notion about how a new program might work or how an existing program might be revised. Typically, such ideas get refined, with more detail added as debate and discussion unfolds. As policy designs enter the political arena, they typically undergo additional changes to attract supporters and mollify opponents. After formal enactment into law, government agencies must then work out the details of implementation. If politicians have been highly prescriptive in the policy, there may be little latitude for additional policy design on the part of government agencies. Conversely, if lawmakers leave things vague, public administrators may have broad discretion to consider alternative designs for the program.

As a policy analyst, you may be asked to support any part of this process. Accordingly, when you're trying to come up with a policy design, it's important to know where you are in the process. You can think of a continuum defined by two end points. In one case, prior to policy enactment and well before implementation, you engage in **design for analysis (DFA)**. In other cases, after policy action becomes certain, you engage in **design for implementation (DFI)**. As Exhibit 14-2 shows, DFI requires more specificity and affords you less freedom to consider alternative designs than does DFA.

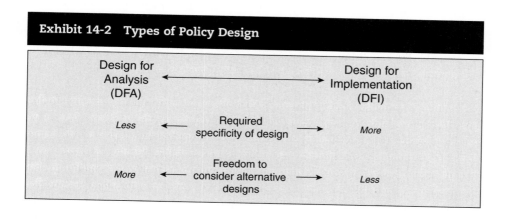

Exhibit 14-2   Types of Policy Design

With DFA, your goal is to develop policy designs that capture the possibilities for action and allow thoughtful analysis of the pros and cons of different paths forward. DFA is most appropriate in the early stages of policy analysis when, for example, you're asked to address a particular policy problem.[2] In such cases, you need to come up with alternative policy options to narrow the gap between the status quo and the state of the world we'd like to see. Similarly, you might be handed an incomplete policy idea and be asked to form it into a coherent policy option for further discussion.

On the other hand, with DFI, you know that a program *will* be implemented, and your objective is to design a specific and detailed approach likely to deliver the policy's

---

[2]Watch out for 'Potemkin Problems,' policy problems strategically defined by a political advocate in such a way that the only obvious solution serves the advocate's self-interest. In such cases, there may not even be a problem.

intended outcomes and impacts. Or you might be dealing with a program that *has been* implemented and where your objective is to apply DFI to the results of a retrospective evaluation and redesign the program. In short, design for analysis is meant to support policy *making* while design for implementation is meant to support policy *delivery*. We'll look again at both types of design work later in the chapter.

A final issue to resolve before diving into policy design reflects the distinction between symbolic and instrumental policies. The former signals that policymakers are aware of and appreciate the gravity of a particular policy issue, despite the fact that policy action may do little to change real world conditions:

> Even if government policies do not succeed in eliminating poverty, preventing crime, and so on, the failure of government to *try* to do these things would be even worse. Individuals, groups, and whole societies frequently judge public policy in terms of its good intentions rather than tangible accomplishments. Sometimes very popular programs have little positive tangible impact. (Dye, 2011, p. 326), *emphasis in original*

While a symbolic policy validates stakeholder concerns, an instrumental policy goes further and aims to have a material impact in mitigating the problem. And, as we saw in Chapter 10, policymakers sometimes feel compelled by a crisis to 'do something' even though a well thought-out policy is not available. Ideally, of course, we'd like all public policies to lead to genuine improvements in real world conditions, but that may not be possible. In such cases, your job is to come up with policy designs that adequately reflect symbolic values or demonstrate action in the face of a crisis, but do so at the least possible cost and with minimal adverse impact on other policy objectives.

14.2 'BORROWING' POLICY OPTIONS FROM ELSEWHERE

Having asked and answered the questions posed in the preceding section, you're ready to start the process of designing policy options.[3] One way to begin is with someone else's policy proposal or an existing policy from another jurisdiction that is then adapted to fit local circumstances. In this section, we'll start with some places to look for ideas, move to the process of extrapolating from one jurisdiction to another, and then talk about how to use an existing policy as a template for building a new design.

---

[3]As discussed in Chapter 1, when it comes to policy analysis, strong options are actionable, specific, descriptive rather than evaluative, and genuinely viable rather than dummy options.

14.2.1 Sources of Policy Options

Issue advocates—lobbyists, interest groups, op-ed writers, bloggers, politicians, and many think tanks—who argue for and against policy changes often offer up their preferred policy alternatives. While such proposals may lack detail, there is often good reason to include them in your analysis. Because they are part of the ongoing debate, you and your client will almost certainly want to understand the pros and cons of these proposals in order to be informed participants in the discussion. That said, a warning is in order. While it's fine to include an advocate's proposal in your analysis, never uncritically accept an advocate's claims about the outcomes of their policy. Advocates are hardly an unbiased source of information; it's your job to figure out whether their claims are true.

A second way to come up with policy alternatives to include in your analysis is to find out what neighboring jurisdictions are doing. Few policy problems are truly unique. If your city or state is wrestling with a policy issue, there's a good chance that another city or state is in a similar situation. Take a look at policies that have been implemented elsewhere (as well as policies that were considered but not implemented). While you can start with web-based research, try to reach out and have a real-time conversation with officials in other jurisdictions who work on the same issues that you do. In many policy areas, there are national networks of professionals working in the same field (e.g., the Association of State and Territorial Solid Waste Management Officials or the Association of State and Territorial Health Officials). Reaching out to these folks will undoubtedly give you some good ideas and help build your personal network at the same time.

A third source of potential policy alternatives for you to consider can be found in libraries of model policies, typically focused on states and localities. Given that the United States comprises tens of thousands of subnational governments, there can be significant economies of scale in policy development when one entity develops a complete and coherent policy template that can be adopted by policymakers in multiple locations. For example, the National League of Cities provides a model ordinance on accelerating broadband deployment at the local level (NLC & NATCO, 2018), the American Society of Heating, Refrigerating and Air-Conditioning Engineers publishes a high-efficiency building code that states and localities can adopt (ASHRAE, 2016), and the Vermont League of Towns and Cities provides a set of model local ordinances on a wide variety of topics (VLTC, 2019).

You should be aware, however, that developers of model policies are not always disinterested participants in the policymaking process. The American Legislative Exchange Council (ALEC), for example, attracted substantial negative press coverage when it was revealed as the source of several conservative policy templates related to, for example, stand-your-ground gun laws, gender-based bathroom rules, and pro-business right-to-work statutes (Rossman, 2019). But ideologically conservative groups are not the only authors of model legislation. A joint investigation by *USA Today*, *The Arizona Republic*, and the *Center for Public Integrity* reviewed thousands of legislative bills introduced mostly between 2010 and 2018 in the 50 states and in Congress for similarities to model legislation drafted by special interests. It found over 10,000 bills that had been copied almost verbatim from the models. About 2,100 of them were enacted into law. About half of the enacted bills matched models drafted by industry, approximately 40% came from conservative groups, and about 7% came from liberal groups (O'Dell & Penzenstadler, 2019). To be clear, I am *not* arguing against ideologically driven policy alternatives or those than originate in the business community; rather, I am simply suggesting that you take care not to unthinkingly accept a model policy without a good understanding of its origin and purpose.

A fourth place to look for ideas about policy alternatives that might belong in your analysis are What Works Clearinghouses maintained by independent researchers and government agencies. We first discussed these sites in Chapter 6 as a source of evidence about the results of existing programs. In this context, browsing through a clearinghouse's content may give you examples of successful policies that could become the basis of a policy design suitable for your jurisdiction.

14.2.2 The Replication Challenge

Once you've found an existing policy to use as a template for a new policy design in your location, what's next? You'll need to correctly understand the basic mechanisms—the program's key features and components—that are responsible for its success in the first location (Bardach, 2004; Bardach & Patashnik, 2016). Doing so requires that you satisfy the tests of both internal and external validity that we talked about in Section 6.3. The former allows you to draw valid conclusions about the causal processes in the program that has been studied, while the latter permits you to generalize those conclusions to other situations. In other words, you need to ensure that you extract the 'right' lesson from the first location so that it can be effectively replicated in the second. The 'right' lesson requires that you not only understand the causal connection between the program and its results in its original setting but that you express that lesson in a suitably generalized form that it can inform action in another setting.

In their book *Evidence-Based Policy*, Cartwright and Hardie illustrate this point with a story of two international nutrition programs, one in Tamil Nadu that succeeded in substantially reducing childhood malnutrition and another in Bangladesh, explicitly modeled on the first, which failed (2012). In Tamil Nadu, nutrition education for mothers was combined with supplemental food for children. Together, these two program components led to the program's success, but when replicated in Bangladesh, it had virtually no effect. According to Cartwright and Hardie, the difference was cultural. In the second case, the role played by husbands and mothers-in-law undermined program success. Because mothers often did not control household food purchases, their enhanced knowledge of nutritional principles did not change consumption patterns. Moreover, they often had little control over allocation of food within the household, meaning that supplemental food was diverted from children to other family members. In short, designers of the Bangladesh program extracted an incomplete causal theory from Tamil Nadu. It wasn't mothers per se who needed nutritional education, it was those who control food purchases and distribution within the family who needed a better knowledge of nutritional principles *and* a willingness to behave differently.

Beyond ensuring that you correctly understand what factors contribute to the success of the policy you're 'borrowing', it's helpful to also understand which program features do not. You need not expend the time or effort to duplicate these nonessential components as you develop your policy design. Moreover, if you see implementation problems in the first case, try to link those problems to specific program features. If you can, adjust these features in your policy design so that you don't inadvertently replicate problems that could have been avoided. The bottom line? While it's a great idea to model your policy design on successful programs operating elsewhere, never lose sight of the fact that simple replication of a successful program in one location doesn't guarantee success in another.

14.2.3 Discerning Design Elements in Existing Policies

Rather than thinking about policies from elsewhere as potential templates to be replicated, you can also think of them as defining the design elements of policy in a particular area. A **design element** is a component of a system that can take on a variety of different forms. Think of the seats in a car; they can be covered in cloth, leather, or vinyl. The seat in need of a covering is the design element. Cloth, leather, and vinyl represent the **design choices** available to specify the nature of the design element. In algebraic terms, a design element is a variable and design choices are the values that the variable can take on.

When you're developing policy designs, you first need a complete set of design elements. For each, you then need to make design choices. If you overlook important elements when coming up with your policy design, you will end up with an incomplete, or not fully specified, result. As a simple example, think of a local property tax system in which the design elements are the types of properties to tax, the tax rate, the assessment system, and the process for making case-specific adjustments. If your policy design is silent about any of these elements, you haven't painted a complete picture of how the policy would work, thus impeding both further analysis of it and actual implementation should it be enacted in its incomplete form.

How can you use existing policies to identify design elements and choices? Through a process of deconstruction and reconstruction. You first deconstruct an existing policy to discern its key design elements and then develop alternative specifications of each element. Finally, you 'mix and match' these choices to reconstruct new policy designs. Exhibit 14-3 illustrates the process with a continuation of the property tax example. Extracting the design elements from a policy in place elsewhere only requires careful study of the tangible features of the other program. By contrast, the specification of design choices in your jurisdiction affords you creative license to imagine alternative ways of specifying each element. You have even more flexibility as you combine choices from across elements to form new policy options. In this simple example, we can choose among 81 options (i.e., the number of permutations when there are three choices for each of four elements) for further analysis.

Exhibit 14-3 Policy Deconstruction and Reconstruction

Design Elements of Program in Their Jurisdiction	Design Choices for a Program in Our Jurisdiction
Element #1: Tax base *Commercial buildings only*	Choice 1A: Commercial buildings only
	Choice 1B: Residential buildings only
	Choice 1C: Residential and commercial buildings
Element #2: Tax rate *$1.00 per $1000 of assessed valuation*	Choice 2A: $1.00 per $1000 of assessed valuation
	Choice 2B: $0.50 per $1000 of assessed valuation
	Choice 2C: $2.00 per $1000 of assessed valuation
Element #3: Assessment system *Buildings assessed at 75% of fair market value (FMV)*	Choice 3A: Buildings assessed at 75% of FMV
	Choice 3B: Buildings assessed at 60% of FMV
	Choice 3C: Buildings assessed at 100% of FMV
Element #4: Adjustments *Service-disabled veterans exempt from taxation*	Choice 4A: Service-disabled veterans exempt
	Choice 4B: Service-disabled veterans and seniors exempt
	Choice 4C: No exemptions

14.3 BUILD POLICIES FROM GENERIC APPROACHES

Rather than looking to other jurisdictions for policy designs to consider, you might opt to build them on your own. The ability to do so is an important skill for policy analysts, since you may not always be able to find analogous cases elsewhere or if you and your client are interested in developing a new approach that hasn't been tried before (Bardach & Patashnik, 2016). Recall from the Introduction to Part I that virtually all public policies take one or more of the approaches shown in Exhibit 14-4. As you think about what alternatives to include in your analysis, scan this list, select two or three items that seem most relevant, and then for each one, spend some time trying to answer questions like these:

- If I built a policy option that fit this category, what would it look like?

- How would it work?

- Who would do what, and by when?

Exhibit 14-4   Types of Government Activity

- Implement infrapolicies to maintain societal systems and facilitate other policies
- Regulate the behavior of individuals, firms, and institutions
- Provide services
- Allocate rights to public resources
- Redistribute wealth and income
- Levy taxes, spend money, and provide subsidies
- Endeavor to foster economic development
- Facilitate the flow of information

As you work iteratively to answer these questions, you'll find yourself designing policy options. Ultimately, successful policy development requires a deep appreciation of the problems of concern, the systems in which they arise, and the needs, motives, and behaviors of those who will be affected by the policy. Nonetheless, you have to start somewhere, and this section provides a broad overview of the policy design process, while subsequent sections offer more specific suggestions.

14.3.1 Choice Architecture

Public policies generally aim to change the behavior of firms, individuals, or institutions. Such behavior, in turn, is the result of decision choices made by these actors over time. Policy design is thus a kind of **choice architecture** that creates the context for, and influences the nature of, the behavioral decisions that people make (Thaler & Sunstein, 2008). In the same way that a building's architecture influences how people use it, the architecture of a public policy influences if and how people will change their behavior in response to it. And just like a residential architect who can design a wide range of different types of houses, a policy analyst can also come up with a variety of different designs intended to serve the same policy purpose.

One way to characterize the choice architecture implicit in a specific policy option is to describe the extent of coercion it exercises over folks' behavior. Some policies are outright **mandates** that leave no room for variation across society. No one is legally allowed to enter the country without a passport, opt out of paying their taxes, or set up a storefront operation to sell hard drugs. Mandates can either compel behavior (e.g., you must appear for jury duty when called) or prohibit behavior (e.g., you may not exceed the speed limit when driving a car).

Other policies impose **tailored mandates**, the effect of which varies based on specific circumstances. A local building code may apply one set of standards to new construction while exempting existing buildings (a process known as grandfathering). Similarly, the stringency of many federal labor laws depends on the size of the firms, with large firms subject to stronger mandates than small firms. Finally, some mandates come with procedures for seeking a variance in a specific case. For example, a zoning ordinance may prohibit the subdivision of one lot into two, but if the landowner seeks and is granted a variance, then the land can be subdivided, but not otherwise.

Prescriptive policies that leave little or no discretion in the hands of regulated firms and individuals are sometimes called **command and control policy instruments**. Such instruments may be easier for governments to implement because compliance (or the lack thereof) is usually readily apparent; public officials don't have to do a great deal of case-specific analysis to determine if a firm or individual has complied with the policy. But because they are blunt instruments—applying the same standard across a regulated community—command and control instruments may lead to inefficiencies in cases where the same policy objective could be achieved more cost-effectively if the regulated entities had been given the flexibility to take a different approach.

Creating a policy-driven choice architecture can be more than simply deciding which activities are permissible and which are not. Public policy can also have a profound impact on the material costs and benefits of alternative decision choices. If a policy increases the cost of doing something, either by imposing a tax or by issuing a regulation that drives up costs, firms and individuals are less likely to engage in the costly activity. For example, taxes on tobacco products are often levied primarily to discourage smoking while capital reserve requirements for banks drive up the cost of doing business but are intended to ensure the stability of the banking system. You are still free to buy cigarettes or operate a bank, but it will cost you more to do so. Conversely, if costs are reduced, perhaps in the form of a direct subsidy or as government provision of a free service, we will likely see more of the activity. Tax credits for renewable energy and technical assistance to farmers from agricultural extension agents are two examples of policies intended to increase the level of a particular activity. Finally, liability law is a form of choice architecture that often motivates firms and individuals to take action to protect others for fear of being held liable and responsible for paying damages to injured parties.

Policies that explicitly use taxes and subsidies to influence behavior are sometimes called **market-based instruments** (MBIs) because, after a new policy leads to changes in the effective price of goods and services, market forces then largely dictate how firms and individuals respond to the policy. In contrast to command and control instruments, MBIs allow regulated entities the flexibility to choose how to respond to public policy. Though they may be more complex to administer, by letting members of the regulated community take account of case-specific costs and benefits, such instruments may lead to more cost-effective attainment of a policy objective than would a command-and-control approach.

A less coercive form of policy design is a **nudge** (Thaler & Sunstein, 2008). Nudges are small changes made in choice architecture to push people toward the policymaker's objectives. Nudges often are built around the decision heuristics we discussed in Chapter 4. For example, knowing that people are apt to leave the status quo intact if nothing is pressing them to make a change, choice architects often set the choice that is presumed to be best for the user as the default. Examples include automatically enrolling new employees in retirement plans, having folks designate their organs for donation when they get a driver's license, or shipping printers preset to double-sided printing to save paper. But users can still easily change the default choice. Philosophically, nudges are a form of **libertarian paternalism** that combines two constructs:

> The *libertarian* aspect of our strategies lies in the straightforward insistence that, in general, people should be free to do what they like – and to opt out of undesirable arrangements if they want to do so. ... The *paternalistic* aspect lies in the claim that it is legitimate for choice architects to try to influence people's behavior in order to make their lives longer, healthier, and better. (Thaler & Sunstein, 2008, p. 5), *emphasis added*

Nudge-based policies are typically targeted at individuals (e.g., workers, drivers, students) rather than at firms or institutions.

Another popular policy instrument is a **public–private partnership** which entails an agreement between government and a private entity. Both parties voluntarily enter the agreement, typically because both see value in doing so. These partnerships span a wide range of policy domains. A local government, for example, may agree to build a sports stadium for a team that then leases it for a long period of time. The locality will collect tax revenue on the associated economic activity and endear itself to fans of the home team while the team will pay less than if it had to build its own stadium. Similarly, the federal government's Energy Star® program is a partnership between the Department of Energy (DOE) and manufacturers of energy-using equipment like appliances, lighting, copiers, computers, and data centers. Participating manufacturers must meet efficiency standards and are in turn allowed to use the Energy Star® brand and logo to market their products. The value to DOE comes in the form of lower energy demand and reduced pollutant emissions—two core elements of the Department's mission.

The least coercive forms of policy-driven choice architecture are **campaigns to inform and influence** action without imposing any incentives for action or disincentives for inaction or requiring folks to formally opt-in or opt-out of a default choice. Public outreach campaigns urging people to get vaccinated, wear their seatbelt, or put on sunscreen aim to change behavior, but there are no government penalties for failing to take action. Some policies contain a **mandate to disclose** information but are silent about how that information is to be used. Mandated truth in lending disclosures, food information labels, and mileage stickers on new cars all help consumers make more informed choices but do not dictate how consumers are to use the disclosed information in making decisions.

14.3.2 Policy Sequencing

In addition to designing policy options to beneficially affect choice architecture, you should also pay attention to issues of timing. For example, to minimize disruption and transition costs, you might phase in a new policy over time rather than make it immediately effective upon enactment. Extra time will allow folks to learn about the new initiative, figure out how they will respond to it, and take preliminary steps to get ready for its implementation. Especially for complex new policies that represent a big change from business as usual (e.g., the Affordable Care Act), firms and individuals may need time to adjust to the new way of doing things. Remember, your goal is to facilitate smooth and effective implementation in order to reap the benefits of the new policy, not to play gotcha and penalize folks who haven't been able to figure it out or who really do need more time to comply. Of course, allowing more time for implementation brings with it the downside that the policy problem will be allowed to persist for a longer period of time while the policy is being put in place.

As you think about phasing policies in (or out), you needn't think only about the passage of time on the calendar as a trigger for policy action. You might also tie changes in policy to real-world conditions. A more formal way of describing this distinction is as a difference between **time-dependent** and **state-dependent policy triggers**. A time-dependent trigger, for example, might end a mandate to wear a mask during a pandemic after six months. By contrast, a state-dependent trigger approach might mandate mask wearing until infection rates drop below a certain number of new cases per day. While a state-dependent policy trigger can make for a more effective policy, it does require that we have ready access to reliable data about the value of the state variable. If, for example, we don't have valid data about infection rates, then it wouldn't make sense to trigger an end to the mask mandate based on infection rates.

We've talked before about a policy problem as a gap between a descriptive as-is condition and a normative to-be condition. In turn, you can think about the policy you're designing as a plan for closing that gap. Sometimes, it's not possible to close the gap (i.e., make the transition from one state of the world to another) all at once with a single policy tool. Sometimes, we need to sequence specific policies over time to create a **transition pathway** from the status quo to the future envisioned in our broad policy (Letzler, 2017; Pahle et al., 2018). Sometimes, the need is political. Perhaps stakeholders are not ready to embrace your full policy proposal at the outset. Starting with a more modest, and less controversial, approach may lead to conditions where a more expansive policy becomes politically acceptable over time. Consider, for example, the progressive expansion of federally funded health care in the United States: first for the poor and elderly in 1965, for disabled persons in 1972, for uninsured children in 1997, for prescription drug coverage in 2006, and for additional low-income and middle-income households in 2010 (CMS, 2021).

Sometimes the need for policy sequencing originates in practical or technological constraints. While, for example, you might want to mandate use of renewable energy to meet 100% of US energy demand, numerous impediments stand in the way. Technological challenges—like grid-scale energy storage with batteries or similar techniques—must be solved first. Moreover, construction of a new nationwide energy infrastructure will take decades, not just a few years. Accordingly, in this example, you need to think sequentially as you design your new energy policy and consider which intermediate policies are appropriate for each stage of the transition process.

On the other hand, you may be constrained by choices made in the past by previous policymakers. Referred to as **path dependency**, this phenomenon limits your choices in the present. If, for example, a highway built in the 1960s led to the breakup of a previously cohesive neighborhood with a diaspora of residents moving elsewhere, it may be difficult to reestablish the neighborhood community, even if the highway is removed. Sometimes, irreversible changes are the inevitable consequence of policy change. The point is not to avoid such policies—their advantages may far exceed their disadvantages—but to be mindful of how the policies designed and implemented today may create path dependencies that constrain policymakers in the future.

14.3.3 Policy Design to Facilitate Learning

As we talked about in Chapter 13, visualizing the future to understand how today's policy choices will affect tomorrow's outcomes is, at best, an imperfect art. Rather than assuming our crystal ball has 20/20 vision and that we'll be able to design the ideal policy from the start, we need to be cautious. Of course, you want to design the best policy you can, but equally important is designing a policy that allows for learning and improvement over time. Two elements of a policy design can help in this regard.

First, as you design a new policy, try to build in features that enable **performance monitoring**. If you can, track outcome and impact measures, as well as metrics related to inputs, activities, and inputs. It's much easier (and less costly) to collect such information in real time as a program is underway than to come back later as part of a retrospective program evaluation and try to reconstruct data that weren't intentionally collected in the first place. Putting resources into monitoring and information collection *will* create an opportunity cost in that fewer resources will be available for program operation. But it's almost certainly a price worth paying since the collected information will enable you to learn from experience and continuously improve the policy.

The second opportunity to learn over time – after policy enactment – is independent of the policy itself and has more to do with the broad context for the policy. The idea here is to design flexible and adaptable policies that can be adjusted as circumstances not directly linked to the policy change. Such policies are sometimes referred to as real options (Linquiti & Vonortas, 2012). Like financial options, they give you the right but not the obligation to take a future action. Suppose you're in a suburban community with a growing population. You're not sure about school enrollments over the next couple of decades. Rather than projecting the number of school kids 20 years from now and building enough schools to accommodate them all, you might build one school now and acquire the land to build a second school in the future if needed. If you don't set aside the land now, it may get used for other purposes and if enrollments grow, you won't have a place to build the new school. In short, procuring the land now creates the option, but not the obligation, to build a school in the future if enrollments grow.

14.4 BUILDING POLICIES INSIDE THE STUDIO: THEORY OF CHANGE AND STRATEGIC ALIGNMENT

Back in Chapter 2, I drew a distinction between working inside the studio and working outside the studio. In the former, your efforts are focused within your own organization and build on the knowledge and expertise that you and your colleagues already possess. In the latter, you reach out to affected stakeholders, subject matter experts, and relevant public servants to assess and fill the gaps in your own knowledge and expertise. Moreover, design for analysis takes place primarily inside the studio while design for implementation mostly happens outside the studio. We'll talk about policy design inside the studio in this section while the next addresses policy design done outside the studio.

Once you decide that a policy option (either borrowed from elsewhere or built from generic tools) might be relevant to the analysis at hand, your next step—inside the studio—is to ensure that its design is based on a credible theory of change and that its component parts are strategically aligned to maximize the chances of success. Let's take a closer look at each objective.

14.4.1 Theory of Change

As noted in Chapter 2, a theory of change is a logical, transparent causal explanation of how we expect to get from our intended policy intervention to the beneficial outcomes we aspire to create. It requires a clear specification of our expected results and of the indicators that would demonstrate success. Logic models—based on causal reasoning—can be used to depict the theory of change implicit in a policy design. We start with inputs and activities (taken together, the policy design) and draw direct causal links from the design to its outputs and then to its results (i.e., its outcomes and impacts).

Because a logic model links policy design, a theory of change, and program results, it can be a useful tool to develop new designs for policy. Exhibit 14-5 depicts an iterative process in which you consider variations in the design by using a theory of change to connect them to the results. You can also work backwards by using the desired results to reverse engineer a policy design potentially capable of generating those results. It may take a few iterations to adjust your policy design and refine your theory of change to produce a logical and internally consistent design that you're happy with. At this point in the process, the design needn't be perfect. If you're engaged in design for analysis, you'll have opportunities during your policy analysis to identify its strengths and weaknesses. And if you're engaged in design for implementation, you can change the design as you go outside the studio to consult with stakeholders and refine the policy's design.

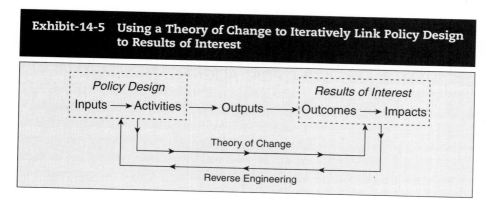

Exhibit-14-5 Using a Theory of Change to Iteratively Link Policy Design to Results of Interest

14.4.2 Strategic Alignment

The success of an organization—public or private—depends in no small measure on the degree of alignment among its components and with the environment in which it operates. If different parts of an organization work at cross-purposes, pursuing different or even contradictory objectives, we shouldn't be surprised if results are unsatisfactory. Moreover, if an organization is out of synch with its environment, perhaps pursuing goals not highly valued by its customers, clients, or citizens, or making poor use of available inputs, its performance will almost certainly suffer. Accordingly, as you develop designs for public policy, you need to come up with designs that are both internally and externally aligned.

There are at least two ways to think about alignment. The first is to ensure that your policy design reflects a coherent integration of mission, strategy, and tactics. There is a hierarchical relationship among these concepts. The **mission** is the overarching purpose of an organization, program, or policy—its reason for existence. A **strategy** broadly explains how the mission will be achieved with an approach that builds on strengths and opportunities and mitigates weaknesses and threats. Finally, **tactics** are the mechanism by which the strategy is executed on a day-to-day basis. In well-run organizations, missions shift only slowly over time, strategies evolve more quickly but nonetheless offer needed stability and serve as a reliable guidepost for tactical decisions. Tactics can be adapted much more frequently to address changing conditions, but ideally, they are always in alignment with the mission and strategy.

Suppose US policymakers decide to take strong action to address climate change. The broad mission might be to reduce greenhouse gas emissions to limit global warming and to encourage other countries to do the same. At a strategic level, policymakers might decide that a market-based mechanism, like a tax on fossil fuels that pushes up the cost of carbon-intensive goods and services, is the best strategy to achieve the mission. Finally, at a tactical level, policymakers would need to decide on, among other things, where in the chain of commerce to tax fossil fuels, what the tax rates should be, and what to do with the tax revenues. Ideally, all elements of the policy would be strategically aligned to achieve the mission. But suppose, for example, policymakers simultaneously subsidize production of ethanol from corn or collect below-market royalties from oil and gas producers on federal land, both policies likely to increase emissions. By doing so, policymakers have created strategic misalignments that undermine achievement of the mission. Sometimes, misalignments must be tolerated as the price of achieving political consensus, but to the extent you can, try to create policy designs where the mission, strategy, and tactics all point in the same direction.

The second perspective on alignment entails consideration of the degree to which a public policy has been designed to create a complementary relationship among its value proposition, its legitimacy and support, and its operational capacity. This vision of strategic alignment originated at the Kennedy School of Government in the 1990s (Moore, 2000). A policy's **value proposition** is an articulation of how its outcomes and impacts are beneficial (i.e., create value) for society. Its **legitimacy and support** reflect the degree to which it is embraced by policymakers who enact it into law and provide funding to keep it going. And its **operational capacity** depends on having sufficient resources and the technical know-how to deliver on the value proposition. If any of these three criteria go unmet, policy success is unlikely.

To illustrate, consider a simple example: local trash collection. Value is created for citizens by virtue of regularly removing an unsightly, smelly, and unhealthy nuisance from homes and neighborhoods. Moreover, trash collection is typically seen by policymakers across the ideological spectrum as an important and legitimate function of local government, worthy of their support and funding. Finally, most localities have figured out how to competently pick up the trash on a regular basis. It's thus no mystery why local trash collection is ubiquitous and has been for decades.

This all seems so straightforward that you could be excused for thinking that the idea that value, support, and capacity need to be aligned is little more than a no brainer:

> At a conceptual level, this simple model is not very challenging. All it says is that in order for a strategy to be a good one, it has to be valuable, authorizable, sustainable, and doable. What could be more obvious than that? Operationally, however, the concept proves to be very challenging indeed. It generally proves quite difficult to lay out a strategy in which all of these bases are touched. Yet, to fail to do so is to court disaster. (Moore, 2000, p. 198)

The political sustainability of public policies often follows predictable patterns (Patashnik & Weaver, 2020). Continuing political support for a policy can be jeopardized under a number of conditions, including, for example, situations where:

- A policy is adopted by a narrow margin in the face of strong opposition;
- There is a long lead time before the policy gets up and running, especially if the policy creates a concentrated group of losers in the short run;
- Operation of the policy demands collaboration among agencies and levels of government, not all of whom support the policy; or
- The policy is costly, and politicians must regularly take explicit action to keep it funded.

To the extent that you can design policies that will attract broad support from the outset, deliver their benefits quickly, ease the burden on those adversely affected by the policy, allocate implementation responsibility to supportive agencies and levels of government, and to the extent possible, rely on a dedicated funding source, you will enhance the political sustainability of your policy design.

As just one example of what can go wrong in the absence of alignment among the three factors, consider the story of the now defunct Office of Technology Assessment (OTA) that we heard back in Chapter 11. Over its two-decade lifespan, OTA produced more than 750 analytic deliverables on science and technology issues; at its peak, OTA had an annual budget of $20 million and a staff of over 200 (CRS, 2020). OTA certainly delivered on two of the three drivers of strategic alignment: it provided its clients with valuable insights not available elsewhere and it repeatedly demonstrated its capability to produce high-quality deliverables. OTA's undoing came when it lost the political support of conservative ideologues unhappy with some of its work and of budget hawks looking to reduce federal spending.

At the same time, however, be careful not to undermine the coherence and logic of your policy design by being too accommodating of political interests. Sometimes, the price of political support may be too high, if it leads you and your client to make changes to the policy that undermine it to the point of rendering it ineffective, and thus unable to deliver on its value proposition. Yes, you want to see your policy garner political support and become law, but you don't want to end up regretting it later (Eggers & O'Leary, 2009; Mead, 2013).

The broad takeaway lesson here for policy design is to pay attention to strategic alignment. Aim to create policy options in which the mission, strategy, and tactics are clear, coherent, and in synch with one another. Moreover, think carefully about a policy's value proposition, its ability to gain political legitimacy and continued support from policymakers, and its operational capacity to deliver on its value proposition. If any of these are in doubt, revisit your policy option and look for ways to adjust its design to overcome such deficiencies.

14.5 BUILDING POLICIES OUTSIDE THE STUDIO: DESIGN THINKING

At this point, you might be done with the policy design process. If you're engaged in design for analysis, you can now subject the policies you've developed to further analysis in which you project their outcomes and identify trade-offs among their pros and cons. On the other hand, if you're engaged in design for implementation, you likely need to develop a more detailed specification of how each policy would work. Doing so requires close attention to the interests of those folks whose support is needed to ensure effective implementation. Moreover, if the policies you're working on provide a public service or regulate a group of firms or consumers, you'll want to develop a good understanding of the needs of the folks who will be served or the interests of those who will be regulated.

14.5.1 Rationale for Stakeholder Consultation

There are at least two reasons why you need to take account of the opinions and interests of folks outside your studio—one normative and one pragmatic. For starters, in a democracy, we tend to think that all points of view deserve a hearing and that people ought not to be subjected to policies that haven't been crafted with their concerns in mind. You might argue that the electoral process meets this requirement and that letting citizens vote officials in and out of office eliminates the need for consultation on specific policy measures. Conversely, you might find elections too blunt an instrument for capturing all viewpoints on all issues; if you fall into this group, you probably view working outside the studio when designing new policies as a normative obligation for public officials.

But even if you don't feel a normative obligation to consult with stakeholders during policy design, I'd like to suggest a couple of pragmatic reasons for doing so. If you ignore stakeholders as you hone your understanding of the problem and plan for implementing new policy measures, you're losing an opportunity to build consensus and support that will later facilitate effective implementation. And, as we talked about in the previous section, if a lack of support turns into outright opposition, your new policy may encounter repeated failure during implementation. Moreover, as a policy analyst working inside the studio, there are inevitably things you don't know—about the issue, about the affected community, and about how your policy design will be received by those who have to deal with it after it's implemented. Failing to consult stakeholders in a meaningful way risks a suboptimal policy design that doesn't work nearly as well as it could have if only you had taken the time to develop a solid understanding of stakeholders' needs and concerns before rolling out your new policy.

In broad terms, you can think about three levels of stakeholder consultation. **Participation** implies that stakeholders are permitted to provide feedback before a policy is finalized. A public agency might publish a draft policy online and allow interested parties to submit comments. Alternatively, members of the public might be given an opportunity to speak about a proposed policy at a public hearing. A more intensive form of consultation is **engagement**, where there is more of a two-way conversation between members of the public and the officials responsible for developing policy. Such conversations entail back and forth discussions about the nature and severity of the problem and about the pros and cons of different ways of addressing it. Participants in the conversation may be self-selected, or public officials may reach out to known stakeholders in an ad hoc fashion to solicit their feedback. Finally, the most collaborative form of stakeholder consultation is **inclusion**, in which public officials intentionally reach out to a wide cross section of the community and work diligently to ensure that a diverse set of voices and perspectives are included in the conversation about how to shape pending public policy.

14.5.2 Emerging Trends in Policy Design Thinking

The past few years have seen a newfound enthusiasm among scholars and public officials for incorporating design thinking into policy analysis and implementation planning (McGuinness & Slaughter, 2019; Olejniczak, Borkowska-Wasak, Domaradzka-Widla, & Park, 2020; van Buuren, Lewis, Peters, & Voorberg, 2020). Several governments have even launched policy design labs—dedicated teams of staff who apply design principles to issues of concern—to support policymaking within their jurisdiction. Not everyone views the concept of design thinking in the same way, but there are some common themes:

> Fundamental to all design thinking approaches is the aim to develop a deepened understanding of stakeholders' contexts, particularly those of the user or citizen for which any service is being designed. … Successful design-oriented conversations are most vividly illustrated perhaps by what they are not. They don't accept obvious and conventional problem definitions, allow extensive debates, or concentrate primarily on evaluating options visible from the start. Instead, they first explore the problem definition itself as a hypothesis, seek to understand rather than to argue with others' differing perspectives in an inquiry-focused conversation, and look for solutions to emerge during the process. (Liedtka & Salzman, 2018, pp. 13–15)

McGuiness and Slaughter (2019) suggest that there are four elements to design thinking. The first is that it is **people-centered**, meaning that even though traditional policy research and analysis still plays a key role, at least as important is a focus on individuals—citizens, users, regulated entities—who are affected by public policy and on their perceptions and experience of policy issues. Getting outside your studio and talking to people is thus an integral element of design thinking.

A second element in design thinking is its **experimental** nature. With problem definitions and claims about the efficacy of new policies always taken—at least initially—as hypotheses to be confirmed, experimentation holds a special place in design thinking. Quick, iterative attempts at small-scale projects allow for trial and error and an acceleration of the learning process about what works and what doesn't (Hermus, van Buuren, & Bekkers, 2020). Moreover, lessons learned are quickly fed back into the analytic process as the problem definition and potential policy choices are updated to reflect the experimental results. The goal is not to conduct an analysis that leads to the *best* policy, but instead it is to work experimentally to find a *better* policy than the one currently under consideration (Liedtka & Salzman, 2018). This constant iteration is quite different from the linear framework of the classical forms of policy analysis that we looked at in Chapters 1 and 2 (Fukayama, 2018).

The third component of design thinking is an **evidence-focused** approach. Although it values folks' firsthand subjective experience with policy issues and government programs, design thinking doesn't dismiss the value of tangible indicators of real-world conditions. For example, the ubiquity of large data sets in an increasingly automated society combined with the analytic power of data sciences means policy designers can understand policy issues in new ways. Moreover, by focusing on the results of policy experimentation and impact evaluation, design thinking aspires to incorporate empirical realities, rather than untested hunches, into the design process.

The final element of design thinking is a long-term perspective on **scalability**. The early stages of design thinking entail pilot projects, small-scale experiments, and close coordination with individuals, but many policy issues are broad in scope and large in scale. It's great if creative, talented social entrepreneurs steeped in design principles can create one-off examples of successful, user-oriented policies, but ultimately the biggest impact will be experienced if success can be scaled up to large applications. A recurrent question that therefore demands an affirmative answer during design is, *can this be scaled?* While design thinking emphasizes starting small and experimentally, its practitioners must always be concerned with whether a proposed approach has the potential to be expanded to serve large numbers of people. If it doesn't, it may not justify a substantial investment of time and resources.

Design thinking is not relevant in all cases. If there are fundamental disagreements among competing political and economic interests, then inclusive, user-oriented conversations may not yield common ground (McGuinness & Slaughter, 2019). Moreover, some aspects of public programs are highly specialized and would benefit less from public consultations than programs with large and diverse communities of affected individuals. But in most areas of public policy, iterative and creative design thinking, with its focus on individuals, experimentation, evidence, and scalability, can help you do a better job of policy development and implementation.

14.6 BUILDING POLICIES OUTSIDE THE STUDIO: STAKEHOLDER ANALYSIS

Consulting with stakeholders—including the public writ large—during the process of policy development can be messy, contentious, and confusing (Liedtka & Salzman, 2018). You might end up in the middle of disputes among groups with decidedly different points of view. Even with a trained facilitator skilled at leading meetings to elicit all points of view, encourage creative collaboration, and create connections among diverse parts of the community, things can still go wrong. You might find public meetings hijacked by special interests or those with the loudest voices. You may face demands to structure a public program in ways that aren't feasible or affordable, or that would create adverse consequences for others. You won't be able to make everyone happy in every situation, but the alternative is not to stay inside the studio and ignore stakeholders.

Stakeholder consultation often works best when it is an iterative process in which you first 'do your homework' inside the studio to understand as much as you can about the issue before going outside the studio to solicit input from stakeholders. Depending how much (or how little) you feel you know about stakeholders' needs, you might start with nothing more than a few talking points to structure the conversation and spend most of your time listening to (rather than talking at) stakeholders. Ideally, you'll hear how they think about the issue and learn more about what they think might work, and what might not, when it comes to the specific features of a policy. On the other hand, if you already know a good bit about the issue and the concerns of stakeholders, you might do more preparatory work and draft a problem statement or policy proposal before meeting with stakeholders to get their reaction to your ideas. Based on the feedback you receive, you would then update your proposed approach to the issue and, if you have time, solicit input on a revised draft. Depending on time and resources, and how successful you are along the way, this iterative process might cycle through multiple loops as you work with stakeholders to create the most effective policy design you can.

It can be hard to stay organized, and to think strategically, as you go through this iterative process of consulting with stakeholders and revising your policy design. Accordingly, the remainder of this section offers some advice based on a framework that a colleague and I created to plan and implement international development assistance projects (Strelneck & Linquiti, 1995).

As shown in Exhibit 14-6, the framework entails four tasks. During the first task, based on your logic model, all key process steps that lie between enactment and successful implementation are identified, with a particular focus on inputs and activities. In the second task, all relevant stakeholders (inside and outside government) are identified. Stakeholders are either potential beneficiaries of the policy who might be persuaded to champion its implementation or potential opponents who might be tempted to thwart successful implementation. The list of process steps is then juxtaposed against the stakeholder list to create a matrix. In the third task, each cell of the matrix is evaluated as to whether the indicated stakeholder may play a role—positive or negative—in that particular step. Fourth, for each cell with a relevant stakeholder, you need to develop a plan for how to gain that stakeholder's support or negate their opposition during implementation. Back in Chapter 10, we heard from the Deputy Mayor of Los Angeles who likened policymaking to driving a bus full of stakeholders, each with a brake pedal at their seat and the power to stop the bus. Now imagine that each seat also has a gas pedal. In this fourth step, you're trying to come up with a plan for each phase of implementation to ensure that as many stakeholders as possible have their foot on the gas pedal and are staying away from the brake pedal.

Exhibit 14-6   Stakeholders and Implementation Planning

1. Identify all process steps between policy enactment and successful implementation

2. List stakeholders whose support must be gained, or opposition mitigated

3. Identify all combinations of stakeholders and process steps relevant to implementation

4. For each combination, develop a plan for managing the stakeholder relationship

Let's look at an example of this four-task approach to implementation planning. It's from my policy analysis class and entails conducting an implementation analysis for an initiative launched by President Obama to address a shortage of science, technology, engineering, and math (STEM) teachers in K-12 education. At the time, it was described as follows:

> [The plan would] invest $100 million to help train 100,000 new educators over the next decade. ... Obama will ask Congress for $80 million to support new Department of Education grants for colleges that provide innovative teacher-training programs. The president also is set to announce a $22 million commitment from private companies that will support the effort. ... The investment is intended to address a problem that the president thinks could ultimately threaten the nation's global competitiveness. U.S. companies have called on the government to help produce more highly skilled workers to keep pace with job openings in new high-tech industries. (Nakamura, 2012)

Given this description, our first task is to characterize the complete path from program implementation to its beneficial impacts (i.e., its implicit theory of change and the associated logic model). In general, each step in the process should display the same level of specificity and detail and be concrete enough to facilitate further analysis. There is no one right formulation of this process, but an example is shown in the left-hand column of Exhibit 14-7. While the first few steps in the process seem obvious, many students overlook the later steps. The point of the program is not simply to train new STEM teachers, but, according to the President, to enhance the nation's global competitiveness. We thus need to use the program's implied theory of change to define all the steps that lead from the start of the logic model to its conclusion.

The second task is to identify the relevant stakeholders. As shown in the right-hand column of Exhibit 14-7, it's best to think expansively about who they might be. Be sure to include self-identified stakeholders who have already expressed an interest

Exhibit 14-7 Logic Model and Stakeholders for Presidential STEM Initiative

Process Steps Implied by Logic Model	Potentially Relevant Stakeholders
1. Secure funding from private donors	1. Private donors
2. Create program management structure within Department of Education	2. Department of Education
3. Design and implement grant program	3. Candidate teacher training entities
4. Identify, recruit, and fund 100 teacher training entities	4. Candidate STEM teachers
5. Recruit students for the teacher training programs	5. School districts that hire STEM teachers
6. Graduate 10,000 STEM teachers from training programs each year	6. Teacher unions
7. Place newly qualified STEM teachers in jobs teaching STEM topics to K-12 students	7. K-12 students and their parents
8. Better educate more K-12 students on STEM topics	8. Colleges that admit better STEM-trained HS students
9. Observe more high school graduates choose STEM fields as career and/or college major	9. US technology firms that hire STEM-trained employees
10. Graduate more STEM-oriented college students	10. Foreign firms that compete with US firms
11. Observe industry hire newly available STEM-oriented HS and college graduates	
12. Observe US technology firms become more globally competitive	

in the policy, as well as invisible stakeholders who could be affected by it but who are as yet unaware of its development. Some stakeholders might be obvious—like the agency running the program or the grantees that it gives money to—while other stakeholders may have only a tangential relationship to the program but might be relevant at a particular step. Remember, we are interested not only in stakeholders who might support the program but also in those who might oppose it. In many school districts, for example, teacher unions are powerful actors whose cooperation would be needed before local school monies are diverted toward STEM education and away from other activities. (Note that the President's initiative doesn't provide funding to school districts to pay the new STEM teachers; it only pays for teacher training.)

Having listed the necessary steps in program implementation and identified key stakeholders, we create the matrix shown in Exhibit 14-8. In the third task, we use a

Exhibit 14-8 Identification of Critical Intersections Between Stakeholder Interests and Steps in the Implementation Process[a]

Process Steps		Stakeholders									
	Donors	Department of Education	STEM Teacher Training Entities	Candidate STEM Teachers	School Districts	Unions	K-12 Students and Parents	Colleges	US Firms	Foreign Firms
Secure private funding	✓	✓								
Set up program management		✓							✓	
Create grant program		✓	✓							
Recruit training entities		✓	✓							
Recruit students		✓	✓	✓						
Graduate STEM teachers			✓	✓						
Place STEM teachers				✓	✓	✓				
Interest K-12 students in STEM				✓	✓		✓	✓	✓	
Observe HS grads focus on STEM				✓	✓		✓	✓	✓	
Observe more STEM college grads							✓	✓	✓	
Observe industry hire STEM grads							✓	✓	✓	
US firms outcompete other firms									✓	✓

[a]This table is not based on detailed study of actual programs or economic conditions, but instead is a hypothetical example meant to illustrate the application of the method described in the text.

checkmark to denote each combination of a process step and stakeholder that we suspect will be relevant to successful implementation. For example, I checked the box at the intersection between US technology firms and the hiring of program graduates in school districts. Because such firms don't hire or pay local teachers, this might seem counterintuitive. But if the new initiative succeeds in training 100,000 teachers in STEM subjects, it seems likely that at least some of them will seek employment not as teachers but as professionals in the tech industry (especially if the President is right that these industries are facing worker shortages). It may not be a bad thing if this happens, but it would certainly undercut the theory of change implied in the program's logic model.

With the matrix in hand, the fourth task is to come up with a plan to address each cell in the matrix where there is a critical combination of a process step and a particular stakeholder (i.e., where there is a checkmark). Such plans may lead to revisions in the policy design. To continue the example from above, we'd want to figure out a way to ensure that the program's graduates end up teaching K-12 students rather than going to work in industry. For example, in exchange for the STEM training they receive, teachers might be required to teach in a K-12 school for five years after program completion. Not all critical intersections between stakeholders and the implementation process will necessitate a change to the policy design. Instead, you may simply need to think about how to maximize stakeholder support, or minimize stakeholder opposition, during each stage of program implementation.

As you work through the matrix, you may find stakeholders with divergent interests who nonetheless are in alignment about a specific policy action, a situation sometimes referred to as the Bootleggers and Baptists phenomenon.[4] This phrase was coined by an economist who worked for the Federal Trade Commission and is the tale of how two groups—one an enthusiastic proponent of alcohol consumption and the other adamantly opposed—might come together in support of a ban on Sunday sales of alcoholic beverages (Yandle, 1999). Bootleggers—unafraid of illegality—are happy to have their competition (i.e., legal liquor stores) forced to close their doors one day a week while the teetotalers of the religious group would be pleased to see their moral instincts codified in law, if only for one day a week. Similarly, during international negotiations in the 1980s to protect stratospheric ozone, a somewhat surprising alignment between environmental groups and chemical manufacturers emerged. Both supported the Montreal Protocol, the former because it banned harmful ozone depleting substances and the latter because it opened the door to the manufacture and sale of more profitable replacement chemicals. In short, as you work through

---

[4]I've always been a bit uncomfortable with this vocabulary as it seems to imply a moral equivalence between the two groups, but Yandle's article has been cited close to 400 times, so I thought you should hear about his ideas.

developing your implementation plan, stay focused on the actions you need stakeholders to take, without insisting that all stakeholders embrace the same rationale for action.

A final thought: As you think about the likely behavior of each stakeholder at each step of the implementation process, remember the advice in Chapter 4 about the risks of mirror imaging and confirmation bias. You're not trying to figure out how you would react at each step in the implementation process but are trying to figure out how stakeholders would behave. That's why you need to get out of your office and away from your laptop to talk to folks. Moreover, if you're intentionally inclusive, hearing voices from across the socioeconomic and ideological spectrums, you'll learn even more. Put yourself in others' shoes, be mindful of the incentives they face and the constraints that affect their actions, figure out how you can design your policy to elicit cooperation, and avoid actions that undermine program effectiveness.

Using this framework for implementation planning won't eradicate opposition to your policy, eliminate implementation difficulties, or guarantee a successful outcome, but it will minimize the risk of unpleasant surprises and improve your chances of having a meaningful impact on the problem you seek to address. Indeed, one scholar goes so far as to claim that implementation planning and stakeholder analysis are "perhaps the most important set of skills" for an aspiring policy analyst to master (Fukayama, 2018, p. 2).

CHAPTER SUMMARY

This chapter described a variety of techniques for developing sound, workable policy designs potentially capable of mitigating policy problems. We started with a series of questions that you need to ask and answer before getting started. Perhaps most importantly, you need to figure out whether you're engaged in design for analysis or design for implementation.

We next looked at processes for finding proposed or existing policies and adapting them for use in a different jurisdiction. Choice architecture was introduced as the context for different types of public policies, including mandates, command and control instruments, market-based instruments, nudges, public–private partnerships, outreach campaigns, and required information disclosure. Policy sequencing was presented as a mechanism for increasing the chances of successful policy implementation.

We then considered how policy designs can be crafted inside the studio, with a focus on designs that facilitate ongoing learning and provide flexibility to future policymakers, as well as on strategically aligned policy designs that are built on a compelling theory of change and reflect careful logic modeling.

We next looked at policy design outside the studio. The principles of user-focused policy design were described, and we reviewed three forms of stakeholder consultation: participation, engagement, and inclusion. We concluded by reviewing how stakeholder mapping and analysis can be used to develop policy designs that engender support and minimize opposition at each stage of implementation.

DISCUSSION QUESTIONS

1. Can you think of a policy that you would like to see enacted? Can you succinctly explain its Theory of Change? Could you draw a logic model to illustrate how it will create outcomes and impacts?

2. Do you think policymakers should rely on models provided by outsiders as the basis of policies they enact? What are the upsides of relying on such templates? How about the downsides?

3. Imagine you've been asked by the City Council to come up with five distinctly different policy options for addressing homelessness. What options would you list? Now suppose the request came from the Secretary of the federal Department of Housing and Urban Development. What options would you list? Are your two lists the same? Why? Why not?

4. How does path dependency affect the policy options available to the United States for reducing greenhouse gas emissions?

5. How do you feel about symbolic policies? Is it ethical for policymakers to adopt policies that they know will have no meaningful impact on people's lives? What are the risks of symbolic policies?

6. Identify a public policy that you think serves an important purpose and is effective at creating impacts. How would you describe its mission, strategy, and tactics? How would you describe the policy's value proposition, the source of its legitimacy and support, and the nature of its operational excellence? What is the level of strategic alignment among these components of the program?

CHAPTER FIFTEEN

HAVING AN IMPACT WHILE PRESERVING YOUR INTEGRITY

The preceding 14 chapters have focused on the cognitive and analytic skills needed to conduct high quality policy analysis. By contrast, this chapter addresses a somewhat disparate collection of practical skills that may enhance your personal effectiveness as a policy analyst on a day-to-day basis. We start in Section 15.1 with a review of how the topic of ethics can be integrated into your work life. From there, we turn in Section 15.2 to a few ideas about how the concept of emotional intelligence can affect your ability to work effectively in team-based settings. Next, Section 15.3 extracts a few principles from the discipline of project management that may help you deliver quality work, on time and within resource constraints. Section 15.4 depicts the policy analyst as an intermediary among multiple actors and gives you some advice about how to be successful in such a role, while Section 15.5 offers a few specific suggestions about how to pick and choose analytic techniques to match the types of assignments you're likely to receive from your client. And, befitting the final section of a final chapter, Section 15.6 offers an afterword that recaps some of the most important takeaways of the book.

15.1 PRESERVING YOUR PROFESSIONAL ETHICS

You can think of ethics as a set of moral principles that guide a person's conduct. You undoubtedly already have a sense of right and wrong in your personal life. The purpose of this discussion is to think more broadly about how to convert personal ethics into a set of professional ethics that apply to your work as a policy analyst. But first a quick caveat: I can't

Learning Objectives

By studying this chapter, you should be able to:

- Explain the content of a typical code of ethics and distinguish ethical behavior based on rule-following from behavior based on ethical reasoning.

- Define the concept of emotional intelligence.

- Explain how the emotional content of interpersonal relationships affects the tangible content of policy analysis.

- Explain the four stages in the lifecycle of a typical project and identify major considerations relevant to the successful execution of each stage.

- Describe how a policy analyst often serves as an intermediary among multiple actors and the steps that can be taken to become more effective in this role.

- For each of about a dozen analytic questions often asked of policy analysts, identify the analytic techniques most likely to be valuable in answering such questions.

- Describe the key takeaway themes of the book as a whole.

give you a definitive set of normative rules by which to conduct your professional life. That's something you need to come up with on your own. This section will introduce some key concepts and highlight a few challenges, but ultimately, you need to personally wrestle with these issues to decide how to conduct your professional life.

There are two basic ways to answer the ethical questions you encounter in your work life: **rule-following** and **ethical reasoning**. Rule-following depends on a codified set of do's and don'ts that tell you which behavior is permissible and which is not. Ethical reasoning, on the other hand, starts with broad principles and applies them to specific circumstances to discern an ethical course of action. In my experience, most folks apply a combination of reasoning and rule-following to address ethical concerns.

When it comes to rule-following, you'll find that many governments, businesses, and professional associations have put in writing a set of standards (i.e., a code) with which they expect their employees or members to comply. To get a sense of what these codes look like, flip to the appendix for this chapter. In it, you'll find four examples of formal ethics codes. Two are directed at folks who work for government; the third is for project management professionals working in both the public and private sectors, and the fourth is for lobbyists whose job is to advocate on behalf of their clients with government policymakers. These four codes are meant to be illustrative: they're not a comprehensive collection of ethical principles applicable to all policy analysts. But you will find several elements that turn up more than once.

- *Tell the truth*: Honesty is a cornerstone of most codes of ethics; although as we'll see in a minute, there is a distinction between a prohibition on lying and a directive to always tell the complete and whole truth.

- *Avoid conflicts of interest*: By virtue of being employed (and paid) as a professional, most codes of ethics presume that you have a duty to put the legitimate interests of your employer ahead of your own personal interest. If, for example, you were doing an analysis of policies to encourage electric vehicles while also owning stock in an electric vehicle manufacturing company, your professional and personal interests might conflict, calling into question the neutrality of your policy recommendations. And if you work in a nonpartisan setting, your personal political preferences shouldn't influence the work you do.

- *Protect confidential information*: Whether it's personally identifiable data about individuals or information provided by someone to you in private, or simply the details of a particular policy analysis project that hasn't been publicly released, the general rule is that such information should be held confidential. I once had a boss who sternly admonished employees to never talk about their work in crowded elevators.

- *Follow the law*: Though you might have thought it obvious, ethics codes often explicitly mandate adherence with the law. The rationale for doing so is that even if undetected by law enforcement, illegal behavior is still a breach of the code and inconsistent with the values of the organization. (Such a provision may also save the organization from being penalized if improper behavior is the result of an individual employee's action, rather than organizational policy.)

- *Report wrongdoing of others*: Not all ethics codes include a duty to report, but many do. The idea is that a professional's obligation goes beyond personally refraining from unethical behavior to include monitoring the behavior of others and alerting appropriate authorities about improper behavior. The goal is to create a culture of accountability in which ethical behavior becomes a social norm, not just a matter of avoiding detection.

- *Treat others equally without regard to identity*: Most ethics codes include a proviso that calls for equal treatment of all individuals across race, gender, and other socioeconomic and identity-based lines, although not all codes call out the same set of groups for protection against discrimination. Professionals are also usually expected to refrain from favoritism and nepotism as they discharge their duties.

If you compare the first pair of ethics codes in Appendix 15-A to the second pair, you'll notice a key differentiator. The first two are targeted at employees who work for government, while the second two are not. You may recall from our review of the legal lens in Chapter 11 that public servants are expected to be good shepherds of governance, with respect for the rule of law, the separation of powers, the principles of federalism, and the rights of citizens. Both the American Society for Public Administration (ASPA) Code of Ethics and the regulations for federal executive branch employees demand loyalty to the constitution and adherence to the law; moreover, both anchor their ethical principles in notions of service to the public and the advancement of the public interest.

> The rule of law is widely held to be a bedrock principle of democracy. ... The rule of law might well be treated as a foundational concept in every introductory course, in every course on administrative ethics and in every course on managing, planning, and policy making. (Lynn, 2009, pp. 803–810)

By contrast, the ethics codes for project management professionals and for lobbyists emphasize the analyst's obligations to his or her clients, rather than to the public writ large. The difference is more than semantic; it has profound implications for the ethics of policy analysis. Back in Chapter 3, I distinguished *analysis as inquiry* from *analysis as advocacy*.[1] If we intersect the two types of analysis with the two types of ethics codes, it seems fair to conclude that policy analysts in the public sector are generally obligated to practice *analysis as inquiry* while those working outside of government have more latitude to practice *analysis as advocacy*. In turn, the ethical standards applicable to an Analytic Specialist or a Public Servant differ from those applicable to a Client Advisor or a Campaigner.[2]

One practical ethical implication of this difference relates to one's obligation to tell the truth. As mentioned above, lying is always impermissible, but the nature of required truth-telling varies based on one's position. According to the lobbying industry's code of ethics, for example, a lobbyist must be truthful when describing the negative impacts of a proposed policy on his or her client but needn't explain the positive impacts on folks who are not the client. In other words, in a democracy grounded in argument and debate, we don't expect advocates to argue both sides of an issue; instead, we expect advocates to take one side and leave it to others to make the counterarguments. By contrast, note the requirement in the ASPA Code that public servants "fully inform" and "provide … comprehensive … information" to those in positions of authority. Such language leaves little room for selective truth-telling and subtle advocacy.

Does that mean there's no role for advocacy within government? Not necessarily. Note that the federal ethics regulations apply to civil servants—career employees in the executive branch—whose positions are, at least notionally, nonpartisan. By contrast, policy analysts working in the role of client advisor to an elected politician or political appointee usually aren't expected to refrain from partisan politics, thereby opening the door for policy analysis as advocacy within government.

This brief discussion—which only scratches the surface of rule-based ethics—is meant to convince you of the need to think carefully about your role as a professional and to consider how applicable standards shape the ethical environment in which you work. Familiarizing yourself with such standards *before* you face an ethical challenge is usually a good idea as it allows you to think about the meaning of the standard in an unhurried way. Doing so can also help you avoid transgressing an ethical standard of which you were unaware.

A shortcoming of rule-based ethics is that you can often find yourself in a situation where there doesn't seem to be an applicable rule. Let's look at three quick examples. Suppose your employer imposes a general prohibition on conflicts of interest, a standard that you embrace and aspire to meet. It seems clear to you that you can't own stock in a company that might be affected by your policy analysis, but what about your

---

[1] See Exhibit 3-5 for a review of the differences between the two types of analysis.
[2] See Chapter 7 for more specific definitions of the four types of policy analyst.

spouse or parents? Or how about investing in a mutual fund with dozens of holdings, only one of which is in the company of concern? The rule isn't specific enough to give you definitive guidance.

Second, consider a situation where two elements of an ethics code point to different actions in the same case. Suppose you are a nonpartisan civil servant working for an elected politician who is planning to implement a policy which, while not unconstitutional or otherwise illegal, will have a profound adverse impact on a disadvantaged community. If word gets out about the plan, political opposition will likely arise and stop the proposal. But if the client attaches the proposal at the last minute to must-pass legislation, it will be enacted. You have a duty to hold nonpublic information confidential, but you also have a duty to serve the public interest. Do you leak the proposal to a sympathetic journalist, or do you stay quiet? Does the fact that you may be fired if you're caught leaking have any bearing on the ethics of the matter?

Third, let's assume you're a government employee in the executive branch personally devoted to the principle of serving the public trust. Further suppose that you are being pulled in multiple directions by equally legitimate sources of political power. Perhaps you're working on a court-ordered regulation being promulgated pursuant to a statutory mandate where your boss—a Senate-confirmed political appointee—has strong opinions about how to proceed:

> In a healthy separation of powers system, Congress, the President, and the courts are constantly struggling to control the mission, objectives, and policy goals of executive departments and agencies … If public organizations operate under the assumption that elected and appointed members of the legislative, executive, and judicial branches are directing them in different directions, resembling a tug-of-war contest, that is par for the course in a separation of powers system. (Newbold, 2008, p. 342)

In all three cases, rule-following cannot give you a definitive answer about how to proceed. Instead, ethical reasoning comes into play as you sort out what to do. As we saw back in Chapter 8, there are two broad schools of thought about how to engage in such reasoning. Some folks anchor ethical principles in rational processes, where careful logical reasoning is used to discern the appropriate course of action (e.g., the type of reasoning used by Bentham, Mill, Kant, and Rawls). Other folks (like Haidt and Hume) argue that moral reasoning is a form of social intuitionism rooted in culture, religion, and social identity.

I won't presume to tell you how to engage in moral reasoning when you're confronted with an ethical challenge. But I will offer you two pieces of advice. First, if your concern is a question of right versus wrong, the answer is easy. Do the right thing. It's when two ethical principles conflict, and you find yourself in a right versus right situation, that things get tricky.[3] Avoid the temptation to oversimplify the matter to save yourself from cognitive dissonance. Instead, try to get comfortable with ambiguity and be ready to consider ethical trade-offs associated with one course of action over another.

Second, if you're facing an ethical challenge, it's often a good idea to seek counsel from friends and colleagues, rather than resolving the matter in the privacy of your own mind. Most public agencies (and many private organizations) have a designated ethics officer or general counsel's office whose job is to help you resolve ethical issues. A robust discussion of an issue will almost always identify important considerations you might have overlooked. As I mentioned earlier, if a course of action seems ethical only if no one else finds out about it, then it's probably not.

15.2 MAXIMIZING YOUR INTERPERSONAL EFFECTIVENESS

Most of the material in the book so far has focused on improving your hard skills—the cognitive and analytic tools you need to conduct policy analysis. Along the way, however, I've hinted at another set of skills that are also important. Chapter 7, for example, defined the mindset of an effective policy analyst as comprising critical thinking, pragmatism, competence, tough mindedness, a service orientation, and cognitive self-awareness. We also saw in Chapter 13 that folks who work constructively in a team setting are often better at forecasting the future than folks who are not team players. Such soft skills can help you work more effectively with others, including clients, colleagues, supervisors, subordinates, stakeholders, and even adversaries. While you certainly need strong cognitive and analytic skills to succeed as a policy analyst, you may find that mastering the soft skills—sometimes referred to as **emotional intelligence**—will make you an even more successful policy analyst.

Salovey and Mayer are typically credited as the first scholars to offer an integrated definition of the concept of emotional intelligence (1990). Daniel Goleman later generated considerable public interest with a best-selling book on the topic (1995). Over subsequent years, permutations of the concept have emerged in the literature, but most definitions are similar and resemble the following:

> [Emotional intelligence is] the set of abilities (verbal and nonverbal) that enable a person to generate, recognize, express, understand, and evaluate their own, and others', emotions in order to guide thinking and action that successfully cope with environmental demands and pressures. (Van Rooy & Viswesvaran, 2004, p. 72)

---

[3]The notion of a right versus right dilemma should ring a bell. We talked about it back in Section 8.7.

You can think of emotional intelligence as comprising four specific elements: self-awareness, self-management, social awareness, and relationship management (Berman & West, 2008). As shown in Exhibit 15-1, the components of emotional intelligence reflect two dimensions: the focus of attention (yourself or others) and the requisite ability (to recognize or to act).[4]

Exhibit 15-1 Components of Emotional Intelligence			
		Required Skill	
		Ability to Recognize	**Ability to Act**
Focus of Attention	You	Self-awareness	Self-management
	Others	Social awareness	Relationship management

- *Self-awareness*: In the same way that metacognition helps you understand your own analytic thinking methods, self-awareness in the context of emotional intelligence refers to your ability to recognize and understand your own feelings, sentiments, and motivations.[5] Emotionally self-aware folks are also adept at identifying the specific situations that trigger changes in their own mood or attitude.

- *Self-management*: Once aware of their emotions, people with high emotional intelligence regulate those emotions in productive ways. By limiting the impact of negative emotions on behavior, strong self-management skills allow you to be more effective in stressful situations. Similarly, such skills may help you channel positive emotions to enhance your performance. You may also find yourself more open-minded and less defensive when receiving critical feedback about your work or your behavior. In short, self-management can help you avoid the mistakes of quick, emotion-driven, System 1 thinking.

- *Social awareness*: While the first two elements are internally focused, the concept of social awareness reflects your ability to perceive and understand the emotional state of others. Doing so requires empathetic

---

[4]Although he uses a somewhat different five-part taxonomy of emotional intelligence, Daniel Goleman (2019) provides further insight into these concepts.
[5]Revisit Section 7.6 if you want to compare cognitive self-awareness to emotional self-awareness.

appreciation of verbal and nonverbal cues, both in one-on-one interactions and in group settings. Moreover, social awareness means that you recognize the effect of your words and actions on the emotions of other people.

- *Relationship management*: The final element of emotional intelligence is the ability to take the insights provided by the first three elements and use them to improve the quality of your relationships with others. By tuning into your own emotions, and the emotions of others, you may be able to develop more effective ways of managing your relationships with others.

Taken together, these four abilities comprise emotional intelligence. Interestingly, a person's level of emotional intelligence isn't fixed for life. As one ages, or matures, emotional intelligence appears to increase. Moreover, people can improve their emotional intelligence through self-reflection, practice, mentoring, and training (Berman & West, 2008; Goleman, 2019). There is a large body of social science evidence that emotional intelligence is predictive of a diverse set of outcomes related to:

> … academic performance, emotional labour, job performance, organizational citizenship behaviour, workplace deviance, leadership, life satisfaction, stress, trust, team process effectiveness, and work-family conflict. (Miao, Humphrey, & Qian, 2017, pp. 177–178), *internal citations omitted*

Several scholars have also argued that emotional intelligence is particularly important in the public sector. Many public sector jobs, such as social work, education, law enforcement, and health care, create emotionally intense work settings where emotional intelligence can be especially valuable (Guy & Lee, 2015). In addition, while they may not refer to it as emotional intelligence, many large US cities have incorporated its core principles in their human resource and professional development training for their workers (Berman & West, 2008). Having emotionally intelligent staff can also help a public agency better serve its public mission. Stakeholders, for example, often bring strong emotions to policy issues and, as we saw in our discussion of social intuitionism as a form of moral reasoning, many normative values have at least partial roots in personal emotions. Because policy analysis entails the analytic integration of emotion-driven concerns and reason-driven concerns, a high level of emotional intelligence can be particularly important for public servants (Vigoda-Gadot & Meisler, 2010).

15.3 MANAGING A POLICY ANALYSIS PROJECT

We touched briefly in Section 7.3 on the idea that you can view policy analysis as a production process where the finished product is the analytic deliverable itself. Except for small projects completed by one person in just a day or two, policy projects can almost always benefit from the application of project management principles. There is a well-established body of knowledge about project management that originated in large engineering and construction projects but has since found its way into the high-tech sector, government procurement, and corporate initiatives of all types (PMI, 2017). Even at the smaller scale of a policy analysis project, application of these management principles increases the likelihood of a successful conclusion to your analysis and minimizes the chances of missed deadlines, shoddy work, or budget overruns.

Accordingly, this section reviews some of the key principles of project management and offers a few suggestions that may help you stay organized. You can start by thinking of a project as having a lifecycle composed of four stages: initiation, planning, execution, and closeout (PMI, 2017). Depending on which project stage you're in, different considerations will be relevant.

1. *Project Initiation*: The initial decision to launch a policy analysis project is an important one. It defines the purpose, scope, and boundaries of the work. A failure to reach agreement on these basic considerations can doom a project before it even starts. Think about questions like the following:

   - Why are we doing this project? What do we hope to learn? What would a successful outcome look like?

   - What are the client's expectations for the project? Who are other relevant stakeholders for the project and what are their expectations?

   - How will differences of opinion about the project—from internal team members and external stakeholders—be handled? Can we address such differences now, before the project starts?

   - How much time and what resources are available to complete the project?

   - What specific deliverables must be produced? What is the required length, format, and content of each deliverable?

2. *Project Planning*: It can be tempting to jump right into a new policy project (especially in a field you care about). But resist that temptation and spend time up front planning the project and mapping out how all its pieces will fit together. Doing so will save you time (and probably wasted effort) later. Do a **premortem** in which you imagine that the project has failed; take steps now

to mitigate the imagined cause of failure. Be sure to reserve time in the schedule to recover from inevitable mistakes and often incomplete first drafts of deliverables. Try to answer questions like these:

- What research questions are we trying to answer? What is already known about these questions?

- What methodologies might we use to answer the research questions? What are the pros and cons of each approach?

- How have similar projects been executed by others in the past? What lessons can we learn from their experience?

- What specific tasks must be executed to achieve a successful result? How are the tasks related? How long will each take? Can all the tasks be executed within the available schedule?

- Who is available to work on the project? Which tasks will each person work on?

- Are we sufficiently skilled and competent to do a good job? Do we need to look outside our organization for the skills needed to do the project?

- Based on the premortem, what could go wrong during the project? What actions can we take—both now and during the project—to mitigate the risks of serious problems?

- What specific steps do we plan to take during the project to ensure that all work is of high quality, finished on time, and completed on budget?

3. *Project Execution*: Once the project is underway, good management can keep things on track. Don't let your project plan gather dust on the shelf; use it on an ongoing basis to monitor progress. If things go awry, be proactive and address problems promptly. Make sure someone is personally responsible for each task, rather than relying on a vague sense of collective responsibility for the whole project. Along the way, you'll need to answer questions like these:

- How will we monitor the progress of each task and ensure the integration of all project components? How will all members of the team be kept informed about other aspects of the project on which they're not directly working?

- How will decisions be made when important issues arise during project execution? Who has the authority to make which decisions?

- What sorts of regular progress reporting is needed? How will performance metrics be collected, analyzed, and reported? To whom will they be reported?

- Should we be creating interim deliverables that are sent to the client or stakeholders for review and feedback (and to build enthusiasm and buy-in for our work)?

- If things go wrong (e.g., interim deadlines get missed, data collection comes up short, a key person gets sick for several days), how will we identify problems with sufficient lead time to develop and take corrective action?

4. *Project Closeout*: It can be easy, in the press of day-to-day business, to send off the final deliverables and then forget about the project. That's often a mistake. Taking time to carefully wrap up a project often pays dividends later. A few months after a project, the client may come back and ask for follow-on work, or you may get assigned a similar project with a different client. If you're working as a consultant for an external client, final payment may be withheld until all closeout activities are completed.

- How will we know the project is done? Might we be expected to continuously revise the project deliverables for an undefined period? Or does submission of a final deliverable define the end of the project?

- What are the logical follow-on projects that might be suggested to the client (or to others) now that this project has finished?

- How will all project materials be archived and remain accessible if needed in the future?

- What lessons did we learn during the project? What worked well and what didn't? If we could do it over, how might we change our approach to better serve our client?

My first boss believed that there were three core elements in any policy analysis project: the speed with which it needed to be completed, the human resources that were available to work on it, along with any prior relevant work, and the rigor and depth of analysis in the final product. These elements, he said, are always in tension and you can't maximize on all three. If you want a top-quality deliverable in a short period of time, you need a lot of smart people working on it or need to tap into a deep trove of directly relevant prior work. At the other extreme, if you only have one part-time junior analyst, you either must give him or her a long time to get the project done or lower your expectations about the quality of the deliverable that can be produced in a limited period of time.

I've come to appreciate my boss's insight: there *is* an inescapable tension among quality, schedule, and budget that can make it hard to achieve all objectives within one policy analysis project. But that doesn't mean success is impossible. For starters, you need to think about project management as conceptually distinct from the policy analysis itself. You need to become proficient at both management and analysis. Moreover, coming up with good answers to the questions posed above—before you launch your policy analysis project—will go a long way toward improving your management of a policy project and the production of a finished product of which you can be proud.

15.4 THE POLICY ANALYST AS AN INTERMEDIARY

One of the most important—and difficult—roles that a policy analyst may be asked to play is that of an intermediary among folks with different political and ideological perspectives, levels of subject matter expertise, and analytic and technical skills. Especially when the role is played under time constraints, a policy analyst can be like a traffic cop dealing with a crowded intersection at rush hour, trying to get everyone quickly on their way without any accidents.

Exhibit 15-2 depicts this situation as one in which the policy analyst receives, processes, and transmits information among multiple actors. Not all situations fit this model. Sometimes it's just you and the client, or you and your boss. But if you find yourself acting as the traffic cop, this stylized model may help you to think about each of these players and how you can work effectively with them.

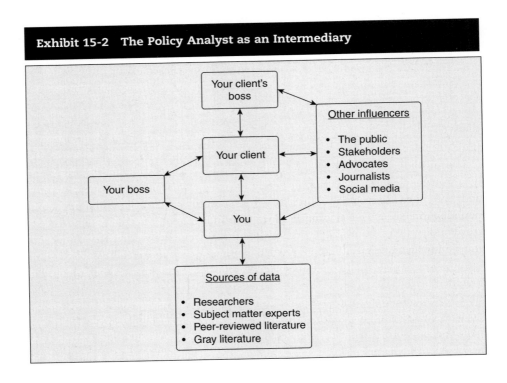

Exhibit 15-2   The Policy Analyst as an Intermediary

When it comes to clients, we've already looked at the processes of discerning their objectives, translating those objectives into research questions to be answered with evidence and logic, and working under time, resource, and information constraints to come up with advice for clients. It's also important to recognize that not all clients are the same. Some are in nonpartisan government positions while others are outside government acting as advocates pursuing a political agenda or as researchers in a think tank or similar organization. Some are political appointees who feel a sense of urgency to enact major policy initiatives before their term of office ends. Others are senior public servants in the middle of a long career. Some know a great deal about the relevant issues; others are novices. Some clients are interested in making a sharp break from their predecessors; others respect precedent and are less interested in going in new directions. Some clients (and bosses) are micromanagers, checking and questioning every aspect of your work; others take a hands-off approach and give you wide latitude to exercise your discretion. And to use the words of Charles Wheelen, some clients are policy wonks and others are political hacks.[6] Taking the time to understand and appreciate your client's motives, capabilities, and even workstyle, can help you play the role of intermediary much more successfully.

There are two other client-like actors who may affect your work: your boss and your client's boss. Let's clarify these roles with an example. Imagine you're an analyst at the Government Accountability Office working on a study for Congress. Your direct supervisor—who is not the client—is a GAO employee. The client is a senior staff person on the Congressional committee that requested the study. That client, in turn, answers to his or her boss—the member of Congress to whom they report. You're likely to have an interactive, two-way, relationship with your client and your boss, but probably not with your client's boss.

Difficulties can arise when these folks give you different, and sometimes conflicting, guidance about your policy analysis. Your boss may think he or she knows what the client needs, but perhaps the client has told you something different. In addition, I've also had the experience of working with a client, diligently answering questions that he or she posed with an agreed-upon methodology, only to find out later that the client's boss had very different ideas about how the policy analysis should have been done. There's no sure way of avoiding such problems, but to the extent you can, seek to build consensus among all these folks by:

- Involving them in framing the research questions,
- Asking for their explicit approval of your approach to data collection and analysis,
- Getting agreement on the specifications for analytic deliverables,

---

[6] If you need a refreshers on the vocabulary of hacks and wonks, see Section 10.1.2.

- Gently asking your client to check with his or her boss to get buy-in on the approach, and
- Sharing interim drafts of deliverables to get feedback while there's still time to act on it.

Another set of actors whose actions may affect your work are folks intentionally trying to influence the conclusions you draw. Typically, they're stakeholders who are either affected by an existing problem or who may be affected by policy changes being debated. They could be members of the general public, or they could be paid lobbyists advocating on behalf of a particular interest. Traditional journalists and social media influencers may also be relevant as they disseminate their views about the issues you're working on. As a policy analyst, you'll want to keep abreast of the latest news on topics that your client cares about, particularly as it relates to your analysis and the research questions you're trying to answer. In Exhibit 15-2, I've depicted this as a one-way relationship in which you monitor, but don't attempt to influence, information coming from these actors. As described in our Section 15.1 discussion of ethics, you almost certainly have a duty of confidentiality to your client that means that unless your client asks you to engage them, you shouldn't be telling outsiders about your work before it's been publicly released. Of course, your client and his or her boss are usually free to engage whomever they like in whatever fashion they choose.

The final source of information you'll need to manage originates with academic researchers, other subject matter experts, and the peer-reviewed and gray literature:

> Policy analysts play critical roles as intermediaries between custodians of knowledge and policymakers. Their training should include the ability to understand the academic literature on a topic at a far deeper level than most journalists have the time or, often, the analytic skill set to uncover. Identifying and connecting pertinent knowledge and analysis should be a core principle of public policy education. (Hird, 2017, p. 76)

Another way to think about this process is that your role is to bridge the gap between policy analysis and policy research. You want your policy analysis to be based as solidly as possible on strong evidence, but you often don't have the time or expertise to do all the relevant research yourself. In turn, you're forced to rely on the expertise of others.

Unfortunately, there's not always a good match between the work of the research community and the needs of policymakers. Sometimes, the work is complex, technical, and inaccessible to the untrained audience; in other cases, it may not be directly on point, providing some but not all the evidence you need. Finally, because real-world policymaking reflects a mix of political considerations, ideological stances, budgetary constraints, and institutional considerations, academic expertise can rarely provide definitive answers about how to address a particular policy issue. That's where you come into the picture; as a policy analyst, your job is to locate and understand the work of relevant experts, and then figure out how to integrate it with the other considerations your client cares about.

And if there are academic researchers who work in your area of interest, don't be shy about suggesting potential topics for their future research. They may not take your suggestion, but I have found that most policy researchers strive to be relevant. The more they know about the needs of policymakers, the more targeted their work can be.

15.5 MATCHING TECHNIQUES TO TASKS

As we talked about in Chapter 3, one of the most persuasive complaints about classical policy analysis models is that they are rarely applied from start to finish in the sequential fashion in which they are taught. Prospective policy analysis, for example, doesn't always begin with a problem definition and proceed step-by-step to a policy recommendation. Similarly, debates about the value and performance of existing programs often don't work methodically from a careful specification of a program's purpose to a blueprint for program reform. Instead, policy analysts often get tasked with assignments that don't fit neatly into the frameworks suggested by classical models. Moreover, even if the assignment generally fits the classical model, policy analysts are routinely given assignments that entail applying a part—and sometimes only a small part—of the model.

Accordingly, this section aims to help you figure out which approaches described in previous chapters may be applicable to a particular policy analysis assignment. Before getting into specifics, however, bear in mind that several considerations will almost always be relevant and applicable to your work as a policy analyst, including:

- The inescapable pathologies of policy analysis in a democracy (Section 3.2),
- The obstacles that often impede use of policy analysis (Section 3.3),
- The importance of metacognition to check your own biases (Chapter 4),
- The need to base policy claims on sound logic and credible evidence (Chapters 5 and 6),
- The need to communicate results in ways that your audience truly understands (Section 7.5),

- The value of bringing the right mindset—critical thinker, pragmatic, competent, tough minded, service-oriented, and self-aware—to your work (Chapter 7.6), and
- The need to look at policy issues through multiple lenses at the same time (Part III).

Beyond these general considerations are several other factors that may come into play depending on which tasks land on your desk or in your inbox. Below are about a dozen short vignettes that describe typical policy analysis assignments using words you might hear from your client. Following each vignette are references to specific parts of the book that may be especially helpful.[7] In each case, I take as given that you and your client are serious about using policy analysis to come up with a response (rather than a public relations strategy that glosses over the issue).

1. *Scope Out a Policy Issue*: I've been hearing more about Issue X. What's going on? Someone just told me that the problem is getting worse quickly and said we need to adopt Policy Q. Are they right?

   - *Deconstruct policy claims made by others to assess their validity (Section 7.2)*

   - *Decide if there is a problem (a gap between a descriptive as-is condition and a normative to-be condition); if so, characterize its magnitude and its causes and effects (Section 1.1)*

   - *Engage in analysis as inquiry rather than analysis as advocacy (Section 3.3)*

   - *Locate the issue within the system in which it occurs (Chapter 12)*

   - *Visualize how relevant events may unfold in the future (Chapter 13)*

2. *Mitigate an Injustice*: Someone, or some group, is being treated unfairly or subjected to discrimination or abuse.

   - *Remind yourself of the risks of mirror-imaging and confirmation bias and of assuming that others' lived experience is the same as yours (Section 4.6)*

   - *Review the principles of moral reasoning (Section 5.4)*

   - *As you gather evidence about the situation, take care to hear all voices in the community, not just those with ready access to policymakers (Section 6.2.1)*

---

[7]For brevity, I identify only those parts of the book most applicable to each vignette. Other considerations, from elsewhere in the text, may also be relevant.

- *While looking at the issue through multiple lenses, pay particular attention to the equity lens (Chapter 8), the political lens (Section 10.1), and the legal lens (Section 11.1)*

- *Apply inclusive, user-focused design principles to ensure that attempts to mitigate the injustice reflect an accurate understanding of the circumstances of the group exposed to the injustice, as well as of groups that may be affected by policy change (Sections 14.5 and 14.6)*

3. *Fix a Dysfunctional Current Policy*: Constituents are constantly complaining about Policy X. What should I do? The program we run just received a disastrous program evaluation. My favorite program just got bad press coverage. What's our next move?

   - *Recall that all policies entail trade-offs between pros and cons (Section 1.5) and be prepared to tolerate cognitive dissonance (Section 4.2)*

   - *Use retrospective analysis to understand how well the current policy is meeting its objectives (Chapter 2)*

   - *Apply the logic of prospective analysis to figure out if there is a better way to address the problem than continuing the current policy (Chapter 1)*

   - *Apply the principles of policy design, including theory of change thinking and strategic alignment, to modify the current policy (Section 14.4)*

4. *Replicate a Successful Policy*: Policy X, from the next town, is really popular with voters. Let's do the same thing here. We can't afford Policy X, from the next town. Give me a cheaper version.

   - *Use the classical model of prospective policy analysis to decide whether Policy X is really a good fit for conditions in this town (Chapter 1)*

   - *Review the requirements for drawing valid inferences from one case and generalizing them to another case (Section 6.3)*

   - *Methodically investigate the policy's operation in the next town and adjust it as appropriate for this town (Section 14.2)*

   - *Think about designing a new policy tailored to this town rather than trying to replicate another policy (Section 14.3)*

5. *Make Sure Nothing Goes Wrong when We Implement Policy X*. I'm up for reelection and can't afford a fiasco.

   - *Remind your client about the intrinsic uncertainty of the future (Chapter 13)*

   - *Ensure that Policy X reflects a solid theory of change and is strategically aligned (Section 14.4)*

- *Apply inclusive, user-focused design principles to stakeholder analysis and implementation planning (Sections 14.5 and 14.6)*

6. *Forecast the Results of a Proposed Policy*: We want to enact Policy X. How much will it cost? Is it a good idea?

   - *Remember that whether Policy X is a good idea depends on how it compares to other policy choices (including sticking with the status quo) and what criteria are used to evaluate it (Chapter 1)*

   - *Apply systems thinking to consider the context into which Policy X will be introduced (Chapter 12)*

   - *Estimate the cost (and other effects) of Policy X (Sections 13.3 and 13.4)*

7. *Figure Out a Way to Say my Policy Proposal Won't Cost Anything.* Otherwise, it won't get enacted because people are complaining that it's too expensive.

   - *Refresh your memory on the ethics of truth-telling (Section 15.1) and review what it means to speak truth to power (Section 5.1.2)*

   - *Remind your client that all policies entail trade-offs between pros and cons (Section 1.5) and that policies with low costs often have little impact (Section 5.7.1)*

   - *While looking at the issue through multiple lenses, pay particular attention to the economics lens to better understand the likely costs and benefits of the proposed policy; the new policy may be costly, but perhaps benefits outweigh costs (Chapter 9)*

   - *If a plausible—but incomplete or uncertain—argument can be made that the proposal has no cost, then make the argument, but don't represent your conclusion as the product of policy analysis as inquiry (Section 3.3)*

8. *Solve a Policy Problem*: I am really worried about Problem X. How should we fix it? My constituents are constantly complaining about Problem X. We have to do something.

   - *Characterize the magnitude of the policy problem; identify the causes and consequences of the problem (Section 1.1)*

   - *Look at the problem through all lenses to better understand the nature of the complaints and understand how folks are experiencing the problem (Part III)*

   - *Locate the problem within the system in which it occurs (Chapter 12)*

   - *Use inclusive consultation with stakeholders and design multiple options for further analysis (Chapter 14)*

   - *Apply the classical model of prospective policy analysis (Chapter 1)*

- Counsel your client to resist the urge to "just do something" to avoid implementing a policy that doesn't work, or worse, has unintended adverse consequences (Section 10.1.2)

9. *Develop an Advocacy Strategy*: I want to get Policy X enacted. Give me the best strategy for a win.

   - Initially, in private, engage your client in policy analysis as inquiry to discern the specific details of the client's preferred course of action, and then switch to policy analysis as advocacy to develop the strategy (Section 3.3.2)

   - Figure out if your client's political opponents are willing to engage in a good faith debate about how best to proceed or are only interested in a political fight (Section 3.3.3)

   - While looking at the issue through multiple lenses, pay particular attention to the political and institutional lenses (Chapter 10) and the legal lens (Section 11.1)

10. *Give me the Answer by the End of the Day (or Week)*: I need to know how much this policy will cost, or how many people it will serve. I don't have time for you to do a big, complicated analysis. Just give me the answer, and it better be right!

    - Review the principles of doing policy analysis under time, resource, and information constraints (Section 7.3), particularly the use of quick analysis, back of the envelope calculations, and Fermi-izing (Section 7.4)

    - Remind your client about the intrinsically uncertain nature of the future (Sections 13.3 and 13.4)

    - Apply a project management mentality to your policy analysis so that you can be as efficient as possible (Section 15.3)

    - Manage your client's expectations carefully about what you will and won't be able to produce by the deadline (Section 15.4)

    - Qualify your conclusions as appropriate to reflect your level of confidence in the available evidence and the certainty you have (or don't have) about your conclusions (Exhibit 6-4)

11. *Rapid Technological Change is Out of Control.* We need to get a handle on the situation and protect folks from invasions of privacy, loss of jobs to automation, and serious environmental consequences.

    - Decide if there is, or will likely be, a significant problem; if there will, characterize its causes and effects and evaluate alternative options for addressing it (Chapter 1)

    - While looking at the issue through multiple lenses, pay particular attention to the economics lens (Chapter 9), the sustainability lens (Section 11.2), and the science and technology lens (Section 11.3)

- *Apply systems thinking to put your client's concern in a broader context (Chapter 12)*

- *Use scenario planning to visualize alternative versions of the future that capture different pathways for scientific and technological change and look for policies that perform well under multiple scenarios (Section 13.4.2)*

12. *Let's Adopt this Package of Policies*: We're facing multiple related problems, and we need to move on multiple fronts at the same time. We can't do this on an incremental basis.

    - *Recognize that the classical model of prospective analysis (Chapter 1) will be of limited use because of its focus on a single problem and identification of a single preferred policy option*

    - *Treat the package of policies as a single option and then develop alternative packages of policies that might be used instead to address the problems of concern; subject all the packages to the classical model of prospective analysis (Chapter 1)*

    - *Combine systems thinking with an influence diagram or causal loop diagram to track multiple related problems and to consider multiple simultaneous interventions in a system (Chapter 12)*

    - *If there are one or two problems among the set under analysis that seem most pressing, narrow your focus to those problems and use the principles of inclusive, user-focused design to come up with potential policy options (Chapter 14)*

13. *I Need you to be my Research Assistant*: I am a policy wonk engaged in policy research, rather than policy analysis. There is no client; I just need your help with this research project, and you have all sorts of great skills.

    - *Refresh your memory on the difference between policy research and policy analysis (Introduction to Part I)*

    - *Recognize that policy research is usually—but not always—conducted within the confines of a single academic discipline, rather than applying a panoptic, multidisciplinary approach (Part III)*

    - *Recognize that policy research usually constitutes analysis as inquiry, but sometimes may be undertaken as analysis as advocacy; make sure you understand the circumstances you're in (Section 3.3.2)*

    - *Know that policy research, like policy analysis, depends on strong evidence and sound reasoning, but with many fewer time and resource constraints; accordingly, policy research is usually held to a higher standard of quality (Section 5.1)*

Over the course of your career, you will almost certainly encounter assignments that differ from these thirteen vignettes. But these assignments are among the most common, and the suggestions offered above are meant to get you started. As you progress in your career, many of these techniques will become second nature.

15.6 AFTERWORD: A DOZEN TAKEAWAYS

Having worked your way through a few hundred pages and dozens of concepts, frameworks, and suggestions, you might be wondering how to prioritize what we've covered over the past fifteen chapters. Several studies suggest that students new to a subject often struggle to identify the most important principles of their chosen field; in turn, it becomes harder than necessary for them to master that field (Angelo, 1993). Accordingly, this section gives you a quick list of what—at least to me—are the twelve most important takeaway messages of the book.

15.6.1 Although Incomplete, the Classical Models Provide a Solid Foundation for Policy Analysis

The classical models give you a reliable framework for organizing your work. They help you stay focused on important issues like the core problem in a prospective analysis or the intended impacts of a program being retrospectively evaluated. They push you to approach policy analysis in a rigorous and consistent fashion, collecting and evaluating the best available evidence. Moreover, the models help you ground your work in sound logic by appropriately applying deductive, causal, inductive, abductive, or Bayesian probabilistic reasoning. And these models focus on the inevitable trade-offs entailed in taking one path rather than another. When confronted with a confusing and complicated policy issue, the classical models are usually a good place to start your analysis.

15.6.2 Policy Analysis Can Help Frame and Clarify Policy Disputes in a Post-Truth World

It can be hard to make sense of the claims, counterclaims, half-truths, and occasional outright lies that you may hear during debates about important policy issues. One of the most valuable contributions you can make as a policy analyst is simply to organize these arguments into a coherent framework. Discounting evidence- and logic-free nonsense is an important first step, although take care not to discount the underlying concerns of those whose voices deserve to be heard in a democracy. Creating a common vocabulary where words are understood in the same way by all concerned is also important, as is deconstructing policy claims to characterize their strengths and weaknesses. Distinguishing descriptive claims where evidence and logic are critical from normative claims that depend on value-oriented moral reasoning can help identify sources of disagreement. And recognizing the difference between *analysis as inquiry* and *analysis as advocacy*, and between a good-faith argument and a fight, can also help keep things sorted.

15.6.3 Policy Analysis Can Never Offer Comprehensive Rationality or the Certainty of the Natural Sciences

Policy analysis is an applied discipline, aimed at providing the best answers that can be developed under time, resource, and information constraints to support policymaking in real time. Triage is an ever-present part of most policy analysts' lives, necessitating trade-offs between analytic rigor and an on-time deliverable. The challenge is made even more difficult because the focus of policy analysis is human affairs rather than the more predictable natural world and because policy analysis aspires to project the future outcomes of today's policies. While the scientific method can guide your analysis, you won't find the precision of fields like chemical engineering or mathematics when it comes to policy analysis.

15.6.4 Policy Analysis Cannot Overcome the Intrinsic Challenges of Democratic Governance

A commitment to a democracy, in which all voices are given equal weight, limits the scope of policy analysis. In the absence of demonstrably correct and formulaic ways of aggregating the preferences of citizens, resolving collective action problems, or solving wicked problems, policy analysis can never deliver a definitive recommendation about the optimal policy. High quality policy analysis can provide policymakers with the best available evidence, logical reasoning, and clarity about the trade-offs of policy choices, but it can never render a final judgment about which public policies are appropriate. Instead, we have to look to the institutions of democracy—elections, the branches and levels of government, and the rule of law—to make such judgments.

15.6.5 Policy Analysis Can Give Voice to the Unheard, Even if No One Listens

Advocates in policy debates sometimes struggle to have their voices heard, but many folks never even get involved in the debate. An important role for policy analysts is thus to surface the perspectives of people who would otherwise not be heard. Unheard voices may be those of folks intentionally excluded from, or too disaffected to participate in, the conversation. In some debates, invisible stakeholders would participate if only they knew that the problems and policies under discussion could directly affect their interests. Future generations (e.g., those impacted by today's climate policies) also have no way to participate (beyond relying on the current generation's empathy for its descendants). And, in many cases, there is no advocate for the counterfactual, no one to ask what would happen if a different policy were enacted. In all these cases, policy analysis may be able to yield insight into what these voices would say if they could be heard. Not being part of the conversation, of course, they often lack political clout; so you shouldn't be surprised if policymakers give their preferences short shrift.

15.6.6 Policy Analysis Is a Mindset as Much as It Is a Collection of Techniques

While there are many analytic techniques that an aspiring policy analyst should master, it's equally important that you develop the right mindset for your work. Metacognition, for example, helps you to understand how emotions can influence cognitive thought processes and in particular, how an aversion to cognitive dissonance may distort your understanding of reality. Moreover, biases and blind spots can creep into your work as the result of fast System 1 thinking, hot cognition, and directionally motivated reasoning. Embracing the right mindset—critical thinker, pragmatic, competent, tough-minded, service-oriented, and self-aware—can go a long way toward making you a more successful policy analyst. Finally, emotional intelligence, an orientation toward ethics, and the ability to serve as an intermediary among multiple actors who may have divergent interests will serve you well during your career.

15.6.7 Without a Panoptic Approach, Policy Analysis Can Be Blind to Important Realities

Most graduate programs in policy analysis focus on microeconomics, quantitative methods, and sometimes, political science. No doubt, these topics are very important. But they are not enough. If you listen to policy debates about, say, the response to COVID-19, policing in communities of color, or the electoral implications of misinformation in social media, you'll quickly conclude that economic efficiency, theories of the political process, and sophisticated statistical analysis often play a limited role in policymaking. Without the multidimensional perspective afforded by a panoptic approach, you can easily overlook policy-relevant considerations that, if integrated into your policy analysis, would allow you to offer your client a more comprehensive and nuanced understanding of the issues. Policy analysis needs to pay as much attention to matters of equity and justice, institutional constraints, the legal regime, sustainability, and science and technology as it does to economics and political science.

15.6.8 A Policy Analysis That Is Not Clearly Understood by Its Target Audience Is a Waste of Time

As an applied discipline, the value of policy analysis is best measured by the quality of its contribution to the decisionmaking process. No matter how rigorous, insightful, and clever a policy analysis is, if its conclusions are not effectively conveyed to and understood by its intended audience, then the analysis won't contribute to policymaking. Aspiring policy analysts should thus pay as much attention to honing their communication skills—in writing, in oral briefings, and in real-time conversations with clients and colleagues—as they do to perfecting their analytic skills. Success is not guaranteed; even if you're a superb communicator, clients may still be unwilling to invest their time and effort in understanding your work. But if your communication skills are weak, then even a motivated client may get little, if anything, out of your work.

15.6.9 A Policy Analyst Using a Simplistic Mental Map of a Complex System Often Gets Lost

In the face of complex policy challenges and time, resource, and information constraints, it can be easy to slip into reductionist thinking, focusing on only a narrow slice of reality. The result can be a simplistic mental map of how a complex world works. But policy problems arise in systems, public policies are themselves interventions in those systems, and to make things even harder, the systems are invisible. Holistic systems thinking can help you to make sense of the multiple lenses in a panoptic framework, to appreciate the interdependent causal relationships that permeate policy-relevant systems, to reassemble the insights you've gleaned from your critical analytic thinking, and to anticipate behavioral responses to public policies. With a flawed map of the system you're analyzing, you shouldn't be surprised if you get lost.

15.6.10 Inclusive, User-Centered Design Can Improve the Quality of Public Policy

Ineffective or dysfunctional public policies have two downsides. They not only waste taxpayer resources and fail to mitigate the problems at which they're targeted, they can exacerbate citizen cynicism about government's ability to address important issues. Learning how to design successful policies is thus an important skill for policy analysts. Putting users—who may be program beneficiaries, regulated firms, citizens being served, or anyone else who interacts with a program—at the center of the policy design process is a great way to start. And intentional inclusion rather than waiting for stakeholders to self-identify can yield both a more democratic process and a more effective program. Built on a sound theory of change, a program in which the mission, strategy, and tactics are well-aligned and where the value proposition, legitimacy and support, and operational capacity are in synch is more likely to succeed than one where its elements are working at cross purposes or where it lacks the capacity to deliver on its value proposition.

15.6.11 High Quality Policy Analysis Captures the Plurality of the Future, Rather Than Obscuring It

Pherson and Heuer's astute observation that the future is plural has profound implications for policy analysis. The fact that public policy is implemented in the present but creates consequences in the future means that policy analysts can't escape the need to contemplate the future. But since your crystal ball lacks 20/20 vision, how can you tell a client what *will* happen if he or she opts for one policy over another? You can't. The best you can do is to describe alternative versions of the future and perhaps offer a judgment about the likelihood of each. Or you might think of alternative futures as scenarios, the likelihood of which cannot be estimated, and instead search for policy choices expected to perform well under multiple scenarios. Either way, your job as a policy analyst is not to pretend that you have perfect foresight but instead to help your client understand how the future may unfold.

15.6.12 Policy Analysis Can, at Best, Speak Only a Provisional Truth to Power

For the many reasons described throughout the book, policy analysis can't yield absolute truth. In the face of competing ideologies, divergent values, the exercise of political power, and inevitable constraints on policymaking, the truth is as much socially constructed as it is based on real-world conditions. But that doesn't mean that everything is relative and that anything goes. When applied to policy analysis, the scientific method with its emphasis on the best available evidence and sound reasoning can yield profound insights. When appropriately qualified, conclusions derived from high quality analysis have the potential to change public policy for the better. While you might have once thought that policy analysis could deliver definitive truth, I hope I've convinced you that it can't. But don't get discouraged. The alternative to provisional truth is not absolute truth. It's usually deceptive rhetoric, uninformed hunches, and the unchecked exercise of political power.

And that's where you come into the picture. My hope is that you are able to take some of the ideas described in this book and integrate them with your innate talent and passion. I also hope that you are better prepared now than you were when you first picked up the book to make a meaningful contribution to resolving the policy issues that you care most about. I wish you the best of luck.

CHAPTER SUMMARY

This chapter focused on practical techniques that can help you become a more effective policy analyst. Such skills are an important complement to the cognitive and analytic techniques described in previous chapters. We started by considering the topic of professional ethics and looked at different codes of ethics. Two ways of answering ethical questions were described: ethics as rule-following and ethical reasoning. We then moved to the topic of emotional intelligence and observed that the emotional aspects of your interactions with others can affect your ability to successfully engage citizens seeking public services, stakeholders trying to influence policymaking, and colleagues with whom you are directly working.

We then turned our attention to the principles of project management and noted that application of such principles to your policy analysis work can improve the quality of the deliverables you produce and the likelihood they will effectively serve your client's needs. We continued our look at management with a review of the ways in which a policy analyst serves as an intermediary among multiple actors and considered some suggestions for being more effective in that role. We saw in earlier chapters that the classical models of policy analysis—both prospective and retrospective—are rarely used in their entirety by policy analysts who are responding to assignments from clients. In this chapter, we therefore looked at about a dozen assignments that policy analysts often *do* receive and talked about specific approaches that might be useful in each case. Finally, this chapter closed with a review of the key themes—the take-aways—of the book as a whole.

DISCUSSION QUESTIONS

1. What do you think about the use of ethics codes in organizations? Do most folks know about and adhere to them? Or are they just compliance exercises that don't have any effect on how the organization works?

2. What ethical standards seem most important to you? What sorts of activities and behaviors seem out of bounds due to ethical concerns? Are there some areas where you think the ethics codes we looked at (in Appendix 15-A) go too far, defining some forms of acceptable behavior as unethical?

3. How do you feel about the concept of emotional intelligence? Is it a useful framework for enhancing teamwork? Or does the concept seem too ephemeral to be of much use? Do you think it could lead to the manipulation of others' emotions for selfish purposes?

4. Think about a group project in which you have participated where the outcome was a good one and another where the outcome was not good. Why did the first project succeed? Why did the second project fail? What's more important: project management skills or substantive policy analysis skills?

5. I suggested that sometimes a policy analyst can be like a traffic cop, trying to keep multiple people happy while moving information back and forth among them. What do you think of this metaphor? Would you enjoy playing such a role? Or does it seem like a thankless task that you'd rather avoid?

6. In Section 15.6, I listed the book's top takeaway messages. What do you think of the list? Are there topics on the list that didn't belong? Were important topics left out? And, what about the book as a whole, did it cover topics it needn't have? Did it overlook topics that it should have addressed?

APPENDIX 15-A ETHICS CODES FROM FOUR ORGANIZATIONS

This appendix provides four illustrative ethics codes that may be relevant to your work as a policy analyst. The first is for US federal government employees; the second, from the American Society for Public Administration, is aimed at public servants in general; the third, from the Project Management Institute, is aimed at managers directing projects on behalf of both public and private sector clients; and the fourth is for government relations professionals lobbying public officials.

Standards of Ethical Conduct for Employees of the Executive Branch (5 U.S. CFR 2635, 2021)

Public service is a public trust. Each employee has a responsibility to the United States Government and its citizens to place loyalty to the Constitution, laws and ethical principles above private gain. To ensure that every citizen can have complete confidence in the integrity of the Federal Government, each employee shall respect and adhere to the principles of ethical conduct set forth in this section …

- Public service is a public trust, requiring employees to place loyalty to the Constitution, the laws, and ethical principles above private gain.

- Employees shall not hold financial interests that conflict with the conscientious performance of duty.

- Employees shall not engage in financial transactions using nonpublic Government information or allow the improper use of such information to further any private interest.

- An employee shall not … solicit or accept any gift or other item of monetary value from any[one] seeking official action from, doing business with, or conducting activities regulated by the employee's agency, or whose interests may be substantially affected by the performance or nonperformance of the employee's duties.

- Employees shall put forth honest effort in the performance of their duties.

- Employees shall not knowingly make unauthorized commitments or promises of any kind purporting to bind the Government.

- Employees shall not use public office for private gain.

- Employees shall act impartially and not give preferential treatment to any private organization or individual.

- Employees shall protect and conserve Federal property and shall not use it for other than authorized activities.

- Employees shall not engage in outside employment or activities, including seeking or negotiating for employment, that conflict with official Government duties and responsibilities.

- Employees shall disclose waste, fraud, abuse, and corruption to appropriate authorities.

- Employees shall satisfy in good faith their obligations as citizens, including all just financial obligations, especially those—such as Federal, State, or local taxes—that are imposed by law.

- Employees shall adhere to all laws and regulations that provide equal opportunity for all Americans regardless of race, color, religion, sex, national origin, age, or handicap.

- Employees shall endeavor to avoid any actions creating the appearance that they are violating the law or the ethical standards set forth in this part. Whether particular circumstances create an appearance that the law or these standards have been violated shall be determined from the perspective of a reasonable person with knowledge of the relevant facts.

American Society for Public Administration Code of Ethics (ASPA, 2013)[8]

The ASPA Code of Ethics is a statement of the aspirations and high expectations of public servants. These practices serve as a guide to behavior for members of ASPA in carrying out its principles. The code and these practices are intended to be used as a whole and in conjunction with one another. An ethical public servant will consider the full range of standards and values that are relevant to handling a specific matter and be committed to upholding both the spirit and the letter of this code. ASPA members are committed to:

- *Advance the Public Interest*: Promote the interests of the public and put service to the public above service to oneself.

- *Uphold the Constitution and the Law*: Respect and support government constitutions and laws, while seeking to improve laws and policies to promote the public good.

---

[8]The 2013 ASPA Code of Ethics is reproduced with the permission of the American Society for Public Administration.

- *Promote Democratic Participation*: Inform the public and encourage active engagement in governance. Be open, transparent and responsive, and respect and assist all persons in their dealings with public organizations.

- *Strengthen Social Equity*: Treat all persons with fairness, justice, and equality and respect individual differences, rights, and freedoms. Promote affirmative action and other initiatives to reduce unfairness, injustice, and inequality in society.

- *Fully Inform and Advise*: Provide accurate, honest, comprehensive, and timely information and advice to elected and appointed officials and governing board members, and to staff members in your organization.

- *Demonstrate Personal Integrity*: Adhere to the highest standards of conduct to inspire public confidence and trust in public service.

- *Promote Ethical Organizations*: Strive to attain the highest standards of ethics, stewardship, and public service in organizations that serve the public.

- *Advance Professional Excellence*: Strengthen personal capabilities to act competently and ethically and encourage the professional development of others.

Project Management Institute Code of Ethics and Professional Conduct (PMI, 2019)[9]

As practitioners of project management, we are committed to doing what is right and honorable. …

Responsibility is our duty to take ownership for the decisions we make or fail to make, the actions we take or fail to take, and the consequences that result. …

- We make decisions and take actions based on the best interests of society, public safety, and the environment.

- We accept only those assignments that are consistent with our background, experience, skills, and qualifications.

- We fulfill the commitments that we undertake …

- When we make errors or omissions, we take ownership and make corrections promptly …

- We protect proprietary or confidential information that has been entrusted to us …

- We inform ourselves and uphold the policies, rules, regulations, and laws that govern our … activities.

- We report unethical or illegal conduct …

- We only file ethics complaints when they are substantiated by facts.

- We pursue disciplinary action against an individual who retaliates against a person raising ethics concerns.

Respect is our duty to show a high regard for ourselves, others, and resources entrusted to us …

- We inform ourselves about the norms and customs of others and avoid engaging in behaviors they might consider disrespectful.

- We listen to others' points of view, seeking to understand them.

- We approach directly those persons with whom we have a conflict or disagreement.

- We conduct ourselves in a professional manner, even when it is not reciprocated.

- We negotiate in good faith.

- We do not exercise the power of our expertise or position to influence … others in order to benefit personally at their expense.

- We do not act in an abusive manner toward others.

- We respect the property rights of others.

Fairness is our duty to make decisions and act impartially and objectively …

- We demonstrate transparency in our decisionmaking process.

- We constantly reexamine our impartiality and objectivity …

- We provide equal access to information …

- We make opportunities equally available to qualified candidates.

- We proactively and fully disclose any real or potential conflicts of interest to the appropriate stakeholders.

- When we realize that we have a … conflict of interest, we refrain from … attempting to influence outcomes … until we have made full disclosure, … have an approved mitigation plan, and … obtained consent to proceed.

- We do not hire or fire, reward or punish, or award or deny contracts based on personal considerations …

- We do not discriminate against others based on, but not limited to, gender, race, age, religion, disability, nationality, or sexual orientation.

- We apply the rules of the organization ... without favoritism or prejudice.

Honesty is our duty to understand the truth and act in a truthful manner both in our communications and in our conduct.

- We earnestly seek to understand the truth.

- We are truthful in our communications and in our conduct.

- We provide accurate information in a timely manner.

- We make commitments and promises, implied or explicit, in good faith.

- We strive to create an environment in which others feel safe to tell the truth.

- We do not engage in or condone behavior that is designed to deceive others ...

- We do not engage in dishonest behavior with the intention of personal gain or at the expense of another.

National Institute for Lobbying & Ethics | Code of Ethics (NILE, 2021)[10]

This professional code of conduct is recognized by the profession, clients, and employers as the standard by which the profession should adhere and conduct itself. Members of our organization are required to accept this code as a condition of membership.

Honesty and Integrity: A lobbyist should conduct lobbying activities with honesty and integrity.

- A lobbyist should be truthful in communicating with public officials and with other interested persons and should seek to provide factually correct, current, and accurate information.

- If a lobbyist determines that the lobbyist has provided a public official or other interested person with factually inaccurate information of a significant, relevant, and material nature, the lobbyist should promptly provide the factually accurate information to the interested person.

- If a material change in factual information that the lobbyist provided previously to a public official causes the information to become inaccurate and the lobbyist knows the public official may still be relying upon the information, the lobbyist should provide accurate and updated information to the public official.

---

[10] The 2021 Lobbyists' Code of Ethics is reproduced with the permission of the National Institute for Lobbying & Ethics.

Compliance with Applicable Laws, Regulations, and Rules: A lobbyist should comply fully with all laws, regulations, and rules applicable to the lobbyist.

- A lobbyist should be familiar with laws, regulations, and rules applicable to the lobbying profession and should not engage in any violation of such laws, regulations, and rules.

- A lobbyist should comply with all campaign finance laws, regulations, and rules. Additionally, a lobbyist should remain informed on updates in campaign finance laws that affect their rights and responsibilities, as a lobbyist and a citizen, under the First Amendment right to participate in the political process.

- A lobbyist should not cause a public official to violate any law, regulation, or rule applicable to such public official.

Professionalism: A lobbyist should conduct lobbying activities in a fair and professional manner.

- A lobbyist should have a basic understanding of the legislative and governmental process and such specialized knowledge as is necessary to represent clients or an employer in a competent, professional manner.

- A lobbyist should maintain the lobbyist's understanding of governmental processes and specialized knowledge through appropriate methods such as continuing study, seminars, and similar sessions in order to represent clients or an employer in a competent, professional manner.

- A lobbyist should treat others—both allies and adversaries—with respect and civility.

- A lobbyist should participate in continuing education and training programs, including those addressing compliance with laws, rules, and ethical standards applicable to the profession, on an annual basis.

Conflicts of Interest: A lobbyist should not continue or undertake representations that may create conflicts of interest without the informed consent of the client or potential client involved.

- A lobbyist should avoid advocating a position on an issue if the lobbyist is also representing another client on the same issue with a conflicting position.

- If a lobbyist's work for one client on an issue may have a significant adverse impact on another client's interests, the lobbyist should inform and obtain consent from the other client whose interests may be affected of this fact even if the lobbyist is not representing the other client on the same issue.

- A lobbyist should disclose all known conflicts to the client or prospective client and discuss and resolve the conflict issues promptly.

- A lobbyist should inform the client if any other person is receiving a direct or indirect referral or consulting fee from the lobbyist due to or in connection with the client's work and the amount of such fee or payment.

Due Diligence and Best Efforts: A lobbyist should vigorously and diligently advance and advocate the client's or employer's interests.

- A lobbyist should devote time, attention, and resources to the client's or employer's interests that are commensurate with client expectations, agreements, and compensation.

- A lobbyist should exercise loyalty to the client's or employer's interests.

- A lobbyist should keep the client or employer informed regarding the work that the lobbyist is undertaking and, to the extent possible, should give the client the opportunity to choose between various options and strategies.

Compensation and Engagement Terms

- A lobbyist who is retained by a client should have a written agreement with the client regarding the terms and conditions for the lobbyist's services, including the amount of and basis for compensation. The agreement should include the subject of expenses, and the lobbyist should charge only those expenditures made on behalf of the client and in furtherance of the objective pursued on the client's behalf.

- The fees charged by a lobbyist should be reasonable, taking into account the facts and circumstances of the engagement.

- A lobbyist shall disclose to other clients and, if requested, to government officials the existence of any agreement for the receipt of contingent fees or bonuses for obtaining or preventing the enactment of legislation.

- Upon termination of representation, a lobbyist should take steps to the extent reasonably practicable to protect an employer's or client's interests, such as giving reasonable notice to the employer or client, allowing time for employment of another lobbyist, and surrendering papers and property to which the employer or client is entitled.

Confidentiality: A lobbyist should maintain appropriate confidentiality of client or employer information.

- A lobbyist should not disclose confidential information without the client's or employer's informed consent.

- A lobbyist should not use confidential client information against the interests of a client or employer or for any purpose not contemplated by the engagement or terms of employment.

Public Education

- A lobbyist should seek to ensure better public understanding and appreciation of the nature, legitimacy, and necessity of lobbying in our democratic governmental process. This includes the First Amendment right to "petition the government for redress of grievances."

- A lobbyist is encouraged to devote a not insubstantial amount of time each year to providing lobbying or related services to persons or organizations that are pursuing objectives that advance the public good but who do not have the resources to compensate lobbyists to represent them in that endeavor.

Duty to Governmental Institutions: In addition to fulfilling duties and responsibilities to the client or employer, a lobbyist should exhibit proper respect for the governmental institutions before which the lobbyist represents and advocates clients' interests.

- A lobbyist should not act in any manner that will undermine public confidence and trust in the democratic governmental process.

- A lobbyist should not act in a manner that shows disrespect for government institutions.

REFERENCES

Abrams, L. (2011). *Fermi questions: A guide for teachers, students, and even supervisors.* Wilmington, DE: DuPont Company. Retrieved November 5, 2020, from https://www.soinc.org/sites/default/files/FermiQuestionsHandout.doc

Abrams, H. (2016). Using mini-cases of real-world quick analyses in analytical techniques courses. *Journal of Public Affairs Education,* 22(4), 531–548.

Acevedo, A. (2021). *Statement for the record.* Washington, DC: Major Cities Chiefs Association. Retrieved June 21, 2021, from https://majorcitieschiefs.com/wp-content/uploads/2021/03/MCCA-Statement-for-the-Record-03.23.21-Senate-Judiciary-Committee-Hearing.pdf

Achenbach, J. (2015, March). Why do many reasonable people doubt science? *National Geographic.* Retrieved September 10, 2020, from https://www.nationalgeographic.com/magazine/2015/03/science-doubters-climate-change-vaccinations-gmos/

Achen, C., & Bartels, L. (2017). *Democracy for realists: Why elections do not produce responsive government.* Princeton, NJ: Princeton University Press.

Al-Khalili, J. (2020, April 21). Doubt is essential for science–But for politicians, it's a sign of weakness. *The Guardian.* Retrieved September 17, 2020, from https://www.theguardian.com/commentisfree/2020/apr/21/doubt-essential-science-politicians-coronavirus

Allcott, H., & Sunstein, C. (2015). Regulating internalities. *Journal of Policy Analysis and Management,* 34(3), 698–704.

Allison, G. (2006). Emergence of schools of public policy: Reflections by a founding dean. In M. Moran, M. Rein, & R. Goodin (Eds.), *The Oxford handbook of public policy* (pp. 58–79). Oxford, UK: Oxford University Press.

Amidzic, O., Riehle, H., Fehr, T., Wienbruch, C., & Elbert, T. (2001). Pattern of focal γ-bursts in chess players. *Nature,* 412(6847), 603.

Angelo, T. (1993). A 'teacher's dozen': Fourteen general, research-based principles for improving higher learning in our classrooms. *AAHE Bulletin,* 45, 3–13.

Anglin, S. (2019). Do beliefs yield to evidence: Examining belief perseverance vs. Changes in response to congruent empirical findings. *Journal of Experimental Social Psychology,* 82, 176–199.

Ansell, C., & Geyer, R. (2017). 'Pragmatic complexity' a new foundation for moving beyond 'evidence-based policy making'? *Policy Studies,* 38, 149–167.

Aronson, E., & Tavris, C. (2020, July 12). The role of cognitive dissonance in the pandemic. *The Atlantic.* Retrieved from https://www.theatlantic.com/ideas/archive/2020/07/role-cognitive-dissonance-pandemic/614074/

Arrow, K. (1951). *Social choice and individual values.* Hobken, NJ: John Wiley & Sons.

Arrow, K. (2010). Personal reflections on applied general equilbrium models. In T. Kehoe, T. Srinivasan, & J. Whalley (Eds.), *Frontiers in applied general equilibrium modelling: In honour of Herbert Scarf* (pp. 13–23). Cambridge, UK: Cambridge University Press.

ASPA. (2013, March 16). *Code of ethics.* Retrieved June 1, 2021, from American Society for Public Administration: https://www.aspanet.org/ASPA/About-ASPA/Code-of-Ethics/ASPA/Code-of-Ethics/Code-of-Ethics.aspx

Badaracco, J. (1997). *Defining moments: When managers must choose between right and right.* Boston, MA: Harvard Business School Press.

Baekgaard, M., Christensen, J., Dahlman, C., Mathiasen, A., & Petersen, N. (2017). The role of evidence in politics: Motivated reasoning and persuasion among politicians. *British Journal of Political Science,* 49(3), 1117–1140.

Balla, J., Heneghan, C., Glasziou, P., Thompson, M., & Balla, M. (2009). A model for reflection for good clinical practice. *Journal of Evaluation in Clinical Practice*, 15(6), 964–969.

Banuri, S., Dercon, S., & Guari, V. (2017). *Biased policy professionals*. Washington, DC: World Bank Group.

Bardach, E. (2004). The extrapolation problem: How can we learn from the experience of others? *Journal of Policy Analysis and Management*, 23(2), 205–220.

Bardach, E., & Patashnik, E. (2016). *A practical guide for policy analysis: The eightfold path to more effective problem solving* (5th ed.). Los Angeles, CA: CQ Press.

Bardon, A. (2020). *The truth about denial: Bias and self-deception in science, politics, and religion*. New York, NY: Oxford University Press.

Bartels, S., Gottschalk, F., Hopp, R., & Nozaki, K. (2017). *Urban farming in Baltimore*. Washington, DC: George Washington University.

Bauman, M. (2016, December 5). *'Truth decay' makes facts subjective and polarization more extreme*. Retrieved July 13, 2019, from https://medium.com/rand-corporationhttps://medium.com/rand-corporation/truth-decay-makes-facts-subjective-and-polarization-more-extreme-9c484d9ddef

BEA. (2019). *The use of commodities by industries*. Bureau of Economic Analysis. Washington, DC: U.S. Department of Commerce. Retrieved January 14, 2021, from https://apps.bea.gov/iTable/iTable.cfm?reqid=52&step=102&isuri=1&table_list=4&aggregation=sum

BEA. (2020). *Gross domestic product, third quarter 2020*. Department of commerce. Washington, DC: Bureau of Economic Analysis.

BEA. (2021, June 24). *Gross domestic product*. Retrieved June 30, 2021, from Bureau of Economic Analysis: https://www.bea.gov/sites/default/files/2021-06/gdp1q21_3rd_0.xlsx

Bell, P. (1981). *Graduate training programs in public policy supported by the Ford Foundation*. New York, NY: Ford Foundation.

Belle, N., Belardinelli, P., & Cantarelli, P. (2018). Prospect theory goes public: Experimental evidence on cognitive biases in public policy and decision making. *Public Administration Review*, 78(6), 828–840.

Benkof, D. (2015, October 13). Why not second-class citizenship for illegal immigrants? *The Daily Caller*. Retrieved July 28, 2019, from https://dailycaller.com/2015/10/13/why-not-second-class-citizenship-for-illegal-immigrants/

Bensen, B. (2017, January 8). *Cognitive bias cheat sheet, simplified*. Retrieved August 28, 2019, from Medium | Thinking is Hard: https://medium.com/thinking-is-hard/4-conundrums-of-intelligence-2ab78d90740f

Benson, B. (2019). *Why are we yelling? The art of productive disagreement*. New York, NY: Portfolio; Penguin.

Bergoglio, J. (2015). *Papal encyclical on climate change and inequality: On care for our common home*. Vatican City. Retrieved August 26, 2020, from http://www.vatican.va/content/francesco/en/encyclicals/documents/papa-francesco_20150524_enciclica-laudato-si.html

Best, J. (2008). *Stat-spotting: A field guide to identifying dubious data*. Berkeley, CA: University of California Press.

Bezos, J. (2017, April 17). *2016 letter to shareholders*. Retrieved November 11, 2020, from Amazon: Company News: https://www.aboutamazon.com/news/company-news/2016-letter-to-shareholders

Biden, J. (2021). *EO 14035: Diversity, equity, inclusion, and accessibility in the federal workforce*. Washington, DC: The White House. Retrieved July 7, 2021, from https://www.govinfo.gov/content/pkg/FR-2021-06-30/pdf/2021-14127.pdf

Binder, S., & Lee, F. (2015). Making deals in Congress. In N. Persily (Ed.), *Solutions to political polarization in America* (pp. 240–261). New York, NY: Cambridge University Press.

BLS. (2019). *Occupational employment and wages*. Washington, DC: U.S. Bureau of Labor Statistics. Retrieved September 26, 2020, from https://www.bls.gov/oes/current/oes291141.htm

BLS. (2021). *Databases, tables & calculators by subject*. Retrieved July 10, 2021, from U.S. Bureau of Labor Statistics https://www.bls.gov/webapps/legacy/cpswktab3.htm

Boardman, A., Greenberg, D., Vining, A., & Weimer, D. (2011). *Cost-benefit analysis: Concepts and practices* (4th ed.). Upper Saddle River, NJ: Prentice Hall.

Bolsen, T., & Palm, R. (2019). Motivated reasoning and political decision making. In W. Thompson (Ed.), *Oxford research encyclopaedia of politics* (pp. 1–25). Oxford, UK: Oxford University Press.

Boyd, J., Bagstad, K., Carter Ingram, J., Shapiro, C., Adkins, J., Casey, C., … Wentland, S. (2018). The natural capital accounting opportunity: Let's really do the numbers. *BioScience*, 68(12), 940–943.

Brady, H. (2019). Dean's message. *Policy Notes*, 2(Fall), 24–25. Retrieved November 25, 2020, from https://gspp.berkeley.edu/assets/uploads/policynotes/policynotes-2019-fall-screen_%281%29.pdf

Brierre, W., Ross-Dyjak, A., Martin, M., Sivulka, C., & Woolford, S. (2019). *Yellow lance mussel habitat in the Hawlings River, Maryland*. Washington, DC: George Washington University.

Bruce, J., & Bennett, M. (2008). Foreign denial and deception: Analytical imperatives. In R. George & J. Bruce (Eds.), *Analyzing intelligence: Origins, obstacles, and innovations* (pp. 122–137). Washington, DC: Georgetown University Press.

Bryant, W. (1997). Conditions for the existence of a market equilibrium. *The Journal of Economic Education*, 28(3), 230–254.

Bucciarelli, M., Khemlani, S., & Johnson-Laird, P. (2008). The psychology of moral reasoning. *Judgment and Decision Making*, 3(2), 121–139.

Bumiller, E. (2010, April 27). We have met the enemy and he is powerpoint. *New York Times*, pp. 1.

Burtraw, D. (2013). The institutional blindspot in environmental economics. *Daedaus*, 142(1), 110–118.

Cairney, P. (2020). *Understanding public policies: Theories and issues*. London, UK: Springer Nature Ltd.

Cairney, P., & Weible, C. (2017). The new policy sciences: Combing the cognitive science of choice, multiple theories of context, and basic and applied analysis. *Policy Sciences*, 9(2), 619–627.

Camillus, J. (2008). Strategy as a wicked problem. *Harvard Business Review*, 86(5), 98–106.

Cammenega, J. (2021, January 6). *State and local sales tax rates*. The Tax Foundation. Retrieved March 15, 2021, from https://taxfoundation.org/2021-sales-taxes/

Card, A. (2017). The problem with '5 whys'. *BMJ Quality & Safety*, 26(8), 671–677.

Carrigan, C., & Shapiro, S. (2017). What's wrong with back of the envelope? A call for simple (and timely) benefit-cost analysis. *Regulation & Governance*, 11(2), 203–212.

Carroll, L. (1865). *Alice's adventures in Wonderland*. London, UK: Macmillan and Co.

Cartwright, N., & Hardie, J. (2012). *Evidence-based policy: A practical guide to doing it better*. Oxford, UK: Oxford University Press.

CBO. (2018a). *How CBO prepares baseline budget projections*. Washington, DC: Congressional Budget Office.

CBO. (2018b). *How CBO prepares cost estimates*. Washington, DC: Congressional Budget Office.

CBO. (2019). *The effects on employment and family income of increasing the federal minimum wage*. Washington, DC: Congressional Budget Office.

CBO. (2020a). *The distribution of household income, 2017*. Washington, DC: Congressional Budget Office.

CBO. (2020b). *Transparency at CBO: Future plans and a review of 2019*. Washington, DC: Congressional Budget Office. Retrieved November 15, 2020, from https://www.cbo.gov/system/files/2020-03/56236-CBO-Transparency.pdf

CBO. (2021a). *An overview of the economic outlook: 2021 to 2031*. Washington, DC: Congressional Budget Office. Retrieved February 1, 2021, from https://www.cbo.gov/system/files/2021-02/56965-Economic-Outlook.pdf

CBO. (2021b). *CBO's support of the U.S. Congress: Presentation to the National Assembly Budget Office, Republic of Korea*. Washington, DC: Congressional Budget Office. Retrieved July 12, 2021, from https://www.cbo.gov

CBO. (2021c). *Transparency at CBO: Future plans and a review of 2020*. Washington, DC: Congressional Budget Office.

Census Bureau. (2020). *The supplemental poverty measure: 2019*. Washington, DC: U.S. Department of Commerce.

Center for Responsive Politics. (2021a, January 11). *Who are the biggest donors?* Retrieved February 9, 2021, from OpenSecrets.org: https://www.opensecrets.org/elections-overview/biggest-donors

Center for Responsible Politics. (2021b, January 11). *Donor demographics*. Retrieved February 9, 2021, from OpenSecrets.org: https://www.opensecrets.org/elections-overview/donor-demographics

Center for Responsible Politics. (2021c, January 23). *Lobbying data summary*. Retrieved February 8, 2021, from OpenSecrets.org: https://www.opensecrets.org/federal-lobbying

Center for Responsible Politics. (2021d, February 8). *Cost of election*. Retrieved February 9, 2021, from OpenSecrets.org: https://www.opensecrets.org/elections-overview/cost-of-election

Chatfield, T. (2018). *Critical thinking: Your guide to effective argument, successful analysis & independent study*. London, UK: SAGE Publications, Ltd.

Chhetri, N., Ghimire, R., Wagner, M., & Wang, M. (2020). Global citizen deliberation: Case of world-wide views on climate. *Energy Policy*, 147, 111892. doi:10.1016/j.enpol.2020.111892

Choi, N., & Jung, K. (2017). Measuring efficiency and effectiveness of highway management in sustainability. *Sustainability*, 9(8), 1347.

Cicero, M. (55BCE/2016). *On the ideal orator* (J. May, Trans.). Princeton, NJ: Princeton University Press.

Cicero, M. (84BCE/2016). *On invention* (J. May, Trans.). Princeton, NJ: Princeton University Press.

Clark, S., & Wallace, R. (2015). Integration and inter-disciplinarity: Concepts, frameworks, and education. *Policy Sciences*, 48, 233–255.

CMS. (2021, May 27). *CMS program hisotry*. Retrieved from Centers for Medicare & Medicaid Servies: https://www.cms.gov/About-CMS/Agency-Information/History

Cogswell, N., Veiga, H., & Li, X. (2015). *Assessing and mapping coastal vulnerability in order to scale up ecosystem-based adaptation in the Philippines*. Washington, DC: George Washington University.

Cohen, S. (2014). *Understanding environmental policy*. New York, NY: Columbia University Press.

Cooper, J. (2007). *Cognitive dissonance: Fifty years of a classic theory*. London, UK: SAGE Publications, Ltd.

Covey, S. (2017). *Covey on trust*. Retrieved April 12, 2017, from Leadership Now: http://www.leadershipnow.com/CoveyOnTrust.html

CPSP. (2021). *Monthly poverty*. Retrieved July 8, 2021, from Center on Poverty and Social Policy | Columbia University: https://www.povertycenter.columbia.edu/forecasting-monthly-poverty-data

Crider, S. (2014). *Aristotle's rhetoric for everybody*. Dallas, TX: Arts of Liberty Project. Retrieved July 25, 2020, from https://artsofliberty.udallas.edu/wp-content/uploads/2017/04/Introductory-Rhetoric.pdf

Crosskerry, P., & Nimmo, G. (2011). Better clinical decision making and reducing diagnostic error. *Journal of the Royal College of Physicians of Edinburgh*, 41(2) 155–162.

CRS. (2013, January 23). *The endangered species act and "sound science"*. Retrieved December 13, 2020, from Congressional Research Service: https://crsreports.congress.gov/product/pdf/RL/RL32992

CRS. (2019a). *Firearms-related appropriations riders*. Washington, DC: Congressional Research Service. Retrieved June 25, 2021, from https://crsreports.congress.gov/product/pdf/IF/IF11371

CRS. (2019b, February 6). *Science and technology issues in the 116th Congress*. Retrieved April 11, 2021, from Congressional Research Service: https://crsreports.congress.gov/product/pdf/R/R45491

CRS. (2019c, November 13). *Presidential directives: An introduction*. Retrieved April 1, 2021, from Congressional Research Service: https://crsreports.congress.gov/product/pdf/IF/IF11358

CRS. (2020a, April 29). *The office of technology assessment: History, authorities, issues, and options*. Retrieved April 8, 2021, from Congressional Research Service: https://crsreports.congress.gov/product/pdf/R/R46327

CRS. (2020b, December 17). *Federal Research and Development (R&D) funding: FY2021*. Retrieved April 8, 2021, from Congressional Research Service: https://crsreports.congress.gov/product/pdf/R/R46341

CRS. (2020c, December 8). *Judicial review under the administrative procedure act*. Retrieved April 1, 2021, from Congressional Research Service: https://crsreports.congress.gov/product/pdf/LSB/LSB10558

CRS. (2021a). *Federal scientific integrity policies: A primer.* Washington, DC: Congressional Research Service. Retrieved June 26, 2021, from https://crsreports.con gress.gov/product/pdf/R/R46614

CRS. (2021b, March 19). *An overview of federal regulations and the rulemaking process.* Retrieved March 30, 2021, from Congressional Research Service: https:// crsreports.congress.gov/product/pdf/IF/IF10003

CRS. (2021c, February 18). *Tribal consultation: Administration guidance and policy consideration.* Retrieved from https://www.everycrsreport.com/files/2021-02-18_IN11 606_066c9da67ab0fa56c557c8fa1a2e9b51421a15e0.pdf

Cunnyngham, K. (2018). *Trends in supplemental nutrition assistance program participation rates: Fiscal year 2010 to fiscal year 2016. Office of policy support, food & nutrition service.* Alexandria, VA: United States Department of Agriculture.

Daviter, F. (2017). Coping, taming, or solving: Alternative approaches to the governance of wicked problems. *Policy Studies*, 38(6), 571–588.

deLeon, P. (2006). The historical roots of the field. In M. Moran, M. Rein, & R. Goodin (Eds.), *The Oxford handbook of public policy* (pp. 39–57). Oxford, UK: Oxford University Press.

deLeon, P., & Martell, C. (2008). Policy sciences approach. In E. Berman (Ed.), *Encyclopaedia of public administration and public policy* (2nd ed., pp. 1495–1498). London, UK: Taylor and Francis.

Denhardt, J., & Denhardt, R. (2007). *The new public service: Serving, not steering.* Armonk, NY: M.E. Sharpe.

Dietz, T., Ostrom, E., & Stern, P. (2003). The struggle to govern the commons. *Science*, 302(5652), 1907–1912.

Ditto, P., Liu, B., Clark, C., Wojcik, S., Chen, E., Grady, R., … Zinger, J. (2019). At least bias in bipartisan: A meta-analytic comparison of bias in liberals and conservatives. *Perspectives on Psychological Science*, 14(2), 273–291.

DOJ. (2021, March 30). *U.S. attorneys listing.* Retrieved from Offices of the United States Attorneys, Department of Justice: https://www.justice.gov/usao/us-attorneys-listing.

Doleželová, H. (2007). *Politika zvyšování míry zaměstnanosti starších osob v České republice (Employment policy for the elderly in the Czech Republic).* Unpublished Master's thesis, Charles University, Faculty of Social Sciences, Prague, CZ.

Donahue, J. (1997). *Disunited States.* New York, NY: Basic Books.

DPIC. (2020). *States with and without the death penalty.* Retrieved March 15, 2021, from Death Penalty Information Center: https://deathpenaltyinfo.org/state-and-federal-info/state-by-state

Dror, Y. (1967). Policy analysts: A new professional role in government services. *Public Administration Review*, 27(3), 197–203.

Drucker, P. (1995, February). Really reinventing government. *The Atlantic Monthly*, 275/2, 49–61.

Drucker, P. (2009). *The effective executive.* New York, NY: HarperCollins e-books.

Dryzek, J. (2002). A post-positivist policy-analytic travelogue. *The Good Society*, 11(1), 32–36.

Dryzek, J. (2006). Policy analysis as critique. In M. Moran & M. G. Rein (Eds.), *The Oxford handbook of public policy* (pp. 190–203). Oxford, UK: Oxford University Press.

Dryzek, J., Nicol, D., Niemeyer, S., Pemberton, S., Curato, N., Bächtiger, A., … Vergne, A. (2020). Global citizen deliberation on genome editing. *Science*, 369(6510), 1435–1437.

Dunn, W. (2018). *Policy analysis: An integrated approach* (6th ed.). New York, NY: Routledge.

Durning, D. (1991). The transition from traditional to postpositivist policy analysis: A role for Q-methodology. *Journal of Policy Analysis and Management*, 18(3), 389–410.

Dwyer, C. (2017, August 25). *18 common logical fallacies and persuasion techniques.* Retrieved from Psychology Today: https://www.psychologytoday.com/us/blog/thoughts-thinking/201708/18-common-logical-fallacies-and-per suasion-techniques

Dwyer, C. (2018, September 7). *12 common biases that affect how we make everyday decisions.* Retrieved from Psychology Today: https://www.psychologytoday.com/us/blog/thoughts-thinking/201809/12-common-biases-affect-how-we-make-everyday-decisions

Dye, T. (2011). *Understanding public policy*. New York, NY: Pearson Education.

Edwards, C. (2015). *Why the federal government fails*. Washington, DC: Cato Institute. Retrieved February 26, 2021, from https://www.cato.org/sites/cato.org/files/pubs/pdf/pa777.pdf

EFSA Scientific Committee. (2017). Guidance on the use of the weight of evidence approach in scientific assessments. *EFSA Journal*, 15, 1–69. doi:10.2903/j.efsa.2017.4971

Eggers, W., & O'Leary, J. (2009). *If we can put a man on the moon: Getting big things done in government*. Boston, MA: Harvard Business Press.

Elliot, L. (2012, March 29). Britain has squandered golden opportunity North Sea oil promised. *The Guardian*. Retrieved March 22, 2021, from https://www.theguardian.com/business/economics-blog/2012/mar/29/north-sea-oil-revenue-squandered

EPA. (2015). *Regulatory impact analysis of the final revisions to the National Ambient Air Quality Standards for ground-level ozone*. Washington, DC: U.S. Environmental Protection Agency. Retrieved January 20, 2021, from https://www3.epa.gov/ttn/naaqs/standards/ozone/data/20151001ria.pdf

EPA/OIG. (2011). *EPA must improve oversight of state enforcement. Office of Inspector General*. Washington, DC: Environmental Protection Agency. Retrieved March 18, 2021, from https://www.epa.gov/sites/production/files/2015-10/documents/20111209-12-p-0113.pdf

Epstein, D. (2019). *Range: Why generalists triumph in a specialized world*. New York, NY: Riverhead Books.

Epstein, S. (1994). Integration of the cognitive and the psychodynamic unconscious. *American Psychologist*, 49(8), 709–724.

Evans, A. (2015). Presidential address: Reflections of an accidental analyst. *Journal of Policy Analysis and Management*, 34(2), 256–266.

Federal Register. (2021, April 1). *Executive orders*. Retrieved from Federal Register: https://www.federalregister.gov/presidential-documents/executive-orders

Federal Reserve Board. (2020, September). Changes in U.S. family finances from 2016 to 2019: Evidence from the Survey of Consumer Finances. *Federal Reserve Bulletin*, 106(5), 1–42.

Festinger, L. (1957). *A theory of cognitive dissonance*. Evanston, IL: Peterson.

Feynman, R. (1974, June). Cargo cult science. *Engineering and Science*, 37(7), 10–13.

Finkel, E., Bail, C., Cikara, M., Ditto, P., Iyengar, S., Klar, S., … Druckman, J. (2020). Political sectarianism in America. *Science*, 370, 533–536.

Fischer, F., & Gottweiss, H. (2012). *The argumentative turn revisited: Public policy as communicative practice*. Durham, NC: Duke University Press.

Fitzgerald, F. (1936, February, March, April). The crack-up: A three part series. *Esquire*. Retrieved July 20, 2019, from https://www.esquire.com/lifestyle/a4310/the-crack-up/

Flynn, D., Nyhan, B., & Reifler, J. (2017). The nature and origins of misperceptions: Understanding false and unsupported beliefs about politics. *Advances in Political Psychology*, 38, 127–150.

Flyvbjerg, B. (1998). Habermas and Foucault: Thinkers for civil society? *The British Journal of Sociology*, 49(2), 210–233.

Flyvbjerg, B. (2001). *Making social science matter: Why social inquiry fails and how it can succeed again*. Cambridge, UK: Cambridge University Press.

Fox, L. (2018, September 6). *What is the supplemental poverty measure and how does it differ from the official measure?* Retrieved February 2, 2021, from U.S. Census Bureau: https://www.census.gov/newsroom/blogs/random-samplings/2018/09/what_is_the_suppleme.html

Fox Business. (2020, October 29). Retrieved from Fox Business News: https://www.foxbusiness.com/economy/us-economy-grew-by-record-shattering-xx-pace-last-quarter

Frank, B. (2012, March 30). *Take the money and run for office*. Retrieved February 9, 2021, from This American Life: https://www.thisamericanlife.org/461/transcript

Franklin, B. (1772). Letter to Joseph Priestley. In W. Bell & Mr. Franklin (Eds.), *A selection from his personal letters*. New Haven, CT: Yale University Press. Retrieved 1956.

Frederick, S. (2005). Cognitive reflection and decision making. *Journal of Economic Perspectives*, 19(4), 25–42.

Freeley, A., & Steinberg, D. (2014). *Argumentation and debate: Critical thinking for reasoned decision making* (13th ed.). Boston, MA: Wadsworth.

Fretwell, E., Rejeski, D., Hendler, J., Peroff, K., & McCord, M. (2019). *Science and technology policy assessment: A congressionally directed review*. Washington, DC: National Academy of Public Administration. Retrieved April 7, 2021, from https://napawash.org/uploads/Academy_Studies/NAPA_FinalReport_forCRS_110119.pdf

Friedman, L. (2002). *The microeconomics of public policy analysis*. Princeton, NJ: Princeton University Press.

Friedman, L. (2017). *Does policy analysis matter: Exploring its effectiveness in theory and practice*. Oakland, CA: University of California Press.

Friendly, H. (1975). Some kind of hearing. *University of Pennsylvania Law Review*, 123(5), 1267–1317.

Fry, B., & Raadschelders, J. (2008). *Mastering public administration: From Max Weber to Dwight Waldo* (2nd ed.). Washington, DC: CQ Press.

Fukayama, F. (2018, August 1). What's wrong with public policy education. *The American Interest*. Retrieved May 23, 2021, from https://www.the-american-interest.com/2018/08/01/whats-wrong-with-public-policy-education/

Funnell, S., & Rogers, P. (2011). *Purposeful program theory: Effective use of theories of change and logic models*. San Francisco, CA: Jossey-Bass.

Gallup. (2020). *In depth: Trust in government*. Retrieved February 28, 2021, from Gallup News: https://news.gallup.com/poll/5392/trust-government.aspx

GAO. (2012). *Designing evaluations*. Washington, DC: Government Accountability Office.

GAO. (2018). *Trends affecting government and society*. Washington, DC: Government Accounability Office. Retrieved April 8, 2021, from https://www.gao.gov/products/gao-18-396sp

GAO. (2019a, September). *Science and tech spotlight: Hypersonic weapons*. Retrieved April 15, 2021, from Government Accountability Office: https://www.gao.gov/products/gao-19-705sp

GAO. (2019b, October 3). *Our new "science & tech spotlights"*. Washington, DC: U.S. Government Accountability Office. Retrieved April 8, 2021, from WatchBlog: Following the Federal Dollar: https://blog.gao.gov/2019/10/03/our-new-science-tech-spotlights/

GAO. (2020, February). *Science & tech spotlight: Deepfakes*. Retrieved April 15, 2021, from Government Accountability Office: https://www.gao.gov/assets/gao-20-379sp.pdf

GAO. (2021a). *Technology assessment design handbook*. Washington, DC: Government Accountability Office. Retrieved April 8, 2021, from https://www.gao.gov/assets/gao-21-347g.pdf

GAO. (2021b, April 8). *Science & tech spotlights*. Retrieved from Government Accountability | Technology and Science: https://www.gao.gov/technology-science

Garner, T., & Gudrais, M. (2018). *Alternative poverty measures for the U.S.: Focus on supplemental poverty measure thresholds. U.S. Department of Labor*. Washington, DC: U.S. Bureau of Labor Statistics.

Garvin, D., & Roberto, M. (2001). What you don't know about making decisions. *Harvard Business Review*, 79(8), 108–116.

GCRP. (2017). *Climate change special report: Fourth national climate assessment* (Vol. I). Washington, DC: U.S. Global Change Research Report.

George, R., & Bruce, J. (2008). *Analyzing intelligence: Origins, obstacles, and innovations*. Washington, DC: Georgetown University Press.

Geva-May, I. (2005). *Thinking like a policy analyst: Policy analysis as a clinical profession*. New York, NY: Palgrave Macmillan.

Ghaffarzadegan, N., Lyneis, J., & Richardson, G. (2011). How small systems dynamics models can help the public policy process. *System Dynamics Review*, 27(1), 22–44.

Gladwell, M. (2006, February 13). *Million-Dollar Murray: Why problems like homelessness may be easier to solve than to manage. The New Yorker*, pp. 96.

Gould, S. (1994). Evolution as fact and theory. In *Hen's teeth and horse's toes* (pp. 253–262). New York, NY: W.W. Norton & Company.

Grossman, P. (2018). Utilizing Ostrom's institutional analysis and development framework toward an understanding of crisis-driven policy. *Policy Sciences*, 52(1), 3–20.

Gupta, D. (2011). *Analyzing public policy: Concepts, tools, & techniques* (2nd ed.). Washington, DC: CQ Press | SAGE Publications.

GW/RSC. (2021, April 1). *Reg stats*. Retrieved from Regulatory Studies Center | George Washington University: https://regulatorystudies.columbian.gwu.edu/reg-stats

Habermas, J. (1990). *Moral consciousness and communicative action* (C. Lenhardt & S. Nicholson, Trans.). Cambridge, MA: The MIT Press.

Haidt, J. (2001). The emotional dog and its rational tail: A social intuitionist approach to moral judgment. *Psychological Review*, 108(4), 814–834.

Haidt, J. (2007). The new synthesis in moral psychology. *Science*, 316, 998–1002.

Haidt, J. (2012). *The righteous mind: Why good people are divided by politics and religion*. New York, NY: Vintage Books.

Haidt, J., & Graham, J. (2007). When morality opposes justice: Conservatives have moral intuitions that liberals may not recognize. *Social Justice Research*, 20(1), 98–116.

Hallsworth, M., Egan, M., Rutter, J., & McCrae, J. (2018). *Behavioural government: Using behavioural science to improve how governments make decisions*. London, UK: Behavioural Insights Ltd.

Hamel, G. (2000). *Leading the revolution*. Boston, MA: Harvard Business School Press.

Hammitt, J. (2021). Accounting for the distribution of benefits and costs in benefit-cost analysis. *Journal of Benefit Cost Analysis*, 12, 1–21.

Hammond, J., Keeney, R., & Raiffa, H. (1999). *Smart choices: A practical guide to making better life decisions*. New York, NY: Broadway Books.

Hansen, J. (2009, February 14). Coal-fired power stations are death factories. Close them. *The Guardian*. Retrieved July 18, 2019, from https://www.theguardian.com/commentisfree/2009/feb/15/james-hansen-power-plants-coal

Hardin, G. (1968). The tragedy of the commons. *Science*, 162, 1243–1248.

Harmon, M. (2006). *Public administration's final exam: A pragmatist restructuring of the profession and the discipline*. Tuscaloosa, AL: The University of Alabama Press.

Hawkins, R. (2009). Collective innovation: A resource book. In *International centre for development oriented research in agriculture*. Wageningen: National Agricultural Research for Development Team. Retrieved April 27, 2021, from http://icra2.sites06.footsteps-cms.nl/file.php/534/sa_resource_book2009_fin2.pdf

Head, B. (2008). Wicked problems in public policy. *Public Policy*, 3(2), 101–118.

Healey, J. (2021, April 2). Opinion: The Supreme Court just opened the robocall floodgates. Call Congress. *The Los Angeles Times*. Retrieved April 3, 2021, from https://www.latimes.com/opinion/story/2021-04-02/opinion-the-supreme-court-just-opened-the-robocall-floodgates-call-congress

Heckelman, J. (2015). Guest editor's introduction to the symposium on the 50th anniversary of Olson's Logic of Collective Action. *Public Choice*, 164(3), 191–193.

Heineman, R., Bluhm, W., Peterson, S., & Kearny, E. (1990). *The world of the policy analyst: Rationality, values, & politics* (3rd ed.). Chatham: Chatham House Publishers.

Heinrichs, J. (2020). *Thank you for arguing: What Aristotle, Lincoln, and Home Simpson can teach us about the art of persuasion*. New York, NY: Broadway Books.

Heller, J. (2018). The required law & public policy courses in the college of William & Mary's master of public policy program: 25 years of lessons. *William & Mary Policy Review*, 9, 73–92.

Hermus, M., van Buuren, A., & Bekkers, V. (2020). Applying design in public administration: A literature review to explore the state of the art. *Policy & Politics*, 48(1), 21–48.

Herweg, N., Zahariadis, N., & Zohlnhofer, R. (2018). The multiple streams framework: Foundations, refinements, and empircal applications. In C. Weible, & P. Sabatier (Eds.), *Theories of the policy process* (4th ed., pp. 17–53). New York, NY: Westview Press | Hachette Book Group.

Hill, C., & Lynn, L. (2016). *Public management: Thinking and acting in three dimensions.* Thousand Oaks, CA: SAGE Publications; CQ Press.

Hird, J. (2017). How effective is policy analysis? In L. Friedman (Ed.), *Does policy analysis matter? Exploring its effectiveness in theory and practice* (pp. 44–84). Oakland, CA: University of California Press.

Honigsberg, P., & Ho, E. (2019). *Lega research, writing & analysis* (13th ed.). St Paul, MN: GIlbert Law Summaries.

Hume, D. (1739/1888). *A treatise on human nature* (L. Selby-Bigge, Ed.). Oxford, UK: The Clarendon Press

Inhofe, J. (2012). *The greatest hoax: How the global warming conspiracy threatens your future.* Washington, DC: WND Books.

IPCC. (2010). *Guidance note for lead authors of the IPCC fifth assessment report on consistent treatment of uncertainty.* Geneva, CH: Intergovernmental Panel on Climate Change. Retrieved September 22, 2020, from https://www.ipcc.ch/site/assets/uploads/2017/08/AR5_Uncertainty_Guidance_Note.pdf

IWG. (2021). Technical support document: Social cost of carbon, methane, and nitrous oxide interim estimates under executive order 13990. In *Interagency working group on social cost of greenhouse gases.* Washington, DC: Executive Office of the President. Retrieved July 1, 2021, from https://www.whitehouse.gov/wp-content/uploads/2021/02/TechnicalSupportDocument_SocialCostofCarbonMethaneNitrousOxide.pdf

Janzwood, S. (2020). Confident, likely, or both? The implementation of the uncertainty language framework in IPCC special reports. *Climatic Change.* Retrieved October 10, 2020, from https://doi.org/10.1007/s10584-020-02746-x

Jenkins-Smith, H. (1982). Professional roles for policy analysts: A critical assessment. *Journal of Policy Analysis and Management,* 2(1), 88–100.

Joselow, M. (2019, July 25). Automakers buck Trump, sign fuel economy deal with Calif. *Greenwire.* Retrieved March 18, 2021, from https://www.eenews.net/greenwire/stories/1060787703/

Jost, J., Hennes, P., & Lavine, H. (2013). "Hot" political cognition: Its self-, group-, and system-serving purposes.

In D. Carlson (Ed.), *The Oxford handbook of social cognition* (pp. 851–875). New York, NY: Oxford University Press.

Justia. (2018, April). *State-level administrative law.* Retrieved April 4, 2021, from Justia.com: https://www.justia.com/administrative-law/state-level-administrative-law/

Kahan, D., Peters, E., Dawson, E., & Slovic, P. (2017). Motivated numeracy and enlightened self-government. *Behavioural Pubic Policy,* 1(1), 54–86.

Kahneman, D. (2011). *Thinking, fast and slow.* New York, NY: Farrar, Straus and Giroux.

Kahneman, D., & Klein, G. (2009). Conditions for intuitive expertise: A failure to disagree. *American Psychologist,* 64, 515–526.

Kelleher Richter, B., Samphantharak, K., & Timmons, J. (2009). Lobbying and taxes. *American Journal of Political Science,* 53, 893–909.

Kellogg Foundation. (2004). *Logic model development guide: Using logic models to bring together planning, evaluation, and action.* Battle Creek, MI: W. K Kellogg Foundation.

Keshav, S. (2007). How to read a paper. *ACM SIGCOMM Computer Communication Review,* 37(3), 83–84.

Kettl, D. (2015). *Politics of the administrative process* (6th ed.). Thousand Oaks, CA: SAGE Publications | CQ Press.

Kettl, D. (2017). The clumsy war against the "administrative state". *Public Administration Review,* 77(5), 639–640.

Kim, D. (2021). *Climate change litigation: An empirical assessment of the role of science in climate change lawsuits.* Washington, DC: ProQuest Dissertations Publishing. Retrieved from https://www-proquest-com.proxygw.wrlc.org/dissertations-theses/climate-change-litigation-empirical-assessment/docview/2480517871/se-2?accountid=11243

Kingdon, J. (2011). *Agendas, alternatives, and public policies.* Glenview, IL: Longman | Pearson.

Knowles, E. (2014). *Oxford dictionary of quotations* (8th ed.). Oxford, UK: Oxford University Press. Retrieved October 26, 2020, from https://global.oup.com/academic/product/oxford-dictionary-of-quotations-9780199668700

Koerth, M. (2019, June 4). *Everyone knows money influences politics … except scientists*. Retrieved February 11, 2021, from from 538.com: https://fivethirtyeight.com/features/everyone-knows-money-influences-politics-except-scientists/

Kraft, P., Lodge, M., & Taber, C. (2015). Why people "don't trust the evidence": Motivated reasoning and scientific beliefs. *The Annals of the American Academy of Political and Social Science*, 658(1), 121–133.

Krayewski, E. (2013, February 7). *5 reasons to grant amnesty to illegal immigrants*. Retrieved from Reason.com: https://reason.com/2013/02/07/5-reasons-for-amnesty-for-illegal-immigr/

Krueger, A. (1974). The political economy of the rent-seeking society. *The American Economic Review*, 64(3), 291–303.

Kruger, J., & Dunning, D. (1999). Unskilled and unaware of it: How difficulties in recognizing one's own incompetence lead to inflated self-assessments. *Journal of Personality and Social Psychology*, 77, 1121–1134.

Kuhn, T. (1996). *The structure of scientific revolutions* (3rd ed.). Chicago, IL: University of Chicago Press.

Kunda, Z. (1990). The case for motivated reasoning. *Psychological Bulletin*, 108(3), 480–498.

Kunda, Z. (1999). *Social cognition: Making sense of people*. Cambridge, MA: The MIT Press.

Lakoff, G. (2009). *The political mind: A cognitive scientist's guide to your brain and its politics*. New York, NY: Penguin Group (USA) Inc.

Lakoff, G. (2014). *Don't think of an elephant!: Know your values and frame the debate*. White River Junction, VT: Chelsea Green Publishing.

Lane, D. (2016). 'Till the muddle in my mind have cleared awa': Can we help shape policy using systems modelling? *Systems Research and Behavioural Science*, 33(5), 633–650.

Lasswell, H. (1951). The policy orientation. In D. Lerner & H. Lasswell (Eds.), *The policy sciences: Recent developments in scope and method* (pp. 3–15). Stanford, CA: Stanford University Press.

Leith, S. (2016). *Words like loaded pistols: Rhetoric from Aristotle to Obama*. New York, NY: Basic Books.

Lempert, R. (2019). Robust decision making (RDM). In V. Marchau, W. Walker, P. Bloemen, & S. Popper (Eds.), *Decision making under deep uncertainty* (pp. 23–51). Cham, CH: Springer.

Letzler, R. (2017, November 3). Strategic incrementalism. In *Presentation at 39th annual fall research conference of teh association for public policy analysis and management, Chicago, IL*.

Levin, K., Cashore, B., Bernstein, S., & Auld, G. (2012). Overcoming the tragedy of super wicked problems: Constraining our future selves to ameliorate global climate change. *Policy Sciences*, 45, 123–152.

Levy, H., Norton, E., & Smith, J. (2017). Tobacco regulation and cost-benefit analysis: How should we value foregone consumer surplus? *American Journal of Health Economics*, 4(1), 1–25.

Liedtka, J., & Salzman, R. (2018). *Applying design thinking to public service delivery*. Washington, DC: IBM Center for the Business of Government. Retrieved May 22, 2021. https://www.businessofgovernment.org/report/applying-design-thinking-public-service-delivery

Light, P. (2019). *The government-industrial complex: The true size of the federal government, 1984–2018*. New York, NY: Oxford University Press.

Lindblom, C. (1977). *Politics and markets: The world's political-economic systems*. New York, NY: Basic Books, Inc.

Lindblom, C. (1979). Still muddling, not yet through. *Public Administration Review*, 39(6), 517–526.

Lindsey, B., Teles, S., Wilkinson, W., & Hammond, S. (2018). *The center can hold: Public policy for an age of extremes*. Washington, DC: Niskanen Center.

Linquiti, P. (2015). *The public sector R&D enterprise: A new approach to portfolio valuation*. New York, NY: Palgrave Macmillan.

Linquiti, P., & Vonortas, N. (2012). The value of flexibility in adapting to climate change: A real options analysis of investments in coastal defense. *Climate Change Economics*, 3(2), 1–33.

Liu, X., Stoutenborough, J., & Vedlitz, A. (2016). Bureaucratic expertise, overconfidence, and policy choice. *Governance*, 30(4), 705–725.

Lovett, F. (2011). *Rawl's a theory of justice*. London, UK: Continuum International Publishing Group.

Lowi, T. (1972). Four systems of policy, politics, and choice. *Public Administration Review*, 32(4), 298–310.

Luzer, D. (2013, November). For some in government, 'effective' is the new 'efficient'. *Governing*. Retrieved June 28, 2020, from https://www.governing.com/topics/mgmt/gov-effective-is-new-efficient.html

Lytle, T. (2019, February 19). Arlington's affordable housing crisis. *Arlington Magazine*.

Lynn, L. (1999). A place at the table: Policy analysis, its postpositive critics, and the future of practice. *Journal of Policy Analysis and Management*, 18(3), 411–424.

Lynn, L. (2009). Restoring the rule of law to public administration: What Frank Goodnow got right and Leonard White didn't. *Public Administration Review*, 69(5), 803–812.

Mach, K., Mastrandrea, M., Freeman, P., & Field, C. (2017). Unleashing expert judgment in assessment. *Global Environmental Change*, 44, 1–14.

Majone, G. (1989). *Evidence, argument, & persuasion in the policy process*. New Haven, CT: Yale University Press.

Malterud, K. (2001). Qualitative research: Standards, challenges, and guidelines. *The Lancet*, 358, 483–488.

Marcum, J. (2012). A integrated model of clinical reasoning: Dual-process theory of cognition and meta-cognition. *Journal of Evaluation in Clinical Practice*, 18, 954–961.

Marrin, S., & Torres, E. (2017). Improving how to think in intelligence analysis and medicine. *Intelligence and National Security*, 32, 649–662.

Mason, J. (2002). *Qualitative reasoning* (2nd ed.). London, UK: SAGE Publications, Ltd.

Matson, F. (1966). *The broken image: Man, science, and society*. New York, NY: Anchor Books.

Mauboussin, A., & Mauboussin, M. (2018). If you say something is "likely," how likely do people think it is? *Harvard Business Review*. Retrieved August 6, 2020, from https://hbr.org/2018/07/if-you-say-something-is-likely-how-likely-do-people-think-it-is

May, J. (2016). *How to win an argument: An ancient guide to the art of persuasion*. Princeton, NJ: Princeton University Press.

McGuinness, T., & Slaughter, A. (2019, Spring). The new practice of public problem solving. *Stanford Social Innovation Review*. Retrieved May 20, 2021, from https://ssir.org/articles/entry/the_new_practice_of_public_problem_solving

McKay, A. (2020). Buying Amendments? Lobbyists' campaign contributions and microlegislation in the creation of the Affordable Care Act. *Legislative Studies Quarterly*, 45, 327–360.

McLaughlin, P., Sherouse, O., Francis, D., & Nels, J. (2018). *State RegData. Mercatus center*. QuantGov. Arlington, VA: George Mason University. Retrieved May 21, 2019, from https://quantgov.org/state-regdata

McNutt, M. (2018, September 10). Evidence-based decision making. *Remarks at Resources for the Future's Policy Leadership Series*. Retrieved September 17, 2020, from https://www.rff.org/events/pls/marcia-mcnutt-on-evidence-based-decisionmaking/

Mead, L. (2013). Teaching public policy: Linking policy and politics. *Journal of Public Affairs Education*, 19(3), 389–403.

Mellers, B., Stone, E., Atanasov, P., Rohrbaugh, N., Emlen Metz, S., Ungar, L., … Tetlock, P. (2015). The psychology of intelligence analysis: Drivers of prediction in world politics. *Journal of Experimental Psychology: Applied*, 21(1), 1–14.

Meltzer, R., & Schwartz, A. (2019). *Policy analysis as problem solving: A flexible and evidence based framework*. New York, NY: Routledge.

Meyerson, H. (2021, March 25). *The Berkeley School. The American Prospect*. Retrieved April 16, 2021, from https://prospect.org/economy/berkeley-school-economics/

Mill, J. (1859/2001). *On liberty*. Kitchener, ON: Batoche Books Limited.

Min Kim, S. (2021, August 1). The quiet Biden-GOP talks behind the infrastructure deal. *Washington Post*. Retrieved from https://www.washingtonpost.com/politics/the-quiet-biden-gop-talks-behind-the-infrastructure-deal/2021/08/01/4f669dea-f165-11eb-81d2-ffae0f931b8f_story.html. Downloaded August 6, 2021.

Mitchell, J. (2007, June 14). Can I really speak truth to power. *Remarks at the CBSA Strategy and Coordination Branch Retreat*. Retrieved September 11, 2020, from http://www.atlas101.ca/pm/wp-content/uploads/2017/02/Can-I-Really-Speak-Truth-to-Power.-James-Mitchell-2007.pdf

Moe, T. (2005). Power and political institutions. *Perspectives on Politics*, 3(2), 215–233.

Moore, M. (2000). Managing for value: Organizational strategy in for-profit, nonprofit, and governmental organizations. *Nonprofit and Voluntary Sector Quarterly*, 29(1), 183–204.

Morgan, R., & Oudekerk, B. (2019). *Criminal victimization: 2018*. Office of Justice Programs, Bureau of Justice Statistics. Washington, DC: U.S. Department of Justice.

NASA. (2020, October 27). *Vital signs of the planet*. Goddard Institute for Space Studies, National Aeronautics and Space Administration. Retrieved October 28, 2020, from Global Climate Change: https://climate.nasa.gov/vital-signs/global-temperature/

NASHP. (2020, December 7). *Where states stand on Medicaid expansion*. Retrieved March 15, 2021, from The National Academy for State Health Policy: https://www.nashp.org/states-stand-medicaid-expansion-decisions/

NASPAA. (2019). *Network of schools of public policy, affairs, and administration*. Retrieved May 9, 2019, from https://www.naspaa.org/schools-search

NCIC. (2006, April 10). *National Center for Interstate Compacts. (The Council of State Governments)*. Retrieved March 10, 2021, from The Council of State Governments: www.csg.org/knowledgecenter/docs/ncic/Fact Sheet.pdf

NCSL. (2021, March 1). *State medical marijuana laws*. Retrieved March 15, 2021, from National Council of State Legislatures: https://www.ncsl.org/research/health/state-medical-marijuana-laws.aspx

Neff Powel, E., & Grimmer, J. (2016). Money in exile: Campaign contributions and committee access. *The Journal of Politics*, 78, 974–988.

Nelson, M., & Ostrander, I. (2016). Keeping appointments: The politics of confirming United States attorneys. *Justice System Journal*, 37(3), 211–231.

Newbold, S. (2008). Teaching orgnization theory from a constitutional perspective: A new twist on an old flame. *Journal of Public Affairs Education*, 14(3), 335–351.

Newbold, S. (2011). No time like the present: Making rule of law and constitutional competence the theoretical and practical foundation for public administration graduate education curriculum. *Journal of Public Affairs Education*, 17(4), 465–481.

Newman, J. (2017). Debating the politics of evidence-based policy. *Public Administration*, 95, 1107–1112.

Newton, I. (1675, February 5). *Isaac Newton letter to Robert Hooke*. Retrieved May 8, 2019, from https://discover.hsp.org/Record/dc-9792/Description#tabnav.

Newzoo. (2020, October 19). *Top countries by smartphone users*. Retrieved April 12, 2021, from https://newzoo.com/insights/rankings/top-countries-by-smartphone-penetration-and-users/

Nienaber, J., & Wildavsky, A. (1973). *The budgeting and evaluation of federal recreation programs or, money doesn't grow on trees*. New York, NY: Basic Books.

NILE. (2021). *Code of ethics*. Retrieved June 2, 2021, from National Institute for Lobbying & Ethics: https://www.lobbyinginstitute.com/ethics

Nixon, R. (1990). *Six crises* (Centennial ed.). New York, NY: Simon & Schuster.

NLC & NATCO. (2018). *Model code for municipalities*. Washington, DC: National League of Cities and National Association of Telecommunications Officers and Advisors. Retrieved May 25, 2019, from https://www.nlc.org/resource/model-code-for-municipalities-0

Norman, G., Monterio, S., Sherbino, J., Ilgen, J., Schmidt, H., & Mamede, S. (2017). The causes of error in clinical reasoning: Cognitive biases, knowledge deficits, and dual process thinking. *Academic Medicine*, 92(1), 23–30.

NRC. (2012). *Using science as evidence in public policy*. National Research Council. Washington, DC: The National Academies Press.

NSF. (2010). *The 2010 user-friendly handbook for project evaluation*. Arlington, VA: National Science Foundation.

NSF. (2020, January). *Glossary*. Retrieved April 8, 2021, from The State of U.S. Science and Engineering 2020: https://ncses.nsf.gov/pubs/nsb20201/glossary

NSF. (2020, January). *Research and development: U.S. trends and international comparisons*. Retrieved November 6, 2020, from Science and Engineering Indicators: https://ncses.nsf.gov/pubs/nsb20203/data

ODNI. (2011). *U.S. National Intelligence: An overview 2011*. Washington, DC: Office of the Director of National Intelligence. Retrieved October 19, 2020, from https://www.dni.gov/files/documents/IC_Consumers_Guide_2011.pdf

ODNI. (2015a). *Intelligence community directive 203: Analytic standards*. Washington, DC: Office of the Director of National Intelligence. Retrieved September 22, 2020, from https://www.dni.gov/files/documents/ICD/ICD%20203%20Analytic%20Standards.pdf

ODNI. (2015b). *Principles of intelligence transparency for the intelligence community*. Washington, DC: Office of the Director of National Intelligence. Retrieved November 15, 2020, from https://www.dni.gov/files/documents/ppd-28/FINAL%20Transparency_poster%20v1.pdf

OECD. (2017). *Trust and public policy: How better governance can help rebuild public trust*. Paris, FR: OECD Publishing.

OECD. (2020). *Trust in government*. Retrieved February 28, 2021, from OECD.org: https://www.oecd.org/gov/trust-in-government.htm

OHRC. (2012). *The Ontario human rights code*. Toronto, CN: Ontario Human Rights Commission. Retrieved December 15, 2020, from http://www.ohrc.on.ca/en/guide-your-rights-and-responsibilities-under-human-rights-code/part-i-%E2%80%93-freedom-discrimination

O'Hare, M. (1989). A typology of governmental action. *Journal of Policy Analysis and Management*, 8(4), 670–672.

OIEA. (1998). *A plain English handbook: How to create clear SEC disclosure documents*. Washington, DC: Office of Investor Education and Assistance, U.S. Securities and Exchange Commission.

Olejniczak, K., Borkowska-Wasak, S., Domaradzka-Widla, A., & Park, Y. (2020). Policy labs: The next frontier of policy design and evaluation? *Policy & Politics*, 48, 89–110.

Olson, M. (1965). *The logic of collective action: Public goods and the theory of groups*. Cambridge, MA: Harvard University Press.

OMB. (2017). *Statistical programs of the United States FY2017*. U.S. Office of Management and Budget. Washington, DC: U.S. Government Publishing Office.

OMB. (2018). *Budget of the U.S. government: Analytical perspectives*. U.S. Office of Management and Budget. Washington, DC: U.S. Government Publishing Office.

OMB. (2020). *Historical tables, budget of the United States government, fiscal year 2021*. Washington, DC: U.S. Office of Management and Budget. Retrieved February 25, 2021, from https://www.govinfo.gov/app/collection/budget/2021

OMB. (2021, June 30). *Evidence-based policymaking: Learning agendas and annual evaluation plans*. Retrieved July 1, 2021, from https://www.whitehouse.gov/wp-content/uploads/2021/06/M-21-27.pdf

Orlinsky, D., Schofield, M., Schroder, T., & Kazantzis, N. (2011). Utilization of personal therapy by psychotherapists: A practice-friendly review and a new study. *Journal of Clinical Psychology*, 67, 828–842.

van Ostaijen, M., & Jhagroe, S. (2015). 'Get those voices at the table!': Interview with Deborah Stone. *Policy Sciences*, 48(1), 127–133.

Oxford University Press. (2001). *The New Oxford American Dictionary* (E. Jewell & F. Abate, Eds.). New York, NY: Oxford University Press.

Oxford University Press. (2016, November 11). *Oxford Dictionary*. Retrieved January 10, 2017, from https://www.oxforddictionaries.com/press/news/2016/11/17/WOTY-16

Pahle, M., Burtraw, D., Flachsland, C., Kelsey, N., Biber, E., Meckling, J., … Zysman, J. (2018). Sequencing to ratchet up climate policy stringency. *Nature Climate Change*, 8, 861–867.

Parsons, W. (1995). *Public policy: An introduction to the theory and practice of policy analysis*. Cheltenham, UK: Edward Elgar Publishing Ltd.

Partnership for Public Service. (2021, March 31). *Political appointee tracker*. Retrieved from The Partnership for Public Service: https://ourpublicservice.org/political-appointee-tracker/

Patashnik, E., & Weaver, R. (2020). Policy analysis and political sustainability. *Policy Studies Journal*, 49, 1110–1134.

Patton, C., Sawicki, D., & Clark, J. (2013). *Basic methods of policy analysis and planning*. Upper Saddle River, NJ: Pearson Education, Inc.

Pauly, D. (1995). Anecdotes and the shifting baseline syndrome of fisheries. *Trends in Ecology and Evolution*, 10, 430.

Pawson, R., Wang, G., & Owen, L. (2011). Known knowns, known unknowns, unknown unknowns: The predicament of evidence-based policy. *American Journal of Evaluation*, 32(4), 518–546.

Peters, E., Vastfjall, D., Garlin, T., & Slovic, P. (2006). Affect and decision making: A "hot" topic. *Journal of Behavioral Decision Making*, 19(2), 79–85.

Pettibone, L. (2014). Sustainability needs citizens but do citizens need sustainability? *Open Citizenship*, 5, 8–19.

Pettijohn, S., & Boris, E. (2013). *Nonprofit-government contracts and grants: Findings from the 2013 national survey*. Washington, DC: Urban Institute.

Pew Research Center. (2018). *The public, the political system and American democracy*. Washington, DC: Pew Research Center. Retrieved February 19, 2021, from https://www.pewresearch.org/politics/2018/04/26/the-public-the-political-system-and-american-democracy/

Pherson, R., & Huer, R. (2021). *Structured analytic techniques for intelligence analysis*. Thousand Oaks, CA: CQ Press | SAGE Publications.

Pietryka, M. (2016). Accuracy motivations, predispositions, and social information in political dicussion networks. *Political Psychology*, 37(3), 367–386.

Piketty, T. (2014). *Capital in the twenty-first century*. Cambridge, MA: Belknap Press of Harvard University Press.

Pindyck, R., & Rubinfeld, D. (2009). *Microeconomics*. Upper Saddle River, NY: Pearson | Prentice Hall.

Pipa, A., & Brown, K. (2019, October 14). *American leadership on the sustainable development goals*. Retrieved March 23, 2021, from The Brookings Institution: https://www.brookings.edu/blog/up-front/2019/10/14/american-leadership-on-the-sustainable-development-goals/

PLAIN. (2011). *Federal plain language guidelines, revision 1*. Washington, DC: Plain Language Action and Information Network.

PMI. (2017). *A guide to the project management body of knowledge (PMBOK® guide)* (6th ed.). Newtown Square, PA: Project Management Institute.

PMI. (2019, November 18). *Code of ethics & professional conduct*. Retrieved June 1, 2021, from Project Management Institute: https://www.pmi.org/about/ethics/code

POST. (2021). Retrieved from https://post.parliament.uk/type/postnote/

Pressman, J., & Wildavsky, A. (1984). *Implementation: How great expectations in Washington are dashed in Oakland* (3rd ed.). Berkeley, CA and Los Angeles, CA: University of California Press.

Productivity Commission. (2013). *On efficiency and effectiveness: Some definitions*. Canberra, ACT: Australian Government.

Pronin, E., & Schmidt, K. (2013). Claims and denials of bias and their implications for policy. In E. Shafir (Ed.), *The behavioral foundations of public policy* (pp. 195–216). Princeton, NJ: Princeton University Press.

Pulitzer Prize Board. (2020, May 4). *Prize winners by category: Public service*. Retrieved October 23, 2020, from The Pulitzer Prizes: https://www.pulitzer.org/prize-winners-by-category/204

Ramirez, R., Churchhouse, S., Palmero, A., & Hoffman, J. (2017, Summer). Using scenario planning to reshape the future. *MIT Sloan Management Review*, 58, 31–37.

Reagan, R. (1981, January 20). *Reagan quotes and speeches*. Retrieved February 28, 2021, from Ronald Reagan Presidential Foundation and Institute: https://www.reaganfoundation.org/ronald-reagan/reagan-quotes-speeches/inaugural-address-2/

Regulatory Studies Center. (2019). *Total pages published in the code of federal regulations*. Washington, DC: George

Washington University. Retrieved May 21, 2019, from https://regulatorystudies.columbian.gwu.edu/reg-stats

Richardson, J. (2017). *24 cognitive biases suffing up your thinking.* (schoolofthought.org). Retrieved from https://yourbias.is

Richardson, J. (2018). *Though shall not commit logical fallacies.* (schoolofthought.org). Retrieved from https://yourlogicalfallacyis.com

Ringhofer, L., & Kohlweg, K. (2019). Has the theory of change established itself as the better alternative to the logical framework approach in development cooperation programmes? *Progress in Development Studies,* 19(2), 112–122.

Rittel, H., & Webber, M. (1973). Dielmmas in a general theory of planning. *Policy Sciences,* 4(2), 155–169.

Robert, C., & Zeckhauser, R. (2011). The methodology of normative policy analysis. *Journal of Policy Analysis and Management,* 30, 613–643.

Roe, E. (2016). Policy messes and their management. *Policy Sciences,* 49(4), 351–372.

Rohr, J. (1990). The constitutional case for public administration. In G. Wamsley, R. Bacher, C. Goodsell, P. Kronenberg, J. Rohr, C. Stivers, … J. Wolf (Eds.), *Refouding public administration* (pp. 52–95). Newbury Park, CA: SAGE Publications.

Rothstein, R. (2017). *The color of law: A forgotten history of how our government segregated America.* New York, NY: Liveright Publishing Corporation.

Rothwell, C. (1951). Foreword. In D. Lerner & H. Lasswell (Eds.), *The policy sciences: Recent developments in scope and method* (pp. vii–xi). Stanford, CA: Stanford University Press.

RWJF. (2006, July). *Qualitative research guidelines project.* Retrieved June 28, 2021, from Robert Wood Johnson Foundation: http://www.qualres.org/HomeRefl-3703.html

Safire, W. (2008). *Safire's political dictionary.* New York, NY: Oxford University Press.

Saiger, A. (2014). Chevron and deference in state law. *Fordham Law Review,* 83(2), 555–585.

Sainsbury, D. (2020). The race to the top. *Issues in Science and Technology,* 36, 81–86.

Salovey, P., & Mayer, J. (1990). *Emotional Intelligence: Imagination, cognition and personality,* 185–211.

Sandel, M. (2020). *The Tyranny of Merit: What's become of the common good.* New York, NY: Farrar, Straus and Giroux.

Sandler, T. (2015). Collective action: Fifty years later. *Public Choice,* 164(3), 195–216.

Sapolsky, H., & Taylor, M. (2011). Politics and the science of science policy. In K. Husbands Feeling, J. Lane, J. Marburger, & S. Shipp (Eds.), *The science of science policy: A handbook* (pp. 31–55). Stanford, CA: Stanford University Press.

Savage, S. (2012). *The flaw of averages: Why we underestimate risk in the face of uncertainty.* Hoboken, NJ: John WIley & Sons, Inc.

Schrage, M. (2005, February 20). What percent is 'Slam Dunk'? *The Washington Post.* Retrieved September 22, 2020, from https://www.washingtonpost.com/archive/opinions/2005/02/20/what-percent-is-slam-dunk/812c1bc6-2f25-4783-a2da-c1256a6d4031/

Schultz, D., Shattuck, D., & Streight, M. (2018). *Assessing land use policies for animal feeding operations in Western Colorado.* Washington, DC: George Washington University.

Schumpeter, J. (1943). *Capitalism, socialism, and democracy.* London: G. Allen & Unwin.

Scoblic, J., & Tetlock, P. (2020, November/December). A better crystal ball: The right way to think about the future. *Foreign Affairs,* 99(6), 10–18.

Serageldin, I., & Steer, A. (1993, December). *Making development sustainable.* Washington, DC: The World Bank.

Sessions, R. (1950, January 8). How a 'difficult' composer gets that way: Harpsichordist. *New York Times,* pp. 89.

Shadish, W., Cook, T., & Campbell, D. (2002). *Experimental and quasi-experimental designs for generalized causal inference.* Boston, MA: Houghton Mifflin Company.

Shafir, E., & LeBoeuf, R. (2002). Rationality. *Annual Review of Psychology,* 53, 491–517.

Shambaugh, J., Nunn, R., Breitwieser, A., & Liu, P. (2018). *The state of competition and dynamism: Facts about concentration, start-ups, and related policies.* Washington,

DC: The Hamilton Project. Retrieved January 9, 2021, from https://www.hamiltonproject.org/papers/the_state_of_competition_and_dynamism_facts_about_concentration_start_

Shapiro, S. (2016). *Analysis and public policy: Successes, failures and directions for reform*. Cheltenham, UK: Edward Elgar Publishing Limited.

Sheffer, L., Loewen, P., Soroka, S., Walgrave, S., & Sheafer, T. (2018). Nonrepresentative representatives: An experimental study of the decision making of elected politicians. *American Political Science Review*, 112(2), 302–321.

Simon, H. (1992). What is an "explanation" of behavior? *Psychological Science*, 3, 150–161.

Simon, H. (1997). *Administrative behavior: A study of decision-making processes in administrative organization* (4th ed.). London, UK: The Free Press.

Sinclair, U. (1935). *I, candidate for governor: And how I got licked*. New York, NY: Farrar & Rhinehart.

Slywotzky, A., Morrison, D., & Andelman, B. (1997). *The profit zone: How strategic business design will lead you to tomorrow's profits*. New York, NY: Times Books.

Smith, A. (1784). *An inquiry into the nature and causes of the wealth of nations* (3rd ed.). London: W Strahan & T Cadell.

Smith, N. (2021, January 20). North Sea oil: A tale of two countries. *Engineering and Technology*. Retrieved March 22, 2021, from https://eandt.theiet.org/content/articles/2021/01/north-sea-oil-a-tale-of-two-countries/

Snow, S. (2018, November 20). A new way to become more open-minded. *Harvard Business Review*.

Solow, R. (1992). *An almost practical step toward sustainability: An invited lecture*. Oxford, UK: Resources for the Future.

Solow, R. (2019). Sustainability: An economist's perspective. In R. Stavins (Ed.), *Economics of the environment: Selected readings* (7th ed., pp. 425–432). Cheltenham, UK: Edward Elgar Publishing.

Spaeth, H., Epstein, L., Martin, A., Segal, J., Ruger, T., & Benesh, S. (2020). *Supreme Court database, version 2020, release 1*. Retrieved July 4, 2021, from http://scdb.wustl.edu/

SPJ. (2014, June 9). *SPJ code of ethics*. Retrieved October 24, 2020, from Society of Professional Journalists: https://www.spj.org/ethicscode.asp

Stanovich, K., & West, R. (2000). Individual differences in reasoning: Implications for the rationality debate. *Behavioural and Brain Sciences*, 23(5), 645–726.

Stapleton, J. (2020). *Exploratory scenario planning (XSP): Navigating an undertain future*. Cambridge, MA: Lincoln Instiute of Land Policy.

Stecker, T. (2015, September 30). Court upholds EPA livestock data rule in win for ag groups. *Greenwire*. Retrieved October 22, 2020, from https://www.ee-news.net/greenwire/stories/1060025610

Sterman, J. (2000). *Business dynamics: Systems thinking and modeling for a complex world*. Boston, MA: The McGraw-Hill Companies, Inc.

Sterman, J. (2006). Learning from evidence in a complex world. *American Journal of Public Health*, 96(3), 505–514.

Sterman, J. (2012). Sustaining sustainability: Creating a systems science in a fragmented academy and polarized world. In M. Weinstein & R. Turner (Eds.), *Sustainability science: The emerging paradigm and the urban environment* (pp. 21–58). New York, NY: Springer Science+Business Media, LLC.

Stern, N. (2007). *The economics of climate change: The stern review*. Cambridge, UK: Cambridge University Press.

Stoker, G., Hay, C., & Barr, M. (2016). Fast thinking: Implications for democratic politics. *European Journal of Political Research*, 55(1), 3–21.

Stokey, E., & Zeckhauser, R. (1978). *A primer for policy analysis*. New York, NY: W.W. Norton & Company, Inc.

Stone, D. (2012). *Policy paradox: The art of political decision making* (3rd ed.). New York, NY: Norton & Company.

Stoneham, A. (2010). Nuclear fission: The interplay of science and technology. *Philosophical Transactions of the Royal Society A: Mathematical, Physical and Engineering Sciences*, 368, 3295–3313.

Szypszak, C. (2011). Teaching law in public affairs education: Synthesizing political theory, decision making, and responsibility. *Journal of Public Affairs Education*, 17(4), 483–499.

Taber, C., & Lodge, M. (2012). Motivated skepticism in the evaluation of political beliefs. *Critical Review: A Journal of Politics and Society*, 24(2), 157–184.

Tarr, A. (2000). *Understanding state constitutions*. Princeton, NJ: Princeton University Press.

Tassey, G. (1997). *The economics of R&D policy*. Westport, CT: Quorum Books.

Tassey, G. (2005). Underinvestment in public good technologies. *Journal of Technology Transfer*, 30, 89–113.

Teamsters Union. (2019, October 11). *Self-driving trucks threaten jobs, especially for minorities*. Retrieved December 23, 2020, from The Teamsters Union: https://teamster.org/

Teovanovic, P. (2019). Individual differences in anchoring effect: Evidence for the role of insufficient adjustment. *Europe's Journal of Psychology*, 15(1), 8–24.

Tetlock, P. (2005). *Expert political judgment: How good is it? How can we know?* Princeton, NJ: Princeton University Press.

Tetlock, P., & Gardner, D. (2015). *Superforecasting: The art and science of prediction*. New York, NY: Crown Publishers.

Thaler, R., & Sunstein, C. (2008). *Nudge: Improving decisions about health, wealth, and happiness*. New Haven, CT: Yale University Press.

Thomson-Devaux, A., Bronner, L., & Damini Sharma, D. (2021, February 22). *Police misconduct costs cities millions every year. But that's where the accountability ends*. Retrieved July 11, 2021, from The Marshall Project: https://www.themarshallproject.org/2021/02/22/police-misconduct-costs-cities-millions-every-year-but-that-s-where-the-accountability-ends

Topiak, M., West, R., & Stanovich, K. (2011). The cognitive reflection test as a predictor of performance on heuristics-and-biases tasks. *Memory and Cognition*, 39, 1275–1289.

Toulmin, S., Ricke, R., & Janik, A. (1979). *An introduction to reasoning*. New York, NY: Macmillan.

Trochim, W. (2007). *The research methods knowledge base* (2nd ed.). Mason, OH: Thomson Custom.

Tversky, A., & Kahneman, D. (1974). Judgment under uncertainty: Heuristics and biases. *Science*, 185, 1124–1131.

UK GOS. (2017). *Tools for futures thinking and foresight across the UK government*. London, UK: The UK Government Office for Science.

UN/DESA. (2019). *SDG summit*. Department of Economic and Social Affairs. New York, NY: United Nations. Retrieved March 23, 2021, from https://www.un.org/en/summits2019/pdf/Climate-Action-Summit.pdf

UN/DESA. (n.d.). *The 17 goals: History*. Retrieved March 23, 2021, from United Nations | Department of Economic and Social Affairs | Sustainable Development: https://sdgs.un.org/goals

UN/WCED. (1987). *Our common future*. United Nations Environment Programme, World Commission on Environment and Development. New York, NY: United Nations General Assembly. Retrieved March 20, 2021, from https://www.un.org/ga/search/view_doc.asp?symbol=A/42/427&Lang=E

UNGA. (2020). *Global indicator framework for the sustainable development goals and targets of the 2030 agenda for sustainable development*. United Nations Department of Economic & Social Affairs | Statistical Commission, Inter-Agency and Expert Group on SDG Indicators. New York, NY: United Nations General Assembly. Retrieved March 20, 2021, from https://unstats.un.org/sdgs/indicators/Global%20Indicator%20Framework%20after%202020%20review_English.xlsx

United States vs. Sioux Nation of Indians, 448 U.S. 371 (U.S. Supreme Court June 30, 1980). Retrieved October 6, 2021, from https://supreme.justia.com/cases/federal/us/448/371/

University of Vermont Libraries. (2017, April 4). *Research guides*. Retrieved 2017, from Gray Literature: http://researchguides.uvm.edu/graylit

USA Facts. (2021, February 24). *Minimum wage in America: How many people are earning $7.25 an hour?* Retrieved March 15, 2021, from USA Facts: https://usafacts.org/articles/minimum-wage-america-how-many-people-are-earning-725-hour/

USCB. (2016). *Reported voting and registration, by sex and single years of age.* Washington, DC: United States Census Bureau. Retrieved October 1, 2020, from https://www.census.gov/data/tables/time-series/demo/voting-and-registration/p20-580.html

USCB. (2017). *Voting and registration in the election of November 2016.* Washington, DC: United State Census Bureau. Retrieved October 1, 2020, from https://www.census.gov/data/tables/time-series/demo/voting-and-registration/p20-580.html

USCB. (2018). *2018 state & local government finance historical datasets and tables. Department of Commerce.* Washington, DC: U.S. Bureau of the Census. Retrieved March 9, 2021, from https://www.census.gov/data/datasets/2018/econ/local/public-use-datasets.html

USCB. (2020). *2017 SUSB annual data tables by establishment industry.* U.S. Census Bureau. Washington, DC: Department of Commerce. Retrieved January 15, 2021, from https://www.census.gov/content/census/en/data/tables/2017/econ/susb/2017-susb-annual.html

U.S. Courts. (2021, January 4). *Authorized judgeships.* Retrieved April 1, 2021, from United States Courts | About Federal Judgeships: https://www.uscourts.gov/judges-judgeships/about-federal-judges

U.S. Forest Service. (2003, May). *Influence of forest structure on wildfire behaviour and the severity of its effects.* Retrieved April 27, 2021, from U.S. Department of Agriculture: https://www.fs.fed.us/projects/hfi/docs/forest_structure_wildfire.pdf

USGCRP. (2018). *Impacts, risks, and adaptation in the United States: Fourth National Climate Assessment, Volume II.* U.S. Global Change Research Program. Washington, DC: U.S. Government Printing Office. doi: 10.7930/NCA4.2018

U.S. Bureau of Census. (2019). *2017 census of governments.* Washington, DC: U.S. Department of Commerce. Retrieved May 8, 2019, from https://census.gov/data/tables/2017/econ/gus/2017-governments.html

U.S. Congress. (1984). *Public law 98-363.* Washington, DC.

U.S. Supreme Court. (2019, December 1). *Federal rules of evidence* Article VII, Rule 702. Online: Cornell Law School. Retrieved October 9, 2020, from https://www.law.cornell.edu/rules/fre/rule_702

van Buuren, A., Lewis, J., Guy Peters, B., & Voorberg, W. (2020). Improving public policy and implementation: Exploring the potential of design. *Politics & Policy,* 3–19.

Veselý, A. (2008). Problem tree: A problem structuring heuristic. *Central European Journal of Public Policy,* 2, 68–81.

VLTC. (2019, May 25). *Vermont league of towns and cities.* Retrieved from Resource Library: https://www.vlct.org/resource-library/mac

Vogel, I. (2012). Review of the use of 'theory of change'. In *International development.* London, UK: UK Department of International Development.

Wallace, R., & Clark, S. (2018). Environmental studies and sciences in a time of chaos: Problems, contexts, and recommendations. *Journal of Environmental Studies and Sciences,* 8, 110–113.

Warrick, J. (2014, August 31). Large dead zone signals continued problems for the Chesapeake Bay. *Washington Post.* Retrieved August 6, 2020, from https://www.washingtonpost.com/national/health-science/large-dead-zone-signals-continued-problems-for-the-chesapeake-bay/2014/08/31/1e0c2024-2fc2-11e4-9b98-848790384093_story.html?utm_term=.7d81798be591

Washington Post. (2020, October 29). Retrieved from WashingtonPost.com: https://www.washingtonpost.com/

Washington Post. (2020, September 12). 1,018 people have been shot and killed by police in the past year. *Washington Post.* Retrieved September 12, 2020, from https://www.washingtonpost.com/graphics/investigations/police-shootings-database/

Watanabe, F. (2008). *Fifteen axioms for intellgience analysts.* Center for the Study of Intelligence. Washington, DC: Central Intelligence Agency. Retrieved September 1, 2020, from https://www.cia.gov/library/center-for-the-study-of-intelligence/csi-publications/csi-studies/studies/97unclass/axioms.html#author

Weber, E. (2013). Doing the right thing willingly. In E. Shafir (Ed.), *The behavioral foundations of public policy* (pp. 380–397). Princeton, NJ: Princeton University Press.

Weible, C. (2017). The scope and focus of policy process research and theory. In C. Weible & P. Sabatier

(Eds.), *Theories of the policy process* (4th ed., pp. 1–13). Boulder, CO: Westview Press.

Weible, C., & Cairney, P. (2018). Practical lessons from policy theories. *Policy & Politics*, 46(2), 183–197.

Weible, C., & Sabatier, P. (Eds.). (2017). *Theories of the policy process* (4th ed.). Boulder, CO: Westview Press.

Weimer, D., & Vining, A. (2017). *Policy analysis: Concepts and practices* (6th ed.). New York, NY: Routledge.

Weiss, C. (1979). The many meaning of research utilization. *Public Administration Review*, 39(5), 426–431.

Weiss, C. (2008). Communicating uncertainty in intelligence and other professions. *International Journal of Intelligence and Counterintelligence*, 27, 57–85.

Wheelen, C. (2011). *Introduction to public policy*. New York, NY: W. W. Norton & Company.

Wikipedia. (2020). *List of ballet companies in the United States*. Wikipedia. Retrieved September 22, 2020, from https://en.wikipedia.org/wiki/List_of_ballet_companies_in_the_United_States

Wildavsky, A. (1979). *Speaking truth to power: The art and craft of policy analysis*. Boston, MA: Little, Brown and Company.

Wilkinson, N., & Klaes, M. (2012). *An introduction to behavioral economics* (2nd ed.). London, UK: Palgrave Macmillan.

Wilson, N., & Thomson, G. (2005). Deaths from international terrorism compared with road crash deaths in OECD countries. *Injury Prevention*, 11, 332–333.

Winship, C. (2006). Policy analysis as problem solving. In E. Moran, M. Rein, & R. Goodin (Eds.), *The Oxford handbook of public policy* (pp. 109–123). Oxford, UK: Oxford University Press.

Wood, T., & Porter, E. (2019). The elusive backfire effect: Mass attitudes' steadfast factual adherence. *Political Behavior*, 41(1), 135–163.

World Bank. (2020). *Gini index (World Bank estimate)*. Retrieved December 30, 2020, from The World Bank | Data: https://data.worldbank.org/indicator/SI.POV.GINI?name_desc=true

Yaakobi, E. (2017). Thinking styles and performance. *Journal of Clinical Psychiatry and Cognitive Psychology*, 1(1), 7–8.

Yackee, S. (2019). The politics of rulemaking in the United States. *Annual Review of Political Science*, 22, 37–55.

Yandle, B. (1999). Bootleggers and Baptists in Retrospect. *Regulation*, 22(3), 5–7.

Yourish, K., Buchanan, L., & Denise Lu, D. (2021, January 7). The 147 republicans who voted to overturn election results. *The New York Times*. Retrieved June 18, 2021, from https://www.nytimes.com/interactive/2021/01/07/us/elections/electoral-college-biden-objectors.html

Zak, P. (2011). The physiology of moral sentiments. *Journal of Economic Behavior & Organization*, 77(1), 53–65.

Zamzow, J. (2018, November 14). Why we can't agree on gun control. *Washington Post*. Retrieved July 21, 2019, from https://www.washingtonpost.com/outlook/2018/11/14/why-we-cant-agree-gun-control

INDEX

Gray literature, 204–205
Group identification process, 136

H

Habermas, J., 98–99
Haidt, J., 136, 277, 278
Hammitt, J., 302
Hansen, J., 110
Hardie, J., 494–495
Hardin, G., 78, 332
Harmon, M., 44
Hayek, Friedrich, 367
Heineman, R., 86, 152
Heller, J., 396
Hird, J., 73
Hitchens, C., 224
Hitler, A., 111
Hot cognition, 127, 128
Huer, R., 471, 543
Human cognition, 116
Hume, D., 183, 277, 278

I

IARPA. *See* Intelligence Advanced Research Programs
    Activity (IARPA)
Impact evaluation, 56, 58, 59
    counterfactual for, 62–65
    difference-in-differences approach, 64
    estimation methods, 65
    program outcomes, 63
    randomized controlled trial (RCT), 64
    students' GPAs, 63
    treatment effect, 63
Imposter syndrome, 141
Income elasticity of demand, 327
Indirect opportunity costs, 24
Inductive reasoning
    by analogy, 164–165, 184
    by classification, 184
    descriptive inference, 164
    by example, 163–164
    by generalization, 184
    logical errors, 183–184
    projective inference, 162
    provisional, 163
Inequity
    criminal justice system, 308
    Criteria-Alternatives matrix, 309

cumulative and systemic, 310–311
    decision making process, 309
    general process/specific case, 307
    intentional, 308
    monetary compensation, 308
    vs. passage of time, 306
    retroactive policies, 307
    sample size, 309–310
    unintentional, 308
Influence diagram, 445–447
Infrapolicies, 5
Inhofe, J., 110
Injustice mitigation, 534–535
Institutional lens, 270
    civil servants, 380
    electoral cycles, 380
    federalism. *See* Intergovernmental governance
    government institutions, 390–393. *See also*
        Government institutions
    institutional blindspot, 372
    principal-agent problem, 379–382
    public policies, 372
    red tape, 381–382
    turfism, 380
Institutional financing, 392
Intellectual agility, 257
Intellectual humility, 256
Intelligence Advanced Research Programs Activity
    (IARPA), 244–245, 483, 484
Intergovernmental governance
    federalism, 382, 383
    public policy, 382
    shared governance, 383–389
    total government spending, 382
Intergovernmental revenue flows, 386–387
Internal validity, 213
International trade policies, 358
Interpersonal effectiveness
    emotional intelligence, 524, 525, 526
    human resource and professional development,
        526
    public servants, 526
    relationship management, 526
    self-awareness, 525
    self-management, 525
    social awareness, 525
Invisible stakeholders, 201

M

MAA. *See* Multiattribute analysis (MAA)
Majone, G., 83, 97, 309
Market-based instruments (MBIs), 499
Market failure
   adverse selection, 336
   Affordable Care Act, 338
   exclusivity and rivalry, 331
   externalities, 334–336
   free-riding, 332
   imperfect information, 336–338
   information asymmetry, 336
   limited competition, 332–334
   monopoly, 333
   nonexclusive and nonrivalrous, 332
   oligopolies, 333
   policy analysis, 331
   public goods, 331–332
   types, 331
Marx, K., 367
Matson, F., 268
Mayer, J., 524
McChrystal, Stanley, 459
Mead, L., 356
Mechanical puzzles, 194–195
Mental map, systems thinking, 441
Mental missteps, cognitive traps, 141–146
Meta-analysis, academic literature, 204
Metacognition, 241
   cognitive dissonance, 120–123
   Cognitive Reflection Test, 117
   cognitive traps. *See* Cognitive traps
   cold cognition, 127–128
   collective welfare demands, 128–129
   definition, 116
   Dual Process Theory (DPT), 129–133
   heuristics, 116
   hot cognition, 127, 128
   motivation, 123–126
   System 1 thinking, 116, 118, 119
   System 2 thinking, 116–117
   valence, 127
Microeconomics, 360, 468, 469
Mill, J., 275, 276, 278, 286, 287
Mirror imaging, 145
Mitchell, J., 152–153
Monte Carlo modeling, 472–473
Montreal Protocol, 514–515

Mood-driven mistakes, cognitive traps, 139–141
Moral reasoning
   authority and respect, 274
   categorical imperative, 276
   fairness and reciprocity, 274
   harm and care, 274
   ingroup loyalty, 274
   normative values, 274
   on-off-the-shelf criterion, 278
   policy issues, 275
   purity and sanctity, 274
   rationalism, 275–276
   social intuitionism, 275, 276–278
   utilitarianism, 275–276
   veil of ignorance, 276, 278–280
Muir, J., 412
Multiattribute analysis (MAA), 35
Multiple streams framework, policymaking, 361–362
Multivariate quantitative analysis, 212, 214
Multivariate relationships, causal reasoning, 161
Murray, P., 192

N

National Environmental Policy Act (NEPA), 400
National Institute for Lobbying & Ethics/Code of
   Ethics (NILE, 2021), 550–553
National-international relationships, 384–385
Newbold, S., 397, 399
Newton, I., 2
Nienaber, J., 23
Nonexcludable resources, 78
Nongovernmental costs, 24
Nongovernmental organizations (NGOs), 3, 204
Nonrivalrous resources, 77–78
Normative policy judgments, analytic conclusion, 197
Normative statements, 89
Normative value judgments, 83
   analytic conclusion, 197

O

Off-the-shelf criteria, 24, 27, 464
O'Hare, M., 4–5
O'Leary, J., 42, 191
Olson, M., 78–79
Open-minded analysts, 231
Opportunity cost, 325
Overconfidence trap, 140
Owen, L., 198
Ozone Air Quality Standard, 341, 342

practical reality, 490
public employees, 489
stakeholder relationships, 489
starting points, 488–492
strategic alignment, 504–506
theory of change, 503
value proposition, 505
Public preferences, 199–201
Public resources, 6
Public servants, good shepherds of governance
    Affordable Care Act, 398
    checks and balances, 397
    duties, 396–397
    dysfunctional public policy, 399
    intergovernmental relations, 398
    rights of citizens, 398–399
    Rule of Law, 397
    separation of powers, 397–398

Q

Qualitative analysis, 210, 211, 212
Qualitative evidence, 220
Quantitative analysis, 210, 211, 212
Quick analysis, 239–240

R

Randomized controlled trial (RCT), 64
Rationalism, 275–276
Rawls, J., 276, 278, 279
Reagan, R., 373
Rebooted policy analysis
    criteria-alternatives matrix, 476
    panoptic analysis, 479
    policy stress-testing, 481
    scenario planning, 478, 481, 482
    societal change, 479, 480
    system map, 477
Recursive reasoning, 197
Redistributive tax policy, 469
Reinforcing (amplifying) loop, 448
Rent control, 22
Reporting, traditional journalism, 206
Researched analysis, 239
Research puzzle, 193–196
Research questions, 197
Retrospective policy analysis, 8, 9, 38, 41, 46
    data collection and analysis, 66
    efficiency and effectiveness, 57, 58
    evaluation question. *See* Evaluation question

formative assessment, 58, 66
impact evaluation, 56, 58, 59
nonprofit group, 56
policy cycle, 42–46
program boundaries, 47–50
program evaluation, 55, 56
program-specific logic model. *See* Program-specific
    logic model
public policy, 57
replicability, 67
summative assessment, 58–59
Revealed preferences, 343
Rhetoric communication, 110
Rich, M., 112
Rogers, P., 51
Romney, M., 98
Rothwell, C., 72
Rule-based ethics, 522

S

Safe Drinking Water Act, 400
Salovey, P., 524
Sandel, M., 349
SCC. *See* Social cost of carbon (SCC)
Schumpeter, J., 423, 424
Science and technology lens, 270
    applied research, 423
    basic research, 423
    Congressional Office of Technology Assessment
        (OTA), 427–428
    convergent technologies, 426
    creative destruction, 423
    disruption, 424
    economics, 430
    ethics, 430
    experimental development, 423
    mobile technology, 421
    novel technologies, 426
    policy analysis, 422
    policy-relevant topics, 424, 425
    privacy, 430
    radical change, 426
    rapid change, 424
    research and development (R&D), 423
    safety, 430
    scientific method, 422
    security, 430
    smartphone technology, 421

societal stability, 430
solve technical problems, 422
tangible manufactured products, 422
typology, 429
widespread change, 426
Scoblic, J., 463
Self-awareness, 262–263, 525
Self-identified stakeholders, 201
Self-management, 525
Shared governance
  Clean Air Act authority, 389
  conditional grant funding, 386
  economic analysis, 386
  environmental protection, 389
  federal-state relationships, 383
  Indian tribes, 383–384
  intergovernmental revenue flows, 386–387
  mandatory obligations, 386
  national-international relationships, 384–385
  operation of, 385
  policy issue, 387–389
  power and authority, 387
  public services, 385
  state-local relationships, 384
  state-to-state relationships, 384
  Terrorism Risk Insurance Program Act, 386
  tribal-federal-state relationships, 383
Simon, H., 83, 84, 242, 256, 458–459
Sinclair, U., 120
Skepticism, 254–255
Slovic, P., 128
Smith, A., 330, 367
SNAP. See Supplemental Nutrition Assistance Program (SNAP)
Social awareness, 525
Social cost of carbon (SCC), 343
Social intuitionism, 275, 276–278, 523
Social media, 207
Social Security and Medicare taxes, 374, 391
Social surplus, 322, 324
Social welfare, 349
Societal inequities, 395
Solow, R., 415
Solution aversion, 125
Sovereign Wealth Fund, 414
Stakeholder analysis, outside the studio
  Federal Trade Commission, 514
  implementation planning, 511

interests and implementation process, 512, 513
  logic model, 511, 512
  Montreal Protocol, 514–515
  policy design, 510
  policy development, 509
  stakeholder consultation, 510
  STEM education, 512, 514
Stakeholder consultation, 507–508, 510
Stakeholder preferences, 201, 216
Standards of Ethical Conduct for Employees of the Executive Branch (5 U.S. CFR 2635, 2021), 546–547
State-dependent policy trigger, 501
Stated preferences, 343
State-local relationships, 384
State-to-state relationships, 384
Statistical conclusion validity, 210
Statutory law, 403
Sterman, J., 443
Stern, N., 141–142
Stokey, E., 76
Stone, D., 25, 83, 84, 88, 97, 99, 199, 274, 360
Student learning, 465
Substantive law, 400
Summative assessment, 58–59
Supplemental Nutrition Assistance Program (SNAP), 301, 366
Supplemental Poverty Measure, 299, 300
Sustainability lens, 270
  benefit flows, 414, 415, 417
  Brundtland Commission, 412
  capital stocks, 414, 415, 417
  complex systems view, 413
  consume/invest, 414
  contested concept, 412–414
  deliberative, collective, purposive, 413
  ecological limits, 413
  long-term outlook, 413
  policy problems, 411
  reflexive management, 413
  sensible sustainability, 416
  Sovereign Wealth Fund, 414
  strong sustainability, 416
  substantial oil reserves, 414
  United Nations Sustainable Development Goals, 417–421
  weak sustainability, 416
Sustainable Development Goals (SDGs), 418–420

aerial firefighting, 474, 475
breakeven analysis, 476
causal theory, 470
classical policy analysis, 467–476
criteria-alternatives matrix, 468–470
cumulative probability distribution, 471
decision tree, 475
evaluation criteria, 464
evidence and experience, 469
exclusive use (EU) basis, 473
expected value analysis, 473
Fermi method, 468
flaw of averages, 470–471
microeconomics, 468, 469
Monte Carlo modeling, 472–473
'off-the-shelf' criteria, 464
policy alternatives, 465, 466
predictive skills, 483–484
program cost, 472
projective inference, 466–467
rebooted policy analysis, 476–483
redistributive tax policy, 469
relevant probability, 474

sensitivity analysis, 476
student learning, 465
systems thinking, 457
tradeoffs, 464
Vouchers, 22

W

Wang, G., 198
Warner, C. D., 367
Wealth and income redistribution, 6
What You See Is All There Is (WYSIATI)
    phenomenon, 145–146
Wheelen, C., 531
Wildavsky, A., 19, 23, 152

Y

Yackee, S., 406

Z

Zeckhauser, R., 76
Zoning laws, 6
Zucman, G., 348